# Police and People in London

# Police and People in London

## The PSI Report

David J. Smith
Jeremy Gray

Gower

Published by
Gower Publishing Company Limited,
Gower House, Croft Road,
Aldershot, Hants GU11 3HR,
England

and

Gower Publishing Company,
Old Post Road, Brookfield,
Vermont 05036,
U.S.A.

ISBN 0 566 00850 5 Case
ISBN 0 566 00851 3 Paperback

Printed and bound in Great Britain by
Biddles Ltd, Guildford and King's Lynn

# CONTENTS

# LIST OF TABLES IN THE TEXT

## FOREWORD TO THE GOWER EDITION

Between 1980 and 1982 the Policy Studies Institute carried out an extensive programme of research on the relations between the police and the public in London and on the Metropolitan Police as an organisation. This research, which was done at the request of the then Commissioner of Police, Sir David McNee, was funded by the Metropolitan Police and the City Parochial Foundation. Since PSI undertakes research in the public interest, it was agreed at the outset that the findings would be published in full and that the contents of the published report would be the responsibility of PSI.

In November 1983 the findings were, accordingly, published by PSI as four volumes under the general title Police and People in London. The four volumes were:

  I A survey of Londoners, by David J. Smith
  II A group of young black people, by Stephen Small
  III A survey of police officers, by David J. Smith
  IV The police in action, by David J. Smith and Jeremy Gray

The present edition consists of the original volumes I and IV with only minor amendments. There is not enough space to include a presentation of the findings of the second and third studies, but the Preface describes the objectives and methods of the whole programme of research in broad terms, and the final chapter summarises the results of our analysis from all parts of the research, and sets out our conclusions and recommendations. Most readers who are coming to this material for the first time will need to look first at the present volume. If there are then further points that they wish to pursue, they should consult volumes II and III of the original series, which are available from PSI. The 19 additional tables in the Appendix to volume I have been omitted from the present edition.

We are grateful to the Metropolitan Police and to the City Parochial Foundation for the financial support that made the study possible. The funding arrangements, the origins of the study and the working relationship between PSI and the Metropolitan Police are explained in some detail in the Preface.

The police in action is based on observational work by the two authors, who accompanied working groups of police officers over a two-year period. A very large number of officers at all ranks in the Metropolitan Police made this research possible by accepting the authors into their working groups, by engaging in discussions and by making themselves available for interviews. The great majority of these officers were frank and welcoming and did their best to help the authors to understand their work. We would like to thank them all very much for everything they did for us and for the research project.

Fieldwork and pre-computer analysis for the survey of Londoners was carried out by Social and Community Planning Research. Our special thanks go to Douglas Wood, who was in charge of the work at SCPR. As well as managing the survey, he made a very large contribution to the design of the questionnaire.

# PREFACE

In the Autumn of 1979, the Commissioner of Police for the Metropolis invited the Policy Studies Institute to put forward proposals for a wide-ranging study of 'the relations between the Metropolitan Police and the community it serves'. The Commissioner indicated his particular concern about relations between the police and members of ethnic minority groups in London.

From the outset, the institute was keen to carry out research on a subject of great and increasing public importance. No sooner had the research begun than a series of events heightened the importance of the issues under study and the amount and intensity of public debate about them. In January 1981 13 young black people were killed and 37 injured in a fire in Deptford that was at first thought to have been caused by a racialist attack. An inquest later brought an open verdict on the cause of the disaster against a background of bitter criticism and demonstrations by black people over the handling of the affair by the police and the coroner's court. In April 1981 there were serious riots in Brixton; the Home Secretary set up a formal inquiry under Lord Scarman, who reported in November of that year. The report criticised the police in Brixton for mounting an intensive stop and search operation without first consulting the 'local community'; made important, though vaguely expressed, recommendations for the establishment of local police committees whom the police would consult in future; criticised the police for not responding quickly enough to the first outbreaks of disorder; and recommended that initial training of police officers should be extended. The Home Secretary accepted the recommendations of the report amid extensive public debate. The Metropolitan Police had already made organisational changes to create the capacity for an immediate response to outbreaks of disorder. Following the publication of the report, they began to make important changes in the field of training and to consult with newly established police committees in some areas. The changes in the field of training largely followed the recommendations of a steering group which reported before the riots of 1981, but were given a further impetus by the publication of Lord Scarman's report.

There was further, serious public disorder in Southall, Liverpool (Toxteth), the Moss Side area of Manchester and the West Midlands in July 1981, which was briefly considered but not fully reviewed in Lord Scarman's report. On the night of the 15 to 16 July the police carried out raids on 11 premises in Railton Road, Brixton, acting on information that stores of petrol bombs were being kept there. A total of 567 officer were used in the operation, more than the total operational strength of some provincial police forces deployed in a single street. One hundred and seventy-six officers actually entered premises. On the following morning serious allegations of police misconduct were made through the media, mostly relating to extensive damage to property. No petrol bombs were found at the time, though the police investigation that followed into the events and allegations found one cache of petrol bombs on waste ground behind one of the properties raided.

In the midst of these developments, the Metropolitan Police made major shifts of deployment to try to ensure that they could respond more swiftly, in future, to outbreaks of public disorder. From April 1981 large numbers of officers were held in reserve at all times in central London (some of these took part in the Brixton raids). This was clearly unsatisfactory since officers in the reserve were bound to be doing nothing most of the time. In the Summer of 1981 the force therefore moved towards establishing locally based 'immediate response units', groups of about a dozen officers equipped with shields and helmets riding in transit vans with reinforced windows. From March 1982 these units were reorganised and encouraged to engage in normal police work when not required to deal with disturbances.

In February 1981, the Home Secretary initiated a study of the incidence of racial attacks, and a report was produced by the Home Office Research Unit in November of that year. In his foreword to that report, the Home Secretary wrote that 'the study has shown quite clearly that the anxieties expressed about racial attacks are justified. Racially motivated attacks, particularly on Asians, are more common that we had supposed; and there are indications that they may be on the increase'. In response to these findings, he intended to adopt new policies for the recording of racial attacks, for training police officers to investigate them and for consultation with representatives of the ethnic minorities affected.

Throughout January and February 1982 the BBC ran a series of documentary films on day-to-day policing in the Thames Valley Force, which attracted 10 million viewers each Monday night and stimulated very extensive comment in the press. In contrast to drama series like 'Z Cars' this series gave most viewers a new, if limited, insight into what police work was really like. In some cases this caused great indignation against the police (particularly the interview of a woman who claimed she had been raped) but public opinion polls suggested that the series as a whole had, if anything, increased public confidence in the police force.

In March 1982 the Metropolitan Police published crime statistics showing analyses, for very limited categories of crime, by the ethnic group of the offender or suspect. This seemed like an effort by the police to rally support for a drive against types of street crime that are often committed by young black people, who had been prominent in the public disturbances over the previous 12 months. This publication was attended by a mass of publicity suggesting, mostly in totally misleading terms, that there was an unprecedented rise in 'serious crime' and that black people were largely responsible. To the more reflective observer, the episode served to highlight the large discretion that the police have to control the flow of information about the nature of crime and the pattern of their own activities.

It is against this background that PSI's programme of research was carried out. In December 1979 PSI produced an outline proposal for the research after a very general discussion of the issues with the Commander, A7 Branch (Community Relations) at Scotland Yard and some of his staff. The proposals were accepted in substance, and after further discussions with A7 Branch, again of a general nature, PSI produced more detailed proposals. The Metropolitan Police did not seek to influence or guide the institute as to the form or substance of the proposals, except by defining at the outset the broad field of 'relations between the Metropolitan Police and the community it serves'. They accepted the proposals without questioning any substantive points. It was formally agreed that PSI would publish the findings in full. Draft reports would be submitted to the Commissioner well in advance of publication. PSI undertook to correct any errors of fact and to remove information from confidential police records if the Commissioner judged that its release would be improper. PSI also undertook to take note of the Commissioner's comments, but it was agreed that the institute would have the final say in deciding on the interpretation and emphasis within the published reports. The Metropolitan Police agreed to grant PSI full access to police buildings, vehicles, personnel and records. The Special Branch was, however, to be excluded from the scope of the study.

In the event PSI was granted access on the agreed terms. In some cases detailed arrangements had to be negotiated with the particular senior officers responsible, but the results of such negotiations were in all cases satisfactory, and no serious blocks were encountered.

In the original proposal, PSI said that it would be strongly in favour of having some funding for the project from an independent source. After the project was well under way, the City Parochial Foundation agreed to make a substantial grant towards the study. The greater part of the expense was covered by the Metropolitan Police.

**General plan of the research**
There was an element of studied ambiguity in the way the

Metropolitan Police defined the broad field of inquiry as to whether they were interested, primarily, in relations with ethnic minority groups. This ambiguity is built into the structure of the organisation itself, since there is a central branch responsible for 'community relations' which may be interpreted broadly to mean relations with the public generally, or more narrowly to mean relations with ethnic minorities (as implied by the names of bodies like Community Relations Councils). In practice, a high proportion of the work of A7 Branch is concerned specifically with ethnic minorities – a much higher proportion than would be expected from their actual numbers in the population of London. PSI took the initiative in placing the emphasis as follows.

> The research will be particularly concerned with relations between the police and members of ethnic minority groups, but this should be seen in the context of relations with the public at large. Policing strategies and practices must be understood in a general way before their implications for relationships with particular communities can be analysed. Also, the responses of individuals to the police may not always critically depend on the ethnic groups to which the two parties belong; it would be wrong to start from the assumption that ethnic differences are paramount. This implies that the research should be designed to provide detailed information about members of ethnic minority groups and their relations with the police, and about areas of medium and high ethnic concentration, but that reliable information about the general public living in all kinds of area within the Metropolitan Police District should also be provided[1].

The chief subjects to be covered were defined as 'policing strategies, as officially prescribed and as carried out on the ground; the factual information, analysis and accepted wisdom on which they are based; how they affect relations with the public at large and with ethnic minority groups' and 'how the police actually behave in situations of contact with the public, and how people respond'. This was to be seen in the context of the attitudes of the police and the public towards one another, taking into account the differences among police officers doing different kinds of job and among people of different ages, living in different areas, and belonging to different groups. The proposal stated clearly that 'It will be an objective of the project to examine the current policies of the Metropolitan Police in the light of the findings ... and to make suggestions for changes of policy as appropriate'.

From the beginning we thought it essential that the research should take account of several different and sometimes conflicting

---

(1)  PSI proposal, December 1979.

perspectives. How the police actually behave in situations of contact with the public and how people respond can be described from the perspective of the police officers concerned, from the perspective of the person or people involved, and from the perspective of an independent observer. The basic plan of the research was that there should be separate but related studies adopting each of these perspectives, and that the final assessment should come from balancing the information from each one against the others.

If we were to make suggestions for changes of policy, it was also essential that we should study the police as an organisation and describe the social setting in which police officers operate. Here we started from the assumption that a study of individual psychology would not be the most useful approach to understanding police behaviour. Even if some aspects of police behaviour can be best understood in terms of the kinds of people who tend to be recruited into the force and the assumptions, attitudes and individual responses that they bring with them, it is unlikely that an understanding in such terms would lead to practical proposals for change in the short or medium term, since the composition of the force can change only slowly if at all and it would be extremely difficult to change the personality or deeply held attitudes of the individuals in the force at any one time. By contrast, even a cursory examination is enough to show that the force does have the capacity to change its structure, systems and management methods in some cases remarkably quickly (even if such changes sometimes turn out to be more superficial than they at first appear). Further, it is very soon evident that the way in which individual police officers behave is heavily dependent on the structures within which they are working: on the ways in which they have to account for their actions, on the goals that they are set (if any), on how the organisation rewards merit and punishes faults, on what the organisation explictly and implicitly defines as good and bad policing, on the structure of the groups in which police officers work and on the ways in which their work is supervised. From the outset we therefore saw a study of the organisation as the key to an understanding of police behaviour that would be both intrinsically enlightening and likely to lead to constructive suggestions for change.

In order to meet the requirements of this general plan, the following four research projects were carried out.

1. A survey of Londoners to establish a set of detailed facts about the extent and nature of contact with the police (from the viewpoint of members of the public) and to relate these actual reported experiences to attitudes towards the police and knowledge of police activities among the same individuals.

2. A study, by means of participant observation, of a group of young black people. Here the objective was to focus on one

particular group who are thought to be often in conflict with the police and hostile towards them. The findings must be set out in the wider context of the findings from the survey of Londoners as a whole. The method of participant observation allows for a deeper and more intensive study of attitudes towards the police and of the experiences and patterns of life that underlie them than is possible by means of a formal survey.

3. A survey of police officers (up to the rank of inspector) by means of a self-completion questionnaire. This survey provides a general description of the pattern of police work, detailed information about recent incidents and the way they were handled, a picture of the career pattern, and an assessment of the constraints and goals which set the framework for police work, seen from the officers' point of view.

4. Study of the police as an organisation and observations of the police at work and of their interactions with the public. The chief methods of research used under this head were:

a)   visits to six police districts by two researchers, who accompanied police officers on the job for long periods, informally interviewed senior officers and looked at local records, statistics and paperwork;
b)   a similar attachment to the Special Patrol Group;
c)   observation of the classes of 60 recruits at Training School during their period of initial training, and formal interviews with all of them; observation of recruit selection boards;
d)   informal interviews of a range of senior officers with specialist functions;
e)   study of reports of the Force Inspectorate and of certain internal statistics;
f)   a study of four examples of major policy changes that occurred during the period of the research, by reading the relevant internal reports and the minutes of the appropriate committees.

The findings from these four studies were published in November 1983 as four volumes under the general title Police and People in London. The present edition brings together Volumes I and VI of the original edition, that is A Survey of Londoners and The Police in Action. The detailed findings from Volume II (A group of young black people) and III (A survey of police officers) are omitted from the present edition. However, the Conclusions and Recommendations at the end of the present volume takes in the findings from all four parts of the study.

6

## Relationship between the Metropolitan Police and the Institute

A7 Branch was responsible for arranging the facilities that the institute required to carry out the research; consequently, there was regular liaison between that branch and the institute. At an early stage there were two meetings between representatives of the institute and the Commissioner (along with other senior officers) when matters of a very general kind were discussed. It became plain that the Commissioner had emphasised his personal authority for the decision that the study should go ahead, and in these circumstances the research team met little, if any, manifest opposition from central departments or at any senior level.

In setting up each district visit, A7 Branch would contact the local Commander and privately explain the nature of the study and of the arrangements being made to facilitate PSI's research. Members of the research team would then meet the Commander, usually with a representative of A7 Branch present, explain the basis of the study in greater detail and make the detailed arrangements for the visit. A similar procedure was followed where the research team required access to central branches or departments (such as Training School, the Force Inspectorate or the Special Patrol Group). Full cooperation was always extended by senior officers at these initial meetings and was followed by genuine efforts to make the facilities available. Where difficulties were encountered it was always at a much lower level in the hierarchy (very rarely above the rank of Inspector).

Formal requests to see records and files were never refused, though because of limitations of time and resources the scope for examining such material was by no means exhausted within the present study.

A7 Branch were sent specific proposals for the survey of Londoners at an early stage, but did not comment in detail. They did comment (along with the Force Psychologist) on draft questionnaires at various stages of their development. While these comments were helpful, they were not a major influence on the design of the questionnaire, and the research team was not persuaded to make any changes that seemed undesirable. Members of A7 Branch attended the briefings of interviewers for this survey but did not speak.

By contrast, the design and planning of the survey of police officers was carried out in close consultation with A7 Branch, and the final plans and questionnaire were only approved after the Assistant Commissioner, A Department had been consulted. The Head of the research team also attended a long meeting with Police Federation representatives. The objective of those involved on the side of the Metropolitan Police seemed to be to arrive at a questionnaire and method of carrying out the survey that would be acceptable to the majority of police officers. Since this objective was shared by the research team, there was no fundamental conflict, although there were different opinions about what most potential respondents to the survey would find acceptable. The

7

result of the negotiations was that the questionnaire was generally much improved, and some highly sensitive questions were omitted(2). It is a moot point whether their inclusion would have been wise or would have produced useful results.

The study of a group of young black people was carried out without any consultation with the Metropolitan Police, although they knew that it was going ahead. Stephen Small, who carried out that study, was arrested while taking part in and observing a march that took place on 2 March 1981 in response to the Deptford fire. He was charged with obstructing a police officer, but after a number of adjournments the case against him was eventually dismissed. The Head of the research team immediately informed the Acting Commissioner (the Commissioner was away in the USA) that Stephen Small had been arrested. In a subsequent meeting between the Director of PSI (John Pinder) the Head of the research team (David Smith) and the Assistant Commissioner, A Department (Mr W H Gibson) the matter was discussed at length. David Smith also discussed the matter extensively with the Commander, A7 Branch, Mr M A Ferguson. It was eventually agreed that all of the research would continue as planned, but PSI undertook that members of the research team would not attend 'public order events' to carry out observations without first informing A7 Branch, who would arrange for them to be accompanied by a police officer in plain clothes. The purpose of these arrangements was to minimise the possibility of a further arrest of a member of the research team during the conduct of the research.

Before the research began, Scotland Yard carried out security checks on members of the research team who were to have access to police facilities (this excluded Stephen Small because he was to have no such access). When the checks had been carried out, A7 Branch said the force had no objections to any members of the team.

### The issues addressed by the study
It is generally accepted wisdom that the police are dependent on the support of the public. One important reason why the Met decided to initiate this study, as we understand it, was that they feared they might be losing support among some sections of the population, and wished to know how far this was true, why it was happening and what could be done about it.

Although there is some truth in the platitude that 'the police are dependent on the support of the public', the formulation is too simple and does not go far enough. The police are not, for the most part, the prime movers, the initiators of the societal pro-

---

(2) These would have asked police officers to say whether they would suppress evidence about police misconduct or fabricate evidence to secure a conviction in certain closely defined circumstances.

cesses that control deviant behaviour; on the contrary, they work, for the most part, at the margins, where the usual processes of control have broken down. Most of the time they are responding to direct requests from individuals or other agencies, and even then they can only act effectively where the assumptions and values that govern their actions are more generally shared. Even within that small proportion of their total activity in which they appear to be taking the initiative, the police act as a continuation and development (by specialists) of more general efforts by the mass of people and institutions to maintain order, control and coherence. In other words, the police are a small but extremely important element within a much larger complex of inter-related systems of control. They require support, though not uncritical support or unthinking obedience; for they themselves are only supporting (not initiating or directing) the wider forms of social control.

## The limited role of the police

Among all the forms of organisation and procedures that combine to control behaviour the police have a limited, yet decisive, role to play. This can best be illustrated by taking a concrete example.

There are $12\frac{1}{2}$ million domestic credit customers of the British Gas Corporation. Most of these receive quarterly bills in arrears, though some have made arrangements for their banks to make monthly payments. A study by Richard Berthoud has shown that three-quarters of these customers pay the bill before receiving a reminder[3]. In one-quarter of cases a procedure is set in motion to 'bring the customer into line'. The first step is to send a final notice. A further 18.8 per cent of customers pay after receiving this notice. The remaining 5.6 per cent are sent a 'disconnection notice' stating that unless the customer pays within seven days the supply will be disconnected. For those who have still not paid within a period generally well in excess of seven days, the next step is that a debt collector (an employee of the Gas Region) calls at the address. In many cases the customer pays on the spot, or promises to pay very shortly and does so or comes to some arrangement with the debt collector. In the very small number of remaining cases the debt collector returns to disconnect the supply. If there is nobody in he leaves a notice stating that the Gas Region will apply for a warrant giving it the authority to effect entry in order to disconnect. If someone present denies entry, the debt collector tells him that the Board will apply for a warrant. In practice, the proportion of cases that lead to disconnection is only 0.074 per cent though the study shows that these cases involve substantial hardship. The debt collector usually goes to the premises alone or with a locksmith or other colleague. Where he has reason to expect physical resistance or abuse from

---

(3)   Richard Berthoud, Fuel Debts and Hardship, Policy Studies Institute, 1981.

the customer, he may ask for a police officer to accompany him. Although we do not know in precisely what proportion of cases a police officer is present, we can be sure that it is very small. Among customers who had been disconnected, only 11 per cent made any comment that implied that they were unhappy about the way in which the disconnection had been carried out, and only three per cent said they had attempted to refuse access or that there had been a struggle. In seems, therefore, that a police officer was likely to be present in less than five per cent of cases where the supply was disconnected, or in less than one in every 30,000 of all cases.

This example shows that a majority of people pay their gas bills without any prompting. The Gas Boards have worked out an elaborate procedure to bring the remainder into line. This procedure is remarkably successful in making nearly everyone conform. In a very small proportion of cases the Gas Region resorts to disconnection, and only in a very small proportion of these cases does it call on the help of the police to enforce the warrant. The first agent of social control is the belief among the great majority of customers that they ought to pay their bills within a reasonable period. The second is the Gas Region, which uses a system of 'rituals' to bring increasing pressure to bear at each stage. The third agent is the police; they are involved very rarely and only at the request of the Gas Region. Of course, the fact that a police officer may ultimately come to help enforce a warrant is an important deterrent, but the less often it is used the more effective it is. If large numbers of people refused to pay after repeated demands, the police would find it difficult to enforce disconnection notices. However, as long as most people conform, at least when some pressure has been brought to bear on them by other agents, the police can effectively deal with the few remaining cases. They are the last resort in a long process of social control.

Another example of the limited, yet decisive, role of the police is in the control of disruptive behaviour in schools. The example is particularly interesting because such a high proportion of the incidents that the police deal with concern children and young people. Many fights and scuffles take place in schools, which might in other circumstances be interpreted as minor assaults. There is also a considerable amount of damage to school property (most of it minor damage) and a fair number of thefts. The schools have their own systems of rewards and punishments for trying to prevent this kind of behaviour and dealing with it when it does occur. They also have links with parents through which they try to use the family to reinforce the codes of conduct applied at school. The vast majority of fights, thefts and incidents involving deliberate damage to property are dealt with by the school procedures and within the family. There is always, implicitly, a threat that a matter may be reported to the police if the offender does not step into line, but in practice the police are informed in a very small proportion of cases (though we do not know what the proportion is). Even when they are informed, they will not take action unless the school or other loser decides to press a charge. Thus, schools and families not only bear the main responsibility for controlling the behaviour of children, but they also largely decide when the police shall be involved and whether or not formal proceedings shall be started.

Examples of this kind show that it is mostly not the police but other agencies and individuals that 'set the agenda' for law enforcement. In examples like the ones that have been quoted, there is little danger that the police will lack support, because it is hard for them to be out of step with the limited and specific demands that are being made, or with the expectations of the people involved (even of the offenders). However, where the police do take the initiative - for example, by stopping and searching a large number of people more or less at random in Brixton - they cannot be responding to a specific request, they are 'defining the agenda' themselves, and there is no built-in mechanism to ensure that what they are doing fits in with the expectations of the majority or with the practices of the other agencies in society that are responsible for controlling deviant behaviour most of the time. The danger is that if the police come to initiate more of their activity themselves they will become detached and isolated from the people they are supposed to be helping, unless ways can be found of involving people outside the police force in the decision-making.

## What comes to be defined as crime

It is commonly said that Parliament and the courts determine what the law is and the police enforce it. This, again, is a description that greatly over-estimates the scope of the role of the police. In practice, it is mainly people and institutions that determine what shall be treated as a crime, that is, what matters will form the subject of criminal proceedings, and the police have to work within the interpretation that originates from the wider society.

Discussion of this matter tends to be obscured by shifting definitions of 'crime'. An important source of confusion is the presentation of the results of victim surveys as showing that there is a large volume of 'unreported crime', by which is meant incidents which, if they had been reported, might have formed the basis for criminal proceedings. This obscures the fact that by not reporting the incident the victim has made one of the all-important decisions that mainly determine what kinds of things will be dealt with by the criminal machinery. In many cases, the victim chose to deal with the matter in some other way and thus tacitly decided not to classify the incident as a crime.

On the narrowest definition, a crime has been committed when a court finds someone guilty of it, or finds that a crime was committed by a person or persons unknown. If we stick to this definition we are saying that an act only becomes a criminal

11

offence when it is declared to be so at the end of a formal legal procedure, just as two people become man and wife only when a valid religious ceremony or civil procedure has been performed.

A much wider definition of criminal offences would be acts which are so defined by common or statute law. However, acts which do not become the subject of legal proceedings can only be called criminal offences in a hypothetical sense. If they are called criminal, then what is being said is that if good evidence were available, if the suspect could be brought to face trial (or an inquest held), if the prosecution were competently conducted and (perhaps) the defence not brilliant, then someone would probably be found guilty of an offence (or an inquest would find that an offence had been committed). Or perhaps, still more broadly, what is being said is that 'this looks like an act which in some circumstances might well form the subject of criminal proceedings'. In the case of victim surveys, anything that a respondent 'thought might be a criminal offence' is generally counted as if it was one.

There is a multitude of reasons why many acts which might be considered criminal in the loosest sense are never found to be so by a court.

a) Nobody knew that the act took place except the 'offender'.

b) Nobody who knew about it interpreted the act as criminal.

c) Though aware that the act might be interpreted as criminal, nobody chose to interpret it that way.

d) The loser found ways of controlling or stopping the unwanted behaviour that were more effective, easier or cheaper than reporting it.

e) The loser could not control the behaviour but considered it a trivial matter.

f) For any other reason, the matter was not reported to the authorities.

g) The police decided not to treat it as a criminal matter although it could have been treated in that way.

h) The police ignored the fact that the act was manifestly taking place or decided to deal with it somehow without taking proceedings.

i) Evidence to support a prosecution was not actively sought.

j) Evidence to support a prosecution could not be obtained after serious attempts.

k) The offender could not be caught.

l) The prosecution failed at some stage.

Because the criminal procedure is complex, lengthy and uncertain there are often strong reasons for individuals, for organisations and for the police to deal with particular incidents in some other way. This applies particularly to relatively minor matters.

12

The number of instances of theft of office supplies, of fraudulent use of the firm's telephone or of minor assaults that 'actually occur' must be very large indeed in relation to the number of cases of that kind that come to court. Police officers ignore motorists who are speeding or who jump traffic lights in a very large number of cases. Private acts that are theoretically offences (for example, sexual offences) will never come to light unless one of the participants objects to them. It does not make much sense to call this 'the dark figure of unreported crime', if only because it is not a definable quantity.

More interesting and important than any of these are offences that are intentionally defined vaguely to give the police discretionary powers or the citizen a recourse to the law in extreme cases. The most obvious examples are 'threatening, abusive or insulting words or behaviour with intent to provoke a breach of the peace, or whereby a breach of the peace may be occasioned'; 'resisting or obstructing a Constable in the execution of his duty'; 'obstructing the free passage along a highway'. These are charges which the police 'use' when they judge that it is necessary - maybe as a last resort. Technically, they could probably be brought much more often than they are, but nobody could ever say how many 'unreported' cases of obstructing a police officer there were. If such charges were used more often, the attitudes of the courts would probably change, so that the chances of conviction would decrease. It is, therefore, impossible to say how many potentially 'good' cases of obstructing a police officer there are which are never brought to court. Offences of this kind make it particularly plain that the criminal law is something that it is open to the police and the citizen to use if they so choose, and not something that classifies all behaviour according to whether it is 'criminal' or not.

A particularly problematic class of behaviour is acts performed by individuals as part of a crowd. At a rowdy football match or demonstration the police may make a number of arrests, but for every person arrested there are generally ten others who have done the same sort of thing or worse. Furthermore, the police decision as to whether to make any arrests and if so how many to make may often be determined by tactical considerations - the objective being to keep the peace - rather than by how many individuals have done things which might be construed as offences. In these circumstances it becomes meaningless to talk about 'how much crime' is committed at a rowdy football match, as opposed to how disorderly it was.

How crime is defined in the philosophical sense is an important question, but what is more important for this study is how it is decided whether incidents shall become the subject of criminal proceedings. What this preliminary discussion has shown is that people and institutions, as opposed to the police, often play the leading role in making this decision, though cases in which the police play the leading role are extremely important. This means

13

that what is to be treated as crime - to be processed through the criminal machinery - is largely determined not by the police but by the wider society (within the framework of the limits set by the law as interpreted in the courts). Secondly, whoever makes the decision, a wide scope for choice or the exercise of discretion is generally available to them. Once the legal process is set in motion, the sequence of moves is largely determined by the rules of the game as defined by the law and interpreted in the courts. But the fundamental point is that the participants very often decide not to play this game at all, and in making these decisions they strongly influence what comes to be treated as crime and hence the nature and pattern of police work.

## Police discretion

It follows from what has already been said that the police, like other citizens, have wide scope for the exercise of discretion in deciding whether a particular incident shall become the subject of criminal proceedings. A superficial look at police work is enough to show that any patrolling police officer ignores a large number of offences or potential offences on every working day. In central London he walks past many illegally parked vehicles, drives behind speeding cars, walks past shops openly selling hard-core pornography, sees prostitutes soliciting, knows of many clubs selling liquor and providing gaming facilities without a licence, goes past unlicensed street traders, and so on, usually without taking any immediate action. Where he does take action over any one of these matters, this will usually occupy him for a considerable period, so that in the meantime he can do nothing about the others. This means that, far from 'enforcing the law' in a straightforward way, every police officer must constantly make decisions about which particular offences he should do something about. The way in which these decisions are taken is of paramount importance, and forms one of the major subjects of study in this project.

A very large area of discretion surrounds the incidents or practices that the police officer observes himself, but discretion is exercised in other important ways as well. Where a matter is reported to the police, or members of the public make a request, the police quite often have considerable scope for choice in deciding how to respond. In a considerable number of cases they may try to deal with the matter to the satisfaction of those concerned without invoking the criminal process, where they could nevertheless have treated the matter as a crime. Again, the way that the officer handles a situation may itself determine whether a crime is committed: for example, if there is a group of young men behaving in a rowdy but not (so far) dangerous manner, a skilful officer may persuade them to disperse, while a less skilful or malicious one may behave in such a way that one of them commits an offence against him and more or less 'has to be' arrested. In any situation involving large crowds, as has already been mentioned, the police have very wide scope for discretion in deciding how many arrests to make and whom to arrest. Also, there are many cases where, given that the police have decided to charge a person with something, they still have considerable scope for choice in deciding what particular charge or charges to bring.

Because this very wide scope for choice exists, and because there are so many more potential offences than the police or the courts could possibly cope with, there is bound to be, implicitly or explicitly, a set of policing policies and strategies that embody a set of priorities. One of the principal objectives of the study is to understand how these priorities are formed and how expressed on the ground. Two particular aspects of this are important. The first is the way in which the structure of the organisation effectively imposes a given pattern of policing: if a large proportion of officers are put in a specialist traffic division, then priority will effectively be given to traffic offences; if officers tend to be rewarded for making arrests for possession of cannabis, then the number of arrests of this kind will tend to increase, particularly if the laboratory facilities for analysing drugs are expanded. To the extent that the organisation tends to impose a pattern, the available discretion is disposed of at a high level by decisions about the structure of the Force. To the extent that it does not, room is left for individual officers to exercise their own discretion, and we have to consider whether there are ways of checking that they do so according to general policy objectives.

The second aspect is the relation between the way that the police exercise their discretion and the assumptions and values within the wider society. It is an important objective of the study to establish how far the assumptions and values implicit in policing policy and practice fit in or conflict with those implicit in the wider socieity, which bears the greater part of the responsibility for deciding when and how the criminal process should be invoked. If there are conflicts, it is important for the study to consider what structures and procedures either within the police force or more widely would help to reconcile such differences. The major difficulty here is that the police have an equal responsibility to every citizen, but the wider society embraces many different groups which may have sharply different expectations and make conflicting demands on them.

### Accountability of the police
There need to be mechanisms that try to achieve a measure of harmony between how the police behave (how they exercise their discretion) and how people expect and wish them to. Enlightened self-interest on the part of the police will tend to bring this about only as long as they share the assumptions and expectations of the majority. If they see themselves as a threatened minority they may not do so.

Whatever the mechanism is, it will tend to be seen within the police force as a means of obtaining public support for the policies and practices that they believe are right; and outside the police force as a means of ensuring that policing policy is adapted to meet public expectations. The outcome will be accommodation, a bargain struck between these different interests.

Discussion of the issue has tended to centre on the idea of accountability: to the law, to a code of practice (the Judges' Rules) and to the police authorities as representatives of the people. It is an important objective of the study to establish what these kinds of accountability mean in practice, that is, how effectively they actually constrain or otherwise influence policing behaviour. However, it is necessary to recognise that account-ability, interpreted in these terms, is largely a set of more or less effective negative constraints. We are concerned, in this study, with how the kind of policing that people want can be encouraged as well as with how the kind of policing they don't want can be stopped or prevented. In this context, the concept of account-ability may be too narrow, especially if it turns out that imposing further external constraints on the police is ineffective or even makes it more difficult to encourage good policing practice.

## Theory and practice of policing

In recent years both academics and senior police officers have begun to put foward ambitious social theories that seek to explain how policing works in terms of cause-and-effect relationships between particular styles of policing and the capacity of the 'community' at large to control and prevent deviant behaviour. All such theories go well beyond the available facts, and will have to wait many years for confirmation or disproof. While they may try to explain too much, such theories do recognise the fact that the police are only a part of a much wider set of social processes. They assume that no method of policing will ever result in the direct detection by police officers of more than a small proportion of crime, and that the police can therefore be effective only by working with, through or on the other mechanisms of control in society. The argument is that appropriate methods of policing can have a catalytic effect in accelerating the development of stronger social norms and of more effective (and pervasive) 'policing' by ordinary citizens and by organisations outside the police force. That this can happen remains to be proved, and that it would be desirable is not self-evident.

More specifically, there is increasing evidence to show how features of the physical and social environment influence the level of crime by extending or denying the opportunity for it and by facilitating or obstructing attempts to prevent it. Among factors that must surely have an influence on the level of crime are the design of housing estates, the planning of transport systems, the layout of shops, the arrangements for car parking, the design and siting of equipment like public telephones and the ways in which salaries, pensions and benefits are paid. New theories of policing seek to show how the police can ensure, through continuing liaison with the appropriate groups and bodies, that crime prevention objectives are built into the decision-making in these fields.

In this study we have no wish to arrive at a general theory of policing. The emphasis is not so much on what kind of policing works as on what kind we have got, how far it is acceptable to people and, perhaps most important, why it is as it is, and hence how it could be changed if changes were required. We make the assumption that the kind of policing we have is largely a function of the way the force is structured and organised and of its relationship with the wider society, and that there is a formidable amount of inertia in the system. Apparently radical changes frequently prove to have made little difference in the end because the basic structure of the organisation has remained the same, and people - police officers - contrive to bend the new procedures to fit their usual practice. We suspect that, without having any ambitious theory, it would be relatively easy to argue coherently in favour of certain priorities and styles of policing, but formidably difficult to introduce them in practice, that is, to change the day-to-day behaviour of the 25,000 officers in the force. At the end of this series of studies we shall try to address the most important question, which is what determines police behaviour, and how can it, in practice, be changed.

# A SURVEY OF LONDONERS

# I INTRODUCTION

There are two main thrusts of inquiry within the survey of Londoners. The first is into the experiences that people have had that might have brought them into contact with the police or actually did so. These include incidents where people were looking to the police for help or advice, where they observed the police in action for example during public disturbances and where they were treated by the police as offenders or suspects; and incidents of social or casual contact. The questioning aims to establish how the police handled the matter and what the individual thought of the way they handled it in that specific instance. The second line of inquiry is into people's attitudes to crime, their willingness to make use of the police, their views about policing methods, priorities and success and their assessment of the standard of police conduct. These two lines of inquiry are brought together in an analysis that shows how people's experiences are related to the views they express.

The likelihood that someone will come into conflict with the police is strongly related to his age and to the kind of area in which he lives, and men are much more likely than women to be in conflict with them. Whatever the actual incidence of conflict, it is widely believed to be higher among ethnic minorities, especially those of West Indian origin, than among whites. The survey was, therefore, designed to provide a separate analysis of the experience and views of men and women belonging to different age and ethnic groups and living in different types of area.

This approach differs from the one used in the many surveys of public opinion, some carried out since the disturbances of 1981, which show that a solid majority of people think that 'the police are doing a good job on the whole' or that police officers are better regarded than engineers, dentists or schoolmasters. The difference lies in the intensiveness of the questioning and analysis and in the specific level on which the discussion takes place. By including exhaustive questioning on personal experience, by tying questioning on matters of opinion to specific aspects of policing policy and practice and by carrying out separate analysis of different groups, we can try to catch the true variety of experience and opinions,

19

which cannot be adequately summarised as 'for' or 'against' or justifiably rolled out into a bland average.

Some limitations are inherent in the survey method, which is why the findings from the present survey must be balanced against those from other parts of this programme of research. The greatest difficulty, particularly in a survey on this subject, is the strong tendency for people to rationalise their experience and rearrange their perceptions to make the world a more comfortable place for them to live in. For some people, and it is a fair assumption that they are a minority, there is a positive need to see the police in an unfavourable light. Revolutionary groups, for example, and those who see themselves as outcasts, regard the present authorities as illegitimate and need to believe that they are violent and corrupt. For the great majority, the pressure is very strongly in the opposite direction. To ask them whether they think the police are fair, honest and moderate in their use of force is rather like asking patients as they are wheeled into the operating theatre whether they think that surgeons are competent. If they are not, we really have a problem, because we all know that we might be 'wheeled into the theatre' at any time, and any lapse from standards by the police officer or surgeon could have extremely serious consequences for ourselves. Beyond that, for a people which particularly prides itself on the maturity of its democratic institutions, any serious criticism of the police force seems like a denial of what is most characteristically British. We can sense the resistance to any such denial in a phrase like 'The British police are still the best in the world', in which the word 'still' is made into the vehicle for an underlying anxiety. The danger is that the survey will record the pious hopes, the rationalisations, the overt expressions of support or condemnation, without catching the inflexions of doubt, if any are there.

Our approach to the problem was to ask many questions that together challenge people to think seriously about their own experience and the issues involved. In practice, people's views do not fall out into the crude dichotomy so clearly projected in the popular press, between the police as corrupt, unjust, violent, and the police as heroic figures who also help old ladies across the road; and the findings do open a small window looking over and beyond the rationalisations towards a more realistic view of what people know, believe and feel.

**Outline of the method**

The survey was carried out among a sample of 2,420 people, designed to be representative of all aged 15 or over in the Metropolitan Police District. This area - the one covered by the Metropolitan Police - includes the whole of Greater London except for the City of London (which has a separate police force) and some areas at the fringes outside the GLC boundaries. The boundaries were originally intended (in 1965) to be the same as those of the GLC, but changes to the GLC boundaries were made after the boundaries of the MPD had been finalised. The area covered by the survey will be referred to as 'London'.

In a straightforward sample the numbers of young people and members of ethnic minority groups would have been too small for separate analysis. For example, people of Asian and West Indian origin account for only 7.6 per cent of the adult population of London, so that a sample of 2,420 Londoners would contain only 184 of them. The representation of ethnic minorities and of young people was therefore radically boosted in relation to population proportions and to a smaller extent the balance was also shifted towards inner London at the expense of outer London. Population proportions were restored by weighting at the analysis stage. Thus, the final weighted sample is representative of the whole population aged 15 or over, while at the same time there are adequate numbers of the smaller groups for separate analysis.

Informants were interviewed between August and October 1981 in their own homes. Most of the interviews were carried out by an established fieldforce of trained interviewers, predominantly female and white, but special arrangements were made to cover Asians who did not speak English fluently. Four bilingual versions of the questionnaire were produced in English and Urdu, Punjabi, Gujerati, and Bengali. Where necessary, Asian informants were interviewed in the appropriate Asian language by interviewers who were mostly recruited and trained specially for this survey. The questionnaire, which was fully structured, took about one hour to administer on average.

The detailed design and administration of the survey was undertaken by Social and Community Planning Research in close consultation with PSI. The computer analysis was carried out by PSI.

### Sampling and response

The whole sample is made up of two separate ones that have been combined in the analysis: a general sample (of the general population) and a special sample (of people of Asian and West Indian origin). The methods of selection used for the two samples were entirely different.

The general sample is based on 80 polling districts, selected (with probability proportionate to the electorate) to be representative of London. An equal number of addresses was drawn within each polling district from the electoral register, with probability proportionate to the number of electors at the address. The selected addresses were randomly divided into three groups (A, B and C). When the interviewer called at the address, she listed all the people aged 15 or over who were living there. If the address was in group A, she then followed a set procedure for selecting one of the listed people at random and interviewed that person. If the address was in group B, she selected one person aged under 45 for interview, if any were present at the address, and if the address was in group C she selected one person aged under 25 if any were present. At group B and C addresses, no-one was selected for interview if a person within the required age group did not live there. By this method, people in the younger age groups were heavily over-represented. An additional procedure was followed in order to include addresses that do not show up on the electoral register at all. A total of 1,411 informants were interviewed within this general sample.

The method used to establish the special sample of Asians and West Indians was one that has been developed by PSI for a national survey that has recently been carried out. The geographical unit on which the sample is based is the enumeration districts (EDs) used in the 1971 census. These are very small areas containing on average 150 households. Data from the 1971 census shows the number of people living in each ED at that time who were born in the West Indies, India, Pakistan or Bangladesh (referred to as immigrants). At the first stage, 246 of these EDs were selected with equal probabilities. The census data showed that in 136 of the selected EDs the proportion of immigrants in 1971 was lower than two per cent. These low-concentration EDs were excluded from the sample, which had the effect of excluding 13 per cent of immigrants present across the whole set of selected EDs in 1971. This introduces a small bias into the sample, since Asians and West Indians living in EDs containing very few other Asians and West Indians have no chance of being selected. Because the definition of 'immigrant' is different from the definition of people of Asian and West Indian origin used in the survey and because of population movements since 1971, we cannot say exactly what proportion of the Asian and West Indian population was excluded, but a reasonable estimate would be 15 per cent.

Fieldwork then took place in two stages. At the first stage, interviewers identified all of the households in the selected EDs that contained anyone of Asian or West Indian origin aged 15 or over. At each such household, the interviewer made a full list of everyone living there aged 15 or over. After the results of the enumeration had been tabulated, the final sample was selected from the Asians and West Indians enumerated at that stage. No more than two people were selected within the same household. The sampling fractions were radically varied so as to maximise the representation of young people. At the second stage of fieldwork, interviewers were issued with the names of selected individuals. Information was obtained at the first stage about the languages spoken by each person in the household, so that where necessary an interviewer speaking the appropriate language could be sent to carry out the interview. A total of 1,009 people were interviewed within this special sample.

The enumeration was carried out differently according to the level of concentration of immigrants in the ED. In EDs where the concentration was ten per cent or more, the interviewer called at every address. In EDs where the concentration was under ten per cent the method of 'focussed enumeration' was used(1). Essentially, calls were made at every fifth address, where the interviewer asked whether there were any people of Asian or West Indian origin living in the five houses to the right and (separately) in the five houses to the left. Where a gap was said to contain Asians or West Indians by the people living on either side, the interviewer called at all of the intervening addresses. Developmental work has shown that this method identifies more than 90 per cent of all Asians and West Indians living in an area.

The response rate achieved at the main fieldwork stage for the general and special samples combined was 70 per cent. In the case of the special sample, there are some losses associated with the enumeration stage. Not all of these can be measured exactly, but we know that there was a refusal to give any information at three per cent of the addresses covered.

For a number of reasons, the sample design gives rise to the need for weighting at the analysis stage to restore the correct population proportions. The weighting procedure adopted allows the two samples to be merged, so that informants can then be sorted into ethnic (or other) groups, regardless of which sample they came from, according to their answers in the main questionnaire.

Because the details of the methods used will not be of interest to most readers, the full description is given in a separate publication(2).

## Definition of ethnic groups

The ethnic groups have been defined in the same way as in other surveys of minority groups carried out by PSI from the 1970s onwards. The definitions use four kinds of information in combination.

a) The interviewer's assessment, by observation, of the 'race' of the informant. The categories used are: white, black, Indian/Pakistani/Bangladeshi; other non-white; mixed/uncertain.
b) The informant's answer to the following question: 'What country does your family come from originally?' If in doubt, informants are told to refer to their father's father.
c) For those born abroad, their answer to the following question: 'Where were you living in the three months before you came to live in the UK?'
d) Country of birth.

---

(1)  See Colin Brown and Jane Ritchie, Focussed Enumeration, Social and Community Planning Research, 1981.
(2)  Douglas Wood, A Survey of Londoners' Relations with the Police: Technical Report, Social and Community Planning Research, 1984.

African Asians are people classified by the interviewer as looking 'Indian/Pakistani/Bangladeshi'; some were born in Africa; some were born in the Indian sub-continent or in Britain, but say that their family originates from Africa or that they were living in Africa immediately before coming to Britain. The rest of those identified as Asian-looking by the interviewer are classified, on the basis of the 'country of origin' question, into Indians, Pakistanis, Bangladeshis and Sri Lankans. West Indians are defined as those identified by the interviewer as other than 'white' and whose families originate from the West Indies or Guyana. There is a small group of other non-whites - people identified as other than white by the interviewer and not falling into one of the previous groups. The remaining group of whites includes a number of people whose families originate from countries outside the UK or who were themselves born abroad, as well as those whose families originate from the UK and who were themselves born there. Because the classification does not primarily depend on country of birth, descendants of immigrants up to the third generation are counted as belonging to the ethnic group of their parents or grandparents.

## Geographical analysis
The main units of organisation within the Metropolitan Police are Districts; in inner London these generally consist of a single borough, while in outer London they consist of two or three boroughs. Because District Commanders have considerable autonomy, policing policies can vary substantially between one District and another. It would be interesting and useful to analyse the results of a survey of the public according to the particular Police District in which the informants lived, especially if these findings could then be related to known differences in policing between the Districts. Unfortunately, an analysis of this kind would require a much larger sample size than was possible within the present study.

Nevertheless, we can carry out analyses in terms of the types of area in which informants live. Surveys of ethnic minorities have shown very large differences between those living in areas of high and low ethnic concentration, for example in terms of educational level, quality of housing, socio-economic group and fluency in English(3). Asians and West Indians living close to many others belonging to the same groups tend to suffer the greatest disadvantage, while at the same time gaining strength from their relationships with other Asians and West Indians living nearby. It therefore seemed worthwhile to analyse the findings of this survey according to some measure of the local ethnic concentration. The sampling points used in the general sample, which were themselves polling districts, have been classified according to the concentration of

---

(3)    See David J. Smith, Racial Disadvantage in Britain, Penguin Books, 1977.

24

ethnic minorities within the ward in which they fall. The source used for this classification was the National Dwelling and Housing Survey carried out in 1977 and the groups counted in the measure of concentration were, broadly, Asians and West Indians. In the case of the special sample, the sampling points were the census enumeration districts used in 1971, and that census shows the number of people in each ED who were born in India, Pakistan, Bangladesh or the West Indies. This has been used to calculate the concentration of 'immigrants' in the ED. Although the data are out of date, they still serve as a good indicator in an analysis of this kind. Because the measure of ethnic concentration has to be different for the two samples, and is based on different geographical units, all analyses by local ethnic concentration are shown for the two samples separately.

We considered the possibility of carrying out an analysis by the 'crime rate' in the local area: that is, the number of recorded crimes in a recent year divided by the local population. We were surprised to find that the Metropolitan Police do not keep any statistics in the form of crime rates, partly because of practical and partly because of conceptual difficulties. The practical difficulty is that they have no up-to-date estimates of the population of Police Districts or Divisions (and early results of the 1981 census show that there have been large population movements in London over the previous ten years). The conceptual difficulty is that crimes are recorded according to where they are committed, but the offender may come from elsewhere. In central London, certainly, it would not make sense to relate the amount of crime to the size of the resident population. In any case, we had to abandon the project of an analysis in terms of local crime rates because the data are not available.

However, we have been able to make use of a classification of the London boroughs devised by Webber and Craig[4]. Using a wide range of indicators from the 1971 census, they arrived at a taxonomy of local authority areas by means of a principal component analysis. We have made use of his first component (that is, the cluster of characteristics found to discriminate most sharply between local authority areas) which they describe as a measure of 'social dependence'. Essentially, the boroughs that score high on this measure are socially and economically deprived, while those that score low have good housing, low unemployment and a strong middle class element in the population. In our analysis, the London boroughs were classified into four groups according to their score on this dimension, so that we can see whether experience of the police differs between deprived and more middle class areas. Because the London boroughs are quite large - their population is of the order of 150,000 - each one contains a considerable variety,

(4)    See Richard Webber and John Craig, Socio-economic classification of local authority areas, HMSO, 1978.

for example in terms of housing and social class composition. This means that the Webber analysis, at the borough level, is a much blunter instrument than our analysis by local ethnic concentration, which is based on far smaller geographical units.

## Terminology

While there are many distinct ethnic minority groups in London, the two most numerous ones are those originating from the Indian sub-continent and from the West Indies. As explained earlier in this chapter, the sample for the survey of Londoners was designed so that findings for these groups could be shown separately. It is not, unfortunately, possible to show separate findings for the many other ethnic minority groups in London: instead, they all have to be grouped together. The term 'ethnic minority groups' is frequently used in this report to refer to the most numerous groups only (those originating from the Indian sub-continent and from the West Indies).

In general, the terminology used is that appropriate to the time when the survey was carried out (the second half of 1981). For example, the 'immediate response units' referred to in this report are now known as district support units'.

The survey provides information about occasions where a person was the victim of something thought to be a crime and about occasions where a person was stopped by the police. These are referred to as 'victim incidents' and 'stops'. It should be remembered that the same victim incident (say, a burglary) would be reported by all of the victims involved (by everyone living in the house). In this survey, victim incidents are therefore counted once for each person affected, and not (as in crime statistics) once for the incident regardless of how many people are affected. This is different from the practice adopted in the British Crime Survey. We have, however, preferred to avoid the obscure (but more strictly accurate) term 'victim experiences'. Similarly, a number of people may be stopped by the police on the same occasion - they may, for example, all be in the same vehicle. The 'stops' referred to in this survey are experiences of being stopped and not occasions on which one or a group of people were stopped.

## Presentation and layout of tables

Tables are shown close to the point where they are discussed in the text, and a list of these tables is given at the beginning of the report. They are numbered within chapters. The 19 additional tables shown in the Appendix to Volume I of the original edition have been omitted from this edition. Where the table reference is 'Table not shown' this table will be found in the original edition.

Unweighted and weighted bases for percentages are normally shown in tables. The unweighted base is the actual number of records that enter into a column or line, and is useful for calculations of statistical significance. However, all of the actual findings and percentages are based on weighted figures, which

26

reflect the true population proportions in various groups. Bases have sometimes been omitted because of lack of space, but in these cases they have usually been shown elsewhere.

In tables the asterisk is used to denote a non-significant quantity (generally more than zero but less than 0.5 per cent). The dash is used to denote an empty cell (zero). The letters 'NA' appear where no data are available (for example, because the number of cases is too small for useful findings to be shown).

# II  ATTITUDES TO CRIME

## Safety on the streets

The most fundamental objective of policing is to help create a society in which it is safe for people to walk on the streets at all times. We therefore start our inquiry by considering the results of some simple and direct questions about the safety of the streets at night. Towards the beginning of the interview, informants were asked:

> Do you think there are risks for women who go out on their own in this area after dark?
> If yes  Are the risks that something might happen to them serious or are they just slight?
> And do you yourself ever feel worried about going out on your own after dark?

All three questions are about night time, and the first pair are about the risks for women. This was quite deliberate. Questions about the risk to young men at noon would have produced quite different answers, but there is cause for concern if the more vulnerable members of society think there are risks at night time.

A substantial proportion of people (41 per cent) thought in the Autumn of 1981 that there were serious risks for women out on their own at night in the area where the informant lived; and a slightly higher proportion (47 per cent) said they were sometimes worried themselves about going out on their own after dark. Thus, there is a very large body of opinion among the general public that London is unsafe. As Table II.1 shows, women have greater fears than men. A much higher proportion of women than of men say they have fears for themselves (70 per cent compared with 20 per cent). Also, women are rather more likely than men to think the streets are unsafe for women generally; in other words, men do not fear for women as much as women do themselves.

It may be that the disturbances of 1981 had some influence on the answers that people gave, though if so it remains to be seen whether confidence will return in future.

Table II.1      Risks in going out after dark, by sex

| Risks for women | Total | Men | Women |
|---|---|---|---|
| Serious | 41 | 34 | 46 |
| Slight | 30 | 30 | 30 |
| None | 25 | 32 | 19 |
| Don't know/not stated | 4 | 5 | 4 |
| Are you ever worried for yourself | | | |
| Yes | 47 | 20 | 70 |
| No | 51 | 79 | 28 |
| Don't know or not stated | 1 | 1 | 2 |
| Base: all informants | | | |
| (unweighted) | 2,420 | 1,161 | 1,259 |
| (weighted) | 13,944 | 6,297 | 7,648 |

As Table II.2 shows, older people are more likely than younger ones to fear for women and for themselves. As many as 57 per cent of those aged 60 or over say that they are sometimes worried themselves about going out after dark.

The ethnic minorities, as defined in this survey, account for about 11 per cent of the population of the Metropolitan Police District, made up of 3.2 per cent West Indians, 4.4 per cent Asians and 3.3 per cent others. Although they are relatively small groups, the design of this survey allows us to show separate analyses of their views and experiences. Table II.2 shows that West Indians are much less likely than other groups (both whites and ethnic minorities) to have fears about the safety of the streets; for example, only 28 per cent of West Indians compared with 48 per cent of whites and 52 per cent of Asians say they are sometimes worried themselves about going out at night. The contrast does not arise mainly because West Indians are a younger group than whites for the difference remains when similar age groups are compared. For example, among those aged 45 or over, 49 per cent of whites compared with only 24 per cent of West Indians say they sometimes fear for themselves. The difference between West Indians and Asians is not connected with age at all, since the two groups have similar age profiles. These findings may reflect a feeling among West Indians that they are being made the scapegoats for street crime; they may wish to deny that a serious problem exists because their own group is held responsible for the problem.

There are strong indications that the safety of the streets at night is a most important aspect of the way that people regard the areas in which they live. At an earlier question, people were asked

Table II.2    Risks in going out after dark, by age and country of origin

Column percentages

| | | | Age | | | | Country of origin | | |
| | 15-19 | 20-24 | 25-44 | 45-59 | 60 and over | Whites | West Indian | Asian | Other non-whites |
|---|---|---|---|---|---|---|---|---|---|
| The risks for women are serious | 25 | 36 | 40 | 40 | 50 | 42 | 24 | 30 | 28 |
| I am sometimes worried for myself | 42 | 42 | 48 | 39 | 57 | 48 | 28 | 52 | 49 |
| Base: all informants | | | | | | | | | |
| (unweighted) | 490 | 494 | 844 | 345 | 247 | 1,252 | 511 | 541 | 116 |
| (weighted) | 1,278 | 1,332 | 5,174 | 2,910 | 3,252 | 12,428 | 450 | 607 | 459 |

Note:    The table shows findings from two separate questions. In each case, the balance of informants
gave one of the other answers shown in Table II.1.

30

Table II.3    Risks in going out after dark, by satisfaction with the area

Column percentages

|  | Very satis- fied | Fairly satis- fied | A bit dissatis- fied | Very dissatis- fied |
|---|---|---|---|---|
| The risks for women are serious | 28 | 44 | 54 | 76 |
| I am sometimes worried for myself | 41 | 47 | 60 | 72 |
| Base: all informants (unweighted) | 869 | 1,166 | 259 | 114 |
| (weighted) | 5,695 | 5,692 | 1,712 | 767 |

whether they felt satisfied or dissatisfied about living in this area of London. The absolute level of satisfaction is not particularly interesting, since there is such a strong tendency for people to make the best of things: in fact, 41 per cent said they were 'very satisfied', a further 41 per cent said they were 'fairly satisfied' and only 12 per cent that they were 'a bit dissatisfied' and 6 per cent that they were 'very dissatisfied'. However, it is useful to look at the relationship between the level of expressed satisfaction and other facts or views about the area. Table II.3 shows that there is a very strong relationship between how satisfied people are with the area and how safe they think the streets are at night; in fact, among those who are 'very dissatisfied' with the area, 76 per cent think there are serious risks for women going out alone at night, compared with only 28 per cent of those who are 'very satisfied'. This remarkably strong relationship suggests that the safety of the streets is central to people's perceptions of the area where they live.

   People's views about the safety of the streets are related not only to what they think of the area but also to the actual characteristics of the area. There is a small but distinct tendency for those in inner London to have more misgivings than those in outer London: for example, 47 per cent of informants in inner London compared with 38 per cent of those in outer London say there are serious risks for women going out alone at night. It is not surprising that the difference is small since both inner and outer London contain a wide variety of areas in terms of socio-economic mix, the level of social stress and crime rate. It is possible to carry out a more refined analysis based on the socio-economic classification of local authority areas worked out by Webber and Craig(1). Table II.4 shows the findings of our questions about the safety of the streets according to the type of borough in which the informant lives. Boroughs with a high index are ones with high levels of housing stress, unemployment and social deprivation, whereas those with a low index are ones with better housing, fewer social problems and a strong middle class element. It is fair to assume, though we have no direct proof of this, that the actual rate of street crime is higher - probably very substantially higher - in the high-scoring than in the low-scoring boroughs. The table shows that there is more anxiety about the risks to women at night in the high-scoring than in the low-scoring boroughs, although there is no difference in the proportion of people who fear for themselves. This is evidence of a small but distinct relationship between the actual characteristics of an area and people's fears about the safety of the streets.

Table II.4    Risks in going out after dark, by type of borough

Column percentages

| | 100 or more | Borough index(a) 0 to 99 | -99 to -1 | -100 or less |
|---|---|---|---|---|
| The risks for women are serious | 51 | 45 | 41 | 33 |
| I am sometimes worried for myself | 44 | 51 | 48 | 45 |
| Base: all informants (unweighted) | 302 | 602 | 1,044 | 470 |
| (weighted) | 1,730 | 2,481 | 5,896 | 3,818 |

(a)    For an explanation of this index, see Chapter I and the discussion in the present section.

Another way of classifying areas is according to the ethnic composition of the local population, and analysis in these terms is highly relevant during a period when the press and television and the Metropolitan Police themselves have created the impression that black people are responsible for a high proportion of crime, especially street crime, in London. In fact we find that white people in areas of high ethnic concentration are twice as likely as those in areas of low ethnic concentration to think that the streets are unsafe for lone women at night (Table II.5), and when we consider people's fears for their own safety the difference is only

(1)    See the discussion in Chapter I.

slightly less striking. These findings indicate a very high level of anxiety in areas of high ethnic concentration. The upper group in our analysis is wards in which 16 per cent or more of the population are of Asian or West Indian origin, and in such areas two-thirds of informants think there are serious risks for women going out alone at night. It should be borne in mind that a few wards have much higher concentrations than 16 per cent, and from the shape of the findings it is likely that the level of anxiety is still higher in such areas.

Among Asians and West Indians, by contrast, the level of anxiety about the safety of the streets is not at all related to the ethnic composition of the local population. This shows that Asians and West Indians do not perceive the presence of other Asians and West Indians in the area as a threat to their safety - they apparently decline to accept that there is a connection between street crime and ethnic minorities. As far as West Indians are concerned, this is entirely to be expected, but the findings also show that Asians decline to accept that ethnic minorities are a threat, although it is not their own group but people of West Indian origin who have been blamed for street crime in most public comment on the matter.

Table II.5    Risks in going out after dark:    whites by local concentration of ethnic minorities

Column percentages

| | Per cent Asians and West Indians in Ward | | | | |
| | Up to 1 | 2-5 | 6-10 | 11-15 | 16 or more |
| --- | --- | --- | --- | --- | --- |
| The risks for women are serious | 32 | 43 | 41 | 52 | 65 |
| I am sometimes worried for myself | 43 | 51 | 41 | 55 | 59 |
| Base:  General sample whites | | | | | |
| (unweighted) | 316 | 289 | 249 | 168 | 161 |
| (weighted) | 3,536 | 2,707 | 2,333 | 1,656 | 1,477 |

These findings certainly show that white people feel much more unsafe in areas of high ethnic concentration than they do in mainly white areas, but it is not certain that it is the presence of the minorities that makes them feel unsafe: it could be argued that it is some of the other characteristics of areas of high ethnic concentration that cause the feeling of insecurity. However, this latter interpretation does not seem very plausible, for two reasons.

33

First, if it is other characteristics of the areas of high ethnic concentration that make white people feel unsafe, we would expect the minorities in these areas to feel unsafe for the same reasons, whereas in fact they feel much safer there than whites do, and no less safe than they do in areas of low concentration. Secondly, the analysis by type of borough shows much less striking differences than the one by ethnic concentrations, which suggests that the fears of white people have something to do with the presence of the ethnic minorities specifically. This second argument cannot be pushed too far, however, because the analysis by type of borough is less powerful than the one by ethnic concentrations, being based on larger geographical units. There is certainly a high level of fear among white people in the areas of ethnic concentration for their own safety and for the safety of women in particular, and the findings suggest that this is connected with a fear of the minority groups specifically.

## The prevalence of crime

Another measure of the success of the police in achieving their overall objectives is public opinion about the prevalence of crime. The difficulty here is that people do not have a view about how much crime there is, because they do not have a concept that would allow them to quantify it. They do, however, have a view about whether various kinds of crime are becoming more or less common, and an advantage of questions about changes is that the findings are relatively easy to interpret: if a substantial majority of people think that the crime rate is going up, this cannot be good. We can also ask people to compare the level of various kinds of crime in their own area with that in other parts of London. This gives an indication of what people think of their own area and may provide a clue as to whether beliefs about changes in the crime rate are based on experience close to home or on conventional wisdom disseminated by the press and television.

The following questions were included at an early stage in the interview (immediately after those about safety on the streets).

Would you say that (people being mugged and robbed in the street) is more common in this area than it was five years ago, less common or about the same?

Would you say that (people being mugged and robbed in the street) is more common in this area, less common or about the same as in other parts of London?

The questions were repeated for the following six kinds of crime:

people being mugged and robbed in the street
people's houses being burgled
people's cars being stolen
fights and disturbances in the street

34

vandalism and deliberate damage to property
drunk driving.

We made a deliberate decision to refer in the questionnaire to 'people being mugged and robbed in the street' even though 'mugging' is an inexact term with a special emotional charge and racial connotations. If 'mugging' can be said to have a definite meaning, it refers to theft from the person involving violence or the threat of violence. In practice, it is often used more loosely to refer to any theft from the person. The effect of this loose use of the term is to attach sinister and violent associations to crimes which are not violent and which do not necessarily cause great distress. It is commonplace for all thefts and robberies from the person to be referred to as 'muggings' and then for statistics on these crimes to be used to 'prove' that the streets are unsafe - whereas in fact, many of the crimes counted in such statistics do not constitute a threat to personal safety. The popular press has also established a firm association in people's minds between 'mugging' and black people; 'mugging' is popularly perceived as a violent crime committed by young black people on old white ladies. In fact (as we shall see later) young people are more at risk from this kind of crime than old people, and black people as much at risk as white people. As later findings from this survey will show, it is true that black people are disproportionately represented among those who commit thefts from the person (including those involving violence). Nevertheless, a majority of these crimes are committed by white people.

We used 'people being mugged and robbed in the street' in the questionnaire because we were concerned, at this point, with public attitudes to crime and we cannot escape from the fact that much public discussion revolves around the concept of 'mugging'. In order to question people effectively about their attitudes we have to adopt their terminology at key points. As things stand, 'mugging' is a necessary term in any discussion about the social psychology of crime, but a term to be strictly avoided in any serious discussion about crime itself.

The results for all informants are shown in Table II.6. There is only a small minority who think that any of the crimes is becoming less prevalent. About 60 per cent of informants think that street robberies, burglary and vandalism are becoming more common, while about five per cent think they are becoming less common in each case. About 40 per cent think that car theft and fights and disturbances are becoming more common. Only in the case of drunk driving is there a degree of complacency; two-thirds of informants think the incidence is staying the same or don't know, while the remaining one-third split two to one in favour of an increase. While some readers may take these findings philosophically on the ground that even at the best of times people tend to think that things are getting worse, others may find them alarming. At any rate the findings do not, by any stretch of the imagination, give cause for reassurance.

Table II.6    Perceived incidence of six kinds of crime

Column percentages

| | Street robberies | Burglary | Car theft | Fights and disturbances | Vandalism | Drunk driving |
|---|---|---|---|---|---|---|
| **Compared with five years ago** | | | | | | |
| More common | 57 | 62 | 44 | 37 | 60 | 22 |
| Less common | 3 | 3 | 6 | 12 | 6 | 11 |
| The same | 29 | 24 | 33 | 41 | 27 | 44 |
| Don't know or not stated | 11 | 10 | 17 | 9 | 7 | 22 |
| **In this area compared with the rest of London** | | | | | | |
| More common | 7 | 14 | 6 | 7 | 8 | 4 |
| Less common | 63 | 35 | 39 | 60 | 46 | 26 |
| The same | 24 | 41 | 43 | 27 | 39 | 51 |
| Don't know or not stated | 6 | 11 | 12 | 7 | 7 | 19 |

36

The final form of the questionnaire was settled, after two stages of piloting, before the first outbreak of rioting in April 1981, and we preferred not to make last-minute changes in the light of recent events. For this reason, there was no question about the prevalence of riots as such, and if there had been the findings would have been trivial, since it is obvious that rioting was more common in 1981 than in previous years. However, informants who were particularly concerned about riots could and would have mentally included them under the heading of 'fights and disturbances in the street'. For this reason the questions as asked do produce a useful indication of the level of concern about riots, along with other disturbances in the streets, in comparison with the concern about other kinds of crime. It is quite clear from the findings that there is more concern about street robberies, burglaries and vandalism than about riots and other disturbances. A probable reason for this is that the questions are about the area where the informant lives; the answers will partly reflect what people have heard about crime in London or in Britain generally, but the questions do make people concentrate on what they think about their own area as far as possible. In spite of the impression that may have been created, rioting was not widespread throughout London, and as we shall show later in this report, comparatively few people actually saw any riots. The findings emphasise that from day to day, street crime, burglaries and vandalism are a greater cause for concern. It is also significant that, in spite of the intense concentration in the media on 'mugging', just as many people think that burglary and vandalism are increasing.

The results of the second question show that very few people think that any of these crimes is particularly common where they live. This is especially striking in the case of street robberies and fights and disturbances, the kinds of crime featured most prominently in the media. While 57 per cent of people think that mugging is becoming more common in London generally, only seven per cent think it is more common where they live than in other parts, and 63 per cent think it is less common. On this second question, the findings are almost identical in the case of fights and disturbances. For each of the kinds of crime, the proportion of people thinking it is less common where they live is much higher than the proportion thinking it is more common, but there are some differences in the balance of answers between 'less common' and 'the same'. Burglary, car theft and vandalism are the crimes that people are most likely to say happen locally as much as elsewhere in London: about 40 per cent give this answer in each case.

Many people think that crime is going up, but most think that where it is happening is somewhere else. There are probably two underlying reasons for this. The first is that people are influenced by what they read and see on television, but do not usually connect it very firmly with their own experience in the area where they live. The second is that most people like to think that they live in a nice area themselves. How much weight should be ascribed to each of these factors we cannot say. There is no actual contra-diction, from the point of view of the individual, in the opinions that they express, but the findings as a whole suggest that general views about rising crime are somewhat detached from personal experience. Nevertheless, there is some connection between the answers that peo ,le give to the two questions. People who think that a kind of crime is going up are markedly more likely than others to think it is particularly common in their own area. This relationship remains fairly constant for each of the six kinds of crime (table not shown). Thus, people's belief that crime is going up is definitely connected with what they think is happening on their own doorstep, but a large component of the belief is about what they think is happening elsewhere.

Table II.7    Perceived incidence of six kinds of crime compared with five years ago, by age

Percentages

|  | Age | | |
|  | 15-24 | 25-44 | 45 and over |
| --- | --- | --- | --- |
| Proportion who think that the crime is more common than five years ago | | | |
| Street robberies | 49 | 53 | 64 |
| Burglary | 54 | 59 | 67 |
| Car theft | 51 | 42 | 43 |
| Fights and disturbances | 46 | 39 | 32 |
| Vandalism | 57 | 57 | 64 |
| Drunk driving | 23 | 26 | 19 |
| | | | |
| Base: all informants | | | |
| (unweighted) | 984 | 844 | 592 |
| (weighted) | 2,609 | 5,174 | 6,162 |

Men and women give much the same answers to these questions, except that women are rather more likely to think that street robbery is becoming more common (61 per cent of women compared with 52 per cent of men). There are some small but distinct differences between age groups. Older people are more likely than younger ones to think that the incidence of street robbery and burglary is going up, whereas the young are more likely than the old to think that car theft and fights and disturbances are on the increase. This probably relfects differences between the age groups in the kinds of crimes that they are victims of, or see or hear about.

38

Table II.8   Perceived incidence of street robberies, by years of residence in the area

Column percentages

| | Years of residence in the area | | | |
| | Less than 2 | 2-6 | 7-19 | 20 or more |
|---|---|---|---|---|
| Compared with five years ago street robbery is | | | | |
| More common | 34 | 49 | 57 | 69 |
| Less common | 3 | 5 | 4 | 3 |
| The same | 25 | 31 | 33 | 24 |
| Don't know | 38 | 15 | 6 | 4 |
| Not stated | 1 | * | * | - |
| Base:  all informants | | | | |
| (unweighted) | 309 | 577 | 992 | 542 |
| (weighted) | 1,571 | 2,889 | 4,426 | 5,039 |

People who have been living in an area for a long time will have a clearer view of changes over time in the local level of crime than those who arrived recently. In practice, we find that this relationship is very strong. Table II.8 gives the findings for street robbery as an example (the pattern is very similar for all six kinds of crime). The proportion who say that street robbery is more common than five years ago rises sharply and consistently with length of residence while the proportion who say they don't know declines in a complementary fashion. Those who have been in the area for less than five years would naturally have some difficulty in answering the question, and this largely accounts for the differences at the lower end, but there is also a difference between those who have been living in the area for 7-19 years and those who have been there for 20 years or more. Long-established residents tend to be older people, but these age differences are not enough to explain the effect. It seems, therefore, that long-established residents are more likely than others to think that crime is going up. It may be that people with a more settled pattern of life tend to think that things in general are changing for the worse, but it may be that they actually have a clearer perspective on the changes that are taking place. In any case the findings show that among long-established residents there is an overwhelming weight of opinion that crime is increasing: among those who have lived in the area for 20 years or more, 69 per cent think street robbery has become more common over the past five years, while only three per cent think it has become less common.

Although West Indians are less likely than other groups to say

they feel unsafe on the streets at night, they are no less likely to
think that the incidence of street robbery and fights and disturbances is going up; further, while about 60 per cent of the other
groups think that these crimes happen more often elsewhere in
London than in their own area, a markedly lower proportion of
West Indians think so (44 per cent in the case of street robbery, and
41 per cent in the case of fights and disturbances). It seems,
therefore, that West Indians are just as likely as other groups to
think that street crimes are increasing in London and more likely
to think there are particular problems of this kind in their own
area; but at the same time, they are less likely to fear that the
streets are unsafe at night. Otherwise the differences between
ethnic groups on the latest questions are not very striking (table
not shown).

Table II.9    Perceived incidence of six kinds of crime compared
             with five years ago: whites by local concentration
             of ethnic minorities

Column percentages

| | Per cent Asians and West Indians in ward | | | | |
| | Up to 1 | 2-5 | 6-10 | 11-15 | 16 or more |
|---|---|---|---|---|---|
| Proportion who think that the crime is more common than five years ago | | | | | |
| Street robbery | 47 | 59 | 61 | 67 | 69 |
| Burglary | 67 | 60 | 56 | 62 | 64 |
| Car theft | 46 | 45 | 38 | 50 | 40 |
| Fights/disturbances | 39 | 33 | 37 | 37 | 42 |
| Vandalism | 63 | 55 | 62 | 64 | 63 |
| Drunk driving | 24 | 21 | 23 | 23 | 22 |
| Base: General sample whites | | | | | |
| (unweighted) | 316 | 289 | 249 | 168 | 161 |
| (weighted) | 3,536 | 2,707 | 2,333 | 1,656 | 1,477 |

We have seen that among white people, fear about the safety
of the streets at night is closely associated with the presence of
ethnic minorities in the local area. We also find that white people
in areas of high ethnic concentration are more likely than those in
areas of low concentration to think that street robbery is on the
increase; Table II.9 shows that among white people in the areas of
highest concentration, 69 per cent say that street robbery is more
common than five years ago, compared with 47 per cent of those
in the areas of lowest concentration. What is particularly

40

interesting is that there are no similar relationships for any of the other five kinds of crime. This is convincing evidence that the findings do point to a specific connection in people's minds between 'mugging' and the ethnic minorities. If the difference arose because areas of high ethnic concentration also tend to be socially deprived, then we would expect to find, for example, that vandalism was also more often thought to be on the increase in areas of high than in areas of low ethnic concentration, but we find no difference of this kind.

When we look at how white people compare their own area with the rest of London, we find much stronger and more general differences according to the level of ethnic concentration locally (Table II.10). For example, among white people in the areas of lowest ethnic concentration, 85 per cent say that street robbery is less common locally than in the rest of London, compared with 32 per cent of those in the areas of highest concentration. But in this case the differences shown for the other kinds of crime are almost as striking.

Table II.10    Perceived incidence of six kinds of crime in this area compared with the rest of London: whites by local concentration of ethnic minorities

Column percentages

|  | Per cent Asians and West Indians in ward | | | | |
|---|---|---|---|---|---|
|  | Up to 1 | 2-5 | 6-10 | 11-15 | 16 or more |
| Proportion who think that the crime is less common in this area than elsewhere |  |  |  |  |  |
| Street robbery | 85 | 64 | 57 | 42 | 32 |
| Burglary | 46 | 36 | 28 | 23 | 17 |
| Car theft | 55 | 36 | 30 | 30 | 21 |
| Fights/disturbances | 74 | 60 | 54 | 48 | 35 |
| Vandalism | 66 | 44 | 40 | 31 | 21 |
| Drunk driving | 33 | 26 | 22 | 23 | 18 |
| Base: General sample whites |  |  |  |  |  |
| (unweighted) | 316 | 289 | 249 | 168 | 161 |
| (weighted) | 3,536 | 2,707 | 2,333 | 1,656 | 1,477 |

The answers of Asians and West Indians to both questions have also been analysed by the level of local ethnic concentration (table not shown). There is some tendency, on the whole, for Asians and West Indians in areas of high ethnic concentration to be more likely than those in areas of low concentration to think that crime is increasing and less likely to think it is relatively uncommon in their own area. However, these relationships are neither very consistent nor very marked. Among Asians, those in the areas of highest concentration are less likely than others to think that fights and disturbances are on the increase, probably because the areas of very high Asian concentration, for example, Southall, were not the scenes of the worst rioting in 1981. What is most striking is that the very strong tendency, among whites, for a belief in the local prevalence of crime to be associated with the presence of ethnic minorities is not reproduced among the minorities themselves either strongly or consistently.

Table II.11 shows large differences between people in inner and outer London in the tendency to associate crime with the local area, consistent with the fact that crime rates are higher in inner than in outer London. Very large differences are also shown according to the type of borough; for example, in the boroughs with

Table II.11    Incidence of six kinds of crime in this area compared with the rest of London: by part of London and type of borough

Column percentages

| | Inner London | Outer London | 100 or more | Borough index 0 to 99 | -99 to -1 | -100 or less |
|---|---|---|---|---|---|---|
| Proportion who think that the crime is less common in this area than elsewhere | | | | | | |
| Street robbery | 43 | 73 | 35 | 49 | 64 | 82 |
| Burglary | 26 | 40 | 19 | 29 | 38 | 42 |
| Car theft | 24 | 47 | 18 | 26 | 43 | 51 |
| Fights and disturbances | 44 | 67 | 35 | 47 | 61 | 77 |
| Vandalism | 30 | 54 | 26 | 33 | 47 | 61 |
| Drunk driving | 19 | 30 | 21 | 18 | 28 | 32 |
| Base: all informants | | | | | | |
| (unweighted) | 1,046 | 1,374 | 302 | 602 | 1,044 | 470 |
| (weighted) | 4,767 | 9,177 | 1,730 | 2,481 | 5,876 | 3,818 |

the highest index of deprivation, only 18 per cent of people think that car theft is less common locally than in the rest of London, compared with 51 per cent of those in the boroughs with the lowest index of deprivation. These findings again demonstrate that people's beliefs about crime do bear a clear relation to the real facts about the areas in which they live. This conclusion applies equally strongly to Asians, West Indians and whites separately (when members of each group are analysed according to the type of borough in which they live). The only exception to this is that Asians in inner London do not differ markedly from those in outer London in their perception of the prevalence of crime locally. Thus, among white people, the perception of the local level of crime is strongly related both to ethnic concentrations and to the more general social and physical characteristics of the area, whereas among the minorities it is equally strongly related to the social and physical characteristics of the area, but only weakly related to its ethnic composition. Both social and physical characteristics of the area and ethnic composition are high significant factors affecting people's perceptions of the level of crime, but ethnic composition has a different and lesser significance for the minorities as opposed to white people.

Two further questions were asked for each of the six kinds of crime.

Do you think any particular sorts of people are mainly responsible for (people being mugged and robbed in the street)?

If yes What particular sorts of people are mainly responsible for (people being mugged and robbed in the street)?

At this point in the questionnaire (and up to a much later stage) there had been no mention of ethnic minority groups, so if anyone were to answer in terms of ethnic groups at the second of these questions, that would be a completely spontaneous response. In practice, we find (Table II.12) that for all kinds of crime except drunk driving, between about one-half and two-thirds of informants think that some particular group or groups are mainly responsible, but the proportion mentioning ethnic minority groups is very small for all crimes except street robberies. Thus, 17 per cent of informants say that ethnic minorities are mainly responsible for street robberies, among whom nine per cent specifically mention West Indians, but for other crimes the proportion who mention ethnic minorities ranges from virtually nil to four per cent (for fights and disturbances). This latter figure is particularly interesting in the light of the riots. It suggests that either people do not mostly have riots in mind when thinking about fights and disturbances, or they think that the minorities were not primarily responsible for the riots.

Young people are the group most often blamed for all kinds of crime except drunk driving. Even in the case of street robbery, young people are mentioned more than twice as often as ethnic minorities. Young people are most often mentioned as the culprits by young people themselves, and there is only a slight tendency for older people to put the blame on the young more often than the

Table II.12   Groups responsible for six kinds of crime

Column percentages

| | Street robberies | Burglary | Car theft | Fights and disturbances | Vandalism | Drunk driving |
|---|---|---|---|---|---|---|
| **Do you think any particular sorts of people are mainly responsible?** | | | | | | |
| Yes | 64 | 43 | 48 | 56 | 68 | 23 |
| **If yes, what particular sorts?** | | | | | | |
| Black/coloured people/ West Indians etc. | 17 | 3 | 1 | 4 | 2 | * |
| Of which, West Indians | 9 | 1 | 1 | 1 | 1 | * |
| Young people | 38 | 25 | 33 | 34 | 57 | 6 |
| Unemployed people | 12 | 9 | 4 | 4 | 5 | * |
| Bored people/trouble makers | 5 | 2 | 12 | 4 | 6 | 1 |
| Punks or skinheads | 2 | * | * | 4 | 2 | * |
| Drunks | 1 | * | 1 | 11 | 1 | 9 |
| Criminals | * | 7 | 4 | * | * | - |
| Other specific groups | 1 | 1 | 1 | 3 | 1 | 3 |
| Vague answers only | 2 | 3 | 2 | 2 | 2 | 4 |
| Don't know | 1 | 1 | * | * | * | * |

Note:   The base for each column is all informants.   Informants could give more than one answer to the second question.

44

young do. On this matter public opinion is right, since a high proportion of all of these crimes are committed by young people. Other groups that are mentioned fairly often are the unemployed and bored people or trouble-makers. Punks and skinheads are mentioned only infrequently. Members of the National Front are mentioned very infrequently (they are included under 'other specific groups' in the table), and other political groups hardly at all.

The most important finding here is that people seldom spontaneously mention the ethnic minorities as those mainly responsible for particular crimes, except in the case of street robberies, and even there less than one-fifth give that kind of answer. At the same time we know that perceptions of crime are strongly related to the presence of ethnic minorities locally, especially among whites, but most people are not prepared to make this connection at a conscious level, or at least it is not the first answer that springs to mind in answer to a general question. Most people do not consciously and actively seek to place the blame for rising crime on West Indians and Asians or else they are not prepared to admit that they do.

Naturally, members of minority groups are less likely than whites to blame street robberies on their own groups, but some of them do so. The proportions saying that ethnic minorities are mainly responsible for street robberies are 18 per cent of white people, four per cent of West Indians, nine per cent of Asians and nine per cent of other non-white people. In the case of fights and disturbances, the proportion who place the responsibility on ethnic minorities is the same for white people, West Indians and Asians (about four per cent in each case).

Among white people there is a strong and consistent tendency for mentions of ethnic minorities as responsible for street robberies to increase with the local level of ethnic concentration. Among white people in the areas of highest concentration 35 per cent say ethnic minorities are mainly responsible for street robberies, compared with eight per cent in the areas of lowest concentration. There is a similar difference in the case of fights and disturbances in the street, but not for the other kinds of crime which are very seldom associated with ethnic minorities in any case. No clear relationship of the same kind is found among the minorities themselves.

## Priorities in fighting crime
As we said in the preface to this series of reports, it is an important question whether the priorities adopted by the police in fighting crime are those shared by the wider society. We shall consider police priorities in later chapters, particularly in Chapter XIV. This section considers the priorities of the general public.

Informants were given a set of 17 cards in random order, each one giving a very brief description of a kind of crime. First they were asked to go through the set and sort out the five crimes which they thought the police should spend the most time and energy in trying to fight. When they had done this, they were asked to go through again and sort out the three crimes which they thought the police should spend the least time and energy in trying to fight. Interviewers ensured that the informant did not make the same crime both a high and a low priority. If the informant could not settle on the required number of top or bottom priorities, a smaller number was accepted, but in practice most informants chose the required number. Where the interview was not being carried out in English the question was not asked, since in most cases the informant would not have been able to cope. This applied to 15 per cent of Asian informants only.

The findings are shown in total in Table II.13. Three crimes stand out as ones to which people think the police should give the highest priority: they are sexual assaults on women, robberies in

Table II.13　Crimes to which the police should give the highest and lowest priority

Column percentages

| | Five highest priorities | Three lowest priorities |
|---|---|---|
| Sexual assaults on women | 79 | 1 |
| Robberies in the street when violence is used | 73 | 1 |
| Crimes in which firearms are used | 72 | 1 |
| Burglary of people's houses | 44 | 2 |
| Racialist attacks | 40 | 3 |
| Use of heroin and other hard drugs | 40 | 5 |
| Vandalism and damage to property | 33 | 3 |
| Drunk driving | 28 | 6 |
| Fighting and rowdyism in streets | 20 | 7 |
| Bag-snatching and pickpocketing | 17 | 8 |
| Violence at football matches | 11 | 8 |
| Use of cannabis | 10 | 30 |
| Burglary of shops and offices | 10 | 6 |
| Theft of motor cars | 8 | 13 |
| Sale of pornography | 6 | 60 |
| Prostitution | 2 | 63 |
| Illegal betting and gaming | 1 | 73 |
| Mean number of choices made | 4.94 | 2.92 |

Base:　informants interviewed in English
　　　　(unweighted)　　　　　　　　2,348
　　　　(weighted)　　　　　　　　　13,849

the street where violence is used and crimes in which firearms are used. About three-quarters of informants chose each of these as one of their top priorities. Next are three crimes given top priority by about 40 per cent of informants each: they are burglary of people's houses, racialist attacks and use of heroin and other hard drugs.

Three crimes stand out very clearly as the ones to which most people would give the lowest priority: illegal betting and gaming (71 per cent), prostitution (63 per cent) and sale of pornography (60 per cent). The only other crime which gets a substantial vote as a low priority is use of cannabis (30 per cent). In general, the low priority choices are the mirror image of the high priority ones, but use of cannabis is the exception to this. There is an appreciable minority (10 per cent) who make fighting use of cannabis one of their five top priorities, while at the same time nearly one-third make it one of their bottom three. This is an indication of a clear conflict of opinion. The same does not apply to any other crime. It is particularly striking that prostitution and pornography both get a high vote as a low priority and a low vote as a high priority, so that there seems to be no sizeable minority that are particularly strongly opposed to them.

More detailed analysis shows that, in general, there is a remarkable degree of agreement among most different sections of the population about priorities in fighting crime. There are no significant differences, for example, between the answers given by men and women; in particular, concern about sexual assaults on women is the same among the two sexes. Differences between age groups are small for the most part, but younger people place much more importance on combating racialist attacks than do older people, while the old are more concerned than the young about bag-snatching and pickpocketing, as the following summary table shows.

| Per cent choosing as a top priority | 15-24 | 25-44 | 45 and over |
|---|---|---|---|
| Racialist attacks | 56 | 46 | 29 |
| Bag snatching and pickpocketing | 11 | 12 | 24 |

Also young people are much more likely than older people to put a low priority on combating use of cannabis and sale of pornography.

| Per cent choosing as a bottom priority | 15-24 | 25-44 | 45 and over |
|---|---|---|---|
| Use of cannabis | 37 | 42 | 18 |
| Sale of pornography | 70 | 63 | 53 |

While there are some differences between ethnic groups, these are not in general large enough to suggest that there is a major divergence of opinion. All of the differences that seem of any importance in the top priority choices are shown in the following summary table.

| Per cent choosing as a top priority | Whites | West Indians | Asians | Other non-whites |
|---|---|---|---|---|
| Sexual assaults on women | 80 | 79 | 70 | 57 |
| Robberies in the street where violence is used | 75 | 64 | 55 | 59 |
| Crimes in which firearms are used | 75 | 54 | 42 | 50 |
| Use of heroin and other hard drugs | 42 | 28 | 19 | 22 |
| Racialist attacks | 37 | 67 | 76 | 56 |
| Fighting and rowdyism in the street | 19 | 14 | 33 | 24 |
| Bag-snatching and pick-pocketing | 16 | 32 | 16 | 26 |

Asians and West Indians are about twice as likely as white people to attach a high priority to combating racialist attacks. Nevertheless, there is a strong body of opinion among white people that action against these attacks should be given a high priority. On the face of it, white people seem more concerned than the minorities that robbery with violence and crimes involving firearms should be combated, but it should be remembered that informants were allowed only five choices. It seems likely that the real difference is in the importance given to combating racialist attacks. Those Asians and West Indians who chose this item had less room left to choose robbery with violence or crimes in which firearms are used. It does seem highly significant, on the other hand, that West Indians are twice as likely as white people or Asians to choose bag-snatching and pickpocketing as a high priority. This shows that a substantial proportion of West Indians react against the accusation that their own group is often responsible for this kind of crime by calling for strong action by the police against the culprits. Further analysis shows that it is older West Indians, in particular, who react in this way: 42 per cent of West Indians aged 45 or over choose bag-snatching and pickpocketing as a high priority, compared with 28 per cent of younger West Indians. The summary table also shows that Asians are about twice as likely as West Indians or white people to make action against fighting and rowdyism a high priority, possibly because they fear that they may be the victims, or possibly because violence on the streets is particularly offensive to them. There seem to be some cultural differences in attitudes towards sexual attacks on women, which are given a higher priority by white people and West Indians than by Asians or other non-white people. Nevertheless, all groups attach a high priority to combating this kind of crime. There are clearly important cultural differences in the attitudes to heroin and other hard drugs, which are more widely accepted in the East

48

than in the West.  Asians put a lower priority on combating use of hard drugs than do white people.

Some other differences between ethnic groups show up when the bottom priority choices are considered.

| Per cent choosing as a bottom priority | Whites | West Indians | Asians | Other non-whites |
|---|---|---|---|---|
| Illegal betting/gaming | 75 | 61 | 58 | 59 |
| Prostitution | 64 | 58 | 44 | 45 |
| Sale of pornography | 61 | 65 | 48 | 57 |
| Use of cannabis | 31 | 39 | 28 | 17 |

As might be expected, West Indians are the group most likely to think that action against users of cannabis should not be given a high priority (among Rastafarians, smoking cannabis is considered a virtue).  However, the difference (though statistically significant) is not very marked, and further analysis shows that even among young West Indians more than half fail to choose use of cannabis as a low priority for action by the police.  From these findings, any idea that the great majority of young West Indians are in favour of cannabis smoking must be rejected.  Also, there is little difference in attitudes between young West Indians and young white people. The proportion choosing action against cannabis smoking as a low priority is 43 per cent for West Indians aged 15 to 24 compared with 37 per cent for whites in the same age group.  The summary table above also shows that Asians are less likely than other groups to give a low priority to action against prostitution and the sale of pornography, which is a clear reflection of the more conservative attitude towards sex among this group.  Finally, the table shows up the particular soft spot for betting, even if illegal, among white British people.

In general, attitudes towards policing priorities among white people are not very much related to the ethnic composition of the local population, but three important differences do appear.

| Per cent choosing as a top priority | Per cent Asians and West Indians in ward | | | | |
|---|---|---|---|---|---|
| | Up to 1 | 2-5 | 6-10 | 11-15 | 16 or more |
| Burglary of people's houses | 40 | 37 | 44 | 48 | 57 |
| Burglary of shops and offices | 8 | 8 | 8 | 12 | 15 |
| Bag-snatching and pick-pocketing | 10 | 14 | 19 | 25 | 24 |

There is considerably more concern about burglary and about bag-snatching and pickpocketing among white people in areas of high ethnic concentration than among those elsewhere.  It is interesting that the level of concern about racialist attacks among white people is not related to the ethnic composition of the local population.

Concern about racialist attacks among the minorities them-selves does not significantly vary, either, according to the local ethnic concentration. Among both Asians and West Indians, a higher priority is given to combating bag-snatching and pickpocket-ing in areas of high than in areas of low concentrat-ion. Thus, in areas of 20 per cent or higher immigrant concentration, 39 per cent of minority group informants choose bag-snatching and pick-pocketing as a high priority for police action, compared with 20 per cent of those in other areas. The analysis by type of borough shows that among all groups there is more concern about this crime in areas of high social deprivation than elsewhere.

Attitudes towards policing priorities do vary substantially, in a number of cases, between socio-economic groups (defined according to the informant's job if in work, or if not according to the present or last main job of the head of the household).

| | Socio-economic group | | | | |
| Per cent choosing as top priority | Profess-ional/manager-ial | White collar | Skilled manual | Semi-skilled manual | Un-skilled manual |
|---|---|---|---|---|---|
| Robberies in the street where violence used | 82 | 76 | 72 | 66 | 62 |
| Crimes in which fire-arms are used | 75 | 77 | 73 | 66 | 58 |
| Racialist attacks | 47 | 45 | 34 | 37 | 25 |
| Use of heroin and other hard drugs | 47 | 39 | 37 | 39 | 34 |
| Burglary of people's houses | 38 | 40 | 53 | 44 | 53 |
| Bag-snatching and pickpocketing | 11 | 15 | 17 | 24 | 21 |
| Use of cannabis | 3 | 9 | 12 | 16 | 19 |

The higher socio-economic groups place much greater emphasis than the lower ones on the need to combat racialist attacks, probably because this kind of crime is thought of as being typically committed by young working class men, whom middle class people feel free to condemn. The higher socio-economic groups also place more emphasis than the lower ones on the need for the police to combat other crimes of violence. The lower socio-economic groups are more concerned than the higher ones about bag-snatching and pickpocketing, probably because they feel more vulnerable and the extent of the loss, to them, would be greater. Attitudes to the use of drugs are related to socio-economic group in an interesting way. The higher groups are more concerned than the lower ones about hard drugs, but much less concerned about cannabis, which is quite fashionable among some middle class people.

While these differences in attitudes towards policing

priorities between various groups make sense in terms of our knowledge of the wider social background, they should not be exaggerated. With a few exceptions, particularly in attitudes towards racialist attacks, the findings show that there is a fair measure of agreement between all major groups about what policing priorities should be. For example, there is no group in which a majority would favour taking action against prostitution, pornography, cannabis or illegal betting and gaming at the expense of bag-snatching or drunk driving.

# III EXPERIENCE AS A VICTIM OF CRIME

In the next four chapters of this report we shall examine in detail the experiences that people have had which might have brought them into contact with the police and describe any encounters with the police that did occur from the point of view of the individual members of the public concerned. The present chapter deals with experiences that people have had in the past twelve months as victims of crime or of acts which they think might have involved a crime, including matters that came to the attention of the police and ones that did not. Chapter IV deals with people's experiences of the police as offenders or suspects, including stops, arrests and arrests of the informant's children. Chapter V deals with experience of crowd trouble and mostly concerns incidents that the informants observed rather than took part in. Chapter VI deals with other occasions of contact with the police, including calls at police stations, conversations with police officers and more casual or social contacts; this chapter also provides a general assessment of the overall pattern of contact with the police.

## The pattern of victimisation
For some years survey techniques have been used in the USA to provide measures of the extent to which people are victims of acts that they consider crimes. In the 1970s Sparks and others developed, tested and validated similar techniques in Britain(1). More recently, the Home Office has published a British Crime Survey, which they intend to carry out regularly. The impetus for all of this research was the belief that the statistics of reported crime give an incomplete picture of the pattern of crime, since many incidents are not reported to the police. Certainly victim surveys give a different perspective from the crime statistics, and one that is useful, though as we pointed out in the Preface the incidents reported in victim surveys cannot necessarily be regarded as crimes, and it is wrong to forget that whether or not an incident

---

(1)　Richard F. Sparks et al, Surveying Victims, John Wiley and Sons, 1977.

is reported is one of the most important facts about it. The work of Sparks and others shows that a fairly high proportion of reported crimes are picked up in victim surveys, together with a large number of other incidents, but that there are inaccuracies in the survey results mostly arising from people's failure to pinpoint when the incident occurred. In spite of such inaccuracies, the evidence shows that the results are good enough to be a very useful source of information.

It was not a prime objective of the present survey to obtain detailed measures of rates of victimisation, but rather to provide a description of contacts with the police, within their proper context. Experience as a victim of crime provides one opportunity among others for contact with the police; it has to be covered, but not in as much detail as within a survey entirely devoted to victimisation. We therefore adopted the questioning approach used by Sparks and others, but simplified it considerably. All the evidence suggests that in this field the results are sensitive to the exact form of the questions. The more questions people are asked and the finer the distinctions that are made, the more incidents will be discovered, if only because the informant will eventually become desperate to say 'yes' to something. Therefore the findings of the present survey will not be directly comparable with those of others, such as the British Crime Survey. At the same time we can be confident that our questioning identifies the vast majority of incidents of victimisation that gave rise to contact with the police, and that is our primary objective.

Informants were asked whether each of the following seven types of incident had happened to them in the past twelve months:

a) burglary, break-in or attempted burglary of your house or flat
b) theft or attempted theft of a car, motor bike or other vehicle for which you were responsible
c) theft from your pocket, briefcase or bag
d) any other theft ('Have you had anything else stolen from you at all?')
e) deliberate damage to property that belonged to you
f) 'Has anyone physically attacked or assaulted you or molested you in any way?'
g) anything else 'which you think might have involved a crime of any sort'

Where they answered 'yes' for a type of incident, informants were asked how many times it had happened to them in the past twelve months. Each of the incidents thus identified then became the subject of a short supplementary questionnaire known as a 'victim sheet'. A maximum of three victim sheets were completed for each informant. If more than three incidents had been mentioned, victim sheets were completed for the three most recent ones.

From the answers to the first set of questions (referred to as the 'filter questions') we can calculate estimates of the rates of victimisation, that is the proportion of people who have been victims of a type of incident over the past twelve months, and the average (mean) number of incidents per person that have occurred. More detailed information about the majority of incidents is available from the victim sheets, and this occasionally conflicts with the information from the filter questions. For example, an incident that was described at the filter question as a physical attack may sound, from the detailed description, more like a theft from the person. However, cross-analysis shows that these conflicts are few. For the purpose of describing the general pattern of victimisation we shall use the information from the filter questions, which can be presented more straightforwardly than the findings from the victim sheets.

Among Londoners generally, 27 per cent said they had been victims of one or more of the seven kinds of act during the past twelve months. The proportion who said they had been victims of each individual offence are shown below.

|  | Per cent |
|---|---|
| House burgled | 6 |
| Theft of vehicle | 6 |
| Theft from pocket, briefcase or bag | 3 |
| Other theft | 7 |
| Deliberate damage to property | 8 |
| Physical attack or assault | 4 |
| Other incidents | 2 |

A higher proportion of women than of men are victims of theft from a pocket, briefcase or bag, and about the same proportion of 'other incidents that might have involved a crime'. For each of the other five types of incident, a higher proportion of men than of women are victims. One reason for this is that a high proportion of crimes involve vehicles, for which men are more often responsible than women. Another is that men are more likely than women to put themselves in situations where they may become victims of crime (this applies particularly to assaults). A third reason is that, as we shall shortly see, victims are often also offenders, and a much higher proportion of men than of women are offenders. These findings can be summarised by considering the proportion of people who have been victims of any of the seven kinds of offence, and the average (mean) number of incidents of all types per person. Thirty-two per cent of men compared with 24 per cent of women were victims of some kind of offence, and the mean number of incidents is 0.54 among men compared with 0.42 among women(2).

54

The rate of victimisation is strongly related to age. It is highest among those aged 20-24, and nearly as high among those aged 25-44, and it is lowest among those aged 60 or over. The rate is also substantially higher among the youngest age group (15-19) than among those aged 45 or over. The extent of these differences can best be expressed by saying that the rate of victimisation is more than three times as high among those aged 20-24 as among those aged 60 and over. The pattern is broadly similar for each of the seven types of incident, except that young people (up to the age of 24) are not very commonly victims of damage to property, presumably because they have relatively little property to be damaged. Also, the victims of physical attacks and assaults are almost exclusively aged under 45. Further, it is mostly young men who are involved in such incidents. The proportion who were victims of physical attacks within each age group is shown for men and women separately below.

|            | Per cent | |
|            | Men | Women |
|------------|-----|-------|
| 15 - 19    | 12  | 5     |
| 20 - 24    | 7   | 6     |
| 25 - 44    | 6   | 6     |
| 45 - 59    | 2   | *     |
| 60 and over| 3   | 1     |

It should be borne in mind that rapes and indecencies would be included under this head, because of the inclusion of the phrase 'or molested in any way' in the question.

The total rate of victimisation is lower for Asians than for other ethnic groups, but about the same for white people, West Indians and 'other non-whites'. Within each ethnic group, the rate of victimisation is higher among men than among women, but the difference is particularly marked in the case of Asians. The rate of victimisation among Asian men is rather lower than among West Indian men or white men; it is much lower among Asian women than among women belonging to other ethnic groups, probably because Asian women tend to live a sheltered and structured life. These findings mean that Asians, and particularly Asian women, will tend to have few occasions to be in contact with the police. Nevertheless, ethnic group is not among the most important determinants of the rate of victimisation. This conclusion is confirmed by the findings for the seven types of incident

---

(2)  The detailed tables on rates of victimisation are not here reproduced from Volume I of the original edition, where they appeared in an appendix. However, the more significant contents of these tables are summarised in this and in succeeding paragraphs.

55

separately, though it is very interesting that, if anything, a higher proportion of West Indians than of white people are victims of theft from a pocket, briefcase or bag (five per cent compared with three per cent). While theft from the person is often described as a crime committed typically by young West Indians on white people, our findings show that West Indians are actually more at risk than whites. The myth that it is mostly old people who are the victims of this kind of crime has already been exploded by other studies; our survey again shows that younger people are far more likely than older people to be the victims (six per cent of those aged 15-24 compared with one per cent of those aged 45 or over).

We have said that the total rate of victimisation is about the same among white people and West Indians, but lower among Asians. However, the age structure of the groups is different: there is a higher proportion of older people among whites than among West Indians or Asians. A more detailed analysis shows that for those aged 25-44 the rate of victimisation is substantially higher among white people than among West Indians, for those aged 15-24 it is a bit higher, while for those aged 45 and over it is about the same. Within certain age groups, therefore, white people are definitely more likely to be victims of crime than West Indians. Also, when comparisons are made within age groups, the contrast in the rate of victimisation between white people and Asians becomes stronger: in particular, young white people are much more likely to be victims of crime than young Asians (37 per cent of white people aged 15-24 compared with 16 per cent of Asians in the same age group were victims of any offence).

As might be expected, rates of victimisation are considerably higher in inner than in outer London, and this contrast is especially marked among West Indians. There is, however, no consistent relationship between the rate of victimisation and the type of borough (classified according to the social class mix and the level of social deprivation). Also, there is no evidence to support the idea that white people are more likely to be victims of crime if they live in areas of high ethnic concentration. However, white people living in such areas are more likely than those in areas of low ethnic concentration to be victims of thefts from the person specifically, as the following summary table shows.

| Per cent of Asians and West Indians in the ward | Per cent of white people who are victims of theft from the person |
|---|---|
| Up to 1 | 3 |
| 2 - 5 | 6 |
| 6 - 10 | 7 |
| 11 - 15 | 10 |
| 16 or more | 9 |

Among Asians and West Indians there seems to be no relationship between the rate of victimisation and the ethnic composition of the local population. Although some differences are apparently shown, they do not follow a consistent pattern, and because of relatively small sample sizes they are on the borderlines of statistical significance.

We found in the last chapter that white people in areas of high ethnic concentration were much more likely than those in areas of low ethnic concentration to think that the streets were unsafe at night and that all kinds of crime were more common where they lived than elsewhere. The present findings show that, except in the case of theft from the person, the actual rates of victimisation do not vary according to local ethnic concentration; thus the perceptions of white people can only be regarded as a reflection of actual differences in crime rates if theft from the person is taken to be supremely important and unusually damaging. In the next section we shall show that it is not. It follows that these responses by white people to the presence of ethnic minorities are not founded on personal experience or other soundly-based knowledge of the areas where they live.

There is a strong and consistent tendency for the rate of victimisation to be higher for the upper than for the lower socio-economic groups. A major reason for this is that much crime involves property; because the upper socio-economic groups have more property than the lower they are therefore more vulnerable. This is strikingly illustrated by the findings for damage to property specifically.

| Socio-economic group | Per cent who are victims of damage to property |
|---|---|
| Professional or managerial | 15 |
| White collar | 8 |
| Skilled manual | 8 |
| Semi-skilled manual | 6 |
| Unskilled manual | 3 |

At the same time, the upper socio-economic groups are at least as likely as the lower ones to be victims of crimes against the person. The proportion who are victims of physical attacks and assaults is five per cent among the non-manual groups compared with three per cent among the manual groups.

There is some evidence that the unemployed are more likely to be the victims of certain types of crime than those who are in full-time work. There is little difference between the two groups when all types of incident are combined, but in the case of burglary, theft from the person and physical attack the unemployed do seem to be particularly vulnerable, while they are most unlikely to have a vehicle stolen since in most cases they do not own one.

| | | Per cent who are victims of | | |
| --- | --- | --- | --- | --- |
| | Burglary | Theft from the person | Physical attack | Theft of vehicle |
| Those working full-time | 7 | 4 | 5 | 9 |
| The unemployed | 14 | 8 | 13 | 2 |

The link between the ownership of property and the tendency to be a victim of crime can be shown most clearly through an analysis by car ownership (or more precisely, whether the informant has the use of a car or van). We shall see in the next section that a high proportion of crimes (damage as well as theft) involve vehicles. We find that 34 per cent of car or motor bike owners have been victims of some incident in the past twelve months, compared with 20 per cent of the rest. Nine per cent of car owners and 13 per cent of motor bike owners claim that their vehicle was stolen or that there was an attempt to steal it (two per cent of non-owners make the same claim, presumably because they had the use of a vehicle at some time in the past twelve months, or else because it was a bicycle that was stolen). Owners of vehicles are also much more likely than non-owners to allege deliberate damage to property, since a vehicle is the kind of property most often damaged. Thus, 12 per cent of car owners and eight per cent of motor bike owners say they have had property deliberately damaged, compared with four per cent of non-owners.

However, there is a more fundamental relationship than any that has been mentioned so far: that is, between people as offenders and people as victims. Those who have been stopped by the police, reported for an offence or arrested are much more likely than others to be also victims of offences. These relationships are strong: if we had to predict, from all the information available, which people had been the victims of offences, we would be able to make the best prediction by considering whether they had committed an offence themselves or been suspected by the police of committing one. For example, among people who have been stopped by the police twice or more in the past year, 59 per cent have also been victims of some offence, and the mean number of cases of victimisation is 1.21; whereas among people who have not come to police notice for any offence or suspected offence, only 18 per cent have been victims, and the mean number of incidents of victimisation is 0.30. There is no superficial or straightforward linkage between being an offender and being a victim; but the findings demonstrate that there is a connection at a deeper level.

One type of explanation would be in terms of a kind of person and a style of life that is associated with both offending and with being a victim. A second type of explanation would be in terms of police practice, and particularly how police officers decide who to stop and question. Both of these factors probably play a part.

According to the first kind of explanation, some people are inadequate or accident-prone, have a style of life that is disorganised and uncontrolled, and tend to associate with others who live in the same kind of way. Within this 'sub-culture' criminality, mostly of a minor kind, is common, so that members of the group tend to be both offenders and victims. This could be elaborated into an account of crime as an aspect of social dislocation among certain rather specific groups, or of what has been called 'anomie' in sociological writings.

However, what would be left out of an explanation of this kind would be the role of the police. Our findings do not, strictly speaking, show that <u>offenders</u> are likely to be also victims, but that <u>offenders who come to police notice</u> and <u>people suspected by the police</u> (whether rightly or wrongly) are likely to be also victims. Also, it is highly significant that the relationship with victimisation is strongest for people who have been frequently stopped by the police (without being subsequently arrested or reported in the great majority of cases) and not for people who have actually been arrested or reported. This suggests that the police tend to concentrate their attention on a limited 'clientele'. Those singled out for police attention will be people already known to the police as offenders, suspects or victims, associates of people known to the police, and others who police officers think resemble those who are known to them, and their associates. In more concrete terms, police officers may tend to stop people whom they know or vaguely recognise without considering too much whether they came across them as victims or as offenders. Again, they may have a concept of a kind of person who is unconventional, living at the margins of society, not 'decent'; and in applying such a concept, they may be as successful in picking out victims as in picking out offenders, or perhaps more successful.

Thus, our findings do support the idea that there are sub-cultures of people who, among other things, tend to 'get into trouble' whether as victims or as offenders. But they also suggest that, by looking out for people like that, the police bring to their notice people whose trouble was hitherto as victims rather than as suspects. By working with the assumption that there is a certain kind of person with whom they mainly deal, they will tend to turn that assumption into an accomplished fact.

**Incidents of victimisation**
The discussion in this chapter so far has been about rates of victimisation, that is the proportion of people who are victims and the average number of incidents per person. We now move from this analysis of people, which shows who is at risk, to an analysis of the incidents themselves. A victim sheet was completed for each incident reported over the past twelve months, except that where an informant reported more than three, victim sheets were completed for the last three incidents only. In practice, only 2.2 per cent of informants reported more than three incidents, and the

incidents not asked about in detail accounted for only 18 per cent of all reported incidents. Therefore our detailed information relates to 82 per cent of all victim incidents reported; for convenience, these will be referred to as 'all victim incidents' from now on, and there are 957 of them (unweighted) in the survey. It is important to realise that the tables are based on incidents rather than people: the total of 957 incidents were reported by only 660 actual people (unweighted).

Details of the incident
At the beginning of the victim sheet, informants were asked to describe the incident, and these descriptions have been used to classify the incidents according to the kind of offence or offences involved. Because the same incident may comprise more than one offence it may be put into more than one category. However, the tables add to only 105 per cent, which means roughly speaking that only five per cent of incidents appear twice. We know which filter question gave rise to each victim sheet, and there are very few cases where the detailed description of the incident given on the victim sheet conflicts with the filter question that gave rise to it. Thus the information used in the first part of this chapter, which derives from the filter questions, proves on further examination to be reliable.

The pattern of the reported incidents according to the kind of offence involved is shown below in a summary form.

|                                    | Per cent of victim incidents |
|------------------------------------|:----------------------------:|
| Theft of motor vehicle             | 11 |
| Damage to motor vehicle            | 14 |
| Theft from motor vehicle           | 8  |
| Bicycle stolen or damaged          | 3  |
| Other vehicle offence              | 3  |
| Burglary or break-in               | 18 |
| Theft from the person              | 13 |
| Other theft                        | 7  |
| Asault (including sexual)          | 12 |
| All other offences                 | 14 |
| Don't know or vague answer only    | 1  |

Theft from the person accounts for 13 per cent of incidents and assault for 12 per cent. There is very little overlap between the two categories: in fact, only four per cent of incidents of theft from the person involved an assault, while five per cent of assaults also involved a theft from the person. Thus, the proportion of all victim incidents that are 'muggings' properly speaking (that is, theft with assault) is extremely low (0.5 per cent). In terms of a rate of victimisation these findings imply that 1.4 per thousand of the adult population in London claim that they have been robbed and attacked in the past twelve months.

Table III.1    Type of victim incident from detailed description

Column percentages

|  | All incidents[a] | |
|---|---|---|
| **Vehicle offence** | | |
| Theft of motor vehicle | 11 | |
| Theft from motor vehicle | 8 | |
| Deliberate damage to motor vehicle | 14 | |
| Bicycle stolen or damaged | 3 | |
| Other vehicle offence | 3 | |
| | | |
| **Burglary or break-in** | | |
| Total burglary or break-in | 18 | |
|    Money, cheque-book or credit cards stolen | | 3 |
|    Other property stolen or damaged | | 10 |
|    No mention of theft or damage | | 7 |
| Theft from the person outdoors | 5 | |
| Theft from the person indoors or on public transport | 8 | |
| Other theft (not of vehicle, nor from vehicle, not burglary or break-in, not from person) | 7 | |
| Assault (excluding sexual assault) | 11 | |
|    Weapon used | | 1 |
|    No mention of weapon | | 10 |
| Sexual assault | 1 | |
| Indecent exposure | 1 | |
| Threatening behaviour | 2 | |
| Blackmail | 1 | |
| Any other offence | 11 | |
| Don't know or vague answer | 1 | |
| | | |
| Base: all victims incidents[a] | | |
|    (unweighted) | 957 | |
|    (weighted) | 5,483 | |

a    In this and subsequent tables, 'all victim incidents' refers to all those for which a 'victim sheet' was completed.

A more detailed classification of the victim incidents is shown in Table III.1. The further information given there about assaults and burglaries comes from people's free descriptions rather than from further questioning, and may not, therefore, be complete. However, it seems that a weapon was used in only a small proportion of assaults (apparently about one in ten). Although this is not shown in the table, the informant mentioned that the assault took place in or near a pub in one out of ten cases, and that the victim or assailant had been drinking in a further one out of ten cases. The further information about burglaries and break-ins shown in the table indicates that in a substantial minority of these cases nothing was stolen or damaged, and that in the remaining cases property other than money or credit cards was usually involved.

From the filter questions supplemented by the detailed descriptions, 17 per cent of the incidents were classified (during the interview) as personal offences, 83 per cent as property offences and two per cent as both. In the case of personal offences, informants were asked whether they had any medical treatment and also whether they stayed in hospital overnight. In the case of property offences, they were asked whether anything was taken or damaged and, if so, what was the value of the loss or damage.

Only 13 per cent of personal offences resulted in the victim having medical treatment, and in only three out of one thousand cases did they result in the victim staying in hospital overnight. Assaults account for three-quarters of offences classified as personal. In 17 per cent of incidents involving an assault the victim received medical treatment and in $4\frac{1}{2}$ out of each one thousand cases of assault the victim stayed in hospital overnight. Along with the indications that in 90 per cent of cases of assault a weapon was not used, these findings show that most assaults are minor. In particular, they show that the risk of being injured as the result of an assault is low in comparison with other risks. According to official statistics, 7,500 people were killed or seriously injured in London in motor accidents during 1981 (the year of our survey), which amounts to a rate of just over 1 per 1,000 of the population. By contrast, the survey findings show that only 0.18 out of every 1,000 Londoners were hospitalised following an assault within the previous twelve months: so broadly the risk of serious injury on the roads is six times as high as the risk of injury from an assault. The risk of injury from an assault combined with a theft is much lower still - so low that it cannot be estimated from the survey which recorded only 10 cases of theft with assault, none of them leading to medical treatment of the victim. Also, as we have already pointed out, robberies account for only five per cent of all assaults and for 0.5 per cent of all incidents of victimisation. In the light of these findings the concentration of public and media attention on 'mugging' cannot be justified, and the feeling among white people that crime is high in areas of high ethnic concentration cannot be said to be soundly based merely because the rate of thefts from the person is higher than average in such areas.

The value of the loss from property offences is shown in Table III.2. In 12 per cent of these cases there was no loss, which is not surprising since attempted burglaries and vehicle thefts are included. The median value of the loss was £44 for property offences overall (taking into account the cases where there was no loss). However, in 23 per cent of cases, the loss was of £200 or

Table III.2    Value of loss from property offences

Column percentages and medians

| Value of what was taken or damaged | Total | Theft of motor vehicle | Damage to motor vehicle | Other vehicle offences | Burglary break-in | Theft from the person | Other theft | Other incidents |
|---|---|---|---|---|---|---|---|---|
| Nil (nothing taken or damaged) | 12 | 9 | 2 | 16 | 26 | 6 | 2 | 8 |
| £1-9 | 13 | - | 10 | 15 | 5 | 22 | 22 | 17 |
| £10-49 | 23 | 6 | 42 | 24 | 8 | 33 | 16 | 26 |
| £50-199 | 19 | 18 | 23 | 18 | 14 | 22 | 17 | 21 |
| £200-999 | 14 | 26 | 11 | 14 | 27 | 10 | 10 | 6 |
| £1000 or more | 7 | 18 | - | * | 13 | - | * | 10 |
| Don't know or not stated | 12 | 21 | 12 | 11 | 6 | 5 | 30 | 12 |
| Median value of loss(a) | £44 | £355 | £40 | £32 | £128 | £34 | £38 | £39 |
| Base: victim incidents: property offences | | | | | | | | |
| (unweighted) | 808 | 94 | 136 | 139 | 183 | 161 | 54 | 88 |
| (weighted) | 4,640 | 584 | 776 | 760 | 1,001 | 712 | 360 | 665 |

(a)    In calculating the median, cases where there was no loss have been included.

63

more. The value of the losses were much higher in the case of theft of a motor vehicle (median £355) and burglary (median £128) than for other types of offence.

## Description of the offender
For just over one-third of incidents the victim was able to give some description of the offender. The kind of knowledge that the victim had can be summarised as follows.

| The offender was | Per cent of all victim incidents |
|---|---|
| A relative | 1 |
| Someone else you previously knew | 10 |
| Not someone you previously knew, but now know who it was | 13 |
| Do not know who it was, but can give some description | 12 |
| Total who can give any description | 36 |
| Can give no description | 64 |

These findings are shown for the different kinds of offence separately in Table III.3. For the great majority of offences the victim does not know who the offender was, and also in the majority of cases can give no description. Assaults are strikingly different from the rest. The victim quite often previously knew the assailant (29 per cent of cases), although assaults by relatives form a fairly small proportion of all those reported (seven per cent). In a further 30 per cent of cases the victim found out subsequently who the assailant was, and in a majority of the remaining cases can give some description. It is only in 17 per cent of cases of assault that the victim can say nothing about the assailant at all. Victims of other offences that have not been separately classified can also give a description in a relatively high proportion of cases (50 per cent), probably because a number of these other offences are personal ones like blackmail, indecency and threatening behaviour.

Overall, the victim could say something about the offender in 36 per cent of cases. For these incidents informants were asked what was the sex, age and race of the offender or offenders. The offender was said to be male in 76 per cent of cases and female in four per cent of cases, while in 14 per cent of cases there were said to be offenders of both sexes. These findings are in agreement with official statistics of reported crime in showing that the great majority of crime is committed by males. Table III.4 shows that this applies to all kinds of offence (though the classification is rather broad, since there are only 342 cases in the survey in which the victim could give some description). According to the victim's reports, about half of the offences were committed by someone up to the age of 25, and 12 per cent by children of school age. Again

Table III.3    Victim incidents: knowledge of who the offender was

Row percentages

| | Someone you previously knew | Now know who it was | Can give some description | Can give no description | Base (a) | (b) |
|---|---|---|---|---|---|---|
| All victim incidents | 11 | 13 | 12 | 64 | 957 | 5,483 |
| Theft of motor vehicle | 3 | 8 | 5 | 79 | 95 | 600 |
| Damage to motor vehicle | 3 | 10 | 4 | 83 | 136 | 776 |
| Other vehicle offence | 2 | 9 | 6 | 83 | 139 | 760 |
| Burglary/break-in | 9 | 7 | 20 | 64 | 183 | 1,001 |
| Theft from the person | 11 | 17 | 11 | 61 | 161 | 712 |
| Other theft | 7 | 12 | 6 | 75 | 54 | 360 |
| Assault | 29 | 30 | 24 | 17 | 127 | 680 |
| Other incidents[c] | 26 | 11 | 13 | 50 | 97 | 756 |

(a)    unweighted
(b)    weighted

65

Table III.4    Victim incidents when the victim can give a description: sex and age of the offender

Column percentages

| | Total | Vehicle[a] offences | Burglary or break-in | Theft from the person | Assault | Others[b] |
|---|---|---|---|---|---|---|
| Sex of offender(s) | | | | | | |
| Male | 76 | 70 | 86 | 79 | 82 | 69 |
| Female | 4 | 5 | * | 12 | 2 | 3 |
| Both sexes | 14 | 7 | 5 | 9 | 16 | 24 |
| Don't know | 5 | 19 | 9 | * | - | 3 |
| Age of offender(s) | | | | | | |
| Of school age | 12 | 12 | 10 | 17 | 6 | 18 |
| 16 – 25 | 41 | 52 | 51 | 57 | 42 | 19 |
| Older than 25 | 32 | 22 | 29 | 21 | 40 | 35 |
| Mixed aged | 10 | 4 | 1 | 1 | 12 | 23 |
| Don't know | 5 | 10 | 10 | 5 | - | 4 |
| Base: unweighted | 342 | 56 | 56 | 69 | 108 | 66 |
| weighted | 1,956 | 362 | 358 | 274 | 563 | 472 |

(a)    Includes theft of motor vehicle, deliberate damage to motor vehicle and offences involving bicycles.

(b)    Includes 'other theft' and all others, except for those too vaguely described to be classifiable.

66

these findings are in agreement with official statistics in showing that a high proportion of crime is committed by children and young people. There is not much variation between the different kinds of offence in this respect, except that assaults and the residual category of 'other offences' are more likely than the rest to be committed by someone over the age of 25.

Table III.5 shows the race of the offender according to the victim's reports. Although the table only includes those 36 per cent of incidents for which the victim could give some description of the offender, the victim could still not describe the offender's race in 10 per cent of cases; also, in eight per cent of cases there were offenders of different races involved. If we exclude these categories and base the table only on incidents where the victim describes an offender or offenders belonging to one racial group only, we find that the pattern overall is as follows.

| Race of the offender | Per cent of incidents |
|---|---|
| White | 72 |
| Black | 24 |
| Asian | 3 |
| Other | 1 |

The list of categories was not read out to informants, who answered the question in their own words, while the interviewer used the list above to classify their answers. It is likely that some of the answers classified as 'black' really meant 'not white' rather than 'West Indian or African looking'. Even so it is quite clear that the proportion of offenders described as black is very high compared with the proportion of black or even of non-white people in the population of London. People of West Indian or African origin account for about five per cent of the population of Greater London. The proportion of the population who 'look black' (as opposed to Asian) might be a bit higher than this - perhaps six or seven per cent. Asians account for about four per cent of the London population. If we take it that when informants said 'black' they meant 'West Indian or African-looking' then the 24 per cent of offenders so described can be compared with the six or seven per cent of the population falling into that group, which on the face of it implies that black people are represented among offenders about four times as strongly as would be expected from their representation in the general population. The representation of Asians among offenders, on the other hand, would be about the same as would be expected from population proportions, or if anything lower. If we assume that informants did not distinguish consistently between black people and Asians, then the 27 per cent of offenders described as black or Asian should be compared with the 10 or 11 per cent of the population belonging to those groups, which would imply that these racial minorities are over-represented among offenders by a factor of about $2\frac{1}{2}$ to 1.

Table III.5   Victim incidents when the victim can give a description: race of offender

Column percentages

| Race of offender(s) | Total | Vehicle[a] offences | Burglary or break-in | Theft from the person | Assault | Others[a] |
|---|---|---|---|---|---|---|
| White | 59 | 42 | 47 | 43 | 73 | 66 |
| Black | 19 | 25 | 18 | 46 | 15 | 10 |
| Asian | 2 | 1 | 2 | 2 | * | 6 |
| Other | 1 | 1 | - | - | 2 | - |
| Different races | 8 | 3 | 4 | 4 | 9 | 18 |
| Don't know | 10 | 28 | 29 | 6 | - | - |
| Base:  unweighted | 342 | 56 | 56 | 69 | 108 | 66 |
|        weighted | 1,956 | 362 | 358 | 274 | 563 | 472 |

(a)   See Table III.4 for the definitions of these categories.

68

Comparisons of this kind are, of course, very crude. For example, a high proportion of crime is committed by children and young people, and West Indians are a young population. Thus, West Indians probably account for about seven per cent of the London population aged 15-24 as compared with five per cent of the population generally. Again, crime rates vary between different areas and socio-economic groups, and West Indians tend to live in the areas and belong to the socio-economic groups in which crime rates are high. In the next chapter we shall show that unemployed men are much more likely to be arrested and charged with offences than those in full-time work, and the rate of unemployment is much higher among West Indians than among whites, and extremely high among young West Indians. We have no means of carrying out a satisfactory analysis to show whether the apparently high representation of blacks among offenders described by the victims can be explained by a combination of factors such as these. However, the effect is so large that in all probability a full analysis would explain some but not all of it.

An entirely different reason for caution is that in two-thirds of cases the victim could not describe the offender, and it may well be that the offender was more often white in these cases: in other words, West Indians may tend to commit kinds of crime - thefts from the person are the obvious example - that give the victim a good chance of being able to come up with a description. Even where the victim does describe the offender, the description may be inaccurate, and if people associate crime with black people they may tend to say that the offender was black when they weren't sure.

In short, from the available information we cannot extimate the actual crime rate among white and black people or make a comparison that takes account of the relevant variables. At the same time, the apparent differences shown by the survey are large, and would probably not entirely disappear if all the qualifications could be fully taken into account. In any case the findings do incontestably have another kind of significance. They show that in one-quarter of cases where a victim can describe the offender they say the offender was black. Presumably, they say this to their friends and acquaintances and they say it to the police. Thus what victims say about their experiences does tend to create or reinforce the impression among the public at large and the police in particular that a relatively high proportion of crimes are committed by black people.

Table III.5 also shows that in cases of theft from the person the proportion of offenders who are said to be black is strikingly high (46 per cent), while it varies between 10 and 25 per cent for the other types of offence. The information compiled by the Metropolitan Police from victim reports shows a similar contrast. It is quite clear from all the available evidence that black people are much more likely to commit theft from the person than other ethnic groups and that this kind of crime forms a much higher proportion of all crimes committed by black people than of crimes committed by other groups.

## Decision to report to the police
Overall 52 per cent of the victim incidents became known to the police in one of the ways shown below.

|                                                    | Per cent of incidents |
|----------------------------------------------------|-----------------------|
| The victim reported the matter                     | 32                    |
| Some other person reported the matter              | 17                    |
| The police were there                              | 1                     |
| The police found out some other way                | 2                     |
| The police did not come to know about the matter   | 48                    |

These findings show something very important - if obvious - about the way that policing works. In only one per cent of cases did the police know about the incident by being there; in the remaining 99 per cent of cases they were dependent on a member of the public to report it, and it was not reported in about half of these cases. The proportion of incidents that the police actually saw happening is even lower than one per cent; for example, in three per cent of cases of damage to a motor vehicle the police were said to have 'been there', but in all probability they would have arrived after the damage was actually done. Burglary and theft from the person are two kinds of offence that the police often try to combat by patrolling in uniform or, more often, in plain clothes, but our findings show that the proportion of incidents for which the police 'were there' was 0.5 per cent for each of these kinds of offence. These findings will form an important background to our discussion of policing strategies in the fourth volume of this series.

Table III.6 shows that there are no differences between ethnic groups in the proportion of victims who reported incidents to the police (the small differences shown are not statistically significant). It is widely thought that West Indians have less confidence in the police than other groups, and later in this report we shall show that this is true. Nevertheless, they are just as likely as other groups to call on the police for help when they require it. This shows that their lack of confidence does not run as deep as might be thought; there is no evidence that they are more inclined than other groups to resort to other methods, in place of the police, for dealing with people who commit offences against them.

The table shows that there is, however, a strong relationship with age. Older people are about twice as likely as young ones to report an incident of victimisation to the police. Where the victim is aged 15-19 the police come to know about the matter in 37 per cent of cases, but in 62 per cent of cases where the victim is aged 60 or over.

Table III.6    Victim incidents: whether and how the police got to know, by ethnic group and age

Row percentages

| | Police told by victim | Police got to know some other way | Police did not get to know | Base unweighted | Base weighted |
|---|---|---|---|---|---|
| All victim incidents | 32 | 20 | 48 | 957 | 5,483 |
| Ethnic group of victim | | | | | |
| White | 32 | 21 | 47 | 593 | 4,995 |
| West Indian | 30 | 13 | 57 | 200 | 159 |
| Asian | 38 | 15 | 47 | 127 | 139 |
| Other non-white | 31 | 5 | 64 | 37 | 189 |
| Age of victim | | | | | |
| 15 – 19 | 19 | 18 | 63 | 168 | 469 |
| 20 – 24 | 29 | 22 | 51 | 265 | 875 |
| 25 – 44 | 33 | 17 | 50 | 399 | 2,918 |
| 45 – 59 | 35 | 29 | 36 | 80 | 727 |
| 60 or over | 39 | 23 | 38 | 45 | 494 |

71

Since a lack of confidence in the police is particularly to be expected among young West Indians, it is also important to compare their response with the response of young white people and young Asians. In fact, the same proportion of young West Indians and young white victims reported the incident to the police. Young Asians may be more inclined to report victim incidents than other young people, though the number of cases is too small to show this conclusively. Within each ethnic group older people are more inclined than younger ones to report incidents to the police (table not shown).

Table III.7    Victim incidents:  proportion that became known to the police by type of offence

|  | Per cent |
|---|---|
| All victim incidents | 52 |
| Theft of motor vehicle | 87 |
| Damage to motor vehicle | 33 |
| Other vehicle offences | 45 |
| Burglary or break-in | 73 |
| Theft from the person | 50 |
| Other theft | 39 |
| Assault | 45 |
| Other offences | 43 |

Note:   The bases for percentages are the same as in Table III.3.

The proportion of incidents that became known to the police varies a good deal according to the type of offence (see Table III.7). The offences that the police are most likely to come to know about are theft of a motor vehicle (87 per cent) and burglary or attempted burglary (73 per cent). In view of the public interest in the offence of theft from the person, it is important to notice that only half of these offences come to police notice. On the one hand this implies that the actual number of such offences is twice as high as the official statistics show. On the other hand it suggests that the crime is often not particularly disturbing to the victim, for there would be no particular reason for a victim not to report a crime of this kind if it were thought to be serious or disturbing (as there would be, for example, in the case of a rape or indecent assault).

As might be expected, the greater the loss in the case of property offences, the more likely it is the matter will be reported to the police (see Table III.8). Only 14 per cent of incidents involving a loss of £200 or more did not come to police notice. In the case of personal offences it is much harder to find a good measure of how serious the matter was from the victim's point of view.  Incidents are more likely to be reported where the victim received medical treatment than where he did not, but the difference is not very large (the statistics here are unreliable, being based on a small number of cases).  Probably the difference is no larger because whether or not there was injury is rather a poor measure of how upsetting the incident was to the victim.

Table III.8    Victim incidents:  proportion that became known to the police by whether the victim received medical treatment and value of the loss

|  | Per cent | Base unweighted | Base weighted |
|---|---|---|---|
| **Personal offences** | | | |
| Victim received medical treatment | 60 | 31 | 120 |
| Victim received no medical treatment | 48 | 133 | 788 |
| **Property offences by loss** | | | |
| No loss | 36 | 106 | 602 |
| £1 - 9 | 17 | 109 | 580 |
| £10 - 49 | 43 | 191 | 1,059 |
| £50 - 199 | 61 | 160 | 862 |
| £200 or over | 86 | 154 | 988 |
| Amount not known | 51 | 85 | 523 |

The police handling of the matter
We have seen that 52 per cent of victim incidents became known to the police; in most of these cases one or more police officers spoke to the victim about the incident; still thinking in terms of all victim incidents, there was a conversation between the victim and one or more police officers in 44 per cent of cases.  Uniform officers were involved in 38 per cent of incidents and plain-clothes officers in 13 per cent (of course in some cases both uniform and plain-clothes officers were involved).

Where police officers were involved, informants were asked whether they were happy with the way the officers spoke to them and, overall, whether they were satisfied or dissatisfied with the way the officers dealt with the matter.  The questions were asked separately for uniform and plain-clothes officers.  The findings (Table III.9) show that about 90 per cent of informants were happy with the way the officers spoke to them regardless of whether the officer was in uniform or in plain clothes.  Victims also expressed a high level of satisfaction overall with the way the police officers dealt with the matter.  In the case of uniform officers, 43 per cent were 'very satisfied' and 33 per cent 'fairly satisfied', while only 12 per cent were 'very dissatisfied'. A similar level of satisfaction was expressed where the officer was in plain clothes. Bearing in mind that a fairly small proportion of these crimes were solved (as we shall see shortly) these findings reflect well on the performance of the police.

Table III.9     Victim incidents: assessment of the way that uniform and plain-clothes officers dealt with the matter

Column percentages

|  | Uniform | Plain-clothes |
|---|---|---|
| **Were you happy about the way they spoke to you?** | | |
| Yes | 89 | 91 |
| No | 10 | 9 |
| Not answered | * | * |
| **Satisfaction with the way they dealt with the matter overall** | | |
| Very satisfied | 43 | 47 |
| Fairly satisfied | 33 | 29 |
| A bit dissatisfied | 10 | 17 |
| Very dissatisfied | 12 | 7 |
| Not answered | 3 | * |
| Base: victim incidents where the victim spoke to a uniform/plain-clothes officer about the matter | | |
| (unweighted) | 340 | 104 |
| (weighted) | 2,095 | 708 |

Table III.10 shows that Asians and West Indians were rather less likely to be satisfied with the performance of the police than white people, but the difference is not large. For example, 84 per cent of West Indians said they were happy with the way the uniform officers spoke to them, and 68 per cent that they were satisfied overall with the way the uniform police dealt with the matter. Thus we have shown that a similar proportion of West Indians as of white people report victim incidents to the police and that a majority of those who do so are satisfied with the service they get, although the level of satisfaction is a little lower than among white people. These findings show that as regards their willingness to make use of the police and their assessment of the service they receive in particular instances, there is no crisis of confidence in the police among West Indians. Surprisingly, the

74

Table III.10    Victim incidents: assessment of the way that uniform officers dealt with the matter by ethnic group and age of the victim

Column percentages

| | Ethnic group | | | | Age | | |
| | White | West Indian | Asian | Other | 15-24 | 25-44 | 45+ |
|---|---|---|---|---|---|---|---|
| **Were you happy about the way they spoke to you?** | | | | | | | |
| Yes | 91 | 84 | 82 | (48) | 84 | 87 | 98 |
| No | 9 | 11 | 16 | (52) | 16 | 13 | 1 |
| Not answered | * | 5 | 2 | (-) | - | 1 | * |
| **Satisfaction with the way they dealt with the matter overall** | | | | | | | |
| Very satisfied | 45 | 36 | 18 | (3) | 29 | 42 | 54 |
| Fairly satisfied | 33 | 32 | 49 | (39) | 47 | 32 | 26 |
| A bit dissatisfied | 10 | 9 | 13 | (-) | 14 | 9 | 8 |
| Very dissatisfied | 10 | 17 | 19 | (58) | 11 | 17 | 2 |
| Not answered | 3 | 5 | - | (-) | - | * | 10 |
| **Base:** victim incidents where the victim spoke to a uniform officer about the matter | | | | | | | |
| (unweighted) | 211 | 61 | 55 | 13 | 128 | 154 | 58 |
| (weighted) | 1,922 | 49 | 61 | 63 | 428 | 1,100 | 566 |

Note:    The percentages in brackets are very unreliable, being based on only 13 cases.

level of satisfaction is lower among Asians than among West Indians (18 per cent of Asians compared with 36 per cent of West Indians say they are very satisfied with the way the uniform officers dealt with the matter).

Differences between age groups are much more marked than those between ethnic groups. Among those aged 45 or more, 54 per cent say they are very satisfied with the way the uniform officer dealt with the matter, compared with 29 per cent of those aged 15-24. Many findings in this study show that older people have warmer feelings towards the police than younger ones, and this may account for the difference. At the same time, it may be that the police try harder to please older people, or that they are better at getting on with them.

For all victim incidents that came to police notice, informants were asked whether the police took any action at that time or later to investigate or deal with the matter. If they answered 'yes' they were asked how full the investigation was, whether the police moved as quickly as could reasonably be expected and whether they caught 'the people who did it'. The findings produced by these questions will not be complete, since the victim will not in all cases know about action taken by the police. They do, however, give some indication of what action was actually taken, and in any case definitely show what the victim knows and thinks about any action taken. In 35 per cent of the cases that came to police notice, the informant says that the police took some action; this amounts to only 18 per cent of all victim incidents. In that rather small number of cases where the police were said to have taken some action, the balance of opinion about the action taken is broadly approving: in 66 per cent of cases the informant thought the police made a full investigation and in 82 per cent of cases that they moved as quickly as could be expected; in 37 per cent of these cases the informant knows that the offender was caught. For the cases where the police are known to have taken some action, these findings reflect well on their performance.

For the purpose of carrying out a more detailed and composite analysis it is better to base all the findings on all cases that came to police notice, regardless of whether they took any action (see Table III.11). Among all of these incidents, the police are said to have taken some action in 35 per cent of cases, to have made a full investigation in 23 per cent of cases and to have moved as quickly as could reasonably be expected in 29 per cent of cases. The informant knows that the offender was caught in 13 per cent of all cases that came to police notice. Expressed in these terms, the success rate of the police seems low - no doubt largely because many of the cases seem to them too trivial to be worth bothering about, and because in many cases there is no hope at all of catching the offender. The numbers are rather small for a detailed analysis, but whether or not the police took action does not seem to depend very critically on the type of offence, except that action was more often known to have been taken over thefts of motor vehicles (56 per cent of cases) than for other offences.

Table III.11 Victim incidents: action taken by the police, by ethnic group and age of victim

Column percentages

| | Total | Ethnic group | | | Age | | |
|---|---|---|---|---|---|---|---|
| | | White | West Indian | Asian | 15-24 | 25-44 | 45+ |
| They took some action | 35 | 36 | 52 | 29 | 49 | 35 | 25 |
| They took no action | 33 | 33 | 34 | 27 | 31 | 32 | 38 |
| Don't know | 32 | 31 | 14 | 43 | 20 | 33 | 37 |
| If they took some action | | | | | | | |
| They made a full investigation | 23 | 24 | 28 | 16 | 28 | 23 | 20 |
| They investigated, but not fully | 6 | 6 | 15 | 4 | 8 | 8 | 3 |
| They did not bother much about it | 3 | 3 | 6 | 5 | 8 | 3 | 3 |
| Not answered | 2 | 2 | 3 | 4 | 4 | 1 | - |
| Did they move as quickly as you could reasonably expect? | | | | | | | |
| Yes | 29 | 29 | 44 | 24 | 39 | 29 | 21 |
| No/not answered | 6 | 7 | 7 | 5 | 10 | 6 | 3 |
| Did they catch those who did it? | | | | | | | |
| Yes | 13 | 13 | 22 | 4 | 19 | 12 | 11 |
| No | 23 | 23 | 30 | 25 | 30 | 23 | 14 |
| Base: victim incidents that came to police notice | | | | | | | |
| (unweighted) | 464 | 298 | 83 | 67 | 193 | 196 | 75 |
| (weighted) | 2,831 | 2,621 | 66 | 74 | 619 | 1,448 | 763 |

Note:    Separate figures are not shown for 'other non-whites' but they are included in the total.

77

Table III.11 shows that where the victim was a West Indian, the police were more likely to take some action, to make a full investigation, to move quickly and to catch the offender than where the victim was white or Asian. The differences shown are quite large. For example, the offender was caught in 22 per cent of cases where the victim was a West Indian compared with 13 per cent of cases where the victim was white. It is where the victim was an Asian that the police action was reported to have been least energetic and successful. For example, the offender was caught in only four per cent of these cases. In interpreting these findings we should beware of assuming that it is the energy and success of the police action that determines how satisfied the victim is. While one line of causation does run that way, it is also likely that the attitude of the victim partly determines the action taken by the police. In other words, the police may make special efforts where the victim is a West Indian because West Indian victims are more often dissatisfied and difficult to fob off. If we look at the matter in this light, there is no conflict between the finding that, on the one hand, West Indian victims are more often dissatisfied with the police efforts than whites and, on the other hand, police efforts on behalf of West Indian victims are more energetic and successful than those on behalf of white victims. In a broader context it does seem likely that the police make greater efforts on behalf of West Indian than other victims because they are conscious of criticism by West Indians as a group, and concerned about the general quality of relations with them.

Table III.11 also shows that where the victim is older, the police are less likely to take action and to catch the offender than where the victim is younger. However, it should be remembered that a much higher proportion of older than of younger victims report the matter to the police, so among incidents reported by older people there is probably a much higher proportion of trivial ones and of cases where there is no hope of catching the offender. Although the police less often take action to investigate and less often catch the offender where the victim is an older person, they still handle the matter in a way that is satisfactory to the victim in the great majority of cases: in fact, older victims are considerably more likely than younger ones to be satisfied with what the police do about the matter. This shows, incidentally, that in many cases it is not necessary for the police to carry out a full investigation or to catch the offender in order to make the victim feel that the matter has been properly dealt with; in many cases what the victim probably wants is for the police officer to talk to him or her in a sympathetic way, or to have words with the 'offender' without bringing charges, and there is evidence from the British Crime Survey to support this interpretation.

**999 calls**
A remarkably high proportion of people - 11 per cent - said they had made a 999 call to the police in the past 12 months. The

majority of these had made only one call, but an appreciable number had made more than one (see Table III.12). In fact, we find that 47 per cent of calls were made by people who had made more than one in the past 12 months, and as many as 16 per cent of calls were made by people who had made five or more, who account for only 0.5 per cent of people. These statistics imply that some people are very much more likely than others to make 999 calls to the police, and that the 'recurrent callers' account for a considerable proportion of the demand for police service. A calculation shows that there are about eight times as many people who have made three or more calls as would be expected on the assumption that the chance of making a call is the same for everyone. Also, about 30 per cent of calls are made by people who call repeatedly and more often than would be expected by chance. This may be partly because some people are in jobs or situations which make it likely that they will get into trouble themselves or observe incidents that require a police presence: examples would be bartenders, bus conductors and managers of ice rinks. But it may also be partly because some people get into the habit of calling the police, sometimes for little or no reason.

Table III.12    Number of 999 calls made to the police in the past twelve months

Column percentages

| Number of calls made | Per cent of people | Per cent of calls made by each group |
|---|---|---|
| None | 88.9 | – |
| Any | 11.1 | 100 |
| One | 8.4 | 53 |
| Two | 1.4 | 17 |
| Three | 0.4 | 8 |
| Four | 0.3 | 6 |
| Five | 0.3 | 9 |
| Six or more | 0.2 | 7 |
| Some, don't know how many | 0.1 | (a) |
| | | |
| Base: all informants | | |
| (unweighted) | 2,420 | |
| (weighted) | 13,944 | |

(a)    Not known

Eight per cent of Asians and West Indians compared with 11 per cent of white people had made a 999 call to the police in the past 12 months. Although this difference may seem small, it is statistically significant, and it implies that the proportion who have made a call among Asians and West Indians is about three-quarters of the level among whites. However, the numbers involved in the survey are so small that we cannot really interpret the difference. It is possible that Asians and West Indians tend to be reluctant to make 999 calls. Equally, however, it is possible that they less often have cause to make a call, or that they are less likely to make a call without good reason. There is no difference between Asians and West Indians in the proportion who have made a call. Older people (aged 60 or over) and young people (aged 15-19) seem less likely to have made 999 calls than those in the intervening age groups.

Table III.13    Reason for last 999 call to the police

|  | Per cent |  |
|---|---|---|
| Reporting offence as victim | 23 | |
| Burglary | | 9 |
| Other theft or damage to property | | 7 |
| Assault | | 5 |
| Vehicle offence | | 5 |
| Other offence | | 2 |
| Call for assistance | 21 | |
| Informant bothered or at risk | | 10 |
| Informant's employer bothered or at risk | | 1 |
| Other call for assistance | | 9 |
| Reporting incidents, not as victims | 50 | |
| Fight or disturbance | | 10 |
| Burglary or theft | | 7 |
| Assault | | 2 |
| Other offence | | 7 |
| Accident involving informant | | 2 |
| Accident not involving informant | | 9 |
| Traffic or road hazard | | 1 |
| Other reports | | |
| Other reasons | 2 | |
| Base: informants who had made a 999 call to the police in the past 12 months | | |
| (unweighted) | | 243 |
| (weighted) | | 1,544 |

Informants were asked the reason for making the last 999 call to the police. In half of all cases, the call was to report an incident where the informant was not a victim; this shows a considerable degree of willingness among people to call the police on behalf of others or for the common good. In about one-quarter of cases the call was to report an incident where the informant was the victim, and in about one-fifth of cases it was a call for assistance.

A more detailed account of the reasons for the last call is shown in Table III.13. The kinds of incident most commonly reported where the informant is not a victim are fights and disturbances (10 per cent of the total) and burglary or theft (7 per cent). Where the informant was reporting an offence as a victim, the most common types of offence were burglary (9 per cent of the total) and other theft or damage to property (7 per cent). Assault (5 per cent) and vehicle offences (5 per cent) are also fairly common. Although the calls for assistance account for 21 per cent of cases in total, it was only in about half of these cases (or 10 per cent of the total) that it was entirely clear that the informant was bothered or at risk.

Table III.14    Proportion satisfied with the way the police treated the last 999 call, by ethnic group

Row percentages

| | Per cent satisfied | Base | |
| | | unweighted | weighted |
|---|---|---|---|
| Total | 83 | 243 | 1,544 |
| | | | |
| Ethnic group | | | |
| Whites | 85 | 139 | 1,373 |
| West Indians | 74 | 44 | 38 |
| Asians | 66 | 47 | 50 |
| Other non-whites | (78) | 13 | 83 |

Note:    The base is informants who had made a 999 call to the police in the past twelve months.

Among those who had made a 999 call, the great majority (83 per cent) were satisfied with the way the police treated the call on the last occasion. Table III.14 shows that Asians and West Indians were less likely than whites to have been satisfied.

## IV EXPERIENCE OF THE POLICE AS OFFENDER OR SUSPECT

### Stops

'Every Constable may stop, search and detain any vessel, boat, cart or carriage in or upon which there shall be reason to suspect that anything stolen or unlawfully obtained may be found, and also any person who may be reasonably suspected of having or conveying in any manner anything stolen or unlawfully obtained (s.66, Metropolitan Police Act 1839).'

'If a Constable has reasonable grounds to suspect that any person is in possession of a controlled drug in contravention of the Act or any regulation made thereunder, the Constable may -

a) search that person and detain him for the purpose;
b) search any vehicle or vessel in which the Constable suspects that the drug may be found;
c) seize and detain for the purposes of proceedings under this Act anything found in the course of the search which appears to the Constable to be evidence of an offence under the Act'.

'A person driving a motor vehicle or riding a pedal cycle on a road must stop the vehicle on being required to do so by a Constable in uniform'.

'A Constable may require any person driving a motor vehicle on a road, or any person reasonably believed to have been the driver of a motor vehicle involved in an accident or to have committed an offence in relation to the use of a motor vehicle, to furnish his name and address and that of the owner, and to produce the relevant certificate' (i.e. of insurance).

'A Constable has power to require any person driving a motor vehicle on a road, or any driver of a motor vehicle reasonably believed to have been involved in an accident or to have committed an offence in relation to the use of a motor vehicle, to produce his driving licence for examination'.

The above extracts from the Instruction Book for the Guidance of the Metropolitan Police Force summarise the powers on which the police in London rely when stopping people on foot or in vehicles, searching the people or the vehicles and requiring them to produce driving documents. These are powers that they use very commonly and extensively. A Constable has power to stop and search someone on foot only where he 'reasonably suspects' that the person has something stolen or unlawfully obtained or a controlled drug. He has power to stop a person driving a vehicle or pedal cycle regardless of whether there is a 'reasonable suspicion' of this kind; and he can, at any time, require a person driving a motor vehicle to produce a driving licence and certificate of insurance.

In Chapter XVI we shall show that the requirement that there should be 'reasonable suspicion' has little effect on police practice. Further guidance given in the Instruction Book suggests that this constraint is not to be taken too seriously.

> These powers are of the greatest value in the prevention and detection of crime and, while care and discretion must be used to prevent annoyance to innocent persons, it is the duty of all officers to exercise them in spite of the inevitable risk of mistakes. (Original emphasis.)

The survey of the public provides a good means of establishing what proportion of people are stopped by the police, what kinds of people are stopped, what proportion of stops lead to the detection of an offence and what the people concerned think about the experience of being stopped in particular instances. This analysis will go a considerable way towards showing how the police use their discretion in this field, and with what results. Whether and if so how far they exceed their powers, for example, by stopping people on foot when they have no grounds for reasonable suspicion, cannot be directly shown from the survey results alone, but these results will at least show how far 'annoyance to innocent persons' is prevented.

## Who is stopped and how often

Our information on who is stopped and how often comes from the following questions.

> The police sometimes stop or approach people in cars, motor-cycles or other vehicles to ask them questions or because they think they may be breaking some of the laws about driving. Has this ever happened to you, whether you were driving or a passenger?
> If yes Has it happened at all in the past twelve months, that is since _____ (current month) 1980?
> If yes How often has it happened in the past twelve months?
> The police sometimes approach people in the street and ask them questions. Has this ever happened to you?
> If yes Has it happened at all in the past twelve months, that is since _____ (current month) 1980?
> If yes How often has it happened in the past twelve months?

It should be noticed that where vehicle stops are concerned all cases where the informant was in the vehicle are included, regardless of whether he or she was driving. Therefore we are throughout talking about the percentage or number of <u>people</u> who have been stopped, and not about the percentage or number of vehicles.

A summary of the findings for all informants is shown below.

<u>In a vehicle</u>

| | |
|---|---|
| Per cent stopped | 14 |
| Mean number of stops overall | 0.21 |
| Mean number of stops among those who have been stopped | 1.54 |

<u>On foot</u>

| | |
|---|---|
| Per cent stopped | 3 |
| Mean number of stops overall | 0.07 |
| Mean number of stops among those who have been stopped | 1.95 |

<u>In a vehicle or on foot</u>

| | |
|---|---|
| Per cent stopped | 16 |
| Mean number of stops overall | 0.28 |
| Mean number of stops among those who have been stopped | 1.71 |

These findings show that a substantial minority of the population (16 per cent) have been stopped by the police one or more times in the past twelve months. The mean number of stops among those who have been stopped at all is much greater than 1, which implies that the same individuals are apt to be stopped on different occasions. A more detailed analysis shows that 12 per cent of people have been stopped just once in the past twelve months, while four per cent have been stopped more than once. If we confine our attention to those who have been stopped at all, we find that a considerable proportion of them have been stopped many times, as the following summary table shows.

| Number of times stopped | Per cent |
|---|---|
| 1 | 75 |
| 2 | 12 |
| 3 | 6 |
| 4 | 2 |
| 5 - 9 | 3 |
| 10 or more | 2 |

People who are stopped repeatedly are a small proportion of the whole population, but account for a substantial proportion of all stops: for example, those who have been stopped four or more times are one per cent of the population, seven per cent of those

Table IV.1    Number of times stopped by the police in the past twelve months, by age

| | 15-19 | 20-24 | 25-44 | 45-59 | 60 and over |
|---|---|---|---|---|---|
| **In a vehicle** | | | | | |
| Per cent stopped | 22 | 27 | 18 | 10 | 3 |
| Mean number of stops overall | 0.56 | 0.42 | 0.24 | 0.12 | 0.03 |
| Mean number of stops among those who have been stopped | 2.51 | 1.58 | 1.36 | 1.23 | 1.00 |
| **On foot** | | | | | |
| Per cent stopped | 18 | 5 | 3 | 1 | 1 |
| Mean number of stops overall | 0.38 | 0.18 | 0.03 | 0.01 | 0.01 |
| Mean number of stops among those who have been stopped | 2.09 | 3.32 | 1.26 | 1.04 | 1.00 |
| **In a vehicle or on foot** | | | | | |
| Per cent stopped | 35 | 29 | 20 | 10 | 3 |
| Mean number of stops overall | 0.94 | 0.60 | 0.27 | 0.13 | 0.03 |
| Mean number of stops among those who have been stopped | 2.67 | 2.05 | 1.38 | 1.22 | 1.00 |
| **Base:** all informants | | | | | |
| (unweighted) | 490 | 494 | 844 | 345 | 247 |
| (weighted) | 1,278 | 1,332 | 5,174 | 2,910 | 3,252 |

85

who have been stopped at all, and account for 30 per cent of stops.

These findings imply that a large number of stops are made. The adult population of London is about $5\frac{1}{2}$ million, and the mean number of stops per person is 0.28; it follows that about $1\frac{1}{2}$ million stops are made by the police over a twelve month period. (This is not the same as the number of stops recorded by the police: we shall see later that in a large proportion of cases the name and address of the person is not taken, and for these a formal record will not be kept.)

Some population groups are many times more likely to be stopped than others. This shows that, by and large, police officers do not make stops randomly, and to the extent that the groups that are likely to be stopped are ones that contain a high proportion of offenders it shows that they are using their powers intelligently. However, membership of a demographic group - that is, being, for example, young, male and black - certainly does not constitute reasonable grounds for suspicion in itself. If a high proportion of any such group has been stopped, then as far as that group are concerned it would seem that the police are failing to use 'care and discretion to prevent annoyance to innocent persons' since it is fair to assume that the great majority of any such group are 'innocent persons'.

Table IV.2    Number of times stopped by the police in the past twelve months, by sex

|  | Men | Women |
|---|---|---|
| **In a vehicle** | | |
| Per cent stopped | 19 | 9 |
| Mean number of stops overall | 0.34 | 0.11 |
| Mean number of stops among those who have been stopped | 1.77 | 1.15 |
| **On foot** | | |
| Per cent stopped | 6 | 2 |
| Mean number of stops overall | 0.11 | 0.03 |
| Mean number of stops among those who have been stopped | 2.01 | 1.78 |
| **In a vehicle or on foot** | | |
| Per cent stopped | 23 | 11 |
| Mean number of stops overall | 0.45 | 0.14 |
| Mean number of stops among those who have been stopped | 1.96 | 1.27 |
| Base:  all informants | | |
| (unweighted) | 1,161 | 1,259 |
| (weighted) | 6,297 | 7,648 |

There are four characteristics that are strongly related to the likelihood of being stopped: age, sex, ethnic group and ownership or use of a vehicle. There are also some further characteristics covered in the survey that have a weaker relationship with the likelihood of being stopped, such as whether or not the person has a job. Of course, not all the relevant characteristics can be covered in a survey of this kind. Our observational work, reported in the fourth volume of this series, shows that people who are of unconventional appearance and those who drive Mark II Ford Cortinas are particularly likely to be stopped, but the survey does not provide information on either of these points. However, even an analysis confined to demographic and socio-economic variables is revealing. We shall first take each of the major variables one by one, then show their effect in combination with each other.

The analysis by age is shown in Table IV.1. Younger people are much more likely to be stopped than older people, by a factor of about 11 to 1 in terms of the proportion of people stopped or about 30 to 1 in terms of the mean number of stops per person. This difference is, of course, clearly related to the very sharp differences in the incidence of criminal activity among different age groups: but it means that an uncomfortably high proportion of young people are stopped. For example, one-third of those aged 15-19 have been stopped in the past twelve months, and, perhaps more important, those young people who have been stopped at all have, on average, been stopped 2.67 times. It is those in the youngest age group (15-19) who are most likely to be stopped on foot - three times as likely as those aged 20-24. However, it is those aged 20-24 who are most likely to be stopped in a vehicle, though the youngest age group is not far behind.

Secondly, men are much more likely to be stopped than women (see Table IV.2). This, again, is clearly related to the incidence of criminal activity, which is much higher among men than women. Men are twice as likely to be stopped as women in terms of the proportion of people involved, and three times as likely in terms of the mean number of stops per person. The difference is stronger for stops of people on foot than for stops of people in vehicles.

Thirdly, the likelihood of being stopped varies according to ethnic group: it is highest for West Indians, lowest for Asians and middling for white people (see Table IV.3). In terms of the proportion who have been stopped, the difference between West Indians and white people is not very striking (24 per cent for West Indians, 17 per cent for white people). However, the mean number of stops is nearly three times as high among West Indians as among white people, and this is largely because those West Indians who are stopped tend to be stopped repeatedly; among those who have been stopped at all, the mean number of stops is 3.19 for West Indians compared with 1.65 among white people. The difference between West Indians and whites is much more marked in the case

Table IV.3  Number of times stopped by the police in the past twelve months, by ethnic group

| | Total | Whites | West Indians | Asians | Other non-whites |
|---|---|---|---|---|---|
| **In a vehicle** | | | | | |
| Per cent stopped | 14 | 14 | 18 | 5 | 4 |
| Mean number of stops overall | 0.21 | 0.21 | 0.56 | 0.08 | 0.06 |
| Mean number of stops among those who have been stopped | 1.54 | 1.46 | 3.19 | 1.59 | 1.56 |
| **On foot** | | | | | |
| Per cent stopped | 3 | 3 | 11 | 2 | 7 |
| Mean number of stops overall | 0.07 | 0.06 | 0.22 | 0.02 | 0.07 |
| Mean number of stops among those who have been stopped | 1.95 | 2.04 | 1.96 | 1.16 | 1.05 |
| **In a vehicle or on foot** | | | | | |
| Per cent stopped | 16 | 17 | 24 | 7 | 11 |
| Mean number of stops overall | 0.28 | 0.27 | 0.78 | 0.10 | 0.13 |
| Mean number of stops among those who have been stopped | 1.71 | 1.65 | 3.19 | 1.58 | 1.24 |
| **Base:** all informants | | | | | |
| (unweighted) | 2,420 | 1,252 | 511 | 541 | 116 |
| (weighted) | 13,944 | 12,428 | 450 | 607 | 459 |

of stops of people on foot than in the case of stops of people in vehicles. Thus, the proportion of people who have been stopped when on foot is nearly four times as high among West Indians as among white people (11 per cent compared with three per cent).

Of course, these differences are to a large degree the reflection of decisions made by police officers about who to stop; but they also partly reflect differences between the habits of various groups. People who are often out on the streets late at night are more likely to be stopped than those who are at home in bed. Factors of this kind will account for some of the differences between age groups, and possibly between the sexes and between ethnic groups; they cannot, for the most part, be measured in a survey. However, there is one such factor that can be measured, that is ownership or use of a vehicle. Table IV.4 shows that 21 per cent of those who own or have the use of a vehicle have been stopped while in a vehicle in the past twelve months, compared with 6 per cent of the rest. A remarkable 41 per cent of motor bike owners and users have been stopped.

Table IV.4    Number of times stopped in a vehicle by the police in the past twelve months, by use of vehicle

|  | Whether own or have use of vehicle | | | |
|  | None | Car or motor bike | Car | Motor bike |
| --- | --- | --- | --- | --- |
| Per cent stopped | 6 | 21 | 20 | 41 |
| Number of stops overall | 0.09 | 0.31 | 0.29 | 0.75 |
| Mean number of stops among those who have been stopped | 1.66 | 1.51 | 1.43 | 1.81 |
| Base: all informants | | | | |
| (unweighted) | 1,297 | 1,123 | 1,082 | 98 |
| (weighted) | 6,445 | 7,500 | 7,264 | 648 |

Note:    412 informants (weighted) have the use of both a car and a motor bike, and are therefore included under both heads.

Each of these four variables has a substantial effect on the likelihood of being stopped; in combination with each other, they have a very powerful effect indeed. The proportion of all adults who have been stopped in a vehicle in the past twelve months is 14 per cent; the proportion of young West Indians who own or have the use of a vehicle who have been stopped in a vehicle is 49 per cent. Unfortunately, the numbers here are rather too small for a separate analysis by sex, but because men are in general much more likely to be stopped than women we can be fairly sure that well over half of young West Indian men who own or have the use of a vehicle will have been stopped.

At the same time, Table IV.5 shows that to some extent the difference between West Indians and white people in the likelihood of being stopped is a function of the different age structure of the two groups. When West Indians and white vehicle owners and users are compared within the same age groups, we find little, if any difference in the proportion who have been stopped, whereas this proportion is radically lower among Asians. However, the number of stops is much higher among young West Indians than among young white people, because the young West Indians tend very strongly to be stopped repeatedly: thus, among young West Indians who have been stopped at all, the mean number of stops is a remarkable 5.06, compared with 1.94 among young white people. What these findings mean is that if you are young and drive a car then, unless you are Asian, you have nearly a 50 per cent chance of being stopped by the police over a twelve-month period, and if you are one of those young West Indian drivers who gets stopped, you can expect to be stopped five times a year on average.

Setting aside ownership or use of a vehicle, we can consider the effect of sex, age and ethnic group in combination (the findings for men are shown in Table IV.6 - the table for women is not shown). Taking the two extreme cases, we find that 63 per cent of West Indian men aged 15-24 have been stopped, compared with none of the Asian women aged 45 or over in the survey. Comparing like with like in Table IV.6, we find that the likelihood of being stopped on foot is radically higher among young West Indian men than among young white men. Here the difference is in the proportion stopped (45 per cent for West Indians compared with 18 per cent for whites) and there is no more tendency among West Indians than among whites for those who are stopped at all to be stopped repeatedly. Thus, police officers are more likely to stop young West Indians than young whites whether they are on foot or in a vehicle; but when they are in a vehicle, they tend to choose the same West Indians again and again, whereas when they are on foot they are more likely to choose a different young West Indian each time. The probable reason for this is that the type of vehicle serves as an important criterion, but there is no similar criterion in the case of people on foot. It is probably the young West Indians in certain types of vehicle, such as Mark II Ford Cortinas, who tend to be stopped repeatedly, whereas for young West Indians on foot this likelihood of being stopped is more uniform, and substantially higher than for young white people.

Of course, the most important finding is that young males are very likely to be stopped, especially if they are West Indian. Sixty-three per cent of young West Indian men and 44 per cent of young white men have been stopped in a twelve-month period, and among those who have been stopped at all the West Indians have been stopped about four times and the whites about $2\frac{1}{2}$ times on average

90

Table IV.5 Number of times stopped in a vehicle by the police: vehicle owners/users by ethnic group and age in combination

| | Whites | | | West Indians | | | Asians | | |
|---|---|---|---|---|---|---|---|---|---|
| | 15-24 | 25-44 | 45 and over | 15-24 | 25-44 | 45 and over | 15-24 | 25-44 | 45 and over |
| Per cent stopped overall | 43 | 24 | 12 | 49 | 27 | 15 | 13 | 7 | 3 |
| Mean number of stops overall | 0.83 | 0.32 | 0.14 | 2.48 | 0.39 | 0.21 | 0.29 | 0.10 | 0.03 |
| Mean number of stops among those who have been stopped | 1.94 | 1.33 | 1.19 | 5.06 | 1.49 | 1.42 | 2.13 | 1.42 | 1.00 |
| Base: informants who own or have the use of a motor vehicle (unweighted) | 222 | 278 | 162 | 50 | 69 | 48 | 72 | 144 | 35 |
| (weighted) | 889 | 3,303 | 2,705 | 40 | 68 | 44 | 55 | 181 | 56 |

91

group in combination

| | Whites | | | West Indians | | | Asians | | |
|---|---|---|---|---|---|---|---|---|---|
| | 15-24 | 25-44 | 45 and over | 15-24 | 25-44 | 45 and over | 15-24 | 25-44 | 45 and over |
| **In a vehicle** | | | | | | | | | |
| Per cent stopped | 35 | 26 | 10 | 34 | 35 | 9 | 15 | 8 | 2 |
| Mean number of stops overall | 0.76 | 0.40 | 0.12 | 1.60 | 0.57 | 0.13 | 0.30 | 0.12 | 0.02 |
| Mean number of stops among those who have been stopped | 2.18 | 1.55 | 1.25 | 4.72 | 1.64 | 1.43 | 2.06 | 1.39 | 1.00 |
| **On foot** | | | | | | | | | |
| Per cent stopped | 18 | 4 | – | 45 | 7 | 4 | 7 | 1 | 2 |
| Mean number of stops overall | 0.43 | 0.06 | – | 0.99 | 0.07 | 0.05 | 0.09 | 0.01 | 0.02 |
| Mean number of stops among those who have been stopped | 2.41 | 1.45 | – | 2.20 | 1.00 | 1.36 | 1.28 | 1.00 | 1.00 |
| **In a vehicle or on foot** | | | | | | | | | |
| Per cent stopped | 44 | 28 | 10 | 63 | 36 | 12 | 18 | 9 | 4 |
| Mean number of stops overall | 1.19 | 0.45 | 0.12 | 2.59 | 0.64 | 0.18 | 0.39 | 0.13 | 0.04 |
| Mean number of stops among those who have been stopped | 2.58 | 1.59 | 1.25 | 4.10 | 1.77 | 1.57 | 2.09 | 1.35 | 1.00 |
| **Base:** men | | | | | | | | | |
| (unweighted) | 243 | 179 | 161 | 101 | 60 | 75 | 103 | 140 | 48 |
| (weighted) | 1,076 | 1,911 | 2,552 | 86 | 68 | 70 | 86 | 164 | 75 |

over the same period. Whether this involves an unacceptable risk of 'causing annoyance to innocent persons' will partly depend on the results in terms of crime detection and the relationship between these groups and the police, which will be considered in the next section.

Two other variables that have some relation to the likelihood of being stopped are whether a person has a job, and socio-economic group. Table IV.7 shows that unemployed men are six times as likely as those who have a job to be stopped when on foot; they are only slightly more likely to be stopped in a vehicle, probably because they often do not have a car to drive. Unemployed men tend to be young, but this accounts for only a small part of the difference. Presumably those who are out of work tend to be out on the streets, and this probably accounts for part of the difference. But it may also be that unemployed men are, to some extent, a recognisable type that tends to attract police suspicion.

Table IV.7    Whether stopped by the police in the past twelve months: men by working status

Percentages

|  | Working | Unemployed | Sick or inactive |
|---|---|---|---|
| Stopped in a vehicle | 24 | 28 | 12 |
| Stopped on foot | 4 | 25 | 15 |
| Stopped in a vehicle or on foot | 28 | 42 | 27 |
| Base: informants aged 15-59 (unweighted) | 772 | 117 | 156 |
| (weighted) | 4,098 | 406 | 447 |

Men in the professional and managerial group are much less likely to be stopped when on foot than men in the other socio-economic groups; the findings for women on this point are inconclusive, probably because of small sample sizes in certain groups (tables not shown). The percentage of vehicle owners and users within each socio-economic group who have been stopped when in a vehicle is shown below (for men and women combined).

|  | Per cent |
|---|---|
| Professional and managerial | 18 |
| White collar | 17 |
| Skilled manual | 28 |
| Semi-skilled manual | 22 |
| Unskilled manual | 36 |

It is clear that the chance of being stopped in a vehicle is higher among the manual than among the non-manual groups, when the comparison is confined to those who own or have the use of a vehicle.

## Circumstances of the stop

A short questionnaire was filled in for each of the incidents in which the informant had been stopped by the police in the past twelve months, except that where the informant had been stopped more than four times, only the last four stops were covered. In practice, 84 per cent of the stops were asked about in detail, and these amounted to 734 incidents (unweighted) altogether. Information in the rest of this section is based on counts of numbers of incidents rather than numbers of people; the 734 incidents happened to a total of 393 people (unweighted) in the survey.

Seventy-eight per cent of these incidents were stops of people in a vehicle (vehicle stops) and the remaining 22 per cent stops of people on foot (foot stops). The proportion that were vehicle stops varies between the age groups as follows:

| Age of informant | Per cent of stops that were vehicle stops |
|---|---|
| 15 - 24 | 66 |
| 25 - 44 | 87 |
| 45 and over | 91 |

Thirty-six per cent of stops involving West Indians, compared with 21 per cent of those involving white people, were foot stops.

The time of the day at which the stops were made is summarised below:

| | Per cent |
|---|---|
| 6am to 1.59pm | 23 |
| 2pm to 9.59pm | 40 |
| 10pm to 5.59am | 34 |

The division of hours shown above is into the three shifts worked by a majority of police officers in London. The stops are fairly evenly divided between the three shifts, although more are made during 'late turn' than 'early turn'. One-third of stops are made during the night shift; although this accounts for one-third of the hours of the day, it is a period when far fewer vehicles and people are on the street than at other times. It follows that a much higher proportion of vehicles and people who are about are stopped at night than at other times. Young people are more likely than older people to have been stopped at night, probably because they are more often about then.

The great majority of stops (93 per cent) were made by

94

officers in uniform; five per cent were made by officers in plain clothes, and two per cent by uniform and plain clothes officers together. About three-quarters of stops (73 per cent) were made by officers in a vehicle, which reflects the largely 'wheels-based' policing of London. In Volume III of this series we shall see that just over one-third of police patrolling time is put in by officers patrolling on foot. The proportion of stops made by officers on foot is less than one-third, probably because it is difficult for an officer on foot to stop a vehicle. In 55 per cent of cases the officers were in a car, in six per cent of cases in a van, in six per cent of cases on one or more motor bikes, and in three per cent of cases several police vehicles were involved. The proportion of stops made by officers on foot was higher in inner London (33 per cent) than in outer London (22 per cent).

Informants were asked the following questions to establish what the reason for the stop might have been and whether a reason was actually given.

a) Were you doing anything out of the ordinary which led to the police approaching you?
b) If yes at (a) What were you doing?
If no at (a)
c) Did the police officer(s) give a reason for approaching you?
d) If they gave a reason What reason did they give?
e) If they did not give a reason Why do you think they approached you?

The most important issue here is whether the informant could be expected to understand that there was a reason for the stop, either because he knew he was doing something out of the ordinary or because the police officer(s) explained what the reason was. Table IV.8 shows that in 28 per cent of cases the person thought he was doing something out of the ordinary, in 52 per cent of cases he did not think so but the officer gave a reason for the stop, and in 19 per cent of cases the person thought he was doing nothing out of the ordinary and no reason for the stop was given. In the case of foot stops the proportion who were left without any understanding of why the stop had been made was rather higher (25 per cent) than in the case of vehicle stops (17 per cent). Two broad conclusions can be drawn from these findings. First, in nearly three-quarters of cases the person stopped thinks that he did not do anything in particular that might have caused the police to stop him; in other words, most people who are stopped do not think that they 'brought it upon themselves'. Secondly, while police officers do often give an explanation, in about one-fifth of cases the person is left thinking that no explanation at all has been given. It could be argued that in some or all of these cases the officer did, in fact, give an explanation, but even if this is true it is beside the point, which is that in one-fifth of cases no explanation got through to the person concerned.

Table IV.8    Stop incidents: informant's behaviour and whether a reason was given for the stop, by type of stop

Column percentages

|  | All stops | Informant was | |
|  |  | In a vehicle | On foot |
| --- | --- | --- | --- |
| **Were you doing anything out of the ordinary?** | | | |
| Yes | 28 | 29 | 24 |
| No | 70 | 69 | 76 |
| Don't know | 2 | 2 | * |
| **If no, did the police officer(s) give a reason for approaching you?** | | | |
| Yes | 52 | 52 | 51 |
| No | 19 | 17 | 25 |
| Base: all stop incidents[a] | | | |
| (unweighted) | 734 | 531 | 203 |
| (weighted) | 3,277 | 2,546 | 731 |

(a)    In this and subsequent tables, 'all stop incidents' refers to those for which a stop sheet was completed.

The summary table below shows what informants said they were doing which led the police to stop them when in a vehicle.

| | Per cent of vehicle stops |
| --- | --- |
| Nothing out of the ordinary | 69 |
| Speeding | 8 |
| Drove through traffic lights | 3 |
| Other offences against traffic signs | 8 |
| Other odd driving | 4 |
| Defect of car | 3 |
| Odd parking | 2 |
| Other odd behaviour | 1 |
| Don't know | 2 |

The following summary table shows the reasons given for vehicle stops.

96

|  | Per cent of vehicle stops |
|---|---|
| Informant was doing something out of the ordinary | 31 |
| No reason for the stop was given though informant not doing anything odd | 17 |
| Reason given | |
| Traffic offence | 18 |
| Stolen car | 7 |
| Illegal contents of car | * |
| Other offence | 7 |
| Road block | 2 |
| Odd driving | 2 |
| 'Routine' | 15 |
| Other reason | 1 |

It is notable that in 15 per cent of cases the reason given was 'just a routine check', which may or may not be acceptable to people but does not amount to a proper reason.

The table below shows what informants said they were doing which led the police to stop them when on foot.

|  | Per cent of foot stops |
|---|---|
| Nothing out of the ordinary | 76 |
| Loitering or hanging about | 7 |
| Carrying property | 4 |
| Drunk | 3 |
| Causing a disturbance | 3 |
| Fighting or causing damage | 1 |
| Running | 1 |
| Odd appearance | * |
| Other odd or suspicious behaviour | 6 |

The following table shows the reasons given for foot stops.

|  | Per cent of foot stops |
|---|---|
| Informant was doing something out of the ordinary | 24 |
| No reason given for the stop though informant not doing anything odd | 25 |
| Reason given | |
| Possible offender in specific offence | 14 |
| Loitering or hanging about | 11 |
| Causing a disturbance | 5 |
| Possible witness in specific offence | 5 |
| Carrying property | 3 |
| Drunk | 2 |
| Odd appearance | 1 |
| Other reason or vague answer | 10 |

Where the police officer gave no reason, informants were asked why they thought they had been approached. The answers are shown below for foot and vehicle stops combined.

|  | Per cent of all stops |
|---|---|
| Informant was doing something out of the ordinary | 30 |
| The police gave a reason | 52 |
| **If neither, what the informant thinks was the reason for the stop** | |
| Routine | 9 |
| Youth | 1 |
| Colour or race | 1 |
| They have nothing else to do | 1 |
| Other specific answer | 2 |
| Vague answer or don't know reason | 5 |

These answers suggest that not many people think they were unfairly picked on. Among West Indians the proportion who volunteered that they were stopped because of their colour or race was six per cent, while no Asian gave this answer. Of course, the proportion who thought that colour might have had something to do with it may be much higher: they were not asked a specific question on this point.

Table IV.9    Vehicle stops:  informant's behaviour and whether a reason was given for the stop, by ethnic group

|  | Whites | West Indians | Asians |
|---|---|---|---|
| **Were you doing anything out of the ordinary?** | | | |
| Yes | 29 | 22 | 31 |
| No | 69 | 69 | 54 |
| Don't know | 2 | 9 | 14 |
| **If no, did the police officer(s) give a reason for approaching you?** | | | |
| Yes | 52 | 44 | 38 |
| No | 17 | 25 | 16 |
| Base:  vehicle stops[a] | | | |
| (unweighted) | 331 | 138 | 47 |
| (weighted) | 2,359 | 118 | 45 |

(a)    Incidents involving 'other non-whites', of which there are only 15 unweighted, are not included in the table.

Table IV.10   Foot stops:   informant's behaviour and whether a reason was given for this stop, by ethnic group

Column percentages

|  | Whites | West Indians |
|---|---|---|
| **Were you doing anything out of the ordinary?** | | |
| Yes | 27 | 8 |
| No | 73 | 88 |
| Don't know | - | 4 |
| | | |
| **If no, did the police officer(s) give a reason for approaching you?** | | |
| Yes | 53 | 52 |
| No | 20 | 36 |
| | | |
| Base: foot stops[a] | | |
| (unweighted) | 110 | 77 |
| (weighted) | 622 | 65 |

(a)    Incidents involving Asians and 'other non-whites' of which there are only 16 unweighted, are not included in the table.

Analysis of the basic information by ethnic group is shown in Tables IV.9 and 10.  In the case of vehicle stops, a slightly higher proportion of West Indians than of white people or Asians say they were left without a reason for the stop, but the difference is too small to be important.  In the case of foot stops the numbers are too small to show separate results for Asians, but there is a definite contrast between the answers of West Indians and white people.  Only eight per cent of West Indians compared with 27 per cent of white people say they were doing something out of the ordinary when they were stopped.  While the proportion of all who say that the officer gave a reason for the stop is the same for the two groups, the question only applies where the informant was not already aware that he was doing something out of the ordinary. Among those who were not aware of this, 72 per cent of the white people compared with 59 per cent of the West Indians say that the officer gave a reason for the stop.  Consequently, 36 per cent(1) of all of the West Indians compared with 20 per cent of the white people think they were left without a reason for being stopped. Whether this is a reflection of different behaviour by police officers towards the two groups or a difference in attitude on the part of the people concerned is an open question.  The difference is

(1)    This difference is just significant at the 5 per cent level of confidence (if we treat the sample as a pure random sample for the purpose of the test).

not a large one, but it does suggest that stops of people on foot have a worse effect on relations with West Indians than with white people.

Table IV.11     <u>Stop incidents: informant's behaviour and whether a</u> <u>reason was given for the stop: ethnic minorities by</u> <u>local ethnic concentration</u>

Column percentages

| | Per cent immigrants in ED | | | |
|---|---|---|---|---|
| | Up to 5 | 6-10 | 11-20 | 21 and over |
| <u>Were you doing anything</u> <u>out of the ordinary?</u> | | | | |
|   Yes | 29 | 26 | 24 | 10 |
|   No, or don't know | 71 | 74 | 76 | 90 |
| <u>If no, did the police officer(s)</u> <u>give a reason for approaching</u> <u>you?</u> | | | | |
|   Yes | 35 | 46 | 44 | 55 |
|   No | 27 | 19 | 20 | 31 |
| Base:  stops involving ethnic       minorities | | | | |
|       (unweighted | 50 | 101 | 64 | 32 |
|       (weighted) | 42 | 89 | 56 | 29 |

In general, analysis of these findings by geographical variables is not very profitable because the stop may not have occurred close to where the informant lives. Analysis by local ethnic concentration shows an apparent difference among ethnic minorities (Table IV.11). Members of minority groups in areas of high ethnic concentration seem less likely than those in areas of low concentration to think that they were doing something out of the ordinary that led to a stop, but more likely to say that the police officer gave an explanation. However, these apparent differences are not statistically significant.

Table IV.12    Stop incidents: assessment of police behaviour, by age

Column percentages

| | Total | Age 15-24 | Age 25-44 | 45 and over |
|---|---|---|---|---|
| **Did the police have good reasons for stopping you?** | | | | |
| Yes | 59 | 54 | 60 | 70 |
| No | 38 | 43 | 34 | 30 |
| Don't know | 4 | 3 | 5 | * |
| **Were they polite or not?** | | | | |
| Yes | 72 | 63 | 76 | 89 |
| No | 24 | 32 | 19 | 11 |
| Don't know | 4 | 4 | 5 | * |
| **Did they behave in a fair and reasonable manner?** | | | | |
| Yes | 79 | 72 | 81 | 95 |
| No | 19 | 26 | 16 | 5 |
| Don't know | 2 | 2 | 3 | * |
| **If no In what way was their behaviour unfair or unreasonable?** | | | | |
| Unpleasant manner | 12 | 18 | 7 | 4 |
| No good reason for stopping | 6 | 5 | 8 | - |
| Used force | 2 | 5 | - | * |
| Disbelieved informant | 2 | 3 | - | - |
| Made accusations | 1 | 2 | 1 | - |
| Other answers | * | * | 1 | * |
| **Base: all stop incidents** | | | | |
| (unweighted) | 734 | 505 | 182 | 47 |
| (weighted) | 3,277 | 1,513 | 1,290 | 474 |

Assessment of police behaviour
      The following questions were included to find out how the informant assessed the behaviour of the police officers who made the stop.

      Would you say the police had good reasons for stopping you and talking to you or not?
      Would you say they were polite or not in the way they treated you?

101

Would you say the police behaved in a fair and reasonable manner on the occasion?
If no  In what way was their behaviour unfair or unreasonable?

The finding are shown in Table IV.12 according to the age of the person stopped. In about three-quarters of incidents the person concerned thinks that the police behaved in a polite, fair and reasonable manner, but the proportion of cases in which the police are thought to have had a good reason for making the stop is lower (59 per cent). The kinds of unfair or unreasonable behaviour that are most commonly mentioned are an unpleasant manner (12 per cent) and the making of a stop without any good reason (six per cent). In two per cent of cases the officers were criticised for using force. These findings show that in a majority of cases the person stopped is happy about the way the incident was handled, but there is still a substantial number of cases where the person is not happy, and a larger number where he can see no good reason for having been stopped in the first place. The proportion who are unhappy about the incident is higher among the younger than among the older age groups; among those aged 45 or over there is very little criticism of the way the police behaved, though 30 per cent even of this group can see no reason for the stop.

The proportion who think there were good reasons for the stop does vary according to whether a reason was given.

|  | Per cent who think there was a good reason for the stop |
|---|---|
| Informant was doing something out of the ordinary | 80 |
| Not doing anything odd, but a reason was given for the stop | 59 |
| Not doing anything odd, no reason given for the stop | 32 |

The reason given for the stop is quite often not found convincing, but police officers clearly create a better impression when they give a reason than when they do not.

Analysis by ethnic group (Table IV.13) shows that West Indians are markedly less happy than other groups with the behaviour of police officers who stopped them. In only 38 per cent of incidents involving West Indians did the person think the police had good reasons for stopping him; the proportion of cases in which the police are thought to have behaved in a fair and reasonable manner is 58 per cent for West Indians compared with 80 per cent for white people. To a small extent these differences are a reflection of the younger age profile of West Indians compared with white people, but if we restrict the comparison to people aged 15-24 very definite differences remain (see Table IV.14). In just 54

Table IV.13    Stop incidents: assessment of police behaviour, by ethnic group

Column percentages

|  | Whites | West Indians | Asians |
|---|---|---|---|
| The police had good reasons for stopping you | 59 | 38 | 62 |
| The police were polite | 73 | 57 | 71 |
| The police behaved in a fair and reasonable manner | 80 | 58 | 77 |
| Base: all stop incidents(a) | | | |
| (unweighted) | 441 | 215 | 58 |
| (weighted) | 2,982 | 183 | 57 |

(a)    Except that 'other non-whites' are not included in the table, since there were only 20 incidents involving them.

per cent of cases young West Indians thought the police who stopped them had behaved in a fair and reasonable manner, compared with 73 per cent of cases for young whites.

It is very interesting to find that West Indians in areas of high ethnic concentration are no more likely to be unhappy about the behaviour of police in stopping them than those in areas of low concentration. In fact, if anything black people in places like

Table IV.14    Stop incidents: assessment of police behaviour: whites and West Indians aged 15-24 compared

Column percentages

|  | Whites | West Indians |
|---|---|---|
| The police had good reasons for stopping you | 55 | 32 |
| The police were polite | 64 | 50 |
| The police behaved in a fair and reasonable manner | 73 | 54 |
| Base: stops involving whites and West Indians aged 15-24 | | |
| (unweighted) | 305 | 153 |
| (weighted) | 1,347 | 121 |

Brixton are happier with the way the police carry out stops than blacks in places like Wimbledon, though the differences are not statistically significant (see Table IV.15). The answers given by West Indians in areas of high ethnic concentration are similar to those given by white people generally. We can suggest two possible reasons for this. The first is that the police may tend to pick on black people in mainly white areas simply because they seem to them to be out of place. During the course of the project, one of the researchers, as a member of the public, reported an incident to a PC in Wimbledon, which involved a black suspect. He was told ... 'Well, they're all at it, the spades'. He later mentioned this to a superintendent, who said, 'In a way the PC was right, because any black face he sees in Wimbledon doesn't really belong'. The second possible explanation is that in areas of high ethnic concentration the police make a greater effort to 'use care and discretion' when stopping black people, or are better at getting on with them (through greater practice) than elsewhere. In any case it is clear that relations between individual black people and police officers who have stopped them on particular occasions are better in places like Brixton than in places like Wimbledon.

Table IV.15    Stop incidents:  assessments of police behaviour: West Indians by local ethnic concentration

Column percentages

|  | Per cent immigrants in ED | | | |
|  | Up to 5 | 6-10 | 11-20 | Over 20 |
| --- | --- | --- | --- | --- |
| The police had good reasons for stopping you | 27 | 38 | 35 | 41 |
| The police were polite | 36 | 60 | 54 | 75 |
| The police behaved in a fair and reasonable manner | 45 | 62 | 50 | 72 |
| Base:  stops involving West Indians | | | | |
| (unweighted) | 35 | 74 | 36 | 30 |
| (weighted) | 27 | 63 | 30 | 28 |

Result of stops

According to standing orders, the details of all persons and vehicles stopped should be recorded in a book kept at the police station. This is not, of course, a legal requirement:  indeed, depending on the circumstances, the person stopped may be entitled, in law, to refuse his name and address. In practice, however, it is rare for people to refuse this information to a police officer, and it is Force

Table IV.16    Whether name and address taken and result of stops, by sex and age

|  | Total | Men | Women | Age 15-24 | Age 25-44 | Age 45 and over |
|---|---|---|---|---|---|---|
| **Whether name and address taken** | | | | | | |
| Yes | 39 | 46 | 22 | 42 | 45 | 16 |
| No | 59 | 52 | 76 | 56 | 52 | 84 |
| Not answered | 2 | 2 | 3 | 2 | 3 | * |
| **Result of stop** | | | — | | | |
| Reported and summonsed | 5 | 7 | 1 | 4 | 7 | 6 |
| Arrested and charged | 3 | 4 | * | 4 | 2 | * |
| **Total any result** | **8** | **11** | **1** | **8** | **9** | **6** |
| Arrested but not charged then or subsequently | 1 | 1 | - | 1 | 1 | - |
| Not reported, summonsed or arrested | 91 | 87 | 99 | 90 | 89 | 94 |
| Not answered | * | 1 | - | 1 | 1 | - |
| **Base:** all stop incidents | | | | | | |
| (unweighted) | 734 | 557 | 177 | 505 | 182 | 47 |
| (weighted) | 3,277 | 2,336 | 941 | 1,513 | 1,290 | 474 |

policy that the information should be sought and recorded whenever a stop is made. We find, however, that the police officer took
the name and address of the person stopped in only 39 per cent of
cases. This is in broad agreement with the findings from our
observational work. There is room for some differing interpretation, at the margins, as to what amounts to a stop; some people
could be reporting as a stop an encounter that the police officer
would describe as a friendly conversation. However, even if we
make some allowance for this, it is still clear that a very
substantial proportion of stops are not recorded at the police
station. This is important, because it means that any estimates of
the number of stops made that come from the police will be radical
under-estimates; we can at least double the numbers shown in
police statistics to arrive at a more realistic figure. Secondly, this
finding shows that a standing instruction to police officers is
disobeyed regularly and as a matter of routine. Supervising
officers know that this is so (see the fourth volume of this series)
but do not attach a high priority to doing anything about it. Also,
PCs are fully aware of the instruction: they often made wry
remarks about having to record their stops because a researcher
was with them. The matter is not important in itself, but it does
show that standing orders may sometimes have a very limited
effect. It is interesting that police officers making stops were
twice as likely to take the names and address of men as of women,
and nearly three times as likely to take the name and address
where the person was aged 15-44 as where he was aged 45 or more.
From the officer's point of view it is important that there should
be a record in the Stop Book if there is subsequently any complaint
about the incident. Probably names and addresses of women and
older people are seldom taken because the officer rarely antic-
ipates any complaint from them.

Table IV.16 shows that five per cent of stops led to an
offence being reported, three per cent to the person being arrested
and charged with an offence, and in one per cent of cases the
person was arrested but not charged then or subsequently with an
offence as a result of the stop. This means that the total strike
rate - the proportion of stops that lead to the detection of an
offence - is about one out of 12. This strike rate varies very
sharply between men and women: 11 per cent of stops of men
produce a 'result' compared with only one per cent of stops of
women. Also, a comparatively small proportion of stops of older
people - only six per cent of stops of people aged 45 or over -
produce a 'result'. The proportion of stops that produce a 'result' is
the same for each ethnic group.

This latter result is important. It shows that the tendency
for the police to stop a higher proportion of West Indians than of
white people is justified in the sense that an equal proportion of
stops of the two groups produces a 'result'. However, this is a
justification only in a narrow sense. The great majority both of
white people and of West Indians who are stopped are not shown to

have committed an offence, and the findings from observational work (see Chapter XVI) show that police are exceeding their formal powers in making many of these stops. Further, we shall show in Chapter X of this report that experience of being stopped - especially of being stopped repeatedly - tends strongly to make people hostile to the police. The relatively high rate of stops of West Indians is <u>understandable</u> in the light of the 'results' produced, but it does not follow that the policy is wise or, in a broad sense, productive when all of the consequences are taken into account.

A difficulty in interpreting these findings is that we do not know, from accounts given by members of the public, what were the powers (if any) under which the officer made the stop, or what was his actual reason or motive for making it. In many cases, the stop was connected with a possible traffic offence, though the officer may have used the opportunity to try to detect other offences. Many of the 'results' are reports for traffic offences, and only 3 per cent of stops resulted in the detection of what police officers would think of as 'crime' (informally, they would not count minor traffic offences under this head).

In any case, the findings clearly show that the great majority of people stopped by the police in London are 'innocent persons'. There is considerable risk of causing annoyance to them; we have seen that a majority of them are happy about the way the incident was handled, but 19 per cent think the officers did not behave in a fair and reasonable manner, and 38 per cent think there was no good reason for them to be stopped. As we shall see in Chapter X there is a strong tendency for people who have been stopped repeatedly to be critical of the police, even though they may not be critical of the way in which the particular stops were handled. Whether the damage caused by pursuing this policy is commensurate with the result in terms of crime detected is a very difficult judgement to make. Although only eight per cent of stops produce a 'result', this still amounts to a large number of offences. Our findings suggest that about $1\frac{1}{2}$ million stops are made in a year (where individuals are counted separately, though they may have been stopped on the same occasion). Roughly speaking, this implies that people are arrested and charged with an offence as a result of a stop on 45,000 occasions a year and reported for an offence (generally a traffic offence) following a stop on 75,000 occasions a year. This is a very significant number of offences detected by means of stops. A fuller assessment would take into account the number of serious offences detected in this way; unfortunately, the number of stops reported in the survey that produced a result is much too small for us to be able to comment on this point.

The findings certainly show that the present stopping policy produces a significant 'yield' and make it clear that there would be a substantial price to be paid if the policy were to be suddenly abandoned and nothing put in its place. At the same time, the cost of the present policy, in terms of the relationship between the police and certain sections of the public, is shown to be substantial, and most stops are wasted effort, if they are seen as purely an attempt to detect crime. The findings therefore suggest that the police should look for other more efficient and less damaging methods of crime detection to replace those stops that are currently carried out for no very specific reason: it may be significant, in this connection, that in some other parts of the country the clear-up rate is higher than in London although many fewer stops are carried out. As well as becoming more discriminating in deciding who to stop, the police could make great improvements by dealing with people more sensitively and by giving a full explanation of the reason for the stop in all cases where this is not already obvious to the person concerned. The implications for policing policy will be discussed more fully in later chapters.

## Arrests

Asking questions about arrests is clearly at the borderline of what is feasible within the context of a formal survey, since there are strong motives for concealment. It is fair to assume that there are people in the survey who have been arrested but deny it. However, there are good reasons for thinking that the great majority have given truthful answers. By the time that arrest was mentioned in the interview it was clear to informants that the purpose of the survey was not to find out whether they were guilty, but to understand their experience and assessment of police behaviour. People who wished to criticise the police therefore had a motive for admitting that they had been arrested. Also, the questioning was intensive and came at the subject of arrests from various different angles. Informants had been asked about crowd trouble, stops and motoring incidents before the subject of arrest was squarely broached, and by that time they would have got the impression that it would be difficult to keep up a consistent line of concealment. It was quite clear to informants that interviewers had no direct connection with the police or legal system, and very firm guarantees of confidentiality had been given. Two stages of questionnaire piloting were carried out; careful questioning of the interviewers who carried out these trial interviews gave very few indications that informants were uncomfortable with the questions about arrest. A refusal to answer these questions was extremely rare. The actual findings of the survey show that a substantial proportion of informants did admit to having been arrested, and the proportion arrested varies between population groups in exactly the way that would be expected from other criminological enquiries. It seems from the findings that those who had been arrested relatively recently - within the past five years - were likely to admit it, but those who had been arrested some time ago but not more recently were likely to deny it in an effort to put their past firmly behind them. This is not an important limitation, since the detailed questioning was confined to arrests in the past five years.

Who has been arrested
These questions were included more than half way through the
interview, when the informant had already been asked about stops,
crowd trouble and motoring incidents that led to their being
reported for an offence.

Including anything you have mentioned already, have you
yourself ever been arrested and taken to a police station?

If yes   And again including anything you have mentioned
already, have you been arrested and taken to a plice station
during the past five years, that is since _____ (current
month), 1976?

Overall, 10 per cent of informants said they had ever been
arrested, and five per cent during the past five years.    As
expected, the findings differ very sharply between men and women
(see Table IV.17).  As many as one out of five men say they have
ever been arrested, while one out of ten say they have been
arrested in the past five years.  Only one out of 50 women say they
have ever been arrested.  Thus, a very substantial minority of men
have the opportunity to form an opinion of the police based on
direct experience of being arrested and taken to a police station.

Table IV.17    Experience of arrest, by sex

Column percentages

|  | Total | | Men | | Women | |
|---|---|---|---|---|---|---|
| Ever arrested | 10 | | 20 | | 2 | |
| In past 5 years | | 5 | | 10 | | 1 |
| Longer ago | | 5 | | 10 | | 1 |
| Never arrested | 90 | | 80 | | 98 | |
| Base: all informants | | | | | | |
| (unweighted) | 2,420 | | 1,161 | | 1,259 | |
| (weighted) | 13,944 | | 6,297 | | 7,648 | |

Analysis by age strongly suggests that people tend not to
report arrests that took place a long time ago if there have been no
subsequent arrests.  Table IV.18 shows that 27 per cent of men
aged 25-44 say they have ever been arrested, compared with nine
per cent of those aged 60 or more.  This may be largely a
reflection of a change over time; for this would imply that the
likelihood of being arrested has increased threefold over a thirty-
year period.  In addition older people may fail to report arrests

Table IV.18    Experience of arrest, by sex and age

Column percentages

|  | Age | | | | |
|---|---|---|---|---|---|
|  | 15-19 | 20-24 | 25-44 | 45-59 | 60 and over |
| **MEN** | | | | | |
| Ever arrested | 21 | 24 | 27 | 14 | 9 |
| In past 5 years | 20 | 18 | 11 | 5 | 4 |
| Longer ago | 1 | 7 | 17 | 9 | 5 |
| Never arrested | 79 | 76 | 73 | 86 | 91 |
| Base: all men | | | | | |
| (unweighted) | 230 | 237 | 400 | 181 | 113 |
| (weighted) | 639 | 655 | 2,239 | 1,371 | 1,393 |
| **WOMEN** | | | | | |
| Ever arrested | 2 | 7 | 3 | - | - |
| In past 5 years | * | 4 | 1 | - | - |
| Longer ago | 2 | 2 | 2 | - | - |
| Never arrested | 98 | 93 | 97 | 100 | 100 |
| Base: all women | | | | | |
| (unweighted) | 260 | 257 | 444 | 164 | 134 |
| (weighted) | 639 | 677 | 2,934 | 1,539 | 1,859 |

that happened many years ago. The proportion who say they have been arrested over the past five years varies according to age in an entirely plausible way; there is a steady decline from 20 per cent of men aged 15-19 to four per cent of men aged 60 and over. We find no women in the sample aged 45 or over who say they have ever been arrested. There are 300 women aged 45 or more in the sample, so this finding will be in error only if the actual proportion of this group who have been arrested is higher than one out of 300, which it may well not be. It is interesting that the rate of arrest among women aged 15-19 is extremely low, whereas it is higher among those aged 20-24. In the case of men there is no such difference between those two age groups: it seems that boys start to get into trouble with the police at an earlier age than girls do.

Table IV.19     Experience of arrest, by ethnic group

Column percentages

|  | Whites | West Indians | Asians | Other non whites |
|---|---|---|---|---|
| Ever arrested | 10 | 12 | 2 | 3 |
| In past 5 years | 5 | 8 | 1 | 1 |
| Longer ago | 5 | 4 | 1 | 2 |
| Never arrested | 90 | 88 | 98 | 97 |
| Base: all informants | | | | |
| (unweighted) | 1,252 | 511 | 541 | 116 |
| (weighted) | 12,428 | 450 | 607 | 459 |

A significantly higher proportion of West Indians than of white people say they have been arrested in the past five years, while the proportion of Asians and non-whites is very much lower (see Table IV.19). If we restrict the comparison to men, we find that 15 per cent of West Indians compared with 10 per cent of whites say they have been arrested in the past five years. Table IV.20 shows the comparison between the three main ethnic groups within each age group, for men and women combined. Among those aged 15-24 a higher proportion of West Indians (17 per cent) than of whites (11 per cent) say they have been arrested in the past five years, while the corresponding proportion for Asians in this age group is virtually nil. Among those aged 25-44 there is no difference between West Indians and whites in the proportion who say they have been arrested. Among those aged 45 and over, a higher proportion of whites (two per cent) than of West Indians (nil) say they have been arrested in the past five years. The nil finding for older West Indians is evidently somewhat in error, but bearing in mind that it is based on only 130 people it may not be seriously

Table IV.20    Whether arrested in the past five years, by ethnic group and age

Column percentages

| | Age | | |
| | 15-24 | 25-44 | 45 and over |
|---|---|---|---|
| **WHITES** | | | |
| Per cent arrested | 11 | 5 | 2 |
| Base: all whites | | | |
| (unweighted) | 497 | 394 | 361 |
| (weighted) | 2,145 | 4,505 | 5,778 |
| **WEST INDIANS** | | | |
| Per cent arrested | 17 | 5 | - |
| Base: all West Indians | | | |
| (unweighted) | 218 | 163 | 130 |
| (weighted) | 173 | 150 | 127 |
| **ASIANS** | | | |
| Per cent arrested | * | 2 | 1 |
| Base: all Asians | | | |
| (unweighted) | 220 | 235 | 86 |
| (weighted) | 169 | 303 | 136 |

wrong. These findings show that there are sharp generational differences among West Indians, and that it is only young West Indians who are more often in trouble with the police than the rest of the population in the same age group.

We found in the last chapter that people who had been the victim of crime were also likely to be suspected by the police of having committed a crime. One possible explanation that we suggested was that the police tend to stop people they know or vaguely recognise, without remembering whether they know them as victims, suspects or offenders. Another possible explanation was that there was a group of people, living at the margins of society, who commit offences mostly on each other, and hence come to be known to the police both as victims and as suspects. We suggested that both of these processes might be at work. In order to pursue this matter further, we can now analyse experience of arrest by experience as a victim of crime. Table IV.21 shows that there is a definite relationship. People who have been repeatedly the victims of crime in the past year are at least twice as likely to have been arrested in the past five years as people who

Table IV.21  Experience of arrest: men by experience as a victim of crime

Column percentages

| | Incidents of victimisation in past year | | | |
| | None | One | Two | Three or more |
|---|---|---|---|---|
| Ever arrested | 18 | 16 | 29 | 39 |
| In past five years | 9 | 8 | 17 | 15 |
| Longer ago | 9 | 8 | 12 | 24 |
| Never arrested | 82 | 84 | 71 | 61 |
| Base: all men | | | | |
| (unweighted) | 801 | 218 | 94 | 48 |
| (weighted) | 4,311 | 1,226 | 479 | 281 |

113

have not repeatedly been the victims of crime. It is particularly interesting that people who have only once been the victim of crime during the past year are no more likely to have been arrested than those who have not been the victims of crime. These findings powerfully suggest that while everyone has a certain chance of being the victim of crime, there is a group of people who have a much higher than average chance of being victims, and these people, who tend to be repeatedly victims, also have a much higher than average chance of being arrested. This supports the hypothesis that to a considerable extent the police deal with a limited clientele of people who tend to be in trouble both as victims and as offenders, without, of course, excluding the hypothesis that some people come to be suspected by the police because they are known to them as victims.

Among men there is a marked variation in the proportion who have been arrested according to socio-economic group. Eleven per cent of men in the manual groups have been arrested in the past five years compared with seven per cent of those in the non-manual groups. There is no difference between the finer socio-economic groupings: for example, the proportion who have been arrested is the same among men in the skilled manual, semi-skilled and unskilled manual groups. While this confirms the traditional view that the police and the law bear down most heavily on the poorer and weaker sections of society, it does not confirm it very strongly: in fact, one-third of men who have been arrested in the past five years are in the non-manual socio-economic groups. The kind of job that someone does is by no means one of the best indicators of whether he will be in trouble with the police: sex and age are far more important indicators, and so is repeated victimisation. If social class is to be assessed by reference to the kind of job that somebody does, we can conclude that being in trouble with the police is less closely connected with social class than with other factors. But perhaps a more valid conclusion would be that the job classification serves as a very inadequate measure of social class.

Our findings would fit very well with the idea that there is an 'underclass' of people who, among other things, are often in trouble with the police, if we asume that this 'underclass' cannot be defined simply by reference to job levels. One likely characteristic of such a group would be that they are marginal to the labour market, do jobs that offer little security of employment and are therefore often in and out of work, so that a relatively high proportion of them are at any one time unemployed. The jobs that they do when in work would not necessarily be low paid or at a low level: for example, scaffolders, construction workers, some of those working in the hotel and restaurant trade and people working in scrap yards might fall into the group, as well as street sweepers and factory cleaners; some of these occupations are semi-skilled or even skilled. According to this view, it would not be low pay that was associated with being in trouble with the police so much as discontinuity, insecurity and rootlessness. We do not have a good enough measure of these things. However, among any such rootless group we would expect to find a high proportion who were unemployed at any one time. It is therefore highly significant that we find that a much higher proportion of the unemployed than of those in full-time work have experience of arrest. Among men aged 15-59, 52 per cent of the unemployed say they have ever been arrested, compared with 22 per cent of those in full-time work; and 32 per cent of the unemployed say they have been arrested in the past five years compared with 10 per cent of those in full-time work. These are very large differences, and much larger than those between socio-economic groups. A subsequent question asked informants how many times they had been arrested in the past five years, and from this we can calculate a mean number of arrests per person. Among men aged 15-59 this mean is six times as high for the unemployed as for those in full-time work (0.6 compared with 0.1). By combining the criterion of socio-economic group with the criterion of whether or not the man is in work we get somewhat closer to a definition of an 'underclass', and analysis of this kind suggests still greater differences, although sample sizes become too small for it to be carried out fully. There are 35 men in the sample aged 15-59 who are unemployed but when in work do semi-skilled or unskilled jobs. Of these an amazing 60 per cent say they have been arrested in the past five years, compared, at the other extreme, with eight per cent of men in work doing non-manual jobs. The mean number of arrests is nine times as high for the first as for the second group.

Analysis of the rate of arrest by geographical variables shows some differences that broadly speaking reflect differences in crime rates between types of area. Thus, 14 per cent of informants in inner London say they have ever been arrested compared with eight per cent of those in outer London. It is very interesting to find, however, that this difference between inner and outer London does not apply to the ethnic minorities: exactly the same proportion both of Asians and of West Indians say they have ever been arrested, and that they have been arrested in the past five years, whether they live in inner or in outer London. Along with other findings, this suggests that differences of geography have a different significance for the ethnic minorities than for white people. In line with this, we find that among the minorities the proportion who have been arrested is not related, or certainly not in a simple way, to the local concentration of Asians and West Indians in the population. If anything, the proportion who have been arrested is higher among Asians and West Indians living in areas of low ethnic concentration than among those living in areas of high concentration. This is not easy to interpret: it may arise because black and brown people in areas of low concentration are conspicuous and more likely to be suspected and therefore arrested. The proportion who have been arrested is higher in boroughs with a high index of 'social dependence' (roughly speaking poverty and housing stress) than in those with a low index, but again the same does not apply to Asians and West Indians when they are analysed separately. Owner occupiers are less likely to have been arrested than those living in rented accommodation, whether it is rented from the council or from a private landlord. Our information about housing is probably not detailed enough to allow us to show strong relationships between types of housing and rates of arrest. The police often claim that crime is strongly associated with particular housing estates, normally ones belonging to the council, but we are not able to classify estates, from the survey, in a way that would allow us to test such claims.

## The experience of arrest in statistics

The sample contains 137 people who say they have been arrested during the past five years. These people were asked detailed questions about each of the occasions on which they were arrested during that period, except that where an informant had been arrested more than three times, only the last three occasions were covered in detail. In practice, 169 actual arrests were asked about and these accounted for 79 per cent of arrests in the past five years. In 93 per cent of these cases the person arrested was a man. In 49 per cent of cases the person arrested was aged 15-24, in 35 per cent aged 25-44 and in 16 per cent aged 45 or over. The arrests were fairly evenly spread over the past five years, with a slight bias towards more recent years because some of the less recent arrests were not covered.

In just under half of cases (48 per cent) informants thought that the police were behaving reasonably in arresting them, in 47 per cent of cases they thought they were behaving unreasonably, and in six per cent of cases they couldn't say. There was no difference here between the answers given by different ethnic groups. The different age groups also gave similar answers.

In 70 per cent of cases the person arrested was charged with an offence either on the first visit to the police station or subsequently. In the remaining cases the person was either cautioned (under the juvenile procedure) or released without charge. It might be thought that those who were arrested but not charged would be inclined to think that the police had behaved unreasonably in arresting them. However, the proportion who think the police had behaved unreasonably is the same among those who were and were not charged with an offence. This suggests that no additional resentment was caused by the police in making an arrest but then not preferring a charge.

In 70 per cent of cases the suspect went to a police station only once in connection with the matter - that is, at the time of the initial arrest; in 19 per cent of cases there was a second visit, and in seven per cent of cases there were three or more visits. The length of time that the suspect was held at the police station on the first visit is shown below.

| Number of hours at police station | Per cent of arrests |
|---|---|
| Up to 1 | 14 |
| 2 | 16 |
| 3 | 19 |
| 4 - 5 | 19 |
| 6 - 12 | 11 |
| 13 - 24 | 3 |
| 25 - 72 | 5 |
| 73 or more | 2 |
| Not answered | 12 |

There is no difference between white people and ethnic minorities in the length of time held. Nearly all of those who were held for more than 12 hours were eventually charged.

In 43 per cent of cases the suspect made a formal signed statement, and in a further five per cent of cases the police made a formal record of questions and answers that the suspect signed. An apparently higher proportion of West Indians than of white people made a signed statement (55 per cent compared with 42 per cent) but the difference is not statistically significant. The proportion of cases in which the suspect either made a statement or signed a record of questions and answers is 68 per cent for West Indians compared with 47 per cent for white people. This difference is just statistically significant.

In 85 per cent of cases where the suspect signed a record of the proceedings, he or she now says that it gave a fair and accurate record of what was said; in 12 per cent of cases the suspect says it did not give a fair and accurate record, and in three per cent of cases no answer was given. Also, in 80 per cent of these cases, the suspect says that the record gave a fair and accurate picture of what actually happened.

While the suspect was being asked questions, making a statement or being charged it was not usual for an independent observer to be present (that is, anyone other than police officers or other suspects). In seven per cent of cases a parent was present, in three per cent of cases a solicitor was present, and in nine per cent of cases some other person (not a police officer or the offender). In no case involving a West Indian was a solicitor present. In a total of 14 per cent of cases involving white people either a solicitor or some other person (not a police officer, other offender or parent) was present, compared with three per cent of cases involving West Indians. (These figures are based on 41 cases involving West Indians and 82 involving white people.)

In 62 per cent of cases the suspect was charged on the first visit to the police station, in eight per cent of cases on a subsequent visit and in 35 per cent of cases the suspect was not charged with an offence (in the remaining four per cent of cases no answer was given). Among those who were not charged, three per cent were cautioned by the police according to the procedure for juveniles. There is no significant difference between white people and members of ethnic minority groups in the proportion who were charged.

The charges have been recorded in detail, but because they are many and varied, the number of cases is too small for the information to be treated statistically.

A total of 62 per cent of arrests gave rise to a court hearing, and 107 cases involving court proceedings were covered in the survey. In 64 per cent of these cases the suspect pleaded guilty and in 82 per cent was found guilty. Seventy of these cases involved white people and 31 involved West Indians. Because these numbers are small, the survey is capable of showing up only very gross differences between the two groups. The proportion who say they were found guilty is apparently higher for white people (83 per cent) than for West Indians (71 per cent) but the difference is not significant. The results suggest that there is no gross difference in the verdicts brought by the courts on suspects belonging to the two groups.

When asked 'Do you have any criticisms of the way the police behaved towards you in this matter at <u>any</u> stage?', informants said they had in 59 per cent of cases. There were, in total, 114 cases involving white people and 46 involving West Indians. In 60 per cent of the cases involving white poeple the informant had criticisms to make of police behaviour, compared with 47 per cent of those involving West Indians. This difference is not statistically significant, but the findings do definitely show that West Indians are no more likely than white people to have criticisms of police behaviour. In the next section, which deals with the comments that people made in their own words, we shall see that a considerable number of very disturbing criticisms were made. But it seems clear that these allegations are not made more frequently by black than by white people.

Informants were further asked a series of questions to establish whether, as they saw it, the police misbehaved towards them in various specific ways. Each of these questions was asked for every case of arrest, regardless of whether or not the informant had already made criticisms of police conduct in the matter in response to the general question. Where informants said that a particular kind of misconduct occurred this was, therefore, not a spontaneous comment, but a response to a specific question.

When asked 'During your dealings with the police in the matter, did any police officer say anything rude or insulting to you at any time?', informants answered 'yes' in 26 per cent of cases. The proportion who thought the police had said something rude or insulting was about the same for cases involving white people and cases involving West Indians (25 per cent and 31 per cent respectively).

When asked 'During your dealings with the police over this matter, did any police officer hit you or use force on you at all at any time?', informants answered 'yes' in 22 per cent of cases; in 14 per cent of cases they said this happened before going to the police station and in eight per cent of cases on the first visit to the police station or later. These figures are again the same for arrests invoving white people and West Indians. Informants were further asked 'Taking into account what you were doing at the time, would you say the police were justified in using force or not?'. Among the 22 per cent who alleged that police officers had used force are 4 per cent who thought this was justified in the circumstances and 18 per cent who thought it was not. None of the West Indians thought that force had justifiably been used.

Table IV.22   Arrests:   overall assessment of treatment by the police, by ethnic group

Column percentages

|  | Total | Whites | West Indians | All minorities |
|---|---|---|---|---|
| The police treated you |  |  |  |  |
| Fairly | 46 | 46 | 57 | 55 |
| A bit unfairly | 21 | 21 | 18 | 18 |
| Very unfairly | 26 | 26 | 24 | 23 |
| Not answered | 7 | 7 | 2 | 5 |
|  |  |  |  |  |
| Base: all arrests |  |  |  |  |
| (unweighted) | 169 | 114 | 46 | 55 |
| (weighted) | 775 | 719 | 47 | 56 |

In addition, informants were asked: 'Apart from anything you have mentioned already, during your dealings with the police over this matter, did they ever threaten you, or put unfair pressure on you in any way?' In 20 per cent of cases the answer was 'yes'. In cases involving white people, 19 per cent thought the police had used threats or unfair pressure, compared with 38 per cent of cases involving West Indians; this difference is unlikely to have arisen by chance (significant at the five per cent level of confidence). However, it is important to notice that the question excludes matters that have been raised already (general criticisms of police behaviour, insults, use of force). The proportion of cases in which white people had already made allegations under one or other of these heads is significantly higher than for West Indians, so the general thrust of the findings is that West Indians tend, if anything, to make less serious allegations than white people.

Finally, informants were asked for their overall assessment of the behaviour of police officers in connection with the incident: 'Overall, taking everything into account, would you say the police treated you fairly or unfairly in this matter? If unfairly  A bit unfairly or very unfairly?' The findings are shown in Table IV.22 above.

In about one-half of cases informants thought they were treated fairly and in about one-half of cases unfairly; in about one-quarter of cases they thought they were treated very unfairly. A higher proportion of West Indians than of white people thought they were treated fairly, but the difference is not statistically significant. Certainly the findings do show that the proportion who think they are treated unfairly is not higher among West Indians than among white people.

## The experience of arrest in people's own words
From time to time reports are produced that give critical accounts of the dealings that individual people have had with the police on particular occasions: an example is the report produced by the Lambeth Council for Community Relations in 1981. Such reports usually consist of a series of serious allegations, some of them of a sensational kind. The response of the police is usually indignant and dismissive. They are able to say that the allegations are unproven; in the vast majority of cases, no formal complaint has been made about the incidents concerned; dates, times and identities of the individuals involved are not given, so that the police are not in a position to start a complaints investigation themselves; the reports may be invented; they may have been stimulated or exaggerated by politically motivated people; and so on. While such arguments may not be conclusive, an independent observer would have to agree that the Lambeth report, for example, is confessedly one-sided; it is put together by people whose prime objective is to criticise the police; most important of all, the information was obtained by inviting people to come forward with accounts of police misconduct, and even if all of these accounts are substantially true, there remains the question as to whether these cases of misconduct are a small or large proportion of the total. The Commissioner could say with some justice that a damning report on garden gnomes or hairdressers might easily be got up by the same method.

The advantage of the present study is that the survey method imposes a certain balance. We have accounts of most of the arrests of a random sample of Londoners over the past five years. There is, of course, some danger of the opposite kind of bias to the one involved in the Lambeth method. We have seen that people living at the margins of society are particularly likely to be arrested: people known in the callous and vivid police slang as 'slag'. The listing in Roget's Thesaurus gives an interesting insight into the associations of this term for human detritus.

> dregs, grounds, lees; sediment; heel-tap; dross; precipitate, ashes, cinders, slag; scum, froth.
> litter, rubbish, lumber, odds and ends, cast-off clothes; shoddy; rags, trash, refuse, sweepings, scourings, off-

scourings, dross, slag, waste, rubble, debris; stubble, leavings; dregs; weeds, tares; rubbish heap, dust hole.

We shall see in the fourth volume of this series that, when there is police misconduct, the explanation for it often lies in this classification by police officers of a large part of their clientele as 'slag'. It is a problem of the survey method that what the police call 'slag' are likely to be under-represented. Dossers, drunks, prostitutes, meths drinkers, people who live in communes, heroin addicts, transvestites, etc., all probably have a less than even chance of inclusion in a survey of this kind, if only because they are less likely than the average to be found at a fixed address. If their experiences of the police tend to be unpleasant, then there is a danger that the survey findings will be biased towards the cosy and reassuring. While this criticism of the survey method cannot be dismissed entirely, we can be sure that the sample does include a considerable number of people whom the police would not regard as respectable. Two informants said they were prostitutes; a number admitted to drug addiction; many said they were thieves; many admitted to drunkenness; many gave accounts of brawls in which they had been involved; and so on. It is probable that people of this kind form a smaller proportion of the sample than of the general population, but the error may be fairly small. Certainly we can provide a far more balanced picture of people's experiences from the survey than we could by any other method.

The accounts of people's experiences of arrest are not here presented as an objective statement of what actually happened, but as how the person saw it. These accounts were given in response to questioning that studiously avoided encouraging people to criticise or to refrain from criticising. They may or may not be true accounts of what actually happened, but they certainly show how the incidents affected the way that people perceive the police. The statistics show that in 47 per cent of cases people thought the police were behaving unreasonably in arresting them; in 59 per cent of cases, people had criticisms to make of the way the police behaved towards them; in 26 per cent of cases they thought a police officer said something rude or insulting to them; in 22 per cent of cases they said that police officers used force or hit them, in 18 per cent of cases unjustifiably in the person's opinion; in 20 per cent of cases people thought the police threatened them or put unfair pressure on them in some other way; and in 47 per cent of cases people thought they were treated unfairly overall in connection with the arrest. We shall now look at the detailed accounts that underlie these statistics.

At an early point, informants were asked how they came to be arrested. We have seen that in about one-half of cases they thought the police were behaving reasonably in arresting them and in the remaining one-half of cases that they were behaving unreasonably. We give, first, examples of cases where from the informant's account the police were behaving reasonably.

I got arrested for burglary. We did a smash-and-grab at the local shop. The police came for me to my house to search. After we did the burglary someone from the flats opposite rang the police. A policeman got out of the car and asked me what we'd got in the bag as we were walking. We ran off. They came for me later that evening.

I'd gone to the wrong station. There was no toilet and I wanted to have a slash, so I went in a corner, had a piss, came back out and a policeman stopped and said it was an offence and arrested me.

A motor bike had been stolen and was lying on waste ground at the top of the road. I was trying to get the bike started. The police came and arrested me.

He charged me with being drunk. He didn't keep me long. I had a few drinks. I'd won a bottle of brandy in the pub and was carrying the bottle on its own in my hand.

Theft of timber. Got involved with another guy on some timber that was going cheap and the owners of the timber called the police and they caught us.

At a football match - drunk - a fight, and got caught.

I was in a stolen car, a passenger. I didn't know it was stolen at the time. It was late at night and a coloured bloke who was known to police was driving. They spotted him and stopped us.
I was fighting in the street.

Carrying and use of an offensive weapon during a fight outside a party. While we were fighting I heard sirens and everyone started to run. The police only caught me.

I was stopped in a car. I was driving. I was breathalysed and found positive. I was taken to the station and charged.

I was seen kicking a car door - a vehicle parked in the street. The police came straight away and took me to the police station.

It was from information given to the police by someone. They said I was harbouring my mate - he'd absconded from open prison. They arrested me in Kentish Town.

Walking in the middle of the street. Arrested for drunk and disorderly.

They caught us shoplifting and took us to the station.

I'd just sprayed a wall and smashed a couple of windows and someone reported me and they came down and caught me as I was walking away.

I was accused of stealing by my employer. They called the police. Two days later the police came to my house and took me to the police station.

I knocked a boy off his bike and left the scene of the accident without giving my name, etc. They came to the house and I wasn't here. I got home and they took me to the police station.

Well, we were out to steal cars that night. What happened, we tried to steal a car but the owner came out of his house. I went back because I thought my mate was caught and I got caught.

We were out one night and my mates were getting into a fight on the street. I went in and helped them. Someone got a punctured liver and he must have recognised me because the police picked me up in a pub a week later. We weren't using any weapons.

Me and a couple of pals went to a warehouse and bought some model horses and carts and some jewellery. We were selling it in the Bromley High Street just before Christmas. I was the look-out. I'd my car parked round the corner. My mate ran off but they got me to the station.

For being a prostitute.

Prostituting, the police came and picked me up in the street.

Fighting with my husband outside in the street in Holloway Road. We'd been drinking a lot and it ended up with arguments like him and I always do. The police came and my husband ran away and I was taken to Hornsey Road police station.

I was driving without insurance. I was driving my boyfriend's car and was involved with another car in an accident which led to the other driver driving off and reporting to the police. The police came round to my house later that evening. They took me and my boyfriend to the police station because we said my boyfriend was driving but the other driver had said I was driving, so they took us both to the police station.

They came to my house and they asked me if I was -- (name given) and I told them yes. They said they are taking me in for being an illegal immigrant.

For cannabis. I was handing it to somebody else. It's outside. I just got caught.

I went to court for another case and when I came out they told me there was a warrant out for me and they arrested me again.

Walking in Finsbury Park. I fitted a description which fitted a guy they were looking for. Handbag snatching.

I was on social security and I was drawing money when I shouldn't have been - call it deception.

I got in with a load of blokes and they were ripping off bikes, so I did have another bike which I'd got from a mate and I had the documents for it, so I gave the documents to these blokes. The police came round by these garages and asked us whose bike it was and we didn't know what to say, so they took the bike and they took us along to the police station.

We were coming out of a pub, three of us, and 20 or 30 blokes run after us and jumped two of my mates. So I got my mates from another pub and we went after them and there was all bricks and bottles flying. Then the police came and they jumped out the van and onto me and they arrested me ...

I was arrested for stealing from my employer. I came out of the shop and they were waiting outside - they arrested me then. My employer thought that I'd stolen a set of fairy lights and had called the police.

I was caught shoplifting. I took a packet of Maltesers from a store. The store detectives grabbed me and took me to the manager's office and told me if I paid for them I wouldn't be arrested. There was a policeman in the store at the time. I denied taking the Maltesers and I had put them in my friend's bag, so they found them in there and she got done for it. I had to go to the police station.

We have quoted extensively from these accounts to show that many informants answered frankly, and freely admitted that they were in the wrong. Other informants gave accounts that suggest that they were wrongfully or unreasonably arrested. The following are examples.

I was walking back from a friend's house. I was stopped by the police and assaulted.

I was a passenger in my brother's car which he had recently bought. We were driving along when several police cars came from all directions and stopped us. When we got out they accused us of being in a stolen car.

(This was probably a genuine mistake on the part of the police; presumably the car showed up as stolen on the computer record.)

I was walking up Charing Cross Road and was about to cross a pedestrian crossing. There was a police van there but I was unaware of it and walked off the crossing. I was stopped and told that I was doing something suspicious.

We came out of a pub and started walking. My mate jumped up and hit a bus shelter with his hand. The police grabbed me and said 'You're drunk and disorderly'. One punched me several times because I would not move because I had done nothing.

I was arrested here in my home. About 7 o'clock in the morning. They came in force, about two police cars, a van and six policemen and one policewoman. They knocked on the door and rushed upstairs with their truncheons. I didn't know who it was and I jumped on them. I was brought to the police station and thrown in a cell for two days without being charged. Bail wasn't accepted so I appeared in court on the fourth day.

I was charged with threatening behaviour and breach of the peace. I can't say what happened because I didn't do anything. It was outside my friend's house. Someone had thrown a brick at someone.

Loitering. I can't remember very well. Picked up in the street. I was just walking along the street and they came along in a car and arrested me.

I was out with my mates (six of us altogether) for the evening and we ended up in a Chinese restaurant, when about ten uniformed PCs rushed in and came straight to our table. They did not take any notice of the others there, just us, and they just grabbed us and with a lot of punching and kicking two of them sat on me, they got us into the van without even telling us what it was about. There was a CID bloke there outside who seemed to be directing them. We did not know what it was all about as we had not done anything. They kept pulling our hair and pushing us around.

I was walking along, I saw this guy coming up to me carrying two bags and he asked if I would help him carry them up the road. I ended up carrying one for him. A police car pulled out of a side street and they saw us. Seeing us they stopped. The other guy put the bag down and walked away and told me to carry on walking. Then I realised I had two stolen bags. The police stopped us, told us to put the bags in the car and took us to the police station.

I was taking part in the annual Gay Pride March. The police were discriminating against this minority group and their arrests were uncalled for as the march was going quite peacefully at the time.

Came out from a club and going to a friend's home. We got to the house before him and was waiting outside. The police came along and thought we were nicking cars and took us down to the station.

We was over waste ground and I got accused of stealing bottles of lemonade from R Whites which we never took.

Sus I got done for. I was just walking down the road with one of my mates and got down the bottom and a plain van and two plain-clothes policemen came up and pulled us both up and said that we were trying to enter vehicles along the street. We were just taken down the police station and put in a cell for about four hours and then my Dad came and we filled in a statement and had my stuff given back to me and went.

I was walking down the road with my girl friend. I was limping as I had sunburnt swollen legs and we heard this crowd behind us and didn't take any notice of it. Then we heard a window smashed and as we turned to have a look two or three police vans pulled up and a policeman jumped out and he ran at me and told me I was nicked for putting the window through and they put me in the back of the police van and took me to the station.

Coming from Wandsworth Common where we were playing football we were going to a chip shop and there was some trouble between two boys who were fighting and I knew one of them and we were standing there and the boy I knew was beating up the other bloke and we thought he was unconscious so I went in to stop it with another boy and we broke up the fight. Then somebody said we'd better go 'cos the police would be there. The police arrived at the scene and we went on walking to the chip shop. The police asked what was going on but we went on walking and then we saw about 12 vehicles

126

go past. After we'd got our chips we went back home and halfway the police van came and two police cars and the police cut our group in half and told half of us to go back. I told the policeman I wanted to go home 'up that way' and pointed. He grabbed my arm and said 'Right, you are arrested'.

I went window shopping at Brent Cross as my Mum was going to buy me a pair of shoes for my birthday. As I was coming out I saw friends from school, the police came behind us and said we were going to be taken in for 'sus'. Attempting to pickpocket.

I went to a pawnbroker's with a friend who was selling a chain his sister had given him. The pawnbroker must have called the police because we were black. The police arrested my friend and me saying we had stolen the jewellery.

They just said 'You're arrested' and took me off in the way I just described and charged me and had photos and finger prints - the lot. Just that I was kept till three in the morning and then told to come back at 10am for the court. It was in Greenwich. We were coming back from a football match after a lot of violence and vandalism to property in the area. I feel the police needed to make some arrests to show they had done something about it.

A bloke in a pub threw a glass outside at the police and they didn't actually see who threw it and they came into the pub and pulled me outside. I tried to tell them I didn't do it but they didn't believe me and took me down the police station.

They thought I was answering them back, but I was only waiting for a lift from my father.

I was in Hastings. A car that was going slowly nearly ran my friend over. His brother was near me and as we crossed the road he tapped the car as if to tell the driver to watch it because they had nearly ran his brother over. The driver made a fuss as there were police on the other side of the road. They called another police car and came up to my friend. He started arguing with the police and I tried to calm him down and the police arrested me for obstructing them, but I was only trying to help to calm my friend down. (This incident did not, of course, involve the Metropolitan Police.)

There was a fight outside a pub and I went to walk in(to) the pub and there was a policeman on the door and he asked me which team I supported and when I said 'West Ham' he said 'You'll do'. And he arrested me for threatening behaviour.

127

(Same person). Football again. It was on the station, Birmingham. That was for nothing. I was going up the escalator to get another train and as I got to the top I felt someone grab my arm and when I turned round and asked what was the matter, they said 'You're nicked'. I asked what for and they didn't answer. When they got us to the mobile police station they said you're nicked for threatening behaviour and threatening words.

| | Number of cases | Per cent of cases where the police were criticised | Per cent of all arrests |
|---|---|---|---|
| Assault or excessive use of force | 22 | 24 | 13 |
| Threatening or abusive behaviour | 12 | 13 | 7 |
| Hectoring, bullying, aggressive, wrong attitude | 24 | 26 | 14 |
| Improper or harsh treatment at police station | 4 | 4 | 2 |
| Fabrication or exaggeration of evidence | 8 | 9 | 5 |
| It was unnecessary to make an arrest | 6 | 6 | 4 |
| The reason for the arrest was not explained | 2 | 2 | 1 |
| Other complaints | 15 | 16 | 9 |

In 93 actual cases (59 per cent of the weighted total) people had some criticism to make of the way the police behaved towards them. It is difficult to classify these answers because each informant usually made several complaints, but the above table shows a classification based on the most serious complaint, taking the first complaint shown in the table as the most serious and working downwards.

The following is a record of all the comments at this point in the interview that mentioned excessive use of force.

They beat me and shouted abuse. They took some of my clothes.

Not so much me but towards my friend. They seemed to pick on him as he was the smallest. Threw him at the car and handcuffed him.

In the station I was physically abused, stripped to my underpants, threatened with violence if I didn't make a statement. They kept trying to wrench my arm off my body. On the way to the police station they sat me in the back of the motor with the police dog. They handcuffed my wrists too tight.

They have done everything wrong. First they didn't show me search warrant. They misbehaved with my wife. They disturbed my children, asked them questions. They took me to police station and locked me in without any food. They did not allow to visit any wife or friend, didn't allow to see my solicitor. One police officer kicked me. I was innocent and they asked to give signature on blank paper. They didn't charge me at that time and they made statement on that blank paper.

The police were holding my arms and another punched me in stomach for no reason - trying to get me in the police car. They were just flash - showing off.

The assault. I was pushed around here, beaten up here, dragged to the police car, handcuffed hands behind my back injuring my arm. I complained and they tightened them. They were abusing me and trying to provoke me. I was put in a cell and not charged and all information was withheld about everything. I wasn't fed. I wasn't given water. I wasn't given a blanket and it was freezing. There was no mattress for me. I ran out and grabbed a civilian and asked him to do something to help, then two or three hours afterwards they fed us and gave us water. I wasn't allowed to wash or change clothes so when we appeared in court, the clerk of the court and the judge took me for a bum in the street.

I was brutally attacked by the police in the back of the police van and beer was thrown over me, cans were thrown at me. I was used as a footrest by the police. I sustained torn muscles in the arm and numb fingers (from which I still suffer) from being hit over the arm with a truncheon. I was threatened in the police cell, refused a doctor when I needed one.

They had no reason to stop me and my friend, let alone arrest us. They behaved very unfairly. They swore at us, threatened us, both on the way to the police station and after we got there. They would not allow us to smoke. They would not allow me to ring my parents to let them know where I was, my mother was very worried. When I got sent to the CID they punched and kicked me. They said that perhaps I didn't do it but I might as well admit to it because they would get me for something. They put me in a cell with three Pakistanis and kept me there all night.

They threatened to kick my head in if I didn't tell them what had happened. They did do in one of my mates but not me.

They were aggressive and pushed us around. We were punched and shouted at. They would not accept that we were not the cause of the ruckus and insisted that they would have us for public disturbance and insulting behaviour. They kept us in a cell for about two hours, then let us go.

I was assaulted - thrown to the floor - when I refused to go to the cells. One policeman wanted five minutes in the cells with me. Water only for 48 hours. No food - afraid of the water.

One police officer was a very nasty person. In the car he lost his temper and started swearing at me. When I got to the police station I was dragged in by my hair. He also gave my mother a lot of verbal abuse and we reported him but nothing was done.

I was hit in the face. I shouldn't have been. (Refused to give more details.) One policeman lost his temper.

The next day he'd left his jacket in my car and I took it to return it and tell him I didn't want to see him again, and the police pounced on the car and yanked me out and made me sit in the back of a police car and take my coat off. I had my car keys in my hand and he tried to grab them and when he did he twisted my arm round the back and gave me a mouthful calling me names.

I didn't like the way they pulled me off the bus, it didn't take five of them to pull me off the bus. One plain-clothes one put my arm behind my back and pulled my hair. The one who said he recognised me after they pulled me off the bus went off and had a little discussion and it seemed obvious that he wasn't sure it was me and when they put me in the car he hesitated and wasn't sure what to charge me with.

When they grabbed hold of me one of them started punching me in the ribs.

When they came to the door at 2am there were uniformed and plain-clothes officers and a dog. It was my brother's house but I opened it. They did not have a warrant. They asked to se my brother. I said he wasn't there. They asked me to come outside. I did and locked the door behind me. Then they got heavy and asked me for the key. They punched me and said they would arrest me if I did not let them in. My brother called out and then they arrested us both. At the station they started to behave more sensibly but they kept me there and then just let me go next afternoon.

Swore at me. Nearly broke my arm first at the time of the actual arrest and then as we were actually entering the police station.

The police just accused me. They were very off-hand. I was not doing anything - just walking. They hurt my hand and arm and I was cut through the force they used on me. They seemed to want to hurt me as much as possible.

When I was arrested, rough handling. If they had asked me to go politely I would have gone, but they didn't give me a chance. I was dragged away by a police officer and a police woman. The way they twisted me arm up me back and they handcuffed me.

I was voluntarily writing the statement as the things occurred, and I was slapped about for no apparent reason by the CID inspector and they put me in custody for the night and did not let me telephone my solicitor or anybody. They did not give me a cup of coffee even in the morning before going to court.

The way they got hold of me and my mate and threw me against the wall as if I was a criminal.

These cases, in which according to the informant's account, excessive or unnecessary force was used, number 22 out of 167, or 13 per cent. It will be recalled that, when directly asked, informants said that force was used in 22 per cent of cases and that it was unjustifiably used in 18 per cent of cases. While there are, therefore, some cases in which there is no detailed backing for the general statement that excessive force was used, there is such detailed backing in a considerable number of cases.

We have made a distinction in the table between descriptions of threatening or abusive behaviour and descriptions of hectoring, bullying or aggressive behaviour of a slightly less disturbing kind. There were 12 cases of the former and 24 of the latter. The distinction is not, however, very secure. Below we quote some examples from these 36 cases.

I think they were very rude and pig-headed. They are a unique unit, seem to think there is nothing the public can do to damage them. The station officer didn't listen to a word I said.

They were effing at me all the time. They denied this later when I accused them.

The attitude in general. After all they are public servants, we pay their wages, you don't expect them to treat you like rubbish in the street. Push you around physically and verbally abusing you, antagonising the situation. Mainly outside the pub. In the station the attitude was appalling. Before this I had the utmost respect, don't have much now.

Too rough. Thought they were 'The Sweeney'.

Too rough. Dragged me by the collar. Kicked the wall with boot cap to get me frightened. Kept calling in other police to get me worried.

First of all the way they treated me. They wouldn't let me phone, he threatened that he was going to hit me. When they searched the house they turned everything upside down and left it like that, and they didn't have a search warrant. Also they harrassed my wife: they are very rude.

They were very harsh, racist, in their behaviour.

I was under duress, they threatened to have my boy in too if we didn't co-operate. One of them threatened to stick three burglaries on us. The statement was misleading. I said one thing and they tried to elaborate on it giving two meanings to my answers to their questions. My wife was there for 36 hours same as me, though they'd promised to let her out that night. The children were here with no-one to look after them.

They threatened me with a night in the cells if I did not give information about my brother (who wasn't there and wasn't wanted by the police) - where he was and what he was doing.

No explanation, just rude and nasty and that is putting it mildly. My father phoned police station, did not tell him what charge was.

They were very rough and off-hand. They did not accept that we were not thieves. They treated us like criminals. They seemed to be the judge as well as prosecutor. They kept accusing me and telling me to admit I had stolen the jewellery.

They treated me very badly. Too aggressive towards me. Threatened me with violence.

Like when we was in the police station one of them asked me if I'd been in trouble before and I said 'No' and he said 'Who's been a good little angel them?' and tried to get me worked up. He did it deliberate like.

132

He said to me I should plead guilty or he'd add more bits to the statement so I pleaded guilty 'cos I didn't want to go to court again.

They kept us too long at the station. One of them started poking me a lot in the ribs.

First and foremost I didn't want to sit down and I was pushed down. Let you go after a couple of hours and they didn't. They had changed officers during the night and he made it clear he was in charge. When in the van they were saying 'Got another one' and jumping up and down, like.

The following are records of the four complaints that were primarily about treatment at the police station.

The way the statement was made and the way I was treated. Not given food and drink for so long.

They put me in a cell for two days. It only had a bench in it, no bed, no blankets. Wouldn't allow me a phone call. I claimed habeas corpus but they said they didn't understand Latin.

They way they kept me up all night. I wasn't allowed to sleep, they kept waking me up. They banged on the cell wall and made me get up and walk around for no reason.

They took a bloody liberty because the bastards refused to let me out in the morning when I wanted a wash. They shouted at me a lot.

The following is a selection of the eight complaints that had mainly to do with fabrication or exaggeration of evidence.

I don't think the police constable told the actual truth. They said I said things that I didn't say.

First of all, when it first started, they called for a police van and a policeman in uniform came up and he said he was watching us from a school down the road and said he saw us doing what we weren't doing. In the court hearing who said he saw us was a different one from the one who said he saw us on the night. What the plain-clothes policeman said was all lies. When we got pulled up by them they said that if we told them we'd done it, they'd let us go. My mate was wearing a Union Jack on his jacket, so the plain-clothes policeman asked him if his old man was in the National Front. My friend replied 'Fuck off' and the point of saying that was that in the court hearing the police officer just said about my mate saying 'Fuck off', he didn't say anything about the National Front. In the court hearing there were quite a lot of questions put to the police and they couldn't really answer. Given the police couldn't really answer some of the questions I couldn't understand why they gave a suspended sentence. In the police cell they tried to get me to put my friend in it but I just said I didn't know.

Very unnecessary. I think I was taken in because I was questioning his authority. Told I shouldn't argue back. Silly procedure to go through all the emptying of pockets and everything at the police station for such a trivial offence. Also, I don't think he was very honest. Because of the statement he gave us to what actually happened was total exaggeration. Size of the pavement what was said between us, saying that people had to step off the pavement to get round me, which simply wasn't true.

They were very rude and offensive. They told lies. For the type of alleged offence they locked us in a cell and I thought was uncalled for.

Made a story up. He told me he saw me doing everything and the police weren't even there. I think they arrested me for nothing instead of getting the ringleaders who were inside the pub.

They arrested us for nothing.

The following are examples of complaints made by people who thought it was unnecessary to arrest them (of which there were six in all).

It was a first offence and they could have let us off with a caution. We were only playing with it (a ball that went into hospital grounds) and had not stolen it and they had a description of the boys (who had committed another offence in the grounds) and they were white.

They had no need to take me to the police station. All they needed to do was to stop and search me.

If they'd bothered to ask us what had happened at the scene, then we needn't have all bothered. They locked me up in a little cell next to the question room and left my mates outside. They tended to believe her at first (the complainant).

It doesn't seem fair that they should be able to fish you up off the street.

Just took me away without giving me a chance to explain.

The following are the complaints from the two people who said the police did not explain to them what the reason for the arrest was (the first has been covered already under the circumstances of the arrest).

They would not tell us what we were supposed to have done. We could not find out. We could not make out why we were taken from the restaurant when they had not taken any notice of the other people there as we were not misbehaving in any way.

When I was getting in the car I asked them 'What's this?'. They didn't tell me why they were arresting us. They didn't tell me what was in the bag or whatever. At the police station the other guy got a bit cheeky and they said 'Shut up or I'll shut you up' or something like that.

The remaining 15 complaints do not fall into any of the previous categories, and mostly do not involve specific or serious allegations. Some examples are given below.

They're two-faced when you are guilty of a crime. They've no respect for nobody. They have only respect for the Queen.

If they had at least said they were sorry they made a mistake. They put me on bail so then I got a letter saying I had no further need to attend when my bail ran out. If only they had said sorry.

From start to finish. The idea basically that you are guilty until proved innocent. I was locked up for the night because the breathalyser bag registered I was over limit. Subsequently the bag was found to be defective and my blood sample showed it was well below the limit.

Takes too long over stupid trivial things. I think there should be someone there to help you out and tell you what your rights are and so on. As soon as you sign a statement you're guilty and they always say that if you sign a statement you get out quicker.

I thought for a small household so many police and dogs were unnecessary. And the strip search we had to go through was quite humiliating.

From the weighted data, in 26 per cent of cases of arrest the suspect claimed that a police officer said something rude or insulting to him or her. There were actually 53 cases (unweighted) in the survey in which such a claim was made. Informants were asked what the police said that was rude or insulting, and from their answers the 53 cases can be classified as shown in the table below.

| | Number of cases | Per cent of cases where insult alleged | Per cent of all arrests |
|---|---|---|---|
| Racist insult | 11 | 21 | 7 |
| Other insult | 24 | 45 | 14 |
| Mild insult | 3 | 6 | 2 |
| Bad language | 4 | 8 | 2 |
| No specific insult or bad language quoted | 11 | 21 | 7 |

The figures in this table are unweighted. There were 18 non-white people who claimed they were insulted, and of these 11 said the insult was racist. There were 55 cases of arrest involving non-white people, and racist insults were alleged in 11 of these cases, or 20 per cent of the total.

Examples of the language used by police officers, according to informants, are given below under the heads shown in the table.

Racist insults
Called me a black bastard.

Using bad language all the time - a black bastard, a wog, on several occasions called me a nigger.

Two women PCs swore at me, told me to shut up and fuck off. Called me names about my colour.

Just called me a black bastard and things like that.

Stupid black cunt. That one stuck in my mind. In the station, I wasn't meant to hear because he turned away and said it.

Other insults
What have you fucking done? You troublemakers are shit.

Every four-letter Anglo-Saxon word in the dictionary plus some I hadn't heard before. Fucking everything. Can't remember it all.

He called me a queer and said 'Go away little boy or we'll

136

arrest you'.

Called me a slut, a tart and a prostitute.

You'll spend the night in the cell, you cocky little fucker.

Swearing at you, telling you to fuck off with no rhyme or reason.

Well they threatened me and what I've just told you, he said 'I've seen scum like you before' - other things as well, but I can't remember.

You useless, junked-out bag of shit.

## Mild insults
They referred to me as a thief and I had only got stolen goods but I had not stolen them. Called me a liar as well.

Generally called me a liar.

Called me 'Porky pies'. (This is rhyming slang for lies.)

## Bad language
You aren't fucking around with juniors here, you're playing with the fucking CID.

I don't want any fucking nonsense from you, we'll get it out of you anyway.

Nothing but swear words, language you might expect from young hooligans.

## No specific insult or bad language quoted
Try to make you attack them, sort of thing. Try to wind you up by insulting you.

They kept saying I was a pest and the sooner I said what had happened I could go. They had me in tears, took my cigarettes away. They gave me the impression they were sure I was guilty.

Just very flash and rude.

In 20 per cent of cases the informant said that the police threatened or put unfair pressure on them (apart from anything that had been mentioned already). The proportion of West Indians who made this claim was significantly higher (38 per cent). There were 43 actual cases in which there were claims of threats or unfair pressure. In most of these cases the claim was that direct threats were used.  Some examples are quoted below.

I was told I wouldn't get bail if I didn't make a statement.  I was intimidated by being made to sit in my underpants with people walking in and out, and past.

They kept me in confinement for a long time.  Said until I speak the truth I would be there and to knock on the door when I was ready to tell the truth.

There were at least six police involved.  The sergeant instructed three men to carry me to the cells.  I was refused my one phone call.  Wife couldn't see me.  I hadn't been charged with a criminal offence.  (There is no claim of a direct threat in this case.)

They kicked me and punched me and said if I did not admit to it they would get me for something.

They threatened to kick my head in if I didn't co-operate.  It was before my brother-in-law came to get me out.

They said if I don't keep calm they'd beat the hell out of me, teach me a lesson.

They asked me to admit to crimes which we committed six or seven months before, and if I didn't tell they'd keep on hitting me which they did.  They took my clothes off, told me to spread my legs and said they'd stick their truncheon up my backside.

I'd never been in trouble with the police before.  He said 'I bet we could find someone of your description to pin something on'.

They threatened to give me a bashing if I didn't say what I had done.

I said what had I done, and one uniformed one said 'How about attempted murder?'

Well two plain-clothes men came down and acted hard and throwing their weight about trying to scare me into saying things.

When I pushed back (they said) 'Ah, assaulting a police officer!'.  But as I was being punched I tried not to fight back but keep within the law.  (One said) 'A hairy cunt' and things like that.

138

They said I would be locked away in the cell for the night if I did not admit I was going out to commit rape. They tried to get me to confess to something I had not done. The pressure was heavy but I did not admit so they could not keep me in. They let me go.

'The longer you leave it the longer you stay, so let's get it over and done with', so I did.

It was a bit frightening. I was in a cell and I didn't know what to expect. The police said they would send us down to the local prison for the night. They said it was not very pleasant there.

Well they said if I said I had done it I could go home. Just nasty to me.

They said if I plead guilty the charges would be less for me and I would probably get off free.

They said if you don't tell us where you got it we will have you for speeding and go over your bike and have you for everything we can find on that as well.

## The experience of arrest: conclusions

Being arrested is inevitably an unpleasant experience. In a substantial minority of cases the person arrested is drunk or behaving violently at the time of the arrest; by the nature of things he is not usually trying to cooperate with the police. However well the police behave, we would not therefore expect the accounts that people give of their arrests to be cheerful reading. Having been through a humiliating experience we would expect people to take every opportunity to shift the blame from themselves and to make accusations against the police.

It is nevertheless extremely disturbing to find that a substantial proportion of people who have been arrested make very specific allegations against the police involving gross misconduct in many cases. How many of these allegations are substantially true can never be finally established. The matter could only be resolved by detailed investigations of each particular case. When such investigations are carried out, as part of the formal complaints procedure, by the police themselves, a very small proportion of the allegations are substantiated. However, the great majority of incidents of the kind reported from the survey never become the subject of formal complaint investigations, and the ones that do may or may not be the worst cases. In the fourth volume of this series we shall, further, argue that the procedure for the investigations is weighted - maybe inevitably so - in favour of the police. We would, therefore, not agree that the findings of the survey can be dismissed by reference to the results of formal complaints investigations.

These findings cannot be swallowed whole either. We shall be able to arrive at a more balanced assessment after considering the results of our observation of the police in action. For the moment it is enough to say that the survey findings strongly suggest that in a considerable minority of cases suspects are assaulted, threatened and verbally abused; and this appears to be not a few isolated incidents, but a pattern of conduct among what must be a substantial minority of police officers.

## Motoring offences

Motoring incidents are one of the commonest occasions of contact between the police and Londoners. Eighteen per cent of all informants said they had ever been reported for a motoring offence by a police officer and received a court summons as a result. Most of these people are men. Exactly one-third of men, compared with five per cent of women said they had ever been reported. Among men and women who own or have the use of a car, 29 per cent said they had ever been reported, compared with 42 per cent of people who own or have the use of a motor bike. Nearly half (45 per cent) of men who own or have the use of a vehicle said they had ever been reported, and seven per cent that they had been reported in the past twelve months. The proportion who say they have been reported within the past twelve months declines sharply with age: among vehicle owners and users, nine per cent of those aged 15-19 compared with two per cent of those aged 60 and over said they had been reported within the past twelve months (tables not shown).

The proportion of motorists who have been reported in the past twelve months is the same for white people and West Indians (five per cent in each case) but rather lower for Asians (three per cent). Those living in inner London are more likely to have been reported than those living in outer London (six per cent compared with four per cent). The proportion reported is higher in boroughs with a high index of social stress than elsewhere (10 per cent within the past twelve months in the top group compared with three per cent in the bottom one). The proportion is higher among those in the skilled manual socio-economic group than among those in other groups. It is rather higher among those in the professional and white collar groups than among those in the semi-skilled and unskilled manual groups. This is undoubtedly the kind of offence that middle-class people are most likely to be accused of.

Informants were asked in detail about the last occasion within the past twelve months on which they were reported. About three-quarters thought that the police dealt with this matter in a fair and reasonable way (72 per cent). Those who thought the police were unfair or unreasonable over the matter were asked to explain further, but there are only 20 such people in the survey, so no very firm conclusions can be drawn from their answers. None of them contains serious allegations against the police, although in a few cases the informant thought the police evidence was exaggerated or adapted to strengthen the case.

# V EXPERIENCE OF CROWD TROUBLE

In relatively peaceful times, a small but significant proportion of the resources of the Metropolitan Police is used in maintaining security and controlling, or trying to control, crowds at football matches, state occasions and processions, demonstrations, political meetings outdoors, carnivals, fairs and so on. Because of the riots in 1981 a larger volume of police resources than before was used in maintaining or restoring 'public order', and new units were created for the purpose. In this chapter we look at the experience people have of occasions when the police came into contact with crowds and at the impressions of police behaviour that they took away with them. Probably the majority of such occasions are largely peaceful. Our questioning was concerned only with occasions 'when there was trouble of any sort between the police and groups of people'. Within a wider context it may be said that this is a biassed approach, since the objective of the police is to prevent 'trouble' and we have only asked about occasions when they failed to do so. However, we shall, in the next chapter, consider other occasions of contact between people and the police, including any at public order events where no conflict was taking place.

The introductory question was as follows.

> Have you yourself ever been present when there was trouble of any sort between the police and groups of people (such as demonstrators, football supporters, gangs of youths or any other groups)? Please include anything you have seen, even if you were not involved.

Further questions established whether the informant had witnessed any such events within the past two years and within the past six months, and how many events of this kind he had witnessed during the past two years. The findings are shown in Table V.1. One-fifth of informants say they have ever witnessed trouble between crowds of people and the police. Most of the interviews were completed by October 1981, so all the riots of that year happened within the six months before the interview of the great majority of cases. We find that eight per cent of informants had

Table V.1  Witnessing of crowd trouble, by sex and age

Column percentages and means

| | Total | Men | Women | Age 15-24 | Age 25-44 | Age 45 and over |
|---|---|---|---|---|---|---|
| Have witnessed crown trouble | | | | | | |
| Within past six months | 8 | 12 | 5 | 17 | 8 | 4 |
| Within past two years | 5 | 8 | 2 | 13 | 4 | 3 |
| Longer ago | 8 | 13 | 5 | 8 | 13 | 5 |
| Never | 79 | 67 | 88 | 62 | 75 | 88 |
| Mean number of occasions within past two years | | | | | | |
| Overall | 0.50 | 0.87 | 0.20 | 0.94 | 0.46 | 0.36 |
| Among those who have witnessed crowd trouble in that period | 3.85 | 4.35 | 2.70 | 3.22 | 3.74 | 5.12 |
| Base: all informants | | | | | | |
| (unweighted) | 2,420 | 1,161 | 1,259 | 984 | 844 | 592 |
| (weighted) | 13,944 | 6,297 | 7,648 | 2,609 | 5,174 | 6,162 |

142

witnessed crowd trouble during the previous six months, during which the riots took place. A total of 13 per cent had witnessed crowd trouble during the previous two years. More detailed questioning shows that many of the events that people witnessed were not riots or directly connected with them.

These findings show that quite a small proportion of Londoners know anything from their own direct observation about the police handling of public order events in which there was trouble; most of their information will come from what they see on television. Also, people have far more experience of the police in other contexts than in the context of public order events. For example, 27 per cent of informants say they have been the victim of crime in the past year only; 40 per cent say they have ever been stopped by police when in a vehicle; 10 per cent say they have ever been arrested; and we shall see in the next chapter that 56 per cent of Londoners say they have spoken with a police officer for some reason or other in the past year. By contrast, only 13 per cent say they have observed trouble between crowds and the police in the past two years, and in most of these cases the person concerned was not directly involved. It may be that experience of police behaviour at public order events, thought not very common, makes a particularly deep impression; also, people will be strongly influenced by the intensive coverage of such events by the press and television. But the findings show that most contacts between people and the police happen outside the public order context.

There is a strong tendency for the same minority of the population to witness crowd trouble repeatedly, because of where they live, where they go or what they do. Among the 13 per cent who have seen any crowd trouble over the past two years, the mean number of occasions on which they have seen it in that period is 3.85. Men are three or four times as likely to have witnessed crowd trouble as women (depending on the exact measure that is used). Also, young people are three or four times as likely as older people to have witnessed it. Three out of ten people aged 15 to 24 say they have witnessed crowd trouble during the previous two years.

Asians and other non-whites are much less likely to have witnessed crowd trouble than either white people or West Indians (see Table V.2). The proportion of white people and West Indians who have seen crowd trouble is the same, but those white people who have seen it are more likely than West Indians to have seen it repeatedly. Thus, none of the ethnic minority groups comes into contact with the police in this kind of situation as often as white people do.

Table V.2    Witnessing of crowd trouble, by ethnic group

Column percentages and means

|  | Whites | West Indians | Asians | Other non-whites |
|---|---|---|---|---|
| **Have witnessed crowd trouble** | | | | |
| With past six months | 9 | 10 | 3 | 3 |
| Within past two years | 5 | 6 | 3 | 5 |
| Longer ago | 9 | 5 | 3 | 1 |
| Never | 77 | 79 | 91 | 91 |
| **Mean number of occasions within past two years** | | | | |
| Overall | 0.55 | 0.28 | 0.17 | 0.11 |
| Among those who have witnessed crowd trouble in that period | 4.03 | 1.76 | 3.03 | 1.42 |
| Base: all informants | | | | |
| (unweighted) | 1,252 | 511 | 541 | 116 |
| (weighted) | 12,428 | 450 | 607 | 459 |

Many public order events happen in central London, and during 1981, riots and disturbances were more common in inner London than in outer London. It is not therefore surprising to find that people living in inner London are more likely to have witnessed crowd trouble than people living in outer London.

| | Per cent of those in | |
| Have witnessed crowd trouble | Inner London | Outer London |
|---|---|---|
| Within past six months | 11 | 7 |
| Within past two years, not past six months | 6 | 5 |

This contrast between those in inner and outer London is much the same among white people and among West Indians, when they are considered separately. However, the proportion of Asians who have witnessed crowd trouble does not vary between those in inner and outer London; it should be remembered that the largest single concentration of Asians is in an outer London borough (Ealing) where there were disturbances in 1981.

The survey shows up no tendency for those living in areas of high ethnic concentration to have witnessed more crowd trouble than those living elsewhere. The only possible exception to this is that 14 per cent of West Indians living in areas of high ethnic concentration say they have witnessed crowd trouble in the past six months, compared with eight per cent of all informants. However, this 14 per cent is based on a sample of only 75 people in the relevant group. The survey is, of course, painting with a broad brush; we are not describing the experience of West Indians in Brixton, but the experience of West Indians generally, and when we speak of West Indians in areas of high ethnic concentration, parts of Brixton are being grouped with many other districts of London. The findings provide a necessary perspective: they show that even among West Indians in areas of high ethnic concentration, experience of any kind of crowd trouble (including many sorts of events as well as riots) is rather uncommon.

The findings show very little relationship between socio-economic group and experience of crowd trouble. It seems that people belonging to all social classes are about equally likely to be present on such occasions. Bearing in mind our previous finding that there is a group of people who tend to come into contact with the police in many and varied circumstances, it comes as no surprise to find that people who have been arrested and people who have repeatedly been stopped by the police are much more likely to have experienced crowd trouble than others. While 13 per cent of all informants have witnessed crowd trouble during the past two years, among those who have been arrested within the past five years the proportion is 33 per cent, and, among those who have not been arrested but have been stopped at least twice in the past year, the proportion is 40 per cent.

Those who had witnessed crowd trouble in the past two years (370 people unweighted) were asked in detail about the last occasion of this sort. This is different from the procedure for stops, arrests and incidents of victimisation, where a number of occasions were asked about. This time there is only one occasion asked about for each informant, and the tables are therefore based on people rather than events. Of these last occasions during the past two years, 62 per cent were in the previous six months - roughly the period of the 1981 riots. This probably indicates that more crowd trouble was observed over the period of the riots than during the previous 18 months, though no precise calculation can be made to prove this, since more distant events will less often be recalled.

Informants were asked who had the trouble with the police on the last occasion, and answered in their own words. As Table V.3 shows, they mentioned 'rioters' in only 10 per cent of cases. Some of the other answers given are consistent with the idea that what was being described was an event connected with the 1981 riots; for example, 12 per cent mentioned 'young people' and four per cent 'blacks'. Also, it is possible that those who said the trouble involved a crowd other than one at a demonstration, sporting event or carnival were in some cases talking about something that could be called a riot. Even if we take all these answers to refer to

145

'riots' - which is certainly an exaggeration - we come to only 38 per cent of last occasions, and this is 38 per cent of 13 per cent of informants, or five per cent of all informants. These findings imply that about one in twenty of Londoners, at most, witnessed any of the riots of 1981. If we take the view that anyone who saw a riot would have said so, then on that definition less than two per cent of Londoners witnessed any of the riots. These findings show that the riots were localised and limited in scale; only a small proportion of the population observed them, and the proportion who were directly involved was very small indeed.

Table V.3    Last occasion of crowd trouble: who were the people involved, by ethnic group

Column percentages

|  | Total | Whites | West Indians | Asians |
|---|---|---|---|---|
| Marchers or demonstrators | 10 | 9 | 12 | 15 |
| Crowd at sporting event | 39 | 41 | 10 | 31 |
| Carnival crowd | 3 | 2 | 26 | - |
| Other crowd | 12 | 12 | 13 | 14 |
| Not any of the above |  |  |  |  |
| Rioters | 10 | 9 | 21 | 11 |
| Young people | 12 | 12 | 12 | 18 |
| Adults | * | * | - | - |
| Drunks, people having a good time | 7 | 7 | 2 | - |
| Skinheads | 3 | 3 | 2 | 10 |
| Gang | 3 | 3 | 1 | - |
| Blacks | 4 | 4 | 3 | - |
| Asians | * | - | - | 12 |
| Whites | * | * | - | 2 |
| Base: informants who have witnessed crowd trouble in the past two years |  |  |  |  |
| (unweighted) | 370 | 238 | 85 | 37 |
| (weighted) | 1,840 | 1,697 | 71 | 35 |

Note:   'Other non-whites' are included in the total but not shown separately. The base for Asians is low.

The kind of occasion at which people have most commonly witnessed crowd trouble is sporting events (39 per cent). Marches and demonstrations account for 10 per cent, carnival crowds for three per cent and other crowds for 12 per cent. These four kinds of crowd or occasion account for two-thirds of the answers. Most of the remaining occasions involved rioters (10 per cent), young people (12 per cent) or drunks or others 'having a good time' (seven per cent). Mentions of skinheads and gangs were at a low level (three per cent each). People seldom answered in terms of ethnic groups; only four per cent mentioned blacks, and less than 0.5 per cent mentioned Asians (though 12 per cent of Asians did so). These findings show that only a very small proportion of incidents of crowd trouble struck observers as primarily involving ethnic minorities.

While crowd trouble at carnivals accounts for a very small proportion of the total (three per cent), it accounts for 26 per cent of the last occasions mentioned by West Indians. This suggests that the police handling of carnivals is likely to be of critical importance for their relations with this particular group. Also, 21 per cent of West Indians compared with nine per cent of white people said the last occasion of crowd trouble they observed involved rioters. This of course reflects the fact that many of the riots took place in areas of high West Indian concentration: even so, riots account for a minority of the occasions of crowd trouble observed by West Indians. A relatively small proportion of West Indians last observed crowd trouble at sporting events (10 per cent, compared with 41 per cent of white people): this may suggest that West Indians tend not to go to football matches because they often face racist abuse when they go, but the point cannot be definitely established since we have no information about attendance at football matches.

Table V.4     Last occasion of crowd trouble:    who caused the trouble, by ethnic group

Column percentages

|  | Total | Whites | West Indians | Asians |
|---|---|---|---|---|
| The crowd or part of the crowd | 80 | 82 | 46 | 74 |
| The police | 9 | 8 | 31 | 10 |
| Other answers | 3 | 3 | 1 | 6 |
| Don't know or not answered | 8 | 8 | 22 | 10 |
| Base: informants who have witnessed crowd trouble in the past two years | | | | |
| (unweighted) | 370 | 238 | 85 | 37 |
| (weighted) | 1,840 | 1,697 | 71 | 35 |

Where the occasion was a march or demonstration, informants were asked whether they were themselves taking part in the event (not necessarily in the trouble). Among the ten per cent who last observed crowd trouble on an occasion of this sort, three per cent were taking part in the march or demonstration; this amounts to less than 0.5 per cent of all informants.

Most informants say that they merely observed the disturbances and did not take part. Only 11 per cent say they were themselves involved in the trouble on the last occasion: this amounts to $1\frac{1}{2}$ per cent of all informants. Thus a small but appreciable minority of Londoners admit that they themselves have been involved in public order disturbances over the past two years; the proportion might rise to two per cent or one in fifty of Londoners if all occasions over the past two years were asked about.

Informants were asked 'In your opinion, who caused the trouble in the first place' and were allowed to answer, without prompting, in their own words. The great majority, 80 per cent, said the trouble was started by the crowd or part of the crowd; nine per cent said it was started by the police and the rest gave other or indefinite answers. Among West Indians, a much higher proportion, 31 per cent, thought the trouble was started by the police, 46 per cent thought it was started by the crowd or part of the crowd and rather a high proportion (23 per cent) gave indefinite answers, probably beause the question for them touched on a conflict of loyalties. The findings for Asians are similar to those for white people (see Table V.4). Young people are more likely than older people to think that the trouble was started by the police. The difference between West Indians and white people may arise partly because the two groups were observing different events; but it probably partly reflects a different assessment by the two groups of the part played by the police, arising from the more hostile attitude to the police among West Indians. The findings show that a small but significant minority of people - just over one per cent of all informants - think they have observed disturbances that were actually started by the police, and describe the event in that way without the idea being put to them. Five per cent of all West Indians think they have observed police-provoked disturbances.

Informants were asked, 'Do you have any criticisms of the way the police acted on that occasion?' and if they answered 'Yes' were asked what their criticisms were (see Table V.5). Overall, 28 per cent said they had criticisms, but 65 per cent of West Indians, compared with 35 per cent of Asians and 26 per cent of white people. Six per cent thought the police used excessive violence, six per cent that they over-reacted in other ways and eight per cent that the police action made the situation worse. All of these answers were given much more often by West Indians than by other groups; in particular, 21 per cent of West Indians thought the police used excessive violence. The only people who specificially stated

148

that the police showed bias or vindictiveness against black people were West Indians, and only three per cent of that group gave such answers. Overwhelmingly the criticisms of the police action, even among West Indians, were not primarily to do with racial prejudice or bias. Nevertheless, criticisms on all counts were much more likely to come from West Indians than from white people or Asians, possibly because the police action was in fact more often directed against West Indians, though possibly for the most part because of greater hostility to the police among West Indian informants.

Table V.5    Last occastion of crowd trouble:    criticisms of police handling, by ethnic group

Column percentages

|  | Total | Whites | West Indians | Asians |
|---|---|---|---|---|
| **Do you have any criticisms?** | | | | |
| Yes | 28 | 26 | 65 | 35 |
| No | 71 | 73 | 33 | 61 |
| Don't know or not answered | 1 | 1 | 2 | 3 |
| | | | | |
| **If yes, what criticisms?** | | | | |
| Anti-black or anti-Asian | * | – | 3 | – |
| Excessive violence | 6 | 6 | 21 | 4 |
| Over-reaction in other ways | 6 | 5 | 26 | 12 |
| Police action made situation worse | 8 | 8 | 19 | 5 |
| Other criticisms of police | 6 | 6 | 5 | 5 |
| Vague answer or don't know | 3 | 3 | 3 | 3 |
| | | | | |
| Base: informants who have witnessed crowd trouble in the past two years | | | | |
| (unweighted) | 370 | 238 | 85 | 37 |
| (weighted) | 1,840 | 1,697 | 71 | 35 |

Informants were asked what they thought about the number of police who were there. Overall, 19 per cent thought there were too many police, 21 per cent that there were too few and 59 per cent that there were about the right number (see Table V.6). Thus, a substantial proportion of informants - 40 per cent - thought that the scale of the police response was wrong, but those who thought the police over-reacted are exactly balanced by those who thought they under-reacted. Of course, different informants were talking about different occasions, but the findings show that people do not have the impression that the police consistently under-react or over-react to public disturbances. However the assessment of the ethnic minorities is entirely different. A majority of West Indians (57 per cent) thought there were too many police present at the last disturbance they observed, and only 30 per cent thought there were about the right number of police. Sixty per cent of Asians thought the police got it wrong, but they were evenly divided between thinking there were too many and too few police.

Table V.6    Last occasion of crowd trouble: number of police and police use of force, by ethnic group

Column percentages

|  | Total | Whites | West Indians | Asians |
|---|---|---|---|---|
| **What do you think about the number of police there?** | | | | |
| Too many | 19 | 16 | 57 | 30 |
| Too few | 21 | 22 | 7 | 30 |
| About right | 59 | 61 | 30 | 36 |
| Don't know or not answered | 1 | 1 | 6 | 3 |
| **Did the police use force at all?** | | | | |
| Yes | 53 | 52 | 74 | 66 |
| No | 43 | 44 | 21 | 31 |
| Don't know or not answered | 4 | 4 | 5 | 3 |
| **If yes, did they only use what force was necessary?** | | | | |
| Only necessary force | 37 | 38 | 18 | 34 |
| Too much force | 15 | 13 | 54 | 32 |
| Don't know or not answered | 2 | 2 | 1 | – |
| Base: informants who have witnessed crowd trouble in the past two years | | | | |
| (unweighted) | 370 | 238 | 85 | 37 |
| (weighted) | 1,840 | 1,697 | 71 | 35 |

We have seen that when asked what criticisms they had of the police action, six per cent of informants said that excessive violence was used. This is not a good measure of the total proportion who held this view, since some people were more concerned to express other criticisms at this point. In order to pursue the matter further, informants were asked the following direct questions about police use of force.

Did the police use force at all to control people or to make arrests?

If yes  From what you saw, would you say they only used what force was necessary or would you say they used too much force?

In just over half of cases (53 per cent) informants said the police used force, and in one out of three of these cases they thought the police used too much force. Bearing in mind that those who have observed crowd trouble over the past two years are 13 per cent of all informants, these findings mean that seven per cent of Londoners have seen the police use force on such occasions and two per cent have seen them use more force than they thought was necessary.  The findings for West Indians and Asians are again sharply different.  Three-quarters of West Indians who had observed crowd trouble said the police used force on the last occasion, and 54 per cent said they used more force than was necessary. Thus when West Indians observe crowd trouble, what they see often convinces them that the police are excessively violent or confirms them in that belief.  If we consider only those who have seen the police use force during a public disturbance, we find that one in three of all Londoners, but three in four of West Indians think that the force used was excessive.  The findings for Asians lie between those for West Indians and white people (though they are here based on only 37 informants, unweighted).  A higher proportion of Asians than of white people (66 per cent compared with 52 per cent) say the police used force on the last occasion, and half of these Asians think the police used too much force (32 per cent of Asians compared with 13 per cent of white people).

Table V.7 shows that in 61 per cent of cases the informant knew or saw that arrests were made, though the informant himself was arrested in only one per cent of cases.  The events observed by West Indians and Asians were rather more likely to have involved arrests than those observed by white people.

Our conclusion from these findings is that public disturbances over the past few years, including the riots of 1981, were directly observed by only a small proportion of the population of London. There is, however, a group of people who have observed a number of disturbances of this kind.  The riots of 1981 account for only a small proportion of the disturbances that people have observed over the past couple of years - perhaps for as little as ten per cent and certainly for no more than one-third.  Disturbances at sporting events are the ones most commonly observed.  Among those who have witnessed public disturbances, a substantial minority of white people but a majority of West Indians have criticisms to make of the action taken by the police.  People who observe public disturbances often see the police using force, usually justifiably in the opinion of white people but unjustifiably in the opinion of West Indians, with Asians taking an intermediate view. It is not clear how

151

Table V.7    Last occasion of crowd trouble: arrests, by ethnic group

Column percentages

|  | Total | | Whites | | West Indians | | Asians |
|---|---|---|---|---|---|---|---|
| Arrests were made | 61 | | 61 | | 72 | | 68 |
| You were arrested | | 1 | | 1 | | 2 | - |
| Only others arrested | 60 | | | 60 | | 70 | 68 |
| No arrests were made | 27 | | 26 | | 26 | | 24 |
| Don't know whether arrests were made | 12 | | 13 | | 2 | | 7 |
| Base: informants who have witnessed crowd trouble in past two years | | | | | | | |
| (unweighted) | 370 | | 238 | | 85 | | 37 |
| (weighted) | 1,840 | | 1,697 | | 71 | | 35 |

far these sharp differences between ethnic groups arise because the different groups were observing different events. While it is a small proportion of all Londoners who have seen the police use force in a way that, to them, was not justifiable, what they saw may have made a deep impression on these witnesses, who have probably described it to many other people. Among West Indians particularly, and to a lesser extent among Asians, this will have created or reinforced a hostile attitude towards the police. Against this, the findings show that a substantial majority of all those who have seen public disturbances are generally happy with the way the police acted on the last occasion.

# VI PATTERN OF CONTACT WITH THE POLICE

In previous chapters we have concentrated in turn on each of a number of ways in which people may come into contact with the police: through being victims of crime, through being treated by the police as offenders or suspected offenders, and through witnessing or taking part in trouble between crowds of people and the police. In this chapter we move towards a general assessment of the whole pattern of contact with the police, whatever the reason for the contact may be. First we consider occasions when people visit police stations, whether of their own accord or when taken there by a police officer. Secondly, we consider the overall pattern of contact, by taking the last occasion of contact as an indicator, and this analysis takes into account all the occasions of contact that have previously been described in greater detail. Finally, we show how this pattern of contact is influenced by the fact that a substantial minority of people have close friends or relatives in the force.

## Visits to police stations

Just over one-quarter of Londoners (27 per cent) say they have been to a police station in the past twelve months. Among these are 17 per cent who have made one visit and 10 per cent who have made more than one. A few people have made a large number of visits, but the mean number of visits made among those who have made any is just under two. These findings imply that about $1\frac{1}{2}$ million adult Londoners have visited a police station in a twelve-month period, and between them they have made about three million visits. This gives some impression of the large scale of the service provided by the police.

Table VI.1 shows that members of ethnic minority groups are markedly less likely to visit police stations than white people. Since most visits to police stations are voluntary (see below) this means that members of ethnic minority groups are less likely to want to make use of the police service than are white people. The difference is striking, and it is particularly strong in the case of Asians, who are exactly half as likely as white people to make visits to police stations. There are also some differences between

153

Table VI.1    Visits to a police station in the past year, by ethnic group

Column percentages

|  | Total | Whites | West Indians | Asians | Other non-whites |
|---|---|---|---|---|---|
| Have visited a police station in past year | 27 | 28 | 18 | 14 | 15 |
| **Number of visits in past year** | | | | | |
| One | 17 | 18 | 12 | 8 | 4 |
| Two | 6 | 6 | 4 | 3 | 11 |
| Three | 2 | 2 | * | 1 | - |
| Four or five | 1 | 1 | 1 | 1 | - |
| Six or more | 1 | 1 | 1 | 1 | - |
| Mean number of visits among those who have made any | 1.98 | 1.98 | 2.03 | 2.26 | 1.72 |
| Base: all informants | | | | | |
| (unweighted) | 2,420 | 1,252 | 511 | 541 | 116 |
| (weighted) | 13,944 | 12,428 | 450 | 607 | 459 |

age groups: the following summary table shows the proportion of each age group who have made a visit to a police station in the past twelve months.

| Age | Per cent |
|---|---|
| 15 - 19 | 26 |
| 20 - 24 | 33 |
| 25 - 44 | 33 |
| 45 - 59 | 25 |
| 60 and over | 16 |

People aged 20-44 are more likely than those who are older or younger to visit police stations. The striking differences between ethnic groups remain when the comparisons are made within particular age groups.

Men are more likely than women to visit police stations (35 per cent compared with 20 per cent), and the contrast is particularly strong among Asians, so that the proportion of Asian women who have visited a police station in the past twelve months is very low (seven per cent).

The fact that the ethnic minorities make less use of the

154

police than white people is not a consequence of the kinds of areas in which they live. This can be shown by a number of types of analysis: by the local ethnic concentration, by inner versus outer London, and by the level of social stress and deprivation in the borough. There is little relationship between the concentration of ethnic minorities in the local population and whether Asians and West Indians have visited police stations. Among Asians there is no consistent relationship at all: in other words Asians in places like Southall and in places like Richmond-on-Thames are equally unlikely to visit police stations. Among West Indians, those in the areas of high immigrant concentration are more likely than those elsewhere to visit police stations: 27 per cent of those in EDs with 20 per cent or more immigrants in 1971 have made a visit in the past twelve months, compared with 16 per cent of those in other EDs. Even so, the likelihood of making a visit among West Indians in areas of high concentration is not particularly high; it is the same as for white people generally. There is little difference in the proportion who have made a visit between those in inner and those in outer London, and again there is little relationship with the level of social stress and deprivation in the borough.

Those in the high socio-economic groups are more likely than those in the lower ones to have had this, mostly voluntary, kind of contact with the police. The following summary table shows the proportion of each socio-economic group who have visited a police station in the past twelve months.

| Socio-economic group | Per cent who have made a visit |
|---|---|
| Professional and managerial | 33 |
| White collar | 26 |
| Skilled manual | 34 |
| Semi-skilled manual | 17 |
| Unskilled manual | 20 |

It is very interesting to find that a high proportion of unemployed men have made visits to police stations.

| | Per cent who have made a visit |
|---|---|
| Unemployed men aged 15-19 | 52 |
| Men in full-time work aged 15-59 | 39 |
| All other men | 22 |
| All women | 20 |

This confirms our earlier finding that unemployed men are likely to fall within that group of people who are in frequent contact with the police for a variety of reasons only some of which are connected with offences or suspected offences on their part.

Informants were asked in detail about the last visit to a

Table VI.2    Reason for last visit to a police station, by ethnic group

Column percentages

|  | Total | | Whites | | West Indians | | Asians | |
|---|---|---|---|---|---|---|---|---|
| **To report offences etc.** | | | | | | | | |
| To report property offence | 22 | | 22 | | 15 | | 27 | |
| To report personal offence | 4 | | 4 | | 7 | | 14 | |
| To report other offence | 6 | | 6 | | 6 | | 3 | |
| To report other matter | 13 | | 13. | | 10 | | 17 | |
| TOTAL | | 45 | | 45 | | 38 | | 61 |
| **Property** | | | | | | | | |
| To report loss | 7 | | 7 | | 5 | | 4 | |
| To report finding | 6 | | 7 | | 1 | | 3 | |
| To recover | 5 | | 5 | | 1 | | 1 | |
| TOTAL | | 18 | | 19 | | 7 | | 8 |
| **Offence or suspected offence by informant or child** | | | | | | | | |
| Arrested or detained | 3 | | 3 | | 13 | | 3 | |
| Child arrested or detained | 2 | | 2 | | 4 | | - | |
| To show documents | 11 | | 10 | | 21 | | 18 | |
| TOTAL | | 16 | | 15 | | 38 | | 21 |
| **Other reasons** | | | | | | | | |
| To identify suspect | 1 | | 1 | | - | | 1 | |
| Other reasons | 18 | | 18 | | 15 | | 8 | |
| Vague answers | 2 | | 2 | | 2 | | 1 | |
| Base: informants who have visited a police station in past 12 months | | | | | | | | |
| (unweighted) | 555 | | 378 | | 92 | | 75 | |
| (weighted) | 3,743 | | 3,512 | | 80 | | 82 | |

Note:   Other non-whites are included in the total but not shown separately

police station.   The reasons for this last visit are shown in Table VI.2.   On a broad classification, they have been grouped into four categories:   reporting offences or other matters, such as accidents, which may or may not have involved an offence (45 per cent of last visits); to report losing or finding property or to recover property (18 per cent); in connection with an offence or suspected offence by the informant or the informant's child (16 per cent); and other matters (21 per cent). The most important thing to notice about these findings is that it is only the third category of visits that involve some kind of conflict between the police and the member of the public; these visits, which were not, broadly speaking, voluntary, account for 16 per cent. In the remaining 84 per cent of cases, the person was seeking help from the police or providing the police with information about crime or less serious matters. Admittedly, among this 84 per cent are 18 per cent of visits not separately classified that include some where the informant was required to make the visit, for example to get a dog or firearms license or to report to the police as an alien; but while such visits are not voluntary, they do not involve conflict.

Secondly, it is striking that among West Indians the proportion of visits that involve some kind of conflict with the police is much higher than among white people. Among West Indians, 38 per cent of last visits were to do with an offence or suspected offence by the informant or the informant's child, compared with 15 per cent among white people. Among Asians, this proportion was about the same, or if anything slightly higher, than among white people. While West Indians are less likely than white people to visit police stations, when they do so the contact is more likely to be of a negative kind.

Table VI.3    Reason for last visit to a police station, by age

Column percentages

|  | Age | | 45 and over |
|  | 15-24 | 25-44 | |
|---|---|---|---|
| To report offences etc. | 35 | 46 | 48 |
| Property lost or found | 20 | 8 | 30 |
| Offence or suspected offence by informant or child | 25 | 20 | 11 |
| Other reasons or vague answer | 20 | 26 | 11 |
| Base: informants who have visited a police station in past 12 months | | | |
| (unweighted) | 238 | 214 | 103 |
| (weighted) | 774 | 1,703 | 1,266 |

Table VI.3 shows that visits to police stations are more likely to be of a negative kind among young people than among older people. However, this is not enough to account for the contrast between white people and West Indians. If we restrict the comparison to those aged 15-24 we find that among young white people 23 per cent of last visits were of a negative kind, whereas among young West Indians the proportion is 42 per cent. The comparable figure for young Asians is based on only 27 informants, but 48 per cent of these last visited a police station because of an offence or suspected offence.

Informants were asked 'How would you describe the police officer's attitude towards you on that (last) occasion?' Three-quarters (74 per cent) made favourable comments, 13 per cent made unfavourable comments, and the remainder gave neutral or mixed answers. The proportion who made favourable comments varied between the ethnic and age groups as follows.

|  | Per cent |
|---|---|
| White people | 75 |
| West Indians | 55 |
| Asians | 56 |
| Age | |
| 15 - 24 | 65 |
| 25 - 44 | 71 |
| 45 and over | 84 |

The difference between the assessments of the minorities and white people is not a consequence of the different age structures of the populations. For example, the proportion making favourable comments is 65 per cent among white people aged 15-24 compared with 47 per cent among West Indians in the same age group. As might be expected, those who went to the police station because of an offence or suspected offence were less likely than others to comment favourably on the police officer's attitude. The proportion who commented favourably was 58 per cent among those who were at the police station because of an offence or suspected offence, compared with 78 per cent among the rest. Again, this does not account for the fact that a smaller proportion of the ethnic minorities commented favourably, especially in the case of Asians, who were about as likely as white people to be at the police station because of an offence or suspected offence. We conclude from these findings that police officers usually make a good impression on white people at police stations, but less often on Asians and West Indians.

**All encounters with police officers**
We have now discussed various kinds of encounter with police officers in some detail. In order to obtain a measure of the level

of contact overall with the police, informants were asked whether they had talked with a police officer for any reason in the past twelve months, and if so how many encounters with police officers they had had in that period. Just over half of Londoners (56 per cent) say they have talked with a police officer for some reason or other in the past twelve months. One-third have had one or two encounters, 11 per cent have had three to five, and 12 per cent six or more. Within this last category there are some people who have had a large number of encounters: five per cent have had 20 or more. Some of these are relatives or close friends of police officers (this point will be discussed further in the next section). In general terms, these findings show that the police come into contact with a large proportion of the population; they therefore have a large opportunity to have a direct influence on what Londoners think of them by the way they behave in these encounters. It is not the case that most people form their impressions of the police entirely from hearsay, myth and rumour and the mass media, though of course the impressions that people get from their mostly mundane encounters with police officers may to some extent tend to fade into insignificance beside the more colourful and dramatic impressions they get in other ways.

Table VI.4    Talks with police officers in past twelve months, by ethnic group

Column percentages

| | Total | Whites | West Indians | Asians | Other non-whites |
|---|---|---|---|---|---|
| Have talked with police officers | 56 | 59 | 42 | 28 | 39 |
| Have not talked | 44 | 41 | 58 | 72 | 61 |
| Number of times | | | | | |
| 1 - 2 | 33 | 34 | 30 | 22 | 25 |
| 3 - 5 | 11 | 11 | 6 | 4 | 10 |
| 6 or more | 12 | 13 | 6 | 2 | * |
| Don't know how many | 1 | 1 | 1 | - | 4 |
| Base: all informants | | | | | |
| (unweighted) | 2,420 | 1,252 | 511 | 541 | 116 |
| (weighted) | 13,944 | 12,428 | 450 | 607 | 459 |

Table VI.4 shows that overall the ethnic minorities have substantially less contact with the police than white people. Asians are about half as likely as white people to have talked with

Table VI.5    Talks with police officers in past twelve months, by sex and age

Column percentages

|  | Men | Women | Age | | | |
|---|---|---|---|---|---|---|
|  |  |  | 15-19 | 20-44 | 45-59 | 65 and over |
| Have talked with police officers | 63 | 51 | 55 | 66 | 57 | 38 |
| Have not talked | 37 | 49 | 45 | 34 | 43 | 62 |
| Number of times |  |  |  |  |  |  |
| 1 - 2 | 32 | 34 | 30 | 38 | 35 | 23 |
| 3 - 5 | 13 | 8 | 12 | 12 | 11 | 7 |
| 6 or more | 16 | 7 | 12 | 15 | 10 | 6 |
| Don't know how many | 2 | 1 | 1 | 1 | 1 | 2 |
| Base: all informants (unweighted) | 1,161 | 1,259 | 490 | 1,338 | 345 | 247 |
| (weighted) | 6,297 | 7,648 | 1,278 | 6,506 | 2,910 | 3,252 |

Table VI.6    Talks with police officers in past twelve months, by socio-economic group

Column percentages

| | Professional/ managerial | White collar | Skilled manual | Semi-skilled manual | Unskilled manual |
|---|---|---|---|---|---|
| Have talked with police officers | 64 | 58 | 61 | 41 | 49 |
| Have not talked | 36 | 42 | 39 | 59 | 51 |
| Number of times | | | | | |
| 1 - 2 | 22 | 35 | 36 | 25 | 33 |
| 3 - 5 | 13 | 12 | 11 | 5 | 9 |
| 6 or more | 17 | 11 | 13 | 10 | 7 |
| Don't know how many | 1 | 1 | 2 | * | 1 |
| Base: all informants | | | | | |
| (unweighted) | 313 | 900 | 556 | 471 | 117 |
| (weighted) | 2,186 | 5,338 | 2,973 | 2,172 | 835 |

161

police officers recently. West Indians have more contact with the police than Asians, but only 42 per cent of them have talked with a police officer in the past twelve months, compared with 59 per cent of white people.

Table VI.5 shows that men have distinctly more contact with the police than women, and people aged 60 and over have less contact than younger people; the age group having the highest level of contact is those aged 20-44 (there are no differences between finer groupings within this broad band). The level of contact is very low among Asian women: only 16 per cent of them have talked to a police officer in a twelve-month period.

The overall level of contact does not vary significantly between types of geographical area: neither between inner and outer London, nor between areas of high and low ethnic concentration, nor between areas of high and low social stress and deprivation. There seems to be a fairly high level of contact with the police throughout the whole of London.

Table VI.7    Talks with police officers in past twelve months: men aged 15-59 by employment status

Column percentages

|  | Working | Unemployed | Sick or economically inactive |
|---|---|---|---|
| Have talked with police officers | 67 | 87 | 63 |
| Have not talked | 33 | 13 | 37 |
| Number of times | | | |
| 1 - 2 | 36 | 39 | 32 |
| 3 - 5 | 12 | 21 | 21 |
| 6 or more | 18 | 23 | 10 |
| Don't know how many | 1 | 4 | * |
| Base: men aged 15-59 | | | |
| (unweighted) | 772 | 117 | 156 |
| (weighted) | 4,048 | 406 | 447 |

It is, perhaps, surprising to find that those in the higher socio-economic groups have more contact with the police overall than those in the lower socio-economic groups. In the great majority of encounters the member of the public is looking for a service from the police or offering to help them or simply having a conversation, and is not in the position of offender or suspected offender. It is probably for this reason that the higher socio-

162

Table VI.8    Reason for the last talk with a police officer, by ethnic group

Column percentages

| | Total | Whites | West Indians | Asians | Other non-whites |
|---|---|---|---|---|---|
| Visit to police station | 28 | 28 | 28 | 39 | 17 |
| 999 call | 9 | 9 | 11 | 18 | 22 |
| Other type of encounter | 63 | 63 | 61 | 43 | 61 |
| Offence or suspected offence by informant | 9 | 9 | 18 | 4 | 19 |
| Reporting offence | 7 | 7 | 6 | 9 | - |
| Witness/giving information about offence | 6 | 7 | 3 | 5 | 1 |
| Accident | 1 | 1 | 1 | 2 | 2 |
| Property lost or found | 2 | 2 | * | * | 1 |
| Asking for information | 9 | 9 | 7 | 12 | 14 |
| Social | 21 | 21 | 18 | 7 | 17 |
| Other reason | 6 | 6 | 6 | 2 | 8 |
| Vague answer or don't know | 1 | 1 | 3 | 2 | - |
| **Base:** informants who have talked with a police officer in past 12 months | | | | | |
| (unweighted) | 1,179 | 768 | 219 | 158 | 34 |
| (weighted) | 7,868 | 7,326 | 191 | 169 | 181 |

economic groups have more contacts, since they are probably more likely to demand a service than members of the lower socio-economic groups.

In agreement with the rest of our findings, we now find that unemployed men have a very high level of contact overall with the police - substantially higher than men who are in work (Table VI.7). This is because they are likely to be victims and offenders and also because they have many encounters with the police which they describe as merely social. In fact, 87 per cent of unemployed men aged 15-59 have talked with a police officer in the past twelve months.

The reasons for the last encounter with a police officer are shown in Table VI.8. The table is based on those who have talked with a police officer in the past twelve months. In 28 per cent of cases the last encounter was a visit to a police station and in nine per cent of cases it arose from a 999 call; these two kinds of encounter have already been considered in detail. In the remaining 63 per cent of cases, the last talk with a police officer did not involve a visit to a police station or a 999 call. The table shows a more detailed breakdown of the reasons for these other kinds of encounter. The proportion of cases in which there was an offence or suspected offence by the informant is fairly small (nine per cent). This figure includes occasions where the informant was stopped by a police officer, if a stop was the occasion for the last talk with a police officer. The findings therefore show that while a large number of stops are made, this kind of encounter forms only a small proportion of all contacts with the police. Stops are greatly outnumbered by occasions where people are seeking help from the police.

A composite analysis of these findings is shown in Table VI.9. All last encounters with a police officer have been classified into six groups regardless of whether they involved a visit to a police station or arose from a 999 call or came about in some other way. Only 14 per cent of all last encounters were connected with an offence or suspected offence by the informant or the informant's child. The largest category of encounter, amounting to 37 per cent of the total, is those in which the informant was giving information to the police or seeking help from them in connection with an offence or other incident. Seven per cent of last encounters were to do with property lost or found, and nine per cent were requests for information (the informant asking the police). One-fifth of last encounters were social.

We have seen that Asians have much less contact and West Indians distinctly less contact with the police than white people do. In the case of Asians, a relatively small proportion of the small number of encounters are social or to do with relatively minor matters (property lost or found, asking for information); a relatively high proportion of the encounters are to do with offences or substantive incidents like accidents; and the proportion of cases in which the Asian is being treated as an offender or suspect is

164

Table VI.9    Reason for the last talk with a police officer in summary, by ethnic group

Column percentages

|  | Total | Whites | West Indians | Asian | Other non-whites |
|---|---|---|---|---|---|
| Offence or suspected offence by informant or informant's child | 14 | 14 | 28 | 12 | 19 |
| Reporting offence or incident, call for assistance, acting as witness, giving information | 37 | 37 | 30 | 57 | 36 |
| Property lost or found | 7 | 6 | 3 | 4 | 1 |
| Asking for information | 9 | 9 | 7 | 12 | 14 |
| Social | 21 | 21 | 18 | 7 | 17 |
| Other reasons, vague answer, don't know | 12 | 13 | 14 | 8 | 13 |
| Base: informants who have talked with a police officer in past 12 months | | | | | |
| (unweighted) | 1,179 | 768 | 219 | 158 | 34 |
| (weighted) | 7,868 | 7,326 | 191 | 169 | 181 |

Note:   This table summarises the reason for the encounter regardless of whether the encounter was a visit to a police station, a 999 call or some other kind.

about the same as for whites. Thus Asians have little contact with the police, and the contact they do have seldom involves conflict but often involves a relatively serious matter.   As with other groups, the contacts between the police and West Indians that involve the West Indian being treated as an offender or suspect are a minority of all contacts, but the proportion is twice as high as for white people (28 per cent compared with 14 per cent).   Thus, contact between the police and West Indians is much more likely to involve conflict than contact between the police and other groups, but even so, amiable encounters between the police and West Indians are more common than ones involving conflict.   It is interesting that 18 per cent of last encounters between West Indians and the police are social - about the same as the proportion of encounters with white people.

165

Table VI.10    Percentage of encounters with the police that have to do with an offence or suspected offence, by age and ethnic group

|  |  | Base[a] | |
|  |  | Unweighted | Weighted |
|---|---|---|---|
| All adults | 14 | 1,179 | 7,863 |
| Whites | 14 | 768 | 7,326 |
| West Indians | 28 | 219 | 191 |
| Asians | 12 | 158 | 169 |
|  |  |  |  |
| White men | 19 | 397 | 3,630 |
| White men aged 15-24 | 35 | 176 | 779 |
| West Indian men | 48 | 116 | 107 |
| West Indian men aged 15-24 | 63 | 62 | 52 |
| Asian men | 14 | 115 | 123 |
| Asian men aged 15-24 | 26 | 42 | 35 |

(a)    The base is informants who have talked with a police officer in the past twelve months.

As might be expected, only a small proportion of police encounters with women (nine per cent) involve the woman being treated as a suspect or offender; the proportion is higher for men (19 per cent). The contrast between West Indians and white people becomes stronger if the comparison is restricted to men (see Table VI.10). Among West Indian men, nearly half of last encounters (48 per cent) involved the person being treated as a suspect or offender, compared with 18 per cent for white men. Thus, there is a very strong tendency for encounters between the police and West Indian men to be likely to reinforce or create negative feelings towards the police. There is also a strong tendency for encounters between the police and young people to be of a negative kind. Consequently, a very high proportion of encounters with young West Indian men involve the person being treated as a suspect or offender (63 per cent for West Indian men aged 15-24, compared with 35 per cent for white men in the same age group). These findings show that while the contacts that most people have with the police are mostly amiable, there are certain small groups whose contacts with the police mostly involve conflict; young West Indian men are one example, but there are probably others that cannot be identified from the survey, for example, skinheads.

In these terms, we do not find much difference in the kind of contact between the police and the public between different kinds of geographical area. It is interesting, however, that social contacts with Asians and with West Indians are a higher proportion of all contacts with these groups in inner than in outer London (inner London 20 per cent, outer London seven per cent). This suggests that the police may have closer and more personal contact with the ethnic minorities in inner London (where the minorities are a larger proportion of the population) than in outer London.

We found in the last section that 74 per cent of people who had visited a police station commented favourably on the attitude of the police officers they spoke to there. Among those who last spoke to a police officer in some other circumstance, a slightly higher proportion (79 per cent) commented favourably on the officer's attitude; among those who were being treated as suspects or offenders on this occasion, 43 per cent commented favourably, and 33 per cent unfavourably, while the remainder gave neutral answers. We can also produce composite findings for the last encounter with a police officer, whether or not this was at a police station (but not here including last encounters that arose from 999 calls). The proportion who commented favourably on the police officer's attitude was as follows for each of the ethnic groups.

|  | Per cent who commented favourably |
|---|---|
| White people | 79 |
| West Indians | 60 |
| Asians | 64 |
| Other non-whites | 61 |

Young people are less likely to comment favourably than older people. Among those aged 15-24, the proportion giving favourable comments is 68 per cent for white people, 64 per cent for Asians and 51 per cent for West Indians.

### Friends and relatives in the police force
Just over one-fifth of informants (22 per cent) say they have close friends or relatives in the police force. The ethnic minorities are much less likely than white people to claim a connection of this kind.

|  | Per cent with close friends or relatives in the police force |
|---|---|
| White people | 24 |
| West Indians | 8 |
| Asians | 6 |
| Other non-whites | 11 |

The police force seems to have strong connections of this kind with all social classes, but rather less strong with people belonging to the semi-skilled and unskilled manual groups than with others: 25 per cent of white people in the skilled manual group and above claim a friend or relative in the force, compared with 20 per cent of those in the semi-skilled and unskilled manual groups. We found earlier that a significant minority of Londoners say they have a very large number of contacts with police officers; five per cent say they have had 20 or more contacts in the past year. Two-thirds of these people have a close friend or relative in the force.

Of course, there are very few police officers in London or elsewhere in Britain who belong to ethnic minority groups. In the Metropolitan Police there were 120 at the time of the survey, or about 0.5 per cent of the force, whereas the minorities account for about 11 per cent of the adult population. It is natural, therefore, that a comparatively small proportion of the ethnic minorities should have close friends or relatives in the force; in fact the proportion who make such a claim is rather higher than might be expected. Contact with friends and relatives in the force is likely to be of a positive and amiable kind, and because of the failure to recruit members of ethnic minorities into the force, these minorities have comparatively little opportunity for contact of that kind. However, our findings suggest that this is not a critical factor. Even among white people it is only a small minority of the population that has regular social contact with police officers, and regular contact with friends or relatives in the force is only a small proportion of all encounters between the police and the public.

# VII WILLINGNESS TO CALL ON AND HELP THE POLICE

In the previous chapters we have considered in some detail the circumstances in which people have, in fact, come into contact with the police. For many people these circumstances do not often arise; there are many kinds of incident that each individual has not come across recently, so that from a purely factual treatment we do not know how that person would react if faced with a particular kind of incident. In this chapter we look at the results of questions about whether the person would call the police or would help the police if asked to do so in various kinds of situation. These hypothetical questions are clearly not about actual behaviour; the answers will partly reflect attitudes to the police, to crime and to danger. But they are not purely about attitudes either: there is probably some relationship, at least, between how a person says he would behave in certain circumstances and how he actually would behave. This chapter therefore forms a bridge between the behavioural and attitudinal parts of the inquiry.

## Willingness to call the police
Informants were asked whether they would call the police in each of the following circumstances.
  a)  If you saw someone being beaten outside a pub.
  b)  If you saw a stranger acting suspiciously outside a neighbour's house.
  c)  If you heard neighbours having a row and thought someone would be injured.
  d)  If you saw someone trying to force their way into a car you thought did not belong to them.
  e)  If you saw people climbing over a back wall into a factory or offices at night.

The answers were in each case classified into three groups: 'Would call the police'; 'It depends'; 'Would not call the police'. Table VII.1 shows that for four out of the five situations, at least two-thirds of informants said they would call the police. The exception was the neighbour's dispute: only 31 per cent said they would call the police in that situation. It is, of course, very old conventional wisdom that domestic disputes are best resolved without outside intervention, and the survey shows that this thinking is still widespread; also, it is shared by police officers (see the fourth volume of this series).

Table VII.1    Whether informant would call the police in five situations

Row percentages

|  | Would call police | It depends | Would not call police |
|---|---|---|---|
| If you saw someone being beaten up outside a pub | 65 | 19 | 16 |
| If you saw a stranger acting suspiciously outside a neighbour's house | 71 | 16 | 13 |
| If you heard neighbours having row and thought someone might be injured | 31 | 27 | 43 |
| If you saw someone trying to force their way into a car | 76 | 12 | 12 |
| If you saw people climbing over a back wall into a factory | 82 | 9 | 9 |

Those who said they would not call the police in any particular case were asked why not (see Table VII.2). In the case of the domestic dispute next door, 70 per cent of those who would not call the police say the matter would be 'none of their business'. Also, a substantial proportion (54 per cent) give this answer in the case of the fight outside a pub, and 32 per cent in the case of people entering a factory. Other reasons given for not calling the police include the chance of making a mistake (40 per cent in the case of the stranger acting suspiciously, 27 per cent in the case of the person breaking into a car, 18 per cent in the case of people seen entering a factory); and the informant's preference for dealing with the matter himself (22 per cent in the case of the stranger acting suspiciously, 14 per cent in the case of the person breaking into a car). However, what is most striking about these findings is that hardly any informants give answers showing a general hostility to the police or an unwillingness to involve them in any situation if it can possibly be avoided. The proportion who explain a decision not to call the police by saying that they don't want any involvement with the police or the law is one per cent or less for each situation. Also, the proportion who say that the situation would not be a matter for the police is fairly small: it is around 10 per cent of those who would not call the police for most of the

Table VII.2   Reasons for not calling the police

Column percentages

| | Fight outside pub | Stranger acting suspiciously | Neigh- bours' row | Breaking into car | People entering factory |
|---|---|---|---|---|---|
| Don't want involvement with police or law | 1 | 1 | * | * | * |
| Not my business | 54 | 17 | 70 | 21 | 32 |
| Not a matter for police | 10 | 4 | 12 | 13 | 1 |
| Could be mistaken | 6 | 40 | 6 | 27 | 18 |
| Fear of reprisals | 5 | 1 | 1 | 4 | 5 |
| Would deal with it myself | 5 | 22 | 6 | 14 | 1 |
| Don't care | 5 | 2 | * | 9 | 14 |
| Other answer | 13 | 13 | 6 | 10 | 18 |
| Don't know | 4 | 2 | 2 | 4 | 11 |
| Base: those who would not call the police (weighted) | 2,231 | 1,823 | 5,956 | 1,690 | 1,314 |

situations, and not more than two per cent of all informants for any situation except the domestic dispute, for which it is five per cent. There is a small minority who say for each situation they would not call the police because they 'don't care', but this does not seem to amount to hostility to the police so much as a self-confessedly irresponsible attitude.

Asians and other non-white people apart from West Indians show about the same willingness to call the police as white people, except that they would be more likely to call the police to a domestic dispute next door (see Table VII.3). This accords with a piece of conventional wisdom in the police force, which holds that ethnic minorities tend to involve the police (to an unwelcome extent) in 'disputes among themselves' or their neighbours. For four out of the five situations, West Indians would be less willing than white people to call the police (the exception is again the domestic dispute). These differences are clear, but not very large; the largest is for the people seen entering a factory, where 65 per cent of West Indians compared with 83 per cent of white people say they would call the police. In all of the situations except the domestic dispute, more than half of West Indians say they would call the police.

Table VII.3    Proportion who would call the police, by ethnic group

Percentages

| | Whites | West Indians | Asians | Other non-whites |
|---|---|---|---|---|
| Fight outside pub | 65 | 54 | 64 | 70 |
| Stranger acting suspiciously | 72 | 58 | 63 | 71 |
| Neighbours having a row | 29 | 31 | 41 | 47 |
| Someone breaking into car | 76 | 69 | 73 | 82 |
| People entering factory | 83 | 65 | 74 | 80 |
| Base: all informants | | | | |
| (unweighted) | 1,252 | 511 | 541 | 116 |
| (weighted) | 12,428 | 450 | 607 | 459 |

Men and women give much the same answers, except that women would be more likely to call the police to a fight outside a pub, probably because they would not try to sort it out themselves (see Table VII.4). Young people would be less willing to call the police than older people in all of the situations; the differences are clear, but not very large.

Table VII.4    Proportion who would call the police, by sex and age

Percentages

| | Men | Women | 15-24 | Age 25-44 | 45 and over |
|---|---|---|---|---|---|
| Fight outside pub | 59 | 70 | 51 | 70 | 67 |
| Stranger acting suspiciously | 69 | 72 | 52 | 72 | 78 |
| Neighbours having a row | 32 | 29 | 23 | 29 | 35 |
| Someone breaking into car | 78 | 75 | 72 | 78 | 76 |
| People entering factory | 81 | 82 | 71 | 82 | 86 |
| Base: all informants | | | | | |
| (unweighted) | 1,161 | 1,259 | 984 | 844 | 592 |
| (weighted) | 6,297 | 7,648 | 2,609 | 5,174 | 6,162 |

Table VII.5    Proportion who would call the police: informants aged 15-24, by ethnic group

Percentages

| | Whites | West Indians | Asians |
|---|---|---|---|
| Fight outside pub | 51 | 40 | 55 |
| Stranger acting suspiciously | 53 | 40 | 48 |
| Neighbours having a row | 22 | 24 | 29 |
| Someone breaking into car | 73 | 62 | 68 |
| People entering factory | 72 | 56 | 73 |
| Base: informants aged 15-24 | | | |
| (unweighted) | 497 | 218 | 220 |
| (weighted) | 2,145 | 173 | 169 |

Young West Indians are the group who would be most reluctant to call the police (see Table VI.5), and they would be definitely more reluctant to do so than young white people, though again the differences are not very large. For three of the situations, well under half of young West Indians say they would call the police. Young Asians, however, give much the same answers as young white people.

Thus, except in the case of domestic disputes, between two-thirds and three-quarters of people are willing to call the police to a range of situations, including some where it is not certain that a crime is being committed. Young people and West Indians are less willing to call the police than others: while these differences are not very striking, in combination the two variables do have a substantial effect, so that young West Indians are considerably less willing to call the police than older white people. This point is illustrated in the summary table below.

|  | Per cent who would call police | |
| --- | --- | --- |
|  | White people aged 45 plus | West Indians 15-24 |
| Fight outside pub | 67 | 40 |
| Stranger acting suspiciously | 78 | 40 |
| Domestic dispute next door | 34 | 24 |
| Someone breaking onto car | 76 | 62 |
| People entering factory | 87 | 56 |

These findings can be summarised by computing a score across the five situations. Where informants would call the police they score 2, where they answer 'it depends' they score 1, and where they would not call the police they score 0, so that the maximum score is 10 and the minimum 0. The distribution of these scores is shown in Table VII.6. More than three-quarters of informants (78 per cent) score at least 7, and only 12 per cent score 4 or less. Overall, the difference between West Indians and white people is small.

It is convenient to use these scores when considering whether willingness to call the police varies between people living in different types of area or belonging to different population groups. From such an analysis we find that there is a fairly high level of willingness to call the police in all parts of London, and we find no significant differences between inner and outer London or according to the level of social stress and deprivation in the borough. The analysis of these findings for Asians and West Indians according to the local level of ethnic concentration is a critical test of certain hypotheses or assumptions about how the grouping together or the dispersion of the minorities relates to their perceptions of the police force, an institution composed mainly of white people and representing a predominantly white population. It is often argued that the ethnic minorities, if grouped together, will tend to emphasise their separate identity, develop alternative social structures and reject the official institutions as representatives of a hostile white authority; while if they disperse they will take on the

Table VII.6    Willingness to call the police: score across five situations, by ethnic group

Column percentages

| | Total | Whites | West Indians | Asians |
|---|---|---|---|---|
| Score | | | | |
| 0 - 2 | 5 | 4 | 9 | 4 |
| 3 - 4 | 7 | 7 | 12 | 5 |
| 5 - 6 | 21 | 21 | 18 | 21 |
| 7 - 8 | 35 | 36 | 35 | 37 |
| 9 - 10 | 33 | 32 | 26 | 34 |
| Base: all informants | | | | |
| (unweighted) | 2,420 | 1,252 | 511 | 541 |
| (weighted) | 13,944 | 12,428 | 450 | 607 |

Note:    'Would call the police' scores 2, 'It depends' scores 1 and 'Would not call the police' scores 0.   Across the five situations the minimum score is 0 and the maximum 10.

values and assumptions of the majority and come to accept the official authorities.   The survey findings conclusively disprove this theory (see Table VII.7).   We find, on the contrary, that willingness to call the police increases as the local ethnic concentration increases:   this applies equally to Asians and West Indians, while among white people willingness to call the police is not related to the ethnic mix of the local population.   This shows that where Asians and West Indians are living close to many others of their own group, far from looking for their own remedies for crime and disputes, they become more willing to make use of the police force.   We can hazard a guess that this is because the local presence of other members of their own group gives them a greater feeling of confidence.

Table VII.7    Willingness to call the police:  proportion scoring 9-10:  Asians and West Indians by local ethnic concentration

Percentages

| Per cent immigrants in ED | Asians | West Indians |
|---|---|---|
| Up to 5 | 29 | 19 |
| Over 5 to 10 | 31 | 24 |
| Over 10 to 20 | 38 | 30 |
| Over 20 | 41 | 36 |

175

## Willingness to help the police

The questions just considered are about people's willingness to call the police to an incident in which they are not themselves involved. In doing so, they would be taking the initiative, but the questioning did not suggest that they might be involved in any subsequent investigation, for example that they might be required to answer police questions, identify the culprits or appear in court. These stages might have followed the incidents described, but the questions were not about that.

Further questions were included to test people's willingness to help the police in the investigation of crime. Here it was assumed that the police would be taking the initiative in seeking information, and the purpose of the questions was to find out whether people would cooperate. The first series was as follows.

> If you had seen a couple of youths smashing up a bus shelter and the police were looking for witnesses, would you be prepared to tell the police what you had seen?
> If yes Would you be prepared to help identify the people who had one it?
> If yes Would you be prepared to give evidence in court about it?

The second series of questions was identical, except that the circumstances were 'If you had seen a couple of youths knock a man down and take his wallet'. The third situation was 'If you had seen a traffic accident in which someone had been badly hurt'. In this third case, informants were not asked whether they would be prepared to help identify the people who had done it, since the imagined situation was not a 'hit and run' accident, and no identification would therefore be necessary; they were, however, asked whether they would be prepared to give evidence in court.

The three situations described differ from each other in various ways. First, there is the kind of offender that would probably be involved. The questions gave no direct clue to the ethnic group of the offenders, but smashing up bus shelters would tend to be associated with white youths - football supporters or skinheads; 'mugging' is strongly associated in people's minds with black youths; anybody might be involved in a serious traffic accident, but in a typical case it might be a white, middle-aged man. A second dimension is the seriousnes of the offence, and particularly the degree of personal injury caused. Smashing up a bus shelter is a crime against public property of a kind that most people do not care much about; street robbery would be perceived as a much more serious crime, though in the example used the victim is not seriously hurt; in the case of the traffic accident, the wording makes it clear that someone has been badly hurt. A third dimension is the degree of culpability of the people involved. In the first two examples, there is clearly a crime and it is assumed that the informant can identify the people who did it; in the case of the traffic accident, it is not clear that there was a crime, or that anyone was to blame, and it is not necessarily clear that the informant's evidence would be the key to a successful prosecution.

Table VII.8    Willingness to help the police, by ethnic group

Column percentages

| | Total | Whites | West Indians | Asians | Other non-whites |
|---|---|---|---|---|---|
| **If you saw youths smashing up a bus shelter** | | | | | |
| Prepared to tell police what you had seen | 83 | 83 | 68 | 81 | 76 |
| Prepared to help identify the culprits | 77 | 78 | 51 | 73 | 67 |
| Prepared to give evidence in court | 71 | 73 | 45 | 66 | 57 |
| **If you saw youths knock a man down and take his wallet** | | | | | |
| Prepared to tell police what you had seen | 96 | 97 | 89 | 92 | 85 |
| Prepared to help identify the culprits | 91 | 92 | 75 | 82 | 81 |
| Prepared to give evidence in court | 84 | 85 | 62 | 75 | 68 |
| **If you had seen a traffic accident in which someone was badly hurt** | | | | | |
| Prepared to tell police what you had seen | 97 | 97 | 96 | 94 | 95 |
| Prepared to give evidence in court | 91 | 91 | 86 | 87 | 84 |
| Base: all informants | | | | | |
| (unweighted) | 2,420 | 1,252 | 511 | 541 | 116 |
| (weighted) | 13,944 | 12,428 | 450 | 607 | 459 |

The findings are shown in Table VII.8, analysed by ethnic group. In all three situations, the great majority of people would be prepared to tell the police what they had seen. There are successively smaller proportions who would be prepared to help identify the culprits and to give evidence in court, but still the proportion who would be prepared to appear in court ranges between 70 and 90 per cent depending on the situation. The case in which the largest proportion of people would help the police is the traffic accident, and the one in which the lowest proportion would help is the damage to the bus shelter; the theft of the wallet lies between. A possible explanation of these differences is that smashing up a bus shelter is perceived as the least serious of the incidents, while the traffic accident involves the most serious injury yet would not necessarily involve the witness is directly identifying the culprit.

Asians and white people give very similar answers, though there may be just slightly less willingness to help the police among Asians. Other non-whites, apart from West Indians, are definitely less willing to help the police than white people, though the differences are fairly small. West Indians are distinctly less willing to help the police than white people or any of the other groups; in the case of the damage to the bus shelter and the theft of the wallet, these differences are marked, for example, less than half of West Indians compared with more than two-thirds of white people would be prepared to give evidence in court about the damage to the bus shelter; but in the case of the traffic accident, the difference between West Indians and white people is small, and a very high proportion of West Indians (86 per cent) would be prepared to appear in court.

For all ethnic groups, willingness to help the police depends on the circumstances and on the kind of help required; there is not among any group a rigid determination to help or not to help, but rather willingness to help varies on a sliding scale depending on the perceived risks and inconveniences and the perceived importance of catching the offenders. Generally speaking, there is considerably more reluctance to help among West Indians than among other groups. It is quite clear that unwillingness to help among West Indians does not arise primarily because the offender may be black, since West Indians are least likely to help in the case of the damage to the bus shelter, where the offenders would probably be white youths; also, they would be much less likely to help in this case than white people would, even though the offenders would probably be white. It is also clear that there is not, among West Indians, a fixed objection to appearing in court to give evidence, because most of them would be prepared to do so in the case of the traffic accident. Further, reluctance to help among West Indians does not arise primarily because of fear of reprisals from the offenders, because they are more reluctant than white people to give information to police officers regardless of whether this involves identifying the offenders; and again, if fear of reprisals were the key, we would expect Asians to be reluctant to help for the same reason. We are therefore left with the explanation that West Indians tend to be more reluctant to help the police because they tend to be more antipathetic or hostile to the police than other groups.

Willingness to help the police varies very little between the sexes, but it does vary between age groups quite markedly. The pattern of these variations is the same for each of the situations: as an example, the proportion of each age group who would be prepared to give evidence in court about the robbery is shown below.

| Age | Per cent |
|---|---|
| 15 - 19 | 63 |
| 20 - 24 | 86 |
| 25 - 44 | 91 |
| 45 - 59 | 87 |
| 60 and over | 76 |

In this, as in the other situations, teenagers are the group that would be least likely to help the police, and people aged 60 and over are also somewhat reluctant. Young people are probably reluctant to help because some of them identify with the offenders and because they tend to be hostile to the police, since a relatively high proportion of them come into conflict with the police. Older people are probably reluctant because of the worry and bother involved and because they may fear reprisals.

It is worth focussing on the answers given by young people, both because they are the group that shows most reluctance to help the police and because they are probably more likely than older people to witness offences in the street.  Table VII.9 shows the findings for people aged 15-24 analysed by ethnic group.  There is again little difference between Asians and white people, though Asians are again rather more reluctant to help the police.  A majority of young Asians and of young white people are prepared to help the police in all three situations; it is only in the case of the damage to the bus shelter that the proportion prepared to give evidence in court falls below 70 per cent.  Young West Indians show much more reluctance to help the police than white people, except in the case of the traffic accident, where the difference is fairly small.   The proportions of young West Indians who would be prepared to appear in court in connection with the first two situations are definitely low:   27 per cent of the bus shelter incident and 46 per cent for the theft of a wallet.  The pattern of the findings is the same as for all age groups combined, but more accentuated.  As in the former case, the answers given by young West Indians do not turn on the likely race of the offender or on fear of reprisals, and there is no fixed reluctance to appear in court.  The findings do seem to indicate a hostility to the police among young West Indians; a hostility that is overcome or outweighed by other considerations in a situation where someone has been seriously injured and giving evidence will not necessarily identify a culprit.

Table VII.9    Willingness to help the police: informants aged 15-24, by ethnic group

Column percentages

|  | Whites | West Indians | Asians |
|---|---|---|---|
| **If you saw youths smashing up a bus shelter** | | | |
| Prepared to tell police what you had seen | 78 | 53 | 80 |
| Prepared to help identify the culprits | 70 | 37 | 70 |
| Prepared to give evidence in court | 63 | 27 | 59 |
| **If you saw youths knock a man down and take his wallet** | | | |
| Prepared to tell police what you had seen | 96 | 80 | 92 |
| Prepared to help identify the culprits | 88 | 60 | 83 |
| Prepared to give evidence in court | 80 | 46 | 70 |
| **If you had seen a traffic accident in which someone was badly hurt** | | | |
| Prepared to tell police what you had seen | 99 | 93 | 96 |
| Prepared to give evidence in court | 89 | 78 | 84 |
| Base:  all informants | | | |
| (unweighted) | 497 | 218 | 220 |
| (weighted) | 2,145 | 173 | 169 |

The pattern of these findings varies slightly between different geographical areas. There is rather more willingness to help the police in outer London than in inner London: for example, 86 per cent of informants in inner London compared with 78 per cent of those in outer London would be prepared to tell the police about what they had seen in the case of the damage to a bus shelter. There is also rather more willingness to help the police in boroughs with low deprivation and social stress than in the opposite kind of borough, as shown in the summary table below.

180

| Index of stress and deprivation in the borough | Bus shelter Per cent prepared to answer police questions |
|---|---|
| 100 or more | 76 |
| 0 to 99 | 79 |
| -99 to -1 | 85 |
| 100 or more | 85 |

Among Asians and West Indians, there are no consistent variations in the proportion who would be prepared to help the police according to the level of local ethnic concentration. Thus, while willingness to <u>call</u> the police <u>increases</u> with the level of ethnic concentration, willingness to <u>help</u> the police remains the same. To the extent that the results of these questions do relate to people's actual behaviour, this suggests that the police have no greater problems in gaining cooperation from Asians and West Indians in areas where they form a relatively high proportion of the local population than they do with Asians and West Indians in mainly white areas.

People in the higher socio-economic groups are distinctly more willing to help the police than those in the lower groups. One example of this pattern is shown in the summary table below.

| | Bus shelter: Per cent prepared to give evidence in court |
|---|---|
| Professional/managerial | 82 |
| White collar | 71 |
| Skilled manual | 70 |
| Semi-skilled manual | 67 |
| Unskilled manual | 66 |

The unemployed are considerably less willing to help the police than those in full-time work: for example 64 per cent of the unemployed would be prepared to answer police questions about the bus shelter incident compared with 86 per cent of those in full-time work. This is presumably connected with the previous findings that a relatively high proportion of the unemployed are victims, are offenders, have been stopped by police and have been arrested.

# VIII POLICING PRIORITIES, METHODS, SUCCESS

In this chapter and the next we consider Londoner's views on policing and the police force. This chapter looks at Londoners' general impression of the police force, as shown by their attitude towards joining themselves, at their assessment of the success of the police in various respects, and at their views on policing policy, for example the number of officers on the streets, the balance between vehicle and foot patrols, the order of priorities in policing and the need for active as opposed to responsive policing. In the next chapter, on standards of police conduct, we come to consider whether people think the police act fairly and responsibly, and how much public concern there is about corruption, fabrication of evidence and excessive use of force.

## Attitudes towards the police as a career

About one per cent of Londoners in the relevant age group (20-44) are in fact police officers. From the survey (which did not include police officers) we find that one-fifth of Londoners aged 15-44 have considered joining the force. Although it is difficult to evaluate this finding without being able to make a comparison with other careers, this seems quite a high proportion, and it suggests that a substantial minority of the population are able to identify very closely with the police force. Although the overall proportion who have considered joining is difficult to interpret, the variations between ethnic groups have a direct and obvious significance. There are still very few black or brown police officers in the Met, at least partly because of a reluctance to join on the part of the minorities. Table VII.1 shows that 13 per cent of West Indians, 10 per cent of Asians and 13 per cent of other non-white people have considered joining, compared with 20 per cent of white people (in all cases the percentages are based on those aged 15-44). This contrast is perhaps not as great as might be expected. Ethnic minorities account for one-half per cent of police officers in the Met, but for about 11 per cent of the population of London, so they are under-represented in the force by a factor of more than 20 to 1. By contrast, the proportion of the ethnic minorities who say they have considered joining is about one-half of the figure for

Table VIII.1    Ideas on joining the police force:  informants aged 15-44, by ethnic group

Column percentages

|  | Total | Whites | West Indians | Asians | Other non-whites |
|---|---|---|---|---|---|
| **Have you ever considered joining the police force?** | | | | | |
| Yes | 19 | 20 | 13 | 10 | 13 |
| No | 81 | 80 | 87 | 90 | 87 |
| **Why have you not joined/ not considered joining?** | | | | | |
| **Physical qualifications** | | | | | |
| Age | 1 | 1 | 2 | 2 | 3 |
| Height | 12 | 12 | 9 | 11 | 8 |
| Other physical disqual- ification | 3 | 4 | 2 | 4 | 1 |
| **Educational qualifications** | | | | | |
| Poor education | 6 | 5 | 5 | 14 | 8 |
| Education too good | 1 | 1 | * | * | - |
| **Nature of work** | | | | | |
| Violence/aggravation | 14 | 15 | 8 | 9 | 6 |
| Money | 2 | 2 | 1 | 1 | 6 |
| Hours | 3 | 4 | 4 | 1 | 1 |
| Prefer other work | 20 | 19 | 12 | 22 | 25 |
| Other objections to nature of work | 20 | 22 | 20 | 11 | 12 |
| **Ethnic reasons** | | | | | |
| Police prejudice | 1 | * | 6 | 2 | 3 |
| Clash with own people | 1 | 1 | 7 | 1 | 1 |
| Against custom | * | * | 1 | 4 | 2 |

Table VIII.1 continued over

Table VIII.1 Continued

Column percentages

| | Total | Whites | West Indians | Asians | Other non-whites |
|---|---|---|---|---|---|
| **Other reasons** | | | | | |
| Hostility to police | 3 | 3 | 8 | 2 | 1 |
| Family respons-ibilities | 3 | 3 | 4 | 3 | 4 |
| Applied & rejected | 1 | 1 | * | 1 | - |
| Deferred the idea | 2 | 3 | 2 | 1 | * |
| Other answers | 2 | 1 | 1 | - | 8 |
| Vague answers or don't know | 24 | 23 | 27 | 27 | 27 |
| Base: informants aged 15-44 | | | | | |
| (unweighted) | 1,828 | 891 | 381 | 455 | 101 |
| (weighted) | 7,783 | 6,650 | 323 | 471 | 339 |

white people. If those who have considered joining can be regarded as potential recruits, on a very wide definition, then there is a potential for greatly increasing the representation of ethnic minorities in the police force, if not to parity with their proportion of the population, at least to six per cent of the strength, which would be half-way towards parity, and would represent a twelve-fold increase on present numbers.

It is interesting that the proportion who have considered joining does not vary significantly between age groups. Young people are more likely to come into conflict with the police than older people, and we shall see in the next chapter that they are more likely to be hostile to them. This may be counterbalanced by a tendency for older people to forget about any consideration that they gave to the police as a career when they were younger. There is also comparatively little difference here between men and women: 22 per cent of men compared with 15 per cent of women aged 15-44 say they have considered the police as a career. This suggests that there is a large pool of potential recruits among women.

From the proportion of people in different socio-economic groups who say they have friends or relatives in the force we concluded earlier that the police is a relatively classless occupation. This conclusion is confirmed by an analysis of the proportion who say they have themselves considered joining by socio-economic group.

| Socio-economic group | Per cent who have considered joining |
|---|---|
| Professional/managerial | 16 |
| White collar | 19 |
| Skilled manual | 21 |
| Semi-skilled manual | 16 |
| Unskilled manual | 20 |

Informants were also asked why they had not considered joining, or if they had, why they had not actually joined (see Table VIII.1). A very wide range of answers was given, but what is most striking is that few answers indicate either a general hostility to the police or, in the case of Asians and West Indians, reservations to do with ethnic differences or racial prejudice. Only three per cent of informants overall gave answers that indicated a general hostility to the police; the proportion is still lower among Asians and other non-white people, and though it is higher among West Indians (eight per cent), it is still a fairly small minority. This does not mean that there is little hostility to the police, but it does mean that general hostility of this kind is not at the forefront of people's minds when thinking about the possibility of a police career. Six per cent of West Indians gave racial prejudice among police officers as a reason for not joining the force, and seven per cent said that to join would bring them into conflict with 'their own people'. These answers were less common among Asians and other non-white people. Twenty-two per cent of young West Indians (aged 15-24) mentioned reservations to do with ethnic differences or police prejudice, compared with six per cent of West Indians aged 25-44.

Twelve per cent of informants said they would not meet the height requirement. It is sometimes argued that this requirement discriminates indirectly against Asians, who perhaps tend to be short. This may be so, but the proportion who mentioned the point is no higher among Asians than among white people.

The bulk of the reasons given for not joining the force relate to the nature of the work; 14 per cent of informants mentioned the violence and aggravation, five per cent the money or hours, and 40 per cent had other objections to the nature of the work or simply said they preferred another job. In general the pattern of the answers is very similar for the different ethnic groups, except of course that white people do not mention the problems connected with ethnic differences or racial prejudice in the force.

**Number of police**
We found in Chapter V that two-fifths of people who had observed crowd trouble thought there were either too many or too few police present, and they divided evenly between thinking the numbers of police were too great and too small. However, a high proportion of West Indians (57 per cent) thought that too many

Table VIII.2    Opinion of the number of police in the area, by age

Column percentages

| | Total | 15-19 | 20-24 | 25-44 | 45-49 | 60 and over |
|---|---|---|---|---|---|---|
| Too many | 3 | 9 | 5 | 3 | 2 | - |
| Too few | 59 | 38 | 48 | 53 | 65 | 76 |
| About the right number | 37 | 50 | 45 | 42 | 33 | 23 |
| Don't know | 1 | 2 | 2 | 2 | 1 | 1 |
| **Base:** all informants (unweighted) | 2,420 | 490 | 494 | 844 | 345 | 247 |
| (weighted) | 13,944 | 1,278 | 1,332 | 5,174 | 2,910 | 3,252 |

186

police were present. These earlier questions were about special events; an entirely different issue is what people think about the numbers of police from day to day in the area where they live. The actual numbers patrolling at any one time are typically low. There are 75 Divisions within the Metropolitan Police District; the average population of a division is about 90,000, but some divisions have populations well above or below this average. In central areas, Divisions cover typically two or three square miles, while in outer areas they can be very large: for example, St Mary Cray Division covers 40 square miles. The typical number of uniform police officers patrolling at any one time in a police Division is around ten. There are parts of London, such as the West End, where anyone who 'is out on the streets for half an hour or so is likely to see police officers in uniform or a police vehicle. But there are large parts of London where it is possible to be out for long periods without seeing the police at all.

A strong police presence from day to day may strike people as oppressive; an absence of a visible police presence may encourage feelings of insecurity. We included the following general question to find out how people assess the current level of policing, making the question as specific as possible to the area where the informant lives.

Thinking about the number of police you see in this area, would you say that, generally, there are too many, too few, or about the right number.

We find that a majority of Londoners (59 per cent) think there are too few police in the area; very few people (three per cent) think there are too many, and just over one-third think there are about the right number. Thus, there is virtually no support for the view that police presence, from day to day, is oppressively high, though there is some support for the view that it is sometimes oppressively high at certain special events. There would be wide support for an increase in the numbers of police patrolling in uniform.

There is marked variation in the answers given according to age (see Table VIII.2). Older people are twice as likely as younger people to think that there are too few police in the area, and half as likely to think there are about the right number. The proportion who think there are too many police, however, remains low for all age groups. Thus, the demand for more police comes particularly from older people, and presumably reflects a feeling of insecurity on their part, but there is little support for the view that there are too many police, even among young people.

The views of the ethnic minorities are sharply different from those of white people (see Table VIII.3). Only 20 per cent of West Indians, compared with 62 per cent of white people, think there are too few police; the findings for Asians and other non-white people are intermediate between those for West Indians and white people.

Table VIII.3     Opinion of the number of police in the area, by ethnic group

Column percentages

|  | Whites | West Indians | Asians | Other non-whites |
|---|---|---|---|---|
| Too many | 2 | 14 | 6 | 4 |
| Too few | 62 | 20 | 38 | 37 |
| About the right number | 34 | 63 | 51 | 56 |
| Don't know | 1 | 3 | 5 | 3 |
| Base: all informants |  |  |  |  |
| (unweighted) | 1,252 | 511 | 541 | 116 |
| (weighted) | 12,428 | 450 | 607 | 459 |

The views of West Indians remain moderate, even though they tend strongly to take a different view from white people; only 14 per cent of West Indians think there are too many police in the area.

Differences between age and ethnic groups have about the same influence on the answers that people give to this question. For example, a comparison between Tables VIII.2 and VIII.3 will show that people of all ethnic groups aged 15-19 give much the same answers as Asians of all age groups. Age and ethnic group in combination have a very large effect, as can be seen by comparing the two extremes, older white people and young West Indians.

| | Per cent of | |
|---|---|---|
| | Whites aged 45 and over | West Indians aged 15-24 |
| Too many | * | 25 |
| Too few | 74 | 17 |
| About the right number | 26 | 55 |
| Don't know | * | 3 |

Although this contrast is marked, still only one-quarter of young West Indians think there are too many police in the area. A much smaller proportion of young Asians (six per cent) hold this view.

Women are just slightly more likely than men to think there are too few police in the area (64 per cent compared with 53 per cent).

There are, in fact, very large differences between areas in the number of police on the ground. In terms of square miles, some Divisions are twenty times as big as others, and there are also considerable (though less extreme) variations in total population, yet the number of police patrolling varies comparatively little between Divisions. These large differences are not much reflected in the answers that people give, possibly because their views are based on a general attitude more than on what they observe, or possibly because the police are thinner on the ground in areas where they are less needed. For all ethnic groups combined, there is hardly any difference between those in inner and those in outer London in their views about the number of police in the area. There is little diffence, too, between Asians in inner and outer London; but a higher proportion of West Indians in inner than in outer London think there are too many police in the area (19 per cent compared with six per cent). It has sometimes been maintained that there is too much policing in areas of high ethnic concentration, but this is not a view that is shared by most Asians and West Indians living in such areas. In the case of Asians, there seems to be no consistent relationship between the views expressed about the number of police in the area and the local level of ethnic concentration; only 10 per cent of Asians in EDs containing more than 10 per cent immigrants in 1971 think there are too many police in the area. In the case of West Indians, however, there is a definite relationship between the answers given and the local level of ethnic concentration, as shown in the summary table below.

| Per cent immigrants in the ED | Per cent of West Indians in each type of area who say there are too many police there |
|---|---|
| Up to 5 | 9 |
| Over 5 to 10 | 13 |
| Over 10 to 20 | 16 |
| Over 20 | 19 |

These findings show that West Indians in areas of high ethnic concentration are more inclined than those elsewhere to think there are too many police in the area, but even among West Indians in areas of high concentration, this is a minority view. Of course, it is quite possible that in certain specific areas, a much higher proportion of West Indians think there are too many police, but the survey provides a necessary perspective by showing that this view is not very common among West Indians in London generally, or even among those in all areas of high ethnic concentration when they are grouped together.

**Wheels versus feet**
A number of important issues in policing policy turn on the use of vehicle versus foot patrols. For the advocates of 'community policing' it is a central article of faith that more police officers should patrol on foot and that vehicles should be used less indiscriminately. The full set of arguments that are put to support

this view amount to quite an elaborate system of thought. If more police officers are put in vehicles it is said that calls will tend to be answered more and more quickly; this will stimulate an increase in demand for service from the police, so that more calls are made and can only be answered quickly if further increases are made in the number of police officers in vehicles, and so on. Meanwhile, these officers, speeding in their vehicles from one call to another, will have little or no opportunity for amiable and relaxed contacts with members of the public. They will get to know little about the people they are supposed to be helping, and will lose interest or competence in handling any situations other than crises. They will constantly be in a high state of tension, either because they are answering an urgent call or because they are bored. When they get out of their police cars after driving to an address at high speed they will assume that the matter they have to deal with is difficult or dangerous, and will tend to turn an innocuous situation into a dangerous one because of their tense attitude. Members of the public will seldom talk to police officers except in circumstances like these, so they will gradually come to form a poor impression of the police. The advocates of 'community policing' maintain that, instead of this, a substantial proportion of police officers should go round a small area on foot, getting to know and to be known by many of the local residents and organisations and building up a relationship of trust based on relaxed, everyday contacts.

These ideas have been skilfully communicated to popular as well as to specialist audiences by John Alderson and others. The popular version of the theory is that what we need is 'more bobbies on the beat'; ideas of policing that are, in fact, radical are represented, so as to appeal to conservatives, as a return to a golden age, in which village or village-like communities functioned each one as an organic whole, with its parson, its squire, its schoolmaster, its doctor, its policeman and its chorus of worthy, if surly, labourers. In this scenario, the policeman, a 'respected member of the local community', knows everyone in the 'village', does not need a personal radio, and can get about quite fast enough on his feet or possibly, in extremis, on a pedal cycle.

Two general questions were included in the survey to test public opinion on this subject. The first aimed to establish whether people do, in fact, have the impression that most police officers they see are in vehicles. The purpose of the second question was to find out whether community policing theories touch a chord in the public consciousness when they call for more police officers on foot rather than in vehicles.

> Some police go about in cars, vans or motorcycles and some go about on foot. In this area would you say that most police you see are on wheels, or most police you see are on foot, or is it about equal?

Do you think that, in this area, too many police are on wheels and too few on foot, or too few police are on wheels and too many on foot, or is the split about right?

More than three-quarters of informants (78 per cent) say that most police they see are on wheels, and most of the remainder (15 per cent) that there are equal numbers on wheels and on foot; only six per cent say that most policemen they see are on foot. Thus, there is a wide measure of agreement with the proposition that the police mainly go about in vehicles. Also, there is wide support for the idea that more police officers should go about on foot. Seven out of ten informants think that too many police are on wheels, and most of the remainder think the balance is about right; only two per cent say that too few police are on wheels. This shows that one of the basic ideas of community policing theories is very attractive to people.

Table VIII.4    Balance between police on foot and in vehicles, by ethnic group

Column percentages

|  | Total | Whites | West Indians | Asians | Other non-whites |
|---|---|---|---|---|---|
| Most police you see are on wheels | 78 | 80 | 56 | 56 | 69 |
| Most police you see are on foot | 6 | 5 | 14 | 12 | 6 |
| About equal | 15 | 14 | 28 | 29 | 19 |
| Don't know | 1 | 1 | 1 | 3 | 6 |
| Too many on wheels | 70 | 72 | 50 | 52 | 52 |
| Too few on wheels | 2 | 2 | 4 | 6 | 3 |
| The split is about right | 26 | 24 | 43 | 37 | 41 |
| Don't know | 2 | 2 | 3 | 6 | 4 |
| Base: all informants (unweighted) | 2,420 | 1,252 | 511 | 541 | 116 |
| (weighted) | 13,944 | 12,428 | 450 | 607 | 459 |

Table VIII.4 shows, however, that the ethnic minorities tend to have a different view of the facts from white people and also that they are less wholehearted in their support for the idea that fewer police officers should go about in vehicles. A first interpretation of these findings would be that the minorities are responding to a different pattern of policing in the areas where they live, but

191

further examination shows that this interpretation cannot be sustained. It is true that in the densely populated areas, where the minorities tend to live, a higher proportion of police officers patrol on foot than in sparsely populated areas. The answers given by the minorities do vary according to the local level of ethnic concentration; in areas of high ethnic concentration, which also tend to be densely populated, the minorities are much less likely to think that most police are in vehicles, and that too many are in vehicles, than in areas of low ethnic concentration, as the following summary table shows.

| Ethnic minorities according to per cent immigrants in the ED | Per cent saying that: | |
|---|---|---|
| | Most police are on wheels | Too many police are on wheels |
| Up to 5 | 59 | 50 |
| Over 5 to 10 | 57 | 54 |
| Over 10 to 20 | 58 | 58 |
| Over 20 | 25 | 25 |

However, it is only those in the areas of highest concentration who give different answers from the rest. Among white people, we find no relationship between the local level of ethnic concentration and the answers given. Because the basis of the geographical analysis is different for the special and general samples, we are not able to make a direct comparison between members of minority groups and white people living in exactly comparable areas, but from the pattern of the findings it is clear that such a comparison would show definite differences. For example, most white people live in EDs containing less than five per cent immigrants. Fifty-nine per cent of the minorities living in such EDs say that most police they see are on wheels, compared with 80 per cent of all white people; 50 per cent of the minorities living in these EDs say that too many police are on wheels compared with 72 per cent of all white people. These comparisons suggest that the difference between the minorities and whites is in the eyes of the beholders and not in the actual pattern of policing in the areas where they live.

There are further indications that the answers that people give are markedly subjective. The actual pattern of policing varies significantly between inner and outer London, but people's perceptions do not vary much. Seventy per cent of informants in inner London say that most police they see are on wheels, compared with 82 per cent in outer London, and there is no difference at all in the proportion who think that too many are on wheels.

These findings show that a majority of Londoners generally think the police patrol mainly in vehicles and would like them to patrol more on foot. On the whole the ethnic minorities incline to the same view, but their perceptions are more mixed, and those in areas of high ethnic concentration definitely tend to take a different view. The pattern of findings suggests that people's perceptions are based perhaps more on their assumptions and preferences than on the actual pattern of policing in the areas where they live. In other words, the preference for foot patrols may be more romantic than practical, and it may be, to a considerable extent, a response to the message of the advocates of 'community policing', who have perhaps succeeded in establishing an association in people's minds between 'more bobbies on the beat' and a golden age of social harmony. It is interesting that older people are much more likely than younger people to think that too many police are on wheels, though they are, admittedly, no more likely to say that most police are, in fact, on wheels, as the following summary table shows.

| | Per cent saying that: | |
| | Most police | Too many police |
| Age | are on wheels | are on wheels |
|---|---|---|
| 15 - 19 | 75 | 55 |
| 20 - 24 | 75 | 65 |
| 25 - 44 | 78 | 69 |
| 45 - 59 | 80 | 73 |
| 60 and over | 77 | 75 |

This suggests that the call for 'more bobbies on the beat' appeals to the conservatism of older people; this may be a clue to why it does not appeal so much to the ethnic minorities. It is interesting that Asians and West Indians in the different age groups, unlike white people, give the same answers. There is also a relationship with views about the rise in crime and the success of the police in combating it. Those who think that crime is increasing and that the police are unsuccessful in combating it also tend to think that most of the police they see are on wheels and that too many are on wheels. Perhaps the best explanation of all of these findings is that the call for a change in the balance of policing in favour of foot patrols is, to some extent, interpreted as a call for more policing; this is strongly supported by older people, those who fear crime and those who think the police are not being successful enough, but less strongly by young white people and by the ethnic minorities, who, as we have already seen, are much less likely than white people to think that we need more police.

**Ethnic minorities in the police force**
At the time when the survey was carried out there were about 120 officers in the Metropolitan Police belonging to ethnic minority groups, or 0.5 per cent of the strength. By October 1983 the number had risen to 206. The Force has not followed a policy of posting black or brown officers to areas where a relatively high proportion of the population is black or brown, and the current distribution of minority group officers across Districts shows an even pattern with apparently random variations.

Recruitment policy in relation to the ethnic minorities will be discussed in the fourth volume in this series. Here we present the findings from two simple questions in the survey of Londoners designed to establish how far black or brown police officers are noticed and how far people think that an increase in their numbers would be desirable.

Do you ever see black or Asian police officers in this area?

On balance, do you think the police would do a better job or a worse job if more of them were black or Asian or would it make no difference?

Only one in five Londoners say that they ever see black or Asian police officers in their area. At the time of the survey, the average police Division had only one or two minority group officers for a population of about 90,000 people, so it is not surprising that a fairly small proportion of Londoners had noticed them. What is, perhaps, surprising is that West Indians are much more likely to have noticed black or brown police officers than white people (50 per cent compared with 17 per cent). The proportion of Asians who have noticed them is higher than for whites (27 per cent) but much lower than for West Indians. It is certain that these differences do not relate to any known facts about the distribution of minority group police officers; they must reflect an interesting difference in psychology between ethnic groups.

Table VIII.5 shows that just over half of Londoners think that more black and brown police officers would make no difference to police performance, and just over one-third think it would lead to an improvement; very few (five per cent) think that an increase in the number of black and brown police officers would have a bad effect. There is little difference, here, in the answers given by the various ethnic groups; if anything, West Indians are rather more in favour of an increase in the number of black and brown police officers than other groups. These findings strongly suggest that the drive to recruit more police officers from the minority groups is soundly based. Since the minorities are greatly under-represented in the force, there are strong reasons, in principle, for increasing the numbers, and the survey findings show that there is very little public resistance to such a policy and a considerable body of public support for it. Furthermore, there is no indication of a difference of opinion between ethnic groups on the issue, and therefore no reason to think that the policy will highlight or exacerbate a conflict of views between members of different ethnic groups. Findings presented earlier in this chapter suggest that there is a considerable pool of potential applicants among the minority groups.

Table VIII.6 shows the findings for Asians and West Indians according to the local level of ethnic concentration. In the case of West Indians, there is a remarkable relationship between the

Table VIII.5     Perception and opinions of black and Asian police
                 officers, by ethnic group

Column percentages

|  | Total | Whites | West Indians | Asians | Other non-whites |
|---|---|---|---|---|---|
| Do you ever see black or Asian police officers in this area? | | | | | |
| Yes | 19 | 17 | 50 | 27 | 21 |
| No | 81 | 83 | 50 | 72 | 79 |
| If more police were black or Asian, would the police do | | | | | |
| A better job | 37 | 37 | 32 | 40 | 39 |
| A worse job | 5 | 5 | 3 | 1 | * |
| No difference | 57 | 57 | 64 | 56 | 59 |
| Don't know | 1 | 1 | 2 | 3 | 2 |
| Base: all informants | | | | | |
| (unweighted) | 2,420 | 1,252 | 511 | 541 | 116 |
| (weighted) | 13,944 | 12,428 | 450 | 607 | 459 |

proportion who have noticed black or brown police officers and the
ethnic mix of the local population.   In areas of high ethnic
concentration, 82 per cent of West Indians have noticed black or
brown police officers, compared with 29 per cent of those in areas
of low concentration.   In the case of Asians, there is a much
smaller difference of the same kind.   The very large difference for
West Indians must reflect an important difference in psychology
between those in areas of high and low concentration, but we
cannot be sure what the underlying psychology is.   One possible
factor is that West Indians in places like Brixton and Lewisham are
much more conscious of the police than those in areas of low
ethnic concentration, and therefore notice the small number of
black or brown officers that are about.   Another possible factor is
that in areas of high concentration, West Indians are far more
colour conscious than in other areas:  this explanation would be not
that black people notice the police in areas of high concentration,
but that they notice whether the police are black.   Yet another
possible explanation would be that there is much more visible
policing in areas of high concentration than elsewhere, but this is
probably not the main factor, since the difference shown for Asians
is much smaller, and a number of the areas of high ethnic
concentration contain both Asians and West Indians.

195

Table VIII.6    Perceptions and opinions of black and Asian police officers: Asians and West Indians by local ethnic concentration

Column percentages

| | West Indians | | | | Asians | | | |
| | Per cent immigrants in ED | | | | Per cent immigrants in ED | | | |
| | Up to 5 | Over 5 to 10 | Over 10 to 20 | Over 20 | Up to 5 | Over 5 to 10 | Over 10 to 20 | Over 20 |
|---|---|---|---|---|---|---|---|---|
| Ever see black or Asian police officers | 29 | 45 | 57 | 82 | 21 | 24 | 26 | 37 |
| If more police were black or Asian, police would do a better job | 21 | 24 | 33 | 33 | 39 | 46 | 41 | 22 |
| Base: Asians and West Indians from the special sample (unweighted) | 93 | 171 | 95 | 75 | 111 | 165 | 170 | 49 |
| (weighted) | 79 | 150 | 85 | 65 | 136 | 182 | 187 | 55 |

196

There is much less variation in opinions about the effects of an increase in the number of black and brown police officers. West Indians in areas of high ethnic concentration are rather more in favour of an increase than those elsewhere. Asians in areas of highest concentration are distinctly less in favour than those elsewhere, but there is no difference between Asians in areas of medium and low concentration. Although the figure is not shown in the table, virtually none of the Asians in areas of high concentration think that an increase in the number of black and brown police officers would make matters worse: it is just that they are less inclined than Asians elsewhere to think that it would lead to an improvement. Therefore, there is no signficant opposition to an increase in the number of minority group police officers among Asians or West Indians anywhere in London, and there is a considerable body of support for the policy among Asians and West Indians in all types of area.

The views of white people do not vary significantly according to the local level of ethnic concentration, except that those in almost exclusively white areas are rather less likely to be positively in favour. White people in areas of very low ethnic concentration are less likely to notice black or brown police officers than those elsewhere.

Views on an increase in the number of black and brown police officers do not vary significantly between age and social class groups.

## Success of the police in various respects

Informants were asked how successful they would say the police were in fighting three kinds of crime: muggings and robberies in the street, burglaries at people's houses and drunk driving. Similarly, they were asked how successful the police are in coping with marches and demonstrations, and with football crowds. Finally they were asked how successful the police are in getting on with people. In each case they chose one of four answers, from 'very successful' to 'not at all successful', though a substantial minority were unable to give a definite answer, ranging from five per cent for marches and demonstrations to 19 per cent for drunk driving. Table VIII.7 shows the percentages giving each answer for all informants, and also a mean score for each aspect of police work. The scores assigned ranged from 3 for 'very successful' to 0 for 'not at all successful'; those who gave no definite answer are excluded from the calculation of the mean score. A score of 1.5 would indicate an even balance of opinion between success and unsuccess.

From the findings, the items fall into two well-defined groups. On the first two aspects of police work - fighting muggings and street robberies and domestic burglaries - the balance of opinion is that the police are not successful, though comparatively few informants think they are 'not at all successful'. On the remaining four aspects of police work - combating drunk

Table VIII.7    Success of the police in various respects

Column percentages and mean scores

|  | Fighting | | | Coping with | | Getting on with people |
|---|---|---|---|---|---|---|
|  | Muggings and street robberies | Domestic burglaries | Drunk driving | Marches and demon-strations | Football crowds |  |
| The police are: | | | | | | |
| Very successful | 5 | 4 | 21 | 38 | 29 | 25 |
| Fairly successful | 27 | 27 | 43 | 42 | 44 | 45 |
| Not very successful | 45 | 45 | 15 | 12 | 14 | 18 |
| Not at all successful | 11 | 12 | 2 | 3 | 3 | 2 |
| Can't say | 13 | 12 | 19 | 5 | 10 | 8 |
| Mean score | 1.29 | 1.26 | 2.02 | 2.21 | 2.10 | 2.02 |

Note:    All columns in the table are based on all informants.

driving, coping with marches and demonstrations and with football crowds and getting on with people - the balance of opinion is that the police are successful; the commonest answer is 'fairly successful', but a substantial proportion of informants, ranging from 21 to 38 per cent, think the police are 'very successful' in these respects. The aspect of their work for which the police gain the highest approval is coping with marches and demonstrations; eight out of ten informants think they handle such events successfully.

Informants do not show a uniform and unthinking tendency to support or criticise the performance of the police; on the contrary, a considerable proportion of informants give different answers depending on which aspect of performance is under consideration. There is clearly a widespread feeling that the police are losing the battle against street crime and burglaries, but much more confidence in the police performance on other fronts. On these other matters, public confidence is not nearly as high as it could be, but it is still at a fairly high level.

Table VIII.8    Success of the police in various respects, by ethnic group

Mean scores

|  | Whites | West Indians | Asians | Other non-whites |
|---|---|---|---|---|
| Muggings and street robberies | 1.28 | 1.48 | 1.31 | 1.35 |
| Domestic burglaries | 1.26 | 1.33 | 1.13 | 1.32 |
| Drunk driving | 2.02 | 2.07 | 2.03 | 2.08 |
| Marches and demonstrations | 2.25 | 1.81 | 1.78 | 1.84 |
| Football crowds | 2.14 | 1.76 | 1.71 | 1.87 |
| Getting on with people | 2.06 | 1.45 | 1.73 | 1.78 |
| Total score | 11.01 | 9.90 | 9.69 | 10.24 |
| Base: all informants (unweighted) | 1,252 | 511 | 541 | 116 |
| (weighted) | 12,428 | 450 | 607 | 459 |

The average scores are shown for the different ethnic groups in Table VIII.8. By totalling the scores across the six items we can arrive at a single measure of the level of confidence expressed by the various groups. This total score is distinctly lower for Asians (9.69) and for West Indians (9.90) than for white people (11.10). It is also rather lower for other non-white people (10.24). However, it is in certain particular respects that the confidence of Asians and West Indians is comparatively low. In the case of muggings and street robberies, burglaries and drunk driving all of the ethnic groups give similar answers, but the minorities are substantially more likely than white people to think the police are unsuccessful in coping with marches and demonstrations and with football crowds and at getting on with people. The detailed answers given by West Indian and white people with regard to the success of the police in getting on with people are shown below.

| Getting on with people | West Indians | Whites |
|---|---|---|
| Very successful | 6 | 27 |
| Fairly successful | 37 | 46 |
| Not very successful | 34 | 17 |
| Not at all successful | 10 | 2 |
| Can't say | 11 | 8 |

Thus, 44 per cent of West Indians are critical of the police in this respect, among whom 10 per cent are strongly critical. While the minorities are by no means uniformly critical of the performance of the police, a substantial proportion of them express important reservations.

There is a general tendency for people aged 45 and over to express more confidence in police performance than younger people, but the differences are not very marked. In the case of street crime and burglaries it is the middle age group (25-44) that expresses the lowest level of confidence; in the case of getting on with people, there is a fairly strong and consistent tendency for approval of the police to increase with age (table not shown).

In general, comparisons between West Indians, Asians and white people within the same age groups lead to the same conclusions as those already drawn from the comparisons for all age groups combined. However, it is noticeable that a relatively high proportion of young West Indians think the police are unsuccessful at getting on with people, as the following summary table shows.

| Getting on with people | West Indians aged 15-24 | Whites aged 15-24 | Whites aged 45 and over |
|---|---|---|---|
| Very successful | 3 | 15 | 37 |
| Fairly successful | 30 | 50 | 42 |
| Not very successful | 40 | 22 | 12 |
| Not at all successful | 16 | 5 | 1 |
| Can't say | 11 | 8 | 8 |

The findings for West Indians and Asians have also been analysed by the local level of ethnic concentration (table not shown). In the case of West Indians, there is a definite tendency for those in areas of high concentration to think the police are more successful than those in areas of low concentration. Among West Indians in EDs containing up to five per cent immigrants in 1971, the total mean score across the six items is 8.97; this compares with 10.93 for West Indians in EDs with concentrations between 10 and 20 per cent and 10.30 for those in EDs with concentrations of over 20 per cent. Among Asians, there is no difference in the views expressed according to the local level of ethnic concentration. These findings fit in with others that have already been reported. They show that it is in the mainly white areas and not in places like Brixton and Lewisham that the police have been least successful in inspiring confidence in West Indians, and that there has been no particular failure to inspire confidence in Asians in places like Ealing. Of course, criticism of the police is more vocal and organised in the main areas of West Indian settlement than elsewhere, because they contain more West Indians, and therefore more critical West Indians, within relatively small areas. But individual West Indians in areas of low concentration are actually more likely to be critical, probably because the police in those areas have made fewer attempts to communicate with them.

We showed in Chapter II that among white people the belief that crime, particularly street crime, was increasing and that it was relatively prevalent in their own area was strongly related to the ethnic mix of the population. From these findings it was clear that white people associate street crime with the presence of ethnic minorities in the area, and if the ethnic concentration is high they think that crime is increasing, especially locally. We also find that white people in areas of high ethnic concentration are rather more likely than those elsewhere to think the police are unsuccessful in combating street crime, as the following summary table shows.

| Per cent Asians and West Indians in the ward | Mean score of white informants' ratings - muggings and street robberies |
|---|---|
| Up to 1 | 1.35 |
| Over 1 to 5 | 1.26 |
| Over 5 to 10 | 1.31 |
| Over 10 to 15 | 1.24 |
| Over 15 | 1.12 |

The ratings given by white people of the success of the police in other respects do not vary according to the local ethnic mix.

The experience that people have had as victims or offenders does seem to influence their views about the success of the police, but this matter will be discussed in Chapter X, which considers the relationship between experience and attitudes. It is worth mentioning here, however, that there is no relationship between whether people think that crime is increasing and whether they think the police are successful. This seems to imply that people do not, in general, hold the police responsible for an increase in crime.

We have pointed out that in a number of respects the police are perceived as relatively classless. We also find that assessments of the success of the police are fairly uniform across the different social classes. The exception to this is that the lower socio-economic groups are more likely than the higher ones to think that the police are successful in combating street crime and burglaries, as the following summary table shows.

| | Mean scores | |
| | Muggings and | |
| Socio-economic group | street robberies | Burglaries |
|---|---|---|
| Professional/managerial | 1.22 | 1.20 |
| White collar | 1.26 | 1.25 |
| Skilled manual | 1.19 | 1.14 |
| Semi-skilled manual | 1.40 | 1.32 |
| Unskilled manual | 1.53 | 1.50 |

**Policing priorities**
Informants were asked how important they thought it was for the police to do each of eight tasks. They were given a choice of four answers from 'very important' to 'not at all important'. The proportion who could not give a definite answer was never higher than seven per cent. The findings are shown as mean scores in Table VIII.9, analysed by ethnic group; as before, the maximum score is 3 and the minimum 0. Informants give the highest priority to catching people committing street crimes and catching burglars; most informants attach the highest possible importance to both of these tasks. Sorting out domestic rows is the task to which the lowest importance is attached; just over one-third of informants (35 per cent) think it is 'not at all important' for the police to do this. The 'social services role' of the police, in helping to run youth clubs or arranging for children to be taken into care, is not given very much importance, but substantially more than the role in sorting out domestic rows. On the other hand, informants do attach great importance to the role of the police in establishing everyday social contact with people in the area, and they also attach fairly high importance to contact between the police and leaders of ethnic or racial groups. Both of these are considered more important than catching people committing motoring offences which is nevertheless thought to be quite important.

Broadly speaking, the ethnic minorities have the same view of policing priorities as white people. Both Asians and West Indians attach greater importance than white peole do to contacts between the police and leaders of ethnic groups; even so, white people do mostly consider that it is important for the police to have contacts of this kind. Other differences between the views of the ethnic groups are incidental.

202

Table VIII.9    Importance of various policing tasks, by ethnic group

Mean scores

|  | Total | Whites | West Indians | Asians | Other non-whites |
|---|---|---|---|---|---|
| Catching people committing muggings and robberies in the street | 2.93 | 2.95 | 2.91 | 2.79 | 2.80 |
| Catching burglars | 2.79 | 2.79 | 2.80 | 2.76 | 2.84 |
| Getting to know people in the area | 2.61 | 2.61 | 2.63 | 2.50 | 2.55 |
| Discussing things with leaders of ethnic or racial groups | 2.29 | 2.27 | 2.61 | 2.52 | 2.22 |
| Catching people committing motoring offences | 2.08 | 2.06 | 2.20 | 2.31 | 2.37 |
| Helping to run youth clubs | 1.82 | 1.84 | 1.98 | 1.54 | 1.53 |
| Arranging for children to be taken into care | 1.72 | 1.73 | 1.51 | 1.78 | 1.59 |
| Sorting out domestic rows between husbands and wives | 0.99 | 0.99 | 1.11 | 0.77 | 1.06 |
| Base: all informants (unweighted) | 2,420 | 1,252 | 511 | 541 | 116 |
| (weighted) | 13,944 | 12,428 | 450 | 607 | 459 |

There is also a consensus of opinion between men and women and between the different age groups on these matters.

There is no strong or consistent pattern of variation in the opinions of Asians and West Indians according to the local level of ethnic concentration. It is particularly important to notice that those in areas of high and low concentration place a high, and an equally high, importance on the need for the police to maintain contacts with leaders of ethnic or racial groups, and also on the need for them to get to know people in the area generally. Thus Asians in places like Southall and West Indians in places like Brixton are asking for regular and close contacts with the police. There are some incidental variations on other items that illustrate cultural differences. For example, Asians in areas of high ethnic concentration place a very low emphasis on the need for the police to help with the arrangements for putting children into care, probably because they are unwilling to countenance the breaking up of a family. By contrast, West Indians in areas of high concentration place a stronger emphasis than those elsewhere on some aspects of the 'social services role' of the police (sorting out domestic rows and arranging for children to be taken into care). Asians in areas of high concentration place less emphasis than those elsewhere on the 'sharp end' of policing (catching people committing street crimes and burglars), but West Indians in all types of area place a very high, and an equally high, emphasis on these tasks. The views of white people are not related to the ethnic mix of the local population.

We have seen that people place a lower emphasis on catching people committing motoring offences than on catching those committing street crimes or burglaries. Non-motorists place a rather stronger emphasis on motoring offences than motorists do, but the differences is not marked (the mean scores are 2.22 among non-motorists and 1.96 among motorists). Those in the lower socio-economic groups are more likely than those in the higher ones to think it is important for the police to catch motoring offenders (professional and managerial 1.86, unskilled manual 2.29).

Our general conclusion from these findings is that while people place the strongest possible emphasis on the 'sharp end' of policing, they also think it is very important indeed for the police to cultivate regular, everyday contacts with people in the area and to make special efforts to establish relations with key members of ethnic minority groups. However, people do not attach a high importance to the 'social services' role of the police, especially where this seems to involve an intrusion into family life.

## Active policing

As we pointed out in the preface to this series, where, as in a high proportion of their work, the police are responding to direct requests from members of the public, the structure of the situation imposes a degree of consonance between the wishes of the public and what the police do. If people judge that the action taken by the police is out of scale or otherwise inappropriate, they will tend not to call on the police in similar circumstances again. Where the police themselves take the initiative, for example by stopping and searching people in the street, there is no mechanism that automatically ensures that their policy has some relation to public demand.

We found, in Chapter IV, that certain groups are much more likely to be stopped, especially to be stopped repeatedly, than others; that the great majority of stops do not directly lead to the detection of an offence or suspected offence, but that a substantial number of offences are nevertheless detected in this way; and that stops are a cause of resentment against the police in a substantial minority of cases, especially where young people or West Indians (and especially young West Indians) are involved. These findings related to that minority of the population who had been stopped by the police in the past year. We now come to consider the views of Londoners as a whole about the policy of the police in this matter. The findings are based on the following pair of questions.

Table VIII.10    Frequency of stops, by ethnic group

Column percentages

| How often do the police make stops in this area? | Total | Whites | West Indians | Asians | Other non-whites |
|---|---|---|---|---|---|
| **Vehicles** | | | | | |
| Very often | 5 | 5 | 12 | 4 | 3 |
| Quite often | 12 | 12 | 15 | 10 | 4 |
| Total often | 17 | 17 | 27 | 14 | 7 |
| Occasionally | 34 | 34 | 34 | 37 | 51 |
| Hardly ever | 33 | 34 | 16 | 32 | 24 |
| Don't know | 16 | 15 | 23 | 17 | 18 |
| **People on foot** | | | | | |
| Very often | 1 | 1 | 10 | 3 | 3 |
| Quite often | 6 | 5 | 18 | 5 | 8 |
| Total often | 7 | 6 | 28 | 8 | 11 |
| Occasionally | 25 | 25 | 29 | 30 | 39 |
| Hardly ever | 54 | 56 | 24 | 45 | 33 |
| Don't know | 14 | 13 | 19 | 17 | 17 |
| Base: all informants | | | | | |
| (unweighted) | 2,420 | 1,252 | 511 | 541 | 116 |
| (weighted) | 13,944 | 12,428 | 450 | 607 | 459 |

How often do police stop and question people in cars or on motor bikes in this area? Do they do it often, quite often, occasionally or hardly ever?

Do you think the police should stop and question more people in cars or on motor bikes, or less people, or is it about right?

These questions were repeated for stops of people on foot. Further questions were included to establish whether people think the police exceed their powers in this matter, and whether they use their discretion fairly, but the findings from these further questions will be considered in the next chapter on standards of police conduct.

Only 17 per cent of informants think the police often stop people in vehicles and only seven per cent that they often stop people on foot. These proportions are rather higher than the proportion who have, in fact, been stopped in the past year (in a vehicle 14 per cent, on foot three per cent). Just as West Indians are more likely to have been stopped than whites, especially on foot, so they are also more likely to think that the police often stop people (see Table VIII.10). A comparison with Table IV.3 will show that the differences in the perceptions of West Indians and white people about the frequency of stops are of the same order as the differences in the actual proportion who have been stopped, though in the case of vehicle stops, the difference in perceptions is rather greater. This suggests that perceptions - and those of West Indians in particular - are closely related to actual police behaviour. Further evidence on this point will be presented in Chapter X, which considers the relation between experience and attitudes. Asians give much the same answers as white people about the frequency of stops, although they are actually stopped much less often. Other non-white people give fairly similar answers to white people, though their estimate of the frequency of vehicle stops is lower, and of foot stops higher.

These findings show that most Londoners see stops by the police as an occasional rather than a regular feature of social life, but just over one-quarter of West Indians take a different view.

A substantial majority of Londoners are content with policing policy in this matter: 70 per cent think that the number of vehicles stopped by the police is about right, or have no definite opinion, and 78 per cent take this view in the case of stops of people on foot. Among the minority of Londoners who would like to see a change in policy, there is a balance of opinion in favour of an increase in the number of stops. Only 11 per cent of informants think the police should stop fewer people in vehicles, and only seven per cent fewer people on foot. The views of West Indians again contrast with those of other Londoners: 27 per cent of West Indians would like the police to stop fewer people in vehicles and 35 per cent fewer people on foot. Nevertheless, a majority of West Indians do not disagree with current policies (65 per cent in

Table VIII.11    Views on stops, by ethnic group

Column percentages

| | Total | Whites | West Indians | Asians | Other non-whites |
|---|---|---|---|---|---|
| **The police should stop** | | | | | |
| **More people in cars or** | | | | | |
| on motor bikes | 18 | 20 | 8 | 10 | 6 |
| Less people | 11 | 10 | 27 | 12 | 9 |
| It is about right | 59 | 59 | 51 | 61 | 66 |
| Don't know | 11 | 11 | 14 | 17 | 19 |
| | | | | | |
| **More people in the** | | | | | |
| street | 14 | 15 | 5 | 7 | 9 |
| Less people | 7 | 6 | 35 | 11 | 12 |
| It is about right | 66 | 67 | 47 | 68 | 62 |
| Don't know | 12 | 12 | 13 | 14 | 17 |
| | | | | | |
| Base: all informants | | | | | |
| (unweighted) | 2,420 | 1,252 | 511 | 541 | 116 |
| (weighted) | 13,944 | 12,428 | 450 | 607 | 459 |

the case of vehicle stops and 60 per cent in the case of foot stops). Among those who are not content with current policies, West Indians are overwhelmingly in favour of fewer stops, white people are strongly in favour of more stops, and Asians and other non-whites are evenly balanced between the two views. (The full findings are shown in Table VIII.11.) Thus there is, among all groups, a large body of people (the majority) who perhaps have no strong feelings in this matter and either say they are happy with present policies or that they have no definite opinion; but among those who would like to see a change of policy, there are strongly conflicting views among the different ethnic groups.

Just as the chances of being stopped are much higher for younger than for older people, so perceptions of the frequency of stops vary between the age groups in the same way (see Table VIII.12). Even so, it is only a minority of young people who think that stops by the police are a frequent occurrence; for example, among those aged 15-19, 32 per cent think the police often stop people in vehicles and 17 per cent that they often stop people on foot. Again, younger people are more inclined than older people to think the police should make fewer stops, but it is still a fairly small minority of young people who hold this view.

Table VIII.12     Frequency of stops and views on stops, by age

Row percentages

| Age | People in vehicles | | People on foot | | Base | |
| | Police often stop | Should stop fewer | Police often stop | Should stop fewer | (a) | (b) |
|---|---|---|---|---|---|---|
| 15-19 | 32 | 16 | 17 | 12 | 490 | 1,278 |
| 20-24 | 28 | 15 | 9 | 9 | 494 | 1,332 |
| 25-44 | 18 | 14 | 8 | 9 | 844 | 5,174 |
| 45-59 | 11 | 8 | 3 | 5 | 345 | 2,910 |
| 60 and over | 8 | 6 | 5 | 4 | 247 | 3,252 |

Note:     the base is all informants
(a)     unweighted
(b)     weighted

Table VIII.13     Views on stops:  men aged 15-24, by ethnic group

Column percentages

| | Whites | West Indians | Asians |
|---|---|---|---|
| The police should stop | | | |
| More people in cars or on motor bikes | 15 | 4 | 14 |
| Less people | 19 | 42 | 11 |
| It is about right | 61 | 48 | 66 |
| Don't know | 5 | 6 | 9 |
| | | | |
| More people in the street | 14 | 2 | 10 |
| Less people | 10 | 43 | 13 |
| It is about right | 71 | 51 | 66 |
| Don't know | 5 | 4 | 10 |
| | | | |
| Base:  all informants | | | |
| (unweighted) | 243 | 101 | 103 |
| (weighted) | 1,076 | 86 | 86 |

The group that is most often stopped is young West Indian men, and they are the group that is most hostile to police policy. Among men aged 15-24, 44 per cent of West Indians think the police often stop people on foot, compared with 14 per cent of whites and 10 per cent of Asians. As Table VIII.13 shows, there is a strong body of opposition to current policies among young West Indian men. Forty-three per cent of them, compared with 10 per cent of young white men, think the police should stop fewer people on foot; 42 per cent, compared with 19 per cent, that they should stop fewer people in vehicles.

These findings show that there is a wide measure of approval for, or possibly indifference to, police policy in this matter among Londoners generally, but that there are sharp differences in perceptions and opinions among specific age and ethnic groups. Groups that are likely to be stopped are aware of it, and are much more likely to be hostile to police policy than other groups. There is very substantial opposition to current policing policies among young West Indians (particularly males). It seems likely that the majority of Londoners are content with current policies or unconcerned about them because they are not personally affected. It is clear that a selective and discriminating stopping policy is divisive; it meets with the support or indifference of the majority who are not affected, but tends to create opposition among the minority who are. The number of people who are opposed to police policy on this matter is small, but the intensity of their feeling may be much greater than the intensity of the feeling of the majority. The police can justifiably point to the views of the majority in support of what they are doing, but this will not help to convince the people who are repeatedly stopped; on the contrary, it will highlight the conflict of views and stimulate greater opposition among those who are affected.

The actual chance of being stopped does not vary between Asians and West Indians in areas of high and low ethnic concentration. Table VIII.14 shows, however, that Asians and West Indians in areas of high concentration are more likely to think that the police often stop people than those in areas of low concentration (though as far as foot stops are concerned, this does not apply to Asians). This seems to point to a difference in awareness: the whole issue probably has more salience for Asians and West Indians in areas of high concentration than for others. However, views about police policy on this matter do not vary in a consistent way among the minorities according to the local ethnic concentration. This may seem surprising, but it fits with a number of other findings that suggest that the relationship between the police and the minority groups is no worse in areas of high concentration than elsewhere, and in some respects is better.

Those in the lowest socio-economic groups are substantially more likely than others to call for the police to make more stops. Twenty-eight per cent of those in the unskilled manual group compared with 13 per cent of others think the police should stop more people on foot; and 41 per cent of them, compared with 16 per cent of others, think they should stop more people in vehicles. Since the call for 'hard policing' tends to come most strongly from the lowest social class, it is clear that the views of West Indians

209

cannot be explained at all by their position in the social class structure, for their social class position tends to be low, yet they are opposed to 'hard policing'.

Table VIII.14     Frequency of stops and views on stops:    West Indians and Asians by local ethnic concentration

Row percentages

| | People in vehicles | | People on foot | | Base (a) (b) | |
|---|---|---|---|---|---|---|
| | Police often stop | Should stop fewer | Police often stop | Should stop fewer | (a) | (b) |
| **WEST INDIANS** | | | | | | |
| Per cent immigrants in ED | | | | | | |
| Up to 5 | 24 | 15 | 18 | 25 | 93 | 79 |
| Over 5 to 10 | 22 | 34 | 25 | 36 | 171 | 150 |
| Over 10 to 20 | 24 | 30 | 38 | 46 | 95 | 85 |
| Over 20 | 38 | 27 | 31 | 26 | 75 | 65 |
| | | | | | | |
| **ASIANS** | | | | | | |
| Per cent immigrants in ED | | | | | | |
| Up to 5 | 9 | 13 | 6 | 7 | 111 | 136 |
| Over 5 to 10 | 11 | 12 | 5 | 10 | 165 | 182 |
| Over 10 to 20 | 22 | 15 | 13 | 17 | 170 | 187 |
| Over 20 | 25 | 5 | 4 | 4 | 49 | 55 |

Note:    the base is Asians and West Indians from the special sample.
(a)      unweighted
(b)      weighted

**Bans on marches and demonstrations**
The complaint is sometimes made that the right of public assembly is too much curtailed by bans on marches, demonstrations and public meetings. The Home Secretary has the power to ban all processions of a specified kind within a specified part of London; this he normally does at the request of the Metropolitan Police Commissioner. He does not have the power to ban any particular procession, though when a ban is imposed it is usually because a particular procession is planned. The organisers of marches and demonstrations usually plan the route in consultation with the police who, although they may not have the power to impose a route, usually succeed in influencing the choice of route to a considerable degree.

We wished, in the survey, to obtain a general indication of the public view as to whether marches and demonstrations are too often prevented. Because most people lack detailed knowledge of the powers of the police and the Home Secretary in these matters, the questions chosen were simple and ignored the complexity of the issues involved.

At the request of the police, the government sometimes bans marches and demonstrations in London. Do you think that, in general, they ban marches and demonstrations too often, or that they ban marches and demonstrations about as often as necessary, or that they do not ban marches and demonstrations often enough?

In a follow-up question, informants were asked if there were particular sorts of marches and demonstrations that were banned too often or not often enough, depending on the answer they had previously given.

Just over half of informants (58 per cent) say that marches and demonstrations are banned about as often as necessary. The balance of opinion among the remainder is strongly that these events are not banned often enough: 35 per cent of informants hold this view, and only five per cent think there are too many bans. Thus, complaints by political or pressure groups that there are too many constraints on public demonstrations have very little public support and there would be considerable support for more constraints on events of this kind. There is a remarkable uniformity of view among different ethnic and age groups. There are no significant differences between the views expressed by different ethnic groups on this matter, and different age groups express similar views, except that those aged 60 and over are more likely than younger people to think that marches and demonstrations are not banned often enough (51 per cent of those aged 60 and over, compared with 31 per cent of those aged 15-59). Young West Indians and Asians express similar views to Londoners generally.

The following is the proportion of informants saying that particular kinds of march or demonstration should be banned more often.

|                                                          | Per cent |
|----------------------------------------------------------|----------|
| No particular kind                                       | 7        |
| National Front/British Movement/fascists                 | 20       |
| International Socialists/Trotskyists/ Workers' Revolutionary Party | 4        |
| Labour Party/Trade Unions                                | 1        |
| Other kinds                                              | 9        |

Thus, far more people object to marches by right-wing than by left-wing organisations. Among the small proportion of informants who think there are too many bans, the marches by right-wing organisations are also mentioned most often as being

211

banned too frequently, but it is only two per cent of all informants who give this answer. These findings show that whether people are in favour of bans or against them, they tend to be thinking in terms of marches organised by right-wing groups.

# IX  VIEWS ABOUT STANDARDS OF POLICE CONDUCT

This chapter reports the responses of Londoners to some very difficult questions about the extent of misconduct by police officers. These questions focus on the main subjects of serious complaints that are made against the police from time to time: exceeding powers to stop and search, unfairness towards particular groups, use of threats, unfair pressure and excessive force, fabrication of evidence, acceptance of bribes and favours. The questions are difficult because nobody actually knows how common these various kinds of misconduct are. Police officers have better information than most, but even they are often unsure for example about the incidence of corruption in the force, not only because they are reluctant to stand in judgement on their colleagues, but also because, except where there has been a prosecution, they have little or no direct knowledge about officers receiving bribes unless they are involved themselves. From our own extensive observation work, over a period of two years, we are able to make an informed judgement on these matters, but not with certainty or precision. Compared with police officers or researchers, most Londoners have very limited knowledge of how the police behave; even the substantial minority who have been stopped or arrested are working on the basis of limited, if intense, experience. Nevertheless, we find that when people are asked, for example, how often they think the police in London use violence on people held at police stations, the great majority give definite answers; this is a kind of issue on which people do have genuine opinions, and ones they are not reluctant to express, even though the information they have to go on is limited, and these opinions must have an important influence on their relations with the police in specific instances.

While our findings are facts about people's opinions, the opinions themselves are based on fact to only a limited extent. This is not only because people have limited information, but also because their answers partly depend on their values and expectations. It is no use, for example, asking people how often police officers hit people - this might be in self-defence or it might be an attack without provocation. The question must be about how often the police use more than necessary or justifiable force.  The

213

questions are therefore about the social meaning of acts, and the answers must incorporate a judgement about the conduct of the police. How the informant describes what happens depends on the values and assumptions through which he perceives the facts that come to his notice.

The questions are more a test of views on specific issues than of general attitudes, in that the answers vary widely according to the exact subject matter. Undoubtedly the answers that people give are influenced by general attitudes towards the police and towards crime: individual people show a tendency to give answers that are either supportive or critical of the police. But this tendency is far from overwhelming, so that the same person is often critical of the police in one respect but not in another. To a considerable extent, therefore, the answers reflect views on issues rather than just the temperature of people's feelings towards the police.

In this chapter we show the findings for all informants and for different age and ethnic groups, and summarise the results of analyses by geographical variables and by social class. In the next chapter we consider how people's views on police misconduct and other matters vary according to their experience of the police. Because there are strong relationships of this kind, it would be wrong to assume that the opinions analysed in this chapter exist independently of people's experience of the police.

**Whether stops are justified**
The powers of the police in London to stop, search and question were summarised at the beginning of Chapter IV. A Constable has the power to stop and search someone on foot only where he 'reasonably suspects' that the person has something stolen or unlawfully obtained or a controlled drug. He has power to stop a person driving a vehicle or pedal cycle regardless of whether there is 'reasonable suspicion' of this kind; and he can, at any time, require a person driving a motor vehicle to produce a driving licence and certificate of insurance. He does not, however, have the power to search the person or the vehicle unless there is 'reasonable suspicion'.

We included some simple questions to find out whether people think that the police exceed their powers in this matter. Because the powers are fairly complex and the interpretation sometimes difficult, we had to allow people to make a judgement about whether the police stop people 'without sufficient reason'; this judgement would not, of course, usually be made on the basis of a knowledge of the law. The question on vehicle stops was as follows.

Do you think the police only stop and question people in cars or on motor bikes if they are acting suspiciously or do you think the police sometimes do it without sufficient reason?

The question was repeated for stops of people on foot.

Table IX.1    Whether stops are justified, by ethnic group

Column percentages

| | Total | Whites | West Indians | Asians | Other non-whites |
|---|---|---|---|---|---|
| Police stop people in vehicles | | | | | |
| Only if acting suspiciously | 58 | 58 | 35 | 66 | 68 |
| Sometimes without sufficient reason | 35 | 35 | 55 | 20 | 21 |
| Don't know | 7 | 7 | 10 | 14 | 11 |
| Police stop people on foot | | | | | |
| Only if acting suspiciously | 71 | 73 | 38 | 72 | 60 |
| Sometimes without sufficient reason | 21 | 20 | 52 | 15 | 25 |
| Don't know | 8 | 7 | 10 | 13 | 15 |
| Base:  all informants | | | | | |
| (unweighted) | 2,420 | 1,252 | 511 | 541 | 116 |
| (weighted) | 13,944 | 12,428 | 450 | 607 | 459 |

One-third of Londoners think the police sometimes stop people in vehicles and one-fifth people on foot without sufficient reason. These answers should perhaps be regarded as only mildly critical, since the question is about what 'sometimes' happens. A majority of Londoners think that the police never exceed their powers in this respect. It is a fairly small minority (seven to eight per cent) who decline to give a definite opinion. A substantially higher proportion of West Indians than of other ethnic groups are critical of the police in this respect; Asians are less critical of the police than white people; other non-whites are less critical of the police than white people in respect of vehicle stops, but rather more critical in respect of foot stops (see Table IX.1). Just over half of West Indians think the police sometimes exceed their powers in respect of each kind of stop. The contrast between the views of West Indians and white people is stronger in the case of stops in the street than in the case of vehicle stops, and this accords with the differences in the actual incidence of stops of the two groups: Table IV.3 (on page 88) shows that the proportion of West Indians who have been stopped when in a vehicle is only slightly higher than the proportion of white people, but the proportion who have been stopped when on foot is nearly four times as high.

Table IX.2    Whether stops are justified, by age

Column percentages

| | 15-19 | 20-24 | 25-44 | 45-59 | 60 and over |
|---|---|---|---|---|---|
| Police stop people in vehicles | | | | | |
| Only if acting suspiciously | 49 | 44 | 52 | 60 | 73 |
| Sometimes without sufficient reason | 46 | 51 | 41 | 32 | 16 |
| Don't know | 5 | 5 | 7 | 8 | 11 |
| Police stop people on foot | | | | | |
| Only if acting suspiciously | 58 | 64 | 67 | 77 | 81 |
| Sometimes without sufficient reason | 38 | 30 | 26 | 15 | 8 |
| Don't know | 4 | 6 | 7 | 8 | 11 |
| Base: all informants (unweighted) | 490 | 494 | 844 | 345 | 247 |
| (weighted) | 1,278 | 1,332 | 5,174 | 2,910 | 3,252 |

Young people are considerably more likely than older people to be critical of the police in this respect (see Table IX.2). Nearly half of people aged 15-24 think the police sometimes stop people in vehicles without sufficient reason, and 38 per cent of those aged 15-19 think they sometimes stop people on foot without sufficient reason. These differences again relate closely to differences in the actual incidence of stops between age groups. In the case of stops in the street, it is the youngest age group (15-19) that is most likely to be stopped, whereas in the case of vehicle stops, those aged 20-24 are most at risk; these are also the groups that are most critical of the police in the two cases.

Ethnic group has a rather stronger influence than age on the answers that people give; thus West Indians are more critical of the police than any single age group. Table IX.3 shows the findings for informants aged 15-24 by ethnic group. About two-thirds of young West Indians think the police make stops without sufficient reason, compared with half of young white people in the case of vehicle stops and one-third in the case of foot stops. Young Asians are

216

Table IX.3    Whether stops are justified: informants aged 15-24,
              by ethnic group

Column percentages

|  | Whites | West Indians | Asians |
|---|---|---|---|
| **Police stop people in vehicles** | | | |
| Only if acting suspiciously | 47 | 23 | 64 |
| Sometimes without sufficient reason | 49 | 70 | 29 |
| Don't know | 4 | 7 | 7 |
| **Police stop people on foot** | | | |
| Only if acting suspiciously | 63 | 27 | 71 |
| Sometimes without sufficient reason | 32 | 66 | 23 |
| Don't know | 5 | 7 | 6 |
| Base: informants aged 15-24 | | | |
| (unweighted) | 497 | 218 | 220 |
| (weighted) | 2,145 | 173 | 169 |

much less critical than either young West Indians or young white people. Thus, a very substantial proportion of young people are critical of the police in this respect, and in the case of young West Indians a solid majority are critical.

The views of the ethnic minorities on this matter do not vary much according to the level of local ethnic concentration, as the following summary table shows.

| | Per cent who think the police sometimes make stops without sufficient reason | | | |
|---|---|---|---|---|
| | West Indians | | Asians | |
| Per cent immigrants in the ED | Vehicle | Foot | Vehicle | Foot |
| Up to 5 | 40 | 42 | 16 | 14 |
| Over 5 to 10 | 58 | 52 | 20 | 18 |
| Over 10 to 20 | 56 | 61 | 26 | 18 |
| Over 20 | 58 | 45 | 14 | 9 |

These findings do not show a consistent pattern, but certainly there is no tendency for Asians and West Indians in areas of high concentration to be more critical of the police than others.

In the case of vehicle stops, there is no difference between the answers given by those in inner and in outer London. However,

217

among those in inner London, the proportion who think the police sometimes stop people on foot without sufficient reason is twice as high as among those in outer London (31 per cent compared with 16 per cent). This is mainly a difference between white people in inner and outer London: there is little difference between the answers given by Asians and West Indians in the two areas. We cannot detect a difference in the actual proportion of people who have been stopped in the street between inner and outer London, but we do find that, in inner London, those who have been stopped tend to have been stopped more often than in outer London, though the numbers here are rather too small for a reliable conclusion to be drawn. It seems possible that the difference in views between those in inner and outer London does relate to a difference in the pattern of policing, though we cannot definitely establish that this is so.

We also find a strong relationship between the index of social stress and deprivation in the borough and the proportion of people who think the police unjustifiably stop people in the street.

| Index of social stress | Per cent who think the police sometimes stop people on foot without sufficient reason |
|---|---|
| 100 or more | 32 |
| 0 to 99 | 26 |
| -99 to -1 | 20 |
| -100 or less | 16 |

The same relationship is shown for Asians and West Indians when they are analysed separately, though less strongly. Views about vehicle stops are not related to the level of social stress and deprivation in the borough. We cannot detect a difference in the incidence of stops between these different types of area, but the more critical views of those in areas of high social stress may reflect a difference in the way that the police behave when making stops.

There is no true relationship between the views expressed and social class. Although people in the semi-skilled and unskilled manual groups are less critical of the police over vehicle stops than those in higher groups, this is explained by the fact that fewer of them have the use of vehicles. (We shall see in the next chapter that motorists are more critical than non-motorists of police practice in stopping vehicles, because they are more likely to have had experience of being stopped.)

### Fairness to different groups
Commenting on the allegation that the police force is motivated by racial prejudice, Lord Scarman had this to say in his report. 'The direction and policies of the Metropolitan Police are not racist'. But 'Racial prejudice does manifest itself occasionally in the

218

behaviour of a few officers on the streets. It may be all too easy for some officers, faced with what they must see as the inexorably rising tide of street crime, to lapse into an unthinking assumption that all young black people are potential criminals'.

We included the following questions in the survey to test public opinion on this issue.

Are there any groups or types of people in London who do not get fair treatment from the police?

If yes Which groups or types of people?

It is important to notice that the second question was open: informants answered in their own words and without prompting from the interviewer, so any who mentioned ethnic minorities did so spontaneously. None of the questioning had made any explicit reference to ethnic minorities up to this point in the interview.

We find that 29 per cent of Londoners overall think there are groups or types of people who do not get fair treatment from the police; nearly half take the opposite view, and one-quarter have no definite opinion. Just over one-fifth of Londoners overall think the ethnic minorities are unfairly treated, and the minorities are far more often mentioned than any other group as the objects of unfair treatment. The summary table below shows the proportion mentioning each particular group, first based on all informants, and secondly based on those who think any group is unfairly treated.

| Groups unfairly treated | Per cent of all informants | Per cent of those thinking some groups are un- fairly treated | |
|---|---|---|---|
| Ethnic minorities | 22 | 78 | |
| Blacks | 9 | | 31 |
| Coloured people | 8 | | 28 |
| 'Ethnic minorities' | 5 | | 19 |
| Asians | 4 | | 12 |
| West Indians | 1 | | 5 |
| Irish people | 1 | | 2 |
| Rastafarians | * | | * |
| White people | 1 | 2 | |
| Young people | 10 | 35 | |
| Skinheads or punks | 3 | 9 | |
| Nazis, NF, BM | * | 1 | |
| People of odd appearance | 1 | 5 | |
| Criminals | 1 | 5 | |
| Poor people | 1 | 3 | |
| Homosexuals (Gays) | * | 2 | |
| Other specific groups | * | * | |

More than three-quarters of those who think some groups are unfairly treated mention ethnic minorities; to a large extent, therefore, the notion of unfair treatment of particular groups by the police is synonymous in people's minds with unfair treatment of the ethnic minorities. From the phrases that people use to describe the minorities, it is unclear whether they are more often thinking of West Indians than of Asians; the most common phrases used are 'blacks' and 'coloured people'. Specific mentions of Rastafarians in this context are very rare, although Lord Scarman in his report does make specific mention of prejudice against this group. The only other group frequently mentioned as the object of unfair treatment by the police is young people, though a significant minority of informants mention skinheads or punks.

Table IX.4    Unfair treatment of particular groups, by ethnic group

Column percentages

| | Total | Whites | West Indians | Asians | Other non-whites |
|---|---|---|---|---|---|
| Are there any groups that do not get fair treatment? | | | | | |
| Yes | 29 | 26 | 62 | 36 | 51 |
| No | 47 | 50 | 13 | 21 | 14 |
| Don't know | 24 | 24 | 25 | 43 | 36 |
| If yes, what groups? | | | | | |
| Any mention of ethnic minorities | 22 | 20 | 48 | 34 | 43 |
| Base: all informants | | | | | |
| (unweighted) | 2,420 | 1,252 | 511 | 541 | 116 |
| (weighted) | 13,944 | 12,428 | 450 | 607 | 459 |

Since unfair treatment is strongly associated in people's minds with the ethnic minorities, it is not surprising to find that the minorities give different answers from white people (see Table IX.4). The differences shown are very striking. Sixty-two per cent of West Indians think some groups are unfairly treated, compared with 26 per cent of white people; 48 per cent of West Indians think ethnic minorities are unfairly treated, compared with 20 per cent of white people. Asians are much less critical of the police in this respect than West Indians, but more critical than white people. The answers given by other non-white people are similar to those given by West Indians, though somewhat less critical. There is some tendency for people to mention their own specific group as the object of unfair treatment by the police rather than other minority groups, but it is not particularly strong. For example, among Asians, 12 per cent say the police are unfair to Asians, but 11 per cent mention 'coloured people' and 16 per cent mention 'blacks', in which group most Asians would not include themselves. Also, one-fifth of white people think the police are unfair to ethnic minorities.

Table IX.5     Unfair treatment of particular groups, by age

Column percentages

| | 15-19 | 20-24 | 25-44 | 45-59 | 60 and over |
|---|---|---|---|---|---|
| Are there any groups that do not get fair treatment? | | | | | |
| Yes | 41 | 43 | 38 | 20 | 11 |
| No | 44 | 38 | 41 | 51 | 57 |
| Don't know | 14 | 19 | 21 | 28 | 32 |
| If yes, what groups? | | | | | |
| Any mention of ethnic minorities | 33 | 37 | 32 | 13 | 6 |
| Base: all informants | | | | | |
| (unweighted) | 490 | 494 | 844 | 345 | 247 |
| (weighted) | 1,278 | 1,332 | 5,174 | 2,910 | 3,252 |

There is little difference in the answers given between the age groups up to 44, but people aged 45 or more are much less likely than younger people to think that any groups, and the minorities in particular, are unfairly treated by the police. Two-fifths of people aged 15-44 think some groups are unfairly treated, and one-third specify the ethnic minorities (see Table IX.5). While Asians generally are much less critical of the police in this respect than West Indians generally, young Asians are nearly as critical as young West Indians (see Table IX.6). Among those aged 15-24, 68 per cent of West Indians think some groups are treated unfairly by the police, compared with 55 per cent of Asians and 39 per cent of white people.

These findings show that a substantial minority of Londoners believe that ethnic minorities are unfairly treated by the police. They also show that there is far more concern, among white people as well as among the minorities, about unfairness towards racial minorities than about unfairness of other kinds. While it is only a

Table IX.6    Unfair treatment of particular groups:  informants
              aged 15-24 by ethnic group

Column percentages

|  | Whites | West Indians | Asians |
|---|---|---|---|
| **Are there any groups that do not get fair treatment?** | | | |
| Yes | 39 | 68 | 55 |
| No | 46 | 15 | 20 |
| Don't know | 15 | 17 | 25 |
| **If yes, what groups?** | | | |
| Any mention of ethnic minorities | 32 | 56 | 51 |
| **Base:  informants aged 15-24** | | | |
| (unweighted) | 497 | 218 | 220 |
| (weighted) | 2,145 | 173 | 169 |

minority of Londoners generally who think the police treat certain groups unfairly, it is a very substantial minority; a higher proportion (still a minority) of young people, but a majority of West Indians hold this view.

We have already found that West Indians in areas of high ethnic concentration are no more likely to be critical of the police than those in areas of low concentration, and in some respects are less critical.  As to unfairness towards certain groups, West Indians in areas of high concentration are definitely less critical than other West Indians, as the following summary table shows.

| West Indians by per cent immigrants in the ED | Per cent saying that some groups are treated unfairly | Per cent who mention ethnic minorities |
|---|---|---|
| 0-5 | 70 | 60 |
| Over 5 to 10 | 65 | 48 |
| Over 10 to 20 | 65 | 46 |
| Over 20 | 50 | 36 |

Among Asians there is little, if any, relationship between the views expressed and the ethnic mix of the local population.  There is definitely no relationship of this kind among white people, which suggests that where white people think the police treat the ethnic minorities unfairly it is not a view they have formed from

222

observing what happens in their local area. White people in inner London are rather more likely to be critical of the police in this respect than those in outer London, but the same does not apply to the minorities.

Forty-two per cent of those in the professional and managerial groups think the police treat certain groups unfairly, compared with 26 per cent of those in lower socio-economic groups. This shows that the criticism is expressed, to a considerable extent, by people who are unlikely to be the objects of unfair treatment themselves, but who are likely to be relatively well-informed and to adopt a generally critical outlook. On the other hand, the unemployed, who are mostly drawn from the lower socio-economic groups, are much more likely than those in work to think that certain groups are treated unfairly (53 per cent of the unemployed compared with 34 per cent of those in work and 30 per cent of the sick and inactive)(1). This relates to our previous findings that the unemployed are likely to be both victims of crime and offenders. Their criticism of the police is likely to be based on experience rather than feelings of altruistic concern for disadvantaged groups.

## Serious misconduct
### The findings among all informants
We included a fairly elaborate series of questions to test people's views about the extent of serious misconduct by police officers in London. The basic question was about whether each type of misconduct happens, and if so how frequently, and it took the following form.

> When the police are questioning people, do you think they ever use threats or unreasonable pressure to get the answers they want?

> If yes  How often does this happen?  From what you have heard, would you say it happens very often, quite often, occasionally or hardly ever?

It should be noticed that this form of question in no way makes the implicit assumption that the misconduct does occur, nor plants the idea in the informant's mind. In some cases, a subsidiary question was included, for those who said a particular kind of misconduct did occur, to find out whether they thought it was increasing or decreasing.

> Does it happen more now than it used to, less, or about the same?

---

(1)   Only those aged 15-59 are included in the analysis by working status.

Table IX.7     Views on the frequency of various kinds of misconduct of various kinds

Column percentages

| | Threats etc. in quest- ioning | False records of inter- views | Excessive force on arrest | Unreason able violence at police station | Fabri- cation of evidence | Accept- ing bribes | Accept- ing favours |
|---|---|---|---|---|---|---|---|
| Often | 25 | 11 | 13 | 12 | 9 | 8 | 14 |
| - Very often | 8 | 3 | 4 | 4 | 2 | 2 | 4 |
| - Quite often | 17 | 8 | 9 | 8 | 7 | 6 | 10 |
| Occasionally | 27 | 16 | 17 | 19 | 29 | 43 | 41 |
| Hardly ever | 4 | 3 | 2 | 4 | 10 | 14 | 8 |
| Sometimes but don't know how often | 1 | - | - | 1 | * | * | * |
| Never | 30 | 56 | 63 | 53 | 40 | 26 | 26 |
| Don't know | 13 | 14 | 5 | 12 | 12 | 8 | 10 |
| **If it happens, is ir more or less than it used to?** | | | | | | | |
| More | NA | NA | 23 | 20 | 19 | 27 | NA |
| Less | NA | NA | * | 1 | 1 | 4 | NA |
| About the same | NA | NA | 8 | 13 | 24 | 31 | NA |
| Don't know | NA | NA | 1 | 2 | 3 | 4 | NA |

NA    Not asked

Note: In the case of accepting bribes and accepting favours, the answers were not as given, but in terms of the <u>number</u> of police officers involved: most police officers at some time, quite a lot of police officers, a few police officers, hardly any police officers, no police officers. The base for each column in this table is all informants.

Some further questions were also included about whether CID or uniform officers were more to blame, and about how the informant had come to know about the kind of misconduct in question. The findings from these further questions will be discussed in a later section.

The questioning covered seven kinds of serious misconduct. Because the exact definitions of these kinds of misconduct are important, the full wording of the introductory questions is given below.

a) When the police are questioning people, do you think they ever use threats or unreasonable pressure to get the answers they want?

b) When the police take written evidence from people, do you think what they write down is always a fair and accurate record of what was said?

c) Police officers sometimes <u>have</u> to use force to defend themselves when they are making arrests or restraining prisoners. Apart from this, do you think the police in London ever use more force than necessary when making arrests?

d) And do you think the police in London ever use violence on people held at police stations without good reason?

e) From what you have heard, do you think police officers in London ever make up evidence or plant evidence on people?

f) From what you have heard, do you think police officers in London ever accept sums of money as bribes?

g) Leaving money aside, from what you have heard do you think police officers in London ever accept goods or favours from people who want to keep on the right side of them?

The findings among all informants are shown in Table IX.7. Perhaps the first thing to notice is that the great majority of Londoners feel able to answer these questions: the proportion who can give no definite answer ranges from eight per cent (bribes) to 14 per cent (false records of interviews). Clearly, people are not speaking from direct experience in the great majority of cases, but they do have views on these issues, and ones they are not reluctant to express.

Secondly, people have different views about the frequency of various kinds of misconduct, so that the various questions produce different answers: for example, 63 per cent of informants think

225

the police officers never use excessive force when making arrests, but only 26 per cent think they never accept bribes.

It is a minority of informants who think that each kind of misconduct often occurs, ranging form 25 per cent (threats etc. in questioning) to eight per cent (accepting bribes). However, a substantial further proportion think each kind of misconduct happens occasionally (or in the case of bribes and favours that a few police officers are involved). Thus, a substantial proportion of informants think that each type of misconduct happens at least occasionally (or among at least a few officers). These findings are summarised below.

|  | Per cent of all informants | |
|---|---|---|
|  | Often or occasionally | Often |
| Accepting favours | 55 | 14 |
| Threats etc. in questioning | 52 | 25 |
| Accepting bribes | 51 | 8 |
| Fabrication of evidence | 38 | 9 |
| Violence at police stations | 31 | 12 |
| Excessive force on arrest | 30 | 13 |
| False records of interviews | 27 | 11 |

Over half of informants think that at least a few (and more than 'hardly any') police officers have accepted bribes, but only eight per cent think that 'quite a lot' or 'most' police officers have done so. The views expressed about accepting goods or favours are similar. Thus, it is a common view that there is some corruption in the police force, but not that it extends to more than a small minority of officers. The use of threats and unfair pressure in questioning people is the kind of misconduct that is thought to be most widespread. About half of informants think it happens at least occasionally, but perhaps more important, one-quarter think that it often happens - that it is a usual pattern of behaviour by police officers. The other kinds of misconduct are thought to happen at least occasionally by a substantial proportion of Londoners, but by well under half, while about one in ten Londoners think police officers often fabricate evidence, make false records of interviews, use excessive force when making arrests, and use violence unjustifiably on people held at police stations. These findings suggest that there is a complete lack of confidence in the police among at least one in ten of Londoners, and that about half of Londoners have serious doubts about the standards of police conduct, though in most cases they do not think there is a pattern of frequent or usual misconduct.

On four of the subjects, informants who said the misconduct ever happened were asked if it now happened more or less than it used to. Very few people think that any of the kinds of misconduct have become less common; the highest proportion thinking that

Table IX.8     Views on the frequency of police misconduct, by ethnic group

Column percentages

| | Whites | West Indians | Asians | Other non-whites |
|---|---|---|---|---|
| **Threats etc. in questioning** | | | | |
| Often | 25 | 52 | 22 | 16 |
| Often or occasionally | 52 | 81 | 36 | 49 |
| **False records of interviews** | | | | |
| Often | 11 | 33 | 10 | 9 |
| Often or occasionally | 26 | 60 | 22 | 28 |
| **Excessive force on arrest** | | | | |
| Often | 12 | 37 | 13 | 23 |
| Often or occasionally | 29 | 64 | 26 | 40 |
| **Unreasonable violence at police station** | | | | |
| Often | 10 | 42 | 10 | 22 |
| Often or occasionally | 30 | 71 | 25 | 33 |
| **Fabrication of evidence** | | | | |
| Often | 8 | 33 | 8 | 6 |
| Often or occasionally | 37 | 73 | 25 | 39 |
| **Accepting bribes** | | | | |
| Most or quite a lot of officers | 7 | 14 | 4 | 7 |
| Most, a lot or a few | 50 | 67 | 26 | 51 |
| **Accepting goods or favours** | | | | |
| Most or quite a lot of officers | 14 | 16 | 5 | 9 |
| Most, a lot or a few | 56 | 65 | 22 | 40 |
| | | | | |
| Base:  all informants | | | | |
| (unweighted) | 1,252 | 511 | 541 | 116 |
| (weighted) | 12,428 | 450 | 607 | 459 |

things are improving is four per cent, in the case of police officers accepting bribes. In two cases (fabrication of evidence and accepting bribes) informants were fairly evenly divided between the view that matters are getting worse and staying the same; in the other two cases (excessive use of force on arrest and unjustifiable violence at police stations) the balance of opinion is definitely that matters are getting worse rather than staying the same. It is interesting that among those who think that the various kinds of misconduct ever occur the most optimistic views about the direction of change are expressed in the case of bribery; the probable reason for this is that Sir Robert Mark was widely known to have initiated special efforts to combat corruption when he was

Commissioner. However, the general conclusion to be drawn from these findings is that where people think that misconduct occurs they rarely think that standards are improving, and as far as force and violence are concerned they are more inclined to think they are getting worse than staying the same. Of course, people who think that misconduct does not occur were not asked this question, and it is plain that they do not think that conduct has deteriorated. Still, it is not encouraging to find that one-fifth of Londoners think the police now use excessive force on arrest or unjustifiable violence at police stations more than they used to.

## Analysis by ethnic group and age

A much higher proportion of West Indians than of white people or of other groups are critical of police conduct (see Table IX.8). The biggest differences between the views of West Indians and white people are in relation to excessive use of force on arrest, unjustifiable use of violence on suspects held at police stations and fabrication of evidence. One-third or more of West Indians think that the police often misbehave in these ways, and two-thirds or more think they do so at least occasionally. In each case, the proportion of West Indians who think the misconduct often occurs is at least three times as high as the proportion of white people. These findings suggest that between one-third and one-half of West Indians have a very low opinion of standards of police conduct and that two-thirds have at least considerable doubts.

Asians definitely tend to be less critical of police conduct than white people, though their views are similar to those of white people on some of the issues (false records of interviews, excessive force on arrest, unjustifiable violence on suspects held at police stations are the issues on which they hold similar views). Asians are much less likely than white people to think that there is a significant amount of corruption in the police force. Other non-white people hold generally similar views to white people, though they are more critical of the police on some points and less critical on others.

Criticism of police conduct decreases sharply with age. The summary table below shows this pattern in the case of threats or unreasonable pressure on people being questioned by police.

|  | Per cent of each age group | |
| --- | --- | --- |
|  | Often or occasionally | Often |
| 15 - 19 | 69 | 36 |
| 20 - 24 | 67 | 36 |
| 25 - 44 | 64 | 33 |
| 45 - 59 | 48 | 19 |
| 60 and over | 24 | 9 |

Up to the age of 44, the different age groups express similar views, but successive age groups from 45 onwards are much less critical. This is the same pattern as the one already described for views about the fairness of the police to different groups. On a few issues, those aged 25-44 are somewhat less critical of the police than younger people, but none of these differences is large.

Table IX.9    Views of the frequency of police misconduct: informants aged 15-24 by ethnic group

Column percentages

| | Whites | West Indians | Asians |
|---|---|---|---|
| Threats etc. in questioning | | | |
| Often | 32 | 62 | 33 |
| Often or occasionally | 66 | 88 | 47 |
| False records of interviews | | | |
| Often | 13 | 41 | 13 |
| Often or occasionally | 30 | 66 | 25 |
| Excessive force on arrest | | | |
| Often | 21 | 53 | 19 |
| Often or occasionally | 42 | 72 | 32 |
| Unreasonable violence at police station | | | |
| Often | 20 | 56 | 17 |
| Often or occasionally | 41 | 82 | 36 |
| Fabrication of evidence | | | |
| Often | 13 | 43 | 11 |
| Often or occasionally | 42 | 75 | 29 |
| Accepting bribes | | | |
| Most or quite a lot of officers | 9 | 20 | 6 |
| Most, a lot or a few | 50 | 71 | 29 |
| Accepting goods or favours | | | |
| Most or quite a lot of officers | 17 | 23 | 9 |
| Most, a lot or a few | 60 | 73 | 31 |
| | | | |
| Base: all informants | | | |
| (unweighted) | 497 | 218 | 220 |
| (weighted) | 2,145 | 173 | 169 |

Looking separately at the views of young people aged 15-24 (Table IX.9) we find that it is a minority, but a substantial minority, of young white people who think there is a pattern of frequent police misconduct. One-third of young white people think the police often use threats or unreasonable pressure in question ing and one-fifth think they often use excessive force on arrest

229

and that they <u>often</u> unjustifiably use force on people held at police stations. Smaller proportions of young white people think that other kinds of misconduct often occur. Young West Indians are far more critical of police conduct than young white people, particularly in relation to false records of interviews, fabrication of evidence and the use of force and violence. The lack of confidence in the police among young West Indians can only be described as disastrous. Sixty-two per cent of them think the police often use threats and unreasonable pressure in questioning, 53 per cent that they often use excessive force on arrest, 56 per cent that they often unjustifiably use violence on people held at police stations, 43 per cent that they often fabricate evidence and 41 per cent that they often make false records of interviews. Just as Asians generally are definitely less critical of the police than white people, so young Asians are less critical than young white people, though again their views are similar on some issues. However, the contrast between young Asians and young white people is less marked than the contrast between Asians and white people of all age groups. This is because the difference in view between the generations is greater among Asians than among white people; consequently, the views of young Asians and young white people tend to converge, while the views of older Asians and older white people diverge sharply. We can therefore expect a tendency for Asians as a group to become more critical of the police - to hold views more like those of white people - as time goes on.

## Mean score analysed by ethnic group, age and sex
We have seen that people hold differentiated views about standards of police conduct depending on what particular kind of misconduct is under consideration. However, cross-analysis shows that there is a considerable degree of correlation between people's views on one kind of misconduct and another; in other words, people show a considerable tendency to be either critical or approving of the police in various respects. Also, the pattern of variation between groups in the views expressed is fairly similar whatever the exact kind of misconduct that is under consideration. When considering the relationship between the views expressed and other factors it is therefore appropriate to use a single measure derived from the answers to all seven questions about serious misconduct. We can produce a single measure of this kind by assigning scores as follows:

| | |
|---|---|
| very often/most police officers | 4 |
| quite often/quite a lot of police officers | 3 |
| occasionally/a few police officers | 2 |
| hardly ever/hardly any police officers | 1 |
| never/no police officers | 0 |
| the misconduct occurs, but don't know how often | 2 |
| don't know whether it occurs | 0 |

Table IX.10    Views on frequency of police misconduct:    overall
              score, by ethnic group
                                        Column percentages and means

|  | Total | Whites | West Indians | Asians | Other non-whites |
|---|---|---|---|---|---|
| Score |  |  |  |  |  |
| 0 | 16 | 15 | 5 | 35 | 15 |
| 1 - 4 | 25 | 25 | 8 | 26 | 26 |
| 5 - 9 | 25 | 26 | 15 | 19 | 30 |
| 10 - 14 | 21 | 21 | 29 | 12 | 18 |
| 15 - 19 | 9 | 9 | 27 | 6 | 5 |
| 20 - 24 | 3 | 3 | 13 | 2 | 5 |
| 25 - 28 | 1 | 1 | 3 | * | * |
| Summary |  |  |  |  |  |
| 0 - 9 | 66 | 66 | 28 | 80 | 71 |
| 10 - 19 | 30 | 30 | 56 | 18 | 23 |
| 20 - 28 | 4 | 4 | 16 | 2 | 5 |
| Mean | 7.4 | 7.3 | 13.1 | 4.8 | 7.1 |
| Base: all informants |  |  |  |  |  |
| (unweighted) | 2,420 | 1,252 | 511 | 541 | 116 |
| (weighted) | 13,944 | 12,428 | 450 | 607 | 459 |

It will be noted that where informants say they don't know whether the misconduct occurs, they are treated as if they said it never occurs. This cautious method of assigning the scores ensures that the measure does not overstate the extent of criticism. Answers to each of the seven questions are scored in this way, so that the maximum possible score is 7x4, or 28. The minimum score is 0. A high score indicates a high level of criticism.

The distribution of these scores is shown in Table IX.10. Sixteen per cent of informants score 0 - that is, they think that no kind of police misconduct ever occurs. Two-thirds of informants score 0-9; a score of 9 would be achieved, for example, by someone who thought that five of the kinds of misconduct 'hardly ever' happened and that two of them happened 'occasionally'. It is fair to say, therefore, that two-thirds of Londoners have no doubts or only minor doubts about the standards of police conduct.    The remaining one-third have some considerable doubts, but most of them (30 per cent) score between 10 and 19, while only four per cent score 20-28.    A typical score for the first of these groups would be 13, and it would be achieved, for example, by someone who thought that all but one of the kinds of misconduct happened 'occasionally' and the other one 'hardly ever'. In order to come into the second group (scoring 20 or more) an informant would have to think that nearly all of the kinds of misconduct happened 'quite often'; it is only one in 25 of Londoners who hold such views.

The scores show, in a summary form, the striking difference

231

between the views of West Indians and white people that has already been noted. The mean score for West Indians is 13.1 compared with 7.3 for white people. Seventy-two per cent of West Indians compared with 34 per cent of white people score 10 or more; 16 per cent of West Indians compared with four per cent of white people score 20 or more. The mean score among Asians is distinctly lower than among white people (4.8 compared with 7.3), while the mean among other-non-whites is about the same as among white people.

Table IX.11 shows the mean scores according to age and ethnic group in combination. Within each age group, West Indians are far more critical of police conduct than white people, whereas Asians are distinctly less critical. The difference between age groups is greater among Asians than among other ethnic groups, and the contrast in views between Asians and white people is less strong among those aged 15-24 than among older people. The variation in views according to ethnic group is greater than that according to age; for example, West Indians aged 45 and over are more critical of police conduct than white people aged 15-24.

Table IX.11    Views on frequency of police misconduct:    mean score by age and ethnic group

Mean scores

|  | Total | 15-24 | Age 25-44 | 45 and over |
|---|---|---|---|---|
| All informants | 7.4 | 9.1 | 8.8 | 5.4 |
| Whites | 7.3 | 8.9 | 9.1 | 5.3 |
| West Indians | 13.1 | 15.2 | 13.2 | 10.3 |
| Asians | 4.8 | 6.1 | 4.9 | 2.9 |
| Other non-whites | 7.1 | NA | NA | NA |

NA    Base too small for analysis.
Note:    The score is derived from the seven questions shown in Tables IX.7-9. For further explanation, see the text.

Table IX.12 shows the mean scores according to sex and ethnic group in combination. Men tend to be more critical of police conduct than women, and this holds for members of each ethnic group. However, these differences between the views of the sexes are not very strong, and are not as important as the age differences. The difference between the views of men and women is smaller among West Indians than among other ethnic groups; thus, West Indian women are almost as critical of police conduct as West Indian men.

232

Table IX.12    Views on frequency of police misconduct:    mean
score by sex and ethnic group

Mean scores

|  | Men | Women |
| --- | --- | --- |
| All informants | 8.5 | 6.4 |
| Whites | 8.4 | 6.4 |
| West Indians | 13.5 | 12.8 |
| Asians | 5.4 | 4.1 |
| Other non-whites | 9.2 | 5.3 |

Analysis by geographical variables

The views of Asians and West Indians about the standards of police
conduct do not vary markedly according to the level of local ethnic
concentration (see Table IX.13). There is, however, some tendency
for those in areas of high ethnic concentration to be less critical of
police conduct than others. This is the same kind of relationship
that we noted in connection with views about the fairness of the
police, and in connection with other measures of the evaluation of
the police by Asians and West Indians. It is quite clear that
criticism of the police is not particularly strong among ethnic
minorities in places like Brixton and Southall: if anything, it is
stronger among those in mainly white areas.

Table IX.13    Views on frequency of police misconduct:    mean
score:    Asians and West Indians by local ethnic
concentration

Mean scores

|  | West Indians | Asians |
| --- | --- | --- |
| Per cent immigrants in ED |  |  |
| 0 - 5 | 12.5 | 4.8 |
| Over 5 to 10 | 14.0 | 4.1 |
| Over 10 to 20 | 13.7 | 5.9 |
| Over 20 | 11.5 | 3.2 |

There is a small, but distinct, tendency for people in inner
London to be more critical of police conduct than those in outer
London (see Table IX.14). While this is true of Londoners generally
and of white people, it is not true of Asians and West Indians. In
the case of West Indians, there is no difference in the views
expressed between those in inner and outer London. In the case of

Table IX.14　Views on frequency of police misconduct:　mean score by part of London and ethnic group

Mean score

|  | Inner London | Outer London |
|---|---|---|
| All ethnic groups | 8.5 | 6.8 |
| Whites | 8.3 | 6.8 |
| West Indians | 13.0 | 13.2 |
| Asians | 3.9 | 5.1 |

Asians, those in outer London are rather more critical than those in inner London. This is perhaps the clearest example of a pattern of findings that recurs on various questions in the survey. Differences of geography do not have the same significance for the different ethnic groups. We are not sure what is the correct interpretation of this pattern of findings. There are indications from the survey that there is a group of people who live unconventional, disorganised lives, and who often come into contact with the police both as offenders or suspects and as victims. These people will probably tend to be critical of the police. They may form a higher proportion of the population of inner than of outer London, which would account for the fact that people in inner London tend to be more critical of the police than those in outer London. On the other hand, Asians and West Indians who belong to this group may be distributed differently - they may not tend to be concentrated in inner London. This would account for the different pattern of views about the police among Asians and West Indians in the two parts of London. This hypothesis is little more than speculation, but for Asians, at least, it does seem likely that the focal points to people living fragmented lives are places like Southall, which are not in inner London.

Analysis by the level of social deprivation in the borough provides another example of the same kind of pattern. Again, views about police conduct are not strongly related to this geographical variable, but there is a distinct tendency, over all ethnic groups, for those in areas of high deprivation to be more critical of police conduct than those in areas of low deprivation (see Table IX.15). This relationship seems entirely understandable, since we would expect people in areas of high deprivation to come into conflict with the police more often than others. However, we again find that the relationship does not hold in the case of Asians and West Indians. Among West Indians, there seems to be no relationship at all, while among Asians there seems, if anything, to be a contrary relationship. What this, perhaps, suggests is that areas of high deprivation are not areas of high deprivation as far as

234

Asians are concerned.

Table IX.15   Views on frequency of police misconduct:   mean score by index of deprivation in the borough and ethnic group

Mean scores

| | Index of deprivation in the borough | | | |
| | 100 or more | 0 to 99 | -99 to -1 | -100 or less |
| --- | --- | --- | --- | --- |
| All ethnic groups | 8.7 | 7.9 | 7.1 | 6.8 |
| Whites | 8.5 | 7.7 | 7.1 | 6.8 |
| West Indians | 12.6 | 13.2 | 13.3 | 13.0 |
| Asians | 2.9 | 4.4 | 5.2 | 4.3 |

Analysis by work-related factors

Although the differences are not large, there is some tendency for those in the higher socio-economic groups to be more critical of police conduct than those in the lower groups (see Table IX.16). The two groups that are most critical are the professional and managerial and the skilled manual; those in the white collar group express views more like those of non-skilled workers than those of professional and managerial workers.  Here the findings for West Indians and Asians follow the same pattern as for white people (though there is some difficulty in tracing them accurately because of small sample sizes in some groups).  Socio-economic group is not a very good measure of social class, and the concept of social class cannot be applied very neatly to Asians and West Indians.  Nevertheless, it is significant that we find some relationship here.  It suggests that among white people and the minorities alike, those who have better jobs, higher incomes, better education and who probably tend to be more socially aware also tend to be more critical of the police than others.  Asians and West Indians of this type probably tend to live in areas of relatively low ethnic concentration.  Certainly, we can show from the survey that there is a tendency, strong in the case of Asians, for those in the higher socio-economic groups to live in areas of lower ethnic concentration than the rest, and nationally there is a strong tendency for 'middle class' Asians, and especially those who are better educated, to live in low-concentration areas.  This may help to explain the fact that those in areas of low ethnic concentration tend, if anything, to be more critical of the police than those elsewhere.  On this argument, better-educated Asians or West Indians, who are more likely to articulate criticism of the police, tend not to live in Brixton or Southall.  At the same time, it is important to emphasise that none of these differences is large:

Table IX.16   <u>Views on frequency of police misconduct: mean</u>
<u>score by socio-economic group and ethnic group</u>

Mean score

| | Professional managerial | White collar | Skilled manual | Semi-skilled manual | Unskilled manual |
|---|---|---|---|---|---|
| All ethnic groups | 8.7 | 7.1 | 8.3 | 6.4 | 5.9 |
| Whites | 8.7 | 7.0 | 8.2 | 6.5 | 5.4 |
| West Indian | (15.9) | 13.9 | 13.4 | 12.2 | (10.3) |
| Asians | 5.5 | 5.8 | 5.1 | 3.1 | (5.4) |

Note:   The means in brackets are based on very small numbers of informants. The unweighted bases are West Indian professional/managerial 17; West Indian unskilled manual 28; Asian unskilled manual 15.

that is, the differences between socio-economic groups, between areas of high and low ethnic concentration and between the demography of these different areas. Making all due allowance for differences of demography, it is still the case that Asians and West Indians in areas of high concentration are <u>no more</u> critical of the police than those elsewhere. Places like Brixton and Lewisham have become flashpoints of police/public relations not because the West Indians living there are particularly hostile to the police, but just because of the weight of numbers of West Indians in such areas.

Table IX.17   <u>Views on frequency of police misconduct: mean</u>
<u>score by working status and sex</u>

Mean scores

| | Men | Women |
|---|---|---|
| Working full-time | 9.4 | 7.9 |
| Working part time | NA | 6.3 |
| Unemployed | 12.7 | 11.3 |
| Sick or inactive | 7.4 | 7.2 |

NA   Base too small for analysis.
Note:   Only informants aged 15-59 are included in the table.

In earlier chapters, we showed that the unemployed tend to come into frequent contact with the police both as suspects or offenders and as victims of crime. We suggested that unemployment itself did not have a direct effect in getting people involved with crime and the police, but rather that a fair proportion of the unemployed belong to a group of people who lead unconventional and disorganised lives, and that these people do tend to be both victims of crime and offenders. Table IX.17 shows, furthermore, that the unemployed are considerably more likely to be critical of police conduct than others. It is interesting that this applies both to men and to women. We have mentioned in earlier chapters that the police tend to categorise people according to whether they are 'respectable' or not. Undoubtedly, many of the unemployed fail to qualify as 'respectable': if they have a low opinion of police conduct, this may arise partly because of the way that people of their type tend to be treated by the police.

## Involvement of uniformed police and CID in misconduct

The drive in the 1970s against corruption in the Metropolitan Police was mainly directed against CID officers, who have far more opportunity than uniform officers to influence what charges are brought against individuals and the result of any prosecution. Sir Robert Mark (then Commissioner) said that the CID had become 'a force within a force' and made it clear that he was determined to break down this separate identity and to bring the CID under the control of the main hierarchy. Among the officers who were prosecuted, were dismissed, suspended or resigned from the Force over this period, a majority belonged to the CID. Organisational changes that were begun during the period when Sir Robert Mark was Commissioner but completed in 1979, when Sir David McNee was in office, made the great majority of CID officers accountable at Chief Superintendent level, to uniform officers and brought about a much larger measure of interchange of personnel between uniform and detective ranks. A great majority of Londoners probably have little detailed knowledge of these events and organisational changes, but we thought it important to find out whether certain kinds of police misconduct are associated in the public mind more with CID than with uniform officers. The following four kinds of misconduct seemed to be the relevant ones: threats, etc. in questioning, fabrication of evidence, accepting bribes and accepting favours. In each case, informants who said that the misconduct occurred were asked whether 'it is mostly uniformed police who do it or mostly CID or don't you know'.

The findings (Table IX.18) show that a majority even of those who think the particular kind of misconduct does occur have no definite opinion as to whether CID or uniformed officers are mostly involved. This demonstrates rather vividly that bad publicity about one particular (and small) section of the force rubs off on the force as a whole. People who do not have close contact with the police probably have no very clear conception of the distinction between CID and uniform officers; if they hear that some CID officers are corrupt, what that means to them is that some police officers are corrupt.

Table IX.18    Whether uniformed police or CID are mostly invol-
               ved in four kinds of misconduct

Column percentages

|  | Threats etc. in questioning | Fabricat- ion of evidence | Accept- ing bribes | Accepting goods or favours |
|---|---|---|---|---|
| **Mostly** | | | | |
| Uniformed police | 13 | 6 | 5 | 10 |
| CID | 28 | 33 | 34 | 20 |
| Don't know | 59 | 60 | 61 | 70 |
| Base:  informants who think the misconduct occurs | | | | |
| (unweighted) | 1,475 | 1,224 | 1,433 | 1,384 |
| (weighted) | 7,786 | 6,688 | 9,086 | 8,873 |

Table IX.19    Use of excessive force on arrest:   how you have
               come to know, by ethnic group

Column percentages

|  | Total | Whites | West Indians | Asians | Other non- whites |
|---|---|---|---|---|---|
| Through it actually happening to you or someone you know | 39 | 38 | 55 | 29 | 27 |
| Through you or someone you know seeing it happen to someone else | 44 | 44 | 56 | 26 | 39 |
| Through seeing news pictures on TV of it happening | 77 | 76 | 77 | 82 | 89 |
| Through hearing it discussed on radio or TV | 78 | 78 | 68 | 86 | 87 |
| Through reading about it in the newspaper | 79 | 79 | 68 | 86 | 87 |
| Base:  informants who think it sometimes happens | | | | | |
| (unweighted) | 992 | 458 | 337 | 153 | 44 |
| (weighted) | 4,486 | 3,838 | 291 | 168 | 189 |

Among those who do express a view, the balance of opinion is that it is mostly CID rather than uniformed officers who are involved in each of the four kinds of misconduct. In the case of fabrication of evidence and accepting bribes, the balance of opinion is overwhelmingly against the CID; between five and seven times as many people think the CID are mostly involved as think it is mostly uniformed officers. In the case of threats etc. in questioning and accepting goods and favours, people divide about two to one in favour of the view that the CID are mostly involved.

These findings show that a fairly small minority of Londoners have a definite view about the standard of conduct of CID compared with uniformed officers, but among those who do have a view, the CID has a much poorer reputation than the uniform branch.

## Source of information about police officers using excessive force

In the next chapter we shall consider how far people's views about the standard of conduct of police offices are related to, and therefore possibly based on, their own personal exprience. We also tried in a limited way to obtain some information on this point by means of direct questioning. The kind of police misconduct about which people are most likely to have information from personal experience or observation is the use of excessive force at the time of arrest. This is because many arrests take place in public, whereas most other occasions of misconduct arise inside police buildings or in private places. These questions were answered by informants who said that police officers do sometimes use more force than necessary when making arrests, that is, by 32 per cent of all informants.

How have you come to know about it? Is it through:
- it actually happening to you or someone you know?
- you or someone you know seeing it happen to someone else?
- seeing news pictures on TV of it happening?
- hearing it discussed on radio or TV?
- reading about it in the newspapers?

Informants definitely stated whether or not they had obtained information about excessive use of force on arrest from each of these sources, but Table IX.19 shows only the proportion saying that they had, in each case. It is important to remember that the findings are based on those who think that this kind of misconduct ever occurs. More than three-quarters of these informants say they have heard about it from television news picures, from radio or television discussions and from newspaper accounts. There is no doubt that the information most widely available comes from the mass media. However, a very substantial proportion of these informants quote personal experience or observation, or the experience or observation of people they know. Thirty-nine per cent say

239

they know about excessive use of force on arrest from it actually happening to them or to people they know; 44 per cent say they know about it from their own observation or the observation of people they know. Although more people quote the mass media than quote personal experience and hearsay, the more immediate kind of information is probably more potent to those who have access to it than the information from the mass media. These findings do not, therefore, lend support to the view that criticisms of police conduct by members of the public are entirely a response to hostile reporting by journalists.

The proportion of all informants who say that they know the police sometimes use excessive force on arresting people 'through it actually happening to you or someone you know' is 12 per cent; and 'through you or someone you know seeing it happen to someone else', 14 per cent. These are not large proportions, but they represent a large number of Londoners - perhaps 700,000 - who will be hard to convince that this kind of misconduct does not occur.

West Indians are distinctly more likely to quote personal experience, observation or hearsay than white people, and are rather less likely to quote the mass media. Asians (and to a lesser extent, other non-white people) are more likely to quote the mass media and less likely to quote personal experience, observation and hearsay than white people. At the same time, of course, a much higher proportion of West Indians than of other groups think this kind of misconduct occurs and are therefore giving answers to this question. In fact, 64 per cent of West Indians think the police sometimes use excessive force on arresting people, and 55 per cent of these West Indians say they have come to know about it through it actually happening to them or someone they know: therefore, 35 per cent of all West Indians say they know about it from personal experience or the experience of someone they know, compared with 12 per cent of white people. These findings suggest that the much higher level of criticism of police conduct among West Indians than among white people is connected with different expriences that West Indians have had or heard about from friends. Of course, if people are generally critical of the police they will tend to interpret their own and their friends' experience in that light; they will look to their own experience and to the experience of people close to them for examples of the kinds of misconduct which, they think, generally tend to occur. In spite of this difficulty, two conclusions can certainly be drawn. First, there is no evidence to support the idea that the critical views of West Indians are based on indirect evidence or general ideas to a greater extent than the approving views of white people; on the contrary, the evidence points the other way. Secondly, more than half of the West Indians who hold critical views think those views are based on experience close to them rather than just on accounts in the mass media; from the West Indians' own perspective, therefore, these views will seem well-founded in a substantial proportion of cases, and will be hard to shake.

**Police use of guns**
Britain is the only industrialised nation in the world in which the police do not normally carry guns, and along with firearms control this is an enormously important factor determining the nature of the relationship in Britain between the police and the public. In the USA, academics measure changes in police/public relations in terms of the number of people shot dead annually by police officers, and the measure has particular significance because, in most cases, it is white police officers who kill black citizens. In Britain, police officers very rarely kill people, and this is a measure of the enormous superiority of policing and of police/public relations in Britain compared with the United States.

We thought it important to find out, in the survey of the public, whether there is still strong public support for the most basic principle of British policing policy - that the police should be normally unarmed. We also thought it important to establish whether there is public concern that the present, limited, use of guns by the police may be excessive. Informants were asked the following questions.

Do you think ordinary policemen on normal duties should carry guns?

The police in London sometimes use guns. From what you have heard, would you say that they use guns too often, or that they should use guns more often, or that it is about right?

Sixteen per cent of informants say that policemen should normally carry guns, 83 per cent that they should not, and two per cent that they don't know. Although there is widespread support for an unarmed police force, it is, perhaps, disturbing to find that a substantial minority of Londoners would like to jettison the best principle of British policing. A higher proportion of women than of men take this view (20 per cent compared with 11 per cent), which suggests that it often springs from a fear of crime. There are no significant differences according to age. West Indians are less likely than white people to be in favour of guns (nine per cent compared with 16 per cent), but a higher proportion of Asians and of other non-white people are in favour (21 per cent and 20 per cent respectively). Although these views are not related to age overall, among Asians and West Indians older people are much more in favour of the police carrying guns than younger people, as the following summary table shows.

| Age | Per cent who think the police should normally carry guns | | |
|-----|--------|--------------|--------|
| | Whites | West Indians | Asians |
| 15 - 24 | 16 | 3 | 15 |
| 25 - 44 | 15 | 10 | 21 |
| 45 and over | 17 | 15 | 27 |

Thus, a very small proportion of young West Indians (three per cent) are in favour of the police normally carrying guns. It looks as though, among the minority groups, those who are most critical of the police (young people) are least likely to think they ought to carry guns, whereas there is no relationship of this kind among white people.

From the second question we find that three-quarters of informants (76 per cent) think that police use guns about as often as they should, but the remainder divide six to one in favour of the view that they should use guns more often (they should use guns more often, 18 per cent; they use guns too often, three per cent). Thus, although a substantial minority of informants criticise the police for using too much force in certain situations, the vast majority believe that they are restrained in their use of guns. Women are rather more inclined than men to think they should use guns more often (21 per cent compared with 15 per cent), probably because they have a greater fear of crime. Also, young people are more likely to think they should use guns more often than older people (25 per cent of those aged 15-24 compared with 17 per cent of those aged 25 and over); this may be because of a greater predilection for violence among the young. White people are more inclined than members of minority groups to think the police should use guns more often (20 per cent compared with nine per cent), but here there are no significant differences between the particular ethnic minority groups. Thus, a higher proportion of Asians and of other non-white people than of West Indians (or white people) think the police should normally carry guns, but a smaller proportion think they should use them more often than they do. It is difficult to explain this pattern, except on the assumption that some Asians and other non-white people assume that the police officers in Britain do carry guns as they do in their countries of origin: many Asians have had absolutely no contact with the police in Britain and live rather culturally enclosed lives.

On the whole, these findings amount to a solid vote of confidence for present police policies on the use of guns. Among a minority of Londoners there is some demand for the police to use guns more than they do; there is very little demand for them to use them less.

## Complaints about police

In recent years, public discussion about standards of police conduct has tended to concentrate on the complaints system, for various reasons: because the system has fairly recently been changed, because Sir Robert Mark made the change a resigning issue and because it is easier to comment on the treatment of complaints than to think constructively about the whole range of factors that influence police behaviour. It is often said that it is supremely important that the public should have confidence in the system for investigating complaints, and, by some, that they do not have that confidence, and will not as long as the system involves the police investigating themselves. In this respect we have not allowed the content and tone of public discussion to shape the design of the survey. We see the complaints system as one of a number of influences on police behaviour, and not necessarily a supremely important one. We also assume that, in spite of the content of public discussion, the most important subjects for investigation are people's actual experiences of the police, and their views on policing policy and police conduct; and we do not believe that what people think of the complaints system is likely to be a very important component of their views about the police. An obvious reason for this is that far more people have had contact with the police than have made, or contemplated making, a complaint; and that most people's knowledge of the complaints system will be slight.

Table IX.20    Proportion who would make a complaint about police, by age, sex and ethnic group

Percentages

|  | Total | Whites | West Indians | Asians | Other non-whites |
|---|---|---|---|---|---|
| All informants | 90 | 90 | 79 | 88 | 80 |
| Sex |  |  |  |  |  |
| Men | 87 | 88 | 79 | 88 | 79 |
| Women | 92 | 93 | 79 | 88 | 80 |
| Age |  |  |  |  |  |
| 15 - 24 | 83 | 84 | 70 | 85 | NA |
| 25 - 44 | 92 | 92 | 82 | 90 | NA |
| 45 and over | 91 | 92 | 87 | 85 | NA |

We did, however, wish to obtain some indication from the survey as to whether there is a lack of confidence in the present complaints system. We felt that the best indicator was whether people would be prepared to use it. We therefore included the following questions.

If you were seriously dissatisfied about something a police officer had done or failed to do, would you make a complaint about it?

If yes To whom would you complain?
If no Why not?

The findings from the first question are shown in Table IX.20. Ninety per cent of informants say they would make a complaint, nine per cent say they would not, and one per cent don't know. Among Londoners generally, therefore, there seems to be a high level of confidence in the present system, although in the vast majority of cases this will not be based on a detailed knowledge of it, still less on experience of using it. Asians give similar answers to white people, but a lower proportion of West Indians (79 per cent) and of other non-white people (80 per cent) say they would complain. Younger people are less likely than older people to say they would make a complaint, thought the differences are not very large. Young West Indians are the group who would be least likely to complain (70 per cent of West Indians aged 15-24). These differences suggest that the groups who have most experience of the police and who are most critical of them would be least likely to make a complaint. Analysis by other variables confirms this interpretation. The pattern of variation is always the mirror image of the pattern for views about police conduct: that is, groups which are more critical than average of police conduct are less likely than average to say they would complain about it. To a certain extent, this supports the argument that a lack of confidence in the complaints system leads to a lack of confidence in the police: cetainly the two are associated, but it may well be that people lose confidence in the complaints system - or at any rate express critical views about it - because they are critical of the police rather than the other way round. But in any case, even among groups, such as young West Indians, who are generally highly critical of the police, a high proportion say they would make use of the complaints system in the appropriate circumstances. It is quite clear, therefore, that a failure of the complaints system is not at the heart of the criticisms that these people have to make.

The original question did not suggest to people that they might complain to the police, but 85 per cent of those who say they would complain are thinking in terms of making a complaint to the police (see Table IX.21). What most people probably have in mind is making a complaint at the local police station; 52 per cent say so explicitly, and a further 20 per cent say they would complain to a senior or supervising officer without mentioning where - in practice they would probably go to the local police station. Only 11 per cent say they would complain to Scotland Yard or to the Complaints Investigation Bureau. Eighteeen per cent say they would make a complaint to someone other than the police, among whom 11 per cent mention a Member of Parliament.

Table IX.21     To whom the informant would complain and reasons for not complaining

Column percentages

| To whom would complain | | Reasons for not complaining | |
|---|---|---|---|
| Senior or supervising officer at local police station | 41 | Ineffective | 34 |
| Senior or supervising officer (no mention of where) | 20 | Police investigating police | 20 |
| | | Don't like to complain | 22 |
| Local police station (no mention of who) | 11 | Afraid | 14 |
| | | Don't know how to complain | 4 |
| Scotland Yard or Complaints Investigation Bureau) | 11 | Other specific answer | 1 |
| | | Vague answer only | 12 |
| Other mentions of the police | 11 | Don't know | 4 |
| MP | 2 | | |
| Solicitor | 11 | Base: those who would not complain | |
| Home Secretary | 5 | (unweighted) | 1,333 |
| Other answer | 2 | (weighted) | |
| Don't know | 1 | | |
| | 3 | | |
| Base: those who would complain (weighted) | 12,501 | | |

Among those who say they would not complain, the reasons given generally reflect the criticisms that are publicly made of the complaints system. Thirty-four per cent say it would be ineffective and 20 per cent that the system involves the police investigating the police. (In fact, about three per cent of complaints are substantiated.) Twenty-two per cent say they 'don't like to complain' and 14 per cent that they would be afraid to do so; these people certainly lack confidence in the strength of their position as complainants, but do not seem to criticise the present complaints system as such. Very few informants (four per cent) confess that they would not complain because of ignorance about how to go about it.

As we pointed out in the preface to this series, it is commonplace for police officers to say that they are dependent on the support of the public.  In previous chapters we have seen that people's experience and views of the police are very complex.  In many ways, the police do have the support of a majority of Londoners, but a substantial minority have serious criticisms to make, and among certain population groups - young people generally and young West Indians in particular - there is a widespread lack of confidence in the police and hostility towards them.  Most people who have been the victims of crime are reasonably happy with the way the police dealt with the matter.  Those who have been stopped by the police or arrested often have substantial criticisms of the way they were treated.  The way in which particular encounters between Londoners and the police develop is based on the perceptions, assumptions and attitudes that both sides bring to these encounters.  Both police officers and members of the public are influenced by what they have read and heard and by the dominant thinking of the groups to which they belong as much as by their own direct previous experience.  If a particular group believes that the police treat them unfairly, or that serious misconduct is common among police officers, they will tend to interpret particular encounters with the police in that light; consequently, they will tend to behave in a way that triggers hostile behaviour by the police officers, and will in any case tend to interpret their behaviour as hostile even if the officer thinks he is being friendly and reasonable.  Similarly, if police officers are apprehensive about the reactions of young West Indians they will tend to interpret their behaviour as hostile even when it is not.  In this way, actual encounters will tend to confirm entrenched expectations on both sides, either because they become hostile as a result of the perceptions and expectations that are brought to them, or because they are interpreted as hostile even when they are not.

There is, in other words, a powerful positive feedback system at work.  Where relations are amiable, they will tend to become more and more amiable, and where they are hostile they will become more and more hostile, because each fresh encounter will tend to conform to expectations, or to be interpreted as doing so. In these circumstances, it is not fruitful to inquire into what originally nudged the relationship into one line of development or the other. What does need to be considered is how the continuing reinforcement of a poor relationship can be stopped. It is difficult to see how there can be coordinated effort on the part of the public, although the development of structures, such as borough Police Committees, through which members of the public can formally express their views, may be helpful. However, it is inevitable that the main responsibility for finding a way forward must lie with the police, even if the development of poor relations with some sections of the public is not altogether 'their fault'. It is therefore extremely important to consider how far critical and hostile views of the police are related to experience of particular kinds of encounter with police officers. Strong relationships of this kind will suggest that the police can change the views and assumptions of the public by changing their own policies and behaviour.

Of course, on a strict intepretation, relationships between views and experience of the police do not 'prove anything'. Many different lines of causation are probably involved as well as the obvious one (that conflict with the police causes people to become critical of them). People who are critical of the police may tend to come into conflict with them, for example because they go on civil rights demonstrations. As we have already pointed out, those who are critical of the police will tend to interpret encounters with them as ones of conflict, and may tend to turn amiable or neutral encounters into hostile ones. Again, there may be a kind of person who is both critical of the police and liable to come into conflict with them, that is, there may be characteristics that have causal links in both directions; a prime example of this is youth: young people tend to be stopped by the police and also to be critical of them, though in theory the two things could be quite independent of one another - they could be stopped because they are young and critical because they are young, and not critical because they are stopped.

In spite of these complexities, it is reasonable to give some credence to the 'obvious' line of causation. If people's views are strongly related to their experience of the police, we still cannot be sure that changes in police policy and behaviour would lead to a change in their views; but in those circumstances a change in police policy and behaviour would look like the best thing to try.

This chapter is arranged according to the different kinds of experience of the police that people have had (for example, stops, arrests, reporting crime as a victim). In each section, we consider how the various views that people express are related to one particular kind of experience of the police. In the final section we summarise these findings and anticipate one of the main conclusions of this report.

**Stops**

We have classified informants into the following five groups according to the experience of being stopped by the police.

Stopped three or more times in the past year.
Stopped two or more times in the past year (this group includes those in the first group).
Stopped once only in the past year.
Have been stopped by the police, but not in the past year.
Have never been stopped by the police.

The classification relates to the total number of stops (whether the informant was in a vehicle or on foot at the time). In practice, vehicle stops greatly outnumber foot stops, and therefore carry more weight in determining the classification.

Table X.1    Views on stops by experience of being stopped

Column percentages

| | Experience of being stopped[a] | | | | |
|---|---|---|---|---|---|
| | 3 or more stops | 2 or more stops | One stop | Not in past year | Never stopped |
| **People in vehicles** | | | | | |
| Police often stop them | 76 | 57 | 27 | 17 | 12 |
| Police should stop fewer | 59 | 39 | 17 | 14 | 6 |
| Police sometimes stop them without sufficient reason | 85 | 71 | 51 | 42 | 24 |
| **People on foot** | | | | | |
| Police often stop them | 26 | 22 | 14 | 8 | 5 |
| Police should stop fewer | 17 | 18 | 14 | 7 | 5 |
| Police sometimes stop them without sufficient reason | 60 | 51 | 28 | 26 | 15 |
| Base: all informants | | | | | |
| (unweighted) | 76 | 157 | 296 | 522 | 1,445 |
| (weighted) | 289 | 561 | 1,706 | 3,939 | 7,739 |

(a)    For a full definition of these categories, see the text.

We first consider the most direct connection: the one between people's views about police policy on stops and their experience of being stopped. Table IX.1 shows that there is an overwhelmingly strong relationship. People's impressions of how often the police stop people are largely based on their personal experience. Among those who have been stopped three or more times in the past year, 76 per cent think the police often stop people in vehicles, compared with 12 per cent of those who have never been stopped. People's impressions of the frequency of foot stops are also strongly related to experience, though foot stops are generally thought to be much less frequent than vehicle stops, even among those who have been stopped several times - this is because a high proportion of these actual stops were vehicle stops. These relationships are so great that it is fair to say that there is a 'great divide' among Londoners between those who are rarely stopped by the police and who are generally unaware that anyone else is, and those who are likely to be stopped and think this is a usual feature of life in London.

People's views about the policy of the police in this matter are equally strongly related to their experience. Among those who have been stopped three or more times in the past year, 59 per cent think the police should stop fewer people in vehicles, compared with six per cent of those who have never been stopped; 85 per cent of the former group compared with 24 per cent of the latter think the police sometimes stop people in vehicles without sufficient reason. Views about policy on stopping people on foot are also strongly related to experience. Furthermore, there is a nice progressive relationship between the amount of experience and the views expressed. Each further stop increases the likelihood that a critical view will be expressed. The table under-estimates the effect of being stopped when on foot, because foot stops tend to be swamped by vehicle stops. Although the numbers in the sample are too small to show it, it is likely that those who have been stopped several times when on foot are overwhelmingly critical of police policy on foot stops specifically.

We now move to consider the relationship between experience of being stopped and views on matters that are less and less directly related to stops. Table X.2 shows the findings for people's views on the fairness of police treatment of different groups. Those who have been stopped several times are more than twice as likely as those who have never been stopped to think there are groups or types of people who do not get fair treatment from the police. Those who thought there were some such groups were asked what groups they were, and answered in their own words. Among those who have been stopped several times, more than twice the propor-tion mention the ethnic minorities as among those who have never been stopped. Thus, people's general views about the fairness of the police to different groups are strongly related to their experience of being stopped, though not as strongly as their views about policy on stopping people.

Table X.2    Views on the fairness of police, by experience of being stopped

Column percentages

| | Experience of being stopped | | | | |
|---|---|---|---|---|---|
| | 3 or more stops | 2 or more stops | One stop | Not in past year | Never stopped |
| There are groups which do not get fair treatment | 51 | 56 | 41 | 34 | 22 |
| Ethnic minorities do not get fair treatment(a) | 44 | 47 | 33 | 26 | 17 |

Base: all informants

(a)    This is the proportion who, when asked 'which groups'? mentioned ethnic minorities without prompting (see Chapter IX for further information about this question).

The questions about the frequency of various kinds of police misconduct are mostly about kinds of behaviour that would not be manifested during a stop (for example, unjustifiable use of force on suspects held at police stations). As Table X.3 shows, there are nevertheless very strong relationships between people's experience of being stopped and their views on these matters. For example, 45 per cent of those who have been stopped three or more times think the police often use unjustifiable violence on people held at police stations, compared with eight per cent of those who have never been stopped, even though the experience of being stopped would not, in itself, give someone any information on this issue. On the other hand, there is no difference in people's views about the number of police officers who have accepted bribes according to their experience of being stopped. What this seems to suggest is that people's views about corruption in the force are not related to their own experience of police officers in any way (by its nature, corruption is clandestine and very few people have offered a bribe to a police officer). Their views on the other kinds of misconduct are related to their experience, in the sense that from the way a police officer behaves during a stop people form an impression of his general pattern of behaviour - if he is rude, the person may think he would beat someone up in a cell. (A substantial minority of those who have been stopped have also been arrested and therefore have experience of what happens in police stations: we shall consider this point in a later section.)

Table X.3     Views on police misconduct, by experience of being stopped

Column percentages and mean scores

| | Experience of being stopped | | | | |
| | 3 or more stops | 2 or more stops | One stop | Not in past year | Never stopped |
|---|---|---|---|---|---|
| The police often |
| Use threats etc. in questioning | 53 | 49 | 42 | 29 | 17 |
| Use excessive force on arrest | 40 | 37 | 18 | 14 | 10 |
| Use unjustifiable violence at police stations | 45 | 40 | 18 | 11 | 8 |
| Fabricate evidence | 33 | 30 | 13 | 9 | 6 |
| Many have accepted bribes | 8 | 12 | 11 | 10 | 6 |
| Mean score on frequency of seven kinds of misconduct | 12.4 | 12.3 | 9.6 | 8.8 | 5.8 |

An important conclusion from the findings shown in Table X.3 is that about half of those who have been stopped several times by the police think there is a pattern of frequent and serious misconduct by police officers. Although views of this kind are not common among the public at large, they are common among those whom the police stop and question. This means that the police will have substantial difficulty in winning the confidence and gaining the cooperation of the people they stop even though the majority are more favourably disposed towards them; and to the extent that police contacts with the public tend to be of this kind, it means that the police will gain the impression that they are misdoubted, disrespected and under attack. The mean score of the seven kinds of misconduct combined is more than twice as high among those who have been stopped several times as among those who have never been stopped.

Expressed willingness to call the police is also strongly related to experience of being stopped (see Table X.4). The questions covered five kinds of situation, and in each case informants were assigned a score of 2 if they said they would call the police, 1 if they said 'it depends' and 0 if they said they would not. This means, for example, that an informant who would call the police in four of the five situations, but not in the fifth would score 8. Among those who have never been stopped, 72 per cent score 7-10, compared with 29 per cent of those who have been stopped three or more times. How we assess these findings depends on whether we think that people's answers to the hypothetical questions (about whether they would call the police) are a good indication of their actual behaviour. If they are, then the findings suggest that active policing diminishes the opportunity for responsive policing. If this were generally true, it would mean that people are less inclined to bring in the police to the extent that the police impose themselves by using stop and search methods; the more these methods were used, the greater would be the pressure to increase their use, because the flow of information from the public would be proportionately reduced.

Table X.4    Willingness to call on and help the police, by experience of being stopped

Column percentages

|  | Experience of being stopped | | | | |
|---|---|---|---|---|---|
|  | 3 or more stops | 2 or more stops | One stop | Not in past year | Never stopped |
| Willingness to call the police Score across five questions |  |  |  |  |  |
| 0 - 4 | 49 | 35 | 13 | 9 | 10 |
| 5 - 6 | 22 | 24 | 23 | 24 | 18 |
| 7 - 10 | 29 | 41 | 64 | 67 | 72 |
| Bus shelter incident Prepared to tell police what you had seen | 61 | 70 | 86 | 86 | 81 |
| Prepared to give evidence in court | 48 | 58 | 77 | 79 | 67 |
| Theft with assault incident Prepared to give evidence in court | 77 | 82 | 90 | 91 | 79 |
| Traffic accident Prepared to give evidence in court | 91 | 92 | 93 | 96 | 98 |

On the other hand, willingness to help the police (in response to their inquiries) is less strongly related to experience of being stopped. In a sense, this is because the great majority of people are prepared to help with police inquiries anyhow, whereas decis ions about whether to call the police into various kinds of situation are more evenly balanced. However, it is an important and substantive point that most people would be prepared to give evidence in court about a theft with assault or a serious traffic accident, regardless of whether they have been stopped by the police several times. In the case of a more minor matter (the 'bus shelter incident') willingness to help the police is quite substantially affected by experience of being stopped.

Table X.5    Views on the success of the police in various respects, by experience of being stopped

Mean scores

| | Experience of being stopped | | | | |
| --- | --- | --- | --- | --- | --- |
| | 3 or more stops | 2 or more stops | One stop | Not in past year | Never stopped |
| Success of the police | | | | | |
| Combating muggings and street crimes | 1.00 | 1.06 | 1.17 | 1.16 | 1.40 |
| Combating burglaries | 1.16 | 1.12 | 1.20 | 1.20 | 1.31 |
| Combating drunk driving | 1.94 | 1.97 | 2.00 | 1.97 | 2.06 |
| Coping with marches and demonstrations | 1.89 | 2.00 | 2.12 | 2.24 | 2.23 |
| Coping with football crowds | 1.95 | 1.99 | 2.09 | 2.14 | 2.09 |
| Getting on with people | 1.41 | 1.46 | 1.85 | 1.95 | 2.14 |
| Total score | 9.35 | 9.60 | 10.43 | 10.66 | 11.23 |

The most indirect kind of relationship is the one between experience of being stopped and views on the success of the police in various respects. Table X.5 shows that, in general, these relationships are much less marked than the ones we have previously considered. However, it seems highly significant that views on the success of the police at getting on with people are more strongly related to experience of being stopped than views on the success of the police in other respects. This counts as a rather specific indication that people's encounters with police officers who have stopped them tend to lower their opinion of the ability of the police to get on with people. The mean score for success at getting on with people is 1.41 among those who have been stopped several times compared with 2.14 among those who have never been stopped.

There is only a slight relationship between whether people say they would make a complaint about police if the occasion arose and their experience of being stopped, as shown in the summary table below.

| Experience of being stopped | Per cent who would make a complaint |
|---|---|
| 3 or more times | 77 |
| 2 or more times | 79 |
| Once only | 88 |
| Not in the past year | 91 |
| Never stopped | 90 |

Thus, confidence in the complaints system is high even among those who have been stopped by the police several times.

Table X.6    Views on police misconduct (overall score) by experience of being stopped and age

| | All informants | Informants aged 15-44 | | |
|---|---|---|---|---|
| | Mean score | Mean score | (a) | (b) |
| Experience of being stopped | | | | |
| 3 or more stops | 12.4 | 13.4 | 74 | 263 |
| 2 or more stops | 12.3 | 13.0 | 151 | 520 |
| One stop | 9.6 | 10.1 | 263 | 1,340 |
| Not in past year | 8.8 | 10.0 | 402 | 2,479 |
| Never stopped | 5.8 | 7.0 | 1,012 | 3,444 |

(a)    Unweighted base
(b)    Weighted base for informants aged 15-44.

As we pointed out in the introduction to this chapter, these relationships between experience and views do not amount to proof that experience of being stopped causes people to have a more critical or hostile view of the police than they otherwise would. A plausible alternative hypothesis is that there is a third variable related both to experience and views, and the most obvious possibility here is age. As we saw in the last chapter, people's views about the police are related fairly strongly to age - younger people tend to be more critical - and it could be argued that being young causes people to be critical and causes them to be stopped, and that there is no causal link between being stopped and being critical. However, further analysis shows that while such an explanation may have some weight, it cannot go very far to explain the pattern of the findings. If we take as an example the overall score on views about the frequency of police misconduct, we find that it does not vary significantly between the age groups up to 44, but that it is substantially lower among people aged 45 and over than among younger people. We can therefore discount the effect of age differences by restricting the analysis to people aged 15-44. Table X.6 shows the mean score for people in this age group according to their experience of being stopped, and also the findings among all informants for comparison. Among people aged 15-44 there is still a very strong relationship between views on police misconduct and experience of being stopped: the score is about twice as high among those who have been stopped three or more times as among those who have never been stopped. In fact, the differences are only slightly less strong among those aged 15-44 than among all informants. This shows quite conclusively that the relationship is not just a function of age differences.

People's views of the police in some other respects are related to age in a slightly different way, and in some cases rather more of the relationship between experience and views may be connected with age differences, but in all cases most of the relationship is unconnected with age. Even to the small extent that the relationships are connected with age, this does not by any means prove that age is the critical factor. Indeed, it seems more plausible to argue that young people tend to be hostile to the police because they have often come into conflict with them.

Of course, it is open to people to argue that there are other variables, not taken account of in the survey, that 'explain' the 'apparent' relationship between being stopped and views about the police. It might be suggested, for example, that people with long hair, unconventional dress or who drive Mark II Ford Cortinas, tend to be critical of the police and to be stopped by them; or more generally that the police recognise and stop a type of person who is both likely to be engaged in criminal activities and likely to be critical of the police. Any particular explanation of this kind could, in principle, be tested from survey data, but if it failed, an unlimited number of further explanations could then be suggested. In our judgement it is likely, from the present survey findings, that there is a strong and genuine link between being stopped and being critical of the police; very laborious experimental research would be required to produce more clear-cut evidence, and it is doubtful whether this would be worthwhile.

## Arrests

It comes as no surprise to find that those who have been arrested are more critical of the police than those who have not. It is, nevertheless, worth looking to see how strong this relationship is in order to show whether being stopped has as much effect on people's perceptions of the police as being arrested. Also, it is important to know, in absolute terms, what are the views of people who have been arrested on matters, such as the use of violence on suspects held at police stations, on which they may have privileged information (and special prejudices).

For the purpose of this analysis, informants are classified into three groups: those who have been arrested in the past five years, those who have been arrested at some time but not in the past five years, and those who have never been arrested. Table X.7 shows that the overall score from the seven questions about the frequency of police misconduct is twice as high among those who have been arrested in the past five years as among those who have never been arrested. The views of those who have been arrested, but longer than five years ago, are closer to the views of those who have more recently been arrested than to the views of those who have never been arrested. If we assume that there is a genuine causal link between experience of arrest and views about police misconduct, this seems to imply that once someone has been arrested this changes his views more or less permanently.

Table X.7     Views on police misconduct, by experience of being arrested

Column percentages and mean scores

|  | | Arrested | |
|  | In past 5 years | Longer ago | Never |
| --- | --- | --- | --- |
| **The police often** | | | |
| **Use threats etc. in** | | | |
|   questioning | 57 | 43 | 22 |
| Use excessive force on arrest | 32 | 24 | 11 |
| Use unjustifiable violence at | | | |
|   police station | 40 | 20 | 10 |
| Fabricate evidence | 36 | 17 | 7 |
| Many have accepted bribes | 18 | 15 | 7 |
| Mean score on frequency of | | | |
|   seven kinds of misconduct | 13.0 | 11.2 | 6.8 |
| Base: all informants | | | |
|   (unweighted) | 137 | 97 | 2,186 |
|   (weighted) | 657 | 695 | 12,592 |

Views about two kinds of misconduct are particularly strongly related to experience of arrest: use of unjustifiable violence on people held at police stations and fabrication of evidence. Among those who have been arrested in the past five years, the proportion who think the police often behave in these ways is four to five times as high as among those who have never been arrested. The proportion of those who have been arrested in the past five years who think the police often use excessive force in making arrests, use unjustifiable violence on people held at police stations and fabricate evidence is at least one-third in each case. More than half (57 per cent) think the police often use threats and unfair pressure in questioning. On the other hand, a comparatively small proportion (18 per cent) think that many police officers have accepted bribes. This completes a pattern of findings that shows that among all groups corruption is thought to be much less pervasive in the Metropolitan Police than excessive use of force or fabrication of evidence.

The relationship between views about police misconduct and experience of arrest is about as strong as, but no stronger than, the relationship with experience of being stopped. It is difficult to express this in quantitative terms, because arrests are rarer events than stops. However, a comparison between Tables X.3 and X.7 will show that people who have been stopped three or more times in the past year hold similar views to people who have been arrested in the past five years. If we adopt a straightforward causal explanation of these relationships, this means that several stops in a year are worth one arrest in five years in terms of the effect on people's views of the police. Of course, matters are really more complex than this because there is considerable overlap between those who have been arrested and those who have been stopped, and we shall consider this point further in the next section.

Table X.8    Views on the fairness of police, by experience of being arrested

Column percentages

|  | Arrested | | |
|  | In past 5 years | Longer ago | Never |
| --- | --- | --- | --- |
| There are groups which do not get fair treatment | 47 | 34 | 28 |
| Ethnic minorities do not get fair treatment | 32 | 27 | 22 |

Views on the fairness of the police are also related to experience of arrest, but not as strongly as views on police misconduct (see Table X.8). In particular, there is only a moderate tendency for people who have been arrested to be more likely than others to think that the police are unfair to ethnic minority groups. Experience of being stopped is much more strongly associated than experience of arrest with the view that the police are unfair to the ethnic minorities, and this counts as strong evidence that it is the police stopping policy specifically that encourages people to think that they act in a racially discriminatory manner.

Table X.9    Willingness to call on and help the police, by experience of being arrested

Column percentages

|  | Arrested | | |
|  | In past 5 years | Longer ago | Never |
| --- | --- | --- | --- |
| Willingness to call the police | | | |
| Score across five questions | | | |
| 0 - 4 | 45 | 12 | 10 |
| 5 - 6 | 14 | 18 | 21 |
| 7 - 10 | 39 | 70 | 70 |
| | | | |
| Bus shelter incident | | | |
| Prepared to tell police what you had seen | 56 | 81 | 84 |
| Prepared to give evidence in court | 45 | 76 | 72 |
| | | | |
| Theft with assault incident | | | |
| Prepared to give evidence in court | 77 | 92 | 84 |
| | | | |
| Traffic accident | | | |
| Prepared to give evidence in court | 92 | 93 | 91 |

People who have been arrested in the past five years are much less willing than people who have never been arrested to call the police to a range of incidents (see Table X.9). However, it is interesting that those who have been arrested but not in the past five years are just as willing to call the police as those who have never been arrested. Whereas experience of arrest seems to have a lasting effect on views of police conduct, it does not have a lasting effect on willingness to call the police. Also, people who have been arrested fairly recently are much less willing than those who have been arrested longer ago (or never) to help the police with inquiries into a minor matter (the bus shelter incident). However, experience of arrest, like experience of being stopped, has little effect on people's willingness to help with inquiries into a theft with assault or a serious traffic accident: in fact, the great majority of those who have been arrested in the past five years would be willing to give evidence in court in each of these two cases.

Views about the success of the police in various respects are only weakly related to experience of arrest, and here the pattern of findings is much the same as for the analysis by experience of being stopped (see Table X.10). Again, the strongest relationship is shown in the case of the success of the police in getting on with people.

Table X.10    Views on the success of the police in various respects, by experience of being arrested

Mean scores

|  | Arrested | | |
|  | In past 5 years | Longer ago | Never |
| --- | --- | --- | --- |
| Success of the police | | | |
| Combating muggings and street crimes | 0.99 | 1.07 | 1.32 |
| Combating burglaries | 1.15 | 1.01 | 1.28 |
| Combating drunk driving | 1.98 | 2.00 | 2.02 |
| Coping with marches and demonstrations | 1.89 | 2.26 | 2.22 |
| Coping with football crowds | 1.93 | 2.21 | 2.10 |
| Getting on with people | 1.52 | 2.01 | 2.05 |
| Total score | 9.46 | 10.56 | 10.99 |

People who have been arrested are more likely than others to have occasion to make a serious complaint about police. Seventy-six per cent of those who have been arrested in the past five years say they would make a complaint if the occasion arose, compared with 89 per cent of those who have been arrested but longer than five years ago, and 90 per cent of those who have never been arrested. Thus, there seems to be a fairly high level of confidence in the complaints system among those who are most likely to have the need to use it.

**Arrests and stops in combination**
We have considered the relationship between people's views of the police and, first, their experience of being stopped, then their experience of being arrested. These two relationships are not

entirely distinct because some of those who have been stopped have also been arrested, and many of those who have been arrested have also been stopped. If we classify people according to their experience of being stopped and arrested in combination, we find the following pattern.

|   |   | Per cent of all informants |
|---|---|---|
| (a) | Stopped two or more times in past year and arrested in past five years | 1.1 |
|   | Stopped once only in past year and arrested in past five yeas | 0.9 |
| (b) | Total stopped in past year and arrested in past five years | 2.0 |
| (c) | Stopped in past year, not arrested in past five years | 14.2 |
| (d) | Arrested in past five years, not stopped in past year | 2.7 |
| (e) | Neither stopped in past year nor arrested in past five years | 81.1 |

It should be noted that the information on arrests covers the past five years, whereas the information on stops covers the past year. Bearing this in mind, we find that a small minority of informants (two per cent) have been both stopped and arrested, and a still smaller proportion (just over one per cent) have been stopped several times and also arrested. It is a very important finding that a very substantial proportion of people (just over 14 per cent) have been stopped but not arrested; this, of course, implies that the great bulk of people who are stopped are not 'criminals'; they have not been arrested, still less been found guilty of any offence, over a fairly lengthy recent period (five years). There is also a considerable minority of informants (just under three per cent) who have been arrested but not stopped; in fact, well over half of people who have been arrested over the past five years have not been stopped over the past year, which shows that 'being known to the police' is not an overwhelmingly important criterion determining whether or not people are stopped. In short, most people who are stopped are innocent of any offence over a lengthy period, and many of those who have committed an offence are nevertheless not stopped.

It is immediately evident from these findings that the strong tendency for those who have been stopped by the police to be critical of them is not purely a consequence of the fact that they have also been arrested, because most of them have not been arrested. We can, however, investigate this matter more thoroughly by considering the views of the police among the groups shown in the summary table above. This analysis is shown in Table

X.11. The columns in the table have been identified by letters to show how they relate to the categories shown in the summary table; the second column includes informants shown separately in the first column.

Table X.11   Views on police misconduct, by experience of being arrested and stopped in combination

Column percentages and mean scores

| | (a)<br>2+<br>stops<br>and<br>arrest | (b)<br>1+<br>stops<br>and<br>arrest | (c)<br>Stop<br>not<br>arrest | (d)<br>Arrest<br>not<br>stop | (e)<br><br><br><br>Neither |
|---|---|---|---|---|---|
| The police often<br>Use threats etc. in<br>   questioning | 76 | 64 | 40 | 52 | 20 |
| Use excessive force<br>   on arrest | 59 | 47 | 19 | 22 | 11 |
| Use unjustifiable<br>   violence at police<br>   station | 77 | 57 | 19 | 26 | 9 |
| Fabricate evidence | 58 | 45 | 14 | 31 | 7 |
| Many have accepted<br>   bribes | 17 | 16 | 10 | 20 | 7 |
| Mean score on frequency<br>   of seven kinds of<br>   misconduct | 16.6 | 14.3 | 9.7 | 12.0 | 6.6 |
| Base:  all informants<br>   (unweighted)<br>   (weighted) | 48<br>156 | 76<br>284 | 377<br>1,983 | 61<br>372 | 1,906<br>11,305 |

(a)-(e)    These letters identify the categories shown in the summary table on the previous page.

Table X.11 shows that experience of arrest and experience of being stopped each have a separate effect on people's views about police misconduct, since those who have been stopped (but not arrested) and also those who have been arrested (but not stopped) are far more critical of the police than those who have neither been stopped nor arrested. Those who have been arrested (but not stopped) are more critical than those who have been stopped (but not arrested); however, although this is not shown in the table, experience of being stopped several times (but without being arrested) has as much effect on people's views as experience of being arrested (without being stopped). These findings therefore confirm the hypothesis that experience of being stopped in itself tends strongly to make people critical of the police.

The table also shows that being stopped and being arrested have an additive effect on people's views, so that those who have both been stopped and arrested are highly critical of the police, and much more critical than those who have just been stopped or just arrested. A high proportion of people with this extensive experience of the police, as offenders and as suspects, believe that there is a pattern of frequent and serious misconduct among police officers. Of those who have been stopped two or more times and also arrested, more than three-quarters think the police often use threats and unfair pressure in questioning, and that they often use unjustifiable violence on people held at police stations; more than half think they often use excessive force on arresting people and that they often fabricate evidence. On the other hand, even among this group, the view that many police officers have accepted bribes is not a common one (it is held by 17 per cent). This again shows that there is less concern about corruption than about other kinds of misconduct, and that extensive experience of the police has comparatively little tendency to persuade people that they are corrupt. This is a key point in helping us to interpret the more general pattern of the findings. It could be argued that experience of being arrested or stopped by the police simply gives people generally negative feelings towards them so that they become likely to agree to any critical statement about them. However, the findings on views about police corruption show that this is not the case. Experience of the police leads people to make a number of specific criticisms, but not to believe that they are corrupt, and this suggests that, to a considerable extent, experience of the police actually gives people information about specific kinds of misconduct or reveals to them a pattern of behaviour that seems consistent with the idea that specific kinds of misconduct (but not others) are commonplace. In other words, because people who have been arrested and stopped do not generally maintain that the police are corrupt, we are more inclined to believe them when they say the police are violent and bullying, and fabricate evidence.

Analysis of views on other matters related to the police shows a similar pattern, according to experience of arrest and of being stopped, as the one shown in Table X.11, except that the relationships are weaker in many cases, as we saw in earlier sections of this chapter.

In Chapter VIII we showed that very few people think there are too many police in their area, while a majority think there are too few; West Indians were less inclined than white people to think there were too few police, but hardly more inclined to think there were too many, and this applied equally to those in areas of high ethnic concentration. It is interesting that even those who have been both stopped by police and arrested do not generally think

Table X.12    Views on the number of police, by experience of being arrested and stopped in combination

Column percentages

| | 2+ stops and arrest | 1+ stops and arrest | Stop not arrest | Arrest not stop | Neither |
|---|---|---|---|---|---|
| **Number of police in this area** | | | | | |
| Too many | 20 | 15 | 4 | 12 | 2 |
| Too few | 16 | 34 | 46 | 35 | 63 |
| About the right number | 63 | 47 | 46 | 53 | 34 |
| Don't know | * | 5 | 3 | 1 | 1 |

there are too many police; only 20 per cent of them take this view, while 16 per cent think there are too few police and 63 per cent that there are about the right number. Although these views vary in the usual way according to experience of being stopped and arrested, it is principally the choice between 'too few' and 'about the right number' that varies; it is a minority view among all groups that there are too many police (see Table X.12). This shows that people who have extensive experience of the police as offenders and as suspects are not, generally speaking, anarchists; they recognise the need for a police force and do not think there are too many police; they are critical of the way the police behave and not of the fact that they are active at all. This suggests that even among those with whom they most often come into conflict, the police do not meet with a uniform and determined opposition, and it leaves open a door to policies which would not necessarily reduce the amount of contact that the police have with people, for example by stopping them, but would seek to make these encounters create and reinforce a more positive view of the police, instead of creating and reinforcing antagonism, as they seem to do at present.

**Experience as a victim of crime**
We might expect that those who have been the victims of crime would be less likely to think the police successful in combating crime than those who have not. Table X.13 shows that this is, in fact, the case. People who have been several times victims of crime in the past year are distinctly less likely than those who have not to think the police are successful in combating muggings and street crime and burglaries. People's views about the success of the police in achieving objectives other than combating crime are

little, if at all, related to whether they have been victimised. In particular, there is no indication that people who have been victims of crime, and who therefore have in many cases come into contact with the police in that connection, have a different opinion from others about the ability of the police to get on with people.

Table X.13    Views on success of the police in various respects, by experience as a victim of crime

Mean scores

| | Number of times a victim in past year | | | |
| | None | One | Two | Three or more |
|---|---|---|---|---|
| **Success of the police** | | | | |
| Combating muggings and street crimes | 1.31 | 1.25 | 0.95 | 0.76 |
| Combating burglaries | 1.30 | 1.20 | 1.13 | 0.92 |
| Combating drunk driving | 2.02 | 2.01 | 1.76 | 1.97 |
| Coping with marches & demonstrations | 2.20 | 2.12 | 2.21 | 1.99 |
| Coping with football crowds | 2.05 | 2.16 | 2.24 | 1.94 |
| Getting on with people | 1.97 | 1.87 | 2.00 | 1.71 |
| Total score | 10.85 | 10.61 | 10.29 | 9.29 |
| Base[a] | | | | |
| (unweighted) | 1,005 | 235 | 80 | 41 |
| (weighted) | 3,882 | 1,161 | 438 | 253 |

(a)    The base is people aged 15-44 who have not been arrested in the past five years nor stopped by police in the past year.

Experience as a victim of crime is related to views about police misconduct in what may seem like a paradoxical way:  the more times people have been victims of crime, the more likely they are to think that serious misconduct by police officers is common.   We found in Chapter III that 52 per cent of victim incidents became known to the police; in fact a number of victims have suffered more than one incident, so the proportion of victims who have been in touch with the police about a crime committed against them is somewhat higher than 52 per cent.  On the face of it, therefore, the findings seem to imply that contact with the police as a victim leads people to believe that police misconduct occurs.  These differences, which are shown in Table X.14, are quite large.    The mean score for views about serious police

265

misconduct is 6.7 among people who have not been victims of crime in the past year, compared with 11.2 among those who have been victims of three or more incidents, and there is a nice progression in the scores according to the number of victim incidents.

It is important to look for an explanation for this startling result, other than that the police deal with victims in such a way as to cause resentment, hostility and a critical attitude. A first possibility is that the relationship is spurious because of age differences. Younger people are considerably more likely to be victims of crime than older ones (contrary to the popular misconception) and they are also more likely to be critical of the police. A second, related, possibility is that the relationship is a product of the association between being a victim and being an offender or suspect that we traced in Chapter IV. On this argument, victims tend to be critical of the police not because of their experience as victims but because they have in many cases also come into conflict with the police as offenders or suspects.

Table X.14    Views about police misconduct, by experience as a victim of crime

Mean scores

|  | Number of times a victim in past year | | | |
| --- | --- | --- | --- | --- |
|  | None | One | Two | Three or more |
| Mean score on views of frequency of seven kinds of misconduct | | | | |
| (a) Among all informants | 6.7 | 8.7 | 9.2 | 11.2 |
| (b) Among informants aged 15-44 who have not been stopped or arrested | 7.5 | 8.9 | 9.1 | 10.3 |
| Base[a] | | | | |
| (unweighted) | 1,761 | 406 | 158 | 95 |
| (weighted) | 10,132 | 2,414 | 873 | 525 |
| Base[b] | | | | |
| (unweighted) | 1,005 | 235 | 80 | 41 |
| (weighted) | 3,822 | 1,161 | 438 | 253 |

It is possible, from the survey data, to test both of these explanations simultaneously. We saw in an earlier section that views about police misconduct do not vary significantly between the age groups up to 44, so that the effect of age differences can be discounted by confining the analysis to people aged 15-44. At the same time, we can exclude people who have been arrested in the past five years and people who have been stopped by police in the past twelve months. This will discount the influence of experience of the police as offender or suspect. The second line in Table X.14 shows the scores for views about police misconduct among the remaining informants, that is among people aged 15-44 who have not been arrested or stopped. Although the differences are reduced, there is still a distinct tendency for criticism of police conduct to increase with the number of incidents of victim- isation in the past year.

The findings are therefore consistent with the hypothesis that contact with the police as a victim of crime causes people to become more critical of them. They do not, of course, prove that this is so. It is possible, for example, that there is a kind of person who both tends to become the victim of crime and tends to be critical of police conduct, and that there is no causal link between the two things. What does seem certain from the findings is that the police do not handle victims of crime in such a way as positively to enhance their reputation with them. On the face of it, this is puzzling, since we know from the direct questions about the police handling of victim incidents that people are reasonably happy and satisfied with it in most cases. Perhaps the solution to this puzzle lies in the fact that police work and police stations inevitably have their unpleasant side. People who have had very little contact with the police or none at all - who have never gone behind the counter at a police station - may have an unrealistic, romanticised picture, more often than not, of what it is like. It may be that any close contact with police work tends to give people a different, and less rosy, perspective on it, even though they are usually satisfied with the treatment that they have personally received.

People's views on other matters related to policing are, at most, weakly related to their experience as victims of crime. However, we cannot find any evidence from any of the questions that victims of crime are more favourably disposed towards the police than others.

## Contact with the police overall
Our measure of the overall level of contact with the police is the number of times the informant has talked with a police officer in the past twelve months. In Chapter VI we showed that in most of these encounters the person is offering or asking for help or information, reporting an offence, or simply having a friendly conversation; only 14 per cent of encounters involve conflict, in that the person is being treated as an offender or suspect. It would be reasonable to hope, therefore, that the more contact people have had with the police, the better-disposed they would be

towards them. Unfortunately, the opposite is the case.

Table X.15 shows that the more contacts people have had with the police, the more likely they are to be critical of police conduct. The differences are not large, and the pattern is not wholly consistent in that people who have had a very large number of contacts (10 or more in the past twelve months) are rather less critical than those who have had rather fewer (5-9). People who have close friends or relatives in the police force have been excluded from the table, since that kind of relationship seems of a different order from normal contacts between the police and the public. In practice, this exclusion makes little difference to the pattern shown.

Table X.15    <u>Views about police misconduct, by amount of contact with the police</u>

Mean scores

| | Number of talks with police officers in past 12 months | | | | | |
| --- | --- | --- | --- | --- | --- | --- |
| | None | 1 | 2 | 3-4 | 5-9 | 10 or more |
| Mean score on views of frequency of seven kinds of misconduct | 6.1 | 8.1 | 8.5 | 9.1 | 10.4 | 9.3 |
| Base[a] | | | | | | |
| (unweighted) | 1,097 | 362 | 245 | 138 | 79 | 87 |
| (weighted) | 4,999 | 2,285 | 1,376 | 883 | 604 | 558 |

(a)    The base is informants who have no close friends or relatives in the police force.

Table X.16 shows, further, that the more contacts people have had with the police the more likely they are to think that they treat some groups unfairly, and that they treat the ethnic minorities unfairly in particular.

We have deliberately abstained, in this case, from presenting further analyses to test possible explanations of the relationship shown (which is not in any case strong). There are so many different kinds of contact with the police that the task of tracing detailed patterns becomes unmanageable, and we have, in any case, already considered some of the most important kinds of contact separately.

In spite of the complexities, the general thrust of the findings presented in this chapter is clear. A majority of Londoners generally have a reasonably favourable view of the police, but those who have come into contact with them, for whatever reason, tend to be more critical. There is a strong tendency for those who have been stopped by police and for those who have been arrested to be critical, but other kinds of contact, where the person is not being treated as offender or suspect, are also associated with critical views. There is overwhelming evidence that people who have been stopped by police (the great majority of whom are not found to have committed any offence) become much more hostile to the police as a result, especially if they have been stopped repeatedly.

Table X.16   Views about the fairness of the police, by amount of contact with the police

Column percentages

| | Number of talks with police officers in past 12 months | | | | | |
| --- | --- | --- | --- | --- | --- | --- |
| | None | 1 | 2 | 3-4 | 5-9 | 10 or more |
| There are groups which do not get fair treatment | 23 | 36 | 30 | 36 | 38 | 42 |
| Ethnic minorities do not get fair treatment | 17 | 27 | 26 | 31 | 34 | 33 |

Note:   The base for this table is informants who do not have close friends or relatives in the police force. The base figures are those shown in Table X.15.

Undoubtedly, one of the underlying reasons for these relationships is that the police tend to seek out, or for other reasons to come across, people who are unsympathetic towards them, while they tend never to meet their strongest supporters. The way that the police often put this is 'We tend to become cynical, because we mostly deal with the worst sort of people, the people who don't like us'. Yet the most careful analysis suggests that this is not the whole explanation. It suggests - and finally it can do no more than suggest - that contact with the police, particularly being stopped, causes people to become much more critical of them.

Two general conclusions can be drawn. The first is that the police should be extremely cautious about adopting policies which would increase the amount of contact they have with people and extend the range of people with whom they come into contact. The hope of the advocates of 'community policing' is that if the police extend the range of their contacts and increase the number of amiable and constructive encounters, this will enhance their reputation and increase people's confidence in them.  The difficulty about this is that we cannot necessarily assume or ensure that these 'extra' encounters will be handled by police officers in a way that will enhance their reputation, and that even if they are intended to be amiable and constructive (on the part of the police officers) they will not necessarily be perceived in that way by the members of the public concerned.  Even allowing for efforts to improve the quality of encounters, it would be a brave person who would assert, from the findings of this study, that an increase in the number of encounters between the police and the public would improve the quality of police/public relations.  This is not just because of the way that the police behave towards people. People's feelings about meeting police officers are bound to be, at best, ambiguous, because they can, in certain circumstances, pose a threat.  There is a natural (perhaps healthy) feeling that one should keep well clear of undertakers, pathologists, brain surgeons, prison walls and police stations.  Children used to touch wood when they saw a Black Maria.

Secondly, the findings strongly suggest that there is an urgent need for the police to use the many purposeful encounters that they do have with people in a more positive way.  Let us accept that people are bound to have inhibitions and fears about being aproached by a police officer - fears that make it difficult for the officer to send them away thinking that the police are doing a good and necessary job:  difficult, but not, perhaps, impossible in the majority of cases.  In later chapters we shall show that what makes it impossible, in current circumstances, is that in the structure of the police force and in the mentality of police officers the different objectives of policing are put into separate compartments.  A police officer making a stop is trying to detect an offence, and if he fails to detect one he is disappointed and afraid that he is being taken for a ride.  The most that he will do is try to minimise any bad feeling the stop may have caused.  The idea that the stop is an opportunity to increase someone's regard for the police force, to engage in conversation about football, or to see if he can be of help to someone who turns out not to be an offender, would not occur to him.  That is the job of another department; or it is the sort of thing he does on another kind of occasion - when he is visiting a local youth club or organising a five-a-side football competition.

But the final word on these findings must draw attention to the views about police misconduct of people with extensive experience as offenders and suspects.  A majority of these people think the police in London are frequently bullying, violent and lying. Here it is hard to escape from the circular argument of the 'Not the Nine O'Clock News' sketch:

'He says you've invented these charges against him'.
'But, Sir, he's a criminal'.

'I know he's a criminal, he's down in the cells at the moment!'

It is not surprising that offenders and (as it were) persistent suspects tend to be critical of the police. Their opinions are not unprejudiced. However, their criticisms are so serious and so frequently expressed that this must give cause for concern.

# XI SUMMARY OF FINDINGS FROM THE SURVEY OF LONDONERS

This survey of Londoners provides a description of police/public relations from the perspective of members of the public. It describes the encounters that people have had with the police as offenders or suspects, as victims of crime and as people seeking information and advice or a casual conversation; it inquires into Londoners' attitudes to crime and their views about policing and the conduct of police officers; and it analyses the relationship between these experiences and these views.

Different perspectives on these issues were provided by the three further projects in this series: the study, by the method of participant observation, of a group of young black people living in a hostel; the survey of police officers; and the study of policing by direct observation, and of the organisational setting in which police officers work. It is only in the final chapter that we shall be able to arrive at a balanced view of the issues involved. At that point, by drawing together the evidence from all four inquiries, we shall be able to consider whether there is a need for changes in policing policy and practice and, if so, how such changes could be brought about. At this point we shall summarise the conclusions from the survey of Londoners alone.

## Attitudes to crime

There is strong evidence that people attach a high importance to safety on the streets, in that their general feelings about the place where they live are closely bound up with how safe they think it is. At the same time, there is a large body of opinion among Londoners generally, and among women in particular, that the streets of London are unsafe at night. Although there are some differences between inner and outer London and between boroughs with high and low levels of social stress, these fears about the safety of the streets are, broadly speaking, common to people living in all types of area.

Very few people think that any kind of crime is becoming less common, though a considerable proportion think that some kinds of

272

crime are continuing at the same level; but a majority believe that street robberies, burglary and vandalism are becoming more common. Analysis of two kinds of question - one about changes in the level of crime in London as a whole, the other about the level of crime in the local area compared with the rest of London - suggests that what people see and hear about in the local area does have an important influence on their more general views. The objective characteristics of the locality in which people live are quite strongly related to their perceptions of the prevalence of crime in the area. However, a large component of people's views is unrelated to local knowledge, and though people are ready to believe that crime is rising in London as a whole, they are much more reluctant to think that their own locality is seriously affected. These findings suggest that people are influenced by the mass media as much as by local experience and knowledge.

There is clear evidence that, among white people, fears about the safety of the streets and the belief that crime is prevalent in the locality are closely linked with a perception of the ethnic minorities as a threat. People in areas of high ethnic concentration are twice as likely as those in areas of low concentration to think the streets are unsafe for lone women at night, and nearly three times as likely to think that certain kinds of crime (street robberies in particular) are prevalent in the locality. The survey also shows that actual rates of victimisation are the same in areas of high and low ethnic concentration, except in the case of theft from the person (seldom involving violence) which is, indeed, much more common in areas of high ethnic concentration than elsewhere. Also, theft from the person is shown to be not a uniquely damaging or disturbing kind of crime. Therefore, the perception of the ethnic minorities as a threat is based only partially on fact. The prevalence of thefts from the person in areas of high ethnic concentration and the publicity given to these crimes, which falsely represents them as usually involving violence, has combined with more deep-seated and vaguer anxieties to make people feel that black people are a threat; though the factual origin relates to thefts from the person, the end product of the psychological process is that people unconsciously associate all kinds of crime - even drunk driving - with the presence of ethnic minorities. People nevertheless hesitate to make this fear explicit. Less than one-fifth of Londoners say that ethnic minorities are mainly responsible for street robberies (identified as 'mugging'), and the proportion who consciously and explicitly blame ethnic minorities for other crimes ranges from virtually nil to four per cent.

The fieldwork took place soon after the major riots of 1981: even at that time, Londoners were more concerned about street robberies, burglaries and vandalism than about riots and other disturbances.

Asians' views about the safety of the streets and the prevalence of crime are similar to those of white people. West Indians also hold generally similar views to white people; they place still more emphasis than white people on the increase in street robberies, the kind of crime with which their own group is particularly associated, and they are more likely to think that all kinds of crime are relatively common in their own locality. However, West Indians are less likely than white people to feel unsafe on the streets at night, possibly because a part of the fear of white people is a response to what they perceive as a threat by black people, which black people themselves do not share. Unlike white people, Asians and West Indians are no more likely to think that crime is prevalent if they live in areas of high ethnic concentration; they do not regard themselves, or members of other minority groups, as a threat.

## Priorities in fighting crime

There is no obvious conflict between the choice that Londoners make of the crimes it is most important for the police to combat and the actual priorities of the police force. Asians and West Indians are about twice as likely as white people to attach a high priority to combating racialist attacks. Nevertheless, there is a strong body of opinion among white people, too, that action against these attacks should be given a high priority. Londoners attach a very low priority to combating illegal betting and gaming, prostitution and the sale of pornography; it may be that there is little public support for the limited action that the police take in these fields, though, strictly speaking, the survey findings do not show that Londoners want the police to do nothing about these things.

There is a conflict of opinion about what action the police should take against the use of cannabis. A significant minority think they should make this a high priority, but three times as many think they should make it a low priority. This conflict of opinion is important, because a considerable amount of active policing, using stop and search methods, is (at least ostensibly) directed at catching people in possession of cannabis. The survey shows that a considerable proportion of Londoners think this kind of police activity is inappropriate, while a significant minority strongly support it. This difference of opinion is not primarily a division between ethnic groups. Although Rastafarians consider that smoking cannabis is a virtue, the proportion of West Indians generally who think that action against cannabis should be given a low priority is only slightly higher than for other ethnic groups. Differences between age groups are far more important (older people are more often opposed to cannabis than younger people) and class differences are notable (the working class are more opposed to cannabis than the middle class).

## Experience as a victim of crime

Crime is not something that affects only a tiny minority of Londoners: in fact, 27 per cent say they have been the victims of some kind of crime (or something they think might have been a crime) in the past twelve months. Groups that have a higher than average chance of being victims are men, young people and those in the higher socio-economic groups (particularly in the case of property crimes). These findings show that, contrary to popular stereotypes, it is the able-bodied, aggressive and richer people who are most likely to be victims. Because much crime is against property, the more property people have the more likely they are to be victims. In the case of crimes against the person, young men are likely to be the victims because they are likely to put themselves into situations where a fight may occur. The myth that it is mostly old people who are the victims of thefts from the person has already been exploded by other studies; our survey again shows that younger people are far more likely than older people to be the victims of this kind of crime. An exception to the rule that it is the strong rather than the weak who tend to be the victims of crime is that the unemployed are considerably more likely than those in full-time work to be victims of burglary, theft from the person and physical attack.

The rate of victimisation is lower among Asians than among other ethnic groups. While there is no difference overall, within certain age groups West Indians are less likely to be victims of crime than white people. Theft from the person is often described as a crime committed by young West Indians on white people, but in fact West Indians are more at risk than whites. This is not surprising, since this kind of crime is particularly common in the areas where West Indians live. Except in the case of theft from the person, rates of victimisation do not vary according to local ethnic concentration. They are, however, considerably higher in inner than in outer London.

From a detailed description of the actual incidents we find that very few of the thefts from the person involved an assault, and very few of the assaults also involved a theft from the person. The proportion of all victim incidents that are 'muggings' properly speaking (that is, theft with assault) is extremely low (1 in 200), which shows that the popular identification of rising crime with 'mugging' is totally unjustified. Londoners who claim that they have been robbed and attacked in the past twelve months account for an estimated 1.4 per thousand of the adult population.

From the detailed descriptions, most of the victim incidents were of a minor nature. Few of the personal offences resulted in the victim having medical treatment, and in only three out of one thousand cases did they result in the victim staying in hospital overnight. The median value of the loss in the case of property offences was £44 though in about one-quarter of cases the loss was of £200 or more.

For one-third of incidents, the victim could describe the race or ethnic group of the offender, who was described as 'black' in 24 per cent of these cases. The proportion of the London population who 'look black' (as opposed to Asian) is about six or seven per cent, so it is clear that black people are represented far more strongly among the offenders described by victims than they are among the population of London generally. Part of the reason for this is that West Indians tend to be concentrated within the age and socio-economic groups in which the crime rate is relatively high. A different reason for caution is that West Indians may tend to commit kinds of crime - thefts from the person are an obvious example - that give the victim a good chance of being able to come up with a description; also, if people associate crime with black people they may tend to say that the offender was black when they weren't sure. For these reasons it would be making a very large leap to say, from our findings, that the crime rate is several times higher among West Indians than among whites. However, these findings do show that in one-quarter of cases where victims can describe the offender, they say the offender was black. What victims say about their experiences will, therefore, tend to create or reinforce the impression among the public at large and the police in particular that a relatively high proportion of crimes are committed by black people. In the case of theft from the person the proportion of offenders who are said to be black is strikingly high (46 per cent), while it varies between 10 and 25 per cent for the other types of offence. It is clear that black people are much more likely to commit theft from the person than members of other ethnic groups, and that this kind of offence forms a much higher proportion of crimes committed by black people than of those committed by other groups.

Overall, 52 per cent of victim incidents became known to the police, and this proportion does not vary according to the ethnic group of the victim. This shows that while Asians and West Indians may, in some respects, have less confidence in the police than other groups, they are just as likely to call on the police for help when they require it. The proportion of incidents that became known to the police varies a good deal according to the seriousness of the offence (as measured by the value of the loss or the extent of personal injury), and also according to the type of offence. Thefts from the person are much less likely to be reported than some other types of offence (theft of motor vehicle and burglary) and only one type of offence is substantially less likely to be reported than theft from the person (damage to motor vehicle). This shows that theft from the person is not a uniquely damaging or disturbing kind of offence.

Where victims had spoken to a police officer about the offence, they were happy with the way they were spoken to in the great majority of cases (90 per cent). They also expressed a high level of satisfaction overall with the way the police officers dealt with the matter. Asians and West Indians were rather less likely to be satisfied with the performance of the police than white people, but the difference is not large; surprisingly, the level of satisfaction is lower among Asians than among West Indians. As regards their willingness to make use of the police and their assessment of the service they receive, as victims in particular instances, there is no crisis of confidence in the police among the ethnic minorities.

276

In one third of cases that came to police notice, the informant says the police took some action; in this rather small number of cases, the balance of opinion about the action taken is broadly approving. However, in only 13 per cent of cases that came to police notice does the informant know that the offender was caught. According to the victim's account of the matter, where the victim was a West Indian, the police were more likely to take some action, to make a full investigation, to move quickly and to catch the offender, than where the victim was white or Asian. The police may make special efforts on behalf of West Indian victims because they are more difficult to fob off (there is evidence that they are more often dissatisfied); also, the police may be conscious of criticism by West Indians as a group, and concerned about the general quality of relations with them.

In many cases it is not necessary for the police to carry out a full investigation or to catch the offender in order to make the victim feel that the matter has been properly dealt with. Older victims are more likely than younger ones to be satisfied with the police's handling of the matter, even though the police are less likely to take any action or to catch the offender in cases involving older victims.

A remarkably high proportion of people - 11 per cent - said they had made a 999 call to the police in the past 12 months. Calls for assistance account for only 21 per cent of cases, but it was in only half of these cases (or 10 per cent of the total) that it was entirely clear that the informant was bothered or at risk. Among those who had made a 999 call, the great majority were satisfied with the way the police treated the call on the last occasion, though Asians and West Indians were distinctly less likely than whites to have been satisfied.

## Experiences of being stopped by the police
Two kinds of question can be asked about police practice in London in stopping, questioning and searching people in vehicles and on foot. The first is whether, and if so how often, the police exceed their formal powers in making stops. The second is what is the balance between the benefits of the practice in terms of the prevention and detection of crime and the ill effects in terms of a worsening of the relationship of the police with the people stopped. The discussion of actual police practice in comparison with their formal powers will be taken up in the fourth volume of this series, when the results of our observational work have been presented; the survey data are relevant to this discussion, but are not enough, on their own, to form a basis for a proper analysis of the issue. The question of the balance between the costs and benefits of current practice can be discussed on the basis of the survey findings, which show what proportion of people are stopped by the police, what kinds of people are stopped, what proportion of stops lead to the detection of an offence and what the people concerned think about the experience of being stopped in particular instances.

A substantial minority of the population (16 per cent) have been stopped by the police one or more times in the past twelve months. Three-quarters of stops are of people in vehicles and one-quarter of people on foot. People who are stopped repeatedly are a small proportion of the whole population, but account for a substantial proportion of all stops: for example, those who have been stopped four or more times are one per cent of the population, seven per cent of those who have been stopped at all, and account for 30 per cent of stops.

However, these figures based on the whole adult population create a misleading impression, because certain population groups are far more likely to be stopped by police than others. Within certain groups, the chance of being stopped in a twelve-month period is well over 50 per cent, and a high proportion of these groups have been stopped several times in that period. There are three demographic characteristics that are strongly related to the likelihood of being stopped: age, sex and ethnic group. Young people, men and West Indians are far more likely to be stopped than others, and young West Indian males are much more likely to be stopped than any other group. The differences shown are enormous. For example, the proportion stopped in the past twelve months varies between young and old people by a factor of 11 to 1, and the mean number of stops per person by a factor of 30 to 1. The difference between men and women is of the order of 2 to 1 in terms of the proportion stopped and 3 to 1 in terms of the mean number of stops. In terms of the proportions stopped, the difference between West Indians and white people is not very striking (24 per cent for West Indians, 17 per cent for white people); but the mean number of stops is nearly three times as high among West Indians as among white people, because West Indians who are stopped at all tend to be stopped repeatedly. Also, the proportion of people who have stopped when on foot is nearly four times as high for West Indians as for white people. Asians are much less likely to be stopped than white people (or, of course, West Indians).

Age, sex and ethnic group in combination have an overwhelming effect on the likelihood of being stopped. Taking the two extreme groups, we find that 63 per cent of West Indian men aged 15-24 have been stopped, compared with none of the Asian women aged 45 or over in the survey. Age is a more important factor than the ethnic group, but differences between the ethnic groups remain when the comparison is restricted to men or women within a particular age group. Among men aged 15-24, the proportion stopped is 63 per cent for West Indians, 44 per cent for whites and 18 per cent for Asians. Those young West Indian males who have been stopped at all over the past twelve months have been stopped four times on average, compared with $2\frac{1}{2}$ times for the whites. Naturally, those who own or have the use of a vehicle are more likely to be stopped when in a vehicle than others, and the frequencies therefore become still higher if this factor is also taken into account.

The findings suggest that unemployed men are, to some extent, a recognisable type that tends to attract police suspicion: they are six times as likely to be stopped when on foot as those who have a job. Also, men in the professional and managerial group are much less likely to be stopped when on foot than men in the other socio-economic groups.

Detailed questions were asked about the occasions on which the informant was stopped in the past twelve months, up to a maximum of three. In nearly three-quarters of cases, the person stopped says he did not do anything in particular that might have caused the police to stop him. Police officers are often said to have given an explanation, but in one-fifth of cases the person says that no explanation at all was given, and, in addition, some of the explanations quoted were unsatisfactory (for example, 'just a routine check'). In the case of foot stops, a distinctly higher proportion of West Indians than of white people think they were left without a reason for being stopped; there is a similar, but smaller, difference in the case of vehicle stops.

In about three-quarters of incidents the person concerned thinks the police behaved in a polite, fair and reasonable manner, but the proportion of cases in which the police are thought to have had a good reason for making the stop is lower (59 per cent). When police officers give an explanation for the stop, this does seem to help; informants who say that a reason was given are more inclined to think that there was, in fact, a good reason. Younger people are more likely to be unhappy about the incident than older people, and West Indians are distinctly more likely to be unhappy than other groups.

It might be expected that Asians and West Indians in areas of high ethnic concentration would be more likely to be stopped and to be unhappy about it than those in areas of low concentration. However, this is not so. There is no variation in the likelihood of being stopped according to the local ethnic concentration (of course, not all of the stops will have happened when people were in their own neighbourhood). More important, West Indians in areas of high ethnic concentration are more likely than those elsewhere to say that a reason was given for the stop and that they were happy about the way it was handled. If there are more problems caused by stops in places like Brixton than in places like Wimbledon, this is because there are more black people there, and not because the police handle the incidents less well or because black people there respond in a more hostile manner.

Three per cent of stops led to the person being arrested and charged with an offence, five per cent to an offence being reported, and in one per cent of cases the person was arrested but not charged then or subsequently with an offence. This means that the total strike rate - the proportion of stops that lead to the detection of an offence - is about one out of 12.

These findings show that a high proportion of certain population groups in London are stopped by the police, many of them repeatedly, and that the great majority of them are 'innocent persons'. The question of whether the police are exceeding their powers in making these stops is a complex one; it depends, in many cases, on whether they 'reasonably suspect' that the person has committed an offence, which cannot be resolved from the survey findings alone but in any case, we regard the balance of costs and benefits attaching to this policy as a more important issue than the relation between the practice and formal powers. On the one hand, our findings show that the stops made in London (amounting to well over a million a year) result in the detection of a very substantial number of offences - perhaps more than 100,000 a year. Even if the police are exceeding their formal powers, it is difficult to argue that a method that leads to the detection of so many offences should be abandoned. On the other hand, since most people who are stopped are innocent, it is clear that current practice runs the serious risk of 'causing offence to innocent persons' (in the words of the Metropolitan Police Instruction Book). In a substantial minority of cases, people are unhappy about the way the police handle the incident; but perhaps more important, the more intelligently the police use their discretion, the more they come to concentrate on certain specific groups, a high proportion of which are stopped and stopped repeatedly. Even if these people have no objections to the way a particular stop is handled, they will come to object to being stopped at all, bearing in mind that most of them are innocent. Indeed, the survey shows that people who have been stopped, and especially those who have been stopped repeatedly, tend to have a much poorer opinion of the police than others: and this is in spite of the fact that they were usually happy with the way in which particular stops were handled.

**Arrests**
As many as one out of five men, but only one out of 50 women, say they have ever been arrested. One out of ten men say they have been arrested within the past five years. Thus, a very substantial minority of men have the opportunity to form an opinion of the police based on direct experience of being arrested and taken to a police station. Young people are, of course, much more likely than older people to have been arrested recently. A higher proportion of young West Indians than of young white people have been arrested in the past five years, but there is no difference of this kind for older people; there are sharp generational differences among West Indians, and it is only the younger generation who are more often in trouble with the police than other ethnic groups. Among all age groups, the proportion of Asians who have been arrested is much lower than the proportion of white people.

The sample contains 137 people who say they have been arrested during the past five years. These people were asked detailed questions about each of the occasions on which they were arrested during that period, up to a maximum of three, and in practice 169 incidents of arrest were covered. The questions studiously avoided encouraging people to criticise or to refrain from criticising the police. Nevertheless, the accounts that people give of their arrests cannot be regarded as objective statements about what actually happened; they are accounts of how the person says he saw it.

Informants answered some of the questions in their own words, but at other questions chose one of a number of specified answers. A statistical analysis of the pre-coded questions shows that in 47 per cent of cases people thought the police were behaving unreasonably in arresting them; in 59 per cent of cases, people had criticisms to make of the way the police behaved towards them; in 26 per cent of cases they thought a police officer said something rude or insulting to them; in 22 per cent of cases they said that police officers used force or hit them, in 18 per cent of cases unjustifiably in the person's opinion; in 20 per cent of cases people thought the police threatened them or put unfair pressure on them in some other way; and in 47 per cent of cases people thought they were treated unfairly overall in connection with the arrest.

It is possible to make a comparison between cases involving West Indians and white people, though the number of cases involving Asians is too small for separate analysis. Although the number of cases involved is rather small, the findings do definitely show that West Indians are no more likely than white people to think they were badly treated by the police in connection with an arrest; if anything, the answers given by the West Indians are more favourable to the police. At the same time, we find that West Indians as a whole are far more critical of the police, in general terms, than white people. It is, of course, possible that the actual treatment of West Indians and white people who have been arrested is different, but that West Indians evaluate their treatment more favourably because they had expected it to be worse than it actually was. Even if that is so, the findings still show that West Indians are more critical of the police than white people not because of the way they feel they are treated on specific occasions when arrested, but for some other reason. This does not mean that their critical views are detached from real experience; a higher proportion of West Indians than of other groups have been stopped by police and arrested, and this may be an important factor.

The accounts that informants give in their own words of the circumstances of their arrest and their treatment by the police give a much fuller picture than the statistics. If is of central importance to the interpretation that in about one-half of cases the person freely admits that he had committed an offence: it is common for people to say they were drunk, brawling, damaging property, committing burglaries, etc. This shows that the answers given are not purely exercises in self-justification, and therefore suggests that some of the allegations made against the police should be taken seriously. It is impossible to summarise the accounts that people give, but it is clear that a substantial proportion of people who have been arrested make very specific allegations against the police, ones involving gross misconduct in many cases. When such allegations are formally investigated, as part of the complaints procedure, by the police themselves, a very small proportion are substantiated. We do not believe that the survey findings can be dismissed for this reason, but a discussion of this issue must be postponed until we have presented the findings from our observational work in the fourth volume of this series.

## Motoring offences

Motoring incidents are a common occasion of contact between the police and Londoners. Nearly half of the men who own or have the use of a vehicle said they had ever been reported for a motoring offence, and seven per cent said they had been reported in the past twelve months. The proportion of women who have been reported is very much lower. When asked about the last occasion within the past twelve months on which they were reported, about three-quarters of the people involved said the police dealt with this matter in a fair and reasonable manner.

## The link between victims, offenders and suspects

Like some previous studies, the survey finds that victims and offenders tend strongly to be the same people. For example, people who have repeatedly been the victims of crime in the past year are at least twice as likely to have been arrested in the past five years as people who have not been repeatedly the victims of crime. It is particularly interesting that people who have only once been the victims of crime during the past year are no more likely to have been arrested than others. These findings powerfully suggest that while everyone has a certain chance of being the victim of crime, there is a group of people who have a much higher than average chance of being victims, and these people also have a much higher than average chance of being arrested.

There is an even stronger relationship between being a victim and being stopped by police (and therefore suspected of an offence). It is people who are repeatedly stopped who are most likely to be also victims. For example, among people who have been stopped by the police twice or more in the past year, 59 per cent have also been victims of some offence, and the mean number of cases of victimisation is 1.21; whereas among people who have not come to police notice for any offence or suspected offence, only 18 per cent have been victims, and the mean number of incidents of victimisation is 0.30.

One type of explanation of this pattern would be in terms of a kind of person and style of life that is associated both with offending and with being a victim. According to this argument, some people are inadequate or accident-prone, have a style of life that is disorganised and uncontrolled, and tend to associate with others who live in the same kind of way. Within this 'sub-culture', criminality, mostly of a minor kind, is common, so that members of the group tend to be both offenders and victims. This could be elaborated into an account of crime as an aspect of social dislocation among certain rather specific groups, or of what has been called 'anomie' in sociological writings.

However, what would be left out of an explanation of this kind would be the role of the police. It is significant that there is a stronger relationship between being a victim and being a suspect than between being a victim and being an offender. This suggests that the police tend to concentrate their attention on a limited 'clientele'. Those singled out for police attention will be people already known to the police, and others who police officers think resemble those who are known to them, and their associates. In more concrete terms, police officers may tend to stop people whom they know or vaguely recognise, and people who strike them as unconventional, living at the margins of society, not 'decent'; in doing so, they may tend to pick out victims as much as suspects.

It is relevant that unemployed men are very likely to be stopped and arrested. Probably a considerable proportion of the unemployed belong to the group of people living unconventional or disorganised lives that we have referred to.

These findings help to explain the tendency among many police officers (described and discussed in Volume IV) to think that many of the people with whom they come into contact are not respectable or worthy of respect. At the same time, this way of thinking obviously carries with it serious dangers. The definition of the group of the non-respectable may be more a reflection of police thinking than of social facts, so that, for example, some people are repeatedly stopped not only for no good reason, but for no real reason at all. We shall return to this issue when discussing the results of our observational work.

### Experience of crowd trouble
Public disturbances over the past few years, including the riots of 1981, were directly observed by only a small proportion of the population of London. Thirteen per cent of informants had observed some kind of public disturbance over the past two years, and eight per cent over the past six months (the period in which the riots took place). However, in most cases, the disturbances observed were not the riots; the kind most commonly observed was disturbances at sporting events. Probably two per cent and certainly no more than five per cent of Londoners directly observed any of the riots of 1981.

Among those who have witnessed public disturbances, a substantial minority of white people but a majority of West Indians have criticisms to make of the action taken by the police. People who observe public disturbances often see the police using force, usually justifiably in the opinion of white people but unjustifiably in the opinion of West Indians, with Asians taking an intermediate view. While it is a small proportion of all Londoners who have seen the police use force in a way that, to them, was not justifiable, what they saw may have made a deep impression on these witnesses, who have probably described it to many other people. Among West Indians particularly, and to a lesser extent among Asians, this will have created or reinforced a hostile attitude towards the police. Against this, the findings show that a substantial majority of all those who have seen public disturbances are generally happy with the way the police acted on the last occasion.

**Visits to police stations**
In more than 80 per cent of cases where people visit police stations the visit is, broadly speaking, voluntary: they make the visit to report offences or other matters, such as accidents (45 per cent), to report losing or finding property or to recover property (18 per cent), or to seek information or advice, to apply for a firearms license, etc. (21 per cent). Only 16 per cent of visits are to do with offences by the informant or the informant's child.

There is a very large amount of contact with the police of this, largely voluntary, kind. Just over one-quarter of Londoners say they have been to a police station in the past twelve months, and 10 per cent have made more than one such visit. The findings imply that about $1\frac{1}{2}$ million adult Londoners have visited a police station in a twelve-month period. Members of ethnic minority groups are markedly less likely to visit police stations than white people, which means that they are less inclined to make use of the police as a service. The difference is striking, particularly in the case of Asians, who are exactly half as likely as white people to have visited a police station in the past twelve months. This is not a consequence of the kinds of area in which the ethnic minorities live, for the pattern of visits is much the same among people living in all kinds of area.

**Overall pattern of contact with the police**
The police come into contact with a large proportion of the population; they therefore have a large opportunity to have a direct influence on what Londoners think of them by the way they behave in these encounters. It is not the case that most people form their impressions of the police entirely from hearsay, myth and rumour and the mass media, though of course the impressions that people get from their mostly mundane encounters with police officers may to some extent tend to fade into insignificance beside the more colourful and dramatic impressions they get in other ways.

Just over half of Londoners say they have talked with a police officer for some reason or other (including those already discussed) in the past twelve months. One-third have had one or two encounters, 11 per cent had had three to five, and 12 per cent six or more. Overall, the ethnic minorities have substantially less contact with the police than white people, Asians about half as much and West Indians about two-thirds. Women have distinctly less contact with the police than men, and Asian women have very little contact with them indeed. The age band within which there is the highest level of contact is 20-44. There are no variations between people in different types of geographical area.

We can show what proportion of all encounters with the police are of different types by taking the last encounter as representative, forgetting whether it arose from a visit to a police station, a talk in the street, a 999 call, a stop by police, etc. We find that only 14 per cent of all encounters were connected with an offence or suspected offence by the informant or the informant's child; the great majority of encounters are, therefore, of a broadly 'positive' kind. One-fifth are purely social. Asians have little contact with the police, and the contact they do have often involves a relatively serious matter, but involves conflict in only 12 per cent of cases (about the same as for white people). West Indians also have relatively little contact with the police, though more than Asians; the proportion of their contacts that are 'negative' is twice as high as for white people (28 per cent compared with 14 per cent). Thus, police contact is much more likely to involve conflict in the case of West Indians than in the case of other groups, but even so, amiable encounters between the police and West Indians are more common than 'negative' ones.

This contrast becomes stronger if the comparison is restricted to men. Nearly half of encounters between the police and West Indian men are 'negative', compared with 18 per cent for white men. Police encounters with young people tend strongly to be 'negative', and a very high proportion of encounters with young West Indian men (63 per cent for West Indian men aged 15-24, compared with 35 per cent for white men in the same age group) involve the person being treated as a suspect or offender. These findings are extremely important in helping to explain the critical view of the police among young people generally, and young West Indians in particular.

**Willingness to call on and help the police**
Informants were asked whether they would call the police in each of five specified situations, and whether they would help the police, if asked, with inquiries into each of three kinds of incident. The answers will partly reflect attitudes to the police, to crime and to danger, but they will also give some indication of how the person actually would behave.

Except in the case of domestic disputes, between two-thirds and three-quarters of people are willing to call the police to a range of situations, including some where it is not certain that a crime is being committed. Young people and West Indians are less willing to call the police than others: while these differences are not very striking, in combination the two variables do have a substantial effect, so that young West Indians are considerably less willing to call the police than older white people. In these imaginary situations, the informant himself was not at risk or the victim of a crime, so the questions test people's willingness to take the initiative on behalf of others. We find that where they are the victims of crime West Indians report the matter to the police in the same proportion of cases as white people, but they seem less inclined than white people to call on the police where they are not themselves threatened.

The findings show that where Asians and West Indians are living close to other members of their own group, they become more willing to call the police to an incident. This may be because the presence of other members of their own group gives them a greater feeling of confidence, and also because they then visualise the loser as a member of their own group, whom they would be more inclined to help than a white person. This is another indication that the relationship of the police with members of minority groups is likely to be better in areas of high concentration than elsewhere.

Informants were asked if they would help the police with inquiries into three imaginary incidents they had seen: youths smashing up a bus shelter, youths knocking a man down and taking his wallet, and a traffic accident in which someone was seriously hurt. The incidents differ in how serious they seem and in whether the informant would expect the offenders to be black (though no direct clue to the ethnic group of the offenders was given). In each case, people were asked whether they would be prepared to tell the police what they had seen, to identify the culprits and to appear in court to give evidence. In all three situations, the great majority of people would be prepared to tell the police what they had seen. There are successively smaller proportions who would be prepared to help identify the culprits and to give evidence in court, but still the proportion who would be prepared to appear in court ranges from 70 to 90 per cent depending on the situation.

Asians and white people give similar answers, but West Indians are distinctly less willing to help the police than other groups. It is quite clear that unwillingness to help among West Indians does not arise primarily because the offender may be black, or primarily because of fear of reprisals, and that there is no fixed reluctance among West Indians to appear in court. They seem to be more reluctant to help simply because they tend to be more antipathetic or hostile to the police than other groups.

Young people are more reluctant to help than those in the middle age range up to 59, probably because some of them identify with the offenders and because they tend to be hostile to the police. People aged 60 and over are also more reluctant to help than middle-aged people, probably because of the worry and bother involved and because they may fear reprisals. Young West Indians show much more reluctance to help the police than young white people, except in the case of the traffic accident, where the difference is fairly small. In the other two situations, the proportion of young West Indians who would be prepared to appear

286

in court is definitely low: 27 per cent for the bus shelter incident and 46 per cent for the street robbery. From the difference between these two percentages it is very unlikely that their reluctance to help springs from the expectation that the offenders would be black.

### Ethnic minorities in the police force
At the time when the survey was carried out there were about 120 officers in the Metropolitan Police belonging to ethnic minority groups, or 0.5 per cent of the strength. The Force has not followed a policy of posting black or brown officers to areas where a relatively high proportion of the population is black or brown, and the current distribution of minority group officers across districts shows an even pattern with apparently random variations.

The survey shows that a fairly small proportion of Londoners have noticed black or brown police officers in their area. For psychological reasons, West Indians and to a lesser extent Asians are much more likely to notice them than white people. They are also more noticed in areas of high ethnic concentration, although there are, in fact, no more black or brown police officers in such areas than elsewhere.

Just over half of Londoners think that more black and brown police officers would make no difference to police performance, and just over one-third think it would lead to an improvement; very few think that an increase in their numbers would have a bad effect. There is little difference between the views of white people, Asians and West Indians on this issue. These findings strongly suggest that the drive to recruit more police officers from the minority groups is soundly based. Since the minorities are greatly under-represented in the Force, there are strong reasons, in principle, for increasing the numbers, and the survey findings show that there is little public resistance to such a policy and a considerable body of public support for it. Furthermore, since there is no difference of opinion between ethnic groups on the issue, there is no reason to think that the policy will highlight or exacerbate a conflict of views between members of different ethnic groups. We also find that there is a considerable pool of potential applicants among the minority groups: although the proportion who have considered joining the police is lower among Asians and West Indians than among white people, it is still substantial.

### Number and deployment of police
The typical number of uniform police officers patrolling at any one time in a police division is about ten for a population of about 90,000 on average. In that context, it is perhaps not surprising that there is virtually no support for the view that the police presence, from day to day, is oppressively high, though there is some support for the view that it is sometimes too high at certain special events. In fact, there would be wide support for an increase in the numbers

of police patrolling in uniform. There are sharp differences in the views expressed by different age and ethnic groups: older people and white people are more likely than others to call for an increase in the number of police, and young West Indians are the people least likely to share this view. Although these differences are very marked, still only one-quarter of young West Indians think there are too many police in the area, and a much smaller proportion of young Asians hold this view. Although the actual number of police patrolling varies quite sharply between types of area, people's views do not vary accordingly: they seem to be based on general attitudes rather than observation of the level of policing locally. Although West Indians in areas of high concentration are more inclined than those elsewhere to think there are too many police in the area, this is still the view of less than one-fifth of West Indians in all types of area.

A majority of Londoners generally think that the police patrol mainly in vehicles and would like them to patrol more on foot. On the whole the ethnic minorities incline to the same view, but their perceptions are more mixed, and those in areas of high concentration definitely tend to take a different view. The pattern of findings suggests that people's perceptions are based more on their assumptions and preferences than on the actual pattern of policing in the areas where they live. In other words, the preference for foot patrols may be more romantic than practical. It may be, to a large extent, a response to the message of the advocates of 'community policing', who seem to have succeeded in establishing an association in people's minds between 'more bobbies on the beat' and a golden age of social harmony. The findings also suggest that the call for a change in the balance of policing in favour of foot patrols is interpreted as a call for more policing; this is strongly supported by older people, those who fear crime and those who think the police are not being successful enough, but less strongly by young white people and by the ethnic minorities.

## Success of the police in various respects
Informants do not show a uniform and unthinking tendency to support or criticise the performance of the police; on the contrary, a considerable proportion of informants give different answers depending on which aspect of performance is under consideration. There is clearly a widespread feeling that the police are losing the battle against street crime and burglaries, but much more confidence in police performance on other fronts. On these other matters, public confidence is not nearly as high as it could be, but it is still at a fairly high level.

In certain particular respects the confidence of Asians and West Indians is comparatively low. In the case of street robberies, burglaries and drunk driving, all of the ethnic groups give similar answers, but the minorities are substantially more likely than white people to think the police are unsuccessful in coping with marches and demonstrations and with football crowds and - most significant - at getting on with people. In fact, 44 per cent of West Indians think the police are unsuccessful at getting on with people, among whom 10 per cent think they are very unsuccessful. Confidence in the success of the police is definitely higher among West Indians in areas of high ethnic concentration than among those elsewhere. This combines with many other findings to show that it is in the mainly white areas, and not in places like Brixton and Lewisham, that the police have been least successful in inspiring confidence in West Indians.

## Policing priorities

While people place the strongest possible emphasis on the 'sharp end' of policing (catching robbers and burglars), they also think it is very important indeed for the police to cultivate regular, everyday contacts with people in the area and to make special efforts to establish relations with key members of ethnic minority groups. However, people do not attach a high priority to the 'social services' role of the police, especially where this seems to involve an intrusion into family life. Broadly speaking, the ethnic minorities have the same view of policing priorities as white people. Both Asians and West Indians attach greater importance than white people do to contacts between the police and leaders of ethnic groups; even so, white people do mostly consider that it is important for the police to have contacts of this kind. Asians and West Indians in areas of high and low concentration place a high, and an equally high, importance on the need for the police to maintain contacts with leaders of ethnic or racial groups, and also on the need for them to get to know people in the area generally. This means that Asians in places like Southall and West Indians in places like Brixton, along with those elsewhere, are asking for regular and close contacts with the police.

## Active policing

Londoners as a whole generally see stops by the police as an occasional rather than a regular feature of social life; among West Indians, it is just over one-quarter who take a different view. On this matter, people's perceptions - and those of West Indians in particular - are closely related to actual police behaviour. Groups that are likely to be stopped are also likely to think that stops are a common occurrence.

A substantial majority of Londoners are content with police policy on stops: 70 per cent think that the number of vehicles stopped by the police is about right, or have no definite opinion, and 78 per cent take this view in the case of stops of people on foot. Among the minority of Londoners who would like to see a change in policy, there is a balance of opinion in favour of an increase in the number of stops. The views of West Indians, and of young West Indians in particular, contrast strongly with those of other Londoners. Although a majority of West Indians are content with current policies, among those who are not the balance of opinion is overwhelmingly in favour of fewer stops. In general, the findings show that there is a wide measure of approval for, or possibly indifference to, police policy in this matter among Londoners, but that there are sharp differences in perceptions and opinions among specific age and ethnic groups. Groups that are likely to be stopped are aware of it, and are much more likely to be hostile to police policy than other groups. It seems likely that the majority of Londoners are content with current policies or unconcerned about them because they are not personally affected. It is clear that a selective discriminating stopping policy is divisive; it meets with the support or indifference of the majority who are not affected, but tends to create opposition among the minority who are. The number of people who are opposed to police policy on this matter is small, but the intensity of their feeling may be much greater than among the majority. The police can justifiably point to the views of the majority in support of what they are doing, but this will not help to convince the people who are repeatedly stopped; on the contrary, it will highlight the conflict of views and stimulate greater opposition among those who are affected.

## Bans on marches and demonstrations

Just over half of informants say that marches and demonstrations are banned about as often as necessary. The balance of opinion among the remainder is strongly that these events are not banned often enough. Complaints by political or pressure groups that there are too many constraints on public demonstrations have very little public support, and there would be considerable support for more constraints on events of this kind. Also, Londoners generally think the police are successful in coping with marches and demonstrations. Whether people are in favour of more bans or fewer bans, they are usually thinking of events organised by right-wing rather than left-wing groups.

## Standards of police conduct

One-third of Londoners think the police sometimes stop people in vehicles and one-fifth people on foot without sufficient reason. These answers should perhaps be regarded as mildly critical, since the question is about what 'sometimes' happens. A majority of Londoners think that the police never exceed their powers in this respect. Young people are considerably more critical of the police in this respect than older people, and West Indians much more critical than Asians or white people. Among those aged 15-24, about two-thirds of West Indians think the police make stops without sufficient reason, compared with half of young white people in the case of vehicle stops and one-third in the case of foot stops. Young Asians are much less critical than either young West Indians or young white people. Thus, a very substantial proportion of young people think the police exceed their powers to stop people, and a solid majority of young West Indians think so.

Twenty-nine per cent of Londoners think there are groups or

types of people who do not get fair treatment from the police; nearly half take the opposite view, and one-quarter have no definite opinion. More than three-quarters of those who think some groups are unfairly treated mention ethnic minorities as the victims (without any prompting); to a large extent, therefore, the notion of unfair treatment of particular groups by the police is synonymous in people's minds with unfair treatment of the ethnic minorities. It is not, therefore, surprising to find that the ethnic minorities give strikingly different answers from white people. Sixty-two per cent of West Indians think some groups are unfairly treated, compared with 26 per cent of white people; Asians are less critical than West Indians, but more critical than white people. In many other respects, young people aged 15-24 are much more critical of the police than others, but not in this one. There is little difference in the answers given between the age groups up to 44, though older people are less critical of the police treatment of different groups. These findings show that the view that the police treat ethnic minorities unfairly is widely held among the minority groups themselves and is held by a substantial minority of white people. In accord with the pattern of findings throughout, West Indians in areas of high concentration are definitely less critical of the police in this respect than West Indians elsewhere.

Informants were asked how frequently they thought seven kinds of serious misconduct by police officers occurred. The findings show that people have different views about the frequency of various kinds of misconduct: they are not either for or against the police on every issue. Over half of informants think that at least a few (and more than 'hardly any') police officers have accepted bribes, but only eight per cent think that 'quite a lot' or 'most' police officers have done so. The views expressed about accepting goods or favours are similar. Thus, it is a common view that there is some corruption in the police force, but not that it extends to more than a small minority of officers. The use of threats and unfair pressure in questioning people is the kind of misconduct that is thought to be most widespread. About half of informants think it happens at least occasionally, but perhaps more important, one-quarter think it often happens - that it is a usual pattern of behaviour by police officers. Fabrication of evidence, violence on suspects held at police stations, excessive use of force on arrest and false records of interviews are all thought to happen at least occasionally by a substantial proportion of Londoners, but by well under half; about one in ten Londoners think each of these kinds of misconduct often occur. These findings suggest that there is a complete lack of confidence in the police among at least one in ten of Londoners, and that about half have serious doubts about the standards of police conduct, though in most cases they do not think there is a pattern of frequent or usual misconduct. Very few people think that any of the kinds of misconduct have become less common; the highest proportion thinking that things are improving is four per cent, in the case of police officers accepting bribes.

One-fifth of Londoners think the police now use excessive force on arrest or unjustifiable violence at police stations more than they used to.

A much higher proportion of West Indians than of white people or of other groups are critical of police conduct. The biggest differences between the view of West Indians and white people are in relation to excessive use of force on arrest, unjustifiable use of violence on suspects held at police stations and fabrication of evidence. One-third or more of West Indians think the police often misbehave in each of these ways, and two-thirds or more think they do so at least occasionally. In each case the proportion of West Indians who think the misconduct often occurs is at least three times as high as the proportion of white people. These findings suggest that between one-third and one-half of West Indians completely lack confidence in the police force, and that two-thirds have at least considerable doubts about standards of police conduct. Asians definitely tend to be less critical of police conduct than white people, though their views are similar to those of white people on some of the issues.

Up to the age of 44, the different age groups express similar views, but successive age groups from 45 onwards are much less critical. Looking separately at the views of young people aged 15-24 we find that it is a minority, but a substantial minority, of young white people who think there is a pattern of frequent police misconduct. One-third of young white people think the police often use threats or unreasonable pressure in questioning and one-fifth think they often use excessive force on arrest and that they often unjustifiably use force on people held at police stations. Young West Indians are far more critical of police conduct than young white people, particularly in relation to false records of interviews, fabrication of evidence and the use of force and violence. The lack of confidence in the police among young West Indians can only be described as disastrous. Sixty-two per cent of them think the police often use threats and unreasonable pressure in questioning, 53 per cent that they often use excessive force on arrest, 56 per cent that they often unjustifiably use violence on people held at police stations, 43 per cent that they often fabricate evidence and 41 per cent that they often make false records of interviews.

A fairly small minority of Londoners have a definite view about the standard of conduct of CID compared with uniformed officers, but among those who do have a view, the CID has a much poorer reputation than the uniform branch.

Ninety per cent of Londoners say that if they were seriously dissatisfied about something a police officer had done or failed to do, they would make a complaint about it; in the great majority of cases, they say they would complain to the police. This suggests that, among Londoners generally, there is a high level of confidence in the present complaints system, although in the vast majority of cases this will not be based on a detailed knowledge of it, still less on experience of using it. Groups which have more experience of the police than the average, and those which are more critical than average of police conduct, are less likely than average to say they would complain about police misconduct. To a certain extent, this supports the argument that a lack of confidence in the complaints system leads to a lack of confidence in the police - at any rate, the two things are associated. But even among groups, such as young West Indians, which are highly critical of the police, a high proportion say they would make use of the complaints system in the appropriate circumstances. It is quite clear, therefore, that a failure of the complaints system is not at the heart of the criticisms that these people have to make.

## Relation between views and experience

A very detailed analysis shows that while a majority of Londoners generally have a reasonably favourable view of the police, those who have come into contact with them, for whatever reason, tend to be more critical. There is a strong tendency for those who have been stopped by police and for those who have been arrested to be critical, but other kinds of contact, where the person is not being treated as offender or suspect, are also associated with critical views. There is overwhelming evidence that people who have been stopped by police (the great majority of whom are not found to have committed any offence) become much more hostile to the police as a result, especially if they have been stopped repeatedly.

# THE POLICE IN ACTION

# XII   OBJECTIVES AND METHODS OF THE RESEARCH

This study describes the results of observation of a wide range of police work by two researchers over a two-year period; it also analyses the structure of the organisation, the methods of management used and the formation of policy, on the basis of informal interviews with senior officers and a study of internal documents.

## Objectives

The distinctive feature of this enquiry is not a particular point of view or theory, but the actual results of long-term observation of police work from the inside.

The questionnaire survey gives a bird's eye view of the pattern of activity of police officers in London up to the rank of inspector(1).   In that survey, the different specialisms and functions, the different ranks and the geographical divisions of the Force are each given their due weight, so that the total activity of police officers in London can be described in quantitative terms. Our first objective within the present project is to give another, more detailed, description of the pattern of activity of selected groups of police officers, but this time filling in the full background: the motivations and personal characteristics of the officers involved, what they think they are trying to achieve, how their objectives and activities relate to the wider structure of the Force. This description will be based on a balanced set of observations of working groups of police officers, carefully chosen so that most kinds of group working in most kinds of area have been included.

Secondly, we hope on the basis of these observations to describe and analyse the psychology of working groups of police officers: to show how individuals, by being part of a group, develop ideas about what counts as success, attitudes towards certain types of person and models of the way in which a police officer should behave. We shall consider how far the expectations built up within the working group amount to an informal code of conduct, and

---

(1)     See Volume III of the original edition.

whether this informal code is in conflict with the formal one set out in internal documents and communicated through the management structure.

Thirdly, we set out to describe how the pattern of policing and the behaviour of police officers is shaped by the internal structure of the organisation in which they work and by the legal and procedural rules imposed from outside. There is certainly a tendency for groups of police officers to develop attitudes, objectives and ways of working that are resistant to attempts to change them, whether by working within the existing structure, by reforming the internal structure of the organisation, or by reshaping the external constraints of law and procedure. We nevertheless assume that the pattern of policing is largely a function of the way the force is structured and of its relationship to the wider society. The organisation, together with the law and rules of criminal procedure, does define the constraints and opportunities that ultimately shape the pattern of policing. Direct attempts by senior officers or legislators to change this pattern may fail, but this is because the context within which groups of police officer work has not really been changed as much as the managers or legislators imagine: because instructions and exhortations are not backed up by substantive changes in the rewards and penalties attaching to different kinds of policing behaviour; or because messages implicit in the way police officers are deployed, commended, disciplined or promoted contradict the explicit messages of the reformers.

**The methods in outline**
Most of the information on which this report is based was obtained in one of two ways: by accompanying, observing and talking to police officers over long periods while they were doing their job; and by carrying out informal interviews, mostly with senior officers. Various other methods were also used, but to a lesser extent: silent observation of classes and selection boards, formal interviews with recruits during their initial training, and study of internal documents (files on policy changes and Force Inspectorate reports).

At the early stages of planning the project, we carefully considered the possibility of observing police work without being with police officers and without the officers knowing that they were being observed. The advantage of this method is that it avoids any influence of the observer on police behaviour. The disadvantage is that it provides a limited insight into everything that underlies the visible behaviour itself. Because police activity, even in London, is not very common, it would be hard to build up many observations even by standing at points where police/public encounters are most likely. It would be very hard to find a way of secretly observing that large part of police behaviour towards the public that takes place inside buildings and vehicles and at police stations. We therefore concluded that this method would have a very limited application, but we did carry out some observation of this kind at public order events.

**Research in Districts and Divisions**
The area covered by the Metropolitan Police (the Metropolitan Police District, or MPD) extends slightly beyond the boundaries of Greater London in some directions, but excludes the City of London. The MPD is divided into 24 Districts, each one headed by a local Commander; these Districts are in turn divided into Divisions, usually three or four to a District, each one headed by a chief-superintendent. The great majority of police officers are attached to these local geographical units. The remainder work in central departments, in central squads (operational groups that may work anywhere in the MPD), or in specialist groups such as traffic or dog handling which have their own geographical units closely allied to the basic district and divisional structure. A few are attached to the four Area offices (the Areas come between the Districts and the central office within the overall structure). It is the Divisions rather than the Districts that are the chief units of organisation. Most operational police officers 'belong to' a Division, while the District office provides a few common services for the group of Divisions that make up the District. For the main body of our research we decided to select six Districts and aimed to cover two Divisions within each selected District.

Selection of Districts and Divisions
Before making the selection, we compiled information on the ethnic and social class composition of the population of the 24 Districts in the MPD (including Webber and Craig's index of social deprivation)(2) and on the pattern of housing tenure. In these respects, the six Districts selected were a balanced set. One was a part of central London, while the other five were spread over the four quarters of the compass, and included areas towards the centre and ones at the periphery.

In consultation with the local Commander, two Divisions were chosen within each of the selected Districts, except that one Division only was covered in one of the Districts. Generally, the two most contrasting Divisions were chosen, in terms of the nature of the population and housing and the type and volume of police work.

Arrangements, explanations, assurances
A7 Branch (Community Relations) was the unit within the Metropolitan Police that was responsible for facilitating the research. It was always a member of A7 Branch who first contacted the local commander to arrange a meeting with the researchers to discuss the visit. At these initial meetings the A7 Branch representative

---

(2)　See Richard Webber and John Craig, Socio-economic classification of local authority areas, HMSO, 1978.

stressed that the study had the personal backing of the Commissioner and that the researchers were to be given full access. Otherwise it was left to the research team to describe the study and say what they wanted. The commander put the researchers in touch with senior officers on the Divisions that had been chosen during the course of the meeting. None of the commanders briefed their divisional officers in detail about the study and in most cases they passed on only the minimum of information to them. It was therefore left to the researchers to make their own explanations at the divisional level.

Each chosen Division was to be covered by one of the two researchers(3), who made the arrangements usually through the chief-superintendent (in charge of the Division) but occasionally through the superintendent or one of the chief-inspectors.

The main points covered by the researchers at these initial meetings were as follows.

a) Each of the main elements of the whole series of research projects was described.

b) It was explained that the Policy Studies Institute exists to carry out social science research on matters of practical importance for public policy, and that the findings of this series of projects would (like all PSI findings) be published.

c) It was explained that the Commissioner had invited PSI to carry out this research, but that he would not be in a position to determine or influence the contents of the reports. Where police officers assumed that the researchers were employed by the Metropolitan Police or by the Home Office, the researchers worked hard to get rid of these misconceptions.

d) Senior officers (and others who expressed an interest) were told that it would be quite impossible to identify individual officers from the published report, and that the researchers would not disclose in conversation any information about individual officers that might be to their discredit. Senior officers tended to assume that any misbehaviour observed would be reported back to them. They were told it would not be, except that there could be circumstances in which a researcher felt bound to lodge a formal complaint against a police officer (in the event this did not arise).

Uniform reliefs
The mainstream of uniform police officers at each Division are

---

(3) Though there were four cases where one researcher carried out some fieldwork on a Division that had earlier been covered by the other.

organised in four groups, or 'reliefs', each one under the command of an inspector, with up to four sergeants and 20 to 40 constables. At any one time one of the four reliefs is responsible for manning the front office and communications at the police station and for patrolling the Division and responding to calls from the public. Each 24-hour period is divided into three shifts operated by a different relief with the fourth relief on weekly leave.

We devoted about half of the time on Divisions to the uniform reliefs. At the early stages (the first two Districts studied) we covered times of the day and night randomly, so that we were working with different reliefs (groups of officers) on different days. We then decided that a better method would be to stick with the same relief throughout, so that we could get to know one particular group of officers well and become fully accepted by them. This method turned out to be more productive than the first. In the best cases, it allowed us to build up a complete picture of the whole working group and of the general pattern of activity of all members of it.

In general we were not able to return to the police station daily over long periods, because this would leave no time for the essential work of writing up notes; we also found it necessary to recuperate from time to time and to restore the sense of our own identity (the norms of working groups are so powerful that they soon begin to impose themselves on the researcher as well as the official in the group). On average, we covered two or three shifts a week during the period that we were with a relief, though one of us (JG) on occasion worked every shift with a single relief over a four-week period. We spread our work fairly evenly between the three shifts (6am to 2pm, 2pm to 10pm, 10pm to 6am) and between the days of the week, but with some bias towards the busier times (Friday and Saturday late turn and nights). We were careful to work some of the shifts considered least attractive, especially 'quick changes', when there is only eight hours between the end of one shift and the beginning of the next. This helped to convince police officers that we were serious about seeing the whole of their job, even though we could not be with them continuously.

Most of the research was carried out by accompanying members of the relief in vehicles or (less usually) on foot. In general, the researcher was attached to a pair of officers or an individual for the whole of a shift, though sometimes a change had to be made during a shift for one reason or another. This naturally led to observation of police work in all settings, including questioning and processing of prisoners at the police station. However, the researchers sometimes spent whole shifts or considerable periods observing inside the police station without being attached to any particular member of the relief. There were almost continuous opportunities for conversation, but the policy was not to use this to carry out informal interviews, but to engage in natural conversation, as a member of the group, arising from events as they unfolded. When nothing was happening (this could be a high proportion of the time) the researcher was more likely than at other times to direct the conversation to matters in which he had a special interest. The researchers accompanied the sergeants and the inspector, on occasion, when they went out, and also found other opportunities to question them directly about various matters.

This method of research worked well. After a time researchers became very fully accepted, and most members of reliefs became quite relaxed in their company. This result was achieved more quickly as the researchers became more experienced; after about six months they had absorbed most of the language, references and mannerisms of uniform police officers, and from this point found it much easier to fit in. There were a few police officers who tried to avoid working with the researchers, and the observer's presence seemed to have some effect on behaviour in certain circumstances: these points are discussed in a later section.

Uniform reliefs at eleven Divisions were covered in this way. Two separate visits were made to two of these Divisions, in the one case to check on a new policing scheme that had been introduced and in the other to take another look at the work of a relief after the riots of 1981 in an area that had been affected.

## Crime squads and 'Q' cars

The crime squads are groups of uniform officers (that is, officers who are not members of the Criminal Investigation Department) but who operate in plain clothes under the general direction of a detective sergeant belonging to a divisional CID office. They typically consist of six to ten young constables with one (uniform) sergeant. These PCs tend to be young and in many cases intend to apply to join CID in future; for those who do intend to join CID, a period in a crime squad is more or less mandatory. There is no very close definition of what these squads should do; they may engage in any of a wide range of activities, but they tend to patrol on foot or in a vehicle, if they can get one (they are not allocated a regular vehicle) and they tend not to investigate individual reported crimes. By contrast, divisional CID officers do very little patrolling and spend a high proportion of their time in investigating reported crimes.

We found that we could carry out research with crime squads in much the same way as with reliefs in most instances. The research was more difficult to the extent that the work of these squads is less structured and predictable than that of uniform reliefs. Nevertheless, the researchers could attach themselves to pairs of officers (occasionally larger groups) who were going out, and follow them around.

'Q' cars are unmarked cars, formally attached to Districts rather than Divisions, that are manned by joint teams of uniform and CID officers (all of them in plain clothes). It was a straightforward matter to join these teams in order to observe their work.

## Divisional CID

In a typical divisional CID office there are about 20 or 30 constables and sergeants with two inspectors under the command of the detective chief-inspector. A large part of their function is to investigate reported crimes (except for the minor ones covered by the beat crimes section) and to process prosecutions through the machinery of criminal procedure. Much of this work is clerical or administrative; a relatively small part involves contact with the public. Another function is to collect information about local crime and criminals. In practice this is mainly done by interrogating people arrested for one offence about other matters they may know about, but also by maintaining contact with local people who for one reason or another have information about local crime and local criminals.

By its nature this kind of work lends itself to observation much less easily than the work of reliefs or crime squads. For much of the time CID officers are sitting writing or reading, or looking things up in files or other records. Perhaps most important, the pace and structure of their work is seldom set by outside events, because they are not usually responding to something that has just happened; instead, most of their time is spent on activities (paperwork, contacting acquaintances and informants, interrogation) which they schedule themselves. This means that, if he was behaving naturally, to follow a CID officer for an entire shift would often be very unproductive, and that the officer has very wide scope to adapt his behaviour to the researcher's presence. If he wants to get rid of the researcher, he can easily do things (paperwork especially) that do not lend themselves to observation; if he does not want the researcher to observe him doing a particular task (say a difficult interrogation) he can usually arrange to carry out that task on another day; if he wants to give the impression of briskness, he can carry out arrests or interrogations that he has been postponing for a while.

These inherent difficulties in observing CID work were just as important as the legendary defensiveness and exclusiveness of the Criminal Investigation Department, or the still-smarting sensitivities caused by Sir Robert Mark's reforms. It would be easier to overcome them if the researcher were to spend a long period (say six months) in the same CID office and if all examples of a particular kind of activity (say interrogations) were to be covered, or as many as practicable. This was the kind of approach used by Barrie Irving in his study of interrogations for the Royal Commission on Criminal Procedure(4). It was not available to us because general conclusions about the CID in the Met could not be based on the study of a single CID office and because we were interested in

---

(4)    Barrie Irving, Police Interrogation: A Case Study of Current Practice, Royal Commission on Criminal Procedure, Research Study, No.2.

the whole pattern of CID work, and not just one aspect of it.

For these reasons, our research on the CID was on the whole less successful than our research on the uniform side. We covered crime squads and CID offices at eight of the eleven Divisions and within five out of the six Districts. We were reasonably satisfied with our research on the crime squads in all of these cases. There were three CID offices that made a determined attempt - largely successful - to prevent us from observing the bulk of their work. These difficulties are further discussed on page 305. In the remaining five Divisions we were reasonably successful and gained the confidence of at least some officers; in three of the five we believe that we overcame nearly all barriers. We spent about 20 working days on crime squads and CID at each Division covered.

<u>Major incident squads</u>
When a 'major incident' such as a murder or suspected murder happens, a district squad is set up <u>ad hoc</u> to investigate it, under the command of the detective chief-superintendent attached to the District, or occasionally under the CID commander for the Area. The personnel for the squad are drawn from the divisional CID offices and crime squads, and also from adjoining Districts if not enough manpower is available locally. We carried out research with two of these squads. One was to investigate a homicide. The other was set up to investigate the fire at 439 New Cross Road, Deptford on the morning of the 18 January 1981, in which 13 people died and a further 30 were injured.

There were no significant difficulties in carrying out research into major incident squads, largely because the work is clearly structured; the researcher can attach himself to officers who have been set specific tasks, study the written evidence emerging from the inquiry, attend briefing and discussion meetings held by the squad and informally interview senior officers. It is interesting that where CID officers are working within a set framework to well-defined objectives there is little difficulty in carrying out research among them; this supports our contention that it is the formlessness of much CID work as well as the attitudes of CID officers that makes research among them difficult.

<u>Other research on Districts and Divisions</u>
The researchers spent a limited amount of time - from one to four days - with home beat officers at each Division covered. It should be emphasised that the bulk of patrolling uniform officers are members of reliefs and not home beat officers: the latter have a specific community relations function.

In four out of the six Districts we informally interviewed the commanders after as well as before the visit. We carried out substantial numbers of informal interviews with senior officers (chief-inspector and above), without, however, systematically covering every senior officer at each District and Divison. Officers with various specialist functions were interviewed on some (but not all) Districts or Divisions. These include officers in the complaints unit (two units covered), the community liaison officer (three covered), juvenile bureaux (two covered), beat crimes officers (one covered thoroughly, others in passing), crime prevention officers (one covered). We carried out observation and informal interviews with an aliens squad that exists on one of the Districts studied.

During 1981 the immediate response units were set up as a permanent standby to control outbreaks of spontaneous public disorder (this is one of the four policy changes that we shall comment on). One of the researchers spent four shifts with one of these units as part of a District visit.

## The influence of the observer

In his report for the Royal Commission on Criminal Procedure, Barrie Irving claims that he became so much accepted by a group of CID officers that his presence did not cause them to modify their behaviour in any way. We believe that an extreme claim of this kind cannot be sustained - certainly it would not be true of our research. What we did aim to do was to allow for the effect of the observer's presence when interpreting the findings.

Certainly, the observer's influence will be much less within a defined situation, such as an interrogation, than outside of it, and this probably explains why Barrie Irving interpreted his experiences in the way he did. Once a police officer is interrogating a particular person, his pattern of behaviour is largely determined by the need to find out certain things, by the way the suspect responds and by the officer's personal and professional resources. In general he will not modify his behaviour much because of the presence of an observer, because he has to achieve certain goals and only knows certain ways of doing it, and he is simply not capable of acting a part for hours on end. This is Barrie Irving's contention, and we agree that it is substantially true.

There are, however, two very important qualifications to be made. The first is that the observer is much more likely to have an influence where the police officer has a choice of activities. As soon as the question arises, 'What shall we do today?' the presence of the observer is bound to be a consideration. Very often police officers respond by trying to think of something to do that they hope will interest the observer; occasionally they may be unco-operative and take the opposite line. The longer the observer is with them, the more the officers tend to settle back into their usual pattern of activity. In any case it is necessary to take this factor into account when interpreting the results of observation of the whole pattern of police work, as opposed to a clearly defined activity such as interrogation.

Secondly, while the police officer will not adopt a whole new pattern of behaviour because the observer is present, he may refrain from doing some things that he would otherwise do because he thinks it is too dangerous to let the observer see them. This is a limitation that exists within the defined situation, such as an interrogation, as well as for the whole pattern of work. As a chief-inspector said to one of us right at the beginning of our research, 'If there are police officers who beat people up in the cells, they're not going to do it while you are watching'. Of course, the presence of another police officer may sometimes be a restraining influence as well. But there is a consensus of opinion in the Force, especially among officers who have investigated complaints, that police officers tend very strongly to back each other up; supposing that an officer has witnessed serious misbehaviour by another officer (for example, an assault) it is again the consensus of opinion that he will usually suppress evidence about it unless he would clearly be risking his own career by taking such a line. Police officers seem to work on the assumption that other officers will support them even when they are in the wrong, within certain informally understood limits. Most of them would say, if pressed, that the job would be impossible or intolerable if they did not back each other up in this way. It is plain to everyone that the observer is not bound by the same reciprocal ties as another police officer: for he does not need to be backed up by police officers should he do something wrong.

No method or procedure can alter this basic fact. We could adduce all the same reasons as Barrie Irving for saying that our presence was accepted. We were often mistaken for police officers by members of the public and other officers. We were often asked to help out (and did so where this did not conflict sharply with our role as researchers). We were often asked for advice and guidance. The jokes and backchat of the group often took us in. Officers frequently broke all sorts of rules in our presence (where, had we reported the matter to their superiors, serious trouble would have been caused), and often behaved in ways that reflected badly on them, or did not enhance their self-esteem. Nevertheless, from the argument a priori, we have to assume that the presence of the researcher was something of a restraining influence; also, there were indications that this was so. For example, when a PC had treated a man arrested for drunk driving rather roughly, his partner said laughingly to someone else on the relief, 'It's a good job David was there, or Kevin might have throttled him!'(5). An experienced sergeant in a crime squad gave the following account of the way he would behave towards the researchers.

You're not a fool. You know that things are not done properly in this job at times. Now I'm not going to do anything seriously wrong in front of you, but you must know that we all have in the past. I'm prepared to be as honest as I

---

(5)     All names used for police officers in this report are always fictitious, though the events or remarks are, of course, real. 'David' was the researcher.

can with you. In other words, I'll give you 90 per cent of the truth.

He went on to explain that he would <u>tell</u> the researcher about his serious misdemeanours, but not make him a witness to any. It was a delicacy of feeling towards the researcher as well as the instinct for self-preservation that acted as a restraint; for this sergeant, like most officers, realised that if the researcher were made a witness to serious criminal behaviour by police officers this would place him in a serious dilemma in which his duty as a citizen would conflict with his duty to complete the research. This does not mean that this officer or others were necessarily likely to do anything seriously criminal in any case, but only that the presence of the researcher would have restrained them had the circumstances arisen. In practice the research was made considerably easier by the fact that police officers came to believe that there would be few repercussions from the researcher observing all but a few kinds of misbehaviour.

After a long period with a group we got to know a great deal about what went on even if we had not seen it all ourselves. Altogether, we believe that the limitations imposed by the influence of the observer have to be constantly borne in mind and allowed for, but that they are not very great except with regard to serious misconduct.

We believe that it was unusual for senior officers to try to ensure that junior ones behaved well during the visit. We know that this did happen at one Division, because a young PC at the neighbouring Division heard about it and told the other researcher.

> Apparently one of the guvnors told them not to use words like 'nigger' but to call them 'clippers' instead ... (While the researcher was there) they didn't go around calling people 'niggers' and hauling them in as they usually do.

The effect of the 'guvnor's' instructions was easily observable. One night a dog handler (not a regular member of the group) spent some time with the relief. He started to tell a racialist joke in the canteen, but was stopped in mid-flow by someone on the relief, and had to rack his brains for jokes that were all right. 'Oh, fuck it,' he said, 'what's left?' In practice, the effect of the senior officer's instructions were not very far-reaching (and were probably not meant to be); they did not seriously affect the research.

We have said that three CID offices tried to prevent us from observing the bulk of their work. In one case this was a concerted campaign worked out at a meeting of all members of the office and involving the detective chief-inspector. In the second case, the 'resistance movement' was led by a detective inspector, but not all members of the office were behind it, and the attitude of the detective chief-inspector was ambivalent. In the third case we believe there was again a coordinated effort to resist the inquiry, largely because the detective chief-inspector was under investigation for serious disciplinary offences. There is no doubt that groups of police officers can shut a researcher out. It is interesting that when this happened to us, officers of inspector and chief-inspector rank were usually involved. We conclude that the more senior officers could obstruct the research, but that where they allowed it to go ahead they did not have much influence on junior officers by asking them to be on their best behaviour.

The roles of the researchers
The research that we carried out on Districts and Divisions cannot be described as participant observation in the strict sense, because we were not police officers, we could not make arrests or carry out interrogations, we were not employed by the Metropolitan Police and we were not subject to the same pressures (for example of the disciplinary system) that police officers are. At the same time, we did take part in the events and the social scene that we were studying to a very considerable extent. We tried to become accepted as temporary or honorary members of the group. Without positively commiting ourselves to the attitudes, opinions and objectives of the group or individuals in it, we nearly always avoided contradicting or opposing them except very gently in order to draw people out. The main change that we had to make in our own behaviour was, therefore, to suppress reactions that we would have made or opinions we would have expressed in other circumstances.

What most helped us to be accepted was simply familiarity - knowing all sorts of detailed things about the organisation, methods of working, terms used, police slang - so that we could follow what people were saying and what was going on as readily as police officers. A symbolic example is that police radios are unintelligible at first, but after a period of adaptation, the ear accommodates to the distortion and to the specialised terminology used.

In detail, the approach of the two researchers had to be somewhat different because of a difference of age. DJS was aged about 40 at the time of the fieldwork, which meant he was a good deal older than most of the operational police officers with whom he was mixing. Consequently, he was not expected to compete with the young men, so that the relationships could be relaxed and friendly, but fairly cool. Young police officers were often looking for reassurance and approval from him, as an independent judge and an older man. JG, on the other hand, was aged about 25 at the time of the fieldwork. Because of his age and strong physique, young men in groups of police officers saw him as being in competition with them. This meant that he had to become more fully a member of the group on equal terms if he was to be accepted at all. Here he was helped by his relatively classless manner. He absorbed the language and mannerisms of the police to the extent that he was usually mistaken for a police officer by those who had not been warned. In order to sustain a relatively

305

close relationship he had on occasion to be more open than DJS: to express his real views, to argue with people who wanted to compete with him. He also had a great deal of social contact with police officers both inside and outside working hours.

To the extent that the observer does have an influence - that the officers are trying to please, to shock or to annoy him - it is an advantage to have two observers of contrasting types who elicit different responses. This allows us to check whether the findings essentially alter according to which observer collects them.

Recording of observations and interviews
When accompanying police officers the researchers did not take notes, since this would have conflicted with the objective of gaining acceptance. The notes were written as soon as possible after the shift, but sometimes several days later. With practice, the researchers became quite good at recalling what had happened and what people had said: we are confident, for example, that virtually all of the incidents that occurred (for example, stops) were recorded. At the same time, of course, smaller events and especially conversations, have been very selectively recalled and recorded; that is, the ones that seemed significant to the researcher are ones that have survived. This means that the process of filtering and analysing the data began before the first notes were made. This may be fortunate since the volume of notes, even though they are selective ones, is difficult to handle. Many quotations are given in this report: since they were recorded hours and sometimes days after the event they are clearly not accurate verbatim records, but we think they are close enough to justify our using them as quotations.

Whenever we carried out informal interviews, we did take notes at the time and reconstructed what was said from our notes soon after. Our records of informal interviews are therefore far more complete than our records of observations, though again they are not accurate word for word.

Special Patrol Group
The SPG is a group of experienced uniform officers which may be used anywhere in London to supplement the local force or to carry out designated tasks. One of the researchers (JG) accompanied an SPG unit for five shifts and informally interviewed the officer in charge of the whole group. In addition, both researchers accompanied SPG units for several shifts when they were deployed on one of the Districts under study.

Public order
It is very difficult to carry out effective observations of the policing of large-scale public order events such as the Notting Hill Carnival: in fact, a large team of researchers would be required to build up really significant observations. We did, however, carry out enough research at events of this kind to understand how the police

306

operation is planned and organised. During the Notting Hill Carnival of 1980 one researcher (DJS) spent two days with the police in the area, while the other observed from the crowd. Similar research was again carried out at the Carnival in 1981, together with some other events that took place during the same weekend. A third member of the research team, Stephen Small, took part, with some young black people with whom he was carrying out research, in the 'Black People's Day of Action' following the Deptford Fire.

During the Brixton riots of April 1981 the other researcher (JG) spent two days with a 'serial' (group of 23 uniform officers) sent to Brixton from the district where he was working at the time. DJS was abroad when rioting broke out in Brixton at this time, but returned to spend two days with police (mostly senior officers) in the area immediately after the rioting itself had ended.

## Research on recruitment and training
We obtained a detailed account of recruitment and selection procedures by informally interviewing the appropriate members of D2 Branch. One of the researchers spent two mornings observing selection boards for applicants to join the Force and had discussions with the members of those particular boards.

We followed the 15-week initial training of a double-class entry of 60 probationers at Peel Centre, Hendon. Researchers attended a balanced selection of the classes (just under half of them) and took detailed notes. The instructors were informally interviewed. Structured interviews, using a set questionnaire, were carried out with the 60 probationers whose classes were being observed. We originally intended to keep contact with these recruits during their probationary period, but we did not, unfortunately, have sufficient resources to be able to do this.

We have collected teaching materials for the new and enlarged initial training course, but we have not been able to study these new arrangements at first hand.

## Use of documents
We have had access to the reports of the Force Inspectorate and used them as a source of information about the structure of parts of the Force and as an indication of the criteria that the Force has used to evaluate its own performance.

We studied four recent policy changes entirely from documentary sources. We called for the files relating to the following changes.

a) The withdrawal of panda cars from inner London.
b) The change in the reporting structure for divisional CID officers whereby detective chief-inspectors came to report to the uniform chief-superintendent in command of the Division.
c) The creation of immediate response units.

307

d)  The development of new arrangements for the recording and collation of information about racial attacks and other racial incidents.

## Presentation

A large body of information underpins this report, but we are concerned with understanding and explanation rather than with description.  The next chapter gives an outline of the organisation and a brief description of what the main groups of police officers do.  Each of the following chapters considers a theme, rather than an organisational unit of the Force, and summarises the evidence that is relevant to that theme and across different types of unit within the Metropolitan Police Force.

Popular conceptions of what the police do and how the organisation works tend to be wrong. For example, the police officer is typically described as 'the man on the beat' and recruiting campaigns are often represented as attempts to increase the number of 'local neighbourhood' or 'beat' or 'home beat' officers. Yet the survey reported in the third volume of this series shows that overall only ten per cent of the time of police officers up to the rank of inspector is spent patrolling on foot, and only 29 per cent patrolling on foot or in a vehicle. Furthermore, 'local beat' or 'home beat' officers are in London a tiny minority of the Force: they account for five per cent of officers. Most of the uniform officers who do patrol are members of reliefs that change from one shift to the next, and individual members of reliefs do not have a responsibility for a particular patch or 'beat' over a continuous period; in fact, they are seldom, in practice, confined to a beat even for the duration of a particular shift. Thus, the whole idea of a continuous, developing relationship growing up between individual police officers and small groups of people living in little areas is based on a false idea of the way the Force is organised. Also, the assumption is too easily made that an increase in the number of police officers will mean a concomitant increase in the number walking about the streets. This could, perhaps, happen if the Force made energetic efforts to encourage foot patrols. But since other activities are far more common than patrolling on foot, it is more likely that an increase in the number of officers will mostly lead to an increase in these other activities.

To set the context for the more detailed description and analysis of police work in later chapters, this chapter gives a general view of the way the Metropolitan Police is organised and of the main activities of police officers in different parts of the organisation.

**Local, central and specialist**
Police officers in the Met can be divided into the following four broad groups.

a) Locally-based officers who are based at Divisions or Districts, the chief geographical and administrative network of the Force. This is three-quarters of all officers.

b) Officers belonging to the four uniform specialist groups: traffic, dog handling, mounted police and Thames (the river police). Each of these groups has its own geographical structure, alongside the main one. Officers in the specialist groups are, therefore, locally based, but they do not report to a divisional chief-superintendent but have a separate command structure for their own specialist group.

c) Central operational branches, that is, operational groups of police officers that are centrally based and which may, therefore, operate anywhere in the MPD. Most of these squads, such as central robbery squad, are to deal with a particular kind of serious crime, and they build up a particular expertise in their own fields. However, one of the central squads, special patrol group, is a mobile reserve that may be used for virtually any purpose.

d) Officers working in central departments, but not in operational jobs. This includes a very wide range of administrative, managerial and public relations functions.

| Per cent posted to | Total | Uniform | CID |
|---|---|---|---|
| Divisions or Districts | 75 | 78 | 55 |
| Uniform specialist groups | 7 | 8 | - |
| Central operational branches | 10 | 6 | 36 |
| Central administrative branches | 8 | 8 | 7 |
| Not known | 1 | 1 | 1 |

Source: PSI survey of police officers (see Volume III of the original edition)
Note: This survey is based on officers up to the rank of inspector.

The percentage distribution of uniform and CID officers between these four broad groups is shown in the table above. This research is mainly concerned with that three-quarters of police officers who are posted to divisions or Districts.

**Police stations, Divisions, Districts**
The MPD is divided into 75 Divisions, which are grouped into 24 Districts, so that most Districts contain three or four divisions.

The work of each Division is focused on a divisional police station; there may be subsidiary police stations, especially in Divisions that cover large areas, but these normally deal with certain aspects of police work only, and lack the facilities of a divisional police station. The mainstream of police officers, both on the uniform and CID side, belong to Divisions and are attached to particular police stations within those Divisions. There are a few officers who belong to the District office, and a few operational units (such as immediate response units) that belong to the District as a whole rather than to a particular Division. Even then, the officers in such units are generally seconded from their own Divisions for a set period. Thus, it is the Divisions rather than the Districts that are the basic geographical units within which the Force is organised. Each Division is, of course, responsible for an area on the map. Sub-divisional stations are responsible for patrolling and taking calls in a part of the Division, although they may not have facilities for charging, or a CID office, so that many matters still have to be handled from the divisional police station. There are also police stations that do not have sub-divisional status; these generally have few police officers based at them and exist mainly as contact points where people can go to report incidents, to ask for information or advice, and so on.

## Deployment on Districts and Divisions

The deployment of police officers based at Districts or Divisions is shown in the table overleaf. The following sections briefly describe the structure and activities of each of these groups.

## Uniform reliefs

The mainstream of uniform police officers at each Division is organised in four groups, or 'reliefs', each one under the command of an inspector, with up to four sergeants and 20 to 40 constables. At any particular time one of the four reliefs is responsible for manning the front office and communications at the police station and for patrolling the Division and responding to calls from the public. Each 24 hour period is divided into three shifts operated by a different relief with the fourth relief on weekly leave. The periods of the three shifts are generally 6am to 2pm, 2pm to 10pm and 10pm to 6am; however, some variations are introduced to ensure that some police vehicles are patrolling at changeover times.

The inspector of the relief on duty is known as the 'duty officer'; he is responsible for supervising and managing the work of the relief and must also deal personally with certain specific matters (for example, fatal accidents). One of the sergeants (exceptionally an inspector) is designated station officer; he is responsible for everything that happens in the front office, the charge room and the cells; for prisoners, including their health, safety and property; for deciding whether a prisoner will be charged and, if so, what the charge will be and for the charging itself. The job of the sergeants not designated station officer is to supervise the constables and to help the station officer at busy times.

Deployment of officers on Districts and Divisions

|  | Per cent of all officers up to inspector rank | |
|---|---|---|
| Uniform reliefs | 44 | |
| Of which, probationers | | 11 |
| Home beat officers | 5 | |
| Immediate response units | 2 | |
| Beat crimes officers | 2 | |
| Crime squads | 3 | |
| Other district or divisional squads | 1 | |
| CID | 8 | |
| Juvenile bureaux | 2 | |
| Crime prevention officers | * | |
| Court officers | 2 | |
| Office or administration | 6 | |
| Other | 1 | |
| Not on Districts and Divisions | 25 | |

* Less than 0.5 per cent
Source:  PSI survey of police officers (see Volume III of the original edition)

Vehicles
In practice, the pattern of policing by uniform reliefs is strongly influenced by the number and type of vehicles available to them. Generally, officers will patrol on foot only if there is no vehicle for them to ride in, and where single officers are assigned to a vehicle they tend to pick up other officers (who are meant to be walking) during the course of the shift. This was recognised by the Force in 1981, when the number of small police cars available in inner London was suddenly reduced in an effort to increase the number of foot patrols.

The number of vehicles available to reliefs now varies considerably between the large, thinly populated Divisions in outer London and the small, densely populated ones in inner London. A common pattern is one area car (a Rover 2.6 litre automatic), one van (a Ford transit), one or two panda or general purpose cars (Austin Allegros or Ford Escorts), with, in some cases, an unmarked car for the use of the inspector, and a marked, small capacity car for the use of 'section sergeants' - that is, sergeants other than the station officer, who should be supervising the constables and may use this car to get about.

In theory, these vehicles have fairly distinct uses, though in practice they may all turn up in response to the same call (along with others such as immediate response units). The area car must be driven by an advanced driver who has had advanced instruction; it carries a 'mainset' radio for direct two-way communication with information room at Scotland Yard. A second police officer, in uniform, sits at the front, operates the radio and logs the calls. There may be a third officer (also from the relief) sitting at the back in plain clothes. He or she may carry out observation work for the crew. The distinctive task of the area car is to go to urgent calls where speed is important. The crew may, however, engage in any kind of police work if they are not called to anything urgent.

The van also carries a mainset radio and can therefore answer calls put out by control room at Scotland Yard. The driver may not be an advanced driver but must have passed a specific test more difficult than the one required for panda car drivers. There are usually one or two other officers in the van besides the driver. The van is specifically used for transporting prisoners, especially when they are violent, excited or drunk. However, prisoners are often carried in other types of vehicle, and the van is used for all sorts of police work as well as carrying prisoners. The van is, of course, used if a number of officers need to be picked up or taken to the same place.

Panda cars do not carry mainset radios. Their only specific use is for humdrum tasks like taking messages (for example, taking papers to court, informing PCs about court appearances the following day). Section pandas (used by sergeants), and general purpose cars and unmarked cars used by inspectors normally carry mainset radios. In practice all of these smaller cars are mostly used for patrolling and for getting about.

### Communications

The radio communication system has an extremely important effect on the pattern of policing and on the way in which the Force responds to the demands that the public makes. It is particularly important to notice that the present system consistently works to the disadvantage of an officer on foot, even if he is much closer to an incident than an officer in a car.

The purpose of the communication system is to establish links between four 'points': members of the public, police stations, police officers moving about in vehicles or on foot and information room at Scotland Yard. Members of the public can contact the police in a number of ways: by stopping a police officer (in a car or on foot); by going to a police station; by telephoning a local police station; and by dialling 999 and asking for the police. These 999 calls are put through to the information room at Scotland Yard and not to local police stations.

Urgent communication between the three 'police' points of the system - moving police officers, police stations and information room - is mostly by radio confirmed a few minutes later by a teleprinter message. Telephones are occasionally used for urgent operational matters, for example if security is an important consideration, since anyone can in practice tune in to the radio messages. The teleprinter is also used for less urgent communications between police stations and central departments.

There are two distinct radio systems: the mainset and the personal radio. The mainset radios, which are not portable, are installed in cars and vans and on the motor cycles used by the traffic patrols. For most purposes, four channels are used (though others are available), the MPD being divided into four parts each covered by a different channel. These 'radio areas' are groups of Districts or Divisions, but do not correspond to the four Areas into which the Force is divided for administrative and management purposes. Although the mainset radios in a given District will normally be tuned to a given channel, the operators may be told to tune to a different channel, for example if the usual one is to be used for some specific purpose; and at slack times (notably the hours after midnight) it is usual for two pairs of channels to be merged, so that for example Channel 1 messages are also heard over Channel 3. (This description applies to the time of our research; in some of its details it has changed since.)

Generally speaking, there are no mainsets installed at police stations. At a few police stations we have found that there is a mainset, but where there is one it may not be on and there is nobody designated to listen to it, log the calls and so on. For practical purposes, therefore, mainsets at police stations, even where they exist, are not a part of the communications system.

When information room at Scotland Yard puts out a radio message on one of the four channels, it will be received by all cars with mainsets tuned to that channel, that is those in roughly one-quarter of the MPD. The message may, of course, be put out over several channels or over all four channels simultaneously. It will not be received by any police station unless information room makes a link, at that moment, with the personal radio system. When someone with a mainset puts out a message, it will normally be received by all mainsets tuned to the channel, as well as by information room.

Messages from information room may be addressed to 'all cars' or to a particular vehicle (identified by a call sign) or they may be asking for units to offer to deal with an incident at a given location. 'All cars' messages generally convey general information or warnings, whereas the remaining messages (the great majority) are generally to do with responding to a particular incident. When a unit accepts a call, information room 'shows' it as 'dealing'. Several units may be shown as dealing, and in addition others may be shown as 'assisting' or 'attending in the vicinity only', which means they are to go to the area and wait to see if their help is needed, but they are not to show themselves at the scene for the time being. In practice, several cars often turn up in response to

314

the same call, often including some that are not shown as 'dealing', 'assisting' or 'attending in the vicinity only'.

After putting out the call on the radio and assigning units to deal with the incident, information room confirms the details by sending a teleprinter message to the police station that covers the place where the incident happened. The unit shown as dealing with the incident then has to report the 'result' along with the teleprinter message. Where information room also needs to record a result (this applies to the more serious incidents) it gets the information from the police station concerned. Thus, local police stations are informed about all incidents happening on their own 'ground', even though the response has been organised by information room through the mainset radio, and they also have to keep a record of the outcome. They are not, however, informed about incidents which their own cars are dealing with but which did not happen on their own 'ground'. In practice, vehicles with mainset radios (the area cars in particular) often deal with incidents in neighbouring Divisions. The only information that their own supervising officers have about this comes from the log book kept by the radio operator in the area car. In general, the police station does not know at a given time where its area car is or what it is doing, because the car is responding to calls from information room on the mainset radio; the police station only gets to know about these calls later (via the teleprinter) and then only if they are on its own ground. If the police station wants to know where the area car is or what it is doing, it has to ask, using the personal radio system.

The personal radio (PR) system allows officers within a particular District to communicate with each other and with their police station. The radios themselves, which are fairly small, are normally worn on the shoulder, but there is a rather bulky rechargeable battery worn on the belt. The normal model of PR used in the Met is not easy to conceal, though it is used fairly widely by officers in plain clothes. (More advanced equipment is used by officers in some central squads.) All members of a relief who are going out will normally use a PR, including those in cars with mainsets as well. This means that officers in cars with mainsets can keep in touch with their own relief and police station (through the PR) as well as with information room (through the mainset). On the other hand, the police station, and members of the relief who are on foot or in cars without mainsets, hear about calls coming out over the mainset only if the crew of a car with a mainset repeats them over the PR.

The PR channels are very localised; generally there will be one channel for a District or Division. All operational officers in a Division normally use PRs on this channel: that is, home beat officers, crime squads, immediate response units, and so on, as well as the uniform reliefs.

In the way that the PR systems are normally used, when anyone speaks everyone with a PR hears the message, so that a PC carrying out some task is often distracted by talk on the radio that has nothing to do with him. However, if the 'talk-through' button is switched off at the police station, then messages from the station will still be heard by everyone with a PR whereas messages from the PRs will be heard only at the station and not by the other PRs. When the system was originally designed it was intended that the 'talk-through' would normally be switched off, so that PCs would not talk directly to each other but pass messages through the station and so that they would be less distracted by radio traffic. In practice, however, it is very rare for the 'talk-through' to be switched off (for example as a sanction because of too much banter and inconsequential talk over the radio) and the PR tends to be used very freely for talk between officers outside as well as between them and the police station.

Someone who dials 999 and asks for the police speaks to an officer in the information room at Scotland Yard. If information room decides to take action in response to the call, they will normally put out a message on the mainset; alternatively, if the matter is not urgent, they may contact the local police station (by radio or by telephone) and instruct them (the relief on duty) to deal with the matter. They will also have to do this if, having put out a call on the mainset, they can find no unit to accept it. Where the police station is required to take action, they will normally assign an officer or officers to the task via the personal radio, though an officer who happens to be in the building at the time may be sent out.

When someone contacts a police station in person or by telephone, the matter may be dealt with entirely at the local level, using the personal radio, but the police station can ask information room to put out a call on the mainset if the circumstances demand it. Equally, where someone contacts a police officer in a car or on foot, the matter may be dealt with by that officer or he may call for others to help him, using the personal radio, or he may very quickly have a call put out on the mainset radio by contacting his police station on the personal radio.

One of the most important aspects of the situation is that nobody knows where anybody else is, and it takes a considerable amount of radio time to find out. This means, of course, that the car assigned to deal with a call is not necessarily the nearest one. Also, there may be an officer on foot or in a car without a mainset who is much closer to the incident than the car with a mainset that accepts the call. In particular, the officer on foot is defined out of being able to answer calls processed through information room that are judged to be at all urgent and which therefore go out over the mainset. It is quite possible for the area car to drive at 70mph from four miles away to a mild domestic dispute when there was an officer on foot just around the corner. PCs will then argue that officers on foot are not much use, because they get to answer fewer calls. Thus, although it may be the policy of the Force at a high level to increase the emphasis on foot patrols, the actual

316

organisation is still pulling in the opposite direction; the radio communication system is only the first of a number of examples of this.

## Communication and message system at the police station
Two members of the relief (or three at very busy Divisions) are required to man the communications at the police station; they are known as the 'communications reserve'. Typically the reserve will consist of two constables, one experienced and the other inexperienced (often a probationer). The experienced officer is designated 'comms 1' and has overall responsibility. These officers sit at consoles with small switchboards; by operating the switches they can take incoming telephone calls, make outgoing telephone calls, listen to messages on the personal radio and transmit on the PR. Everything that comes in to the reserve, whether from a member of the public (normally a telephone call) or from information room or another police station (normally a teleprinter message) is treated as a 'message' - if it is recorded at all. Essentially, messages are something for which there must be an outcome, or 'result'. They are recorded on a standard form and the forms numbered and kept together on a 'message pad'. Normally, a 'result' must be recorded on the form for each message, and it is the job of the constable in charge of the reserve to try to ensure that by the end of the shift a result has been shown for each message; any still outstanding have to be carried over to the next shift and shown as still requiring action. Teleprinter messages sent to 'all stations' are kept separately from the rest, since unlike the others they may not require action from an individual station.

The reserve (who are constables) take three very important kinds of decision: first, whether to treat a communication as a message or to make no record of it; secondly, who to send to deal with an incident; and thirdly, what other action to take about messages, especially steps to inform senior officers or other reliefs.

This message system is designed to ensure that once anything has been fed in, something will be done and an outcome recorded. The system is efficient in that respect; but because a 'result' must always be shown, there is strong pressure on the officer to avoid making any record of a communication if he does not propose to do anything about it. If, for example, a father telephones at midnight saying his fifteen year-old son was due back from a party at 10pm and has not returned, the officer on the reserve will probably suggest that it is too early to report the son as a missing person, and ask the father to telephone again later if the boy has still not returned. This is a perfectly reasonable response. However, if the officer were to record this as a message, the only 'result' he could show would be that the father had been persuaded to wait for his son to return. If he were to record such a message and something happened to the boy, he would expose himself to serious criticism; so he will make no record of the conversation at all. The effect is

317

that, while the reserve officer is expected to make decisions, the decision-making is submerged and remains invisible. The important decision is taken before the matter enters the system; it determines whether it will enter or not. For many purposes this may not matter, but it does matter when senior officers are trying to assess what demands are being made and how the Force is coping with them: in that context it means that the messages actually recorded are an inadequate source of information.

On the second point - the decision about what is to be done once a message has been recorded - it is important to notice that a high proportion of the work of the relief is in response to calls, and that the allocation of this work is largely out of the control of supervising officers. As regards mainset calls, they are put out by a unit (information room) that has no connection at all with local management. Calls on the local, personal radio network are put out by a constable (the reserve), and in the normal run of things the sergeants and the inspector do not interest themselves in how he allocates them; it is up to this constable to decide whether to send a probationer on foot, an experienced PC on foot, a panda car or an area car. Also, the pattern of work is much influenced by the constables' decisions about what calls to accept. When a call comes up, whether on the mainset or on the personal radio, constables generally have a choice as to whether or not to respond. Even if the call is for them personally or for their vehicle, they can generally avoid responding with impunity if they consider the matter is 'weary' (tedious and unlikely to produce what they would consider a positive result) or 'grief' (likely to lead to trouble). One reason for this is that, because of the defects of the radio transmissions, it is always difficult to prove that a call was actually received. Equally, constables choose to respond very quickly to calls that interest them, and the ones who respond most quickly are generally allocated to the call. The allocation of work among members of the relief is therefore very much a matter for shop-floor management. In spite of the hierarchical nature of the organisation, industrial democracy reigns, because it is only a constable who is doing the allocation, and the other constables can largely choose the work they accept to do.

The third point - decisions about the dissemination of information - also emphasise the key role of the reserve officer. If he judges that all reliefs should know about something sent out as a teleprinter message, he can paste the message to a page of the parade book (see below) so that it will be read out to reliefs at the beginning of their shift. He makes similar decisions about whether to inform senior officers.

One of the officers allocated to communications will normally be a qualified VDU (visual display unit) operator. Every police station has a VDU which is 'on line' to the police computer at Hendon. Through the VDU the operator can use the computer to carry out car checks - that is, show the recorded description of a car with a given index number and its registered keeper - and checks to establish whether an individual, or someone very like him, has some kind of criminal record. These checks are very often carried out at the request of officers outside who radio in (some young constables seem to carry out endless car checks). Sometimes an officer in the station will ask for a check, but on many reliefs officers use the VDU themselves to cary out their checks even though they are not accredited operators (this is against regulations). One of the reserve officers is also meant to be responsible for sending out all teleprinter messages, though again officers who have not had the required training often send their own messages instead of pestering the person nominally responsible.

## Deployment of officers on uniform reliefs

For any given shift, a number of members of the relief must be posted to jobs inside. Of the supervising officers, only the station officer (normally a sergeant) must remain inside, but in practice the other sergeants and the inspector often spend a high proportion of their time at the police station. At least two officers are required to man the communications. At busy police stations, one member of the relief will act as gaoler and another as assistant station officer. The gaoler is responsible for the cells and prisoners - for example, for seeing that they are fed. The assistant station officer usually spends most of his time dealing with members of the public who come to the front counter, while the station officer is 'processing' and charging prisoners.

Although the theoretical strength of a relief may be anything from 20 to 40, it is unusual for more than 20 officers to be on duty for a particular shift, and the most common number is 10 to 15. Among the factors leading to the depletion of the effective strength of the reliefs are leave, sickness, courses, secondment to other duties on the Division or District, aid to other Districts (for example, for policing football matches) and deployment at special events in central London. During the course of our research we would typically find a dozen PCs on duty from the relief. Three or four of these would be inside, two in the area car, two in the van and two (at least) in GP or panda cars, leaving two or three (normally probationers) to patrol on foot. This is broadly in agreement with the findings of the police officer survey, which show that among officers posted to a relief, 36 per cent carried out station duties during their last full shift, and 57 per cent went about in a vehicle for at least some part of it.

Of course, the numbers on duty fluctuate considerably, depending on the other commitments drawing them away. There are probably _more_ relief officers on duty during night shifts than during the day, because the other commitments tend to be daytime ones; whereas, of course, the night between 12pm and 5am is the least busy time, and a time when many kinds of police work cannot be carried out at all.

These effective strengths mean that a Divison - typically an area of about five square miles - will normally be covered by nine patrolling officers of which six are in vehicles and three on foot. This may seem thin, but on some shifts it can be much worse, as a commander who had recently come from another force pointed out to us.

> As a commander in this job you have to buy your own uniform. After I had been here a few weeks I realised that I had got it all together, so I put it on and decided to parade the afternoon relief here. Do you know how many there were? There was only one man!

(The area car crew come on duty at a different time and those posted to station duties do not attend the parade, so this meant there would be one man outside in addition to the area car crew.)

Pattern of work

Much of the following chapters is about what members of uniform reliefs do in detail, but it is worth making a few preliminary remarks about the pattern of their activity. Three very general points can be made. First, police officers, whether in cars or on foot, are inactive for much of the time. Even the crew of a powerful radio car may easily take no calls for a couple of hours together, especially in the middle of the night, and may spend the time gently driving around without stopping or talking to anyone outside the car, or even stationary in a quiet side road. An officer on foot, particularly an inexperienced one (and most officers on foot are inexperienced) may easily spend a whole shift without talking to anyone except to answer enquiries about the time or the way. We have shown in the last section that there are really very few police officers patrolling at any one time. Even so, many of them are not very busy. On the other hand, there can at certain times be a large number of calls to be dealt with simultaneously, and at such times there tend to be too few police officers to cope adequately. The fluctuations in demand are partly random and partly predictable: for example, chucking out time on a Saturday night is nearly always busy for the police, and warm summer evenings tend to be busier than cold winter ones. An important implication of these extreme fluctuations in the demands being made is that the time of police officers will be very inefficiently used if they do little except respond to calls; for if there are enough of them to cope more or less with the peak demands, then they will be idle most of the time unless they can generate their own work and pursue defined objectives instead of patrolling aimlessly.

A second point is that most of the activity of patrolling police officers is, in fact, in response to a call or some other demand. If there are no calls they find it hard to think of something useful to do. A few officers try to avoid doing anything, but it is much more common for them to become bored and to hope for a call, preferably something exciting, to break the tedium and (if they are in a car) to allow them to drive fast with the siren or horn going. The researchers came to share this attitude very quickly. Just as glaziers hope for broken windows, so police officers (and any researchers accompanying them) look forward to news of a punch up, a burglary or a rape.

Thirdly, to the extent that patrolling officers do choose their own activity, rather than simply responding to calls, they do this mainly on their individual initiative, and usually have only short-term objectives in mind. In other words, the relief does not, as a group, decide to do something about vandalism on a particular council estate, or about indecent assaults committed on children on their way to a couple of schools. Instead, one individual officer says to himself 'I think I'll go down to the such-and-such estate and take a look around', or 'I bet it's so-and-so who's doing these indecencies, I think I'll take a look outside his house'. Half-formulated plans of this kind tend not to be followed through because coordinated action would be required to have an impact and because the individual officer is likely to be interrupted by a call and therefore to give up his original intention. Consequently, the only kinds of activity that officers are likely to initiate themselves are ones that do not require planning or follow-through, and which can be started on the spur of the moment: stopping and questioning people on foot or in vehicles is a prime example.

The unplanned nature of the activity of reliefs can be seen from the very limited use that is generally made of parade. At the beginning of the shift, members of the relief gather in the parade room to be briefed by the inspector or one of the sergeants. Unfortunately, not all members of the relief do parade, and this reduces the usefulness of the occasion; those posted to station duties go straight to their jobs inside, and the area car crew (sometimes others as well) start an hour later than the rest of the relief. Each member of the relief is told what duty he is assigned for the shift: if he is walking he is generally told to cover a particular beat, if he is driving a panda car he may be told to cover a particular panda beat. The 'ground' (area covered by the police station) will generally be divided into about eight walking beats and four panda beats (larger areas superimposed on the walking beats) but only a few of these beats can be covered during a particular shift unless there is an exceptional turn-out. Apart from assigning the duties the inspector or sergeant will read out new items in the parade book; this is a way in which members of one relief can leave messages for another one and more generally a 'notice board' that anyone can use. Finally, the inspector or sergeant may draw attention to a pattern of recent offences, or to particular notable offences, and suggest that officers should therefore keep a lookout for such-and-such; and he may commend somebody on the relief for a good piece of police work, say on the previous shift. However, many parades are extremely desultory and informal. It is very rare indeed for the sergeant or inspector to suggest a particular pattern of activity to any of the officers present, or to set them a particular objective for that shift. It is also very rare for there to be any discussion by the group as a whole. This would be made difficult by the sub-military style of the proceedings. The format is that the officer in charge gives orders, so that attempts to have discussion tend to be embarrassing and out of place. This may be a difficulty, since the formulation of plans would probably have to involve some participation by the more experienced members of the group, at least.

After parade, officers who are going out normally adjourn to the canteen for a cup of tea. The amount of time spent in the canteen varies considerably between reliefs and also according to the number of calls being received. On some reliefs it is not uncommon for officers to spend a total of three hours or more in the canteen out of an eight hour shift, but they have their personal radios with them and they are always ready to rush out if there is an urgent call. On other reliefs the inspector smartly chucks his officers out of the canteen after ten minutes or so and also ensures that they do not spend more than about an hour for their meal (they are officially allowed 45 minutes). Inspectors who behave like this tend to be resented.

The pattern of patrolling varies between the different types of unit. Area cars are meant to patrol their Division, but often accept calls in other Divisions, sometimes a long way from their own police station. Even when they are not going to a call they often stray outside their own Division. Patrolling, for an area car, means driving about any part of the Division, an area of typically five square miles, with extended forays into adjoining areas. No pattern of patrolling is imposed; it is entirely up to the driver to decide where to go next unless and until the car accepts a call. Also, most drivers do not patrol according to a pattern of their own, though they tend to have their favourite areas (places where they think there may be trouble or crime of some kind) and to avoid other areas altogether. Needless to say, this is not based on any systematic information or analysis of the pattern of crime in the area.

The van is never assigned a beat - it has to be available on any part of the Division to transport prisoners - and it tends to be used to patrol anywhere in the Division, again without any particular pattern. Panda cars are often assigned to 'panda beats', but this limitation is not taken seriously. On one shift that we observed the driver of one panda car made three separate arrests on the beat assigned to another panda. The inspector took no notice of the fact that this driver had not stuck to his beat, and the complaints of the driver whose beat had been poached were humorous and ritualistic. Officers on foot are nearly always officially assigned to a beat, but in many reliefs they are not seriously expected to keep to it. Where they are given something specific to do during the course of a shift, it is often at a location outside the beat to which they have been assigned. It is not much

322

of an exaggeration to say that in many areas the beats have almost ceased to exist. One of the researchers went out walking one day with a PC having five years' experience. As they were going out of the front entrance of the police station, the researcher asked what beat they were assigned to. 'Let me see', said the PC, trying hard to be helpful, 'which one was it, now? I'm not sure'. The researcher said 'Don't you take any notice of which beat you are on?' The PC replied, 'When there are so few (officers) on, you just go anywhere because the ground is not being covered'. Essentially, the beats are not relevant to policing by uniform reliefs as currently practised, but they have not been replaced by any other unit or method of management, and they linger on, giving the impression that there is still a system of patrolling when in fact there is not.

## Home beat officers

Most Divisions operate a home beat system. Typically the Division is divided into eight to sixteen beats, each one covered by a single home beat officer. However, in some cases there are two home beat officers for a particularly troublesome area or council estate. At most Divisions there is little contact between the home beat officers and the reliefs. Home beat officers decide their own hours of working (though officially in consultation with a supervising officer). They very rarely work nights, but quite often work in the evenings.

The conception of what home beat officers are supposed to do is fairly flexible and their activity may vary considerably between one Division and another. What is special about them is that they do all of their work (or virtually all of it) in a particular beat, and therefore have the opportunity to get to know the area and the people there very well. While people outside the police force often think that this pattern of policing is the norm, home beat officers actually account for only five per cent of officers up to inspector rank in the Met, or seven per cent of those posted to Districts and Divisions.

Getting to know people in the area and putting over a friendly image of the police are certainly considered, within the Force, to be prime functions of home beat officers; also, these officers have a specific responsibility to make regular visits to primary schools on their beat as part of the schools involvement programme. Beyond that, there are fairly wide variations in thinking and practice. Some home beat officers make considerable numbers of arrests, answer calls on the personal radio, investigate minor ('beat') crimes, help to trace missing persons, help to curb traffic offences (by reporting motorists for traffic process) and use their local contacts to provide information to the Division about local criminals and the pattern of local crime. Others do few, if any, of these things. One view is that home beat officers should be basically public relations men or glad-handers; the opposite view is that they should be closely involved in all the main kinds of policing on their beat. Both views exist in the Force. It is quite common for officers on reliefs to dismiss home beat officers as useless on the ground that they don't make arrests (though, of course, some of them do). On the other hand, the view that they provide valuable information is also common.

The uncertainty about what home beat officers are supposed to do and the variability in actual practice arise partly because they are little supervised and are therefore free to go their own way. Being outside the relief system they normally report to the chief-inspector (the one responsible for 'operations'), who does not usually take a detailed interest in what they do. Where they do not report to sergeants or inspectors, as is usually the case, they are virtually unsupervised.

## Beat crimes
Of course, all crimes happen on somebody's beat, but the term 'beat crime' is, rather confusingly, used for minor crime that is to be investigated by uniform officers without the involvement of the CID. The officer who deals with the first report of a crime starts a 'crime sheet' for it; this sheet goes into the 'beat crime book' or into the 'major crime book' depending on the nature of the crime. CID are responsible for investigating the major crimes, and the major crime book is kept in the CID office. Beat crimes are normally investigated by a small group of uniform officers under a sergeant, who reports to the chief-inspector (operations). At some Divisions the actual investigation is always carried out by an officer in this group; in others, the work of investigation is often delegated to home beat officers and PCs on reliefs and the beat crimes office coordinates these efforts rather than doing all of the work. The beat crimes book is kept in the beat crimes office. Details of the investigation and result are later added to the original entry on each crime sheet (and the same applies to entries in the major crime book kept in the CID office).

Beat crimes are defined as criminal damage, thefts of articles to the value of under £500, thefts of motor vehicles where no contents are involved, and simple assaults(1).

The intention of the beat crimes system is to allow CID to concentrate on investigating the more serious offences. There may, however, be scope for taking the investigation of beat crimes more seriously by putting more resources on the uniform side into investigating them, especially since this is a kind of activity that lends itself to planning and naturally leads to an analysis and awareness of patterns of crime in the locality. These points will be discussed later in this report.

---

(1)    That is, assaults involving injury amounting to actual bodily harm and punishable under s.47 of the Offences Against the Person Act, 1961.

## Immediate response units

These units were created, following the riots of 1981, to respond very quickly to spontaneous public disorder. The IRUs (renamed district support units since the research was carried out) belong to Districts rather than Divisions. In detail the way in which they are organised has gone through a number of phases, but under the current arrangements there are two units of about 11 PCs and a sergeant in each District, each unit having its own carrier. These two units are under the command of a single inspector and can be regarded as jointly forming an additional relief. The members of these units are all young or youngish men who have had recent training in the use of shields; more recently, the units have undergone regular shield training together as a group. The carriers always have on board a protective helmet and either a long or a short shield for each member of the unit. The vehicles are reinforced and protected in various ways.

In the early days of IRUs, men were drafted to them from the reliefs, often without their being first consulted and usually for short periods (say a week or two). Although the men had to be shield trained, the unit had not trained together. The current arrangement is that the places are filled by volunteers who are normally posted to the IRU for a period of three months; also, each unit now trains together as a group.

From Monday to Friday the two units work overlapping early and late turn (9am to 5pm and 4pm to 12pm) so there is no cover between midnight and 9am. At weekends there may also be a third unit of men drafted temporarily from the reliefs and there may be cover overnight or at least until 2am.

The problem with these units is that most of the time there is no public disorder for them to deal with, and there is therefore a difficulty in finding them something to do. Also there is a conflict between the requirement for units of this kind to act together in response to orders in a military fashion and the individualistic nature of most other police work. These points will be discussed in a later chapter.

## Crime squads and other local squads

At the time of the research, there was one crime squad on each Division, or 75 in the Met as a whole. More recently, the crime squads within each District have been combined into a single unit (so that there are 24 in all) and the numbers of officers in them have been somewhat reduced. As we explained in the last chapter, the Divisional crime squads were groups of uniform officers operating in plain clothes under the general direction of a detective sergeant belonging to the divisional CID office. They typically consisted of six to ten constables with one (uniform) sergeant, who acted as their main supervisor from day to day (the detective-sergeant involved also had normal CID work to carry out and was not usually continuously involved with the crime squad from day to day). These squads tend to patrol on foot or, less often, in a vehicle, and aim to make arrests, and they tend not to investigate individual reported crimes. They sometimes carry out lengthy investigations of a group of criminals or a pattern of crimes, and mount observations in connection with such investigations. If CID officers need to carry out a 'raid' - a search with warrant, with good prospects of making a number of arrests - they will often call in the crime squad to help them, since otherwise not enough officers could be mustered.

Crime squads are, in part, a training ground for future CID officers; as such, they have evolved out of the old Temporary Detective Constable system. However, not all members of crime squads want to join CID, and a number of those who do are never successful. It was not entirely clear which senior officer had responsibility for the Divisional crime squad, though ultimately they of course reported to the divisional chief-superintendent. The detective chief-inspector was responsible for their training in CID work, and since many members of the squads hope to join CID they tended to think they were more under CID than uniform control. On the other hand, some uniform chief-inspectors (operations) thought they had responsibility for the crime squad, and this seemed logical in that the squad was from day to day under the supervision of a uniform sergeant. It is an interesting comment on the nature of supervision that it can remain unclear who the supervising officers are.

District crime cars ('Q' cars) are unmarked cars, formally attached to Districts rather than Divisions, that are manned by joint teams of uniform and CID officers (all of them in plain clothes). These officers, who are drawn from the reliefs and CID offices, normally do a tour of duty on the 'Q' car of four weeks. These cars are equipped with mainset radios and often answer calls alongside or instead of area cars. On the whole, though, they initiate more of their own work than area car crews, and because the officers are in plain clothes and the cars unmarked they are better able to carry out observations and to arrest people in the act of committing a crime.

Various other squads exist on Districts or Divisions from time to time, or on certain Districts but not others. For example, 'L' District (the London Borough of Lambeth) has had a fairly large District robbery squad for some years, though no similar squads exist anywhere else. Various Districts have from time to time had squads called 'District support units': a group of ten officers or so who patrol in fairly small areas on foot, or go about in a van. Some Districts or Divisions have 'vice squads', usually very small groups (two or three officers) devoted to catching prostitutes and pimps. In a Division where hotel burglaries are a particular problem, a 'hotel squad' may be set up to investigate them. Some 'aliens squads' exist to catch and initiate proceedings against people who are staying in the country illegally. The attraction of creating these squads is that their purpose is built into their definition, so that they generally know what they are trying to achieve, which is much less true of the generalists on the reliefs. The disadvantage is a lack of flexibility and the tendency not to review the priorities that led (at a time that no one any longer remembers) to the establishment of the squad in the first place. However, these other local squads account for a very small proportion of manpower (for one per cent of officers based at Districts and Divisions).

## Divisional CID officers
One way of describing the CID is to say that it is a specialism on a par with traffic or dog handling. As in the case of other specialisms, officers can apply to join CID only after a period as 'ordinary' constables; there is a fairly elaborate selection procedure, and the officer's status as a CID officer is only confirmed after he has attended a course and passed an exam. There were, historically, important differences between the CID and other specialisms, however. There was a separate, but parallel rank structure, and even now the prefix 'Detective' is used for officers in the CID. Secondly, the CID was and is the largest of the specialisms in the Force: CID officers account for 14 per cent of the total, while officers in the next largest specialism, traffic, account for only four per cent. Thirdly, the CID cultivated a separate and exclusive identity to a greater extent than the other specialist groups. In the Met, the term 'uniform officer' means 'not a member of the CID' (many uniform officers' actually patrol in plain clothes, for example members of crime squads). Historically, the CID had a separate reporting structure from the uniform side, so that the boss of every CID officer, even his ultimate boss at a very high level, was always another CID officer. In an effort to break down the separateness and exclusiveness of the CID this has now been changed for divisional CID officers (though not for the 45 per cent of CID officers who are posted to central squads and departments). Ironically, it is now only the uniform specialisms that have separate reporting structures at a local level.

In every Division there is a group of CID officers under the command of a detective chief-inspector. Very often these officers all work in the same CID office at one police station; where there are sub-divisional police stations these usually have no CID office, but as a reaction against earlier centralising reorganisations there have been a few moves recently to open small CID offices at sub-divisional stations. Typically, there are about 20 or 30 detective constables and detective sergeants in a Division; the sergeants very rarely exercise any supervisory function; although, formally, they should supervise a number of detective constables, they are in practice simply rather more senior (though they may easily be less experienced in CID work than the detective constables with whom they are working). There are generally two detective inspectors, whose job is largely supervisory and administrative. Where there is a single divisional office, though the DCs and DSs may be formally arranged in two groups reporting to the two inspectors, the supervisory and reporting structure remains fluid in practice.

Divisional CID officers normally work two overlapping shifts (9am to 5pm, 2pm to 10pm), but considerably more work on the earlier than on the later shift. There are normally just two CID officers on night duty for the whole District. Hours are quite often varied in response to the pattern of work: for example, a number of officers may start work at 6am to make some dawn arrests, and they may well not be allowed to work the three hours before 9am as overtime, so they will in that case finish work at 2pm.

Much CID work is clerical or administrative. A considerable proportion is a response to entries in the major crime book - an attempt to investigate particular reported crimes - but CID officers also devote a substantial amount of time to obtaining information about local crime and criminals from informants, local people and (especially) suspects who are under arrest.

## Collator

At all divisional police stations, and at some sub-divisional ones, there is a collator's office where information about local crime is gathered and files are kept on all local criminals and suspects. The office is generally staffed by a PC and a civilian assistant. Police officers are encouraged to record any useful information they obtain in a 'collator's book'. From these entries and from other sources the collator produces a weekly bulletin, as well as keeping an extensive set of reference files up to date. Police officers do refer to these files regularly, especially to make a quick check on the 'form' (previous criminal record) of someone they have arrested. (It would take time to get a copy of the entry at the Criminal Records Office, which would not contain details of matters not brought to court, though these may be shown in the collator's records.) These local records are used for checking up on individual people or incidents rather than to show a pattern of events or to plan coordinated police activity.

## Community liaison officers and juvenile bureaux

On each District there is a community liaison officer who, according to the official job description, is 'responsible to his commander for the coordination and encouragement of activities affecting community relations and the promotion and maintenance of good relationships with the local community and their organisations, with special emphasis on those concerned with ethnic minority groups'. CLOs are either chief-inspectors or superintendents, and since they normally remain in the post for a minimum of three years, they are often promoted to superintendent during their period of tenure. Since this is a District post, the single officer has a large area and a wide range of organisations, events and interests to cover; in practice he has to concentrate on the parts of the District or on the organisations or groups that he considers important or sensitive from the police point of view. For example, the CLO in 'L' District (Lambeth) tends to concentrate on Brixton and on black groups; the CLO in 'B' District (Kensington and

Chelsea) spends a considerable part of the year preparing for the Notting Hill Carnival. CLOs have no responsibility for operational policing, except that they take their turn as the senior officer on late duty; if they are effective, the advice they give to their commander may be very influential, but they do not usually have a direct influence on the detail of policing at the Divisional level. Thus, the specialist function of 'creating good community relations' is, to an extent, separated from police work itself. A7 Branch at Scotland Yard provides a back-up of information and advice to CLOs and a channel of communication between them; to some extent it coordinates their activities by formulating general policy guidelines, but it remains quite clear that CLOs are primarily responsible to their District commanders, and report directly to them.

On each District there is also a juvenile bureau headed by an inspector. This inspector reports to the CLO but in practice the CLO's other responsibilities are very demanding, and he usually leaves the running of the juvenile bureau in the hands of the inspector without taking a detailed interest in it. The juvenile bureaux normally consist of about eight PCs with two sergeants and the inspector. Their main function is to look after the arrangements for dealing with juvenile offenders other than by charging them and taking them to court. They are also concerned with arrangements for taking children into care for their own safety or protection. Both of these roles bring them into contact with the other local agencies, particularly social workers and social services departments and schools and education departments. As part of the Force's 'schools involvement programme', they visit all secondary schools in the District on a regular basis (the primary schools are visited by home beat officers).

The juvenile procedures, whereby the police decide to caution rather than to charge juveniles in many cases, amount to a very large exercise of police discretion; the way in which this discretion is used has a considerable impact on the criminal justice system, and the juvenile bureaux may therefore be regarded as a rather critical part of the police force. They are also important because they are effectively the only part of the Force which is in close and regular contact with other local agencies.

### Divisional and District command structure
Each District is headed by a commander who has a chief-superintendent as his deputy. The (district) chief-superintendent does not have a separate and different job from the commander, but acts for him when he is away (bearing in mind that policing continues around the clock). It is only in the arrangements for hearing discipline cases that the duties of the (district) chief-superintendent are distinct from those of the commander.

Each Division is headed by a chief-superintendent who reports to the commander (or, when he is away, to the district chief-superintendent as acting commander). The divisional chief-superintendent has a superintendent as deputy, and again this superintendent's job is not distinct, except in certain disciplinary matters, from that of his boss. All four of the officers mentioned so far are 'uniform' officers. It is only from the chief-inspector level down that the line of command diverges between uniform and CID.

The rest of the divisional structure has already been described from the bottom upwards. At large or busy Divisions there are two uniform chief-inspectors, one in charge of 'operations', the other in charge of 'administration'; at smaller or less busy divisions the two functions are performed by a single chief-inspector; where there are two, they are responsible for different aspects of the same officers' work rather than responsible for entirely different groups of officers. For example, the chief-inspector (administration) is in charge of the paperwork arising from traffic process carried out be uniform reliefs, but not for deciding whether they should carry out a road block - that is the job of the chief-inspector (operations). All of the CID officers on the Division report to the detective chief-inspector. The uniform and CID chief-inspectors report to the divisional chief-superintendent who is, of course, a uniform officer. Thus, the divisional CID no longer have a separate chain of command leading to a central Criminal Investigation Department. Instead they report through the divisional command structure, which is controlled by uniform officers.

However, there is on each District a detective superintendent and a detective chief-superintendent. These officers are attached to the District and not to any particular Division. Before the change introduced in January 1980 the detective chief-inspector on the Divisions reported to these senior District CID officers, but formally they no longer do so, and in fact nobody at all reports to the detective chief-superintendent or his deputy. Informally, divisional CID officers may go to these senior CID officers for help or guidance, and the senior CID officers may still be able to exert some power or influence. Since the change in command structure, the position of the detective chief-superintendent and his deputy is undoubtedly anomalous, though it is very difficult to see what can be done about it. When there is a succession of murders and other major incidents to be investigated, the district CID officers are kept busy: they take personal charge of the investigations carried out by major incident squads set up ad hoc at the district level. Outside of such investigations they do not have a clear role, especially since the Divisions rather than the Districts are the effective management units.

## Specialist groups

There are four specialist groups in the Met which have their own local network separate from and superimposed on the main network of Districts and Divisions. They are traffic (4 per cent of officers); dog handling (1.5 per cent); mounted police and river police (0.5 per cent).

The traffic patrols are based at 11 garages all of them outside the central and usually congested area. Between one and four of the Districts are covered from each of these garages. They operate motor cycle patrols on the main roads leading to London between 7 am and 11 pm, whose main job is to facilitate the flow of traffic; operate patrols of traffic accident cars (specially equipped Rovers with two blue lights), normally one to a District in inner London and one to a Division in outer London, with a reduced coverage during the night; and vehicle removal teams which concentrate on cars causing serious obstruction in central London. The patrols carry out a substantial amount of law enforcement work, mainly outside the hours of greatest traffic congestion. Traffic patrols deal with many accidents but many are dealt with by the normal uniform reliefs. They now use the mainset channel for the area where they are working, so that they are kept informed about other police activity on the ground, and can offer to help where appropriate. The eleven garages are grouped into a divisional structure, each division being headed by a chief-superintendent who reports to the commander in charge of traffic patrols as a whole. Formally speaking, this commander is said to be in charge of an additional, notional 'District'. Thus, the local traffic patrols are not at all under the control of the local commander.

The other specialist groups, though much smaller than traffic, have a similar structure of locally-based officers reporting through a separate command structure and not to the local commander. Dog handlers normally patrol in pairs in special vans; they often liaise quite closely with uniform reliefs on duty at the same time; because they are thinly spread, they often have to travel long distances to calls. The mounted police are based at stables at a very few police stations. Thames police mainly use boats and their operations are therefore quite separate from those of the rest of the Force.

Officers apply to join these specialisms after experience on Divisions with uniform reliefs, and each of the specialist groups has its own selection procedure. Moving from a relief to a specialist group is regarded as career progress, especially for PCs who do not hope to move up the rank structure. For constables who do not become area car drivers, working on a uniform relief is regarded as a job with a relatively low status.

## Central squads
There are a number of operational groups that are centrally based and may, therefore, work anywhere in the MPD. The Special Patrol Group is a mobile reserve of uniform officers. Two separate uniform groups exist for the protection of royalty and of diplomats. The remaining central squads are specialist CID units; as pointed out at the beginning of this chapter, a substantial proportion of CID officers (16 per cent) work in these central squads. The main groups are as follows.

Uniform groups
Special patrol group
Royalty protection group
Diplomatic protection group

CID groups
Serious crime squads
Company fraud department (joint with the City Police)
Flying squad and robbery squad
Stolen motor vehicle investigation branch
Regional crime squads (joint with other forces)
Anti-terrorist branch
Criminal intelligence branch (observation and surveillance)
Special branch (national security)

Postings to these central squads are considered highly desirable because of the prestige attaching to them, because of the intrinsic interest of the work in many cases, and because of the opportunity to boost earnings by working substantial overtime.

## Higher command and management structure

We have concentrated in this chapter on describing the operational groups of police officers in the Met working from the bottom upwards. As well as these operational groups, most of which are locally based, there is an enormous apparatus of central branches which provide technical or specialist services, perform some regulatory function, or run some aspect of the Force that has been hived off and centralised (for example, selection and training). It is not necessary to list these branches here, though some of their functions such as selection and training, will be discussed in some detail in later chapters. It is, however, important to describe the general structure at the centre and to show how the operational groups slot into a command and management structure that also takes in the branches with a service or regulatory function. For this purpose it is best to reverse the earlier procedure and work from the top downwards.

The Metropolitan Police employs 17,000 civilians as well as 27,000 police officers. On the civilian side, the line of command runs from the Commissioner through the Receiver to the heads of the civilian departments. On the police side, it runs from the Commissioner through the Deputy Commissioner to the four assistant commissioners, who are each in charge of one of the following police departments.

A Department. For most purposes, the line of command from the Commissioner to the Districts and Divisions can be regarded as passing through the Assistant Commissioner, A Department. In addition, various of the (uniform) operational groups outside the District and Divisional structure are, formally, branches within A Department; for example, special patrol group is A9 Branch. A Department also contains six branches that provide support of some kind to operational groups; for example, A7 Branch provides support and guidance in race and community relations and in matters affecting juveniles.

B Department covers traffic and technical services. The traffic patrols are, formally, a branch within B Department (B8), and two further branches supply and service the vehicles used by the whole of the Force. Four civilian branches deal with the administrative and clerical procedures in connection with prosecutions for traffic offences. Five police branches provide technical services (photographic, computing, communications, fingerprints, criminal records, indices of juvenile offenders, prostitutes and missing persons).

C Department is what used to be called the criminal investigation department. Six of the branches are central CID squads. A seventh, C11, is an operational group that collects criminal intelligence (often by observation) and collates it, but essentially it provides a service to other groups, which always carry out the actual arrests. There are five further C Department branches that provide support principally to CID officers. The special branch also falls within C Department.

D Department deals with recruitment, training, the promotion system and personnel matters.

Each branch of a department, whether it is support or operational group, is headed by a commander. Between the Assistant Commissioner, who is the head of the department, and the commanders of the individual branches there are two or three deputy assistant commissioners, each one responsible for a proportion of the branches in the department.

The relationship between the Districts and Divisions and the central departmental structure is not entirely straightforward or clear cut. The 24 Districts are grouped into four Areas, each with its own headquarters office headed by a deputy assistant commissioner (DAC). The officers at area headquarters, apart from the DAC, are a CID commander and a superintendent acting as staff officer. With such a small staff, the area headquarters are clearly not able to supervise the management of Districts and Divisions in any detail. They concern themselves with matters of general policy, and the DAC and commander may take command at a Division or District in special circumstances: for example, the Area DAC took command in 'L' District at the time of the riots in April 1981 in rotation with the district commander, and the CID commander for the Area took charge of the investigation into the Deptford fire in January 1981.

Moving upwards from the Area DACs it is not possible to

trace a single line of command. The channels of communication run through all four assistant commissioners: which one is consulted or gives instructions depends on the matter under consideration; in a decision about the communication system, for example, the Assistant Commissioner, B Department would have the strongest say, whereas in a decision about training the Assistant Commissioner, D Department would have the clearest responsibility. At the same time, the different assistant commissioners will usually have some interest in any important matter, and their interests may well conflict. For example, B Department has direct responsibility for running the traffic patrols, together with a general responsiblity for the pattern of vehicle use in the force and for monitoring police accidents and trying to reduce their numbers. B Department therefore had a double interest in reducing the number of police cars used in inner London (a means of reducing the number of police accidents and of reducing expenditure on general purpose police cars, possibly allowing leeway for more expenditure on special police cars, for example those used by traffic patrols). But A Department, which is responsible for day-to-day policing operations, must also have a legitimate interest in this matter and is likely to want to maintain or increase the number of vehicles available for ordinary patrolling and general purposes.

Conflicts of this kind can be resolved by agreement between the six most senior officers (the assistant commissioners, the Deputy Commissioner and the Commissioner), by the Policy Committee (a body that includes the Receiver and some others as well as the six most senior officers), or by a decision on the part of the Commissioner alone. The high-level structure creates plenty of potential for conflicts especially between A Department and the rest, because the main operational network and the network of services backing it up have not really been combined into a coherent whole. In other words there is a local structure of Areas, Districts and Divisions through which most of the operational police work is actually carried out; and, separately, there is a structure of central departments which primarily service the operational network, but which are also directly responsible for certain operational groups (traffic, special patrol group). These two sets of structures do not slot together in a simple way. On paper the 'service' departments - all of them at once - are responsible for the local operational network. This is bound to lead to tensions, whether destructive or creative we shall leave for discussion later in this report.

The central complaints investigation bureau lies outside the departmental structure; it is headed by a DAC. The public information department, also headed by a DAC and lying outside the departmental structure, is in charge of public relations and the release of information through the press and broadcasting.

A solicitor's department deals with legal matters. There are further civilian departments to deal with finance, administration, catering, buildings and computing. A chief engineer's department deals with purchase and maintenance of vehicles, radios and other technical equipment (B Department deals with these matters in their policing rather than their engineering aspect).

## Set procedures
This structure, in its enormous complexity, is held together by an immense apparatus of set procedures. In accordance with the quasi-military style of the organisation, these are codified as 'standing orders' in a huge reference book known as 'General Orders'. To an outsider the detailed way in which General Orders specifies how everything should be done is simply amazing. It describes every form used by the Force, specifies the circumstances in which it should be filled in, who should complete it, who should countersign and check it, to whom it should next be passed, and so on; and it specifies, for example, when officers are permitted to wear shirtsleeves without their tunics and how the sleeves should be rolled.

A glance at General Orders or the shorter Instruction Book (for the guidance of constables) creates the strong impression that the freedom of action of senior officers must be very limited: that it must be difficult for them to take initiatives, because these would require a greater flexibility in Force-wide procedures than exists. In practice, this inflexibility of the system may be somewhat illusory; such a Byzantine codex of regulations only exists as a reference point in certain circumstances rather than a guide to everyday behaviour. Even so, the background of set procedures means that when things go badly everyone, including the senior officers 'responsible', can blame pervasive features of the system in which they are working: and this may largely account for the frank and outspoken criticisms of the police force that are so characteristic of senior police officers talking about their job in private.

That same glance at the regulations also creates the strong impression of a concentration on procedures rather than objectives, on form rather than content. What individual police officers do is governed by a sense of trying to achieve various things, but these objectives grow up informally from the lower levels of the organisation. That is the subject that we turn to in the next chapter.

# XIV OBJECTIVES AND NORMS

The Metropolitan Police is a very large and inevitably bureaucratic organisation in which there tends to be more emphasis on form than on content, more concern with following a procedure than with achieving an end result. When talking to senior officers it was difficult to get a clear statement of objectives or priorities except in the most general terms. Yet, whether or not they are explicitly stated and discussed, there must be a set of objectives implicit in the pattern of policing. In the absence of a continuing attempt, within the organisation, to define objectives explicitly, the vacuum has been filled by the preoccupations, perceptions and prejudices that develop among groups of constables and sergeants in response to the people and the problems they have to deal with. Though the organisation may not have a clear idea of what they should be trying to achieve (as it did not at the time of the research), constables do have goals of their own, which shape their behaviour. Where their behaviour is not much organised in terms of goals, it is still strongly influenced by 'norms' - by custom, precedent, the expectations of the group - that have grown up informally and are distinct from the formal rules and regulations. In this chapter we shall describe and define these informally understood objectives and norms and show how they influence the general pattern of policing and the detail of police behaviour.

From a distance it may look as though the objectives of the police force are either imposed on them by the demands made of the public or else are otherwise clear and unambiguous. However, this is not really so. Although a great deal of what the police do is a direct response to calls, the way in which they deal with these incidents must strongly affect the future pattern of demand. The overall speed and efficiency of response will affect the total amount of demand (the better the service the more people will want to use it). Beyond that, the response to particular kinds of incident will affect the pattern of demand: for example, allegations of rape will tend not to be made if the victims are insensitively treated, wives will not make allegations of assault

336

against their husbands (or prostitutes against their ponces) if the police are always reluctant to get involved in cases of 'family violence', ethnic minorities will tend not to complain about racial attacks if the police tend not to take their complaints very seriously. Victim surveys show that among the incidents not reported to the police some are apparently just as 'serious' as those that are reported. The pattern of demand for police services is elastic: it depends not only on objective facts about incidents that are going on 'out there' but also on how people decide to cope with these incidents (indeed, how they perceive and classify them). Whether they decide to bring in the police depends on how they think the police would respond, and this must be partly a function of past experience. It may not be much of an exaggeration to say that, far from simply responding to demands, the police actually create the demand by the way they respond, in much the same way that a manufacturer creates the demand for a particular product.

Of course, the police force also expresses its objectives and priorities in more direct ways. By allocating police officers to various types of unit, particularly the specialist groups, the Force creates a capacity for a certain kind of policing and limits the capacity in other directions. For example, the larger the number of police officers in vice squads or aliens squads the larger will be the numbers of prostitutes arrested for soliciting or aliens arrested for staying in the country illegally. Equally, the amount of action taken against parked cars causing an obstruction reaches an absolute limit depending on the number of police officers allocated to vehicle removal teams. Even if we confine our attention to police officers posted to more general duties, a significant proportion of their activity involves them in taking an initiative (for example, by stopping and questioning a member of the public).

Although objectives are inescapable for individual police officers and for the police force as a whole, 'police culture' has not traditionally been a favourable medium for the growth of an explicit and thought-out set of objectives and priorities. One reason for this is the insistence inside and outside the Force on the sturdy independence and impartiality of the individual police officer, whose duty is (apparently) to enforce all of the laws with equal enthusiasm and without fear or favour. Of course, police officers are effectively told to enforce certain laws rather than others according to the duties they are allocated; besides, an individual police officer frequently ignores all sorts of offence or irregularity in order to concentrate on others (or just do nothing). Nevertheless, ideas of impartiality, of applying the law, of therefore following the correct procedures, do sit uneasily with the idea of pursuing priorities and policy objectives in law enforcement. To a police officer, pursuing an objective often sounds as if it conflicts with doing what is 'correct'; trying hard to reach a goal is often associated with improperly bending the rules and regulations. This is another reason why the objectives and norms that actually shape police behaviour tend to be unofficial, unacknowledged and implicit. It is more comfortable for the organisation to pretend that it simply works to the law and the regulations, and to keep its objectives to itself. Hence it is only within the last year that the need to develop explicit objectives has been fully recognised within the Metropolitan Police.

The objectives and norms that informally develop tend to be those of a group rather than those of individuals; members of the group feel that there is considerable pressure on them to adopt or appear to adopt them. Many of these norms are similar to those that develop in any male-dominated group (for example, in the army) especially where the need for loyalty and solidarity is paramount. One of the effects of the group psychology is that certain themes tend to be emphasised in conversation in an exaggerated way: the prime examples are male dominance (combined with a denigration of women), the glamour (but not the reality) of violence, and racial prejudice. Conversation often emphasises such themes as a means of relieving tension: for example, a policeman may say, after dealing with an awkward or obstructive prisoner, that he would have liked to hit him and nearly did. This may be a way of relieving his feelings while at the same time showing his solidarity with group norms. It does not necessarily show that he would, in fact, hit a prisoner: the group norm may require officers to talk about violence rather than indulge in it. This distinction between words (often strongly influenced by group psychology) and deeds is particularly plain in the case of racial prejudice, which we find is expressed in action much less than might be expected from listening to what officers say.

### Interest, excitement, sensation

For a police officer, patrolling tends to be boring, not only because it is often uneventful, but also because it is rather aimless. A considerable amount of police behaviour can best be understood as a search for some interest, excitement or sensation. An officer on foot will often spend a whole shift without doing any police work, and without talking to anyone except to greet them and provide simple information. At night it is common for a 'walker' to spend a whole shift without talking to anyone at all. Even officers in cars with mainsets can spend several hours without responding to a call and without finding something to do on their own account. Of course, there are times when a car rushes straight from one call to another one, but overall these are definitely unusual except in certain very restricted areas.

The importance of boredom and aimlessness is very much obscured by most popular treatments of police work, whether in fictional or in documentary style. They naturally concentrate on the interesting bits, and, so, of course, do the police themselves. The first time that DJS ever interviewed a police officer, he asked what he had been doing in the past few days. The PC answered by describing a hair-raising car chase which ended with a crash and the PC arresting the driver as he ran off. After some further

338

questioning it turned out that this was the only car chase that the PC had ever been involved in and that it had happened two years before. The PC concluded by saying 'That's just about the best thing that's happened to me in the job'. When members of a relief come together at tea breaks or meal times they recount interesting things that have happened during the shift, and if things have been dull (which they usually have) quite trivial incidents will be inflated and described like dog-fights by RAF pilots during the Battle of Britain. The researchers quickly came to share this perspective. Sensing this, police officers would always tease us, if we were away for a shift, by maintaining that 'all hell broke loose' while we were away. On one occasion an area car crew that DJS had spent a long time with told him that 'things had gone really mad' the night before when he was away. 'You should have seen' said the WPC plain-clothes observer 'this bloke who got stabbed in the belly, and his guts had all spilled out and his intestine was draped all over the pavement'. This was, admittedly, a more dramatic event than was usual, though the account was highly exaggerated and it turned out to be the only incident that had happened all night.

Because of the boredom, car crews strongly compete with each other to answer calls that sound interesting (what counts as interesting depends on how bored they are). In one area car the (young) radio operator would grab the microphone as soon as a call started to come over the radio, his thumb hovering over the button (which you have to press to make a transmission) and would look tensely at the driver to see if he wanted to accept the call or considered it 'weary'; if the driver wanted to accept it he would try hard to answer before another crew, and if another one got in first he would be 'slagged off' remorselessly by the rest of the crew and given advice on his radio technique; then the next time, the driver would grab the microphone and answer the call to prevent the operator from bungling it.

Car chases offer a kind of excitement that police officers particularly hanker after. Joining a particular area car crew for the first time, JG spent a completely uneventful six hours during which time the car drove round apparently aimlessly without answering a call and without the crew ever speaking to any member of the public. At four o'clock they stopped an old and battered car with seven youths in it (they were punks), breathalised the driver, searched the car and the occupants and sent them on their way. At four-thirty the crew stopped an Asian couple leaving a car, again without any 'result'. They then went into a police station to 'book the stops in' (record them in the 'stop book'). JG stayed in the car and heard a great commotion break out in the mainset radio. He ran into the police station to alert the crew who were just running out, having heard the transmission on their personal radios, because information room had linked the personal radio to the mainset channel. They drove out of the yard knowing that the car was coming towards them. Within a few seconds a Ford Fiesta appeared round the corner going very fast towards them with another area car in pursuit. The driver of JG's car made the roadway narrow, hoping to make the driver stop, but he squeezed between the area car and the kerb and went off again at great speed. JG's car joined the chase. The area car in front of them kept up a running commentary as the Fiesta was chased for some fourteen miles (it had already driven several miles from another district). As dawn came up, four area cars had joined the chase, which became more and more hair-raising, the cars reaching speeds of 90mph and over in fairly narrow suburban streets. The driver eventually came to a halt in a dead-end by a recreation ground and made a run for a council estate. The crews of the four area cars on his tail jumped out and chased him, and JG came upon the suspect just as he was being arrested rather roughly, but without real violence. He was taken back to where he had dumped the car. By this time the whole recreation ground was surrounded by police vehicles. JG counted seven area cars, four panda cars and two vans, a total of thirteen. One of the area cars, which had come from a District a considerable distance away, had tried to drive across the recreation ground and was stuck in the mud: JG and some of the many police officers there managed to shift it.

By the end of the chase, most of the police cars from about six Divisions were concentrated in a recreation ground a long way from their home patch. At about 5.30 am this may not have mattered too much, but it illustrated the magnetic attraction of a chase like this one for all police vehicles that have any chance of joining in. Everyone who had taken part in the chase found it intensely satisfying. They stood around in the charge room at the police station in small groups swapping exaggerated and self-congratulatory accounts of what had happened for some time afterwards. As JG's crew drove back to their own police station, the driver said to him: 'You don't know how lucky you are: some blokes wait twenty-five years in the job to see what you've seen on your first night here'.

One crew that DJS was with, when it got bored, would chase after any police car that it saw driving fast or with the light or siren on, without knowing at all what the call was about. Apart from chases, a good deal of driving by PCs in the Met is explained by the need for interest and excitement. When one relief found itself with a brand new van one night, the van driver drove it flat out down a dual carriageway for a while and blew the gasket. At night when nothing had happened for a long time one area car driver was in the habit of suddenly accelerating up to about 100 mph if he was on an urban motorway or up to about 80 mph on a normal road and then driving for 10 to 20 miles at very high speed.

Of course, there are other sources of excitement and interest apart from driving fast in cars. Most constables would like to have a reasonable number of dramatic or at least interesting crimes to deal with. One PC complained at length to a sergeant that the 'ground' where they both worked had become much quieter; he looked back with nostalgia to the old days when the ground was much 'harder' and 'you could literally be strolling past a pub and a bloke would come staggering out with a knife in his back'. The sergeant, who was new to the area, said 'Hmm, it sounds as though it used to be a really tasty ground, nice and varied. You know, I feel sorry for some of the younger ones now who come out here - it's so dead. I mean, their staple diet is accidents, drunks and motor vehicle crime.' He went on to explain that his first posting had been very boring. 'It really wasn't what I joined for. When I left training school I wanted excitement and variety.' A bit later, the PC talked about crime prevention, saying 'Ideally I'd like a zero crime rate', but the sergeant replied 'It might be a bit boring'.

A considerable number of stops are carried out mainly for something to do. When DJS spent a whole night walking with a probationer who could find nothing at all to do, the probationer eventually waited on a main road where there was virtually no traffic and stopped the first two cars that came by. Both were young men on their way to work, and both said they were very frequently stopped by police at about 5am as they went to work. One of them, who was ultra-respectable working class, had stream-lined the whole procedure to such an extent that he recited the index number of his car and spelt out his name using the police code-words for the letters (alpha, bravo, charlie, etc.). The few people out on the road at 5am are very likely to be stopped by bored police officers, which partly explains why the same people tend to be stopped over and over again (see Chapter IV).

The prospect of a violent disturbance or a riot is something that is certainly found interesting and exciting by many police officers, though if they are in small groups they may not look forward to it through finding it too frightening. However, larger groups such as immediate response units certainly look forward to disturbances and, in fact, tend to find anything else boring by comparison. On one evening when DJS was with an IRU, the group had worked out a plan to keep itself occupied (in the expectation that there would not be any disturbances to deal with). The idea was to try to catch burglars who had been concentrating on commercial premises in a particular network of small streets. One member of the group had spent the early hours of the shift making copies of a map of the area and planning observation posts at strategic points. Because they had set themselves a defined task (unlike patrolling vehicles) the group were quite looking forward to their evening's work. As they got into the carrier (in plain clothes since they were to be doing observation work) there was activity over the radio from another District where petrol bombs had been used by a group of black people. The IRU belonging to the District was dealing with the incident, together with some other local units. Immediately everyone in the group pricked up their ears and started to say things like: 'That's it, it's starting, we'll have to go to U District to help with the operation against the riot. Hoi, hoi, hoi! Away we go, that's what we're really here for. Sergeant, shall we get into our uniforms?' The sergeant, very much respected and rather a thoughtful man, considered for a moment then said 'Right, everybody into your uniforms'. One or two said 'What about the burglaries, then?' The sergeant said 'We'll have to abandon it. We must be on hand in case they need us in U District.' One member of the group said 'Look, Sergeant, that's miles away, we would take ages to get there.' There was an argument about how long it would take, but the driver said it would only take 10 minutes and his word was taken to be authoritative. Only two members of the group were disappointed. The other 10 were all pleased to be having the chance of dealing with a real disturbance. There was just one man who remained firmly convinced that the group would not be needed. He said 'All right, I don't mind, but I bet you that by the end of the evening we won't have gone to U District.' He was right, of course. A part of the reason for the group's response, in this case, was that they had been trained to deal with disturbances, and they regarded the IRU as primarily existing for that purpose: hence, as long as there was no disturbance, the group had no purpose, whereas it came into its own as soon as a disturbance happened. But, apart from that, there was also the simple feeling that something really dangerous must be more exciting than just trying to catch some burglars. The researcher found it quite easy to share this feeling.

It would be wrong to give the impression that patrolling officers are completely aimless until they have a call to respond to. The more experienced ones, especially those with talents as 'thief takers', are looking out for signs or bits of behaviour around them that will act as cues and give them a chance to make a 'good arrest'. Analysis of the arrests that we observed in the research shows that a significant minority of them were made because a patrolling officer saw something - for example saw someone drop a plastic bag over a wall. Still, a great deal of the time, patrolling officers do not see anything of that kind, and have lost hope of seeing anything in the current shift. Instead, they look forward to some kind of excitement arising from a call, and therefore they listen hard to the radio. When nothing does happen, they may try to persuade themselves that by being there, by 'showing the flag', they are doing something useful, that is, preventing crime. But preventing crime without having anything to show for it is the last thing they really want to do.

Whether more police officers could be carrying out defined tasks instead of patrolling and waiting to respond, and whether the satisfaction to be derived from these tasks could compete with the high (if rare) excitement of car chases and riots is a question we shall discuss later in this report.

**'Figures'**

'Figures' is the disparaging term used by police officers for the evaluation of their performance in terms of numbers: typically, the number of traffic process reports or the number of arrests made in a particular period. There are a number of reasons for the contempt associated with the term. One is resentment at what is seen as a crude attempt by senior officers to get constables to do something useful. Another is the conviction that certain kinds of arrest are far more valuable than others, and that assessment in terms of 'figures' confounds good and bad police work. Thirdly, police officers never fully accept without misgivings the idea that making arrests or doing traffic process reports should be taken as the objectives of police work: they argue that this will produce wrongful or unnecessary arrests and pointless traffic process reports.

We shall consider this matter from the viewpoint of supervising officers in Chapter XVIII. Their problem is that they find it difficult to conceive of any useful measure of performance other than 'figures' since objectives of police work other than making arrests and so on are hard to define and, if defined, are hard to recognise when achieved.

Looking at the matter from the viewpoint of the constables, 'figures' are not an objective that they recognise as springing from their own conception of police work; they are something you may have to get, on occasion, to satisfy more senior officers. It would, however, be a gross exaggeration to say that most constables are motivated from day to day by a need to get 'figures'. This only applies to probationers, to others who are at transitional stage (for example, trying to get into CID or a specialist group) and to officers working in units which they fear may be wound up unless they continue to show good results. Also, 'figures' have no relevance at all to promotion.

Probationers (officers in their first two years of service) have three-monthly meetings with their chief-superintendents when they are expected to produce returns of work and show that they have had experience of a range of policing activities. The sanction is that their appointment as police officers cannot be confirmed (even if they pass the final examination) without the support of their chief-superintendent. Few constables think that this system works to ensure that probationers undertake a reasonable balance of work. The usual view is that they tend to carry out certain simple operations in a mechanical fashion in order to produce 'figures'. In particular, most traffic process work that is done by officers outside the specialist traffic group is done by probationers, because it is easy to build up 'figures' that way, and because there is no pressure on confirmed constables to undertake this kind of work. A young PC who was two years out of probation put it this way.

When you're a probationer you must get 'figures' so that you have something to show at your meeting with God's deputy (the chief-superintendent). You have to build up the figures with traffic process. But once you have passed your final exam, nobody cares whether you do one or a hundred traffic processes a month.

DJS: Could you get away with doing nothing?
PC: You probably could do, but luckily there is nobody on our relief like that, except for one who is not with us at the moment - he's in the Coroner's office.

That same night this PC took a probationer with him in his panda car, and at about 3 am they went down a long residential road while the probationer wrote out a process report for every car he found without an up-to-date tax disc. There were twelve of these cars in the single road, which was as many as the probationer needed to keep up his 'figures'. Of course, this was a purely clerical exercise that provided no experience of police work at all, since the probationer did not meet or talk to anyone. Not all chief-superintendents would give any credit for simply 'writing out tickets': in fact some told us plainly that they considered this kind of activity to be totally useless from every point of view. But this probationer would not have behaved like this if his own chief-superintendent had not encouraged him to.

On another District, the probationers said they were set a target of two process or arrests and five stops a day. A popular way of getting the process 'figures' was to stand by a bus lane and report the motorists driving in it. Once an officer was out of probation he would be very unlikely to do anything of this kind.

Probationers are responsible for keeping their own records of the work they have done so that they have something to show to the Chief-Superintendent. However, once they are out of probation, uniform officers are not expected to keep a record of this kind, and there is no ready way in which senior officers can pull out statistics, from all the forms filled in, showing the number of arrests, stops or traffic process reports done by an individual officer. (CID officers do, however, keep a record of their arrests at the back of their diaries.) Apart from probationers, the officers who have to show 'figures' are those working in crime squads and hoping to be selected for CID, and those trying to get into a uniform specialism. In both cases there is a selection procedure including a method of finding out what the officer's experience is and what kind of work he has been doing recently. Under the old system, whereby officers worked as Temporary Detective Constables for about two years before being selected for CID, this pressure was probably greater than it is now (though some of the stories told are exaggerated and romanticised).

At one Division the members of the crime squad thought that senior officers were less than fully committed to the continuance of the squad. All of them wanted to stay working in the squad either because they hoped to join CID or because they liked the nature of the work and the more flexible working environment (compared with a relief). They thought that their places on the squad were assured as long as they continued to make 5-10 arrests a week, but worried if they failed to achieve this 'quota'.

It is widely believed that 'figures' are a bad criterion of

performances and that the use of such a criterion leads to unnecessary or unjustified arrests and stops. Police officers will prove that the criterion is crude and mechanical by finding ways of distorting the 'figures'. As the uniform sergeant in charge of a crime squad put it:

> It's really quite simple. If anyone in the crime squad comes under attack for not getting figures, the rest of us make sure that anyone nicked for a two or three-day period is shown to the person criticised.

Unfortunately, the mildly mischievous practice of misleading a supervising officer can lead to the far more serious one of misleading a court: for 'showing the arrests to the person criticised' can mean fabricating evidence to make it appear that this person actually made the arrests when he did not (for example, see pages 473-474). It is significant that the motive has to do with the internal management of a police force rather than with any desire to increase the chance of conviction.

At the same Division, concern was suddenly expressed somewhere high up in the hierarchy about the numbers of burglaries, which had steeply increased in a large part of the ground. The message bumped all the way down to the sergeant in charge of the crime squad, which was expected to do something about it. When members of the squad heard about this, one of them immediately volunteered a suspect who 'might be good for one or two jobs'. His solution to the problem was 'Let's go round and nick Danny'. The only justification for doing so was that Danny 'had form' for burglary, that a particular shop had been burgled three nights running and that Danny was the only local criminal who was stupid enough to do a burglary three times in the same place. The sergeant thought this was a good idea, and he went (with JG) to arrest Danny at a building site, but could not find him there. To the annoyance of the crime squad, someone on a uniform relief did arrest Danny later that same day, and Danny did admit to the shop burglaries. We did not find out how or why Danny came to be arrested.

We did not see police officers making unnecessary or wrongful arrests for the sake of the 'figures', though we did hear stories about it, mostly going back to the old Temporary Detective Constable system. A PC who had at one time been in the CID said that when he was trying to get in, he and the other TDCs had worked on a quota system, which meant that they had to achieve a certain number of arrests a week.

> If you got to Friday and that space at the back of your diary wasn't filling up, you used to go out or were sent out in search of bodies (arrests). People got nicked for things like sus, just to make everything look right. I just couldn't do it and the DI (detective inspector) used to say to me 'Why have

345

you got so few arrests and everybody else seems to be able to manage to get X per week?' I would say 'I just didn't see the crimes committed, Sir'. He would say 'Either you're calling your colleagues liars or you're just not looking hard enough'.

A uniform sergeant boasted about the success of his recent posting to the Q car in terms of the number of arrests made: 'We had 64 bodies in eight weeks'. At the same time he strongly criticised the use of arrests as a criterion of performance by management. He had at one time been an aide to CID (a TDC) under the old system and told rather lurid stories about the methods used to get 'figures'.

There was a space in the back of your diary for arrests. The quota was two per week. If you didn't get the quota come Friday you had to grab just anyone or buy the DI a bottle of Scotch. It was wicked in those days - you could be back in a top hat on the Monday. What some of the aides at X Police Station used to do was suspend a jemmy from an archway by a piece of twine. The paddies would come out of the local pub, pissed, and one of them would grab the jemmy. Then he'd be nicked with his dabs all over it for the old offence of going equipped for house-breaking. I used to know an old DS (detective sergeant). When he worked in the Q car he used to carry a briefcase. In this briefcase he carried a Luger and ten rounds. They'd go out and pick up the first old drunk they saw and put him in the back of the car. The DS would say 'What are you going to have? (What charge are you going to admit to?) You can have a bit of sus, a bit of burglary... or you can have this Luger and ten rounds.' So the bloke would put his hands up to something and the Q car had its body for the day. Mind you, I'm talking about some time ago.
J.G: Does it still happen?
Sergeant: Of course it does. But it isn't as bad as the old days.

However exaggerated these stories are, they show that the junior ranks are extremely sceptical about 'management by figures' and hostile towards it. This is partly because they resent any attempt to set targets which may mean that they have to work harder; but it is partly because of genuine misgivings about the nature of the criterion and the abuse it could lead to.

### 'Good arrest', 'good result', 'good villain', 'rubbish'

Whereas 'figures' is a disparaging term for a crude method of evaluating performance used by senior officers, terms like 'good arrest' and 'good result' are used to descibe what the lower ranks see as the objectives of police work; and such terms are also adopted by senior officers when making judgements about performance.

A 'good arrest' is one which demonstrated skill, determination or physical strength. It might be considered 'good', for example, because the officer noticed something apparently insignificant that led to the arrest, sensed that someone was uneasy, afraid or out of place and therefore suspected him, or had the physical speed or strength to catch and hold onto someone who might have got away. A 'good result' is similar, except that the emphasis is on building a good case against someone in connection with a reported crime rather than catching someone in the act. A 'good villain is a successful criminal who, therefore, counts as a worthy antagonist; arresting a 'good villian' is counted a much greater success than arresting an incompetent or occasional law-breaker, even if the offence committed by the latter is fairly serious. 'Rubbish' is a matter that the police are required to deal with but which will result either in no arrest or in an arrest of a kind that is not valued.

The following is an example of a 'good arrest' combined with a 'good result'. One night two PCs on a relief that DJS was working with stopped a youngish man of fairly conventional appearance. The PCs would claim that they sensed there was something suspicious about him, though in fact they were keen to make arrests and considered that any young person walking in that area late at night was likely to have cannabis on him. When they questioned him about where he had come from and where he was going to they did genuinely sense that he was uneasy. They therefore searched him very thoroughly. Most people would not have found anything, but these PCs were sure that the man was worried about something, were determined to find something if possible, and were good lookers. Eventually they found a single cannabis seed. Many PCs, even if they had noticed the seed, would not have known what it was, but these PCs did know. They then went with the suspect to his flat, which they searched (without a warrant). They found a large quantity of cannabis worth several thousand pounds and quantities of cocaine. It was evident that the man must be a drugs dealer. He was of course arrested, but in addition the relief inspector decided to mount a continuous observation on the flat. Early the next morning a respectable looking man came to call. When he was stopped and searched he was found to be carrying a large quantity of drugs. The case was then taken over by a central drugs squad, who may have been able to catch several more drugs dealers through the two already arrested. This was considered by everyone on the relief to be a very good arrest and result because many police officers would have missed the small initial clues, because the first stop was followed up intelligently and effectively, because it led to a further arrest, and (perhaps most of all) because a specialist central squad took an interest in the case and benefited from the spadework done by members of an ordinary uniform relief. (An interesting point to notice about this case is that if the original suspect had refused to let the PCs into his flat they could not legally have gained entry without first getting a warrant. They could probably have legally detained the suspect for long enough to get a warrant, but as very often happens they 'fronted' their way in without one.)

Although this was undoubtedly a 'good arrest' and a 'good result', the suspects were not referred to as 'good villains' probably because drug dealers do not really fall into this category: they are not the kind of criminal that a police officer normally respects. The prototype of the 'good villain' would be a skilful safe-breaker or jewel burglar. However, most police officers have to settle for 'good villains' of a lower order: any young man who had done a large number of burglaries, or his 'fence', would qualify. An active and pushy PC on a relief that JG worked with made a 'good arrest' of a man considered to be a 'good villain'. JG was not with the PC at the time of the arrest but heard a detailed account of it soon afterwards. The PC spotted a man driving a car whom he had arrested before, stopped the car, questioned and arrested the man without difficulty. The reason for the arrest was that the man was wanted after escaping from prison. The PC's inspector put in a 'good arrest report' on the incident (the beginning of a procedure for encouragement and commendation). The reasons for thinking that this was a good arrest were that the man was considered dangerous (he had convictions for causing grievous bodily harm) and daring (he had escaped from prison) and that the PC did well to spot him. The man, who was small and muscular, had at one time been a 'good cat burglar', but also had convictions for various other offences, such as car theft, as well as for serious assaults. JG accompanied three PCs (including the one who had made the arrest) when they transported him to prison. The PCs spent the whole journey in animated conversation with the offender; they wanted to know about his most outstanding crimes and to hear the story of his escape from prison in detail. They all got on very well with the prisoner and very much enjoyed the conversation and the feeling that they had a valuable relationship with him; the fact that he was looking out for a way of escaping from them, and that they had to be careful to hang on to him did not interfere with this relationship at all. Afterwards the PC who had made the arrest said 'Allessandro is a diamond, but he's a villain'.

Although many of their activities do not involve making arrests at all, uniform officers on reliefs and crime squads generally gain greater satisfaction from making 'good arrests' than from anything else. The officers within these groups who make 'good arrests' tend to be the more respected ones even if they are unattractive in other ways. Among CID officers, the values are rather different. This is partly because the emphasis is more on investigation or in other words getting a 'good result', which usually turns, in the end, on getting an admission of guilt. Also, there is value placed on collecting information from local contacts (especially contacts with criminals). At best, the CID officer who does well and gets 'good results' is one who has the knack of talking to people, especially criminals, and of getting them to unburden

348

themselves to him or take him into their confidence. At worst, it is the successful bully who is admired. In addition, CID officers often seem to have preoccupations, such as the cultivation of a special idea of manliness, that have little to do with achieving results in terms of practical police work.

The clearest examples of what PCs call 'rubbish' are domestic disputes and disturbances. A typical piece of 'rubbish' was a call to a 'domestic disturbance' that was answered by a 22-year old PC driving a panda car and accompanied by DJS. They were met outside the house by a girl aged about twenty who seemed upset and said she had called the police. The PC immediately recognised the girl and remembered going to the house before. On that occasion the girl had called the police because a man whom she had taken home after meeting him in a restaurant was firing blank cartridges from a gun. So the PC started by asking 'What's the trouble this time? Is there a man inside waving a gun?' The girl said 'Everything's happening', and the PC asked her what she meant. She did not explain very clearly but the PC gathered that there was a quarrel between her mother and a man. 'Is the man your mother's husband?' he asked, probably more out of prurience than anything else. 'No', said the girl, 'he's, sort of, my mum's boyfriend. He's been staying in the house for a while'.

The PC, the girl and DJS went into the front room of the house, where there was a loud argument going on between the mother and her Irish lodger. Both of them were drunk. The man said the woman had insulted him by calling him an 'Irish bastard' and other things of that kind. He also said she had hit him and kept pointing to a small mark on his mouth. He was rather embarassed about not having hit her back. 'In my young days I would have flattened anyone who insulted me, but I'm not so young any more, that's the trouble.' (He looked about 45.) The daughter said she felt she had to call the police because things had gone too far, and left the room. The PC went into another room with the mother, leaving DJS with the man. He asked whether he should have hit the mother on being insulted, given that she was a woman. He calmed down a bit when asked about his job, but then soon became very emotional, burst into tears from time to time and went over to the sink to wash his face afterwards. 'What would you do?' he asked. DJS suggested leaving the house and going to live somewhere else. The man made it clear that he didn't want to leave and considered this to be just a temporary quarrel. He then burst into tears again.

The PC came back into the front room to talk to the man. Unfortunately he was soon joined by the mother, who was determined to join in. She began to shout at the man and insulted him on the grounds of his Irishness. 'Don't you dare call my daughter a whore!' she screamed. 'I don't mind if you say anything like that to me, but I won't have you insult my daughters!' From this it appeared that the man had started the quarrel by calling the daughters whores and the woman had retaliated by calling him an

Irish bastard. The PC managed to persuade the woman to leave the room for a short time so that he could speak to the man. 'I hope you don't mind me saying it plain in my own language', said the man, 'but I didn't call you, and I'd be quite happy if you would fuck off out of here.' At this the PC became very grave and white and drawing himself up said 'That may be your language, but it isn't my language and I object to it, and another thing is you should show some respect for the uniform.' At this the man apologised quite meekly, saying that all he meant was that the PC could not do anything to help (which was, of course, quite true). At this point the woman came back into the room and she and the man engaged in a shouting match for a while. The woman made a great point of offering to have her daughters medically examined to prove that they were virgins.

After a while, the PC, who had remained calm and self-controlled, persuaded the man to put on his jacket and leave the house for a while. He left most reluctantly, saying, 'I admit that I am drunk, but she, she called me an Irish bastard!' The PC now explained to the woman what steps she should take if she wanted to make the man leave the house permanently. By saying that she had tried to do all that before and it hadn't worked, she made it clear that she did not want to turn the man out in any case. Altogether she was not very friendly. On leaving the house, the PC and DJS found the man skulking around outside and had another talk with him. When the PC asked whether it was true that he had called the daughter 'a slag' the man replied sharply that it was 'none of your business'. When one of the woman's sons arrived and went into the house, the man insisted on going in again although the PC tried to dissuade him; he said that the son would have a calming influence.

As the PC and DJS went back to the car, DJS suggested that the quarrel would probably start again now. The PC agreed but did not seem to be concerned. He made it clear that he did not regard this as proper police work, chiefly because the people involved did not want or require any help from the police. If the daughter had not called the police, he thought the pair would probably just have hit each other a few times and then given up. DJS suggested that there might be a danger of injury, but the PC was not concerned about that. On the whole, his attitude was rational and unprejudiced. Of course, he did not respect the people, and that contributed to his view that the call was 'rubbish', but his more important reasons for thinking so were that there was nothing that he should or could do about the matter and that there could not possibly be any 'result'. He was (privately) prejudiced in that he took sides with the man, but he hardly showed it at the time. He argued that the man was in the right because the daughters were, in fact, 'slags' (after all one of them had picked up a man in a restaurant). Also, he thought that men should be allowed to win arguments with women.

350

## Dominance and not losing face

It flows from the nature of police work that it is important for officers to keep control in any encounter. It is not true, however, that the most effective method of keeping control is for the officer to be self-assertive or aggressively dominant, or that he needs to be preoccupied with the risk of losing face. At the time when we observed classes at training school (Autumn 1980) instructors gave some emphasis to the need to demand respect and not to accept any slight or humiliation:  one instructor said, 'You must remember that if people show disrespect for you they are showing disrespect for the uniform'.  Yet there was no fully worked out instruction in strategies for gaining and keeping control, so that recruits might well have been left with the impression that vigorous self-assertion and a refusal to accept any slight was what was expected.  More recently, the 'human awareness training' has tried to tackle the problem of giving recruits the means of managing an encounter without being unduly or unnecessarily self-assertive.  The relevant skills are of central importance to police work, and the success of the Force will depend, to a considerable extent, on whether they can be identified and transmitted.

Within the norms of working groups of police officers, a high value is placed on being seen to be dominant and not being seen to lose face or be 'had over' (deceived).  This does not necessarily have any unwelcome consequences in itself, but it does for an officer who lacks confidence or does not know how to control an encounter without being unduly assertive. The problem arises from a combination of the high value placed on dominance and a lack of the skills needed to achieve it legitimately.

The strategies used by the best police officers are the ones that would emerge from a social psychology textbook.  They remain impassive and show by the slowness of their responses that they only speak or act after consideration and from choice, so that they are not under the control of the other person. They are not voluble.  They are prepared to wait and to put the onus on the other person to say something.  As far as possible, they ignore foolish or hysterical behaviour rather than drawing attention to it. They are watchful and sceptical, always placing the onus on the other person to convince them of something rather than jumping to a conclusion.  They maintain close eye contact with the person they are talking to, making him feel that he wants to look away. They never allow a slight or insult to go unremarked, but respond in a measured way so as to re-establish control without raising the emotional temperature.

Essentially, these strategies work, and the difficulties come when a police officer departs from them.  But a further problem arises because police officers who do not use the best strategies can usually get by without losing control altogether, so that they are not usually faced with the necessity of changing their approach.  Our observations show that police officers - even inexperienced ones - very rarely lose control altogether in an encounter; there is quite often some threat to their authority, but this can usually be dealt with without much difficulty. Also, where an officer does respond more sharply to a threat than he needs to, or deliberately 'winds someone up' instead of lowering the temperature, he usually gets away with it without losing control. The simple fact of being a police officer (especially one in uniform) gives someone an enormous advantage in any encounter, and most of the time, unless he does something really silly, he is unlikely to lose contol completely. Sooner or later an officer who always over-reacts to any challenge to his authority will be physically attacked, but this retribution may not catch up with him for some considerable time, and when it does the rest of the relief will rush to his defence, and he may be cast in the role of hero.

Running through the whole of police behaviour there is a fear of being 'had over' (deceived) or losing face. Much canteen banter turns on the idea that an officer let a suspect go although he had just committed a crime, or was 'wound up' by a suspect but 'lost his bottle' and therefore did nothing about it.

One evening DJS accompanied a group of uniform officers carrying out a road block by a notorious council estate known to the relief as 'the rat farm'. A number of people with serious criminal records live on this estate, and a much larger number with a record of minor offences. The plan was to stop cars coming out of the estate in the hope of catching someone carrying stolen goods. Unfortunately, there was hardly any traffic when the road block started, and very soon it began to rain. The local 'yobs' who were drinking in a pub opposite noticed what was going on, and came out with their beer mugs to send up derisive cheers from time to time. The group of police officers included the home beat officer for the area, who felt a special responsibility, and who was losing face severely through being jeered by his own 'yobs' on his own patch in front of a whole party of other officers. He was a middle-aged, heavily built man with a special line in coarse raillery exchanged mainly with his special friend, of a similar age and build, who was with him at this incident. The two of them went off towards the pub, saying they were going to 'sort out the yobs'. They would do this by 'winding up' a 'yob' so that he would hit one of the officers and could then be arrested. Because DJS was there, the others in the group tried to dissuade the pair from doing this. At this point the men outside the pub started to jeer 'It's raining! You're getting wet!' which was too much for the home beat officer and his friend. Ignoring what the others said they set off to 'sort out' the louts, but at this moment the inspector who was organising the road blocks that evening arrived in a car and got out. The men in front of the pub jeered again 'It's raining, you're going to get wet!', this time at the inspector. He replied 'So are you getting wet, but I'm getting paid for it', turned on his heel and walked away. When the home beat officer and his friend again started to go towards the pub, he stopped them by giving them another task to perform. The inspector told DJS afterwards that if neither of them had been there these two PCs would have started a fight in order to be able to make arrests. The other officers who saw what happened said the same. Also, most of the officers, although they discouraged the pair from starting something, found their attitudes quite understandable, and several of them said things like 'It's all right for us, but Barry has got to make sure that he keeps control of his patch'. What they had not chosen to notice, of course, was that after their encounter with the inspector the 'yobs' had gradually drifted off back into the pub.

Another incident also shows how police officers react much more strongly than they need to, on occasion, to a challenge to their authority because of their need to 'save face', and that they can get away with it without losing control completely. At 3 am on a Sunday morning, JG was with an area car crew who went to assist officers arresting a drunk driver (who turned out to be Asian). Two friends of the driver were standing about on the pavement trying to find out from the police officers what was going on, but none of the officers would speak to them. They became agitated when their friend was arrested and his car driven off, leaving them stranded. When the other police cars had left, and the crew JG was with got back into their car and started to drive off, one of the friends of the arrested man made a mildly obscene gesture. The driver of the area car (a PC with about eight years' experience) stopped the car, reversed at speed and jumped out, looking as if he was about to hit the Asian man. As it was, he seemed to restrain himself with difficulty, grabbed hold of the man and said 'I don't need that kind of behaviour from your sort ... from people like you'. ('Your sort' may have been a reference to the man's race.) Because the two men accepted this quite passively, the unnecessary response from the PC, which was purely a matter of 'saving face', did not get him into any difficulty. It is interesting to notice that in this case it was the behaviour of the police that had caused the two men to be upset in the first place: if one of the officers had explained to them what was happening and suggested that they took a cab home, they would not have been so upset and annoyed as to have deliberately provoked the PC.

In another case that we came across, an experienced PC became very upset and was only prevented by good supervision from assaulting a prisoner who challenged his authority in a clever way. The prisoner was a black man aged about 20 who had been arrested along with three others on suspicion of theft (they had been seen hanging about a jeweller's shop). First of all Rodney (the suspect) denied everything that the PCs said about how they had been behaving in the street. Then one of them called one PC 'sunshine' and another 'a cunt'. As he was being put into a cell to await an interview, Rodney claimed that he had 'already been tried and found guilty'. Then (rather contradicting the earlier remark) he said 'You've got nothing on us and you know it. You'll have to let us go.' The PCs were already very irritated by Rodney's behaviour. One of them said, 'That Rodney's always a leery

bastard. He was just like that when SPG arrested him for TDA.'
(Checks showed that while he had been arrested several times, he
had never been convicted of an offence.) After Rodney had been
interviewed and had made no admission it was decided to release
him without charge. The PC acting as gaoler (who had, of course,
had nothing to do with the arrest) went to get him from the cell,
but came back looking very angry and saying, 'I don't think Mr.
Rodney wants to go'. He explained that Rodney had damaged his
cell. The inspector and JG went to take a look and found that a
long, heavy strip of metal had been removed from the radiator.
Rodney insisted that he knew nothing about it, but the gaoler said
he was sure that the radiator was intact when Rodney was put in
the cell. Rodney was then strip-searched to find the implement he
had used to prise off the metal strip. He told the PC's to wash
their hands before they touched him, and kept up a stream of
objections to the searching procedure. Nothing was found. On the
way to the charge room, Rodney claimed that £1 had been stolen
from his trouser pocket (impossible, because all prisoner's property
is put in a sealed bag when the prisoner is checked into the police
station). While the release procedure was being gone through,
Rodney spotted three cold prisoner's meals. A PC was picking at
the chips. Rodney asked if the meals had been intended for him
and his friend. The gaoler told him he was going out now, so he
didn't need a meal. 'Did I ask for it?' said Rodney. By this time
the gaoler was furious. He stood up very close to Rodney and said
'You ain't half got a lot of fucking mouth, haven't you?'. It was
only because the inspector intervened at this point that a serious
confrontation was prevented. When Rodney and his two friends had
been shown out, the gaoler said to JG, 'I'd love to have belted that
Rodney, you can put that in your report'. JG asked why. 'Because
he scared the shit out of me. That lump of metal could have killed
someone.'

The PC responded in this way because Rodney had deliberately set out to 'wind him up' and had succeeded rather well. One
way he could have got over the humiliation, or made up for it,
would have been to hit Rodney.

### Backing up others in the group
The solidarity among police officers generally, and particularly
among small groups who work together, is extremely strong. This
shows in the very high priority given to going to the aid of any
police officer who is under (physical) attack or in danger; in the
lengths to which officers will go to defend a member of the group
who is threatened in some other way (for example, by allegations
of misconduct made against him); and in the 'rituals' and 'initiation
ceremonies' imposed on any outsider who wishes to join the group.

We found that calls for urgent assistance from PCs always
met with a massive response; if there was any indication that a PC
was being physically attacked, every police car within a radius of
about two miles would race to answer the call, regardless of

whether they were shown as dealing with the incident or assisting. DJS spend one shift with a car having a specific assignment to deal with any bomb threats. During the late afternoon there was a call to a pub about two miles away (through heavy traffic) where an off-duty PC was said to be under attack. About four cars accepted the call on the radio. The bomb car did not, but the driver went there at very high speed. On arrival there were six other police cars outside the pub, including three areas cars, but no sign of any disturbance or of any off-duty PC. DJS mentioned to the crew that he had counted six vehicles. The driver said 'Quite right, too. We would all have needed to be there if a PC had been having his head kicked in. It was a very good response, wasn't it?' This answer also illustrated another point: that for the driver of a police car, simply getting quickly to the location counts as achieving an objective, and whether there is anything when he gets there can be a secondary consideration.

During the early period of our research, information room were not usually strict about the number of cars assigned to a call. In January 1982 there was a change of policy. From that time they normally allowed only two units to be assigned to a call, but if the matter was particularly urgent or the incident violent they would send two units and instruct one or two others to be in the immediate vicinity. This policy was applied quite strictly when it was first introduced, although there was some slackening later on. When the new rule was first introduced there was no general instruction or memorandum issued that the ordinary PCs were aware of. They simply found that the operator repeatedly refused to assign them to calls. This caused a great number of comments over the radio. For example, in response to a simple disturbance (youths fighting) the operator allowed two units and refused permission to attend to four others. There were many comments such as 'I hope the other lot aren't getting a kicking'. Eventually, the operator got tired of this and said 'Look, information room have received instructions on this from the DAC B Department. That is why attendance is being restricted'. The comment that came back over the mainset was 'Yeah, well he's a cunt then'. JG found out that it was a PC at the Division where he was working who said this.

We were told many times that an officer who had done something wrong would always, or almost always, be backed up by other officers, even if they didn't like him. Perhaps the clearest statement on this was made by a uniform sergeant in charge of a crime squad. JG asked him whether he would 'shop' one of his mates who had committed a serious assault on a prisoner. He said 'No, I never would. If one of the boys working for me got himself into trouble, I would get all of us together and I would literally script him out of it. I would write all the parts out and if we followed them closely we couldn't be defeated. And believe me, I would do it'. JG asked if he didn't think it was wrong for police officers to get away with assaulting prisoners, especially as this would involve a conspiracy to cover up the evidence. He said, 'Oh yes, but when it was all over, I wouldn't want to work with that bloke ever again. I wouldn't want anything to do with him'. We never heard anyone contradict this point of view at the level of constable or sergeant. This sergeant obviously thought that internal justice administered informally by colleagues was far preferable to justice through the machinery of the complaints and disciplinary system of the Force. When he was asked about this he said that the disciplinary system was inflexible and unfair and that the penalties it imposed were too severe: 'I'd never stand by and let a bloke lose his job'. Underlying his thinking there was also the feeling that the machinery of Force discipline was something that attacked the in-group from outside and which the group could not control in any way once it built up a momentum. Control from within the group was not only less damaging to the officer concerned, but also less threatening to the group as a whole.

The officers who investigate complaints - for example, the chief-inspectors in charge of complaints units on Districts - accept that police officers in the lower ranks almost always back each other up. The following are the exact words used by a chief-inspector in charge of the complaints unit on one of the Districts that we studied.

> If I have to 'not substantiate' an allegation for lack of evidence and yet am almost certain the officer is guilty, I let him know. Recently I had a case where some officers were accused of stopping a black man, calling him a black bastard, and one of them punched him in the mouth. He lost a couple of teeth. One of the other officers cooled him down. They all denied this incident, but I'm almost certain it happened. Before they left my office I made it clear that I thought they were guilty, and they didn't look too comfortable.

Since membership of the group has important implications, entry into the group has to be marked by observances and rituals so that the new member is made aware of the obligations he is taking on. It may be misleading, in this context, to talk about 'the group'. Everyone who becomes a police officer and wears the uniform qualifies for membership of a broadly defined group and gains a minimum of acceptance. In the past, probationers and other young officers did not become fully accepted by experienced officers for some considerable time. Older policemen commonly maintain that the 'parent constables' who took them round when they were probationers would not speak to them at all, and would leave them outside in the cold when they went to their 'tea holes' for refreshment. More recently, the younger and less experienced officers have become a much higher proportion of the total; probably because of this, their relations with the older officers have become more informal. Even so, there are very clearly defined 'inner groups' of PCs who tend to work together and avoid close relations with 'outgroups'. The 'inner groups' tend to be more experienced and a bit older (say 25 or more) and may centre on two or three officers who have a common experience (for example, having worked together in a central or specialist group or squad). In practice, police officers very often work together (on a given shift) in pairs or small groups. Those who feel comfortable together tend to work together - it is rare for the management to impose a grouping that cuts across these invisible categories. Where, for some reason, a member of an 'inner group' does have to work with a member of the 'outgroup' whom he definitely does not trust, he will simply try to avoid doing serious police work. For example, an area car driver told DJS that he had just finished a tour of duty with the 'Q' car, a unit that normally makes many arrests. He said that over the four-week period they made very few arrests (and, what was worse, earned very little overtime) because, of the other two members of the crew, one did not trust the other and therefore refused to work. Because there are, in detail, many groupings among PCs, it would be wrong to talk of a single 'initiation ceremony'. Instead, a new person gains an increasing degree of acceptance in a number of stages and into successive groups of more respected and more experienced officers.

Like police officers, the researchers were tested out before being given a measure of acceptance. Because he belonged to the same age group as the PCs, JG was much more fully subjected to these tests than was DJS. One whole set of tests relates to death, corpses, gory injuries and horrifying violence. Every opportunity is taken to see if new entrants can be shocked or shaken by any of these things. Canteen conversations suggest that for a young PC the first sudden death he or she has to deal with is always some kind of milestone. DJS once listened to more than an hour's conversation about corpses on a Sunday night, some of it going to extremes of coarseness and gallows humour: this seemed to be partly a release of tension by the PCs who had dealt with corpses and very much disliked doing so, but it was also an attempt to shock some probationers and DJS in particular. On three separate occasions DJS on his first introduction to a group of police officers was immediately shown horrifying photographs of victims who had in two cases been raped then murdered (very messily) and in the third, burnt to death. JG was also subjected to the ritual of the gory photographs on several occasions, and senior officers told us that PCs also do it to them. In practice, police officers do not deal with corpses or seriously injured people very often; unlike surgeons or ambulance men they remain almost as squeamish as the ordinary person. For example, a PC who took part in the 'corpse conversation' went with DJS to a mortuary to take a ring from the finger of a dead man; he clearly had great difficulty in bringing himself to touch the corpse. JG accompanied a PC when he dealt with the case of a woman who committed suicide by throwing herself in front of a train. This case was emotionally disturbing not only because of the physical state of the body but also because of the history that led to the suicide and the need to inform the mother of the dead woman, who had been completely dependent on her daughter. Working on this case initiated JG very fully into the group of police officers concerned. On one occasion, DJS saw a probationer vomiting in the yard of the police station after helping to deal with a 'sudden death'. On mentioning this later to the PCs he was working with he was told many stories about the 'initiation antics' of older PCs. 'Soon after I went on District I had to deal with a fatal accident with an old PC who was a real devil. The bloke had had the top of his skull knocked off and his brains were spilling out. I was not too happy about it at all. When we got back to the police station, the old devil took me to the canteen and he deliberately ordered spaghetti Bolognese and sat there eating it in front of me'.

Otherwise the most common forms of initiation are trial by alcohol, physical contest and verbal attack. The three were combined in an evening and all-night session that JG spent with Terry (a PC) and some of his friends. First, Terry took him to his old section house (police residence) and showed him round. When they got to the weights room, Terry asked JG to lift a weight on the bench press, and when he declined, lifted it easily himself. He again asked JG to try; this time he did try but failed to lift the weight. Later in the evening Terry made a great point of this to his friends in the pub while JG was present. Later they were joined by another PC, Derek, who insisted that JG should take him on in various contests of strength, including arm wrestling. JG gained points by winning some of these contests. They were joined by a third PC, Steve, and JG was taken drinking in a pub until closing time, then in a hotel bar and finally in two clubs, finishing at 6 am. Everyone became fairly drunk, but the police officers tried to remain slightly more sober than JG at all times and kept up a fairly continuous verbal attack. Steve repeated many times that JG could not be trusted, so that he had to keep trying to justify himself. When JG eventually showed some weakness, the PCs suddenly became sympathetic and friendly. They told their inspector the story of the night out; one was quite remorseful, thinking he had gone too far, 'got out of order' and been too aggressive towards JG. The inspector thought JG would now be fully accepted by the group, and he turned out to be right.

## Punishment and retribution

Formally, penalties are imposed by the courts on those who have been found guilty of an offence; in principle, reporting people for offences, arresting and charging them, interrogating them or taking statements from them, holding them in custody while these enquiries are made - these are no part of the punishment for any offence. In practice, however, the process of being arrested, held at a police station, questioned and then charged may often be a much more serious punishment than the penalty (if any) that is subsequently imposed by the court. This is not intended as a criticism either of the police or of the courts. It is simply a statement of fact. For most people, being arrested and taken to a police station is a disturbing and humiliating experience, assuming that the police behave towards them in a way that they (the police) would consider normal and correct. If the police behave badly it is, of course, worse still. On the other hand, a considerable number of these people will not be charged with an offence, and a further proportion will be found not guilty. Among those found guilty, a majority will not be given a custodial sentence. For many, perhaps most, therefore, the process of arrest is probably worse than the sentence imposed by the court.

Naturally, police officers are perfectly well aware that they are not, formally, supposed to be punishing people. They are equally well aware that in effect arrest is a kind of punishment, especially because of the disproportionately small gravity of the sentence of the courts in many cases. In any case, it is the police who handle the early stages of a process which ends in formal punishments being imposed, and it is difficult for them to separate the end result of the whole process from the objectives of police work itself. To put it at its lowest, the idea of punishing people is closely bound up with the criminal justice system, of which the police are a part; to put it rather more strongly, most police officers see it as a part of their own function to punish, at least in certain circumstances, and this is one of the underlying motivations of their behaviour.

This view of the function of the police is given weight by the system of cautioning that is used for juveniles. For less serious offences the Met does not normally charge juveniles if they admit the offence and if they have not previously offended a large number of times. Instead they are 'cautioned' by a senior police officer in the presence of their parents, which means they are given some kind of stern moral lecture and warning. Within this procedure, it is the police who are responsible for the whole of the process of dealing with an offender. Formally there is no punishment, but informally it is quite clear that the process of being arrested, questioned, admitting the offence and being cautioned is intended to 'scare the living daylights out of' the child. Admittedly, the intention is to enlist the parents as allies in achieving this.

JG saw a chief-inspector administering a caution to three boys aged 11-13 in the presence of their three fathers. They had admitted exposing themselves to a housewife. To the authors of this report, amusement and ridicule would be the most appropriate response to behaviour of this kind by such young boys, but unlike us the chief-inspector did not regard the case as 'rubbish'. He delivered a long monologue, lasting for nearly 20 minutes, in which the main theme was a scarcely repressed wish to be violent towards the boys because of their open expression of a sexual impulse. JG was not able to take notes, but the following is a precis of some of the chief-inspector's remarks.

You have been very lucky.  If I'd been that woman's husband I might have dealt with you myself whether or not I'd called the police.  You were lucky - he simply called us.  Every man has nothing but contempt for what you've done and if you go on doing it someone will give you a damn good hiding one day.  People who molest ladies and children have to be kept separately in prisons.  Do you know why?  Because all the other prisoners might do them a very serious injury if they were allowed to mix.  Next time you fancy doing this why don't you do it to your sisters ...  your 22 year-old sister (looking throught the papers) your 18 year-old sister, your 17-year old sister.  Then you see what your fathers and brothers think of you.  Or do it to your mum, eh?  Why not do it to your mothers?  It's not funny!

In this situation, the police officer takes the place of the magistrate who delivers solemn words on sentencing, with the difference that there is no sentence.  Because this kind of performance is integrated into police work, the line between apprehension and punishment is blurred, and there is encouragement for the idea that what the police do is legitimately regarded as retribution.

There was also, of course, a violently retributive undertone in what the chief-inspector actually said.  The 'very serious injury' hinted at was castration - possibly rather a strong warning for a eleven year-old.  This makes the link between the police as moral tutors and the idea of violent retribution; this link is extremely important, because it means that where the police are tempted to use violence, they may feel they are doing it from the best possible motives.  Hence it is not unusual for police officers to think that although it is formally forbidden it is justifiable for sexual offenders to be beaten up on arrest, or that it is justifiable to hit a man who has taken someone's car and driven it dangerously with police cars chasing after him.

While the chief-inspector's hint was veiled, more direct references to castration recur again and again in talk about retribution among police officers.  For example, DJS was more an audience that a participant in a long conversation between a home beat officer and a crime prevention officer, which kept coming back to the question of how to deal with rapists.  The crime prevention officer said that if his daughter were raped and he caught the man he would 'spend half an hour doing him over before turning him in, and make sure he could never put his whatsit anywhere again', and the home beat officer later suggested that one could 'set police dogs on them to bite them in the bollocks'.

Another occasion on which police officers sometimes warn, admonish or give stern advice is when dealing with prisoner in the charge room.  JG was with an area car when they were called to deal with a youth (aged 15) who had snatched a woman's purse, had been caught by a neighbour, and was being held.  On searching the boy the PC found money from the purse in his sock, and the boy seemed to be admitting to the offence. The driver had arrested the boy before. When they got him into the charge room, the station officer came in to deal with him. He stood very close to the boy, with their two faces two inches apart, and delivered a long speech. The gist of it was as follows.

Why don't you try it on me? If that had been my old lady I'd have knocked seven different kinds of it out of you and you'd have trouble snatching a purse again, wouldn't you? You'd better give it up or one day you'll come across a bloke like me ...

Warnings of this kind are delivered to juveniles rather than to adults, and the sergeant's approach in this case may have been just what the parents of the boy would want and expect. (In the case of the formal caution quoted earlier, one of the fathers approved of the way it was done; the other two appeared to disapprove strongly.) The point that we wish to establish here is that for many police officers punishment and retribution are legitimately aspects of what they themselves do, and, whatever the formal position, it is in practice difficult to separate police work from the retributive objectives of the whole criminal justice system of which it is a part.

## Overtime

One of the objectives of police officers is to increase their earnings by working overtime, and this can have a substantial effect on the pattern of police work. A good deal of overtime arises because the officers are asked or required to work the extra hours (as, for example, at the time of the 1981 riots, or each year at the Notting Hill Carnival). However, a fair proportion of overtime arises because the individual officer is doing something that he himself needs to complete, and for which he needs to stay on beyond the normal eight hours. Because there is always a tendency for this 'discretionary' overtime to increase, the Force cracks down on it from time to time, as it did in October 1980 towards the beginning of our research. All overtime worked has to be authorised by a supervising officer; at the time of a crackdown, every rank will be subject to strong criticism from the rank above if the amount of overtime worked is more than is considered acceptable. In fact, the authorisation of overtime and the check-ing of claims is perhaps the best example of what is meant by 'supervision' in the Met. It has an effect, in the sense that the amount of overtime worked is substantially reduced at the time of a crackdown, and presumably if the routine level of 'supervision' were reduced, the overtime would go up. All the same, the supervision is not very effective, in the sense that the people who work the overtime are not necessarily those who need to. It is often fairly easy for those working in crime squads or CID offices to arrange their day so that they still have something vital to do when their normal shift is coming to an end, or to make it look as if that is so. In addition, there is a good deal of blatant abuse (working overtime in the pub) that is not picked up. When there is a crackdown, it suddenly becomes much more difficult for everyone to get authority to work overtime, regardless of the strength of their case. This may mean that important work is not done and may damage the morale of officers who genuinely need to stay on to do a job properly.

One of the implications of the payment system is that certain postings are sought after because they offer good opportunities for overtime. This is one of the chief attractions of central squads, major incident squads set up on Districts to investigate murders and other serious crimes, and postings to the 'Q' car. By contrast, a posting to a home beat, a juvenile bureau or a relief offers much poorer overtime opportunities, so that the 'softer' and more generalist police functions are lower in this very important scale of values. At a very early stage of the investigation into the Deptford fire, officers in the squad were already looking forward to boosting their earnings.

> I like working on major incident squads. We've been on now for four hours here at time and a half, I should be on weekly leave today, and I might be able to work on Friday as well when I should be off ... I reckon this inquiry should bring in about 250 quid in overtime this month, which can't be bad. Mind you, it's nothing to what you'd get in industry.

In an investigation of this kind, the officers do have closely defined tasks to carry out, and there is more opportunity for management by results (say, number of witness interviews carried out) than in most police work. Even so, members of a squad are able to work long but not hard - to delay for a couple of hours before setting off for an interview so that they will be able to work a few hours overtime later. Members of a major incident squad tend to become very upset if the overtime that they expect does not materialise. On another murder squad that we worked with, eight arrests were made at a very early stage - in fact, before the squad had been assembled. Members of the squad expected the men arrested to be held in custody for several days before charges were made, and hoped to be able to interrogate them repeatedly over that period (which would have included a weekend) thus earning substantial amounts of overtime. They were extremely disappointed when the officer in charge of the investigation decided to release seven of the eight suspects on police bail. One reason for their disappointment was their belief that once the suspects were released the chances of obtaining confessions from them would be much reduced. A second consideration was that the officers were sent home at 6pm every day and had no chance of working overtime over the weekend.

Among PCs on reliefs, overtime payments tend to encourage them to make arrests rather than engage in other kinds of police work.  When a PC makes an arrest he will often generate a couple of hours work for himself in 'processing' the arrest at the police station.  Generally it will not be possible for another PC to take over from him, so if an arrest is made towards the end of the shift this tends to produce overtime.  The amount of time required depends on how simple the case is: an ordinary drunk would take very little time to deal with, but a juvenile arrested for taking and driving away a motor vehicle could generate several hours' work for the arresting officer.  There are few activities involving 'positive' contacts with members of the public that lead to overtime, though there may be some.

The most general point to be made about the system is that payment is only tenuously connected with achieving a useful objective.  This was vividly illustrated by a small incident on a relief which DJS was working with.  Two PCs had to go to court on a Monday morning after the last Sunday in a week of night shifts.  After a 'quick change', the relief then came on duty again for the late turn at 2pm on the Monday.  After coming back from the court (which was a long way away) the two PCs were back on duty with the relief at about 7pm If they worked the rest of the shift they would by the end of it have been awake for more than 24 hours continuously.  They hung about the police station taking advice from the other PCs about what payment they would receive if they remained on duty.  They knew that they should get an extra payment for 'working off nights' - that is, going to court straight after the end of the night shift.  They also thought they should get a further payment for 'continuous working' over a long period.  They thought that for continuous working combined with working off nights they might hit the jackpot, in which case they thought it would be worth while to stay for the rest of the shift.  Eventually, advice was sought from the sergeant acting as station officer.  He considered the question very carefully, calculated what the maximum payment would be and explained that since the PCs were already getting this for working 'off nights' they would not get any further increase for 'continuous working'.  He was not concerned in the slightest with the question of whether the PCs were fit to carry out any work, nor did he consider whether there was anything for them to do.  He simply advised on the question of payment, and assumed that the PCs would make their decision on this basis alone.  When they heard what the payment would be for remaining on duty the PCs decided to go home to bed because they could hardly keep their eyes open, and they felt that a really exceptional payment was needed to make up for the discomfort of staying awake for another four hours.

## Alcohol
Drinking seems to have a great importance in the lives of police officers.  In the case of the CID, it is an integral part of their

working lives, whereas among uniform officers it is the focal point for the continued social life of the group outside working hours. A part of the explanation for this emphasis on drinking is that police officers use alcohol as a way of coping with the tension and stress associated with the job. (Both the long hours of boredom and the occasional excitement of police work are causes of stress). Another part of the explanation is that drinking with members of the working group is charged with a special symbolic meaning for police officers, who need to find colleagues whom they feel they can trust. A particular reason for drinking among the CID is that on occasion they need to do it in order to make contact with 'villains' or others who can give them information, and to gain their confidence. Since CID officers may have a legitimate reason for drinking in a pub it is difficult for them or anyone else to regulate the number of hours they spend there. Beyond that, although they may start off thinking that they need to drink with people, on occasion, to gain their confidence or obtain some information, they often end up believing that regular hard drinking is the passport to acceptance by a whole world of villains and informers.

As to the actual facts, our present study can only give broad indications of the extent of drinking among police officers. We do not know, for example, whether alcoholism is more of a problem among the police than among other groups, although we have the strong impression that it is. On three occasions during the course of the research we came across police officers in uniform who were clearly drunk, though in all cases they could walk fairly steadily. This is not a very high count, but not a low one either. We often saw officers in plain clothes who were drunk while formally 'on duty' - but that is partly a comment on the procedures whereby they were shown on duty at the time. Other officers were said to be alcoholics, although they never seemed to be obviously drunk. Many officers, especially in the CID, appear to be extremely unfit and sometimes unhealthy because of drink. The survey of police officers confirms other findings showing that the rate of divorce is higher among police officers than among the rest of the population, and informal conversations suggest that drink is often one of the factors associated with the breakdown of policemen's marriages. All of these are impressions - some of them very strong impressions - rather than quantitative statements of fact. Nevertheless, they are enough to make us believe that alcoholism is a serious occupational hazard for police officers and that the resources of preventive medicine (rather than the discipline system) need to be brought to bear on the problem. It might be a start if all officers were given regular fitness tests.

Many of the working days of CID officers include a substantial period in the pub; and while drinking in pubs, CID officers are often 'on duty' or 'working overtime'. CID parties are frequently arranged in pubs to celebrate special events, such as farewells to officers with long service who are leaving the Division. Also, CID officers at all ranks often drink in the office; in many CID offices there is a regular drinking session, often on a Friday. Uniform officers working in plain clothes (such as members of crime squads) tend to develop the same habits as CID officers. Officers actually in uniform rarely drink while on duty, but often meet after a shift or working day and drink heavily then. However, not all of them do this. Uniform officers can avoid drinking with their colleagues, and a considerable number of them do. CID officers can hardly avoid it. A CID officer who did not drink with his colleagues would be an oddball.

The fact that CID officers are expected and required to drink can be shown by a story an inspector tells about himself. All police officers have annual qualification reports completed by their supervising officers; these reports constitute the official record of an officer's career, and may have a considerable influence on postings, selection for specialist branches and promotion. An inspector (who is marked out for rapid promotion) said that when he was previously a detective sergeant he decided to turn over a new leaf and cut down on his drinking; he made this resolution on his first posting to a particular police station. His first annual qualification report after this was very poor: he was considered to be far too aloof and not to be 'part of the team'. As soon as he started drinking again, his reports improved.

An incident that we observed illustrated the same point. On one Division, the detective chief-inspector had arranged a farewell party for a detective sergeant; the arrangements involved buying some of the drink (the participants were expected to bring more with them) and fixing it so that everyone would be shown on overtime while the party took place. One of the detective constables who had been expected at the party (and who had been shown as working overtime) did not turn up. The next day he came into the office for a brief visit before going off on holiday. He had to meet a hail of insults from his colleagues, who were extremely annoyed that the detective chief-inspector had arranged overtime for him but he hadn't turned up. 'The man puts your overtime in for you and you don't even come here and put a bottle on.' The detective superintendent had been elsewhere on his own and had insisted that he should drink with him. Finding himself caught between two obligations, he had decided to drink with the detective superintendent in view of his superior rank.

As well as farewell and anniversary parties, the CID on many Divisions also organise regular lunches (say four times a year) which normally continue all afternoon. Particular groups of uniform officers (for example, a number of officers from a relief) often meet fairly regularly to go drinking; for example, it is common on some reliefs for groups to go to pubs near the London markets to drink (legally) after late turn or the night shift. Also, uniform officers often organise special outings (for example, day-trips to the French coast) that are essentially drinking parties. On these sorts of occasion, officers often deliberately set out to get drunk. This is partly taken as a proof of masculinity - it is interesting, in this connection, that many of the special day-trips organised are for men only. In addition, these occasions provide a context in which men can legitimately show their true feelings, compete in a playful manner, allow their weaknesses to show and establish relationships of trust. This last point is particularly important. The idea behind JG's 'initiation ceremony' described earlier was that by breaking down his defences through drink the officers would be able to tell whether they could trust him; and in any case, until they had got drunk with him they would not be able to feel completely at ease in his company. One crime squad sergeant actually said to JG, 'You only get to know a man in drink' and, 'Now we've had a few drinks I know how far I can trust you'. Drinking with colleagues is used both to test their loyalty, trustworthiness, masculinity, and to symbolise and reinforce the links between the members of the group. It is important to recognise that police officers do not automatically assume that they can trust all other officers; on the contrary, they are constantly wary of their colleagues and afraid of misplacing their confidence. Consequently there is always a need to test them out again and to re-establish feelings of mutual trust.

CID officers often justify time spent in the pub as a way of gaining information about local crime. This kind of justification is not always intended to be taken seriously, but up to a point CID officers do believe it themselves, and the occasion for going to a pub is quite often the idea of finding a particular informant or villain, or getting the latest gossip from the landlord. There are occasions when trips to pubs are purely 'functional' in this sort of way. For example, JG one day went with two officers to a pub where one of the officers expected to meet a 'snout' (informant). The informant was there. After some general conversation, the second officer and JG had to leave the other officer to talk privately with the informant. This visit to a pub did not turn into a long drinking session.

There are also occasions when there is a practical reason for going to a pub, but this is soon forgotten and a long drinking session follows. For example, JG spent a day with an officer who was looking for a drug pusher in order to arrest him. He had seen the pusher at a pub ten days before with a 'minder' who was very heavily built. He had arrested the 'minder' but the alleged pusher meanwhile got away. They went back to this pub to look for him. Not finding him there they took the opportunity to re-establish good relations with the landlord, since the arrest ten days before had interrupted a function taking place in the pub. They drank three pints with him and left well after closing time in the afternoon. They then went to the pusher's house, but after failing to find him there went on to another pub. The officer explained that even if the pusher wasn't there, there was a good chance of finding another man he wanted to arrest. As it turned out, neither of the two men was in the pub (where everything went quiet when the officer walked in with a colleague and JG). However, the officer and the landlord were great friends; they drank four or five pints together, most of it paid for by the pub. The landlord showed great familiarity with the local police, referring to some officers by nicknames (such as 'Big Harry'), and exchanged information about local crime using criminal jargon, or an imitation of it. However, most of the talk was saloon bar philosophising about recent events (the Iranian siege), social security scroungers and the prevalence of violence in society. The officer and his colleague were rather drunk when they left the pub at 2am, saying thay they intended to claim three hours of overtime. However, they genuinely thought they had done some work, since they had gone to the pub in the hope of making an arrest and had talked to the landlord about local crime and criminals.

In a sense, police officers, especially those in the CID, esteem and admire the successful 'villains' they are trying to catch (of course, they do not admire the obvious inadequates and petty offenders). 'Good villains' often see ostentatious hard drinking as a way of showing their dominance and success, and they often frequent pubs. Thus, one attraction of pubs and hard drinking, for police officers, is the association with the world of 'good villains' with which they have such an equivocal relationship. JG went with two police officers, to a club where drinks were (legally) served at very unusual hours. The officers immediately began to tell him, in rather awed tones, that this club was known as a 'villain's drinker'. They pointed to a chair where McLoughlan, one of the 'tastiest' of the local villains, had been sitting only a week before. One of the officers told how he had once arrested McLoughlan on his own, implying that he had been brave (though scared) because McLoughlan was such a dangerous man. These were uniform police officers off duty, and they had no practical reason for going to the club at the time, but they were clearly pleased at being fully accepted in a place where important and violent criminals were in the habit of drinking.

The link between CID officers and pubs is strengthened further when ex-CID officers become publicans. On one of the Divisions that we covered, most of the CID and some of the uniform officers drink in a pub that is run by an ex-detective constable who used to work in a central squad. According to the local officers, when he first moved into the area he was very quick to establish relations with the police because he 'doesn't want to run a yobby place' and therefore wants to have plenty of police officers frequenting it. One of the officers said that he gets a great deal of information from this publican, though JG did not ever hear any information being exchanged. When the officers stayed drinking in the pub after hours, the publican was at first worried that JG was there, but changed his attitude after one of the officers had reassured him.

A few senior officers would like to see a change in attitudes towards drinking within the Force, but most participate in present patterns of behaviour. DJS spent a night observing raids on eight 'drinkers' (parties where drink is sold without a license). The raids were organised by a chief-inspector, but his superintendent also came along for companionship and to lend his moral support. About 50 uniformed police officers were involved, including some drawn from a neighbouring District. When DJS arrived he chatted for about half an hour with the two senior officers over a couple of glasses of whisky in the superintendent's office. They then went down to the canteen to brief the PCs and sergeants who were to carry out the raids. Everyone then set off and carried out successful raids on four 'drinkers', confiscating large quantities of alcohol and also making some arrests for possession of cannabis. When they got back to the police station, the senior officers decided to carry out four more raids that night, while they had the officers available. They returned with DJS to the superintendent's office where they gave instructions for two PCs to call on a magistrate to obtain warrants for the additional raids, and one of them telephoned the magistrate. Then they drank whisky with DJS for an hour and a half, before setting off to carry out the raids on four more drinkers. Drinking in circumstances like these is considered by most senior officers to be quite normal. Equally, the drinks parties in CID offices are often attended (usually for fairly brief periods) by the (uniform) superintendent or chief-superintendent. A few senior officers take a sharply different line and definitely avoid going to drinks parties in the office; we do not know of any who stop any such occasions from taking place.

Many police officers do recognise that drinking in the police force is a problem. This shows itself, for example, when uniform officers say that they do not want to join the CID because it would involve them in too much drinking; although only 5 per cent gave this answer in the survey of police officers, a substantial number make remarks of that kind in informal conversations. A PC who had been in the CID but had transferred back to uniform explained that 'in the Department, drinking is a way of life'. He had gone back to uniform because he had decided, after the break-up of his marriage, that he wanted a quieter life. Because of drinking, police officers tend to be put in equivocal positions, or ones where they are clearly breaking the law. They often break licensing regulations (by drinking in pubs after hours) but can generally get away with it. A greater problem is that drinking can lead to motoring offences. A young PC who was two years out of probation told DJS:

> My first drunk driver was in a terrible state. He was weaving all over the road, and when I got him out of the car he could hardly stand up. He turned out to be a CID man.
> DJS: What did you do about it?
> PC: I told him to leave the car and take a minicab home, but when I had gone he probably got back into his car and drove off.

If the officer has an accident, the matter cannot be so easily overlooked, and a considerable number of discipline cases arise in this way.

**Attitudes to violence**
In a later chapter we shall discuss in what circumstances and how far police officers actually use force, and how often they are actually involved in violent situations. Although these situations do occur, and although some police officers use force on occasion when they don't need to, fighting and violence are not a regular occurrence in the working lives of most police officers; in fact for many they are really quite rare events. In contrast to these realities, we find that the idea of violence is often central to the conceptions that police officers have of their work. This is partly because the central meaning of the job for most police officers is the exercise of authority, and force (rather than knowledge or understanding) is for them the main symbol of authority and power, even if they actually impose their authority in other ways. Also, it is because many police officers see violence as a source of excitement and glamour. As already pointed out (page 338) group norms require talk about violence rather than violent deeds.

Stories of fighting and violence tend to come up in conversation alongside and mixed in with talk of sexual conquests and feats of drinking: all three combine together into a kind of cult of masculinity. For example, DJS spent an early turn in a van with three experienced PCs, all of them influential in their relief and considered to be good policemen who made 'good arrests'. There was a great deal of conversation about sex, in very gross language, in which the men were always conquerors and the women 'slags' and 'whores'. One of the three PCs in particular boasted about his drinking; he claimed that he drank twelve pints a day and felt none the worse for it. He said he was not an alcoholic because an alcoholic was someone who 'has to have a drink as soon as he gets up in the morning', whereas he did not normally have his first drink until later. This talk about sex, women and drink was interspersed with descriptions of violent incidents that the PCs had witnessed, heard about or taken part in. The PC who drank twelve pints a day told a long story about a man who had smashed a beer glass then rammed it into a police officer's face five times before the officer's 'mates' had been able to restrain him. 'You can imagine what happened to him then', he added. He described in great detail how the flesh of the man's face had been cut to the bone, said that his wounds had required 200 stitches and described his disfigurement afterwards. This story did not illustrate any point or arise in any way from the previous conversation (which had been about fellatio). The PC just thought it was interesting in itself, and he told it with relish.

This led on to a discussion about violence at demonstrations. Another of the PCs gave an account of 'the only time I have ever hit a woman'. This was at a political demonstration where a

369

particular woman had made a practice of 'tugging and kicking the bollocks of the blokes in the front line'. The PC said that he told her not to do it again 'and she did do it again, so I hit her and she was most upset, screaming at me and asking me how I could bring myself to hit a woman'. The main point about this story seemed to be that the PC had, for once, found a situation in which it was legitimate to triumph over a woman by physical force. He did not seem to be making a confession, but to be recounting a notable success. He went on to talk with deliberate humour and exaggeration about the Grunwick dispute.

> That Grunwick dispute, I liked that one best of all. It was such a fair, clean fight. The unions got all these blokes in from all over the country, they were a really tough lot, not rubbish mind you, but a really good class of demonstrator. They had a go at us and we had a go at them. If someone was hurt, both sides made a gangway so that the corpse could be carried out to the ambulance. Then as soon as the injured person had been taken off, the two sides got straight back to fighting each other again. It was a really good one, that, I liked it. When it was all over I felt like shaking hands with the opposition and thanking them for such a good contest.

This kind of comment about large scale events at which violence occurs is quite common. A PC on a different Division told JG on three separate occasions how much he had enjoyed the Southall disturbances in July 1981. He was part of a serial belonging to the central London reserve at the time. 'We went wanging down there, jumped out of the van and just started fighting.' He said that Southall was 'better' than the Brixton riots because no petrol bombs were being used. 'My bottle does tend to go a bit when petrol bombs come over.' Although conceding that flares were used against police at Southall, he concluded 'It was a great day out, fighting the Pakis. It ought to be an annual fixture. I thoroughly enjoyed myself'.

Similarly, the sporting metaphor was used in a long conversation among police officers (including a chief-inspector) after the 'Day of Action' in April 1981 when there were skirmishes between black people marching over Blackfriars Bridge and the police. On this occasion, the police thought they had come off worst, but the chief-inspector looked forward to the 'second leg' or 'return match' when he thought they would achieve a much better score. Unlike the comments about Grunwick and Southall, this was an entirely serious remark. Where comments about violence were partly jocular or facetious, they still revealed an interest in the subject and showed that one of the chief ways in which police officers can boost their egos is by claiming to have taken part in violent incidents. Also, most conversations of this kind did not involve the researcher much; the officers appeared to be showing off mainly to each other. Sometimes, when talking about other officers' exploits rather than their own, they were not showing off at all. For example, one PC said quite seriously, 'A lot of blokes in the job love a bit of violence' and he went on to talk about a big PC on his relief in particular. 'During the riots he was jumping into crowds and grabbing people and just handing them out. Very strong bloke. You need some people like that.'

DJS spent a shift with two CID officers, both in their mid-twenties; after driving round aimlessly in the CID car they ended up in a pub. After much talk about sexual and drinking exploits, the conversation turned to the old days (which the two young officers had only heard about) when 'the villains and the CID were almost the same thing, there was only one per cent difference between them'. The two officers agreed that that was the way in which the CID could operate most effectively, though they conceded that the CID had had to change and was now further removed from the criminal world. They showed some nostalgia for the days (which they had never known) when the CID officer was really someone among the villains. One of them then began to talk about tough villains' pubs, in particular about one pub he went into with another CID officer 'who likes a fight'. He said they were attacked the moment they went in the door and described the ensuing fight in great detail. 'We ended up kicking and punching while we were splashing about in the urinals.' The Detective Constable was very proud that he and his colleague had not called for assistance. He said that when it was finished, there were a lot of 'bruised ribs', but everyone stood together at the bar and drank together in a spirit of fellowship, having settled their differences in the time-honoured fashion. He went on to describe another fight with great relish, in which an officer had 'unfortunately' got his face slashed. This conversation shows that some CID officers see violence as a way of showing their credentials to villains who, they think, respect a show of force. More generally, it shows how ideas about sex, drinking and violence are linked together in a cult of masculinity which is thought to provide the key to the criminal world.

It should be emphasised that we are not commenting here on the actual amount of force used by police officers, but on the attitudes towards violence which, among groups of police officers, it is normal and acceptable to express. There is no doubt that the norm is to talk about violence as something interesting and exciting, to exaggerate the extent and frequency of violent incidents in police work and to tell tall stories about one's own violent exploits. On the whole, police officers are much less inclined to visualise themselves triumphing in some other way, for example, by conclusively winning an argument or by successfully manipulating someone else's behaviour.

Although police officers do not talk about it much, fear of violence and dislike of the stress associated with it are also important influences. A considerable number of police officers find their way (often at a later rather than an earlier stage of their careers) into jobs in which they will not encounter violence and conflict; thus, the survey of police officers shows that many older officers do purely office or administrative jobs. Also, some younger officers transfer to specialist groups in order to avoid 'aggro'. For example, an area car driver (aged about 30) said that he hoped to transfer to Traffic and had already taken his motorbike course. He explained (spontaneously) that he was fed up with his present Division because 'I keep on getting slapped'. He went on to describe a run of incidents where a suspect had hit him so that he had got involved in a punch-up. He mentioned one in particular where two black men had been seen doing a robbery in the street. The area car driver and one other PC had gone up to the group of five men to arrest the two culprits. He said they had immediately started swearing and shouting and attacked the two PCs, who called for assistance. Eventually about five PCs made the arrests. It took five of them, he said, to hold one of the men down. When the case came to court it was thrown out on the ground that the policemen had started the fight. This, said the driver, was ridiculous, since two PCs would never start a fight with five men. The whole tone of this account was quite different from that of the ones quoted earlier. The PC was describing, without relish, the kind of thing that he was trying to get away from. Although this kind of talk is much less common than the sensational talk about violence as something attractive, the underlying feelings are probably just as common.

## Sex, women, sexual offences

Although nine per cent of police officers (up to the rank of inspector) are women, the dominant values of the Force are still in many ways those of an all-male institution such as a rugby club or boys' school. This shows itself in many of the attitudes and norms that have already been discussed: in the emphasis on remaining dominant in any encounter and not losing face, the emphasis placed on masculine solidarity and on backing up other men in the group especially when they are in the wrong, the stress on drinking as a test of manliness and a basis for good fellowship, the importance given to physical courage and the glamour attached to violence. This set of attitudes and norms amounts to a 'cult of masculinity' which also has a strong influence on policemen's behaviour towards women, towards victims of sexual offences and towards sexual offenders.

In groups of policemen a certain pattern of talk about sex and women is expected, much as it is in the army. The underlying attitudes are, however, more significant in the police force than in the army, for a number of reasons. The most important point is that policemen are expected to work closely with policewomen as colleagues. Policewomen now pursue careers formally on an equal footing with policemen, but find it difficult to fit in with an organisation that still has much of the culture of a male preserve. Also, police work involves dealing with people (including women) in a sensitive and sympathetic manner on occasion; the denigration of women implicit in canteen talk is also a devaluing of qualities associated with women that are actually required in much police work.

Bawdy talk is a kind of game among groups of men in which they play, in their imagination, the role of a man triumphing over a woman. For example, an older PC said that 'in the old days' WPCs when they first arrived at a police station were always stamped 'on the bare bum' with the station rubber stamp. This fantasy neatly symbolises the three chief impulses that animate this kind of conversational game: the treatment of a woman as a thing (like a form to be filled in or rubber-stamped), the humiliation of a woman and sexual assault on her. Talk about women on this level is pervasive among groups of men in the Met; much of it is far more lurid and extreme than the small example quoted. It often continues when women are present, though the men may then switch to competing for the attention of the woman (if she is considered attractive).

Policemen show anxiety about their own sexual make-up in various ways. For example, at one police station the main subject of jokes for a considerable time was a story about two young PCs who were supposed to have 'had it for free' with a prostitute while working a night shift in a panda car. For the story to have become current, they must have boasted that they had picked up the prostitute and taken her back to her flat, where they 'accepted her invitation'. When all this was repeated, with endless variations, the two PCs made no attempt to deny it. Whether or not it actually happened, it is hard to explain why the two PCs boasted about it unless it was to reassure themselves about their own potency. Again, we find that some PCs take every opportunity to give detailed accounts of reported rape cases. Sometimes there is a reason or an occasion for telling these stories. For example, as they drove past a particular night club, a PC started to tell DJS a long story about the rape of the barmaid there. He told it without gloating and his account was entirely sympathetic to the victim. DJS asked if she had got over the experience and the PC said she had not altogether and probably never would. This contrasted with an account of the same incident given by another PC on the same relief, later the same day in the canteen. This time there was no particular occasion for telling the story (which the PC told not to DJS but to the company at large). He ended by saying that the woman was not really all that upset and strongly implied that she had thoroughly enjoyed the whole experience.

The men involved in this kind of conversation sometimes imply not only that the woman probably enjoyed the experience but also that they would like to have committed the offence them-selves. For example, a CID officer went to interview two teenage girls (the younger one aged 14) who alleged that they had been sexually assaulted in the flat where they lived. He came back saying that they had played the man along and that he found the two girls very 'tasty' himself. Yet on other occasions, officers will tell stories of sexual assaults or other sexual offences (for example homosexual practices between men and boys) in a way that is calculated to shock and intended to produce the strongest possible condemnation of the offenders. It does seem that guilt at sharing the impulses of certain sexual offenders can easily turn into a vindictive attitude towards these offenders and an exaggerated attitude of condemnation. After listening to a tale of local paedophilia, DJS experimented by refusing to condemn the offender (he said the impulse to do that sort of thing was not very unusual). The officers who had been telling the story then became disoriented; when they did not obtain the usual response they seemed to be forced to ask themselves why they were telling the story in the first place.

Insecurity about sex is also shown by homosexual jokes, which are fairly common. In one group of uniform officers who were working together in a carrier there was a big and husky PC who had an incongruously high pitched voice. It was a running joke to pretend that he was homosexual. Other men in the group would often undo his collar and put their hands down the neck of his shirt, saying things like 'Oh, Steve, why won't you be nice to me?' in an imitation of his high voice, and would kiss and hug him, all apparently as part of the teasing. On one occasion they actually debagged him in the yard of a police station. In another Division, one of the men posted to inside duties was standing and leaning forward onto the counter in a position reminiscent of a sexual invitation, while he wrote in a book. When a PC came up behind him and made as if to take advantage of the invitation, everyone in the police station was convulsed with laughter for several minutes. Again, the complement to this is a very strong condemnation of homosexuals among many policemen. The jokes and the condemnation arise from the same anxiety.

In all of these ways, policemen are adopting the pattern of values and responses that they think is expected within what still remains essentially a group of men. At a minimum they are expected not to show dissent. Of course, as individuals these policemen have very varied characteristics, and in other contexts (for example, with their families) they probably behave quite differently. However, it is the group values of the men that have the greatest effect on the women in the Force. What women police officers say is amply confirmed by our observations of the way in which they are treated. In informal conversations, most of them say that policemen are prejudiced against them, that they greatly over-emphasise the importance of physical strength in the job so as to argue that women cannot do it adequately, that women are effectively excluded from some of the more interesting kinds of work and that the men will not accept them as full members of the working group or as colleagues on an equal basis. They make a particular complaint about prejudice against women at training school. There is no doubt that a majority of policemen do have

374

broadly the attitudes that policewomen ascribe to them. For example, the survey of police officers shows that 62 per cent of policemen think 'Policewomen should not do the same work as policemen, but should specialise, for example in duties concerning women and children'. Only 22 per cent of policewomen hold this view. Although women are formally colleagues on an equal basis with men, many of the men manage to put their views into practice: for example, area car drivers often succeed in refusing to have a woman as operator.

Many women police officers accommodate to the attitudes of their male colleagues. For example, a WPC with four years' service said she had accepted long ago that she 'couldn't do the same job as the men' and she felt that this made for better relations with the men on her relief. She thought it was better not to react to 'prejudiced criticism': if you ignored it, it would just go away. As an illustration of this, she mentioned that an inspector at training school had come up to her and said: 'Why don't you admit it, you're only here to get a husband, aren't you? Why don't you resign and save us a lot of time and money?' She had stayed cool and 'let it run off her back'.

Women complain about the atmosphere at training school, not only on the initial training course, but also on subsequent courses which they may attend after obtaining considerable experience in the job. For example, a WPC who seemed to be good at her job complained bitterly to JG about the way women are treated in the Met. She criticised Hendon (the training centre) particularly, saying 'I hate the place'. She said she had gone back to Hendon recently for a course and that she had been shouted down whenever she had opened her mouth by jeers like 'Yah, what do you know, you're just a plonk!' ('Plonk' is a derisory slang word for a woman in the Force.) She was exasperated and upset by this attitude on the part of the men. 'I've been on a vagrancy squad and I've done some horrible jobs. I've nicked more bodies than some of those blokes put together.'

A WPC with five years' experience was much more tolerant about the attitudes of men towards women in the job. She said that she had originally wanted to do the advanced driving course but had given up the idea because it was almost impossible for women to get a place on a course. At the same time, she did not seem to be bitter about this alleged discrimination. For example, she said that most of the men were 'anti-women' because women were weaker, and she agreed with them on that point; those who carried out the recruitment and selection were far too easy-going about the physical strength of women, and many of those now selected were tiny. All the same, she did not find these arguments very conclusive. She thought that many of the men were also 'weedy' nowadays, and claimed that she could 'handle herself' better than many of the men. She said she had dealt with many pub punch-ups on her own or with another WPC. 'The fighters are so amazed to see women arrive that they quieten down and do what they're told.' This WPC, who had accommodated to the difficulties faced by women in the Force, only hinted at the way in which women tend to be excluded from groups of male officers. 'When they thought they could trust you, the older ones would help you and work with you, but they had to be sure of you - that you'd back them up in court and not drop them in it.'

Another WPC with about five years' experience was fairly well respected by the men on her relief, although she still had to take the usual anti-women jokes, for example about her driving (which was in fact very good). She had not yet given up the idea of becoming an area car driver, though she also believed it was very difficult for a woman to get a place on the necessary driving courses. The way in which she explained this was that 'the Job' thinks that women may go off to have children, so it is not worthwhile to train them to be advanced drivers. She thought that quite a few WPCs fitted this assessment: they do not expect to stay in the job for long and do not take it seriously, and they give the others a bad name. She had accepted this part of the criticism as a defensive measure (in order to make it clear that the criticism did not apply to her) but otherwise remained strongly feminist.

Comparatively few women have managed to get into the CID (four per cent of CID officers are women compared with nine per cent of uniform officers). This is, broadly, because the 'cult of masculinity' is stronger in the CID than elsewhere in the Force, and in line with this we find that women in crime squads and in the CID make particularly strong complaints about their treatment by men. When JG worked with one crime squad one of the first things the (uniform) sergeant told him was that he thought he would have to get rid of the WPC in the squad, since none of the men wanted to work with her. Some of their objections to this WPC were that if you worked with her you could not make the usual number of arrests, that 'she can't get up in the morning for an early job' and that 'she can't work in a team'. Two weeks later a long discussion developed in the office about women police, when the WPC was present. The men argued strongly against women in the Force, placing the usual emphasis on physical danger. Eventually the discussion became quite heated and the WPC was personally criticised. Afterwards she spoke separately to JG. She confessed that she would 'never be able to do the job the way the men do it, not quite the same,' but was nonetheless bitter about her experience in the crime squad. She said that for the first two months in the squad she had been miserable - that she had been 'left out in the cold'. 'They would refuse to take me out on patrol ... I am the first WPC to be allowed into this crime squad and they're trying to make sure that I'll be the last ... Eventually I decided to go out on patrol by myself. I started bringing bodies in on my own!' Although she gained some respect from the men by doing this, the sergeant was still preparing to throw her off the squad.

On the same Division there was a woman detective constable who to some extent specialised in offences involving women and children because her detective inspector saw her in that role. She thought that male CID officers treated women detectives badly because they felt threatened by them. 'They can't admit that a woman, someone who they normally think of as a dumb sex object, can do the job as well as they can.' In answer to the argument that women do not have the necessary physical strength to deal with violent or threatening people, she said that she strongly objected to the way the men dealt with people: they were often rude and 'physical' without cause and thereby provoked the violent behaviour which, they said, only they as men could deal with.

A woman detective sergeant immediately lit up with interest when DJS suggested to her that women tend to be 'put down' in the police force. She agreed wholeheartedly, saying that the police is one of those professions - 'if you can call it a profession' - where women are not accepted on equal terms. 'You have to work much harder to prove yourself if you're a woman.' DJS suggested that the problem might be the masculine tradition, particularly in the CID, that went with drinking, coarse jokes, and so on. She immediately said that there were particular problems for women in the CID (as opposed to the rest of the Force); the Department simply did not welcome women, and this was certainly tied up with an 'old fashioned machismo' which had no relevance to present day policing. CID officers liked to think that it was important to be a hard drinker to be able to do the job, but in fact it wasn't. Also, there was very little need of brawn and muscles in ·the job, especially in the CID. She said that very often if a woman police officer were handling a situation, people would not be so violent, whereas they would be if a man were handling it, particularly if he was a 'physical type' himself. Although this woman was not obviously 'militant' and appeared outwardly conventional, her views about the treatment of women in the Force were very definite and most forthrightly expressed. It was also interesting that she seemed to be considerably more skilled in many aspects of the job (for example, interviewing witnesses and suspects) than most male CID officers. Later DJS spoke to a PC working on the crime squad in the same Division. When asked about women in the Force, he immediately said that women could not work on an equal footing with men because they were physically inferior, though he reluctantly made an exception of clerical jobs. DJS mentioned that the woman detective sergeant in the same Division seemed to manage all right. The PC was doubtful about her; he thought she could not do the job properly, although in the judgement of DJS she was far more intelligent and competent in every way than the PC himself.

In general, the complaints made by women in the Force about their treatment are amply borne out by our observations. For example, it is true that many area car drivers try to avoid having a woman as operator and often succeed. One area car driver mentioned spontaneously that he was adamantly opposed to having a woman as operator. 'I don't want to go into a sticky situation without back-up. I'd be worried about her but even more worried about myself.' He had been given a woman as operator on one or two occasions ('You always get one or two that are dead obstinate') but had managed to kick up such a fuss that they were removed. On another Division, DJS worked for two weeks with an area car crew including a woman as plain clothes observer, but with a man as operator. On the following tour of duty there was a large man as plain clothes observer; several members of the relief spontaneously commented that 'it doesn't half make a difference when you have a man as observer', although the crew that included the woman had worked very successfully and had (incidentally) made a considerable number of arrests. In the attitudes and talk of the men, ideas about the limitations of women specifically as police officers merge imperceptibly into general views about the inferiority of women which again merge into sexual boasting and horseplay. Something of this mixture is caught in a single remark by an older PC, who said that 'a young girl will be no good in restraining a violent man as long as she has a hole in her arse'.

## Help, advice, sympathy, support

What police officers generally regard as most characteristic of police work is the element of conflict. By intervening to resolve conflicts they see themselves as helping the innocent parties; they may also, in these circumstances, offer sympathy and support, though they vary very much in their ability to do so and in the importance they attach to it. Where the element of conflict is not present or is very much in the background, police officers tend to regard the matter as 'not proper police work'. They are less likely to offer sympathy and support in those circumstances, though whether or not they do so will partly depend on whether the people involved seem to them to be normal and deserving rather than deviant, crazy or the cause of their own troubles.

From the observations that we have made, it is difficult to prove that the norms or objectives of police officers (with regard to offering help, sympathy or support) are as we have just stated; some of the difficulties are that the kinds of incidents involved are very varied and that the behaviour of police officers depends not only on the kind of incident and the kind of people involved but also on the individual officer and his mood. What we can say with certainty is that how police officers behave in this respect varies a great deal. There are many occasions when they see it as their duty and as 'normal' to offer help and sympathy, but there are also many occasions when no sympathy or support is given even though it seems to have been expected or would have been welcome. At present it is worth giving a few examples of each type of behaviour, but we shall return to this question later in the report.

The clearest example of a kind of encounter where a police officer is most likely to show the kind of sympathy expected is when dealing (immediately after the event) with the victim of a theft or robbery from the person. An example of this was an incident dealt with by an area car driver with whom DJS worked tor a considerable period. This man had a very effective manner, rather dry and reserved, but very pleasant; the impression he conveyed was that he would do what was necessary without making a fuss. One afternoon the car answered a call about an old woman who had been robbed of her handbag by two young boys (aged between 10 and 12) on the elevated walkway of a large council estate. The address given was the flat of a Burmese family where the woman of the house was looking after the old lady following the incident. When the area car driver arrived (with DJS) the Burmese woman was feeding the old woman with tea and sympathy; she had never met her before but had come to her aid immediately after the incident. The victim, who was aged 81 and rather deaf though not infirm, had recovered quite well from the shock and was fairly clear-headed, though she was still very upset. It seemed significant that the Burmese woman knew one of the home beat officers for the estate; this seemed to encourage her to help the old woman.

The PC began by asking the old woman some simple questions about how she was now feeling and whether she was at all hurt. In this way, and by smaller signs, he conveyed his concern without being effusive and without patronising the old woman in any way. He then questioned her cogently about what had happened. When she didn't catch the question he did not become irritated. He carefully found out that the keys to her flat had been taken with the bag. After looking around to see if the bag had been dumped and drawing a blank, he telephoned the council to ask them to change the lock of the old woman's flat and made arrangements for her to let her into her flat later on in the day. He encouraged the Burmese woman to help out by taking the old woman back to her own flat later, after the council had called back. By his practical and businesslike approach he encouraged the victim to be realistic and practical, so that she had become quite herself by the time he left. He also encouraged the other helper to do what was necessary instead of doing everything himself. Although this particular officer was exceptionally skilled, most officers behave in this kind of way in circumstances like these.

Suicides and sudden deaths are also incidents that officers try to handle with sensitivity. An example was a suicide dealt with by Mike, a PC aged about 35 and with 15 years' service. JG was with Mike in the canteen when the call came over the personal radio: it was not a popular assignment - nobody else on the relief volunteered to take it on. The call was to a railway station where a woman had been killed by falling under the wheels of a train. As Mike and JG arrived (in a panda car) the ambulance crew was getting the body onto a stretcher; it was a woman aged about 50 who had died from very severe head injuries. The main point about Mike's handling of the case was that he took great care about the way in which he broke the news to the dead woman's relatives, particularly her aged mother who had relied on her daughter to look after her. After finding a suicide note and an address book in the dead woman's handbag, he went to see a sister and some of the closest friends of the family and persuaded them to come with him to break the news to the mother. They agreed not to explain at first how or why the woman had died. When the party got to the mother's house it was the 'friends of the family' who said that the daughter was dead. When the mother asked how she had died they told her not to worry about that at the moment. The mother was spared having to identify her daughter's body: she was asked to identify her handbag instead. Mike quickly removed the handbag as soon as it had been identified. He did not read the suicide note or disclose its existence for the time being. Before leaving the house he had some short words of comfort for the mother who had wept for a time but had now recovered her composure.

As in the previous example, Mike was able to show his concern and sympathy in a practical way: by finding friends who would be able to comfort and support the old woman, by encouraging them to help and by taking trouble to break the news gently and in stages (clearly the old woman would eventually have to know how her daughter had died). Mike himself felt under a considerable strain during the handling of this incident, partly because the corpse was horribly mutilated and partly because the emotional turmoil of the woman who had killed herself communicated itself to everyone involved in the immediate aftermath.

In general, assaults or threats of assault seem to evoke sympathy and concern from police officers where the victim is thought to be weak or defenceless, but not if the victim is thought to be strong or not entirely blameless in the matter. DJS was with an experienced area car driver and a probationer acting as radio operator when they dealt with a Bengali woman who had been assaulted by her husband and with a threatened assault on a woman and her family by her estranged husband. In both cases the victims were treated very sympathetically. The Bengali woman had been kicked in the stomach and hit on the head with something heavy. She was in a state of shock (her teeth were chattering) but was at first very reluctant to go to hospital because there were two young children in the flat. The PC persuaded the neighbours to look after the two children for the time being and by being firm and kindly managed to get the woman to agree to go to hospital. She turned out to be quite badly hurt. Later that day the crew answered another call to the flat, where they found the husband drunk on the landing. They arrested him for being drunk and disorderly with the intention of charging him with assault later when the full extent of his wife's injuries had been revealed. It was interesting that the police officers had no hesitation in taking decisive action in a case of domestic violence, even though accepted wisdom in the Force is that such cases are 'weary' because they often end with the injured party withdrawing charges. The area car driver was able to convey his concern and sympathy to the woman and to the neighbours in all sorts of small ways, as well as providing practical help.

The same crew earlier answered a call from a woman whose

estranged husband had telephoned her to threaten that he would come back, smash up the flat and take away his son. The driver parked up outside the flats for a while as a preventive measure in case the husband did, in fact, turn up. After half an hour he knocked on the door of the flat. The family were so frightened that they would not answer the door until the driver shouted through the letter box that it was the police; they were then very glad to welcome the officers in. They showed their concern by listening gravely to what the wife had to say, and by small gestures and remarks. The driver emphasised that if there was any hint of any more trouble she should call them again and they would come round very quickly. He should, perhaps, have advised the woman to have her telephone number changed - she probably did not know that this could be done very quickly in the special circumstances. He could, perhaps, have gone to find the husband and talked to him, but this would not necessarily have solved the problem in any case. He did, at any rate, manage to convey sympathy and offer support in future if it was required.

These two cases contrast with an incident covered by an area car on another District. The crew (accompanied by JG) accepted a call on a neighbouring Division because there was no response from the local area car. The incident was described on the mainset as 'disturbance and criminal damage'. It took the car between 15 and 20 minutes to get to the address, where they found a white man aged about 32 standing in the doorway of his council house. He had an inch-long cut on his forehead raised on an egg-shaped lump. He looked scruffy, though this could have been partly because he was in the middle of redecorating his sitting room, which had numerous spots of blood on the bare floorboards. There was also a considerable amount of blood on his clothing. The glass panelled front door had been badly smashed. The man's wife sat crying in an armchair. The victim explained that last week he had caught some white 'yobs' trying to break into his car. He had called the local police who had taken the youths' names and addresses. The victim had declined to go to court and give evidence: 'I thought, well, as they didn't actually nick anything...' That night he had answered a knock at his door to find one of the 'yobs' standing there. 'About last week...' said the 'yob', then he struck the victim with an iron bar, smashed the door and made off.

The two PCs did not seem to be particularly interested or concerned. They advised the victim to go to hospital. The wife immediately said he couldn't leave her alone and that there was a baby upstairs. The driver said he could go to hospital in the morning: 'It needs stitches'. The victim said 'So will he if I get hold of him'. The second PC said, 'Probably the best thing'. The two PCs did not offer to run the victim to hospital or to get the local police to help out. JG gained the impression from what the officers said that part of the reason for their attitude was that they were not on their own 'ground': since the local officers had dealt with the matter previously the present crew, from a neighbouring Division, thought they should not intervene. However, they did ensure that the matter was handed back to the local police: having dealt with the incident they drove directly to the local station and entered a short written report. A more important reason for their behaviour emerged as they left, when one PC said to the other, 'This is mostly white slag living up here'. (This very important criterion, by which people are judged to be 'not respectable', will be discussed in the next chapter.) A further reason for the lack of sympathy was that the victim was a man in the prime of life. Because of this the officers thought that he should be able to defend himself and encouraged him to take his private revenge instead of bothering the police; also, because he was a youngish man they suspected that he might be partly to blame by having provoked his assailant.

Police officers seem to vary very widely in their ability or inclination to show sympathy and concern to people who are behaving abnormally. We can quote two clear examples of cases where sympathy was and was not shown. On one occasion two PCs who were patrolling in the van during a late turn answered a call concerning a woman who was making false telephone calls to the fire brigade. JG went with them. The fire brigade kept the woman talking until the crew got to her address. The two officers tried to persuade her to come to the door. At first she did not reply. Eventually she gave up the telephone call, but refused to let the police in. It was clear from her speech that she was mentally unstable and probably senile. The two officers decided to kick the door in (although they accepted that they had no 'right' or 'power' to do so). One of them pretended that he could smell gas, to give him a spurious reason for kicking down the door. He warned the woman to stand back, took several hefty kicks at the door and managed to open it, doing considerable damage to the jamb and ruining the lock.

Once inside the two PCs engaged the woman, who was in her sixties, in sympathetic and humorous conversation. They turned out to be very good at this. It was clear that the woman was disturbed; she was probably ringing the fire brigade partly out of loneliness, partly from a desire to draw attention to herself (as in classic cases of hysteria). The PCs impressed on her the need to leave the fire brigade alone because they were so busy and needed to put out real fires. They gave her the telephone number of their own police station as a substitute and told her to ring any time she wanted to. She did telephone the station later on, and one of the PCs told the communications reserve to humour her, which they did uncomplainingly. The two PCs spent 40 minutes talking to the woman. They tried to secure her shattered door and told her the police would pay for the repairs, though they did not help her to make a claim. One of the PCs made a call to a social worker and notified the local social services department about the woman's condition.

This contrasts very sharply with the treatment of another

incident involving abnormal behaviour which was observed by DJS. The call was to a 'disturbance'. DJS was with an experienced PC, Terry, in a van. When they got to the area (part of a council estate) they found a group of people outside a house, and went inside. The house was not well kept, but was not in a very bad state. Inside was a woman in late middle age, drunk and tearful, her daughter, Mary, another daughter, that daughter's boyfriend, a large dog, the mother's father (who came in and went out periodically) and various neighbours who also came and went. The family were white, except for one daughter, Mary, who looked partly black. The mother was in a hysterical state. She said that Mary was epileptic, and the daughter herself confirmed that this was so. She also said that Mary was 'nutty', 'crazy' and 'mad'. According to both mother and daughter, the daughter had been brought to a terrible state because of constant rows with the neighbour, an Asian man, who was in the habit of deliberately provoking and insulting her. (It was this man who had called the police.) Mary said that this man was constantly complaining about noise, although they were very careful to be reasonably quiet, and was always insulting her by calling her nutty. This made her mother upset (as she was at present) and the mother explained in between fits of weeping that when she was upset on her daughter's account Mary would try to commit suicide or mutilate herself. The daughter currently had ugly scars on her neck.

As the mother was explaining matters, she dissolved into a wail and became incoherent, at which Tracy (the second daughter) was very loving to her and tried to comfort her. When the same thing happened a second time, and when the mother started saying that she 'couldn't stand it any longer', Mary disappeared upstairs, saying she would kill herself. By this time two more PCs had arrived: Kevin, a man of about 30 but with only two years' experience in the Force, and John, a young probationer. Terry, the experienced PC, went to see the Asian man next door. DJS had to step out of his role as researcher to suggest to Kevin that he should go upstairs to see whether Mary was actually killing herself. At this point, Tracy's boyfriend came downstairs, saying that Mary was sticking needles into herself. DJS went upstairs with Kevin, where they found the girl cowering in the corner and forcing a needle into her neck close to the artery. Kevin was clearly nonplussed by this unusual behaviour and became very indecisive. He tried very tentatively to talk to the girl and to persuade her that she should stop sticking the needle into her neck. She did not respond at all to this approach, partly because she was in a very abnormal state, partly because Kevin failed to express either sympathy or authority by what he said. Eventually, after about two minutes during which the girl was forcing the needle further and further in and stirring it about, Kevin made a grab for her arm and pulled the needle out himself. DJS now saw that the wounds on the girl's neck from previous insertions were quite extensive and that her wrists had recently been slashed.

Kevin, Mary and DJS went downstairs and Kevin tried to talk to the mother along with a neighbour (a woman) who had appeared. Kevin was completely out of his depth and only conveyed his own confusion about what was going on. The mother soon began to be badly upset again; as soon as she started wailing, Mary dashed out of the house. By this time an ambulance had arrived. The ambulance crew told Kevin that they had taken the same girl to hospital several times after her attempted suicides. After a while, Tracy's boyfriend came back down the road saying that he had found the girl, who had stuck another needle into her neck. Soon after, she came back down the street and was persuaded (by the ambulance crew) to get into the ambulance. Terry came back from talking to the Asian neighbour, who had complained about the noise and disorderly way of life of the family next door and said that Mary was crazy, although he denied insulting her. As the girl got into the ambulance, the police officers were preparing to leave; none of them was talking to the girl's family, who were not given any suggestions or advice. DJS decided to go to the hospital in the ambulance, along with John (the young probationer), Mary and an ambulancewoman.

In the ambulance, John sat on one side of the girl and the ambulancewoman on the other. A broken needle was still lodged in the girl's neck. John sat rigidly staring straight in front of him; he neither touched the girl, nor looked at her nor made any attempt to speak to her. The ambulancewoman began to scold the girl gently, saying, 'We're only trying to help you'.

'I don't want your help.'
'You know it costs money for us to call on you and take you to hospital.'
'I didn't ask you to come.'
'What are you doing, sticking things in your neck for?'
'I've got a birthmark.'

After a while, the ambulancewoman asked to look at the wound, caught the girl's head and held it firmly, then ordered John (who was rigid with fear and embarrassment) to take the needle out, which he managed to do with signs of great distaste. The girl had blook trickling all over her chest and was annoyed about ruining her tee shirt. Neither the ambulancewoman nor John made any attempt to speak after this.

Since it was quite clear that John was not going to say or do anything, DJS decided to talk to the girl. She responded straight away to simple questions and they kept up a continuous conversation for five or ten minutes on the way to the hospital. She said that everything was all right at home and everyone was happy as long as there were only white people in the neighbourhood, but that ever since the Asian people had moved in next door her life had been a misery. The Asian man taunted and insulted her because she had fits. He made her feel that she was not safe in her own home; if she went out into the garden he would come out and start insulting her. When her mother became upset, she felt that there was nothing to be done, so she tried to kill herself. She insisted that she would kill herself as soon as she got the chance. It became clear that everyone around her hated the Asian man because he was not white (maybe because of his behaviour as well) and that this put the girl into an acute state of conflict since the Asian man was also her greatest enemy (he taunted her) yet she was herself partly black. She explained that she stuck the needles in her neck to take away her birthmark. Although it was difficult to tell because of all the wounds, there did not seem to be any birthmark; she seemed to be trying to get rid of the 'birthmark' of being black.

After the girl had been examined, the hospital sister said the psychiatrist refused to admit her to hospital, it was not clear why, but probably because she was not willing to stay and would have had to have been committed. Soon the mother and the sister's boyfriend arrived at the hospital under their own steam, and the girl was discharged and went home with them. The mother was still drunk and somewhat hysterical. The PC, John, did not speak to the relatives or to the girl.

None of the police officers involved in this incident either expressed or demonstrated sympathy or support. They behaved towards the girl as if she was taboo: that is, not to be touched, approached or spoken to because of her abnormal state. They tried to talk to the mother, but were not at all successful (largely through not adopting a brisk, practical approach). There was a range of things that they might have considered doing, but they did not actually do anything to help, apart from calling the ambulance. They did not help the mother to get to the hospital. They did not inform the housing department of the council with a view to having the family or the neighbours moved. They did not find out whether the girl or the family had a social worker, or therefore make any contact with any social worker. They did not inform the social services department. They probably did not persuade the Asian neighbour to stop causing trouble (Terry took the view that he was quite within his rights and that it was natural for him to taunt the girl since she was abnormal). Finally, the police officers did not find out why the hospital would not provide psychiatric treatment for someone who was clearly mentally ill.

Another member of the relief told DJS afterwards that he had recently called at the same house after a suicide attempt by the daughter when she had taken 100 paracetemol tablets and locked herself in the garden shed. She had by chance been found there long before she was dead, and the family had laid her out on the kitchen table, stripped her and poured cold water over her in the attempt to revive her. She had been got to hospital in time to be saved. The officers who dealt with the current incident, although belonging to the same relief, had not known about these earlier suicide attempts, but no one on the relief considered that it would be important to take some preventive action so that they would not be repeatedly called to the house.

Why the officers were so much more helpful in the case of the woman telephoning the fire brigade than in the case of the suicidal girl is not entirely clear. It was probably partly a question of the individual characteristics of the officers involved. Perhaps equally important, the whole family in the second case was in turmoil, several family members were behaving abnormally, and the girl's behaviour was more extreme than that of the woman who telephoned the fire brigade. Consequently, the police officers seemed to give up the idea of trying to relate to these people or to do something constructive for them.

When calling on the victims of burglaries, the response of police officers is surprisingly variable. In general they would like to offer sympathy, but they seem on occasion to be inhibited because of embarrassment at how little they are able to do to help. Also, as we shall discuss in the next chapter, their response partly depends on how 'respectable' they think the victims are. DJS observed a case where a uniform police officer signally failed to show the sympathy and concern that was expected. The burglary had taken place at a cheap hotel with a tatty reception manned by a surly youth in jeans, and with long narrow corridors and winding stairs. Two parties of Danish schoolchildren had come back from an evening out at about midnight and found that the doors of all their rooms had been forced and their belongings rifled. A couple of the children were in tears. The leader of one of the two parties acted as spokesman; he and several of the children had excellent English. The leader was extremely punctilious; he had ensured that none of the children should touch anything until the police arrived, and made each child search his or her belongings in the presence of the officer to find out what was missing. As the children discovered their losses, several more of them burst into tears. The PC dealing with the matter was experienced, aged about 35, generally competent but rather reserved. His approach was correct, but completely lacked any warmth or sympathy. The leader kept saying, 'Yes, but, you see, it is very upsetting', and 'This is the first time they have been away from their parents'. The PC simply ignored remarks of this kind and ploughed on with asking the routine questions. Eventually the attitude of the leader became one of barely suppressed resentment. After he had left the hotel, the PC said that he felt embarrassed at the conditions in which the Danes were lodged on their trip to London. 'Even the meanest hotel on the continent would have some semblance of order about it,' he pointed out. It seemed to be this embarrassment that prevented him from showing any real sympathy. Also, he felt he could do nothing for the Danes, and that the burglar would almost certainly not be caught, not least because the people running the hotel were not at all anxious to help. However, he did not appreciate that on this occasion what was expected was not any practical help - the Danes did not really expect to get their purses back - but a show of sympathy.

Police officers are generally reluctant to show sympathy towards people affected by the actions of the police themselves. DJS observed a striking example of this following a raid on a West Indian drinking party. The organiser of the party, a middle-aged man, was not arrested but merely reported for illegally selling alcohol. However, his sixteen year old son was arrested for possession of cannabis (everyone at the party was searched). As the large number of police officers left the house, the boy's mother stood on the pavement in tears. 'Take me to the station too!' she said. 'Jail me as well! Why do you have to do that to the boy? He's only sixteen!' All of the officers completely ignored her. The chief-inspector in command got briskly into his vehicle and drove off and when asked what the woman was upset about said he didn't know. It would have been quite easy for him or one of the other officers to explain to the mother that the boy would be back home in an hour or two after the procedures had been gone through at the police station, and to reassure her. There was not the remotest chance that they would do this because they saw the raid as an aggressive or punitive act, and if the woman was upset that proved that they had achieved their objective.

# XV   RACE AND CLASS

On beginning this project, neither of the researchers had any experience of the police force, or more than a passing acquaintance with any police officers. Our first impression after being attached to groups of police officers in areas having a substantial ethnic minority population was that racialist language and racial prejudice were prominent and pervasive and that many individual officers and also whole groups were preoccupied with ethnic differences. At the same time, on accompanying these officers as they went about their work we found that their relations with black and brown people were often relaxed or friendly and that the degree of tension between them and black people from day to day was much less than might have been expected either from their own conversation or from accounts in the newspapers and on television. Just as police officers dwelt on the violent and dangerous parts of their job, so they tended to exaggerate, in conversation, the extent of hostility between them and black people in their everyday relations; also, some of them seemed to cultivate a rhetoric of abuse of black people which did not carry through into action at any rate in normal circumstances. This rhetoric, which was seldom accompanied by hostile behaviour towards black people, was encouraged by the norms of working groups.

On the whole, our further research confirmed these initial impressions. Longer experience showed that the prominence of racialist talk varies greatly between individuals and between groups of police officers; also, it seems to be more common in areas with a substantial ethnic population than elsewhere. The aftermath of the Deptford fire and the riots of 1981 provided a focus for racialist talk within the Force: it became more prominent and more general at that time. All of this suggests that racialist talk is partly a response by police officers to the feeling that they under attack from black people.

These variations in the extent of racialist talk and racial prejudice are important, but our initial impression (that these things are pervasive) was correct in the sense that they are, on the whole, expected, accepted and even fashionable. Where someone in a group of police officers started on a line of racialist talk we never heard a member of the group explicitly oppose his views or saw the person made to feel that he was being a bore, speaking out of turn or erring against unspoken conventions or inhibitions. The only serious attempt that we saw by senior officers to set a different tone or establish a different set of values in this respect was in response to our visit: this had a degree of success, in that a particular group of officers would drop a line of racialist talk in the middle when they suddenly remembered their instruction and that DJS was present. This was an interesting demonstration of the ability of a senior officer to exert an influence, though whether or not this influence could have been sustained in the longer term is an open question.

Some aspects of policing behaviour seem to be clearly correlated with colour, though not necessarily with racial prejudice. For example, one criterion that police officers use for stopping people (especially in areas of relatively low ethnic concentration) is that they are black. Thus, from the survey of police officers we find that 20 per cent of people recently stopped were black (and not Asian), whereas about six per cent of the London population 'look black'. In two senses, this does not seem to be very closely related to racial prejudice on the part of the police. First, it is not only or mostly the officers who express prejudiced views who behave in this way. Secondly, the chance of getting a 'result' from a stop may, in fact be higher if black people are stopped. Thus, the survey of Londoners shows that in about one-third of cases people who have been the victims of crime in the past year can describe the offender, and in 24 per cent of these cases they say the offender was 'black'. Police stopping behaviour and the reports of victims are, therefore, roughly in step.

Where police officers behave badly towards black people after stopping or arresting them it is usually very hard to say whether or not their bad behaviour was 'switched on' by the race of the suspect or connected with it in any way. Generally speaking, police officers do not reserve a special kind of bad behaviour for black people; they did not openly direct racialist insults or language towards black people in the presence of the researchers. Racial prejudice is presumably one of a number of factors conducive towards bad behaviour by police officers, but it is probably not a fundamental one. Police behaviour is best explained by the structure of rewards and constraints within which police officers operate; only at exceptional times (such as the riots of 1981) does retribution against a particular ethnic group become an end in itself for police officers.

A special conception of social class, mixed with an idea of conventional or proper behaviour, is just as important to police officers as racial or ethnic group. In this scale, the 'respectable' working class and the suburban middle class stand highest, while the 'underclass' of the poor and rootless, together with groups regarded as deviant, such as homosexuals or hippies, stand lowest. The attitude of the police towards upper class people seems ambivalent: they seem ready to admire but quick to condemn them if they fail to live up to expectations. To a considerable extent, police hostility towards people of West Indian origin is connected with the belief that they are rootless, alienated, poor, unable to cope and deviant in various ways.

In the rest of this chapter we expand and illustrate these general points.

## Attitudes towards racial minorities

Police officers often use racialist language (among themselves) for effect, but it is the more casual or automatic use of such language that is the most telling. On one occasion, DJS was with two officers who were dealing with a suspected bomb in a mailbag. Of the two postmen who had noticed a sound coming from the bag in the back of their van, one was white and aged about 50 and the other was black, presumably of West Indian origin, aged about 45 and speaking with a perfect cockney accent with all the mannerisms to go with it. The black man was the driver, and the white man deferred to him for this reason: for example, if he was asked a question, he often said, 'I don't know about that, you'll have to ask my driver'. It was obvious that the two men worked together often and were good friends; they stood together chatting in a relaxed fashion as they waited for the police officers to come back to them and allow them to leave. Later, the officers questioned the black man in a friendly manner and the answers were given with clarity, common sense and courtesy. As they got back into the police car afterwards, one of the officers, checking through his notes, said to the other, 'Was it the coon who called us out?' The other replied, 'Yes, believe it or not, it was the coon that was the driver'.

Similarly, racialist language is quite commonly used over the personal radio. For example, JG heard the inspector of the relief with which he was working say over the personal radio, 'Look, I've got a bunch of coons in sight'. The inspector was standing in a public place at the time, and of course this message came up over the radios of all police officers on the Division, many of whom would have been in public places at the time. Racialist language is also used over the mainset radio on occasion.

About five terms are casually used to refer to black people.

Hello, she's a nigger. Almost unheard of, a nigger in Esher.

He's very good at parking is Geoff (another policeman). He parked right up a nigger's arse once.

I think I'll do a check on the bunch of satchies in the old 1100. (This officer later stopped the car but without getting a 'result'.)

The sooties are giving us a bit of trouble. We'll have to work hard to get statements. (To JG) Oh, we're not supposed to call them sooties, are we?

There was this West Indian club by the section house, and when I got back late I had to run the gauntlet through all these coons shouting 'Here comes the pigs, get the pigs!'

Both the boy and the girl that we're going to arrest this morning are spades.

The object of these patrols is to protect property, because when these monkeys get through they can cause a great deal of damage ...

Most of these terms are interchangeable and are simply used to refer to black people, but 'monkeys' is specifically used to describe black people behaving in a ludicrous and mischievous manner, for example:

You must brief your constables: they must not say 'Look at those monkeys!' even if they may think they look like that jumping up and down. We don't want to spoil everything with stupid remarks.

'Monkeys' can be used in various ways, for example, to describe anyone monkeying about. However, we never heard a police officer refer to a white person as a monkey.

Another term occasionally used for black people is 'spooks', but we did not come across its being used casually; whenever used it seemed to carry a higher emotional charge.

None of the terms so far quoted is used to describe Asians, and in general a parallel vocabulary for Asians does not exist. Occasionally police officers refer to Asians as 'Pakis', which is a kind of racialist term especially when the person who uses it knows that the people he is talking about are not actually of Pakistani origin. However, the extent of genuine ignorance about the origins of Asians can be astounding. In an area where the local population are mostly of Bengali origin, an inspector referred to them not as 'Pakis', but as 'Pakistanis'; bearing in mind that he would speak to these people more or less every day, this was a colossal mistake to make. However, what is most significant is that the police have a limited abusive vocabulary to describe a group - Asians - with which their relations are fairly good, but an extensive vocabulary to describe black people, with whom their relations are much poorer.

Although the terms by which police officers refer to black people are in common use in various other social contexts, they seem to be more commonly used within the Met than in most other groups: there can be few other groups in which it is normal, automatic, habitual to refer to black people as 'coons', 'niggers' and so on. This point was underlined by a woman detective constable who had joined the force after working for some years in other jobs. She told JG that before she joined she used to wince when people used words like 'coon', 'wog' and 'nigger'; she had pledged to herself that she would never use such terms. She pointed out that the habitual use of words like these, as part of police jargon, was uniform throughout the Force, and admitted that she herself now said 'spade' and 'spook' constantly, though she couldn't explain why.

Apart from these casually abusive references, there is a vein of deliberately hostile and bitter comment on black people by police officers. In the autumn of 1981 we saw the following inscriptions in a lavatory at a police station in an area of high ethnic concentration.

> Fight racialism - smash a nigger in the gob today.
>
> Q: What's the difference between a nigger and a bucket of shit?
> A: The bucket.

These lavatories were only used by police officers and civilian staff of the Met. The two examples quoted are taken from the large number that covered the lavatory doors, most of them racialist, but some of them against women or WPCs. It is very unusual to see inscriptions in lavatories in police buildings. Effective managers would have noticed the inscriptions themselves or come to know about them, and once they knew they would have had them removed immediately.

In extended conversations, hostile comments about black people are occasionally related to a race theory and to neo-Fascist politics. For example, during a drinks party in a CID office, JG talked at length with two detective constables, Stan and Vic. Stan brought the conversation round to ethnic minorities by making a racialist remark, so JG asked why he felt that way. Vic answered for him, 'Because they're all thieving toe-ragging little niggers, the ones we deal with'. This jogged Stan into coming up with a more general theory. 'I think it's because they've only just come over here and it's bred into them,' he said.

> JG: What's bred into them?
> Stan: Well, they're used to running round in the jungle, plucking what they want from the trees and off the floor and killing someone for it if necessary. When they get here it's all different. They don't know how to behave.

JG laughed and said Stan was 'taking the piss'. Stan insisted that he wasn't. He said he was in favour of the NF's policy - Britain for the British. 'You mean white British', said JG. 'Well, of course I do.' Stan went on to explain that 'they' take our jobs they take our houses ... at this point Vic interrupted to say:

This country has become the dumping ground of the world because of its past moral culpability. Isn't that only fair? No, it isn't! Because we've let all these people be dumped here, there'll be war out there one day. (He meant in the streets outside the police station.)

Stan then continued with his own train of thought. He said that the black world wasn't fit to rule itself - you only had to look at Africa. He asked JG whether he 'believed in 1984'. JG asked what he meant, and he made it clear that he thought of 1984 as the year of cataclysm brought about by black uprising. He said, 'That man was right and he paid for telling the truth'. It turned out that he meant Enoch Powell rather than George Orwell. He went on to explain that he didn't mind the first generation of black people, but was hostile to the young black people, whom he described as 'the legacy'. As though they were still talking about the same subject, Stan and Vic then went on to complain about light sentencing by the courts: 'Who ever thinks about the victim?' Vic argued that the victim should be able to appeal against an acquittal or for a harsher sentence and proudly stated, 'I'm somewhere to the right of Genghis Khan'. Stan then supported (as he saw it) his arguments about stiffer sentencing by saying that in his army days he and his mates had beaten up his wife's lover. This whole conversation shows how hostility to black people is linked, in the minds of these police officers, with racialist theories, right wing politics, fear of violence and disorder caused by black people, a psychological need for retribution and the view that violent retribution is legitimate.

Police officers who expressed a racist ideology are certainly a small minority. Those who initiate racialist talk (without referring to a racist ideology) may be a minority too, but since they are rarely contradicted or opposed they tend to shape the norms of the group. A young probationer WPC put it like this.

Blacks today are repaying whites for their bad treatment in colonial days. They aren't just against police but against all white people. The police are an obvious target because they represent white supremacy. Really, until blacks have taken over and evened up the score, the problem won't be solved. I don't blame them really, when they get stuck in places like Brixton. I know that PCs call them spooks, niggers and sooties, but deep down the majority of PCs aren't really against them, although there are some who really hate them and will go out of their way to get them. I call them niggers myself now, but I don't really mean it. I think a relief takes on a personality of its own. Although you still have your own personality you lose a lot of it to the relief group personality.

This quotation gives a vivid insight into how someone who is basically sympathetic towards black people can come to adopt racialist language in order to conform to the expectations of the group, which are set by a minority of active racists.

The Deptford Fire and its aftermath had the effect of focusing racialist attitudes within the Met. When a PC heard that JG had spent some time looking at the police investigation into the fire, he asked conversationally: 'How many of these niggers actually fried in this barbecue at Deptford, then?'. After that shift, a group of eight officers went to the pub, accompanied by JG. The only WPC, who wanted to attract the attention of the area car driver, tried to shine by telling the following racialist joke. 'Do you know what they've renamed Deptford?' 'No, what have they renamed it?' 'Blackfriars.' Later, at a drinks party in a CID office on a different District, DJS heard a series of anti-IRA jokes (Bobby Sands was buried in a billiard cue case, he got the slimmer of the year award, and so on), followed by a series of racialist jokes of which the Blackfriars joke was one. A much longer conversation took place on an outer Division the day after the protest march, known as the 'Black People's Day of Action', that was organised in response to the Deptford Fire. The conversation began when one PC scoffed at the press coverage of the march as he looked at his newspaper. He had been there, and said it had been 'chaos' and that there had been 'a lot of fighting at times'. Other officers suggested that the march was staged by black people so that they could have a punch up with police. The first speaker said that one PC had taken a brick in the face and suffered a broken jaw. Others mentioned officers they knew who had been injured, one with a broken jaw, another with a stomach injury.

As soon as the temperature had been raised in this way, racialist comments abounded. Someone described the march as 'hundreds of rampaging niggers'. The first speaker made it clear that the march had been a 'defeat' for the police 'though I managed to hit a nigger in the mouth. (Holding out his hand to show a small mark) This is where the nigger's teeth went in'. Someone else commented, 'I hope you've had your tetanus jab' to general laughter. The discussion ended with the officers agreeing that 'they' were 'animals' and that 'they should be shot'.

There was another long discussion among a group of about eight officers later that day at the same police station. Two officers who had been at the march started the talk by describing what had happened. They said the command was 'rubbish'; men had been wrongly deployed and orders were contradictory and lacked clarity. They described how the demonstrators' lorry had broken through the police cordon on Blackfriars Bridge and claimed that the lorry had only been used because of its value in fighting the police. They then described the fighting that broke out as soon as the cordon had been broken. This (like the description of police injuries in the morning) triggered a flood of racialist comments. One of the PCs who had been at the march said that the blacks were 'animals'; the words 'nigger' and 'spade' were continually used. The second PC who had been present said, 'They're not like white

394

people, you're always afraid you'll be stabbed by a nigger'. A WPC agreed that 'they' were 'animals', at which JG gently remonstrated. She became heated and said, 'Yes, they are, they're all animals!'.

An argument then developed about the quality of command on the police side. A chief-inspector who was present argued that the police would not have been 'beaten' if orders had been properly followed. The two PCs who had been at the march insisted that it was senior officers who were at fault.

> It should be up to the PCs to decide when they should draw truncheons. 'Course, we weren't allowed to do yesterday, were we? 'Cause they were black. I mean, they wouldn't even keep to the fucking route.

There was then further talk about blacks being 'animals' and 'bestial'. Again, JG registered gentle disagreement. The chief-inspector then said;

> The American, when they were dealing with their, what they call little banana republic, they had to invent the Colt .45, because that's the only thing that would stop a spade. If a nigger's coming straight at you, you can put a .38 straight through him and he'll keep coming.

In order to keep control of himself, JG had to move away from the group at this point, but he returned to it as the conversation was ending. By this time, one of the PCs and the chief-inspector were talking about the 'return match' or 'second leg' at which they hoped the police would get a better score. This was another march then scheduled for the following Saturday (but which never in fact took place). The chief-inspector was saying that, if presented with a problem like the one on Blackfriars Bridge, he would have the entire street cleared. 'I'd get everyone with their truncheons out and they'd move up the road slowly and <u>anything</u> that didn't get out of the way they'd hit, and hard.' The PC objected, 'What about the press?', but the chief-inspector brushed such objections aside.

In between the casual use of racialist language and the very hostile racialist comments of the kind just quoted, there is a considerable amount of explicitly racialist comment in which the hostility is moderated, or in many cases, clothed in a joke. For example, as a group of officers were driving about at night in a van they entered an area where all the lamp-posts were out of action. 'Cor, isn't it dark round here!' a WPC said. The driver, who was a constant source of jokes, replied, 'Yeah, that's why all the spooks round here have flat noses'. A more coldly hostile joke was told by a detective constable (in the pub): 'What's a racist? Someone who hates niggers more than is necessary'. More straightforward hostility was shown by a uniform sergeant in charge of a crime squad when a black person crossed the road in front of the car he was travelling in (with DJS in the back). He said, 'Get out of the way, you fat nigger, if you don't want to be run over'.

It is unusual to find a similar level of hostility against Asians. On one occasion an area car crew stopped several Asians in a car, and on finding a crowbar in it kept the people talking for some time and carried out various checks before deciding to let them go. At one point, the driver became upset, but was calmed by placatory noises made by his friends. As the police officers got back into their car, the driver said to his operator, 'No problem, Paki filth, just blow into this', meaning that he was not prepared to countenance any complaints from the driver since he had been generous in not breathalysing him. Far more common than open hostility of this kind is for police officers to say that Asians or 'Pakis' are devious, sly or unreliable, and in particular that they don't tell the truth. A sober statement of this point of view was given by a detective chief-inspector in an informal interview. He said, 'Asians are incapable of telling the truth. If it's to their advantage, they'll lie'. An example of the racier version of this saying is a spontaneous remark by a uniform sergeant: 'Course, the Bengalis wouldn't know the truth if it jumped up and hit them in the face'.

Police officers show their attitudes towards ethnic minorities in an entirely different way when they reflect on their work and philosophise about it. On one occasion a uniform sergeant started talking about a special posting to a district support unit of twelve officers whose job was to make a large number of crime arrests over a one-month period. He said the group had had a wonderful time.

> Almost every other stop produced a good crime arrest for drugs, offensive weapon or something like that. We had so many bodies it was unbelievable. Most of them were black. They must have been getting away with it for years. The crime rate fell dramatically while we were there. Admittedly some of the villains went to ground, but we nicked a lot of them too. We only had a couple of tugs of war with a crowd (over a prisoner) because usually we jumped out, stuck him in the back of the van and were back in and away sharpish. Some of the blacks thought we were SPG and asked us why we didn't have CO on our shoulders. I usually explained to them. Actually I found one or two reasonable ones who accepted what we were doing. But when you see so much violent crime perpetrated by blacks and so much of it is against elderly whites, your broad-minded bit goes out of the window.

From this, the sergeant went on to talk more generally about race relations. He was outraged that some black people thought they had been given a poor deal by this country. 'The poor old whites are shelling out for this lot to be on the dole.' He said that black people were ill-educated, but was not sure whether this was because they had problems with the school system or because they were 'thick'. He said, 'Whilst not being very intelligent, they have this low animal cunning'. None of this was said aggressively, and the sergeant would probably have been deeply offended if anyone had suggested he was showing a racial prejudice.

Another example of this more expansive vein of commentary comes from a conversation with a detective constable.

> The minority communities have to split up unless we want a race war. They should be dispersed across the land. Indians and Pakistanis are industrious people who will fit in quickly anywhere. But the West Indian - well, he's used to wine, women and song and that's all he's used to. That's what they taught them out there on the plantations.

A conversation about apartheid developed between three PCs sitting around at court waiting for a case to come up.

> First PC: You know like you have golf-driving ranges? Well, over there (in South Africa) they have little coons to go round picking the balls up. My brother says it's a good game over there - they try and hit them - 50 points for the head, 25 for the body.

> Second PC: Yeah, but it's a terrible system, isn't it? They haven't got any rights. They're told what to do all through their lives.

> First PC: Apparently they all get dead pissed at night because they're made to work so hard during the day. They're not used to the alcohol. They just get drunk and fall down. Then a lorry comes round and they're slung in the back, taken to a compound and dumped until they're sober.

> Third PC: But they're so stupid, aren't they? Someone told me that if they fancy a kip they just lie down where they are, even if it's in the middle of the road. And if they get too hot in the sun they put more clothes on.

> First PC: Shouldn't mistreat them though, just 'cause they're stupid.

> Third PC: Oh no, no.

We cannot produce examples of police officers objecting to racialist language or arguing with others who express racialist views. This, of course, says more about the fashion or expectations within groups of police officers than about the views of individual members of the groups. In private conversations, police officers spoke up in favour of black people or against racialism; it was much more common for them to make racialist comments than the opposite, but this could be because destructive and hostile remarks tend to make better conversation than expressions of support or affection. A PC with ten years experience said to JG, 'As far as I'm concerned the coloureds have had such a bad deal over here, a black is more likely to get lenient treatment from me than anything else'. It is significant that this officer was known among the other members of his relief for having progressive views.

JG accompanied an area car driver with fifteen years' experience shortly after he had spent some days in Brixton in the aftermath of the riots of April 1981. He was now back in his own (outer) Division. He said he was fed up with the racism of some of the policemen who had been in Brixton. He blamed 'the Job' (the hierarchy) to the extent that nobody had properly informed the PCs about what was going on so that rumours had been rife. One rumour was that a PC had died from his injuries but that this was not being made public. The area car driver said that this was 'bullshit' but that everybody believed it, and it had the effect of sharpening the hostility of the police to blacks. He said he was 'amazed and shocked' to see black people in Brixton looking at him 'with hate in their eyes'. It unsettled him greatly to be hated so much when he did not know the people who were staring at him. He thought that the police must bear a large part of the responsibility for what happened in Brixton and he said that there must have been malpractice in the area for so much hatred to develop. He was highly critical of Force policy in sending young PCs straight out of training school to Brixton: 'It's no wonder they become racist, is it, sent there at nineteen with no experience and just being flung into the deep end'. This was effectively a private conversation in an area car (the radio operator was asleep at the time); the driver did not speak like this when he was in a group of police officers.

Perhaps the strongest opposition to racial prejudice that we heard came from a WPC in the special patrol group; she made the remarks in the presence of other officers from her unit, but not in contradiction of anything they had said. She said that 'racial prejudice in this job is dreadful' and most other members of the unit agreed. She said that she became angry about PCs saying 'spook', 'coon', 'spade' and 'nigger'. 'I've got a lot of young coloured friends. How can I explain to them why a PC calls them spades?' The driver said, 'Yeah, but you don't hear it on this unit, do you?' The WPC replied, 'Oh, tell the truth! Yes, I've heard it on this unit. If I was a sergeant and one of my PCs used those terms in front of me he'd be straight up before the guvnor'.

In a private conversation with DJS, a very experienced PC made a careful distinction between words and deeds in connection with racialism. He first explained that he had once been accused of being a racist in his annual qualification report, had objected and had succeeded in having the report withdrawn. After showing how deeply offended he had been at being called a racist, he went on to reflect on the matter further.

I was talking to a policeman not long ago, one of these who says he hates black people, they're the scum of the earth and all of those things. I said to him, 'Suppose you're on a street and two skinheads are doing over a black man, putting the boot in, what would you do?' 'You know what I would do,' he said. 'Tell me what you would do, would you intervene?' 'Of course I would,' he said. 'Well, what would you do, would you join in kicking the black man?' 'Of course I wouldn't,' he said, 'I would come to his aid and sort out the skinheads.' 'Well then,' I said, 'when you say you hate blacks, you don't mean it, you're just going through a phase.' It's a recognised thing, you know, that people do go through phases like that. In America they have found that policemen who are dealing with crap all day can get upset about it and go round the twist.

In fact, this PC's relations with the few black people that he dealt with over a couple of working days were very good. It seemed that the senior officer who had done his annual qualification report had made the mistake of thinking that because he was conservative and authoritarian he must be a racist. The PC's view that many of the racialist views expressed by police officers do not carry over into action seems to be correct, as we shall suggest later in this chapter.

### Senior officers and ethnic minorities
We shall discuss the nature of supervision in the Met and the extent to which senior officers influence the behaviour of PCs in a later chapter. Here we briefly consider how far senior officers share the attitudes of the lower ranks towards ethnic minorities and how far they try to change these attitudes.

It is very difficult to make a general statement on this matter because of the great variety of attitudes and views expressed. This is partly because of the marked differences between the personal views and character of different senior officers, but it is also partly a matter of social context: what senior officers say in the 'senior common room' atmosphere of a discussion with DJS tends to be different from what they say in the canteen. In spite of these difficulties, the following points can be made with some confidence. There are substantial numbers of senior officers who are strongly opposed to racial discrimination and prejudice, and if they do not succeed in influencing the officers under their command in this regard that is because of the limitations of their influence generally and not because of a lack of sincerity on the part of the senior officers concerned. Equally, there are senior officers - we have met several in the course of the research - who show quite clearly that they have strong racial prejudices.

In one of the Divisions that we studied, the senior management team (chief-superintendent and superintendent) were clearly very anxious to establish and maintain good relations with members of ethnic minority groups locally. They showed this by giving their own attention to any events or incidents that might act as a focus for racial tensions. They also spent a considerable amount of their time getting to know prominent people belonging to the ethnic minority groups locally. They were well aware that there was a great deal of racialist talk among PCs on the reliefs; they certainly did not appear to condone it and they made a (partly successful) attempt to stop it while the researcher was there. Although the racialist talk continued (except in the exceptional circumstances of the research) the PCs were well aware of the policy of the senior management, especially their insistence on giving support to the Asians when under threat from skinheads and supporters of extreme right wing organisations. This policy was often commented on, was resented by some, but was put into action. It was significant that DJS saw a potentially explosive incident involving West Indians successfully defused on this Division (this incident will be described in a later section).

In the other nine Divisions that we visited, the senior management team was much less active in all of these ways. A majority of senior officers showed, in conversation, that they could be sensitive to racial issues, but in general they had not themselves devoted substantial energies to making contact with ethnic minority groups locally and they had not impressed the PCs on the reliefs either by their views or by the force of example. This was, however, more a consequence of the nature of management and supervision generally than a reflection of the views or attitudes of the senior officers or their interest in race relations issues.

In some cases senior officers undoubtedly overlooked racialism or racial prejudice when it was manifest, or participated in racialist talk themselves. It was a chief-inspector who (in the aftermath of the Black People's Day of Action) worked himself up into a frenzy of hatred against black people and orchestrated a session of absurd racialist talk with a large group of PCs in the canteen. (His remark about the kind of gun needed to stop a charge from a black man was quoted in the last section.) On another occasion, a superintendent indulged in saloon bar philosophising about black people in the company of a chief-inspector and a PC (as well as JG).

> I was never prejudiced before I came into this job, but now ... I mean I had coloured friends in the forces before it was trendy to have coloured friends. Everything was all right in the army - everyone knew what was expected of them and acted accordingly. No one got preferential treatment. Now the blacks want it both ways - they want to live in the white man's country and still have their own lifestyle, so they come into conflict with the law. When in Rome, do what the Romans do, that's what I say. These do-gooders never change people's minds by law. They're just making it worse.

It was a detective chief-inspector who said (in an interview) that 'Asians are incapable of telling the truth', a remark that was not made with great hostility, but which shows a degree of ethnocentrism and a capacity to make unwise generalisations that is quite startling for someone at this level in the Force. Again, a detective chief-inspector was present at a CID drinks party when a series of extremely callous racialist jokes were made (including the one about renaming Deptford as Blackfriars). He clearly found the jokes amusing, but looked uneasily at DJS after laughing each time to see how he was responding. He made no attempt to turn the conversation, still less did he show any disapproval. One of the officers giving the briefing for a large 'public order event' managed to indicate that he sympathised with PCs who found black people ridiculous even while he was saying that the PCs should not call them 'monkeys' as this might cause trouble. A commander in a sensitive area spontaneously spoke at length (to DJS) about the alien, unintelligible and threatening nature of the West Indian way of life; while some of the points that he made were, individually, valid, what he had to say was, taken as a whole, an expression of hostility towards West Indians especially since he had nothing to say in their favour. It was quite clear that this commander had little sense of a common humanity with the West Indians who formed an important part of local population.

In general we had little opportunity to observe senior officers actually dealing with incidents, but on one occasion DJS watched a chief-inspector dealing with black people at an illegal drinking party. Most of the guests were quite good humoured and made no protest about the raid or about being searched (for drugs) but a young boy of about 16 started saying, 'Why are you doing this?' Almost immediately the chief-inspector began to lose his temper. He replied very sharply, 'Because it's against the law'. The boy started to say, 'But in our country...' but before he could go on the chief-inspector interjected, very angrily, 'Well, when you come to a different country, you have to obey the laws of the country that you're in. And if I go to Jamaica or somewhere, I would have to obey the laws of Jamaica, and that's that!' By this time the boy was almost in tears and said again, 'But why are you doing it? Jesus Christ, I mean...' but could not express himself any further. The chief-inspector began to question him very brusquely about who his parents were, where he was born (in London) and so on. His crushing response to the boy's rather pathetic enquiry was quite unnecessary; the house was swarming with police officers and the guests were extremely well behaved. It seemed to be triggered by indignation that the boy should appeal to a different and foreign tradition together with irritation at any challenge to his authority.

Essentially, racialist attitudes, like other norms, develop informally among groups of working police officers at the lower ranks. Thus, senior officers are certainly not the initiators of racialist attitudes in the Force, but except in one of the Divisions that we visited, they were not effectively counteracting them either, while in some cases prejudiced senior officers reinforce racialism or seem to give it the seal of approval by letting racialist remarks pass without comment.

## Behaviour of police officers towards ethnic minority groups
It has often been shown that the relationship between racial prejudice and discriminatory or hostile behaviour towards ethnic minorities is far from straightforward. In a general sense, the relation between what people say and what they do is indirect; both people and organisations often do not do what they say they would do, as shown by a classic experiment carried out in the 1930s which showed that hotels that claimed they would refuse to admit Chinese people actually admitted a Chinese couple without demur when put to the test. Beyond that, racialist talk is itself a pattern of behaviour that satisfies certain individual psychological needs and serves the needs of the group - it helps to reinforce the identity, security and solidarity of the group against a clearly perceived external threat. A well-known example of this mechanism is the identification, by a disunited country, of a foreign enemy as a means of finding a greater sense of national purpose. The police do go through moods and through periods when they feel themselves to be unfairly attacked and criticised from many directions - witness the stock question put to us as researchers by many police officers, 'Have you considered the problems of the police as a minority group?' When they are in this kind of mood, the police may sometimes indulge in racialist talk as a kind of ritual to help to restore their self-confidence. When police officers actually come into contact with members of minority groups, a different set of needs comes into play: very often the officer is forced to look on the person as a person - as someone whose support is required or who must be manipulated - rather than as a member of a particular ethnic group. For these reasons, it would be quite wrong to assume that, because there is a good deal of racialist talk in the Metropolitan Police, it follows that the police discriminate against members of minority groups or regularly behave towards them in a hostile manner.

The contrast between words and deeds was shown very clearly by a relief that JG worked with. Racialist talk was very common in this group, together with a line of reasoned argument intended to justify an attitude of resentment towards minority groups (they can't expect to get on in this country if they don't adopt our habits and standards). This outlook was reinforced by the Divisional chief-superintendent in the following terms.

> They were originally guests in this country. Now of course some of them are born here, unfortunately. You've got to feel sorry for some of the old people up there. There are some white people who've lived in London for 30 years or more - real Londoners. They've been swallowed up by all this. They'll help and support the police. When you come to another country you have to live by its rules.

402

The terms 'nigger', 'coon', 'spade' and 'spook' were commonly used by members of the relief. There was also prejudice against Asians: a PC with four years' experience said to JG, 'I hate Pakis'. JG asked him why. 'Because you always know a spade'll lie to you, but you can never tell with a Paki.' However, when JG went out with the area car crew, they were anxious to point out that they would not use the term 'spade' to a black man's face in the normal course of duty. Because black men are renowned for their speed, they said, 'What we should do when we nick these spades is spend the money on feeding them up, make them really fat: that'll slow them down'. Almost immediately the car answered a call to a tube station where a drunk white man was hurling Nazi-style racialist abuse at a black ticket collector, and refusing to move on. The PC who had talked about 'making them fat' dealt with the situation very well. Every time the drunk called the ticket collector 'filth', or 'scum', or a 'spade', the PC referred to him as 'this gentleman'. He did not arrest the white man but persuaded him to go away. The ticket collector was clearly pleased by the service the police had given, and happy about the way he had been spoken to. To the PC, the fact that the black ticket collector was being 'as good as gold' while the drunken white man was making a nuisance of himself was far more important (despite all his racialist talk) than the race of the two people involved.

Police officers themselves often draw the distinction between words and behaviour and claim that they won't let their views about black people affect the way they treat them. The most vivid statement of this kind was made by an area car driver.

> I freely admit that I hate, loathe and despise niggers. I can't stand them. I don't let it affect my job though. There are some decent ones, though, like that bloke we've just dealt with. Not the African cunt, the other one.

On another occasion a detective sergeant, who was talking to a woman detective constable, said, 'Oh, come on, they're nothing if not a bloody lazy race. How many West Indian businesses can you name, how many West Indian restaurants? See? I mean, when we had the Jewish invasion they became powers in the community and worked hard'. But immediately after, both officers insisted that nothing that they had said about their attitudes to West Indians could possibly affect their police work.

A detective inspector who was being interviewed by DJS insisted repeatedly that it was impossible not to be racially prejudiced 'although it's wrong, you shouldn't be'. But the example that he gave made it clear that the prejudice would really be incidental to any bad behaviour.

> Let's face it, if a black man is lying to you, you say, 'You lying black bastard!' and that is prejudice, really, because if it was a white man you'd just say, 'You lying bastard!', you wouldn't say, 'You lying white bastard!'.

The impression sometimes given in the press and on television is that most encounters between police officers and black people are 'confrontations' involving clear hostility on each side. This is definitely not so. Even in the six months preceding the riots and in some of the areas where riots later broke out, most encounters between police officers and black people were fairly relaxed; after the riots, there was naturally a higher level of tension for some time. The survey of Londoners shows that black people evaluate their encounters with the police no more unfavourably than do white people.

Although the detective inspector quoted above said that he would call someone 'a lying black bastard' in what he thought were the appropriate circumstances, we did not observe police officers using racial insults to members of the public. The presence of the observer may have had an influence, here. Even so, our more general impression is, very strongly, that police officers rarely behave badly in such a way as to make it obvious that a person's ethnic group is the reason for their bad behaviour. It is still possible that police officers behave differently and more badly towards black people (and maybe Asians) without making it plain that they are motivated by a racial prejudice. It is difficult for us to establish whether or not this is so by analysis of our observations, because a large number of factors comes into play in each incident, so that we cannot easily isolate the effect of the ethnic group of the people involved. However, although the thing cannot definitely be proved, we are fairly confident that there is no widespread tendency for black or Asian people to be given greatly inferior treatment by the police. That broad statement has to be qualified in the following ways.

1.  It has been proved (see Chapter IV) that black people (but not Asians) are much more likely to be stopped by police than are white people; there are strong indications that this has a substantial influence on the attitudes of black people towards the police.

2.  Police officers tend to make a crude equation between crime and black people, to assume that suspects are black and to justify stopping people in these terms.

3.  Police officers sometimes show reluctance to act energetically in matters involving Asians because they feel that they are a 'closed community' and do not really welcome a resolution of conflicts by the police. This may extend to a reluctance to act over matters that could turn out to be racist attacks.

4.  Police officers may well treat members of different ethnic groups differently, but the motive for this is not usually racial prejudice: for example, they may tend to

404

be careful in their encounters with black people because they fear repercussions if they mishandle the matter.

5.  Where the police are engaged in a big confrontation with large numbers of people, as during the 1981 riots, the ethnic factor will be a focus for police hostility if the people are black, but this does not mean that racial prejudice is the cause of the hostility. If the police were faced by large numbers of skinheads armed with petrol bombs, their feelings would focus, for the time being, on a hatred of skinheads.

6.  For some officers, racial prejudice may be the chief reason for their bad behaviour on occasion. The best we can do is quote some examples so that the reader can form his own opinion on this point.

## Colour as a criterion for stops

On the extent to which colour is used as a criterion for stopping people, the best kind of evidence comes from statistical analysis of experience of being stopped among a random sample of Londoners and of stops recently carried out by a random sample of police officers. However, our observational work provides some incidental confirmation of these findings. On a relief that DJS was working with, three relatively experienced PCs were the most respected officers, primarily because they were thought to make 'good arrests'. One of these, a heavily built, hard drinking man about 26 years old, was asked to give a talk to the probationers on a street duties course about stopping, searching and questioning people. (Since the summer of 1981, probationers have attended street duties courses organised on their Divisions as part of their training; these courses are largely practical and represent an attempt to introduce a greater element of training on the job.) The PC was not used to giving a talk to a group of people, and even though the audience were to be probationers he was clearly rather nervous about it. He sat in the canteen among his friends (including the two other experienced PCs) with a notebook and a pencil trying to think what to say and asking for suggestions. Various joking suggestions were made about the technique of questioning suspects in the street. 'If you're Harry (the PC who was to give the talk) you just rock back on your heels, sniff a few times, then grab hold of the man with both hands, shake him like a sack of onions and say "You're nicked!" ' Then Harry decided what advice he was going to give.

How does an experienced policeman decide who to stop? Well, the one that you stop is often wearing a woolly hat, he is dark in complexion, he has thick lips and he usually has dark fuzzy hair.

This group of officers indulged in a great deal of racialist talk, but they also gave what they regarded as reasoned justifications for stopping black people. All three insisted that it was reasonable to stop any black people in cars because nine times out of ten they would have drugs. (In fact, 3 per cent of stops lead to an arrest and charge and a further 5 per cent lead to an offence being reported.) The same point was made by a different group of officers at the same Division, this time to JG: 'If so many IC3s are involved in crime, why shouldn't we give them disproportionate attention?' (Identity Code 3 - hence 'IC3' is used on police forms to describe people who look 'negroid'.) Though most police officers do not spontaneously make frank statements of this kind, many probably share the same basic view. A more qualified version of the same view was put by a PC who worked in a Division containing areas of high and low ethnic concentration.

> If I saw a black man walking through Wimbledon High Street I would definitely stop him. 'Course, down here it's a common sight, so there's no point.

## Black people associated with crime

This stopping policy is inseparable from a tendency to assume that black people have committed crimes and that whoever has committed a crime must be black. For example, JG saw an inspector dealing with an accident. A bread van had struck a black cyclist as it was turning into a side road. The bicycle had been damaged beyond repair, though the cyclist was not hurt. Explaining to JG what had happened, the inspector said, 'He was a young West Indian gentleman on the bike, so I presume it's stolen, although he says he got it from a friend'. On another occasion, a detective constable who was looking over a house after a burglary said to the householder, 'I usually associate this type of crime with young blacks. Though, of course, if we catch them it won't be their fault, there'll be all sorts of reasons why they're deprived and why they did it'.

DJS was once walking through a market with two PCs when there was a call over the personal radio about two youths who had done a robbery at a shop then damaged a milkman's float; all this had happened nearby. Only one of the two PCs listened to the call – the other was not paying attention. The first one relayed it to the second, giving the description as two black youths, one in a burgundy jerkin, the other in a blue pullover, and so on. The PCs spent ten minutes looking for the suspects and questioning one or two people who might have seen them pass. Then the area car crew relayed a more detailed description over the personal radio (they had got it from the mainset radio). In this description, the youths were white. The first PC said, 'I was wrong for once,' meaning to acknowledge that the first description had not mentioned the colour of the suspects. He had simply assumed that two youths who robbed a shop would be black - he hardly thought it worth while stopping to check up on the matter. On another occasion DJS was with a group of officers who were called to a break-in at a nursery school. When they arrived a telephone worker shouted to them from the top floor of a telephone exchange that overlooked the nursery school. He said he had seen the break-in and started to shout a decription of two boys. The sergeant shouted up to him, 'They were black?'. In fact, all three of the boys involved were white.

## Reluctance to investigate crime involving Asians

In most cases where crimes were reported by Asian people there was little or no indication that the police were reluctant to take action about the matter. Cases involving Asians were likely to be regarded as 'weary' because of the extra difficulties involved, but this did not usually seem to prevent the appropriate action from being taken. For example, a detective constable who had to deal with an alleged assault on an Asian boy at school certainly regarded the whole affair as a nuisance, especially in view of the need to find interpreters and the special care needed to communicate with the various people involved. Nevertheless, he dealt with the matter very successfully and built up a good case against the suspect. There was, however, one case covered by JG where the police had delayed for a considerable time before taking action, maybe because it involved Asians. A Bengali woman in her 40s had reported assault and indecent behaviour by two Bengali men in their 30s. Specifically, she claimed that on two occasions the men had beaten and kicked her, and that on one of the occasions one of them had exposed hmself and said, 'See, I am a man. You know what I can do'. She was advised to obtain warrants for the arrest of the two men, which she had done. However, the police held these warrants for five months before executing them. The probable reason for the delay emerges from a remark made by the detective sergeant dealing with the case. 'This really is a load of grief for me and there's not much chance of a result at the end - especially as they're Pakis'. As the case developed, this detective sergeant in fact handled it well, though he was constantly looking for an opportunity to resolve the matter without bringing charges and several times came close to putting pressure on the victim to retract.

The area car crew arrested two Bengali men with the warrants that had been issued. As they were brought into the charge room, the operator said, 'I've given them the full works, you know, Rule 2 caution and everything. Well, in view of recent events you never know if someone's watching'. The 'recent event' referred to was the arrest of a local Bengali community worker which had upset the relations of the police with the Bengalis generally. The operator went on to say that the older of the two Bengali men had only decided he could not speak English when he realised he had been arrested. 'Well, you know what lying shits they are.' The detective sergeant quickly established that one of the men arrested was not the man named on the warrant. (Close comparison of the passport and the warrant showed that the names were not exactly the same.) Nevertheless, both men were put in a detention room while the area car went to fetch the victim. While he was waiting, the detective sergeant explained why he did not relish having to deal with the case. He said that 'Pakis' always took up more time than 'ordinary' prisoners because of the language problems and because of the 'Pakis' ' inability to tell the truth. He explained that he very much hoped the victim would retract her allegations and 'cancel' the warrants. This would involve taking her to a magistrates court, where she would have to make a statement. The detective sergeant consulted with another CID officer on the exact method to be followed in doing this. This second officer said he had had a similar case at West Ham once. 'For fuck's sake don't charge them till you're sure she wants to know. Mine changed her mind at court and I had a terrible job sorting it all out.' On hearing this the detective sergeant said, 'Typical Pakis'. 'No,' replied the other officer, 'my lot were white.'

Before the victim had arrived an Asian PC was asked to speak to the two men. They told him that the elders of the Bengali community, through their representative association, had met as 'arbitrators' in this case, that the victim had accepted apologies, and that everything had been settled informally. This encouraged the detective sergeant to think that the victim could easily be persuaded to retract her allegations. Although this was what he wanted, he still grumbled about it: 'They get police involved, then they sort it out between themselves. Course, she doesn't bother to inform us, does she?' Also, the man who had been arrested by mistake gave the present working address and nickname of the man cited on the second warrant, and he was prepared to identify the man to police. The response of the detective sergeant to this was, 'Yeah, but not today'. He told both detective inspectors (in JG's presence) that he intended to try to get the victim to retract. Neither of them disagreed with him.

When the victim arrived it was clear that she could speak no English at all. (A CID officer later commented, 'They shouldn't let them in the country unless they can speak the language'.) An interpreter was called and he turned out to be very much on the side of the suspect; he was trying to persuade the victim to retract. However, when it came to the point, the detective sergeant dealt with the victim very fairly, and did not put pressure on her to retract. She began by saying that she was not satisfied with the informal ruling of the community association, and wanted the matter to go to court, but she did not seem very firm and could probably have been swayed. The detective sergeant pointed out that the suspect had been arrested and 'told off' and said he was quite happy to leave the matter there, especially if the victim was satisfied with the verdict of the arbitrator. But he added, with equal weight, that if the victim still felt that she wanted to proceed with charges, she should do so. He had the warrants and there would be no problem. The victim confirmed that she realised she would have to appear in court. She said that she was very much afraid the same thing would happen again unless the two men were charged. Unless there was something else the police could do to ensure that it wouldn't happen again... she suggested that the men should write out and sign a declaration to the effect that they would not harm her. The detective sergeant firmly refused to take any action other than proceeding with the charges - it seemed that the victim expected or hoped that he would dish out some kind of rough justice. However, the detective sergeant made it clear that if the suspects were not to be charged, the most he could do was to warn them not to interfere with the victim, on pain of arrest. Eventually, the suspect who had been correctly arrested was charged and the second suspect later arrested. The officer who dealt with this case continually showed prejudice and resentment against Bengalis: for example, he was annoyed by the fact that the caution was available in Bengali in the charge room. This made him ask why we should bend over backwards to help these people when they make so many difficulties for us and behave in such a devious manner. Apart from the fact that it involved Bengalis, the case came close to being 'rubbish' in the estimate of the detective constable: it was a minor matter best resolved by the people concerned, in his way of thinking, and not really a matter for the police. All the same, though strongly tempted to persuade the victim to retract, he actually dealt with her very fairly. This again illustrates the contrast between words and deeds, but it also suggests that there may be cases involving Asians which the police avoid dealing with.

Investigation of racialist attacks
In the course of our observations, we covered the investigation of four incidents that were probably or certainly racialist attacks. Three of the four incidents were very thoroughly investigated (by CID as well as uniform officers); in one of these cases, the officers dealing with the matter were reluctant to believe that there had been a racial motive for the attack, but this did not affect the way in which they investigated the matter. In the fourth case, one of the officers dealing with the matter was very reluctant to think there might be a racial motive, showed bias against the victims and probably failed to investigate the matter as thoroughly as he might have done. It is worth describing this case to illustrate these points.

JG was with an area car which answered a call to an address where a man alleged that his windows were being stoned. The driver (Bob) took the lead in dealing with this incident, but his operator (Ian) showed that he disagreed with some of Bob's decisions and views. On arriving at the address, the officers found a Nigerian man in his late twenties who had been studying at the kitchen table when a milk bottle was thrown through the window (which now had a hole in it). The Nigerian told the story evenly and quietly. (It turned out that he did not live at the address, but was babysitting for the householder.) Just after the bottle had come through the window, he thought he had heard laughing from a nearby back garden. Bob and Ian asked a few questions. As a conversational point, Bob asked the Nigerian what he was studying, only to receive the rather pompous and humourless reply, 'Is it relevant?'. This rebuff seemed to turn Bob very much against the man. Later he described the man as 'the African cunt' in a racialist tirade quoted earlier, said that Nigerians 'talk down to people', and remarked 'They're all illegal immigrants, these Africans'. However, for the time being he made it clear to the man that what had happened was 'well out of order'. The two officers went out to have a quick look around the area. In the back garden that the Nigerian had indicated they found five white children aged between 11 and 14 years. They were tinkering with their bicycles.

When Bob questioned them, these boys said they had heard the crash of the bottle going through the window. Just before that they had seen one or two youths flitting about. They said they did not recognise these youths, and on further questioning could give no description of them at all: for example, they didn't know whether they were white or black. When they heard the breaking glass, they had looked over the fence and seen another black man, two doors down, come out of his house, say something, then go back in again. Two of the boys were wearing union jack badges on their jackets (the National Front and British Movement symbol). Ian pointed this out, but Bob thought the badges were not significant.

The officers went to speak to the man two doors down, who turned out to be West Indian. He was very clearly spoken and helpful - on opening the door he said, 'Good evening sir, can I help you'. He said he had had problems with the kids before: they had taken his milk bottles. He said, 'I must admit, I didn't see them steal the milk bottle tonight, nor did I see them throw it, but when I looked out they were climbing over the fence there'. Bob brought the boys and asked the West Indian to repeat what he had said when they were there. This led to an argument (not a heated one) between the boys and the West Indian, without the matter being resolved. Bob thanked the West Indians and took the boys back to the garden, where he spoke to them as follows.

> Now I don't know whether you threw this bottle or not. I can't be sure. But I'll tell you something in the way of advice. Don't hang around here as you have been doing because either he (indicating the West Indian) or he (indicating the Nigerian) is gonna fit you up. (The boys agreed.) And I'll tell you something else. If his (the West Indian's) window goes in the next couple of days, you'll be the first people I come and see, all right?

410

This speech was largely an honest attempt to give the boys a warning, though in saying that one of the two men would 'fit you up', Bob implied that the boys were not really the culprits and that the black people would try to pin the blame on them falsely. As the officers left, a white woman told them she could vouch for the boys. 'They've been doing their bikes all day, love, they're not the ones.' The PCs did not find her very convincing and suspected her motives for saying this.

Half an hour later, the area car crew were called back to the address because it was said that the stone throwing had started again. The couple who lived in the house had now returned; they also were Nigerians in their late twenties or early thirties. The man discussed the problem quietly and at length with Bob, who pointed out that it was difficult to catch people 'at it' and mentioned that children on this estate even vandalised police cars. Finally he urged the couple to form a tenants' association. The wife seemed dissatisfied. She made it clear that she regarded the attacks as racially motivated. Bob said, 'Look, my dear, I'm quite sure they didn't do this just because you're black'. The woman made a movement of disagreement. 'Well, form yourselves into a black tenants' association, then. Get something done.' Ian quietly disagreed, saying he thought this would make matters worse. Bob continued, 'And look, if you can actually catch the people responsible and hold on to them until we arrive, all well and good. But remember, you can only use as much force as is reasonable to detain him. I don't want you to go beating his head against a wall'. The man seemed happy with this advice, but the woman remained sullen, said again that these attacks were racist, and did not thank the PCs. When the officers had got back into the car, Bob said, 'All African women are a pain in the arse'. He went on to argue fiercely against the idea that black people on council estates were attacked because of their colour. Ian took the opposite point of view. At one point, Bob said, 'All black people talk down to you. They've obviously been winding the kids up'. He had taken against the Nigerian babysitter in the first instance (because of his pompous reply to a friendly question) and then against the woman. He seemed to be saying that the white children had probably thrown the milk bottle, but that the Nigerians had provoked them by 'talking down' to them in just the way that one of them had to him.

Nine days later Bob asked Ian to tell JG that the same family had had their window smashed again. The following day JG saw Bob and thanked him for passing on the new information. Bob said, 'The PC who came with me the second time asked me if she (the Nigerian woman) wound the kids up. I told him she did. She deserves to have her window smashed if she talks to them that way'.

In all his commentary on this case, Bob showed strong prejudice against the Nigerians, and it was because of this prejudice that he was reluctant to think or say that there might be

411

a racial motive ('Look, my dear, I'm quite sure they didn't do this just because you're black'). This reluctance to consider the possibility that attacks might be racially motivated does not enhance the reputation of the police in the eyes of black people. It may also be connected with a failure to investigate thoroughly, through a prior belief that black people may make unjustified complaints ('Either he (indicating the Nigerian) or he (indicating the West Indian) is gonna fit you up'). In view of his expressed prejudices, Bob did, in fact, carry out a reasonably thorough invesigation, though if his attitude had been different he might have pressed the boys harder, and he was probably not as enthusiastic in his approach to the case as he would have been if the victims had been white. Finally, the case illustrates the need for a more strategic approach to a pattern of incidents of a certain type. Bob's suggestion of forming a tenants' association may have been a good one, but it would need to be nurtured and facilitated by the police in a more orderly manner.

## Three incidents involving black people

Many of the incidents that we observed involved black people as victims or as suspects. In most cases it would be difficult to identify aspects of police behaviour that were clearly a response to the race of the people involved. We shall now give three examples of possible exceptions to this generalisation. In the first incident we suggest that the police handling was more careful because West Indians were involved than it otherwise would have been. The other two cases provide examples of bad behaviour by police officers towards West Indian suspects. There is no proof that the race of the suspects was a reason for the bad behaviour, but this seems likely. In particular, it seems significant that some of the worst police behaviour we have observed (in the last example to be described here) was towards black suspects.

The first incident occurred during a night shift that DJS spent in a van with the driver and a probationer. The Division was one with a large Asian and smaller West Indian population. At about 3am the van answered a call for urgent assistance in a mainly Asian area. When the crew arrived, all of the other officers on patrol from the relief were already there (about a dozen in all) together with the inspector. There was a lorry parked outside a club with about five black people standing in the back and looking out over the tailboard. About ten more black people were spilling out of the club onto the pavement and were arguing with the group in the lorry. A number of the black people involved had dreadlocks, most were men, few were older than 25. As matters developed, more people came out of the club and others went back into it. The inspector was talking to a black man who appeared to be the spokesman for those in the club. The rest of the police officers present were standing well back (the inspector later said this was at his orders). There was quite a commotion, with people talking in loud voices or shouting. It was raining hard. It became

412

clear that the man from the club accused those on the lorry of taking some of his equipment (a loudspeaker). The people on the lorry implied they didn't have it without actually saying so.

The inspector remained completely calm, though his manner was very firm. He spoke in a loud voice, with great emphasis. To the people on the lorry he said, 'He says you have taken his loud-speaker. Will you give it back to him?' In reply, the people on the lorry smiled in a menacing way and said things that were not relevant. To the man in the club the inspector said, 'I'll shine the torch into the lorry and you can get up and look for your equipment'. The man was understandably reluctant to do this, since the people on the lorry seemed very hostile. The inspector told the people on the lorry to put the tailboard down. After some protests, they did so. Then one of them said, 'You're not going to search this lorry. You can't search it without a warrant'. The police would, in fact, have been perfectly entitled to search the lorry, since there was reason to think it was carrying stolen property. However, there was a total of about 15 people who belonged to the party on the lorry, so even with 12 officers, searching the lorry could have been difficult if the people resisted. Besides, the people in the club (probably about 50 of them) might then have joined in against the police. At this point, DJS was scared.

The inspector ignored the man's remark about needing a search warrant to search the lorry. He shone his torch into the back of the lorry and urged the man from the club to search for his equipment. But there was a line of five men standing inside the lorry and peering out, so he could not see in very far, and he would have had to get up onto the lorry to search it. He was not willing to do so. After the torch had been shone for a minute or two, the man from the club may have caught a glimpse of his loudspeaker. In any case, those in the lorry suddenly disappeared to the back and roughly bundled a loudspeaker out. It was quickly taken into the club by a group including the spokesman, who shortly came out again, saying, 'Wait, I think they've got our record box'. At this, the people on the lorry said, 'Right, we'll be off, then'. The inspector quickly stepped in and said, 'No, you bloody well won't. You're not going anywhere until I say so'. At this point DJS realised that he had taken possession of the keys of the lorry on arriving (about one minute before the van and DJS). After about a minute, people spilled out of the club, saying, 'Yes, they've got our record box'. Again, the people on the lorry denied it by implic-ation.

The inspector said to the man from the club, 'Are you prepared to charge these people with the theft of your record box?' The man did not reply. A man with dreadlocks on the lorry said to him, 'Look, what do you mean by calling in the pigs like this? What do you want to do with these supporters of the National Front, they're a load of Nazis'. The inspector ignored this, and said to the man from the club, 'The law says that I can't charge these people

413

with theft unless you are prepared to sign the charge sheet. Tell me yes or no whether you are prepared to sign it'. The man said, 'I suppose so'. The inspector said, 'I'm sorry but that's not good enough for me. Let me make this absolutely clear. If you will say that you will definitely sign the charge sheet, I will take this lorry into the police station and I will arrest everyone on it and charge them all with theft. Is that clear?' There was a pause, during which an Asian man came out of the club - the only man DJS saw on either side who was not black. He started to tell the people on the lorry to give back the record box. At this, a man with dreadlocks on the lorry said, 'Who are you anyway, some kind of Paki bastard? What have you got to do with us? You're some kind of Paki, aren't you?' The inspector said, 'Never mind about that,' very firmly, thus putting an end to this racialist talk for the time being. He turned again to the man from the club, saying, 'Are you willing to sign the charge sheet, yes or no? I've explained to you that if you are, all these people will be arrested'. After a further pause, he said, 'All right, yes'. For a moment, there was another diversion as the man with dreadlocks on the lorry saw that the Asian was wearing a badge (probably a 'fight racism' badge) and said, 'Why are you wearing that badge? What does that badge defend?' Ignoring this, the inspector said, 'Freddie!' and the area car driver came running forward, 'take it in!' The inspector tossed the keys to Freddie, who went forward to sit in the driver's seat of the lorry. At this, the men on the back of the lorry suddenly disappeared into the darkness behind and then re-emerged with a very large record box which they bundled out of the lorry. This box was holding about 200 records. It was quickly taken into the club.

The inspector immediately restored the keys of the lorry to the group and they were allowed to go. The man from the club came up to him and said, 'Thank you very much, I'm very grateful for your help'. The inspector just said, 'All right, then'. The other officers helped the lorry to manoeuvre out of the tight space it was in. In discussion afterwards the inspector said that he thought the people on the lorry wanted to tempt the police 'into a situation in which they would lose'. If the police had searched the lorry, he thought the people on the lorry would have provoked a fight in which those from the club might have joined in against the police as the situation became confused. This was exactly what DJS feared would happen at the time.

In our judgement, this was an excellent piece of police work. First, the relief inspector had gone out to deal with it himself; if he had not, there would have been the possibility of confusion. Secondly, there were enough police officers there to make the people on the lorry think twice before causing a disturbance, but they stood well back and offered no provocation. Thirdly, the inspector kept control in the classic manner by remaining calm, speaking slowly and clearly and ignoring attempts to cause disruption. Fourthly, he was very careful to avoid provoking a fight. One of the reasons for this was that he had his priorities right and preferred to resolve the matter peaceably if possible. However, a powerful reason was that he thought that all of the black people would stick together in a fight, so that the police would be heavily outnumbered. In this part of this thinking he was strongly influenced by the fact that the people were black: if they had been white, he would have considered that he had only 15 people (those on the lorry) to contend with. A further reason for caution was that he saw himself starting a new set of 'race riots' if he was not careful (indeed, a riot could be started by a far more trivial incident than this). Finally, it was interesting that the inspector squashed the expressions of racial hostility towards the Asian man.

At about 4.15am after nothing had happened for several hours, JG was with a panda car as it passed the area car from the adjoining Division going the other way. The WPC operator in the area car said over the personal radio that she had just seen someone duck behind a balcony wall in a block of flats nearby. Within a few minutes, four police vehicles had arrived on the scene, presumably because the crews had all had a boring night and were looking for something to do. JG and a group of officers walked up to the landing where the figure had been seen. On the stairs they found a black man, aged about 22, smartly dressed and wearing a felt hat. He had a small holdall with him. The police officers approached him very ungraciously. One of them said, 'What are you doing here, then? Why did you duck behind that wall?' He replied, in a very soft and polite manner, that he didn't want to disturb anybody. The policeman leading the questioning said, 'Don't give me that. What are you doing up here?' Immediately they started to look through his belongings and search him. As he was searched he was questioned by three officers at the same time, none of them bothering to listen to what he said, each frequently repeating the others' questions, none of them taking down the answers. He seemed confused by this procedure. He said he had come down to London from Birmingham to stay with friends. He had arrived (by coach) too late to disturb them. He was therefore waiting on the balcony until the morning when his friends would be going to work. He showed the police officers his bus ticket from Birmingham.

The officers rudely sorted through the suspect's holdall, which was beautifully packed with clean clothes. With a bay of triumph, the policeman searching the bag said, 'Ah, now what's this?' He pulled out a flick knife. Delroy (the suspect) said, 'Well...', but before he could answer he was asked again, 'What is it?' Delroy looked very worried and said he had found it. The policeman said, 'That's rubbish!' very violently, then 'That'll do to take him in. Let's take him in'. On the way to the police station, JG was not in the same car as Delroy, but he arrived at the charge room at about the same time.

Once in the charge room, Delroy was strip searched while he was again asked questions by several different officers, who took down what he said only partly or incorrectly and who did not communicate between one another. He was therefore asked the same questions again and again. He looked confused and frightened. He offered no resistance and was being very compliant indeed. He mentioned districts of Birmingham (such as Sparkbrook and Smallheath) that the police officers had not heard of; they thought he was making it up until JG told them the places were real. As the questioning continued, the demeanour and attitude of the officers began to change. The station officer became genial and polite, several of the others became reasonably relaxed, but the driver and operator of one of the area cars continued to treat Delroy somewhat contemptuously.

When he was asked again about the knife, Delroy said he used it in his work (there was in fact paint on it). One of the officers asked him, 'Would you use it against someone if they attacked you?' He said that he might brandish it to scare off attackers. The officer said, 'That's good enough. We'll take him to court in the morning on that'. The others agreed, and the station officer made no objection. Delroy was therefore charged with carrying an offensive weapon. The routine checks showed that he had one conviction for a minor traffic offence. When JG spoke to him privately it became clear that Delroy did not understand what had happened or what was going to happen: for example, he asked if he would be charged in the morning, not realising that he had been charged already, and he had no clear conception of what offence he was accused. He would not talk freely to JG because he did not believe him when he said he was not a police officer.

The reason the officers originally stopped Delroy was that they suspected him of loitering with intent to commit burglary. When this suspicion was not confirmed they looked for some other reason to arrest him, settling on the charge of carrying an offensive weapon. The arrest itself was highly irregular: the officers did not clearly state that they were arresting Delroy, they did not say why they were arresting him in so many words, and they did not caution him. They treated him contemptuously and oppressively in spite of his continual good behaviour. Their confused and amateurish questioning, through unintentional repetitions, gave the impression of being harassing. They did not bother to check his story, which was probably true: for example, none of the officers showed any inclination to find out whether his friends really did live in the nearby flat that he indicated. In all this, they made no reference to Delroy's colour, and there is no means of knowing whether they would have treated a white young man in the same way.

The third case that we shall describe in this section involved misjudgements and bad behaviour by several officers. JG was working with a uniform relief that came on duty at 2pm for the late turn. However, as is usual, the area car crew belonging to JG's relief did not come on duty until 3pm, and the early turn area car crew towards the end of its shift answered a call to a council estate where a woman aged 27 had been pushed to the ground, punched and robbed of her handbag. The assailants were described as IC3 (that is, looking black, like West Indians or Africans) and between 15 and 17 years old. One was tall, had hollow cheeks and was wearing a blue duffle coat and a floppy hat; the other was wearing a yellow cap, a brown cord jacket and blue jeans. JG spent the first hour of the late turn (from 2 to 3pm) out with the inspector. He heard about the robbery when two PCs from his relief reported over the personal radio that they had stopped three 'IC3s' as likely suspects for the crime. He and the inspector were not far from where the stop had been made, so quickly arrived at the spot.

The three boys who had been stopped were all aged about 14 (younger, therefore, than the 15-17 years quoted for the assailants). They were of slim build, and none of the three was tall (one of the assailants was described as tall). One of the three who had been stopped was wearing a yellow hat (like the description of one of the assailants) but was wearing a tweed jacket rather than a cord jacket. One of his friends had a floppy hat and a blue coat (like one of the assailants) but the coat was not a duffle coat and the boy was not tall. It was clear that the PCs had done well to stop and question these boys: they had a number of points in common with the description of the assailants, and it was certainly justifiable to arrest them while the original descriptions were checked and further enquiries made. One of the two PCs who had made the stop checked the descriptions over the radio with the WPC radio operator on the early turn area car. It was evident that the fit was by no means exact.

As the inspector and JG transported Steven (the boy with the yellow hat) to the police station, each commented to the other that the boys looked too young for the description. In the car, the inspector asked Steven a few gentle questions about where he had been and what they had been doing. He protested that he had been at home with his mother until quite recently; the robbery had taken place at 2.30pm and it was now 3.30pm. Steven then started to cry and said, 'I don't beat up old ladies, I don't do that sort of thing'. This comment could not have been calculated to deceive; Steven had lost control of himself at the time when he made it. It therefore very strongly suggested his innocence, since the victim was a 27 year old woman. The inspector did not notice how significant Steven's remark was. No attempt was made to check his alibi with his mother.

At the police station the two PCs who had made the arrests (Barry and Bill) were taking the lead in handling the matter. The station officer performed purely administrative tasks in connection with the processing of the prisoners; he did not supervise or control the actions of the PCs. Although they (voluntarily) gave him a brief explanation of the circumstances of the arrest, he did not ask any further questions, or take any steps to satisfy himself that the matter was being appropriately dealt with. The inspector kept himself informed from time to time about what was going on, but did not intervene decisively at any point.

JG asked the two PCs whether the other two boys had said anything on the way back to the police station; apparently, they had not. As the boys were searched and asked routine questions (for example, the names and addresses of their parents) they were largely cooperative. Steven seemed genuinely frightened and was very compliant. Royston (who had a blue coat and floppy hat) was relaxed and friendly. Donald (the smallest of the three) was a bit cocky. When Barry (the PC who was taking the leading role) explained that he would arrange for the boy's parents to be contacted, Royston said, 'My mum said if I got into any more trouble she wouldn't come down'. He was therefore admitting that he already had a record. In fact, Barry knew him from having arrested him before.

When Steven was asked to sign for his property (as it was taken from him and sealed in a bag) he could only print his first name with the greatest difficulty.

The boys were then locked up separately, one in a detention room, the other two in cells. According to regulations, juveniles should only be put in detention rooms, but the PCs wanted to ensure that they could not talk to each other, and there was only one detention room at the police station. Donald said, 'My sister says I can't go in a cell', referring to this regulation. One of the PCs was sure that he said 'My solicitor says I can't go in a cell', but JG is sure that he didn't.

The PCs found cards for all three boys in the collator's records. Steven had been in trouble twice before (criminal damage and carrying an offensive weapon). Royston had similar convictions and one for theft from the person. Donald had a considerable criminal record, including two convictions for robbery. Steven had so far told the truth about his previous record.

On searching the boys, the PCs had found plastic carrier bags on all of them (neatly folded in their back pockets). The PCs were convinced that the bags were for carrying stolen property, or for coats discarded to prevent being recognised.

Barry and Bill now interviewed the three boys one after the other in an unstructured way, hopping from one cell to another, often repeating questions and forgetting the answers that had previously been given. According to the rules of procedure with juvenile prisoners, no interviews should have been carried out except in the presence of the parents or other responsible adult. Acknowledging this, Barry said to JG, 'You realise what you've just seen is quite illegal'. (In fact, it offends against rules of procedure that do not have the force of law.) Also, according to police regulations, what was said during the interviews on both sides should have been taken down, but in fact nothing was recorded at the time.

Barry went in to see Steven first. He asked him what he had been doing during the day. Steven insisted that he didn't do 'that sort of thing' (while admitting that he did other sorts of things that

418

were illegal). Barry raised his voice and said, 'You think about it. If you've done it, you tell me! Now think about it!' This little speech gives a fair impression of the level of subtlety that Barry used throughout the questioning. He and Bill carried out similar interviews with the other boys, though with Royston they were rather more friendly and used the opportunity to pick up information about local characters with criminal records, and to check their knowledge of their nicknames (such as 'Starboy', 'Ratman' or 'Gums') against the real names of the people concerned.

Barry and Bill had not obtained any useful information about the case from these interviews. However, when they discussed with each other what the boys had said they became convinced that two of them (Steven and one of the others) were responsible for the robbery. Although they did not try to justify their opinion in a rational way, their reasons were presumably that

1. the boys had something in common with the descriptions;
2. they were picked up not far from the scene of the crime (but 45 minutes after it was committed);
3. they had criminal records.

At this point, the WPC who was operator on the early turn area car came into the police station. She said that while she was talking to the victim and walking through the estate, the victim thought she had spotted one of her two assailants five to ten yards away. The WPC approached the youth, who ran away, and the WPC lost him. She had now taken a look at the three boys arrested, and told Barry that Steven was the one she had chased. She did not seem to be entirely sure about this, and became aggressive when JG questioned her more closely about it. Arrangements were being made to bring the victim in, but the PCs did not wait until they had got a full statement from her before questioning the suspects further. The inspector checked up on what was happening, but did not prevent further questioning of the boys without their parents being present, and he did not advise the PCs to wait until the victim had made a statement.

Barry and Bill told JG that there had been two or three robberies or thefts from the person per week on this council estate for some months. They thought a team was at work. Barry said, 'I know this lot are at it'. JG asked how, and he said, "Cause I keep my ears and eyes open and I just know'. This illustrated a very important point about the approach of these two PCs. They had very little real evidence, so far, to implicate these youths in this particular crime, and they more or less realised that this was so. On the other hand, these boys had criminal records and were carrying plastic bags, and the PCs were quite convinced that they were engaged in criminal activities of some kind, probably theft from the person, possibly burglary. They were therefore willing to adopt a very low standard of evidence with regard to this particular crime on the argument that they 'knew that this lot were at it'. Whether or not they had committed this particular crime was, morally speaking, a matter of secondary importance - in fact, it was trivial. It was because they were locked into this mental set that the PCs did not attend to the details of the evidence about this particular incident and the possibility of the boys' involvement. It was not so much that they wanted to falsify the evidence as that they were not really intererested in what that detailed evidence was.

The home beat officers for the estate (Matt) now came into the police station. He was an experienced and tough policeman who had acted as home beat officer for this estate for a number of years, but had lost none of his appetite for arresting people. He had with him a file on the spate of robberies and thefts from the person, which showed that nearly all of the victims alleged that the offenders were black. Matt pointed out (triumphantly) that very few of the victims were black, although a high proportion of the population of the estate was black. Many of the victims were, however, Asians. Matt now visited each of the three boys two or three times, in rotation, to 'interview' them. The parents were not, of course, present. A fair example of his behaviour was his first interview with Steven. He put his face very close to Steven's and said,

> You're a fucking little cunt, aren't you? You've been at it, haven't you, you little bastard? You know what I'm gonna do, don't you? I'm going to nail your fucking hide to the wall! You'll stay here as long as I want you to. You'll stay here all weekend if necessary, until you tell me what you've done.

Matt's 'interviews' with the other suspects were similar.

By this time, Steven's parents had arrived and were left in a room to wait for 40 minutes. Meanwhile further interviews of their son took place. At no time were relatives of any of the boys present while they were interviewed.

The CID were contacted and a detective sergeant came down. JG was not in the charge room when he arrived, but saw him for the first time when he was concluding an 'interview' with Steven, who was crying. The detective sergeant said, 'And you'd better stop crying or I'll give you something to cry about!' As he left the cell, he saw JG and asked 'Who's this?' After the explanations, the detective sergeant took Barry on one side to have a private word, making it clear he did not want JG to hear. Barry returned from this conversation full of resentment. He explained that the detective sergeant was not interested in interviewing the boys and going over crime book entries with them to see if they might admit to earlier offences. Not surprisingly, the PCs were annoyed that the CID officer did not want to do his job. Apparently his only contribution had been to bully one of the boys.

Matt and Barry tried again to hasten the arrival of the victim. JG left the charge room for twenty minutes at this time.

When he returned, the inspector told him that Steven had 'put his hands up'. JG asked Barry how and why this had happened, and Barry said, 'Well, he's not so sure now'.

At last the victim arrived. She was quite sure she would recognise the two assailants again. She went over the descriptions, which were the same as before. JG asked her (while police were out of the room) whether she was quite sure that one was wearing a cord jacket. 'Positive', she replied. When Barry returned, JG pointed this out to him. He indicated that he began to see the case slipping away from him. The victim also emphasised that one of the assailants was very tall and had very hollow cheeks. None of the boys arrested fitted this description at all. Also, the victim was quite sure she had bitten one of the assailants on the hand - quite hard, because he had let out a yell. Matt went to check Steven's hands. He found one small dark mark, rather like a skin blemish. He suggested to JG that this was a bite mark, but JG disagreed. Five minutes later Barry went to check Steven's hands, not knowing that Matt had already done so (this was typical of the uncoordinated nature of the investigation). He came back saying there were no bite marks. Various other details of the victim's description did not fit the suspects. Though Royston was wearing a blue coat, it was nothing like a duffle coat, while the victim insisted on the duffle coat description; also, Royston's coat had red flashes on it, while the victim insisted that there was no red.

For the first time, the inspector made a positive decision about the investigation of the case. He decided they must let the victim and the suspects see one another and ask the victim whether she recognised them. First, they showed Steven's tweed jacket to the victim. She was sure it wasn't the one worn by her assailant. Apparently the parents or relatives were consulted about the 'confrontation' and agreed (JG did not witness the consultation). Steven's parents were led into the charge room and sat on the bench. Steven was produced and asked to stand against a wall; JG reminded the officers that he should be wearing his hat, which was an integral part of the description. The hat was accordingly produced and put on. The victim was brought in; she was rather nervous but firmly in control of herself. The inspector said, 'This is the young lady who was robbed today. Do you see one of the boys that attacked you in this room?' She answered 'No', and was quite sure about it. The procedure was repeated for Royston, whose mother muttered that this was all a 'disgrace' and that he shouldn't mix with those 'bad boys'. The victim was quite sure that Royston was not involved. When they presented Donald to her, she had to stifle a laugh, because he was so small compared with her attackers. As Royston was released and in the presence of his parents, Matt said to him, 'You don't shit on your own doorstep, all right?' The parents made no objection, and afterwards even thanked the inspector.

Throughout the handling of the case, the PCs involved made complaints to JG about the cumbersome nature of juvenile procedures, although they were not sticking to the procedures anyway. The inspector afterwards wrote up the 'persons at stations' sheet 'professionally' as he put it to JG. His account made it seem that events had turned on the victim's uncertain and changeable descriptions. In fact, the victim had given very clear descriptions, stuck to them consistently and always maintained that she would recognise the attackers. The official record finished with the words '...apologies tendered and no resentment noted', although Royston was sent on his way with the words 'Don't shit on your own doorstep, all right?', and no hint of an apology was offered to either of the other two boys or to their parents. The PCs consoled themselves by saying, 'Never mind, they'll come another day'; this illustrated again that they were concerned to get the boys for something and not to establish their guilt or innocence of some particular offence.

JG could not definitely establish whether the victim thought that Steven was the person she had pointed out to the WPC on the scene, but she gave no indication at all that she had seen him before. What probably happened was that the WPC thought Steven was a bit like the boy who had been pointed out and whom she had chased, and decided to say she was sure it was him because, like the PCs, she had no concern with being particular about the evidence. She was extremely uncomfortable when JG questioned her about the matter (before the victim had arrived at the police station). She would have stood by her identification of Steven if she had not (by implication) been contradicted.

The chief shortcomings in the handling of this particular case were as follows.

1.  The decisions were taken in an uncoordinated way by the PCs; there was no effective direction by more senior officers, even though the inspector and, to a lesser extent, the station officer, kept themselves informed about the case.

2.  All of the officers involved failed to pay proper attention to the evidence as it emerged.

3.  One of the officers involved (the WPC) came close to fabricating evidence, by her false identification.

4.  Four of the officers involved (the two PCs, the home beat officer and the detective sergeant) used grossly oppressive bullying tactics in the effort to get confessions; at one stage, one of the suspects did confess, in response to these tactics, though it was later proved beyond doubt that he was not guilty.

5.  The existence of rules is no guarantee of acceptable behaviour by police officers; the officers involved broke

rules with impunity and quite without compunction, with the knowledge of their inspector.

6. The officers attached more importance to the pattern of crime on the estate and to their belief that the suspects 'were at it' than to any facts that might link the suspects with this particular crime.

It remains to consider how far the ethnic group of the suspects influenced the way the officers behaved. On the whole it seems likely that there was a considerable influence of this kind. Matt was particularly concerned to emphasise the racial dimension of crime on the estate and was triumphant in his assertion that virtually none of the victims were black. More generally, JG formed the strong impression that the hostility towards the three suspects, and their conviction that they were 'at it', were connected with a hostility towards black people.

**Racial minorities in the Force**
At the time of our observations, there were about 120 officers in the Force belonging to ethnic minority groups, all except a handful being constables (by the Autumn of 1983 there were 216). We got to know six of these officers reasonably well during the course of our research. Of the six, five were black (all ultimately of West Indian origin) and one was Asian. One of the six was a woman. Two had been promoted beyond the rank of constable. Although our observations are here based on rather small numbers, we can still draw certain conclusions with considerable confidence, because they emerge consistently from what we saw and heard.

Those who work with black or brown officers on the same reliefs say that they face special difficulties, because of their race, in dealing with the public; observation and the accounts given by minority group officers themselves confirm that this is true. For example, a PC told DJS that the Asian officer on his relief normally had to take an enormous amount of racialist abuse from anyone he arrested. This conversation was soon followed by a call for assistance from the area car in which the Asian officer was a plain clothes observer. When the PC and DJS got there (they were in a car) the area car crew were in the process of arresting a very heavily-built man, who was drunk, some of whose companions were hanging around jeering at the police. All were white men. There was a struggle as the man was bundled into the area car (with one PC sitting on either side of him) and the man called the Asian officer a 'Paki bastard', told him that this was not his country and asked why he thought he could go around arresting 'English people', and so on.

One of the black PCs was posted to an area with a large West Indian population. He made it clear to JG that black people in the area tended to dislike or hate him (as being a black person who had 'gone over to the other side'). He said that black prostitutes had been instructed by their pimps to tell local police officers that he (the black PC) would end up with a knife in his back one day. He also gave accounts of several occasions when he had been involved in fights with black people in the area and where his race had been a factor contributing to the fight being started. The other black officers had not had the same difficulties, or if they had did not talk about it.

Racialism within the Force causes considerable embarrassment, distress and difficulty to black and brown police officers. A relief that DJS worked with contained both a black and an Asian officer. There was a group of three experienced officers on the relief who engaged in quite extreme racialist talk when they were in the threesome or with members of the relief other than the black and Asian officer. When these two officers were present, the racialist talk and jokes continued, but were considerably moderated. The white members of the relief thought that the Asian and black officers didn't mind the racialist talk too much. One of them even said that 'he (the black officer) thinks of himself as a white person really'. They were quite mistaken about this. When the relief made racialist jokes, the two who were in a minority would look watchful and defensive; they had learnt by experience not to protest, but to be on their guard. In some cases, they would forestall the jokes. For example, a PC driving a car only slowed down at the last minute when the black PC was crossing the road in front of him. Afterwards, the black PC said, 'I know, you couldn't see me because I didn't stand out against the tarmac'. All this was purely defensive. Both the black and the Asian PCs told DJS that they resented the racialist talk of the relief very much. The Asian strongly resented jokes about his English (which was excellent) and said that he tried to avoid speaking over the personal radio as far as possible so as to dodge the inevitable jokes. After a reference to the abuse that the Asian took from members of the public, one PC said that the relief tried to make sure that he got used to racialist abuse by giving him plenty of practice; this was not so much a joke as a shamefaced justification of the relief's attitude.

A probationer at one Division during an informal interview said she often wondered how the two black PCs on the Division managed, what with all the anti-black jokes and comments in the canteen, but 'they seem to get along'. The inspector in charge of the relief that JG was with at this Division said on one occasion, 'John (the black PC) takes a terrible hammering from the blacks out there - they insult him and call him "raas claat". It's very difficult for him'. Five minutes later, he said, 'The other day I said, "Fucking niggers", and then realised I was standing next to John. I had to give him a friendly shove and say, "Except you, John"'. The inspector said that John was inclined to be violent because he was often challenged by black people. John himself tended to confirm this by what he said. One afternoon when JG was with him in the area car, he spotted a black youth he knew. 'I gave that bloke a right pasting once,' he said. He had been on a bus, just off duty, when some black youths had started 'winding him up' about being a copper. He had told one, 'Shut it, or I'll fill it'. It had ended with John beating the youth up. The inspector gave another indication of his attitude to John, when he told JG that John had never known his father, who had left his mother high and dry. After explaining this history, the inspector commented, 'Typical nigger'.

John told JG that he did not enjoy his time at training school, partly because of the racialism of the other recruits and of the instructors. He told of an occasion when a fellow probationer at training school had told him to get out of the lift and walk up the stairs because he was a 'fucking nigger'. John hit this man and then had to explain himself to his inspector. The Asian PC also told DJS that he found it very tough when he got to training school, especially since he had encountered little or no racialism in his previous job or before that at college. He said that at training school the instructors made a deliberate effort to 'get at' him continually with racialist remarks, so that he was several times on the point of giving up. Later, when he had gone through with it, the instructors maintained that they had put him through a test to make sure he could stand it, because they knew he would have to put up with a lot of racialist abuse from police officers. The Asian PC thought this was merely a convenient justification of the instructors' own racialism. (Certainly, if instructors behave this way, it shows that they consider racialism to be legitimate; only those blacks and Asians who can put up with it without protest are acceptable to them.) It was interesting that this PC was as acceptable to English policemen as any Asian could possibly be. He was a good sportsman, physically quite tough and solidly built, very light-skinned and in fact hardly more physically distinct from most English people than a Devonian or a Welshman. He was humorous and affable, not at all religious, and frequently ate hamburgers and chips. His (slightly accented) English was excellent. In spite of this stunning evidence of normality, together with qualities as a policeman well above average, he was still the butt of many bad jokes and generally given quite a hard time, even though he was fairly fully accepted as a 'proper' policeman and a full member of the relief.

Two of the black officers we got to know had progressed beyond the rank of PC and both were clearly exceptionally good at their jobs. We saw no indication that one of these encountered any special difficulties with his colleagues because of his race. Considerable resentment was expressed against the other one, often in racialist terms.

The presence of black and brown officers - in the present small numbers - seems to have only a mild effect on the level of racialist talk and probably has no effect on actual policing behaviour. The limited effect on racialist talk is evident from examples already quoted. On this point, John told a story about a car chase in which he had taken part. The operator in the police car immediately behind the car that was trying to get away said 'There's one white guy and three spooks in this motor' over the mainset radio. A PC in John's car replied 'They are not spooks, they're IC3s, so call them that. We've got an IC3 on our relief'. Several people (anonymously) made jokes or scathing remarks at John's expense over the radio before the operator at information room backed up John's friend and told them to cut it out. Thus, John's own relief would make jokes at his expense, but they resented any explicit or implicit insult from outside the relief. Like the relief with the two minority group officers, they probably also moderated their own racialist language in John's presence.

One of the black supervising officers made a point of objecting to racialist language on the personal radio. One day at parade, he said:

> Yesterday I overheard an officer say on the PR that he'd 'fallen on his fucking arse' and that there were 'two spades' being chased. He should have said he'd fallen over and that he was chasing IC3s. I might be standing right next to a member of the public when you say that.

This admonishment was deeply resented by the officer concerned. He could hardly bring himself to look at the supervising officer all night. Our general conclusion is that some reduction in racialist language is achieved by the introduction of black and brown police officers, especially in supervisory positions, but that there is little change, at least in the short term, in the underlying attitudes.

There are some things that black and brown police officers can do, but which could not be done by a white officer. Thus the Asian PC was regularly used as an interpreter and go-between when the police were dealing with the local Asians, and all police officers strongly appreciated his help in this respect. Although the black police officers often meet with hostility from other black people, particularly those who are young or politicised, they are often more successful at talking to black people than other officers. For example, when a West Indian man was arrested after damaging a social security office, the black supervising officer was much better able to calm him down and get him to talk in the charge room than was anyone else. He was also much more able to offer him support and sympathy.

Overall, it is clear that for most black and brown people, being a police officer puts them under considerable strain. They have to take abuse from the public and put up with racialist language and jokes from their colleagues, and they are subject to a conflict of loyalties. Most of the six that we got to know were, however, coping with these difficulties remarkably well. One was responding in a way that was potentially dangerous.

We conclude that the modest increase in the number of police officers belonging to ethnic minority groups that can be expected in the short term is unlikely to make a fundamental difference to the norms or behaviour of working groups of police officers.

## A note on community liaison officers and juvenile bureaux

As explained in Chapter XIII, community liaison officers are chief-inspectors or superintendents whose responsibility extends over a whole District - often two London boroughs. They report to the District commander, but they also have a looser relationship with A7 Branch at Scotland Yard, which coordinates their activities. There was a time (ten years ago) when CLOs were despised by 'operational' police officers, and regarded as soft-centred do-gooders or public relations men. This attitude is no longer common. the CLOs that we have met are high fliers - men (all of them were men) who are likely to be promoted much further and quickly, and who adopt a very practical approach to policing. This is because being a CLO is now regarded as a 'good' posting for someone expecting to gain promotion to a high rank. Another reason for the change of attitude is that police officers see that CLOs are useful: they provide intelligence and they help the police to win over various groups.

In areas containing any significant populations belonging to minority groups, the CLOs regard it as a high priority to make contact with prominent or influential members of these groups. They see it as a large part of their function to act as a channel of communication between minority groups and the local management of the police force (the commander and his deputy and, to a lesser extent, the divisional chief-superintendents). They seem to perform this function effectively, the main limitations being imposed by factors outside their control, namely the difficulty of finding people who can in any real sense represent or speak for the minority groups and the reluctance of local police management to adapt their policing strategies in the light of local opinion. (The attitudes of local police management may now have begun to change in response to the recently established consultative committees.)

Although CLOs are effective within these limits, they have little or no influence on the aspects of policing that we have been discussing in this chapter: on the attitudes and behaviour of police officers towards members of ethnic minority groups. They are much too thin on the ground to have an influence of this kind. They have little, if any, contact with uniform reliefs and CID offices. They cannot keep continuous contact with local minority groups in each of the Divisions - this can only be done by the local management team (chief-superintendent and superintendent). The best that they can do is to provide a central advisory service for the District and a central repository of information. They may be consulted about operational matters that would particularly affect community relations (for example, raids on illegal drinking parties), but the local management are not obliged to consult them and if they do they are not obliged to heed their advice, especially since the CLO will be outranked by the divisional chief-superintendent. They do keep a list of 'sensitive premises' in the District. They will certainly be involved in trying to cope with any local race relations disaster (such as the Deptford fire) and will be extremely useful in this capacity, but this will not affect the day-to-day attitudes and behaviour of police officers.

Some of the activities of juvenile bureaux have a particular effect on the relations of the police with minority groups. As part of the schools involvement programme, members of the bureaux engage in a regular round of visits to secondary schools and in many areas they also visit local youth clubs. With the help of officers on the reliefs, they organise various special events such as the annual five-a-side football competition, in which a very large number of black and brown children take part. This kind of activity presumably has a background 'drip' effect, particularly since it is carried out on a considerable scale. Its main limitation is that it is not essentially policing activity for the most part. Responses developed in both police officers and young people within a purely social context will not necessarily carry over into contexts where the officer is acting as an officer.

## The Deptford fire
The fire at 439 New Cross Road on the morning of 18 January 1981 caused the deaths of thirteen young black people and caused injury and disfigurement to at least 30 others. This was a disaster not only for those who died and were injured and for their families and friends, but also for relations between black people and the police in London. Many black people (and some white sympathisers) came to believe that this fire was the result of an attack by white racialists, and was the culminating point in a long-established pattern of persecution of black people. The police investigation, whilst not ruling out other possibilities, tended to suggest that the fire was started by black people at the party taking place at the house that night, probably not intending the consequences that occurred. Black people made strongly worded and widely public-ised allegations that the police were not carrying out a thorough and impartial investigation. In late February the police arrested eight boys who had been at the party and some of whom made statements, in the presence of independent witnesses, to the effect that shortly before the fire started there had been a dispute and a fight; these boys were not charged with any offence in connection with the incident; they later retracted their statements when questioned at the inquest, alleging that they had made them under pressure. A 'Massacre Action Committee' was formed to organise a protest movement. A mass demonstration was held on 2 March in which ten to fifteen thousand people took part. This was a demonstration of sympathy towards the families of those who had died and suffered in the fire, a demonstration of more general solidarity among black people and also a way of showing opposition and hostility to the police and criticism of their handling of the investigation. Although the march was largely peaceful, there were significant clashes between demonstrators and the police, and at least 28 arrests were made. These events acted as a focus for

hostility towards black people among police officers generally, as described on pages 111 onwards. The inquest was the occasion for further demonstrations against the police; it failed to resolve the question as to how the fire was started (it arrived at an open verdict). This bald summary of a complex sequence of events is enough to give some impression of the widespread damage caused to relations between the police and black people in London by the repercussions of the fire. It seems reasonable to assume that this added substantially to the tension underlying the riots of April in the same year.

Although a book could be written about the Deptford fire, we can only devote a few pages here to considering whether the police could have handled the investigation and the aftermath of the fire in such a way as to prevent or to limit more effectively the damage caused to their relations with black people in London. Within the framework of our study as a whole, we were able to devote only very modest resources to looking at the police handling of this affair.

The fire happened very early on a Sunday morning. By the Monday morning a large major incident squad had been established and was working from Brockley police office. JG spent that Monday with the squad. DJS spent four days with the squad during the first two weeks and returned on two subsequent occasions to interview senior officers. JG interviewed the community liaison officer for P District (within which Deptford falls) on 23 January and also interviewed black people prominent in local community relations. DJS and JG again interviewed the community liaison officer well after the events (but before the inquest) and JG interviewed the Commander of P District. During his visits to the squad, DJS had full access to the statements of witnesses, spoke at length with the officers in charge of the inquiry, attended the briefings regularly held for members of the squad and was present at an inevitably small number of interviews with witnesses. He also interviewed 24 members of the squad, using a short questionnaire. JG attended (up to the point where the few white people present were asked to leave) the first meeting held in the Pagnell Street centre on 25 January to discuss the fire. Stephen Small attended this meeting (in its entirety) and a number of subsequent ones organised under the auspices of the Massacre Action Committee. At this time, Stephen Small was working with a group of young black people in a hostel (see volume 2 of this series) and was able to observe the response of this particular group to the news of the fire. Along with some members of this group, he attended the demonstration on 2 March.

By this mixture of methods, we were able to obtain some information about each of the main aspects of the situation: the police investigation, the activities of senior police officers and community relations specialists, the responses of young black people who were not particularly politicised and the meetings of the organised protest movement. On the other hand, we were not able to carry out a thorough study of any of these aspects.

From the beginning, the police gave a very high priority to the investigation and showed that they were fully aware of its importance and of the possible repercussions of the fire - in fact the mood of senior officers was pessimistic at a very early stage: whatever the outcome they thought the affair would be damaging to the police. The importance attached to the investigation was shown by the fact that the CID commander based at the Area office took charge (in place of the detective chief-superintendent for the District, who worked to the commander in the squad). A large number of officers (about 50) was drafted into the investigation. From our visits to the squad it was quite clear that the police were giving their best efforts to trying to find out what had actually happened.

The community liaison officer and the local commander were very active in making contact with prominent or influential black people and with the families of the victims. They also met and spoke to leaders of the protest movement on several occasions.

For the most part, the response of black people to the fire was an expression of feelings of persecution. Over the years there have been many objective facts to justify these feelings and make them intelligible to white people and to the police (substantial racial discrimination, increasingly restrictive immigration policies, political parties with openly racialist policies, racialist attacks). Whether or not the fire itself was an attack from outside has still not been resolved, but it is entirely understandable that it should have been interpreted in that way by many black people. This would be brought home to anyone who read the letters that Mrs Ruddock (whose house was burnt down and who lost a son and daughter in the fire) received shortly afterwards. These letters, which were highly offensive and racialist, gloated over the deaths and saw the fire as a first step in ridding Britain of black people.

In addition to the feelings of persecution, there were also some feelings of guilt, especially among the small circle of people who had been at the party; whatever the precise cause of the fire, they felt that they would be blamed, for example for allowing the party to go on late: one way of coping with such feelings was to find an external enemy to blame (the police).

The earliest newspaper reports suggested that the fire was started by a petrol bomb thrown through the dowstairs front window. The origin of these reports was a remark by a PC on the scene soon after the fire. They were supported by statements by some witnesses, particularly Carl Wright, but further investigations strongly suggested that what these witnesses had seen was the man who shortly afterwards raised the alarm, and that he was shielding his face from the flames, or waving, rather than throwing something. In their public information from a very early stage the police tried to change the impression created by the initial reports: specifically, they stated that the man seen by Carl Wright had been traced and was not responsible. In reply to questioning on radio, the head of the inquiry gave the impression that he reluctantly agreed that the police were considering every possible explanation of the fire, including an attack from outside. He did not come out saying that the police were actively considering the possibity that this could have been a racialist attack. In general, the treatment in the media gave the impression that the police thought the fire had been started by someone at the party and were strenuously playing down the idea that it could have been a racialist attack.

In fact, by the first day that DJS spent with the squad (the Tuesday two days after the fire), the three senior members of the squad were already fairly sure in their own minds that the fire was not caused by an attack from outside though other lines of inquiry were still being pursued. They may well have been right in this instance (in our judgement they probably were) but this attitude could, in principle, lead to a failure to investigate evidence pointing in a different direction.

We have said that the response of black people was the expression of feelings of persecution. Up to a point, the response of the police was also the expression of similar feelings. From the beginning the police felt that they would be blamed whatever the outcome. If they found that the fire was caused by a black person, black people would never believe it and would conclude that they were being persecuted by the police as well as by whoever started the fire. They would therefore mount a hostile and probably effective campaign against the police. If the police found that a white person had caused the fire, they thought there would be a serious risk of reprisals by black people against whites followed by a spread of racial conflict. In either case, as a senior member of the squad said, 'we (the police) stand to lose'.

Also, police officers generally and those working on the squad in particular felt threatened by the hostility shown to them by black militants and therefore not unnaturally resented it. There was immediate evidence of this hostility. On the Tuesday evening, Commander P District and his community liaison officer had to withdraw from a meeting with black people at the Pagnell Street centre because they thought they would otherwise be physically ejected. Within the week the police were being accused of covering up evidence that the fire was a racialist attack and trying to frame innocent black people who had been at the party. Although they tried not to show it, members of the squad (especially the senior officers) were deeply offended by these allegations. To say that they felt persecuted would be going too far, but they certainly felt that they were being put under very unfair pressure. There were two important consequences of this. First, at briefings, by pointing out the difficulties that investigators might face, senior officers reinforced and possibly created the expectation that black witnesses would be hostile, obstructive or untruthful. Secondly, senior officers found it very hard to give the impression that the theory of a racialist attack was being taken seriously. Because this was the theory of people who were unreasonably

431

criticising them, as they saw it, they felt they must distance themselves from it as far as possible. In our view, this strategy was dictated by emotion rather than by a cool analysis of how the police could best present themselves in the difficult circumstances.

It was clear from the early briefings that senior officers were encouraging the squad to expect hostility from black people. At the Tuesday briefing (two days after the fire) senior officers already strongly put across the idea that black people were being obstructive and emphasised to members of the squad that they would have to 'dig hard' to get at the truth. On the following day, they reported that the Commander and the CLO had withdrawn from the meeting at the Pagnell Street centre as an illustration of black hostility.

Interviews carried out with officers in the squad showed that there was a sharp division of opinion between one group (about two-fifths of the total) who thought black witnesses were trying to avoid being seen by police officers, were reluctant to answer questions or were withholding information, and a group of about the same size who thought that few black witnesses were making any of these difficulties and that officers were encountering no more problems than they would expect on a similar enquiry involving white people. Officers on the squad were allocated people to be interviewed more or less randomly, yet several said that none of their witnesses had been difficult or reluctant, while at the same time several said that all or nearly all of theirs had been. These answers seem to reflect the expectations and attitudes of the officers rather than the responses of the black people they had interviewed. In the small number of interviews that we observed, we saw little or no manifest obstructiveness or reluctance to give information and no real hostility: certainly, the attitude of black people in these private encounters was quite different from that shown in public, for example at the Pagnell Street meetings (a point not made at the squad briefings). A number of witnesses changed their stories or gave further information when they were interviewed again, so some witnesses were undoubtedly reluctant or obstructive; but this kind of behaviour can probably be expected on any investigation of this kind.

We conclude that a substantial proportion of the officers on the squad went to interview black people expecting them to obstruct the enquiry, and they were conditioned in this by the attitude of senior officers. This was a response by police to the feeling that they were threatened. A conscious attempt to cultivate a more positive and relaxed attitude would probably have produced better results - it would not be inconsistent with pressing questions hard when necessary.

Similarly, it is hard to see that there was any need for the police to resist or publicly play down the suggestion that the fire might have been a racialist attack. Mrs Ruddock had received some vicious letters from racists. The police could have made it public that they had taken every step to establish whether these people were in any way connected with the fire. It was not revealed until the inquest that an unexploded and highly amateurish incendiary device was found outside the house. The police could have made it public that some kind of incendiary device had been found (without, of course, describing it in detail) and could have said they were energetically trying to trace where it had come from. From discussions with the local commander it was clear that this possibility had been considered, but he referred to the conventional wisdom that some details should not be made public so that anyone falsely confessing to the act would betray his ignorance of the facts. However, this condition could have been met by making public only the broadest description of the incendiary device. There are political organisations that have advocated attacks on black people from time to time. The police could have made a point of examining the possibility that any such organisations (particularly local ones) might have been involved.

We do not suggest that such initiatives would have affected the outcome of the investigation. The police were right to put most of their resources into contacting and interviewing people who had been at the party and other witnesses, together with analysis of the physical remains and testing of the physical possibility of an object being thrown through the downstairs front window to start the fire. But without changing these priorities, the team could still have taken the initiatives mentioned in the last paragraph; equally important, senior officers could have appeared open and enthusiastic about investigating the possibility that the fire was caused by a racialist attack. It is possible, of course, that the feelings of persecution among black people at the time were so strong that nothing in what the police did would have made any difference to their response - but it might still have been worth trying.

In their private comments on the protest among black people, senior police officers were always anxious to emphasise that political activists were trying to take advantage of the situation to create an effective black political movement. They found the idea of such a movement threatening because opposition to the police would be one of its central motivating principles; but they argued that it would not be a legitimate expression of the feelings and thinking of significant numbers of black people, who were in danger of being manipulated by extremists for their own ends. It was partly because of this political analysis of what was going on that senior officers were so opposed to taking seriously the suggestion that the fire was the result of a racialist attack. To encourage this theory in any way would, in their eyes, be to encourage the political movement whose theory it was. Even if we adopt this perspective and think for a moment of the police as being in conflict with a bunch of extremists manipulating a large, emotional, confused group of black people, the smartest tactic in the propaganda war could be for the police to place the theory of a racialist attack at the centre of the stage and examine it thoroughly from every angle. Of course, the other possibilities would also have had to be vigorously pursued. But in any case, the political analysis put forward by senior officers embodies a considerable exaggeration. Some black militants from outside the area (notably Darcus Howe and John La Rose) tried to channel the feelings aroused by the fire into an organised political movement, but in fact there was never anything more than a protest movement - it did not develop into a persisting political movement with a range of objectives. The militants from outside the area were not in full control of the meetings, were viewed with some scepticism by many of the people participating, and were certainly not in a position to manipulate the movement of protest for their own political ends. The community liaison officer recognised this, and others within the Force with specialist knowledge probably did so, but the crude political analysis we have outlined was probably more influential in deciding the general 'public relations stance' that the police would adopt.

## Class

Many police officers have sharply defined attitudes towards people belonging to different social classes, and these attitudes seem to be quite closely related to some aspects of policing behaviour, for example, decisions as to whether to stop and search people. The system of class distinctions recognised by police officers seems to be related to the system that would be recognised by most people, but different in some respects. The two groups most clearly identified by police officers are 'slag' or 'rubbish' and 'respectable people', and these are groups defined partly, but not entirely, in terms of social class. There is strong disapproval of people regarded as 'slag' or 'rubbish' and, separately, a specific racial prejudice among many police officers; however, there is some link between colour and slag in the minds of some. For example, JG was on his first shift with a particular area car when the crew answered a call to a large council estate where three black men had been seen 'lurking suspiciously' at the back of some flats. On the way there, the driver explained, 'The estate is full of rubbish and toe-rags. All the decent people have moved out and now it's 60 per cent black'. Part of the connotation of the word 'slag' is people who live disorganised or unconventional lives and who are thought, as a consequence, to have a tendency to be involved in crime. This is fairly close to the idea that police officers often have of the style of life of West Indians. This came out in the remarks of a detective inspector, who explained to DJS that 'The way of life of West Indians is quite different from ours. If you go into their houses you'll often find that the wife is out for the time being, and the husband is in bed with one of his totties. You'll find there are three people sleeping in the same room and they are taking the electricity from the street lamp'.

Although the class origins of police officers themselves are fairly diverse, there is a strong tendency for them to come from the upper working class or lower middle class. Many of the values of the Force seem to have evolved from 'respectable working class' values and the norms among police officers in terms of dress (when in plain clothes), manner and speech are derived from working class norms. It is a milieu in which people who do not speak with a London or other regional accent and men who do not dress like football managers are definitely made to feel out of place. We came across one detective constable who came from an upper class background and went to a well known public school. His parents had been mortified when he had joined the police force. He said that to start with he had had difficulty in getting rid of his 'plummy' accent, but, with time, had managed to cultivate a cockney alternative, which he thought was essential. Two other police officers present also thought he could not have survived without changing his accent. Now that he had four years' service he found it hard to turn the cockney off, so that his mother was 'disgusted' by the way he spoke.

Police officers' perspective on social class is partly explained by their own class origins. Coming predominantly from the 'respectable working class', they are preoccupied with establishing the firm distinction between that group and parts of the working class that are not considered respectable. However, the 'definition' of 'slag' is only partly in terms of social class indicators such as occupation, education and accent. For example, people who are dependent on drugs, people living in communes or squats, people with extreme or unusual political views and (possibly) people with unusual sexual habits may all be regarded as 'slag'. There is a strong association between certain council housing estates and 'slag'. Finally, the assessment may be partly in terms of attitudes to the police. Generally, police officers like people to behave towards them with slight deference but without subservience. They strongly criticise people who are 'cocky' or 'lippy' but they also criticise those who humble themselves too much ('snivelling little toe-rag' is a phrase we have heard used to describe people who behave like this). People who are servile or who show no respect are liable to be classified as 'slag'.

We found some indications that police officers admire the 'real aristocracy' and the 'solid middle class' but despise the vulgar, flashy or newly-rich. It may be that vulgarly rich people are akin to villains in their eyes. It is true that in certain contexts or moods they also admire successful villains - we are dealing with a shifting scale of values. Thus, a couple of older PCs who had worked in the diplomatic protection group in the past were immensely proud of having spoken to members of the nobility such as Lord Mountbatten, and spoke in tones of fervent admiration of all the 'nobs' they had had to deal with. In contrast with this, where PCs came into contact with famous and rich sporting personalities whose origins were working class, they showed an aristocratic distaste for their vulgarity and flamboyance and (in two instances) told stories about the criminal associations of these

435

people. For example, a famous sporting personality who had a large house on one of the Divisions we visited was described as a 'jumped up little scrote' with family and friends who had some minor 'form'.

A broad indication of the way the term 'slag' is used is given by the talk of an area car driver on his first trip out with JG in the back.

> We only deal with five to ten per cent of the population, and that's the slag. Ordinary people don't need to have anything to do with us ... 'Course, there's a lot of prostitutes round here and all the pimps and filth that goes with them ... It's all very well trying to understand why these things happen and why people think they're harrassed but we are the police force and we've got a right to stop people and ask them questions.

It is strongly implied in this kind of talk that 'slag' and 'filth' do not have the same rights as 'ordinary people' and that the police need not stick to the same rules in dealing with them: this is the dangerous part of the philosophy. A justification sometimes given for this outlook is that ratepayers and property owners contribute to society, whereas 'slag' give nothing. When JG was with a PC who was searching some back gardens for traces of a burglar, they noticed curtains twitching at the windows of the (owner-occupied) houses. The PC said,

> I don't mind them being nosey. After all, they pay our wages, the ratepayers and property-owners. They've got a right to expect a return. You'll find that policemen get fed up with dealing with the rubbish, you know, the slag. They don't contribute anything, do they?

That people who are unconventional in some way tend to be put into the same category as 'slag', or a similar one, can best be illustrated by the response of a group of police officers to a 'troops out of Northern Ireland' demonstration. The march aroused considerable hostility among people (other than police officers) who saw it passing by. There were shouts of 'scum' and 'murdering bastards'; a chant of 'Bobby Sands is dead' was taken up by some of the onlookers. The marchers responded by chanting on one occasion, 'One, two, three, four, Argentina win the war' (it was at the time of the Falklands campaign). Some of the police officers wondered whether they could arrest the marchers for treason. A typical comment was, 'It's the scum of the earth. Why should we protect that?' The officers very much regretted that one or two of the people heckling the marchers were arrested.

It is a cliche for police officers to say that their 'ground' is a good one because it contains a varied social mix living in varied housing. JG was with a PC who received a call about 'squatters breaking in' at an address. When they got there the door was secure, but a white man in his late 50s came out from his house across the road and explained that he and his friends had chased the squatters off. He had also secured the door. As the PC and JG drove away, the PC explained that he liked the Division because there was a good mix of people: 'A lot of slag, obviously, but also a lot of people like that bloke - you know, your genuine East Ender'. This kind of remark makes particularly clear the distinction between 'slag' and the 'respectable' working class.

Analysis of the survey of Londoners shows that the same people tend to come into contact with the police in different contexts, and that certain people are stopped, questioned and searched repeatedly by the police. These findings are mirrored by the tendency of the police to classify a minority of the lower working class as 'slag', and by their expectation that most of their dealings will be with this group. Naturally, there is no hope of identifying a 'final cause' in this chain of influences. One type of argument (favoured by the police) is that the behaviour of the group they informally classify as 'slag' brings members of the group to the attention of police, and that the attention is legitimate and deserved. The opposing type of argument is that the police work with a crude model of the type of person who is likely to be 'up to something' and so direct their attention to large numbers of people who are like the model but do not commit offences. It does not seem very important to resolve the issue between these two arguments. It is, in any case, clear that the weight of police activity bears much more heavily on sections of the lower working class and others whom the police tend to lump with them than on other groups; much police activity is a way of 'dealing with' the mostly petty offences committed within this social milieu. Secondly, whatever the link between actual anti-social or criminal behaviour and the definition by the police of the group that they see as their clientele, the important point is that the term 'slag' is contemptuous. If it embodies a way of thinking that allows police officers to justify to themselves behaviour that the rest of us would consider unacceptable, then it is dangerous.

As in the case of racial prejudice, it is difficult to assess how far the attitudes of police officers (in this case to 'slag') influence actual policing behaviour. There is clear statistical evidence that certain social groups (unskilled workers, the young, the unemployed) are more likely than others to be stopped. How far bad behaviour by police officers towards suspects is associated with their classifying them as 'slag' is much harder to establish. We quoted a case in the last chapter where two uniform officers did nothing to help a youngish white man who had been the victim of a fairly serious assault. Among the reasons for the officers' unhelpful response was that 'This is mostly white slag living up here' (on what they considered to be a notorious council estate).

An intricate but essentially petty case observed by JG illustrates police behaviour that probably turned on the social classification of two boys. The incident started from a call to a disturbance on a council estate. It involved a 'respectable' family (the estate caretaker and his wife, who help to run a youth club, and their son) and a group of teenage boys, including one called Chas who was aged 17, rather drunk and definitely classified as 'slag' by the police officers dealing with the incident. The respectable couple had found the side window of their car broken, and some boys who were hanging around suggested that Chas had done it. The couple thought he had not done it, but there had been the beginnings of a fight between their son and Chas when a group of youths accused Chas of breaking the car window. During this confrontation, the son had looked as if he was going to hit Chas, and Chas had responded by picking up a milk bottle, breaking it and brandishing the sharp end.

After a confused and inadequate investigation, the officers arrested Chas. They treated him contemptuously throughout, questioned him in a blundering fashion, and failed to attend to evidence that was in his favour. At the time of the arrest, one of the officers said to Chas, 'And you can take that smirk off your face or I'll come over there and wipe it off for you, you little scrote!' - which gives a fair impression of the tone they adopted towards him. When giving their account of the incident to the station officer, the PCs either deliberately or through unconscious prejudice changed the details to make it appear that Chas had suddenly gone berserk without any explanation or the slightest provocation. They maintained that the son denied going to strike Chas, which was not true. Later, when they interviewed Chas they failed to pay attention to important points that he made: for example, he repeatedly said that there were many witnesses to the fact that he was threatened, and that a number of youths had been shouting (to the son) 'Don't hit him! Don't hit him!' The PC's only response to this was, 'Witnesses? Witnesses? I bet they're all little scrotes like you!' Again, Chas repeatedly said that the wife had poked him in the chest and shouted at him while the husband held him. The PC ignored these remarks until they were made for the third time, then he pretended Chas was changing his story and said, 'Oh, she's poking you now, is she?' - though Chas had said this all along. Later the PC said to the mother that Chas's story was changing all the time, 'Now he's saying you poked him in the chest', and smiled as if to say, 'How ridiculous!' The mother replied, 'Quite right, I poked him in the chest...' Eventually, Chas was charged with carrying an offensive weapon. Since the matter had been resolved without a fight it was not inevitable that a charge should be brought, and in deciding to charge the officers may have been influenced by the fact that they regarded Chas as a 'slag'. It may not, however, have been the decisive factor. The officers might, possibly, have charged the son if he had been the one who brandished the bottle.

We cannot identify any cases where the social classification of the people involved was clearly the decisive factor determining police behaviour.   Nevertheless, these social attitudes do probably have an influence.

# XVI  RULES, PROCEDURES AND PRACTICE

People inside and outside the Force generally think of policing behaviour as being shaped chiefly by the application of rules and set procedure.  Some of these originate from the law and the Judges' Rules, for example the requirement that suspects should be formally cautioned in certain circumstances; others originate from within the Force, for example the requirement that officers in uniform should not buy a drink in a pub.  In both cases they act as a set of negative constraints.  Formally, they are intended to limit the area of individual initiative: by ensuring that certain things are forbidden or done to a formula, they are meant to reduce the chance that things will be done badly or wrongly, or not at all.

It is, of course, true that a complex network of rules and set procedures is a central feature of the way the Force is organised, but there are dangers in taking too superficial a view of the way that this works.  It is important to recognise that these rules are almost purely negative in their effect:  that is, police officers may be disciplined, prosecuted or otherwise get into difficulties if they are seen to break the rules, but they will not necessarily be praised, enjoy their work or achieve their career objectives if they keep to them.  As we argued in Chapter XIV, the positive objectives of police officers are much more informal and difficult to define than the framework of rules within which they operate, but may have an equally important influence.  Consequently the view that policing behaviour is chiefly shaped by the rules may well be wrong.

Because a rule exists, it does not follow that it automatically and rigidly governs day-to-day policing behaviour.  At the extreme, a rule may be universally ignored and never invoked to discipline anyone.  More important are the intermediate cases where a rule is invoked only in certain circumstances and where it has some effect on policing behaviour, but not the simple and direct influence that might be imagined.  There are many reasons why this should happen.  There is usually considerable scope for different interpretation and application of the rule (for example, that officers should only use what force is necessary to make an arrest).

Information about what the officer actually did is usually very limited because of a lack of independent witnesses, the strong tendency for officers to back each other up and the small amount of direct supervision. Also, there may be a very sharp conflict between 'doing the job well' - that is, achieving objectives that are widely recognised inside and outside the Force as being desirable - and sticking rigidly to the rules. For all of these reasons, a gap opens up between the formal rules and procedures and the kind of behaviour that police officers generally recognise as being acceptable.

One way of putting this is to say that while police officers know what the rules are and bear in mind the consequences of being found to have broken them, not all the rules become internalised into guiding principles of their behaviour. To take a minor example, an area car is formally forbidden to drive at high speed, with siren going and light flashing, to a call to which it has not been assigned (where other cars have been assigned instead). The driver may not think it is wrong to do this, he may not blame himself for doing it, but he knows that if he crashes the car on the way he is liable to be disciplined. In that case, the rule has an influence as an external hazard with which the driver has to contend and not as a personal rule of conduct. The driver has to weigh up the chances of coming unstuck if he goes to the call, but may well decide to risk it, especially if he feels (according to a different code) that he is expected to go because another police officer is in danger.

Where the rules are internalised, they are likely to have a far more consistent controlling influence. For example, if officers believe that it is wrong to behave oppressively towards suspects in order to get confessions, they will never, or almost never, do so; if they do not believe it is wrong, at any rate in certain circumstances, but regard the rule as a hazard to be taken into account in deciding how to behave, they will still be restrained to some extent by the rule, but may behave oppressively if they personally feel it is justified and if they think they can get away with it.

A third kind of function of rules is to put a gloss on policing behaviour so as to make it acceptable to the wider public. We would argue, for example, that the limitation by law of police powers to stop and search people on foot amounts to a set of rules with a largely cosmetic function. In theory, police officers may only stop and search people who they reasonably suspect to be in possession of stolen goods or controlled drugs; in practice they can stop and search virtually anyone, and a police officer will rarely be disciplined or reprimanded for making a stop where he was not entitled by law to do so (though he may be criticised for making a stop that is most unlikely to produce a 'result').

A convenient way of summarising this analysis is to distinguish three kinds of rules. Working rules are those that are internalised by police officers to become guiding principles of their conduct. Inhibitory rules are those which are not internalised, but

441

which police officers take into account when deciding how to act and which tend to discourage them from behaving in certain ways in case they should be caught and the rule invoked against them. Presentational rules are ones that exist to give an acceptable appearance to the way that police work is carried out. It is important to realise that it is not only or even mainly the police who seek to put this gloss on the reality of policing behaviour and interactions between the police and the public. Most of the presentational rules derive from the law and are part of a (successful) attempt by the wider society to deceive itself about the realities of policing.

In practice, the distinction to be made is often between three functions of rules rather than between three types of rule, because the same rule may perform more than one function, or may be used differently by different officers or at different times. For example, inhibitory rules often perform a presentational function as well: if people criticise the police for charging about in cars at high speeds when they don't need to and thereby causing accidents, the police can point to the existence of the rule restricting the number of cars assigned to a call and mention that some drivers have recently been disciplined for going to calls to which they were not assigned.

None of this means that rules are unimportant: it does mean that they have a very variable influence on policing behaviour, depending on what kind of rule they are taken to be, on how they are interpreted and used by senior officers, on how they interact with the norms and objectives of working groups of police officers, and so on. There are therefore considerable dangers in the simple response to accounts of bad policing behaviour: that is, just suggesting more rules. If these additional rules turn out to be presentational ones, then this is a way of pretending to take action without willing the means. It may even make matters worse by increasing the defensiveness and self-protective activity of the police without any concomitant gain.

In the rest of this chapter we look at policing practice in the Met in relation to the rules on the use of force, the collection of evidence, the treatment of suspects at police stations, the records to be kept of hours worked and activities when on duty, and various other matters. In this field, the limitations of any method of research become fairly severe. It seems likely that police officers will tend to follow the rules more closely when an observer is present than they otherwise would; even the presence of another officer of the same rank whom they do not know or trust will have some effect on their behaviour. This means that research can provide little direct evidence about the extent of serious kinds of misbehaviour - kinds which police officers feel the need to conceal from any observer. We have no evidence at all (apart from what is public knowledge already) about the extent of corruption in the Met, unless smaller misdemeanours such as accepting favours are included under this head. This is partly because officers would try hard to prevent anyone who was not also implicated from having access to any evidence about bribery; it is also because this kind of activity is planned, so the officer can easily arrange to do it when nobody from outside the group is there. For most other kinds of rule-breaking practices, observation provides a certain amount of direct evidence, because these practices are part of the flow of policing activities in response to events as they develop. Officers have to go on dealing with the work while the observer is there and it is much easier for them to deal with it in something like their usual style than to change their whole pattern of behaviour. Our research also provides a considerable amount of indirect evidence - essentially from what police officers say - about rule-breaking, though this has to be treated critically because of the habitual bragging and exaggeration of police officers that we have emphasised in Chapter XIV.

This research cannot provide a quantitative assessment of the extent to which rules are broken. However, it can provide broad indications of this and, perhaps more important, an understanding of the part played by different kinds of rules in shaping policing behaviour.

## Use of force

The essential principle that runs through the law as it affects the use of force by constables is that they may only use what force is necessary, in the execution of their duty, to detain or arrest someone, to prevent someone from escaping from custody, or to restrain a prisoner who is behaving violently. In detail, the interpretation of this principle, in all the varied circumstances in which it has to be applied, is very complex, but the Metropolitan Police Instruction Book does not go into such details and police officers themselves, while always familiar with the general principle, usually have little knowledge of the legal ramifications.

Our general conclusion from this research is that the great majority of police officers treat this principle as a 'working rule' which shapes their day-to-day policing behaviour and which they use to evaluate the behaviour of other officers. This means that the great majority of police officers habitually try to avoid using more force than is necessary, in spite of the glamour attaching to violence and the tendency to brag about being in fights and winning them that we have described in Chapter XIV.

However, two very important qualifications have to be made to this general conclusion. First, a minority of officers treat the principle about the use of force as merely an 'inhibitory rule'. These officers will use excessive force if they think they have a good chance of getting away with it, either because they have a taste for violence or because they see the use of force as the best available means to achieve an objective (maybe because they lack the skills to achieve their objectives in other ways). We also conclude that these officers have a very good chance of 'getting away with it' in most individual instances, though this is partly balanced by the knowledge that if they are caught the penalties are likely to be severe.

The second qualification is that officers at all levels in the Force operate with different working rules when dealing with a major public disturbance or riot. For example, during the Brixton riots of April 1981 large groups of officers mounted 'baton charges' on groups of rioters, in which the object was to clear a street by hitting anyone who tried to stay there, and where force was used not primarily to make arrests but primarily to disperse a crowd. In circumstances like the Brixton riots, officers seem to switch into a different 'mode' in which they think the normal principle no longer applies. Although it is hard to see how this can be justified in the law, it may be what most citizens, and even the rioters themselves, expect; in other words, it seems to be generally accepted that the police should behave in this kind of way, and there is little chance of proceedings being taken against the officers involved.

Some of our information comes from direct observation, some from what officers said about specific incidents that they had taken part in or observed and some from more general conversation about patterns of police behaviour rather than about particular incidents. During the course of our research we came across nine specific incidents where we can be certain that excessive force was used, in most cases through direct observation but in some cases through very reliable reports. The reader will form his own judgements from the descriptions of the incidents, but in our judgement there were no more than four cases in which the degree of force was such as to cause serious distress. To place this in context, we covered about 100 incidents involving one or more arrests and 129 stops: we saw a large number of prisoners being dealt with in the charge room (many more than those whose arrests we followed). In addition, we heard from police officers about at least 19 incidents where excessive force had been used, but this figure cannot be set in any context, since officers were recalling things that happened at various times. There are also some important conversations to be reported about the general approach of officers towards the use of force and the pattern of their behaviour in this respect.

Incidents covered where there is certain knowledge that excessive force was used

A brief summary of each of these incidents is given below. There is considerable variation in the nature of the incidents: in some cases (perhaps four) the police officer's behaviour caused serious distress, but in others the harm done was fairly slight.

1.  A thirteen year old boy who had taken and driven away a car was chased by police vehicles and arrested after being tracked by a police dog. The boy fell onto the live rail on a railway line; he was unconscious when found and had a bad burn on his arm. Shortly after the arrest, JG saw the dog

handler treating the boy very roughly as he brought him back to the police cars. He was shouting and swearing at him and shoving him around although the boy was offering no resistance. When they got back to the yard of the police station, JG saw the boy dragged from the car and swung into the charge room by an officer holding each of his arms. Although the boy was handled much more roughly than was necessary, JG did not see an officer hit him.

2.  A suicidal young woman was arrested after protesting about the arrest of her boyfriend. She was in a hysterical state. When the van reached the yard of the police station, JG saw the girl dragged out of it and hauled into the charge room as she continued to scream. JG followed her in and saw a PC take her into a corridor leading towards the cells. After a few seconds, the girl was face down on the floor of the corridor with the PC holding her arms behind her and kneeling on her back. This PC did not know JG. Looking up and seeing him he said, 'Who's this bloke?', then, as JG began to reply, told another PC to close the door leading from the charge room, which the PC did. When the door was shut, JG could only hear what was going on. The girl said, 'I can't help it, my mother made me mental' in a hysterical wail. There was then a thump and she started to scream and to shout 'Get off me!' When the girl had been got into a cell, the inspector of the relief appeared and explained who JG was, saying, 'It's all right, he's one of the good guys' to the PC who had apparently hit the girl. Later, the PC said laughingly, 'There I was with that girl on the floor and this bloke's watching me. I didn't know who the fuck he was'.

3.  JG was with three officers belonging to a crime squad patrolling in a car when they stopped and searched a small man in his early 20s. One of the officers (Geoff) took the lead in deciding to stop the man, in searching and in questioning him. The search was thorough and rather rough. The young man, whose legs began to shake, would not remove his hand from his left coat pocket. Geoff pulled it out, and there was a struggle as the suspect tried to break away while Geoff held onto his arm, shouting to another PC in the car to help him. The other two PCs got out of the car quickly and arrested the man as Geoff wrestled half a 'joint' from his left hand. The suspect was put in the back of the police car. Geoff got in next to him and kicked him hard and deliberately on the leg as he did so, saying, 'Go on, get over!' The suspect yelped when kicked.

4.  DJS was with two officers in a panda car when they answered a call for urgent assistance to officers making an arrest in a restaurant. A large, muscular Asian man, who was very

drunk, was shouting and struggling with a group of three policemen who were trying to hold him down. He was dragged out of the restaurant with difficulty, especially since his friend, a large muscular white man with a scar on his face, was holding onto him and tugging in the opposite direction. DJS did not see anyone hit the Asian man at this stage. He was shouting abuse at the policemen. He was handcuffed and bundled with difficulty into the back of the van. One of the officers from the panda car (a probationer) went back in the van to the police station, while DJS continued to patrol in the panda car. Later in the canteen, the probationer sat down purposely opposite the van driver and said, in a half joking fashion, 'I want to have a word with you'. After a pause, he went on, 'You've been very naughty, winding up a prisoner like that in the van. You know you shouldn't do that'. The van driver smiled sheepishly. Then the probationer told DJS that the van driver had wound up (verbally taunted) the Asian man very successfully, so that the man became very agitated, hurled more abuse at the policemen, then suddenly butted the probationer in the chest. The probationer said that he punched the Asian man hard in the face in retaliation. Later, in the charge room, the Asian man was calling for a doctor to attend to his nose; the station officer did not take this request seriously. Later still the same night, the van driver told another officer on the relief that he had been in a bad mood, explained why, and volunteered that he had 'wound up' a prisoner in the van 'very successfully' just because of the mood he was in.

DJS was with an area car crew which stopped a car that was weaving about slightly. The driver was obviously drunk. The area car driver got him into the back of the area car and the operator gave him a breath test, which was positive. Then the driver needed to get the keys of the suspect's car so that he could drive it back to the police station. He asked him, 'Where are the keys of your car?' The man said, 'I don't know'. He was asked again, roughly. He said, 'They're in the ignition'. The driver said, 'They're not in the ignition because I've looked, now will you give them to me?' The man said nothing and the driver began to lose his temper. He said, 'Look, stop pissing me about, you cunt', reached into the back of the area car and grabbed the man's arms, shook him about (he was much larger than the suspect) and wrenched the keys from one of his hands, insulting him again. Later, as they were hanging about in the charge room, the radio operator said to another officer on the relief, 'It's a good thing that David was there, otherwise Harry (the driver) might have throttled him'.

446

6.    JG saw a suspect in the fingerprint room at the police station and on making enquiries was told by officers on the relief he was with that he had been arrested for assaulting a dog handler and taking his flat cap. He had been wearing the flat cap when he was arrested by an off-duty PC. Later that night, the two PCs with whom JG was working said that this prisoner had been assaulted by the detective constable on night duty. One of the PCs said that this detective constable was 'out of order' because the PC who had gone down as the arresting officer and the station sergeant would 'receive 163s' if the man complained, not the detective constable. (The '163' is the formal notification to an officer that a complaint has been made against him.) In other words, the uniform officers would be in danger of taking the blame for an assault on a prisoner in custody by someone else (the detective constable). Also, the PC maintained that if the detective constable wanted to assault prisoners 'he should do it outside, not in the police station' where he was more likely to be caught, and where there was a danger of implicating other officers. Although JG showed no disapproval, the other PC said, 'Well, I don't hold with hitting people anyway'. Soon after this conversation, the PCs came across the same detective constable at the scene of a crime. The detective put his head into their car and said, 'Your station officer's really got the hump with me'. One of the PCs said, 'Well, you can't really blame him, can you?' The detective said, 'Just because I gave that bloke a slap', then grinned. He did not know JG, but assumed he was a police officer.

7.    JG was with a PC in a GP car which answered a call for assistance from a WPC: a man was becoming violent in the casualty department at a hospital. Many other officers (at least six) went to the call. The van had arrived before the GP car with JG in it. As JG and the PC went into the entrance of the hospital they could hear screams and shouts from down the corridor. As they turned a corner they found Neil, a large and muscular PC from the relief, holding a man's arm up his back. The man was white and in his late thirties. He was screaming, 'All right, let go, you're breaking me arm!' The PCs said that he had come into the casualty ward, started swearing at people and then had taken a swing at someone. Neil kept saying to him, 'Now, you gonna be quiet? Sure? Honest?', punctuating each question with a twist of the arm up the man's back. Each time the man shouted 'Yes!' Suddenly, Neil let go of him and he fell to the floor and just lay there. From his voice, behaviour and facial expression, he seemed to be mentally disturbed. Neil and others hauled him to his feet and, as he remained limp, dragged him out. One of the PCs put his cap on the suspect's head and all of the PCs began to lark about. When he got out

447

into the fresh air, the suspect suddenly woke up and behaved normally for a few moments. He asked, 'What's going to happen to me now, lads?' One of the PCs told him he could go. 'What, not going to take me down to the police station?' he asked. The PC said 'No'. The suspect began to walk away. Then his manner changed. he kicked one of the PCs in the backside (not very hard) and scuttled off, cackling, 'Stupid cunt! Not going to take me in. Got all the cameras and tapes as well - it's wasted. Cunt'. He seemed to believe that the whole incident was being filmed. One of the PCs ran after him and rugby tackled him. There was then a serious fight between the suspect and eight PCs, who took some time to subdue him. He was eventually led to the van by two PCs, one on each side twisting his arms, while a WPC (quite unnecessarily) held him by the hair. The suspect was screaming, 'You see this, George, eight on to one. Fucking disgusting!'

When the PCs put him in the van, he ran through and tried to come out at the front. One of them stopped him and said later that he 'gave him a kick up the arse' in return. As one of the PCs tried to climb back into the van, a foot whistled out of the back door and narrowly missed his head. He eventually got in. JG, watching from outside, heard screams and sounds of a struggle. JG and 'his' PC then resumed patrolling in the GP car, but were called into the police station by some of the PCs involved in making this arrest. When they arrived, the suspect was in a cell and had reverted to his semi-comatose state. By doing a computer check the PCs established that the suspect was a violent epileptic who had not long been released from jail. From his recent behaviour he seemed to be insane. Half a dozen police officers now began to behave towards him in a way calculated to make him more disturbed and cause him to become violent again. They sat him up in his cell (he remained in his stupor for the time being) and read the charge to him (assault on police). Towards the end of this procedure, he started thrashing about and tried to kick a PC in the crutch, but hardly caught him. JG thought the PCs would leave it there, but ten minutes later he heard a tremendous commotion from the charge room and when he went to investigate found that a group of six PCs were trying to take the suspect's fingerprints. Neil and the PC whom the suspect had tried to kick in the crutch were restraining him. Eventually he agreed to have his prints taken by Neil alone, but six other PCs stood around watching, so the suspect talked to them and started to abuse one of them in particular by calling him a 'nancy boy'. This PC, who was keen on weightlifting and keeping fit, became very upset at this abuse although the man was obviously mad. He handled him very roughly indeed the next

448

time he had a chance to restrain him. When the PCs tried to take his photograph, the suspect seemed to go berserk. He nearly wrecked the equipment, dropped his trousers and tried to expose himself to a WPC, then dangled his penis in front of the camera. A sergeant leapt forward and slashed at his penis with a bunch of keys, but fortunately missed. He said, 'Next time you put that out you'll get it chopped off'. The suspect had by this time climbed onto the seat in front of the camera. Neil pulled him off, and he tumbled onto the floor and hit his head on the door. At this point he went back into his stupor. He was taken back to his cell. The sergeant turned to JG and said, 'Trouble is, that's the sort of lunatic who'll top your five year old daughter'.

The sergeant then tried to find a PC who would agree that the suspect had assaulted him (so that the charge of assaulting a police officer could be proceeded with). Neil would not agree (he had been kicked, but it hadn't hurt), but another PC did. Not only was the man insane, but the police officers had deliberately provoked him and then used far more force than was necessary to restrain him.

8.   JG was with a panda car that backed up a number of other units that were answering a call to 'suspects on premises'. When he arrived, a very large PC had a black youth aged about 16 pinned against some railings. He was holding the railings with his two hands and crushing the youth as hard as he could with the whole of his body. This was more than was necessary to prevent the youth from escaping, especially as he was very cooperative: he even apologised as he climbed into the area car when his foot accidentally bumped against the 'seek and search' lamp.

9.   JG heard accounts of this incident from the PC concerned and from his inspector, and the two accounts tally closely except in certain details that will be noted. The PC (Michael) was acting as plain clothes observer with an area car. According to the inspector (who heard about the incident afterwards) the area car crew 'pulled a mini full of yobs' who 'got a bit lippy' with the officers and were very rude to Michael. He 'lost his head', grabbed one of the 'yobs' (who was very small) round the neck very fiercely and half throttled him. Michael's description (given privately to JG) was that he 'put his hand round the guy's throat and held him over the bonnet of the area car'. The inspector said that it wasn't so much the assault that was wrong, it was the fact that Michael had 'let the side down in front of members of the public and made prime prosecution witnesses of two fellow officers. Then, of course, he had to go and tell the truth to a senior officer (the superintendent). There's nothing

worse than telling the truth'. The man who was assaulted made a complaint. There was the evidence of the marks on his neck, although Michael said he had made them worse. He also produced an independent witness, but Michael maintained that (contrary to the inspector's account) members of the public had not witnessed the incident, and that the witness was 'arranged'. However, Michael confirmed that he had assaulted the man and that he told the superintendent that he assaulted him. The inspector said that at the time of the incident and in early meetings the complainant was 'adamant' that he wanted to press the complaint. He was well known to police, with convictions for burglary, but 'He was quite sure he wanted to go through with it, this villain. He said that he'd been nicked a few times but never had any violence used on him. He wasn't going to wear it. But eventually he decided, as he was known to police, it would do him no good to continue and that he'd get a hard time if he did, so he dropped it'. Michael said that he was told by the chief-inspector that the complaint had been withdrawn, and that the chief-inspector did not say why. Michael added, 'Course, I know that -- -- (the chief-inspector) put the squeeze on him (the complainant)'. Michael also said the chief-inspector asked him to make a case as to why he should not be disciplined internally. Michael said he couldn't and that he 'wouldn't crawl'. According to Michael, the chief-inspector replied, 'All right, you've convinced me because you've been honest' and left it at that.

Reported incidents where excessive force was used
Under this head we include incidents that officers talked about but without giving very specific information; many of these incidents happened well outside the time period of the research.

1. DJS got to know Peter (a PC) very well, and considered him to be skilled and professional in his approach. However, Peter said that there had been occasions when, because he was in a bad mood, he had hit someone when he could easily have avoided it. He did not seem to be proud of this, but seemed to be well aware of the advantages of 'talking people down' rather than 'lashing out'. That same evening he dealt with a dispute between a husband and wife. The woman was belabouring the man with a plank in the street when Peter arrived. Peter resolved the matter without making any arrests and without using force at all.

2. A detective constable handled a long series of interrogations of a burglar very effectively. He did not use force or threats of force. Afterwards JG asked him whether he 'saw any mileage' in assaulting prisoners. He said he had assaulted

450

prisoners in the past but had given it up. 'I think all you lose is your self-respect, but you very rarely gain anything. A good class villain knows full well that the moment you start hitting him, you've got a very weak case and that as long as he can take a beating, he's home and dry.'

3.  A conversation started between the sergeant in charge of a crime squad and one of the PCs on the squad, with JG also taking part from time to time. The talk turned to assaulting prisoners. The PC said he'd never done it but that he could understand why people did. The sergeant jumped in to say, 'Tell the man (JG) the truth. It can't do you any harm'. The PC said, 'Well, if somebody hits you, you're going to have a go back, aren't, you?' He went on to describe an incident that happened when he had been on duty at a football match. In a struggle with a football fan who had a lot of friends with him, the PC had been knocked over and pushed down the terracing. He said, 'It's all right when he's got hundreds of his mates behind him, isn't it? So when he was finally nicked and I got him in the van, I gave him a hiding'.

4.  A uniform sergeant told JG that on the previous evening a man had been arrested for sexually assaulting or committing indecencies with children. The sergeant said, 'Apparently, he's been arrested before at -- (police station) and they gave him a right beating there. He was very frightened that he was going to receive the same thing here'. JG made no comment and there was a pause before the sergeant said, 'You may not agree, but I think that's right'. He went on to say that the suspect had not received the beating he was expecting this time, but his tone when he said this was not very convincing. When the topic came up in conversation again among the same group, a detective constable said that it was foolish to beat up sexual offenders in police cells as they were bound to get beaten in prison anyway. However, most members of the group agreed with the proposition that it was right for police officers to deal out 'summary justice' in these cases.

5.  A PC told JG that when he first joined the group he was currently working with they went to a football match. 'A lot of people (police officers) were getting involved - in fact, we probably caused more fights than we sorted out. And a senior officer - well, there's only one inspector on the unit - he was urging people to get stuck in. I did because I was new and thought I had to. A lot of the more experienced blokes refused to have anything to do with it. And people weren't being nicked, they were just being thrown out of the ground. I don't see any point in doing that'. Another PC mentioned, in response to this account, that they used to have an officer in

the group who was often violent. 'He used to nut people - I've seen him do it. You'd been arresting someone, talking to them, and he'd come up and kick them in the bollocks.'

6. JG went with two PCs to arrest a man (Bill) on a warrant for failing to appear in connection with a charge of assault. They arrested the man at his home and just before they left, Bill said, 'I'm not going to get a kicking this time, am I? One of the PCs responded angrily, 'You know me, Bill, I've arrested you before. You're my prisoner and that's not going to happen'. Bill continued, 'Only that other officer said I'd get a kicking...' He did not mean the other PC involved in making this arrest, but described the 'other officer' as fat with a beard. The PC said he knew who he was and added, 'Well, it's a good job I arrested you, Bill, isn't it? Otherwise you'd have got a kicking, wouldn't you?'

7. A PC told a story of how he and Fred (another PC) had arrested a National Front supporter; he told it to a group including JG in the canteen. 'So me and Fred stopped this bloke and he got really lippy. Fred told him to shut up and panned (punched) him. We nicked him and searched him. He had NF stickers in his pocket so we nicked him for sticking them up. Fred is crazy sometimes - there was a whole crowd of NF standing nearby.'

8. Two PCs stopped two youths whom they recognised, but were annoyed not to be able to arrest them for anything. Once they had got back into the car, one PC said to the other, 'What a fucking little toe-rag. I wouldn't have minded thumping him'. The other PC agreed and went on to talk about the way in which the dog handler in that area treated kids like these. 'If they give him any lip he justs belts them. That shuts 'em up quick. He says, "Either the dog's got to bite 'em or I've got to hit 'em. If the dog bites 'em there's a load of fucking writing to do..."' The other PC said, 'Yeah, he's one of the old school, knows how to deal with the little shits round here'. In talking like this the PCs seemed to be bragging to JG; however, these particular PCs did behave rudely and roughly to people themselves and it was clear that, for them, the principle of using no more force than is necessary was not a 'working rule'.

9. A PC said to JG, 'I've only ever hit three prisoners without cause, and I've felt bad each time'.

10. Two PCs transported two prisoners in a van from the head-quarters of a major incident squad where they had been questioned in connection with a murder to a police station. One was a white man in his early twenties who was described

452

as a 'violent prisoner'. His face was puffy and reddened as if he had been repeatedly hit. The PC driving the van pointed this out to JG, saying, 'I wonder who did that?' The prisoner was defiant, angry and distressed.

11. Two PCs agreed with each other in conversation that villains and rioters didn't mind a 'pasting' out on the streets, because that was 'part of the game'. It was when they got beaten up in the cells that they complained. One of these PCs said that when he was posted to a different Division (a few years before) a PC had hit one of his prisoners in the charge room. He had demanded that the station officer reprimand the PC on the spot, otherwise he would make an official complaint. 'In many ways I was more pissed off with the station officer than with the PC. He'd already told me off for telling the prisoner to shut up. Then this PC pans him. I wasn't standing for that - I have to account for any injuries to my prisoners.' This account incidentally illustrates the proprietary interest that police officers have in 'their' prisoners.

12. A PC spoke of an arrest that he and a number of other PCs had made two to three months before. They had gone to arrest a large, black man at his home. He had started brandishing a knife and for a time the police officers 'played cat and mouse'. 'Eventually Dave, the dog handler, turned up totally pissed and told this bloke to put the knife down or he'd set the fucking dog on him.' The PC said that the dog gave the man a number of nasty bites. 'Once we'd got him on the ground, one of the U District heroes came over and punched this bloke on the head - hurt his hand. We'd already sticked him a couple of times.' At length, the man was brought to the police station. 'By this time he was as good as gold.' Then the two night duty CID officers appeared. According to the PC, they said, 'What's all this about a nigger giving you some trouble?' The PC went on, 'They asked the station officer for the keys and went down to this bloke's cell. All you could hear was thumps and shouts. They did this bloke up a treat. They came back from the cell saying, "There you are, he won't give you any more trouble", and they left'.

13. A PC gave an account of an incident that happened during some of the riots of 1981. A woman journalist had been shown round the police station by some senior officers. At one point she arrived at the back gate to find two PCs who had just given a black man 'a belting' as he was forced right up against the gate. 'They'd already tried to open the charge room door with his head' which was covered with blood. The PC who told the story and others present were amused that they found no reference to this incident in the papers.

14. One PC, backed up by a number of others, gave accounts of several incidents during the riots of April 1981.

a) He was part of a serial travelling about in a transit van. The driver deliberately drove at a black youth, who turned round to see the van bearing down on him. The van struck him with some force. 'He went right up on to the roof and slithered back down the windscreen again.' The PC did not say what the extent of the youth's injuries were.

b) 'I remember once we drew sticks and charged a group of blacks who'd been stoning us. It was as though telepathy took over: about ten sticks converged on this one head. I saw the back of this bloke's head just open up.'

c) A number of PCs spoke about an occasion when a group of rioters had been trapped by police who had sealed off both ends of a street, leaving no way of escaping. Everyone in the crowd was 'relentlessly beaten'.

d) The PCs said that a very senior officer ordered a charge down one particular street, saying 'No sticks, no prisoners'. One PC said, 'There was no one left standing after they'd been through'.

e) 'During the riots, I was sat up here (in the canteen) eating my breakfast when I saw a U District PC on aid bring a prisoner into the yard. This prisoner got just far enough away from the PC and made a bolt for the gate. There were two more U District blokes on the gate. The shout went up - 'Stop him!' - and they just sort of collected this bloke and rammed him into the gate. Then the first PC walked over, grabbed the guy's collar and dragged him into the charge room.'

15. The same group of PCs told a story about an incident that was not connected with the riots. A WPC in a panda car stopped to deal with three white youths who were beating up a black youth. 'She got a thumping for her pains.' Other officers reached the scene and captured two of the assailants. The PC telling the story said that the officers beat them up. Two dog handlers went to look for the assailant who had escaped. 'They were just about to give up when they found this bloke in a bush. There wasn't much left of the geezer when they dragged him in. And, the WPC's husband was an ex-PC at --- nick, so you can imagine what happened to those blokes.'

454

16. A PC told JG that a chief-inspector on the Division had been an inspector at another Division when the PC was posted there. 'Once he really badly beat up a prisoner of mine in the charge room, mad bastard. I was only five weeks out of training school.' JG asked the PC why he didn't stop the inspector as the prisoner (arrested for taking and driving away a car) was his. The PC said he couldn't imagine a new recruit remonstrating with an inspector over such a matter, but he disliked the man very much because of the incident: he called him 'an evil fucker'.

17. A uniform sergeant told JG that he had broken a man's arm and dislocated his shoulder whilst arresting him for drunk driving.

18. A PC told a story (when being interviewed by JG) of an incident that had taken place shortly before when a group of officers were carrying out a drugs raid. Michael (who was telling the story) and another PC were guarding a door to prevent people from escaping when a Rastafarian man tried to run out. Michael caught him and searched him with the help of another PC. They found a knife, which the Rasta said he used 'to cut up oranges and bananas'. Just then, Michael saw someone else escaping and started to go after this second man, at which the Rasta kicked the other PC in the crutch and ran. Michael chased after the Rasta, who stopped briefly, smacked Michael in the mouth, then ran on. Eventually the two PCs caught the man and Michael got him on to the ground. While he was lying on the ground, the second PC hit him about the head with a truncheon. Michael tried to stop him. A small crowd of black people had gathered and started throwing bricks at the two PCs. Michael called on the personal radio for urgent assistance as the other PC was dragged to the ground. Michael said that the other PC was afterwards bruised but was not badly hurt. Several units of officers arrived to help. An inspector came up to Michael, asked him if he was all right, then he asked the Rasta, 'Are you gonna behave?', punched him and repeated the question.

19. The same PC reported two further cases where excessive force was used. The first was at a football match. He said that fighting broke out and the SPG were sent in to deal with it, backed up by Michael's serial. After a while, Michael noticed the SPG inspector, ringed by other SPG officers with their backs to him, beating a girl about the head and shoulders with his truncheon. The PCs in the ring were saying, 'Go on, guv, give it to her'.

20. When JG said he could not understand why prisoners should be beaten in the charge room, Michael said he had only inter-

vened once (in such a situation) when 'six of another relief were beating up a mentally deficient black guy in the charge room'.

## Threats of violence
In two of the cases quoted in the last chapter, officers strongly threatened prisoners with violence in the presence of the resarcher (the black boys wrongly suspected of robbing a young woman, and the white boy who brandished a milk bottle). There was a third occasion on which a threat of violence was made. JG was with an area car that took part in a chase of a Rover containing two black suspects. The chase ended when the Rover crashed with the driver's door wedged against a wall. The driver could not get out and was quickly arrested, but his passenger escaped. The car was full of stolen leather coats. JG went off with his crew to look for the passenger who had escaped, but without success. When they returned to the scene of the crash, an officer in plain clothes was interviewing the man who had been arrested (both men were sitting in a police car). As JG started to listen to this interview from outside the car, the officer said, 'Come on, mate. You'd better start telling us the truth. You've been treated very well up to now, but if you don't start coming across, I'll take you down --- nick and I'll give you the biggest hiding of your life'.

## Other information on the use of force
In a case observed by DJS, two CID officers arrested a black boy in connection with the theft of a ring and later arrested the boy who had committed the theft on the basis of information given by the first boy arrested. This first boy was to be released without charge (he had not had any part in the theft) but first made a statement in the presence of his mother. Just as he was about to start taking the statement, one of the officers said to the boy, 'You have been very foolish, haven't you?', and then, after some more talk along these lines, 'You know, you're very lucky. Have I mistreated you?' 'No,' said the boy. The officer went on, 'Well, you're very lucky. You might have come across a policeman who would have knocked you about, who would have given you a cuff behind the ear, mightn't you? You're very lucky that I wouldn't do a thing like that'. The boy's mother said, 'That would have been illegal'. The officer said, 'Of course it would. Of course it would have been illegal, but it still might have happened, mightn't it?' The mother said nothing further, but looked shocked. This was an example of an officer creating a violent image of the police without behaving violently himself and in circumstances where there would be no point in frightening the prisoner because he had already said everything he knew. It seemed to be the officer's way of scolding the child. He seemed to be taking the part of a parent and behaving as he thought a parent would.

In a number of the examples we have already quoted, officers have wanted to dissociate themselves from excessive use of force by other officers. This kind of remark was quite common in general conversation (when no specific incident was under discussion). For example, a detective constable said he had never been assaulted in nine years' of service. He always tried to talk prisoners into the police station. 'Some officers prefer to punch them in the head first and that's why they are always reporting assault on police'. A uniform sergeant who had transferred (as a sergeant) from another force and was now posted to an inner Division said that the PCs there were much rougher with prisoners than he was used to from his experience in the provincial force. He was careful to say that he did not mean 'beatings', but said that 'pushing and shoving and bad language' were commonplace. He mentioned an incident where a prisoner was held flat on the charge room table because he was 'a bit stroppy', which he thought quite unnecessary. In his previous force he said the prisoner would simply be locked up till he quietened down.

There is considerable evidence from our research that when suspects (usually boys) have taken and driven away a car and have been caught after a chase, many police officers expect them to be beaten: this seems to be a particular circumstance in which the principle that no more force than is necessary should be used ceases to be a 'working rule' for a significant number of officers. This conclusion is not based on direct observation of beating or rough treatment of suspects, and is not, therefore, fully established, but the indications are fairly strong. JG walked into the yard of a police station one evening and saw an area car driver sitting in a car listening to the mainset radio. A car chase was taking place. JG sat next to the driver to listen with him. The suspect car, which had been chased by an area car for about half an hour, eventually got itself jammed between a lamp post and a wall. Both occupants were caught. The officer sitting with JG sent an anonymous message ending with 'Give them what for'. When JG showed slight surprise at this, the PC he was with said it was quite right that people like the suspects who had just been caught should get rough handling because of all the lives that they had endangered.

On another occasion, JG was with three officers from a crime squad who were patrolling in a car and took part in a chase. The suspects were arrested by officers in another car and were known to the crew JG was with. When they heard who the suspects were, one of the PCs in JG's crew (referring to one of these boys) said, 'Oh, I bet he's had a right seeing to'. He then seemed to remember that JG was there, gulped and looked embarrassed. On a third occasion, JG told two PCs about a long chase he had taken part in, where the suspect was eventually arrested. One of the PCs said, 'I bet he got a right panning - the adrenalin pumping round' and the other made a similar remark. On a fourth occasion, during a conversation in a pub, a PC became quite heated while arguing that it was correct to beat up 'TDA merchants' after a chase. 'These toe-rags have driven like maniacs, could have wiped up <u>your</u>

wife and <u>your</u> kid. 'Course it's right to give them a whacking.' Whether or not suspects are actually beaten in these circumstances, it seems that a considerable number of officers think it is acceptable that they should be and do not accept the minimum use of force as a working rule in this case.

On getting into a panda car on an outer Division, JG stumbled over a pick-axe handle with a large metal implement on the end. The officers present (including a uniform sergeant) made some jokes about this. The PC driver said, 'Well, it does get pretty lonely out here, you know'. He did not seem to be an aggressive person.

## Summary
In the account just given, we have been concentrating on evidence from our research that police officers have, on occasion, used more force than was necessary. We have not, therefore, given detailed examples of the (many) cases where no more force than was necessary was used. As we said at the outset, our findings cannot be analysed quantitatively, but it is important to bear in mind that we observed or got to know about a large number of incidents: we covered 100 arrests and 129 stops, and we saw a large number of people dealt with in the charge room, though it would not be appropriate to give a count since some of these prisoners were observed for short and some for long periods of time. We have come up with nine cases where we are certain that excessive force was used, including about four where this was enough to cause serious distress. We have, in addition, heard officers give fairly specific information about at least 20 other incidents where excessive force was used, but these were incidents that had stuck in the memory of police officers and may have taken place as long as two years before in some cases: they are therefore selected from a very large number of arrests and stops that these officers had made or observed.

These findings suggest that the great majority of cases are dealt with by police officers without the excessive use of force, but that police behave violently in an important minority of cases. The fairly large number of incidents mentioned by officers (but not observed by the researchers) is probably explained by a tendency to dwell on violent incidents in conversation and by the large pool from which these 'interesting' incidents have been selected to become the subjects of conversation. If it is thought that officers tended to use force much less than usual because of the presence of the observer, then these findings will be an understatement.

Not surprisingly, the rules that govern police officers' use of force vary to some extent according to the context. For most officers most of the time, the principle of seeking to use the minimum amount of force is a working rule. There is evidence that they tend to 'waive' the rule when dealing with suspects caught after a car chase. Officers are probably quite strongly influenced in their behaviour by their assessment of the chance of being disciplined. One reason for the provocative and very rough behaviour of a group of officers towards a suspect who appeared to be insane was probably that these officers knew the man would not be in a position to make a formal complaint. Another reason was that they did not know how to respond to his abnormal behaviour (another illustration of this was given in Chapter XIV).

We have little or no observational evidence about the behaviour of police officers during outbreaks of serious public disorder. From what police officers said about the riots of 1981 it was quite clear that in those circumstances they 'switched into a different mode'. They saw themselves as being engaged in a battle with large numbers of people conceived of as a group and not as individuals who might or might not have committed an offence. Because they saw themselves as fighting a crowd rather than trying to arrest individuals or defending themselves from individual attackers, the principle of using no more force than is necessary could not be applied in the usual way. From what officers said, there were many cases where officers beat people whom they were not at that time trying to arrest or to disperse (since the street was sealed off) and who were not at that moment attacking them. This kind of policing cannot be justified within the terms of the law, which balances the force used by an officer against that used by the individual person whom he is trying to arrest or who is attacking him, and which provides no justification for any degree of force except in self-defence or in making an arrest. On the other hand, there is no serious attempt by the wider society to enforce the law on the police in circumstances like these; their 'switching into another mode' is tacitly accepted by a large number of people.

One PC accused senior officers of hypocrisy in this matter. He said he found it infuriating that in the riots 'they (the guvnors) thought all was fair in love and war' and made it clear to PCs that it was all right to use indiscriminate violence, even if they (the guvnors) knew about it or saw it; whereas now, in 'peace time', you had to be careful not to be caught.

In a sense, this PC's protest indicates the danger that habits acquired at the time of riots or serious public disorder will carry over into day-to-day policing. It also underlines the point that the behaviour of the police during events like the 1981 riots is much less constrained by the law and the discipline code than at normal times because there is little chance of evidence about the behaviour of individual officers emerging from the confused situation of a riot. It follows that effective control of police behaviour at such times must depend on officers being trained to act in disciplined groups and on the quality of command by senior officers on the day. It is necessary that this should be an activity quite distinct from 'normal' policing and requiring quite a different attitude; but, contrary to the PC's account of 1981, these groups of officers should be acting under orders at all times, and these orders should ensure that they use the minimum amount of force that is necessary.

## Power of arrest

It is often said that, in granting police officers wide-ranging powers to arrest and detain people suspected of having committed various offences, we (the people) place a heavy reliance on their honesty and judgement. It is, indeed, often stressed to recruits at training school that to deprive someone of his liberty is to take a grave step, and we have already pointed out in Chapter XIV that in many cases the experience of being arrested is a more unpleasant and disturbing thing than the penalty exacted by the courts in the case of a conviction. This is not a comment on any bad behaviour by the police: it is so primarily because it comes as a shock to most people to be deprived of their liberty for any appreciable length of time (where the sentence of the courts will often be at worst a fine rather than imprisonment), because the process of being arrested and questioned is at best deeply humiliating and because police stations are at best an unpleasant environment for those at the receiving end.

Where the police make an arrest under a warrant the decision is not entirely theirs. In a few cases a private individual has applied for the warrant, though in most cases it is the police who made the application; either way, the warrant is proof that a body outside the police force is satisfied that adequate grounds for the arrest exist. However, the great majority of arrests are made without a warrant - in only a handful of the 100 cases of arrest covered in this research was a warrant involved. The police derive their powers of arrest without a warrant from a wide range of Acts of Parliament and from common law. The common principles underlying these powers are that the police may arrest someone who is in the act of committing a specified offence (partly in order to stop them) and that they may arrest someone whom they 'reasonably suspect' has committed a specified offence. The question of what amounts to proper grounds for reasonable suspicion is very complex, but the essential point is that the evidence required is much less than a court would require to convict. In many cases, therefore, an arrest is regarded as a step in the process of bringing a case to court. It is fully accepted that at the time of arrest the constable may not have all of the evidence required to secure a conviction and in fact the arrest itself and the subsequent questioning of the suspect in custody are seen as one of the means whereby this evidence may be obtained.

It is easy to see why the law and criminal procedure have developed broadly in this way. In most circumstances, enforcement of the law would be impossible if the police had to have enough evidence to secure a conviction before they could make an arrest. At the same time, it would clearly be intolerable if there were no constraints on the police in deciding whom to arrest (in other words, if they could just arrest anyone). The law has therefore tried to develop a set of criteria sufficient to justify arrest that are much weaker than those required for conviction but which will nevertheless set an effective limit to the exercise of discretion by the police.

However, the constraints imposed by the formal limitation of powers of arrest are not, perhaps, as great as most people think. Without going into the considerable case law on the subject, it will be generally accepted that the criterion of 'reasonable suspicion' is fairly weak and (perhaps inevitably) vague. Perhaps more important, the likely consequences where a police officer does arrest someone without reasonable suspicion are not very grave. Such an officer will not have committed a criminal offence. If it is shown that the arrest was not lawful, then the suspect will not be convicted on any charge arising from the affair. The person may bring a civil action for wrongful arrest against the Commissioner; even setting aside the financial risks involved in doing this and the difficulty of establishing evidence where (as is usually the case) there are no independent witnesses, if such an action is successful there will simply be an award of damages to the person which will be paid out of police funds. Any penalty for the individual officer involved would depend on the working of the internal discipline system.

The best way of putting this is to say that the constraints imposed by law on police officers in this field operate in a very indirect manner. The officer has to bear in mind that if he is seen to have exceeded his powers of arrest he will spoil his chances of getting a conviction. The Force at a senior level may see successful actions for wrongful arrest as seriously damaging to its reputation and (therefore) its ability to achieve objectives to do with law enforcement; to that extent, the management of the Force may see it as being in their own interest to discourage officers from exceeding their powers. All the same, the chance that an individual officer will get into difficulty through exceeding his powers of arrest in a particular case is probably low, though a persistent pattern of behaviour of this kind would be more likely to come to light.

What this shows is that the law on its own cannot be an adequate or sufficient control. The constraints imposed by the law have tangible consequences - administer an actual kick to the police - in a few cases only. In order to achieve a consistent pattern of policing behaviour such that the discretion to make arrests is reasonably exercised most of the time, it is necessary that police officers should genuinely accept the norms inherent in the law, and for this we are dependent on the way that the Force is supervised, managed and organised. Ultimately the sanction on which we rely is that a breakdown of confidence in the police will make it impossible for them to achieve their own objectives, but for this to work the management must be able to take a long view of the ultimate consequences of a failure to impose the constraints of the law on themselves.

We conclude from our observations that when making arrests most police officers do operate within 'working rules' which broadly approximate to powers of arrest defined by law. Among the 100 incidents involving arrests that we covered, there were four cases in which the powers of arrest were clearly exceeded. In two of these cases officers arrested someone who they thought had not committed an offence. In each of these cases the officers thought the person arrested knew something about an offence they were investigating and made the arrest in order to put pressure on the person to give evidence. They thought they were acting within their powers because, although they did not personally believe that the person arrested had committed an offence, this person was closely enough associated with it for the arrest to be justified (they could persuade a court that a reasonable man might have suspected them). In both of these cases, the officers personally thought it was 'fair' to make the arrest, though they accepted that their 'working rule' departed from the formal rule slightly. In the third case, two aliens were arrested on insufficient grounds (because they did not have their certificate of registration with them); the officers thought this was 'fair' but their 'working rule' departed widely from their formal powers in the matter, probably because they thought the chance of any 'come-back' would be minimal. In a fourth case, three black youths were arrested on suspicion of having committed a street robbery, but there was no evidence at all to connect them with the offence. It is worth describing each of these cases to illustrate the thinking of the officers involved.

In the first case a white boy aged 14 reported that a black boy had stolen a gold ring from him. DJS followed the whole investigation of this case, which was handled by a detective sergeant and a detective constable working together. They first had an appointment to see the loser with his father and a school friend who had been with him when the incident took place. The detectives questioned the two boys in the presence of the father. Their story was that they had gone to sit on an empty bus during the lunch break. Three black boys came along; one had a grievance against them because he thought they had taken his keys. In retaliation he told one of the white boys to give him the gold chain around his neck and threatened him with his fist until he did so. However, when he found it was only 'rolled gold' he gave it back. He then told the other white boy to give him his gold ring and when he did so went off with it accompanied by the other two black boys. It was the white boy's father who had reported the matter to police, and he pressed the officers very hard to take action. The black boys had been wearing overalls and were seen going back to the nearby training workshop, so there was some prospect of finding them.

The detectives went to the workshop with the boys, spoke to the organiser there, and walked round to see if the boys could identify the culprit. They did not see any of the three boys who had come onto the bus, but on leaving they did see a boy who, they said, had come off a second bus parked behind and had walked back to the workshop with the other three. This boy (Daniel) was brought out of the workshop and interviewed at length on the pavement. At first he said he had not been on the buses at all the previous day (when the incident took place). The detective sergeant told him that he knew he had been on the buses, that if he was cooperative and told him all he knew he would not get into any trouble, but that if he did not cooperate he might get into serious trouble. After about ten minutes Daniel said he had been on the buses but he had not seen anything and did not know anything about the theft of the ring. The detective constable now took up the questioning. He told Daniel that by his own admission he had earlier been lying, and that this gave him a low opinion of his character and made him think he might have had something to do with the theft (of course, the detectives did not really think this since the two white boys were quite positive that Daniel had not even boarded their bus). He went on, 'Anyway, we know that you've lied to us once, so we have to assume that you're going to lie to us again. In fact, we can't really trust a word that you say'. He suggested that the three black boys must have told him what had happened on the way back to the workshop. Daniel went on denying this for about five minutes. Then the detective sergeant took up the questioning again and became much more aggressive. He leaned over and spoke with his face about six inches from the boy's. After another five minutes of this, Daniel admitted that one of the boys had said something about taking a ring from the white boy because he had eaten his Swiss roll (the difference between this and the story of their taking his keys was never resolved). But under heavy pressure, Daniel insisted that he didn't know the names of any of the three black boys involved. After another five minutes the detectives began to get impatient. The sergeant said,

> So far, we've had three stages of the truth, but we still haven't got at the whole truth. First of all you lied to us when you told us that you weren't near the buses at all. Then you said that you had been near the buses but you didn't see anything or hear anything about a ring being taken. That was the second stage of lying, although it was a bit closer to the truth. Now you say that you didn't see anything but you asked the black boys what had happened and one of them told you about a ring having been taken because one of the white boys had eaten a Swiss roll. That's the third stage. It still isn't the complete truth, is it, Daniel?

Daniel again said, 'I've told you everything that I know, there's nothing else to say'. The sergeant then delivered a long speech.

> The boys picked you out because they knew that you'd been somewhere near the buses. They thought you'd got off a bus behind. They didn't say you were involved in taking the ring. They just said that you were around at the time. We didn't think that you were involved, but now you've kept on lying to us. You've told us all sorts of lies in three different stages,

we can't really trust a word that you say. You're really giving us no option. You're making us think that you may have been involved in some way. All that we want is for you to tell us the truth. Is that really so difficult? If you tell us the truth, you're not going to be in any trouble because you weren't involved in any way, but if you don't tell us the truth we're going to think that you may have been involved. Then you could find that you're in really big trouble. You're trying to protect the other boys at the workshop, aren't you? You don't want to squeal on them, do you? You're worried that they might cause you some trouble. Well, I can tell you that you'll get into a lot more trouble if you don't tell us the truth now, because we're going to have to take you down to the police station. I'll give you one more chance to tell us the truth, otherwise I'll have to take you straight down to the police station now.

Daniel still said there was nothing more to tell. The detective sergeant said, 'You're a very stupid and foolish young man. Now get into the car!' When they arrived at the charge room, the detective sergeant told the station officer that they had arrested 'this young man' because they thought he might have been involved with the theft of a ring. They said they would want to put him in a detention room. The station officer agreed without asking any questions, and left the room. The detective sergeant then said to Daniel,

You've got just three minutes before we put you in that detention room. Now wouldn't it have been much easier if you had told us the truth, and then you could have avoided all this? Now we've brought you here, we're going to have to telephone your mother and tell her to come, so she's going to have to know all about it. What's she going to say when she hears about it? You've got just three minutes before we put you in the detention room to tell us the truth. What is the name of the boy who told you about the ring being taken?

Daniel put his hand to his forehead and made sidewise glances. After a pause he said, 'I think he's known as Digby' and then he went on to tell the whole story in detail. It was clear that he was telling the truth because he said that Digby had first taken the gold chain and then given it back, which was something the detectives had never mentioned to him. In the meantime, the organiser of the workshop had managed to get back the ring by saying, 'I'm going to go away for five minutes and by the time I'm back, that ring is going to be on this shelf here'. Digby and one of his friends were arrested; Digby was charged (with robbery rather than theft), but his friend was released without charge. Daniel was released without charge after the detectives had taken a statement from him in the presence of his mother.

After Daniel had given his detailed account of what had happened (before his mother arrived) he was put in a detention room and the detectives went to the canteen with DJS to have something to eat. Over this lunch, DJS said to the detective sergeant, 'I just want to check on the technicalities of what has happened this morning so far. I am right in thinking that you have arrested Daniel, aren't I?' The sergeant agreed that they had arrested him. DJS said, 'As a matter of interest, what have you arrested him for?' The sergeant said, 'On suspicion of having stolen the ring, because we suspect him'. DJS said, 'But none of us think that Daniel did steal the ring, do we?' The sergeant said, 'It's a pain in the bum, really, it's a pain in the arse. But unfortunately he gave us no option'. The constable chimed in, 'He gave us no option at all'. When DJS looked a bit doubtful, the sergeant said,

> Look, in practical terms, I can arrest anyone. I could arrest you, David, now, if I wanted to. I wouldn't exactly have to invent anything. There'd be something I was trying to solve and I'd just have to say that I suspected that you had something to do with it, then I could arrest you.

At the end of the day the detective sergeant looked to DJS for some reassurance about the way he had handled the case. 'Tell me your honest opinion, David,' he said, 'was I fair or not?' In his own terms, and according to his own 'working rules', he considered the arrest of Daniel to have been entirely justified; also, although he was exaggerating when he said 'I can arrest anyone', he would see no difficulty in defending the decision to make the arrest within the terms of the law, although he regarded the possibility of any challenge as extremely remote. At the same time, he felt uneasy because he thought the arrest was not actually justified within the formal terms of the law, even though he would have no difficulty in making it look as if it were, and because DJS had pointed this out. When DJS spoke privately to Daniel's mother it became clear that she was disturbed by what had happened. When asked whether she thought Daniel had been treated reasonably, she first said she couldn't judge because she had not been there and had not yet heard Daniel's account of what had happened. Then she said it was difficult to say whether it was reasonable because something might seem reasonable to the police or to somebody else but not to her or to the person affected.

The second example essentially illustrates the same point as the first, although the crime (a stabbing) was a more serious one. It was interesting that in this case a detective sergeant pointedly avoided making the arrest of a girl who was with the attacker but took no part in the attack, though the girl was still eventually arrested. Two incidents were involved in the case. A black boy, Eddy, and his girlfriend, Miriam, had had repeated skirmishes and arguments with a particular family on a council estate. In the final incident, Eddy had hit the mother over the head with a tennis racket. She was not badly hurt, but had to have stitches in a wound. A very consistent set of witness statements showed that Eddy had been provoked by the mother, who had tried to hit him with a piece of wood but missed. The second incident happened when Eddy and Miriam were queuing up in sub-post office. Eddy started to mess about with the scales, and the sub-postmaster (a Pakistani) told him to leave the scales alone. Eddy at first ignored him, then, after an altercation, got out a knife and stabbed him in the stomach. The injury was serious enough to put the man in hospital for some time, especially since he was not in the best of health before the attack. Eddy and Miriam ran away in different directions afterwards, chased by police officers, who lost them in a nearby housing estate. Again, a very consistent set of witness statements described this incident, and one witness was present at both incidents and was certain that the same black boy was involved in each case. For a considerable time, the police did not know who this boy was, but while DJS was in the CID office, a woman came into the police station to offer information which pointed to Eddy as the person responsible for the stabbing in the post office.

After making enquiries to establish who Eddy was and where he lived, and after finding that he had a criminal record, the detective constable in charge of the case decided to arrest him and Miriam early one morning at their homes. The witness statements describing the two incidents made it perfectly clear that Miriam had not been involved at all except that she was with Eddy when both attacks took place. Since they were clearly not planned attacks, there was no reason to think that Miriam was in any way implicated. The detective decided to arrest her (without even pausing to think about the matter) because he thought she might give evidence that would incriminate her boyfriend and that she would be more likely to give evidence of this kind if she was in custody. He decided, when making the arrests, to mention only the first, less serious incident, in the hope that Eddy would first admit to this and then be in a mood to admit to the stabbing. DJS went with the party that went to Eddy's house and made the arrest without difficulty. At the same time a party went to Miriam's house, headed by a detective sergeant. When DJS's group got back to the police station with Eddy, they found that the other party had come back empty-handed. They had gone to the house and found that Miriam was there, but the detective sergeant had decided not to make the arrest. When he was asked about it he said it occurred to him that if the other party did not find Eddy at home, it would be embarrassing to have arrested Miriam, so he decided not to. The members of the other party thought this explanation was ridiculous. One of them told DJS that the detective sergeant was notorious for getting out of doing things and particularly for refusing to take responsibility. One of the Eddy party said to one of the Miriam party, 'Couldn't you persuade DS Hughes to see sense?' The other replied (tongue-in-cheek), 'I wasn't really very keen myself on arresting this poor young girl who hasn't done anything'. The detective constable in charge of the case had a private word with DS Hughes, who then agreed to go back and arrest Miriam, and his party duly set off again. However, whether or not he himself 'laid hands on' the girl (DJS was not present), he was careful to 'give the arrest' to another member of his party. DJS saw him disappearing fast from the charge room after the girl was brought in, without signing the 'persons at station' sheet. The others involved attributed DS Hughes' behaviour to laziness and a lack of moral fibre, but on talking to him later DJS found that he explicitly objected to the way some of his colleagues approached the job and considered that his own 'working rules' were different from theirs.

Eddy admitted to both crimes, and Miriam gave evidence that clearly implicated him. Although she was shaking with fear or shock during the whole of the questioning, she did not protest her innocence or query her arrest. It is important to emphasise that the detective constable handled the whole case - both the earlier investigation and the later questioning of Eddy and Miriam - in an impressively professional and effective manner and showed restraint throughout. The great majority of officers would share the thinking underlying his decision to arrest Miriam even though he definitely knew that she was not implicated (she was, of course, released without charge).

An entirely different kind of police behaviour is the arrest of people on the off chance that they might have committed a reported crime, but where there is no real evidence to connect them with it. From our observations, this is not at all common, but we did come across one clear case where it happened. JG was with an area car that answered a call to part of a council estate where a member of the public had seen three black boys 'lurking suspiciously' at the back of some flats. The witness had called the police by telephone and presumably gave no description of the boys: at any rate, no description was given over the radio to the area car crew. The area car, along with two panda cars, searched the area for about ten minutes. One of the pandas then reported (over the PR) that they had stopped three black boys. The local home beat officer who was out in plain clothes went to assist this panda and immediately made the decision to arrest the three boys. They put up no resistance. The eye witness refused to give evidence. From the police station records, nothing was found on the boys except a pen-knife (because JG was not present at the time of the arrest, we do not know whether they were searched then, but they probably were). There was, therefore, no prospect of charging the boys with any offence unless they would make an admission, which they did not. When JG questioned the home beat officer, he made it clear that the boys had been arrested only because they had been in the area mentioned by the member of the public who made the telephone call. There was nothing to show that the boys arrested were the same as those seen by the witness, except that there were three of them, they were black and they were boys: but since more than half of the families on the estate were black this was hardly significant. Furthermore, at the time of the arrest all the police had was a brief telephone call from a member of the public (who subsequently refused to cooperate any further) and this witness did not describe anything that amounted to clear evidence that an offence was being committed ('lurking suspiciously' could mean 'just being there' or 'quietly going home'). Presumably the home beat officer hoped that the boys would 'put their hands up' to something under questioning - though what offence he thought they might admit to remained unclear. The boys were later released without charge.

The fourth incident in which powers of arrest were exceeded happened when JG was with an 'aliens squad', whose main objective is to catch people who entered the country illegally or have stayed longer than their terms of entry allowed. An arrest was made by a PC who was not a member of this squad but was based at the same police station, was aware of their activity and made the arrest because he thought the squad might be interested in the people arrested. He had stopped two Iranians in their car and arrested them on finding that they did not have their 'certificate of registration' with them, though they had been required on entering the country to register with the police within seven days. JG was not present at the time of the arrest and only caught up with the case in the charge room after the Iranians had been questioned for some time. It was not clear exactly why the PC had made the arrest. Under the immigration acts aliens who have to register with the police are required to produce their certificate of registration when required to do so by a constable, or to bring it in to a police station within 48 hours if they cannot produce it at the time. There is clearly no power to arrest an alien who does not immediately produce the certificate. There is a power to arrest someone who is reasonably suspected of having committed one of various offences against the immigration acts (for example, illegally entering the country or overstaying). There was no reason to suspect that the Iranians had committed any such offence, except that they did not have their certificate of registration with them, but that cannot be admitted as a reason, since there is a provision for the certificate to be produced within 48 hours. It is fair to say, therefore, that there was no valid reason for arresting these Iranians at all. Checks with the Home Office register showed that they were legally in Britain and they were released without charge. The officer dealing with the matter (a member of the aliens squad and not the arresting officer) spoke to them brusquely as he prepared to release them, although they were polite and apologetic. He did not apologise for the arrest: instead he gave them a lecture about the need to carry their registration certificates at all times.

Although we have little direct evidence about it, an entirely different kind of circumstance in which we believe that police officers quite often exceed their formal powers of arrest is during outbreaks of public disorder. We argued in the last section that at such times officers apply a different set of 'working rules' from their usual ones. This probably applies to the decision to arrest as well as to the use of force (which was discussed in the last section). The clearest evidence that we have of this is the arrest of Stephen Small, a member of our research team, during the 'Black People's Day of Action' in March 1981. The full circumstances are explained in volume II of the original edition, but the best explanation of his arrest is that he was in a place where clashes between the police and demonstrators were taking place. A number of officers with whom DJS discussed the incident seemed to think that if the researcher was in the area where the 'trouble' was taking place then he naturally had a good chance of being arrested regardless of what he was actually doing. Unfortunately it is extremely difficult to make observations of exactly what happens leading up to an arrest in the confused circumstances of public disorder, and because of this difficulty we have no further firm evidence on this matter. There was a case where a number of football supporters had caused a disturbance late on a Saturday afternoon by shouting, running down pavements and kicking litter bins (none of them was actually violent). DJS did not get to the scene in time to see the incident, but he later spoke at length to a 14-year old boy who had been arrested for threatening behaviour. When DJS asked what had happened, the boy (Vince) said a 'copper' had taken his 'stick' out and run at him, so 'naturally' he had turned and fled, and after being chased for a while was grabbed from behind and bundled into a van. The conversation continued as follows.

DJS: Was the one who grabbed you the same as the one who came at you with his stick out?
Vince: No, it was two different coppers. The silly thing is I didn't used to hate coppers until today.
DJS: What were you doing just before you saw the copper coming at you?
Vince: I was just standing on the pavement with some other Arsenal supporters.
DJS: Why did you go to X Street in the first place?
Vince: To kick the shit out of the Spurs supporters, because they're a load of cunts. They are, they're cunts, and I don't care what anybody says.
DJS: Did you find any Spurs supporters in X Street?
Vince: No, unfortunately.
DJS: Were you fighting with anyone when the police came?
Vince: No, because we didn't find them, did we?
DJS: Were you running about making a fuss?
Vince: No, we were just standing on the pavement.
DJS: Have you ever been arrested before?
Vince: No.

DJS: If that is true things probably won't be too bad for you.

Vince: Yes, but my father's going to have to come, isn't he? I probably won't be allowed to go to football for the rest of this year.

DJS: Well, I wouldn't let you if I were your father.

Vince: Do you work here?

DJS: No, I'm observing what goes on so I can write a book about it.

Vince: Well, I suppose someone's got to do it.

Seeing this conversation going on in the charge room, the relief inspector became obviously nervous (though he could not hear what was being said). DJS told the inspector that the boy was upset because he was frightened of his father, and asked to speak to the arresting officer. This turned out to be a sergeant, who behaved in a very stiff and formal manner (he came from another Division and was not previously known to DJS). DJS read through the incident report book (which gave the sergeant's account of the arrest) while talking to him. The report said that he (the sergeant) saw Vince standing on the pavement and 'shouting obscenities', in the company of a large group of youths. The sergeant remonstrated with him, and Vince shouted further abuse and ran off. The sergeant chased after him and caught him, and as Vince was still 'behaving in an unseemly manner', he found it necessary to arrest him for threatening behaviour, in order to prevent a breach of the peace. The report also said that as the sergeant got out of the van he found an elderly man lying on the pavement near where Vince was, and helped him to his feet. It was vaguely implied that Vince might have knocked the man over, but when DJS asked the sergeant about it, he said that he didn't 'honestly' know whether Vince had anything to do with the elderly man being on the pavement. Later the report said that as Vince ran off, his fist swung close to the sergeant's face, without hitting him. When DJS questioned the sergeant about this, he said that 'quite honestly' he didn't know whether Vince had really intended to hit him, but he didn't really think so. It became clear that both of these details were just bits of colouring that might help to make it look as if Vince had been behaving badly.

Vince's parents had not yet come. DJS said that he would like to be present when Vince was formally dealt with in the presence of his parents. Whether by mistake or deliberately, DJS was not informed when the parents arrived and therefore missed the formal procedure. The arresting officer was not present either, but the station officer said that Vince seemed to be terrified of his father, had acted in a very contrite manner, had 'more or less admitted to having done something he shouldn't have', and had said he was prepared to admit to an offence in order to get a caution instead of being charged.

DJS formed the strong impression that Vince was arrested because he was with a group of boys some of whom were behaving in a threatening manner and not because of anything he had himself done, though it will be evident that the matter cannot be proved one way or the other. Vince seemed to be contrite because that afternoon he had been looking for trouble, but he seemed to be telling the truth when he said he hadn't found any. Faced with an angry father who immediately accepted the police version of what had happened, it is not surprising at all that Vince was prepared to admit to an offence, especially since this would allow him to escape with a caution (bearing in mind his feeling that he was, broadly speaking, in the wrong because he had been up to no good).

It is difficult to generalise from our findings about how the police interpret their powers of arrest. Certainly, if we consider all arrests in a single lump, it is clear that the police were acting within their powers to make the arrests in the great majority of cases. However, we believe that the case of the stolen ring and the post office stabbing are quite typical of their kind, and that people who are known not to have committed an offence will normally be arrested where they have information about an offence that they are unwilling to divulge, in order to put pressure on them to divulge it. We also believe that anyone who is close to the seat of a public disturbance is at risk of being arrested, regardless of what he is actually doing as an individual. However, these are informed opinions rather than fully substantiated conclusions.

## Cautions

The Judges' rules are a set of guidelines to police officers questioning suspects or people in custody. Although they do not have the force of law, they have an influence in the sense that the courts are generally unwilling to convict where it is shown that any of the Judges' rules are broken.

One of the principles underlying these rules is that while the police are entitled to question anybody (whether in custody or not) as part of an investigation to find out whether a crime has been committed, or who committed it, the person being questioned is entitled to know whether he is being treated as a suspect or not. One of the chief reasons why he is entitled to know this is that he has the right to remain silent so as to avoid incriminating himself. Accordingly, the Judges' rules set out the following formal procedure.

> II.  As soon as a police officer has evidence which would afford reasonable grounds for suspecting that a person has committed an offence, he shall caution that person or cause him to be cautioned before putting to him any questions or further questions, relating to that offence.
> The caution shall be in the following terms:-
> 'You are not obliged to say anything unless you wish to do so but what you say may be put into writing and given in evidence.'

Rule III provides that a similar caution should be given when a person is charged with an offence or informed that he may be prosecuted for an offence. However, since it is only in exceptional circumstances that questioning is (formally) allowed to continue after charging, the Rule III caution has less significance than the Rule II caution.

It used to be thought that the observance of these rules was of paramount importance to our system of justice. However, research by Barrie Irving has shown that suspects (even after having been cautioned) virtually never 'exercise' their right of silence, because the psychological pressure brought to bear by being in custody and under interrogation (however correctly it is conducted) is overwhelming to most people. In the course of our research we never saw anyone remain silent under questioning. Furthermore, a high proportion of suspects made statements incriminating themselves or provided incriminating information in answer to questions.

In the terms explained earlier in this chapter, we would describe the Judges' rules on cautions as 'presentational'. They exist to give the appearance of a kind of balance and fairness that cannot be achieved in practice (as long as the evidence required to arrest is much less than that required to convict). People who are arrested are, in many cases, being put under pressure to provide incriminating evidence, and the recital of the caution by a police officer does little, if anything, to change this.

It follows that there is little motive for the police not to caution people, except laziness. In practice we found that officers rarely cautioned people formally on arrest (though in the majority of cases they should have done, because they had, at that stage, reasonable grounds for suspecting that the person had committed an offence, and they nearly always asked some questions before getting back to the police station). On the other hand, we found that officers nearly always cautioned suspects at the beginning of a formal interrogation at the police station, wrote the caution down as part of the record of the interview, and got the suspect to initial it. Suspects seemed to take this as a piece of ritual or administration (like giving their date of birth or home address for the umpteenth time) and generally showed no sign of noting the content of the caution. We found that Rule III cautions were always given when a person was charged or told he would be reported for an offence.

An important point to notice is that officers do not use a set formula of words when making arrests other than the caution, and they often do not use the caution. Consequently, it can be unclear even to the researcher whether or not someone has been arrested. For example, police from an aliens squad were told by a college that one of their students, a Nigerian girl, was probably an overstayer. The officers found the student at the college; she said that all her documents were in order but did not have them with her. The officers took her to her flat where she showed them the documents which were, in fact, in order. The police then left. Whether or not this girl was arrested depends on whether she would have gone with the officers to her flat had she not been required to do so. (The officers left her without offering any kind of apology for disrupting her day.) A second example arose from a search (with warrant) of a yard apparently used for storing goods, which the police thought might be connected with large-scale robberies. The owner, who lived in a caravan on the site with his family, was taken into the police station, where he was questioned, but there was never any kind of specific evidence against him, the officers did not give any apparent indication that they were arresting him, and he seemed to be 'agreeing' to go in to answer some questions; he was not recorded on a 'person at station' sheet, which means there was no official record of his having been arrested. On the other hand, he would probably not have gone to the police station to answer questions if he thought he could avoid doing so, and if that interpretation is correct he was, in fact, arrested.

From many of the cases that we have followed it is evident that the suspect did not understand the procedures. A necessary first step in doing something about this would be to make it clear to people at the time of the arrest that they are being arrested, and why. That this is often not done at present seems to be partly because there is no prescribed formula of words to be used when making an arrest, partly because of sloppiness about the use of the cautioning formula, and partly because officers vaguely feel that there is more pressure on suspects if they do not entirely understand what is going on.

## Evidence
### Arresting officer
For various reasons, working groups of police officers tend to share out arrests between them. There may be one or two members of the group who tend to make many more arrests than the others, but do not have the time to 'process' all of the resulting prisoners. Because of their different private circumstances, some members of the group will usually need or welcome the overtime associated with 'processing' arrests more than others. Young or inexperienced members of the group will tend to be 'given' arrests for training. As mentioned in Chapter XIV, if one member of the group is under threat from the management because he has not made enough arrests, other members will 'give him' some.

There are ways of sharing work and boosting the 'figures' of an officer that do not involve adjustment of evidence. The same arrest may be 'shown' on the charge sheet to several officers without affecting the account of how the arrest was made, and there is no reason, in principle, why an officer other than the one who made the arrest, should not 'process' the prisoner, without the evidence being altered, as happens not infrequently. However, work sharing can lead to the adjustment of evidence in some cases. A good example was a case observed by DJS where two white

473

teenage boys were arrested as they broke out of a house where they had been committing a burglary. DJS was with an area car crew who had answered a call to 'suspects on premises'. When they arrived, another area car was already there. Three of the four officers went to the back of the house, while the fourth, an older man on the point of retirement (not one of DJS's crew) remained at the front with DJS. After a few minutes the glass panel of the front door was smashed from the inside and two boys came out (one of them badly cutting his leg in the process). The older officer grabbed hold of the two boys one with each arm and they offered no resistance. He stayed there holding them until the other officers returned from the back. One boy was then put in each area car and there was a little conference between the policemen. The older PC explained that he was retiring in a week and did not want to deal with the 'bodies' because that would mean going to court after his retirement. One of his crew was a WPC who looked fairly young and inexperienced. She was asked if she wanted to 'have the bodies' but declined. DJS's crew were then asked if they wanted them and readily agreed - they seemed to be keen to get the 'figures'. The other crew took one of the boys to the local police station and then left, so that DJS's crew had to deal with the whole of the 'processing'. After the boys had been charged, DJS sat with the PCs while they wrote up their incident report books and the case history folders. They falsified these records to make it look as if they had 'made the arrests'; this meant they had to say they were at the front of the house when the boys broke out, and were the first to lay hands on them. They consulted DJS about the details as they wrote the reports and one said, 'I'm going to have to change this a bit to make it that we arrested them'. They had no compunction at all about doing this because the boys had been caught in the act, they had subsequently admitted to the burglary, they seemed to have no complaints about the way they had been treated and the officers thought that who had laid hands on the boys had no evidential significance.

In other cases that we observed, the swapping of prisoners between officers did not involve the adjustment of evidence. JG was with an area car crew of three officers when the driver decided to stop a car containing five black youths after he saw one of them throw a 'reefer' out of the window. The driver carried out all of the questioning and searching, made the decision to arrest the driver (for possession of cannabis) and physically led him to the area car. However, it was the operator who did all the paperwork and was shown as the arresting officer. The driver commented that he did not need the overtime for court appearances. 'My wife's in the Job and our salaries are quite enough without overtime. All overtime would mean is that I see her less.'

In the case of a stolen ring described earlier in this chapter, the two detectives were sitting in the canteen having a meal with DJS and wondering what 'transport' they could use to go and arrest the two boys named by Daniel as having stolen the ring. A group of

Special Patrol Group officers came into the canteen, and the detective constables suggested that they might be persuaded to bring the boys back in their van after the detectives had made the arrests. The detective sergeant thought that was a 'dumb' idea. 'They'd nick the bodies from us, wouldn't they?' he said. 'Oh, I wouldn't have thought so,' said the constable. 'You bet they would, said the sergeant, so the idea was squashed.

This swapping of prisoners between officers does not always involve the adjustment of evidence and when it does the adjustments do not usually seem significant to the officers involved and do not usually affect matters that are vital to the case. Nevertheless, it establishes a habit among officers of regarding evidence as to some extent flexible and negotiable; it is apt to make them defensive in court; if discovered in court it will destroy the case and erode the confidence of the courts in police evidence; and if officers are used to making what they regard as innocuous adjustments to evidence, it is only a small step for them to take before they make adjustments that affect the essence of a case.

## Questioning of juveniles

The administrative directions to the Judges' rules state that 'As far as practicable, children (whether suspected of a crime or not) should only be interviewed in the presence of a parent or guardian, or, in their absence, some person who is not a police officer and is of the same sex as the child'. Within the Judges' Rules, a 'child' is a person under the age of 17. Our observations show that this direction is frequently ignored. In all, or nearly all, cases where a child has been arrested, police officers do succeed in getting a parent, guardian or other responsible adult to come to the police station (often a social worker if no parent or guardian is available). However, the children are often questioned before the responsible adult arrives or separately from the adult when the adult is at the police station. This happened in several of the cases already described (for example, Daniel in the case of the stolen ring, the three boys wrongly suspected of having snatched a woman's handbag). Where the whole of an interview is being taken down in contemporaneous notes for use as evidence in court, or where the child is giving a statement, a responsible adult is almost always present, because the procedures require that those present sign the contemporaneous notes or statement form, and the evidence will almost certainly be treated as inadmissible if this is not done. However, lengthy questioning may well take place beforehand, and if so it is normally during these earlier sessions that efforts are made (to which the responsible adult might object) to make the child 'come across'. In that case, by the time that the formal questioning takes place or a statement is taken in the presence of the adult, what the child is going to say has already essentially been settled. In most of the cases we are talking about, it would be quite 'practicable' (to use the word in the administrative directions) for all of the questioning to happen while the adult is there.

In some cases there could be some doubt about what constitutes 'questioning' or an 'interview' as opposed to a conversation between police officers and the child. No doubt the directions should not be interpreted to mean that an officer should not talk to the child at all unless the adult is there. However, in a number of the cases we have observed (including the two mentioned above) there was no doubt that what happened constituted 'questioning' or 'interrogation', with considerable pressure being put on the child.

The presence of an adult is certainly important, since officers tend to be more restrained in their manner and questioning method when an adult is there than otherwise. However, it would be dangerous to assume that this is necessarily an effective guarantee of fairness, for two reasons. First, the adult usually has little or no knowledge of what kinds of approach or questioning are allowable and consequently says nothing and does not interfere with any questioning or behaviour by the officers that he disapproves of. Thus, it is common for the adult to acquiesce in hectoring questioning, thinking it is 'normal', or to sign the record of an interview without drawing attention to inaccuracies in what has been recorded. Secondly, it is not uncommon for the adult to be 'on the side of' the police: the parent's presence may often bring an additional pressure to bear on the child, if the parent has made up his mind that the child is guilty.

## Recording of interviews and statements

It should be clear from what has just been said that many interrogations or interviews are not recorded at all. The Judges' rules require that 'when after being cautioned a person is being questioned, or elects to make a statement, a record shall be kept of the time and place at which any such questioning or statement began and ended and of the persons present'. Our experience is that interviews quite often take place without any record being kept (for example, the crucial questioning of Daniel took place before he was put in the detention room, but there was no official record to show that it had taken place). But even if the rule is adhered to, there may still be no record of what was said during the interview, and certainly many interviews take place without any notes being kept, at the time, of what is said. It is usual for there to be an informal exchange, or a series of informal exchanges, between officers and the suspect before the final interview takes place at which a record is kept. Officers do not generally use what was said in the earlier, informal interviews as evidence to be presented to a court, but they may be able to overcome the suspect's resistance to questioning at that stage, so that the later, formal interview will be more fruitful; also, they may use the informal interviews to obtain information (for example about other crimes that the suspect knows about) that is useful to them but which they will not plan to use in court. Of course, they may use evidence from informal interviews in court in some cases, for example if a suspect makes an admission in the car on the way back to the police station, or on the way to the cell, but later withdraws the admission during formal questioning.

There are procedures for recording when an interview began and ended and who was present, even though a record of what was said is not to be kept, but these procedures are far from foolproof. Where a CID officer takes a prisoner out of a cell to interview him, the station officer should record the fact, and usually does, and the CID officer should make a note about the interview in his notebook; we did not see CID officers make a record at the time, but they may have done so later. However, it is fairly easy for a CID officer to talk to a prisoner in his cell without any record being kept and, as already pointed out, suspects are often questioned quite extensively (by uniform as well as CID officers) after they get to the police station but before being put in a cell, and there is usually no record that these interviews took place.

Where a detailed record is kept, it will be either in the form of a statement, or in the form of a verbatim record of the questions and answers. In the case of statements under caution (that is, by people suspected of having committed an offence) the judges' rules state that they should always be given the option of writing out the statement themselves. In practice, statements are written out by a police officer in the vast majority of cases; although suspects are often not explicitly asked whether they wish to write out the statement themselves, it is usually fairly clear that they do not wish to (because they would not be able to cope). The rules state that 'Whenever a police officer writes the statement, he shall take down the exact words spoken by the person making the statement, without putting any questions other than such as may be needed to make the statement coherent, intelligent and relevant to the material matters; he shall not prompt him'. It would be extremely difficult for officers to adhere to this rule in a literal sense. The exact words spoken by the person are not usually 'coherent, intelligent and relevant to material matters', since most people do not have the skills required to dictate a statement that meets these requirements. Consequently, statements seldom even approximate to 'the exact words spoken by the person making the statement'. What happens, in practice, is that the officer has previously spoken to the person at length and formed a 'draft' in his own mind of what the person is saying. He then suggests sentences to the person as he writes, making changes in response to the person's observations and asking further questions as he goes along. Thus the statement (inevitably) arises from a process of interaction between the officer and the suspect. While this is often done skilfully and in good faith by the officer, because of the nature of the encounter he cannot avoid making suggestions to the suspect, and it is simply not true that statements are spontaneous accounts given in the suspect's own words. Of course, the officer is in a stronger position than the suspect because he is aware of the evidential significance of different emphases and forms of words, while the suspect may not be. We conclude that when the officer takes a statement in good faith and with the intention of being fair, he will still tend to frame it in a way that is helpful to the prosecution and if he wishes to bend the evidence to some extent, it is fairly easy for him to do so while still drafting the statement in a form that the suspect will be ready to approve.

Where a verbatim record is kept of the questions and answers, the interview is often handled by two officers, one to ask the questions and the other to keep the record. This procedure tends to be very stilted and artificial. Most of these interviews are carried out by junior officers (generally constables) who are not highly literate. Quite often they write painfully slowly, have to stop to consider spelling and grammar, miss out words, are not sure how to phrase things, and so on. By contrast, they usually speak vividly and fluently and often show a quick intelligence which does not easily translate onto paper. This means that they find the process of writing down the questions and answers extremely inhibiting. There usually has to be a long pause after each question is asked for it to be written down before the suspect is allowed to answer. If the suspect speaks naturally, he has to be stopped repeatedly in mid-flow while the scribe tries to write down a version of what he has said. When we have watched these interviews, what has been written has usually been a reasonably fair indication of what was said, though by no means an accurate verbatim record. But, even to achieve this level of accuracy, it is necessary for the flow of the interview to be completely disrupted so that it is quite impossible for the questioner to pursue a particular line of questioning swiftly and effectively as soon as an opening is indicated by a previous answer. It is, of course, because of the very stilted nature of these formal interviews that officers often carry out informal interviews first in which the substance of the suspect's story is established. In many cases their job would be impossible if they did not work in this way. On occasion, officers also lapse into the informal mode in the middle of a formal interview: that is, they ask some questions that are not recorded and enter into a rapid exchange of question and answer which there is no time to write down, then revert to the formal procedure incorporating any material that has emerged in the informal interlude.

It is worth giving two examples to illustrate the way in which the content and wording of statements can be influenced by the officer taking them. The first arose in the case of the post office stabbing already described. The detective constable handling the case had arranged for Miriam to be arrested because she was the girlfriend of Eddy, who was suspected of having committed the crime and was thought to have been with him at the time. This detective was one of the most skilful officers we came across at his rank and was basically fair-minded in his approach to the case. After Eddy had admitted to the stabbing, Miriam was brought from her cell to the interviewing room and the detective questioned her informally for about half an hour without any record being kept. Miriam answered quite readily and clearly incriminated Eddy by the answers she gave. The detective then began to write out a summary of what she had said (Miriam's 'statement'), reading it out as he went along. In general it was an accurate summary, though mainly in the detective's words rather than Miriam's (after all, he had spoken to her for half an hour without taking notes and couldn't in any case remember exactly what she had said). During the questioning, the detective had asked Miriam, 'Would you say that Eddy is quick to get angry with people?' Miriam said, 'Yes, he argues with people if they pick on him'. (DJS was not taking notes, so this is only an approximation to what was said and not a true verbatim record.) When the detective came to write the statement, he put down 'Eddy gets annoyed when someone picks on him'. When he read this out, Miriam explained further by saying that Eddy would argue in words with somebody who attacked him in words, and that if somebody wanted to fight him, he would fight them back, but if somebody attacked him in words he would not fight them physically. The detective did not put this down. When he read through the whole statement again, at the end, Miriam drew attention to the sentence for a second time, and repeated her qualification, but the detective still made no change and Miriam eventually signed the statement as it was. The detective did not ostensibly put any pressure on Miriam about this: he just ignored the distinction she was trying to make.

A second case observed by DJS was to do with the smashing of the glass panel of a pub door by one of two young men whom the publican had tried to shut out. DJS was in a general purpose car with a PC with seven years' service when he was stopped by a young Arab man, who said that two young men had just broken the window of a pub nearby. The PC took the Arab into the back of the car so that he could show him the pub and identify the culprits if necessary. He did not take a detailed description of the two men from the Arab. He got to the pub and spoke to the publican, who was very excited and told him which way the young men had gone: he did not ask the publican to describe them in detail. He got back into the car and went in the direction indicated for about 100 yards, when the Arab man pointed out two young men on the pavement. He got out of the car and arrested one of them, while the other ran away. The PC sent out a message on the PR and the area car arrived within about one minute and searched the area for the young man who had escaped, but without success. The PC also called up the van, which took the suspect back to the police station. He then went back to the pub, picked up the publican, who was willing to make a statement, took the Arab back to the hotel where he was staying and left him there without taking down a note of his full name or establishing how to contact him (he would be leaving the country before long). He went on to the police station and left the publican in an interviewing room while he spoke to the suspect, who said that he did not know the man who

479

had run away, had not been with him, but had been about to go into the pub when he (the one who had run away) smashed the glass panel.

The PC's problem was that he didn't know whether the man he had arrested or the one who had run away was the one who had smashed the glass panel; he assumed (probably correctly) that one of them had, and that they had been drinking together. After consulting with the station officer he decided to take a statement from the publican. He soon found out that the publican was a very confused witness. His story was that he had seen two obviously drunk young men heading towards his pub as he stood by the door at opening time. Because he had just been sawing a plank of wood in the cellar he happened to be holding a saw in his hand (an obvious lie). As he saw the two men come along the pavement, he put the latch on the door to stop them getting in. They approached the door, looking very ugly. One said, 'I'm coming in' and the other took off his anorak, wrapped it around his right arm and shoulder and elbowed in the glass. The publican was very frightened, thought they were coming to get him, and tried to hit one (the one who said 'I'm coming in') with the saw on the shoulder and across the body. The men then went off and the police car arrived shortly afterwards.

This story emerged from informal questioning of the publican, but when the PC started to write out the statement he found that the publican gave different descriptions of the two men at different times. After writing a few sentences of the statement he found he had something of a description and went off to look at the suspect in the cell because he couldn't remember what he looked like. He could not remember, for example, whether or not the man had a moustache or what colour his anorak was. He came back after finding that he was wearing a green anorak and asked the publican which of the two men was wearing a green anorak. When something else occurred to him he went back to look at the suspect again and then returned to ask a further question. He went back to look at the suspect three times altogether. After this had been going on for about an hour he thought of asking the publican whether he had torn the man's anorak with his saw. The publican wasn't sure, but thought he might have done, so the PC went off to see if his suspect had a torn anorak, which he hadn't. DJS had to point out to him that the man the publican had hit with the saw was the one who had <u>not</u> smashed the glass panel, as the PC had become confused about this. He eventually completed a statement for the publican which gave descriptions of the two men that coincided with what the publican had said at certain times but conflicted with what he had said at others. DJS pointed out to him that it contained an unfinished sentence (where he had broken off to have a look at the suspect). The publican signed it without reading it or having it read over to him and the PC crossed out the unfinished sentence afterwards. The man in custody could not be clearly identified as either of the men described in the statement, so had to be released without charge.

The main characteristic of this investigation was incompetence. The PC should have got a description of the two men from both the Arab and the publican as soon as possible. He lost track of the Arab altogether and by the time he had finished questioning the publican 1½ hours had elapsed so that he had forgotten what the men looked like. By his procedure in taking the statement, the PC created a strong danger that there would be a false identification. Far from taking down the description in the man's own words (which were admittedly confusing) he did his best to get him to give a description that would fit the man in custody. The main reason why he did not succeed in getting such a description was that he was confused himself about what this man looked like, and he was also confused about which of the two men that the publican was describing was the one he said had smashed the glass panel.

It is also worth giving an example of an interview that was recorded in question and answer form, but where a part of the interview was left unrecorded because the approach used by the detectives at that point was 'improper'. DJS followed a major incident squad set up to investigate a killing that happened in a fight outside a pub. Eight young men had been arrested shortly after the killing, and DJS accompanied a pair of detectives (one a constable and the other a sergeant) while they interviewed two of these suspects. Evidence given by several of the young men arrested suggested that Jack (the second of the suspects to be interviewed in the presence of DJS) had picked up a leather coat on leaving the pub and refused to give it back to its owner (a blond youth) when asked. The fight started when the blond youth hit Jack; it involved a considerable number of young men. There was fighting outside the pub at the front (where the killing took place), in the car park at the back and in a garage building opening off the car park. There was no evidence so far that Jack had been involved in the fighting or that he had hit or kicked the man who had died. Jack had already been interviewed once. He denied that he had refused to hand the coat back to the blond youth; he said he had offered the coat back when asked but been hit in return, that he had remained outside the back entrance of the pub while the fighting took place and taken no part in it, and that on leaving he had seen a man lying on the ground at the front of the pub but had not seen anyone hit or kick him. The detectives assumed that he knew much more than he had said about what had happened but they had an open mind about whether he had been involved in the fighting. A slow and stilted interview was carried out with the questions and answers being written down in full and reasonably accurately. Jack told exactly the same story as before. He rejected all suggestions that he had taken part in the fighting, that he had been anywhere but outside the back entrance while the fighting took place, that he had seen who hit or kicked the man who had died, or that he had heard anything more about it from the

481

others involved (with whom he had talked as they walked away from the pub). When the formal interview had continued for about half an hour without producing anything new, the detective who was doing the writing put down his pen and said, 'We have been speaking to your friend Harry, and Harry has told us a different story from the one you are telling us. He says you were involved in the fighting and that you went to the garage and that you were involved in a fight with the blond boy there'. Jack said this was not true. The detective went on, 'We have been talking to other people as well as your friend Harry and we are building up a picture that is quite different from what you are saying'. Jack still insisted that his version was correct. The detective then said, 'It suits us fine if you go on like that. We don't mind, because we have other information and what you are saying is just making matters worse for you'. None of this was recorded. It made no difference to Jack, who did not change his story.

This example shows why many police officers are opposed to tape-recording of interviews. On one occasion, DJS suggested to a chief-superintendent that if interviews were tape-recorded they could then be far more flowing so that it would be easier for the officer to get the information he wanted. He replied, 'The problem is that the recordings would show hints of impropriety that would then have the cases thrown out'. The example that he gave was that it would be easy for the suspect to smack the table and say 'Stop hitting me!', but a more real difficulty is that officers use interrogation tactics that would not be acceptable to the courts; as long as interviews are partially and manually recorded, this is largely concealed in the official records.

## Interrogation tactics

The Judges' rules state it as a general principle 'That it is a fundamental condition of the admissability in evidence against any person, equally of any oral answer given by that person to a question put by a police officer and of any statement made by that person, that it shall have been voluntary, in the sense that it has not been obtained from him by fear of prejudice or hope of advantage, exercised or held out by a person in authority, or by oppression'. In its notes on the Judges' rules, the Metropolitan Police instruction book adds, 'In addition to complying with the rules, interrogating officers should always try to be fair to the person who is being questioned, and scrupulously avoid any method which could be regarded as in any way unfair or oppressive'.

From our observations, we conclude that many police officers - probably a majority - do not take this to be a 'working rule', but rather treat it as an 'inhibitory rule'; they bear in mind the difficulty of getting a conviction if it is shown in court that evidence has been obtained 'by fear of prejudice or hope of advantage ... or by oppression', but they do not themselves believe that it is wrong to offer inducements or make threats in order to get someone to talk, and also they do not believe that their supervising officers seriously expect them to refrain from using threats and inducements. The rule, through the decisions of the courts, still exerts a restraining influence, but only to the extent that there is good evidence that threats or inducements were used. From our analysis of the way in which interviews and statements are recorded it should be clear that officers have good opportunities to make threats and inducements without this appearing in the official record.

We have already described several cases in which physical threats were made or bullying tactics used, together with two cases where people were arrested (although they were not suspected of any offence) so as to bring pressure to bear on them to give evidence. Of course, an interrogation of somebody in custody is inherently a situation in which the interrogator is putting pressure on the person to overcome his resistance to telling the truth. Although the Judges' rules do not face up to the issue, the real problem is to decide what kind and level of pressure is acceptable; it is absurd to pretend, as the rules appear to, that there should be no pressure at all. Thus, the behaviour of police officers can be explained partly as a response to the imposition of a rule which is out of step with the reality that they have to deal with. The detectives who arrested Daniel in the case of the stolen ring, and bullied him quite a bit, recognised that what they were doing was strictly against the rules, knew that they could make it look as if it was within the rules (and hence were not inhibited by the rules) yet wanted to be reassured that they had been 'fair', because they recognised a concept of 'fairness' underlying the rules and wanted to adhere to it even though they thought the rules themselves were impracticable.

However, where gross bullying tactics are used, the reasons tend to be entirely different. In the case, described in Chapter XV, where three black boys were (wrongly) suspected of taking a handbag, the motivation of the home beat officer (who was responsible for much of the oppressive questioning) was fairly clear. First, he considered that the boys were 'toe-rags' and 'knew' they had committed crimes; whether or not they had committed this crime was not very important to him; it was a matter of 'getting them for something'. Secondly, he had no questioning skills. He put his face two inches from the suspect's and shouted threats and abuse from that distance because more refined and effective questioning techniques were beyond his capacities.

A lack of skills in questioning is probably an extremely important factor. Another illustration of this was the questioning of Jack in the case of the killing outside a pub. DJS formed the strong impression that Jack was not telling the whole truth, but he was not being asked very penetrating questions. When they saw they were not getting anywhere the best the detectives could do was to pretend that other suspects had incriminated Jack and hope this would put pressure on him. They had to resort to this because they did not have the sharpness of wit required to work away at the small details of what Jack had said. Their lack of sharpness was vividly demonstrated during the two interviews they had previously carried out with another suspect, William. William maintained that he had taken no part in the fighting but said he had lost one of his shoes at the scene and that he had gone home with one shoe on and without the othe . The detectives knew that the dead man had been killed by a kick delivered to his head. In these circumstances it was highly significant that William said he had 'lost a shoe' (maybe the missing shoe had blood and hair on it). Also, William gave no explanation of <u>how</u> he came to lose his shoe if he had not been engaged in any fighting or other vigorous physical activity. Besides, it was hard to see why he should not have <u>picked up</u> his shoe again and put it on before going home, unless he had needed to get away from the scene as soon as possible (it's very uncomfortable to walk two miles with one shoe on and one shoe off). The detectives didn't notice the particular importance of missing shoes in a case where someone had been kicked to death, and they didn't see that they could work on William by getting him to explain <u>how</u> he had come to lose his shoe. It was partly because they couldn't see the soft spots in an account, where it was necessary to press for precise explanations, that these detectives tended to have to resort to making vague threats.

The rule quoted at the beginning of this section mentions 'hope of advantage' as well as 'fear of prejudice' and 'oppression'. The Metropolitan Police instruction book spells out what this means in the case of confessions, and this explanation applies equally to other evidence.

> If a person is induced to confess by some promise or threat by the prosecutor, a police officer or other person in authority, such as 'It will be better for you if you tell the truth' or 'You may see your wife if you tell me where you hid the stolen property', the confession is not admissable.

This is a field in which we have made rather few useful observations, but from those we have made we have formed the strong impression that it is accepted behaviour, especially among CID officers, to offer inducements to suspects to provide evidence. Where the bargaining power of the police officer derives from his ability to decide whether or not to prefer particular charges, it can be difficult to say whether the pressure is best described as a threat or an inducement. It is a threat if he says he will bring a certain charge against the suspect unless he comes forward with certain evidence or information, an inducement if he offers to waive a certain charge on the same condition. If the evidence that the suspect is to produce in return is to be used in court, then the threat or inducement has to be concealed for the evidence to seem admissable. Of course, in many cases the police officer does not plan to use the information in court. For example, the suspect may be able to tell the officer who he thinks did a particular robbery.

This (hearsay) evidence would probably be useless in court anyway, but it may be a very valuable starting point for the officer's investigation into the robbery. It may seem, therefore, that the officer who enters into a bargain of this kind (where the information he receives in return for not preferring a charge is to be used only as criminal intelligence) is not breaking any rule. However, this is not the case, because the general principles of the Judges' rules state 'That when a police officer who is making enquiries of any person about an offence has enough evidence to prefer a charge against that person for the offence, he should without delay cause that person to be charged or informed that he may be prosecuted for the offence'. According to the rules, therefore, a police officer must not say, 'I will not charge you with X if you tell me about Y' because he should have charged the suspect with X already if he had the necessary evidence.

We believe that most CID officers do not accept these principles as working rules. The true attitude of the CID emerges clearly from a conversation that DJS had with a detective inspector in charge of a CID squad. This was a thoughtful man, who took his job seriously, wanted to do was what 'fair' and 'right', but also wanted to catch criminals. The conversation began with a discussion about the relationship of the police with black people. The detective inspector said that he was not against black people and had some understanding of their problems. From the police point of view, the difficulty was that they stuck together and that one would not give evidence that incriminated another. The same was also true of white people to some extent. The detective said he had worked in the East End, where working class white people had also tended to 'cover' for one another, but black people did it more. He thought this was understandable, because their whole way of life was different from 'ours' and because they felt that they had little in common with 'us', but it meant that the job of a CID was to find ways of putting enough pressure on witnesses to make them come up with evidence. This often meant doing things that were 'strictly against the book'.

The detective said it was usual practice to find someone who had committed a minor offence and then to use him as a source of information about some more important crime. He said it was done by offering to help him in various ways. In practice, CID usually had to exaggerate the amount of help that they could give. It didn't mean dropping charges against the person altogether. It meant, perhaps, preferring a more minor charge or speaking up for him in court and trying to get a smaller sentence. The detective said, 'We have been told not to do this, but we do it'. DJS asked what he meant, and he explained that his chief superintendent would not encourage him to do it (he meant the detective chief superintendent). DJS asked whether the chief superintendent knew that it happened. The inspector said he did know, and he put pressure on the squad to get convictions. Here he corrected himself, and said they 'were always told' that it was not the job of the police to get a conviction. Whether or not a man was convicted was up to the court, but the detective added that this was an unrealistic view, since if the CID officers put in a lot of work and then 'at the end of the day' the man was 'let off by the courts', they would feel extremely frustrated. In practice, therefore, the detective chief superintendent knew how they operated and put pressure on them to get convictions.

DJS asked the detective whether he would agree that there were conflicting messages coming to him from above. On the one hand they were told not to bargain with potential witnesses (trading the charges to be brought or a good prospect of bail against evidence). On the other hand, there was pressure to get convictions, and the chief superintendent did not enquire too closely into how the evidence was obtained. Did this mean that he would be quite happy if the squad did bargain with potential witnesses, provided that he did not get to know about it, and that it was quite clear it was not done on his instructions? The detective inspector thought this was exactly the right way of putting it.

DJS got to know about two cases that illustrated this way of working while he was with this detective inspector on different occasions. The first case turned on two assaults connected with drug dealing. One man had a quantity of cannabis and agreed to sell it to another man for £10,000 at an appointed place and time. When he arrived he was beaten up and the cannabis taken from him. Two people had been arrested in connection with this assault, but had not yet been charged. Subsequently, a group of young men had turned up at a cafe with bayonets and a shotgun and had badly wounded one man in the cafe with shots and by stabbing. The wounded man had said that the second incident was a reprisal for the earlier beating up and had given some information about drug dealing in the area. The two men arrested in connection with the first incident had not yet been charged because the detective hoped that he 'might be able to make them see that it would be in their interest to provide information' about others involved in the drug dealing: in other words, the police would prefer lesser charges or try to get bail for the suspects if they provided information. In connection with the same incidents, an informer had agreed to risk his life in order to find out who was involved. The detective inspector said he was doing this in order to avoid prosecution on another charge.

On another occasion when DJS spoke to this detective inspector, he had recently received a letter from someone in prison in which he offered to provide information; a central squad were interested, because they thought this man might know about the people who were organising a stolen car racket. The detective inspector said that if the prisoner could provide useful information, he might be able to offer to speak on his behalf to the parole board.

In one case we had the opportunity to observe the bargaining process. JG was working with a crime squad which had obtained information (probably from several informants) suggesting that large quantities of cannabis and heroin were changing hands regularly at a particular hotel. They obtained a warrant and carried out a well-organised raid which resulted in seven arrests, four for possession of drugs and three for other matters. The (uniform) sergeant in charge of the squad, who had planned the operation, was rather disappointed with this outcome, since he believed that large quantities of drugs were changing hands at the hotel, but only small amounts had been found, and the people arrested seemed to be 'punters' rather than 'pushers' - certainly none of them seemed to be a drug dealer on any substantial scale. He was therefore anxious to get information from those arrested that would point the way towards dealers or other 'good villains'.

After going to court in the morning following the raid and spending the three hours from 1 to 4pm in the pub, the sergeant prepared to carry out his first interrogation of those arrested in the morning. He was to be helped by a PC who was a particular friend of his, and who was running the probationer training squad on the Division. The PC went off to bring the first prisoner from the cell and did not return for some time. The sergeant explained, 'What's happening now is that Jock (the PC) is giving this geezer some chat about how I'm a very hard man and how I'm his guvnor and how I want to make life difficult'. The object of this was to make the prisoner feel that he needed to come up with some information and that he could trust Jock, who said he would put in a good word for him with the sergeant (Dave). As Jock approached the door of the interviewing room with the prisoner, JG heard him talking to him in just the terms that Dave had predicted he would.

The suspect was a young man aged 22 for whom a warrant of arrest had been issued by another Division in connection with a burglary. Dave (the sergeant) quickly came to the point. He explained that because of the warrant he could easily keep the suspect in custody over the weekend (it was now Friday afternoon). Also, he pointed out that a 'bent' (forged) driving license had been found in the suspect's room, and said that he would have to consider whether to press charges in connection with that. The prisoner confessed that he 'had business to attend to' and 'wanted out badly'. Dave indicated that he was prepared to help provided he could offer something in return. At this point, Jock left the room. The prisoner immediately made efforts to check what Jock had told him. He asked what Dave's rank was and who were the other people in the room (JG and some probationers in the 'training squad'). Dave said that he was a detective inspector and that JG and the probationers were trainee detectives. The prisoner believed this and seemed to be satisfied that Dave was in charge and that he needed to make a deal in order to be released that day (he had already been in custody for eight hours).

After a while, the prisoner gave Dave the name and address of someone he said was a drug pusher of some standing. Dave asked questions to find out what motive the prisoner had for incriminating this person.  He said he was 'a bit gay' and that a boyfriend of his had ben ruined by addiction to this man's drugs. The prisoner was taken back to his cell while Dave checked up on the alleged pusher.  It turned out that he had a criminal record for taking motor cars, but not for drug dealing.  Jock and Dave thought he must have supplied the prisoner with the 'bent' driving license. They decided to accept the prisoner's offer.  He was brought back and questioned at length to test his information.  When Dave was satisfied that it was genuine, he got in touch with the Division that had issued the arrest warrant, and persuaded them to agree to the release of the prisoner on bail.   Later, information given by another man arrested during the raid confirmed the information given by this suspect; both prisoners independently named the same man as a pusher.

After he had taken the prisoner back to his cell prior to his release, Jock asked JG, 'Do you think what we did is wrong? Letting a bloke get away with a poxy bent driving license and softening X Division up so as to catch a drug pusher? ' JG gave a non-commital reply, and Jock said, 'We'd have no problems showing outsiders round what we do if they were all as balanced as you, Jerry'.  This comment showed that the officers were somewhat anxious because their method was in conflict with the formal rules, but did not think it was wrong for that reason, and wanted to be reassured that it was all right, really.  Immediately afterwards, the same officers interrogated a heroin addict who had been picked up in the raid, and who badly wanted to get out so that he could get a 'fix', take his anti-depressants and have a drink.  They threatened to keep him in custody over the weekend if he did not provide information but made little progress because he didn't seem to know much.  In the end they decided to release him without having obtained any useful information from him.

### 'Gilding the lily'
'Fitting people up' and 'gilding the lily' are two phrases used in the Force for the fabrication of evidence.  The difference of emphasis is that where someone is 'fitted up', the whole of a case against him is fabricated, whereas 'gilding the lily' is adjusting or 'improving' existing evidence against someone to make it more conclusive. It would be unrealistic to expect our research to come up with conclusive findings on the extent to which evidence is adjusted, or the proportion of officers who adjust evidence in the Met.  However, the survey of police officers shows that the officers themselves think a significant proportion of their number adjust evidence.  There are also indications from our observational work that this is a significant problem.

An early version of the questionnaire for the survey of police officers included a question that described circumstances in which 'gilding the lily' would be most likely to occur.

Here is an imaginary case. A PC is patrolling on foot near some council flats. He hears the sound of breaking glass coming from the first floor balcony. Running up the steps to the balcony he meets a large, very drunk man coming down. Twenty-six windows have been broken. The man says 'I've got the bastards'. He does not live on the estate and when sober can give no explanation for being there. The PC is convinced that the man broke the windows. In court he says he saw him break the last one. Do you know of any cases where evidence was adjusted in this kind of way?

JG showed this question to a detective sergeant who had commented on some difficulties he was currently having in gaining acceptance in a CID office. He said, 'Of course they'd all say they saw him break a window. But they're not gonna tell you that'. Of course, this was the opinion of only one detective. The question was not finally included in the survey, partly because of the difficulty in obtaining frank answers that was pointed out by this detective and by other officers.

On another occasion, JG had a long conversation with a detective constable who expressed what may be quite a common view in the CID. He protested about the increasing number of regulations governing CID behaviour. He thought that rules and regulations were fine, 'but abiding by them means that villains get away by playing the system'. He thought the right of silence should be abolished: if someone was brought into a police station, the police had a good reason to detain him and he should be required to explain himself. He went on to refer to 'gilding the lily' and 'verballing' the prisoner. He argued that a detective might 'know' that a man had committed an offence but not be able to raise conclusive proof. 'Why shouldn't the detective write out the man's confession?' He mentioned a notorious local criminal who had recently escaped from custody. 'He's as guilty as sin, so why not fit him up? He's a dangerous, violent animal'.

In a number of cases already quoted there was some element of adjustment of evidence. Thus, in the case of the post office stabbing (which was generally well handled) what Miriam said about her boyfriend Eddy was slightly altered; she insisted that Eddy would not physically attack people unless physically attacked himself, but this was excluded from her statement. In the case of the broken glass panel in the pub door, the PC tried to get the publican to give a description that would identify the man in custody as the culprit, and recorded his description highly selectively in order to achieve this. In a case not yet described, JG was in a car with two officers in plain clothes. One of them saw a white man drop a plastic bag over a wall, and on retrieving the bag found that it contained a fur coat. The suspect said nothing until he was brought to the charge room at the police station. There the arresting officer said, 'Right, where did you nick the coat?' and the suspect replied, 'You're a cunt mate, you're making a right cunt of yourself. The coat's fucking straight'. The officer pushed him around and looked very angry. The suspect said, 'Don't push me around, you cunt, you're a cunt for wearing a uniform'. He was forcibly pushed down onto the bench, half sitting and half stretched out. In this position he was again asked how he had got hold of the coat. He replied, 'You're so fucking clever, you find out'. The arresting officer recorded in his incident report book that he had said this on arrest, whereas he said nothing until he was brought to the charge room. The officer clearly thought this adjustment was significant because when JG read the report book he said, 'Fair and accurate record?'

On another occasion, JG was in a marked police car with a sergeant and a probationer in uniform when they saw a young white man walking along the pavement and holding his hand, which was bleeding from a cut. He said he had been 'larking about with some mates' and had cut his hand on a broken bottle. He had been drinking heavily. The officers took this man to hospital for the cut to be treated, then returned to the place where they had found him to investigate. Shortly they noticed a man walking towards them carrying a strip of metal. He also had been drinking heavily. He was arrested for having an offensive weapon. The officers thought that there had been a fight between him and the man with the cut hand. The man with the strip of metal admitted that he had been in a fight, though he could remember little about it, but it later became clear that he did not know the man with the cut hand and there was no reason to think the fight had been with him. On being brought back from the hospital, the man with the cut hand stuck to his original story. JG went back to the place where he had been picked up with a PC and the suspect, where he (JG) found a broken vodka bottle in exactly the place indicated by the suspect. When they got back to the charge room, the PC told the inspector and the CID that the suspect had 'obviously been up to something' and that he could not find any glass on the scene, which was a straightforward lie. When JG pointed out that he had found the broken vodka bottle, the PC did not seem to be unduly perturbed.

The clearest case that we observed where evidence was adjusted involved an officer saying he had seen something he could not have seen. DJS was with a 'Q' car manned by three uniform officers in plain clothes at about 1 am when they passed a group of six young men with long hair and black leather jackets ('Hell's Angels') on the pavement by a belisha beacon. The driver backed the car into a side road at least fifty yards beyond the group to watch them. From this distance they appeared almost as silhouettes - it was impossible to see their faces, and they were all dressed alike in what amounted to a uniform. One got onto the shoulders of another and knocked the shade off the beacon, then the whole group went up an alleyway with one or more of them kicking the shade as a football as they went. The driver drove up to the entrance of the alleyway, and the whole crew with DJS got out to follow the group. Before the car had reached the belisha beacon, all but one of the group were out of sight down the alley. The one who had knocked off the shade had led and was well out of sight by this time. The officers and DJS followed at a steady walking pace and saw some members of the group kicking the shade from one to another. One of the officers (Geoff) now put his hand on the collar of one of the youths and said, 'You're nicked'. He asked what for, and Geoff said, 'For knocking off that belisha beacon'. The youth said, 'I didn't, I didn't take it off'. The other youths backed him up, saying, 'It wasn't him'. Geoff said, 'It was you because I saw you do it' and the driver said the same in a very cocksure manner. There seemed to be no danger of violence because the youths were in quite a happy mood, but the crew had called for back-up before leaving the car, so a panda car drew up, and the youths said, 'Oh, I see, you've called up reinforcements!' The man arrested was put into the 'Q' car while the others gathered round insisting that he hadn't done it. The driver said, 'Look, you tell that to the court, don't tell it to me, I know he did it because I saw him do it. OK?

DJS went back to the police station in the panda car but arrived in the charge room at the same time as the suspect. The station officer quickly asked what it was about. Geoff, holding the damaged shade, said 'I saw this man get up on the lampstand for the belisha beacon, knock this shade off, then kick it down an alley, and as you see it is damaged. I followed him down the alley and arrested him for criminal damage'. The sergeant asked the youth what he had to say. He said, 'I didn't do it. I didn't knock it off the stand'. The sergeant said, 'And how did it come to be damaged?' The youth said, 'Well, a group of us were kicking it about'. 'So you were kicking it about?' 'I joined in, yes, with the rest of us'. The sergeant said, 'Oh, well, that's good enough'. He meant that it didn't matter whether the youth had knocked the shade off or not, because kicking it about amounted to criminal damage, and he admitted to that. Afterwards DJS said to the crew, 'I couldn't tell which one it was who took the shade off', and the driver said, 'Quite honestly, neither could I', though he had been adamant to the youth that he saw him do it and could identify him. But Geoff, the arresting officer, said quickly, 'Oh, I kept my eye on him, so I knew it was him'. DJS was sure that he meant he had not lost sight of the youth from the time when the cover was knocked off to the time when he was arrested, which would have been impossible since the youths were out of sight for a time after the shade had been knocked off. In principle, he could have meant that he was able to recognise the youth he had seen (from a distance) knocking off the beacon. In the judgement of DJS, this would also have been impossible. This was, therefore, a clear case of fabrication of evidence, admitted in the case of the driver. It was not particularly significant in this instance, since the youth was guilty of criminal damage in kicking the shade, but it was evidence of a habit which could have far more important consequences in other cases.

These few examples show that police officers adjust or fabricate evidence in some cases. On the other hand, bearing in mind the amount of time that the researchers spent with police officers, and the amount of policing activity they observed, the findings are perfectly consistent with the view that in the great majority of cases, police officers provide accurate evidence to the best of their ability. Of course, the limitations of this (or any) research method have to be borne in mind. We believe that we saw a fair cross-section of the work of uniform reliefs, but CID officers were much more able to control what part of their work became visible to us. It is possible, therefore, that there is a pattern of fabrication by some CID officers which we were not able to observe - in a number of offices, CID encouraged such doubts by their conspiratorial air and defensive attitude.

General conclusion
Our general conclusion is that outright fabrication of evidence is probably rare - that is, cases where an officer says he saw something he did not see or that a suspect said something that he did not say. This has to be qualified in various ways.

1.    Our access to some aspects of the work of the CID was limited.

2.    In order to share work, one officer frequently 'gives' an arrest to another, and this may involve adjustment of evidence, but not usually in a way that the non-legal mind would think material (though, if known to the courts, it would often cause them to acquit).

3.    We believe that police officers will normally tell lies to prevent another officer from being disciplined or prosecuted, and this is the belief of senior officers who handle complaints and discipline cases. Of course, there are important exceptions, where officers do give incriminating evidence about their fellows.

However, our findings strongly suggest that departure from rules and procedure affecting evidence are far more common than outright fabrication and have a far more significant effect on the quality of the evidence that goes before the courts. At the time of arrest suspects are frequently neither cautioned nor told they are being arrested. Juveniles are often questioned without a responsible adult being present. The process of arrest is frequently seen as a way of bringing pressure to bear on a suspect to provide evidence against himself or others; while a degree of pressure is implicit in the fact of being arrested (at a point where the evidence that a court would require to convict does not exist) it is not uncommon for officers to use bullying tactics in interrogation and to use threats, especially the threat of being kept in custody for a time.  These kinds of pressure go well beyond what is necessary or inevitable within the current framework of procedure. In many cases, there is no record of the 'informal' interviews during which tough questions are asked, or merely a record to show that the interview took place.  Statements are produced by a process of interaction between an officer and a suspect (or other person); they are generally not a record of what the suspect said in his own words.  They may amount to a highly selective summary of what was said.  We believe that it is common for officers to make 'bargains' with suspects in which an offer not to press charges or to help the suspect to get bail is traded for evidence or (perhaps more commonly) information.

These departures from the rules are important for the effect they may have on the evidence in particular cases.  They also have a wider significance.  Taken as a whole our findings show that a gap has opened up between the 'working rules' of officers and the formal rules of procedure affecting evidence.  This means that the Force has come to work within a framework of double standards, which ultimately threatens the self-confidence of police officers, the confidence that the public have in them, and the confidence of the courts in the evidence they provide.

There will be no fundamental change as long as many police officers believe that the job cannot be done effectively within the rules.  What our findings show most clearly is that rules on their own will not be effective, without a collective effort by the Force to make them work.  This means that those who would like to see a change in police behaviour must interest themselves in the management of the Force, and not just in making more rules.

Finally, it is extremely important to recognise that a lack of skills may be the main reason for breaking rules.  The officer who has failed to get a description of a suspect at the earliest possible opportunity from someone who saw him is likely to end up bending the confused description he gets much later to fit the suspect he has arrested.  The officer who does not assimilate information or notice the weak points in a suspect's story is unable to ask the decisive questions that would expose the suspect's prevarication or lies; he is likely, because of this inadequacy, to resort to bullying tactics.  In many cases, therefore, an improvement in policing skills would be a shorter way to better police behaviour than punitive action in connection with rule-breaking.  This is not to say that the rules are unimportant.  But if police officers can do the job well and achieve their objectives within the rules, the task of enforcing the rules will be a great deal easier.

## Stops

The powers of the police in London to stop and search people on foot and in vehicles are set out in Chapter IV.  In brief, a constable has power to stop and search someone on foot or in a vehicle where he 'reasonably suspects' that the person has something stolen or unlawfully obtained or a controlled drug.  He has power to stop a person driving a vehicle or pedal cycle regardless of whether there is a 'reasonable suspicion' of this kind and he can at any time require a person driving a motor vehicle to produce a driving licence and certificate of insurance. But, having stopped a person in a vehicle, a constable does not have the power to search the person or the vehicle unless there is 'reasonable suspicion'.

Two interpretations of the criterion of 'reasonable suspicion', as it applies to stops, can be suggested. On the first interpretation, there must be a specific reason for suspecting the individual person concerned, and this reason would normally be connected with the person's behaviour at the time or the immediate circumstances. On the second, much broader, interpretation, it would only be necessary to show that there was a higher than average chance that the person had committed an offence, for example because the person belonged to a group within which offenders of a certain type were relatively common, or because he was in an area in which offences of a certain type were relatively common, or because of a combination of factors like these. It was, broadly, the view of the Royal Commission on Criminal Procedure that the first and narrower interpretation of the criterion is the correct one. At the same time, the Royal Commission weakened its stated view by proposing that the power to stop should be extended to circumstances where there was reasonable suspicion that a person was carrying an offensive weapon: many commentators have pointed out that it is hard to see what <u>specific</u> reason there could be for suspecting that an <u>individual</u> was carrying an offensive weapon if the weapon itself was not visible, so that reasonable suspicion, if extended to offensive weapons, might have to be interpreted in the weaker sense. On this weaker interpretation it would, for example, be reasonable to suspect that any youth attending a football match might be carrying an offensive weapon even though there was no specific reason to suspect that any particular youth was carrying one.

It is not any part of the purpose of this report to arrive at a judgement as to the correct interpretation of the law on this point. However, it must be said that it is difficult to comment on the relation between the law and the actual behaviour of police officers in stopping people if the weaker interpretation is accepted. The reason is that on this interpretation the criterion of reasonable suspicion is so weak that it would be difficult to discern its effect, since the police could be said to 'reasonably suspect' any young man who was out on the streets in an area where burglary or theft was relatively common. Since young black people are mostly to be found in such areas, this would effectively mean that the police would be justified in stopping and searching most young black people that they enountered, especially since it has been shown that the proportion of young black people who are arrested and convicted of burglary and theft is higher than the proportion of other groups who are arrested and convicted of such offences.

In the following analysis we shall therefore evaluate the

behaviour of police officers in stopping people against the first and narrower interpretation of the present powers. We shall see that if this interpretation is adopted then a substantial proportion of stops are carried out where the criterion of reasonable suspicion has not been met. If the broader interpretation is adopted, then the police are acting within their powers when making stops in the great majority of cases, but what this means is only that police officers rarely stop people belonging to groups for which the rate of arrest reason to suspect the individual person concerned.

We saw police officers make 129 stops in the course of the present research. In 23 of these cases (18 per cent) the person was seen to commit a traffic offence; this provided a watertight reason for the stop, even though the person was often subsequently questioned about other matters as well. We have tried to classify the remaining 106 cases according to whether or not there was a 'reasonable suspicion' (on the narrower interpretation). We found it extremely difficult to do this, which tends to show how vague is the criterion imposed by the law. On the interpretation of 'reasonable suspicion' that we adopted, behaviour or circumstances that are unusual or odd, without being necessarily suspicious, are taken in by the definition. The following types of behaviour or circumstance have been counted as giving rise to a reasonable suspicion.

1. Odd driving, for example, quick acceleration away from traffic lights, or unusually slow driving (where no traffic offence is involved).
2. Running or moving quickly.
3. Behaving aimlessly ('hanging about'), moving very slowly, especially at night.
4. Specific odd circumstances, for example a man following a woman 20 yards behind at 3am.
5. Carrying valuable property by hand or in a vehicle (it is often possible to see, say, a television set in the back of a car).
6. Being out on foot in the small hours of the morning (this is, of course, a very weak reason for suspicion on its own, but we have counted it in some cases).
7. Having something in common with the description of suspects in a recently reported crime in the area.

On this basis, we find that there was a reason to make the stop in 44 per cent of cases (in addition to the 23 per cent where a traffic offence was committed). There was no specific reason to make the stop in 34 per cent of the cases, though among these are five per cent where the person stopped was 'known to police' - had, according to the officer, been recently arrested or convicted of an offence. These findings are summarised in the table overleaf.

|                                  | Number | Per cent |
|----------------------------------|--------|----------|
| All stops                        | 129    | 100      |
| Seen to commit traffic offence   | 23     | 18       |
| Reasonable suspicion             | 63     | 49       |
| No good reason to stop           | 43     | 33       |
| Of which, known to police        | 6      | 5        |

Although the stops observed cannot be regarded as a statistically representative sample, there is a good fit between these findings and the results of the survey of Londoners. That survey shows, for example, that for 38 per cent of stops the person involved thinks the police had no good reason for making the stop, which is very close to the 33 per cent of observed stops where we judge that there was no 'reasonable suspicion' and that the person had not been seen to commit a traffic offence.

These findings show that the criterion of 'reasonable suspicion' does not act as an effective constraint on police officers in deciding whether to make a stop. It is true that in the case of people in vehicles there is a power to stop without 'reasonable suspicion', but there is no power to search; yet in many cases the person and vehicle was searched. Further, it is clear from the way that police officers talk about stops that the question of what their legal powers may be does not enter into their decision-making except in the case of rare individuals. They do, of course, consider the chance of getting a 'result', but factors that they associate with the chance of getting a 'result' are often unconnected with the concept of 'reasonable suspicion' on the narrower interpretation. Thus, they strongly tend to choose young males, especially young black males. Other groups that they tend to single out are people who look scruffy or poor ('slag'), people who have long hair or unconventional dress (who, they think, may use drugs) and homosexuals. We observed two cases where men were stopped purely because they appeared to be homosexual. In a few cases there appear to be no criteria at all, and the stop is completely random; this happens especially in the early hours of the morning when police officers tend to be bored.

One reason why the legal powers have little relevance is that most people do not know what they are. We never saw anyone openly challenge the right of the police to stop, search and question them, nor did anyone ever refuse to answer questions. In a very small number of cases the person tried to move away, but soon gave up when the officer made it clear that he would not allow it. Thus, a few people thought they might be able to 'escape' without answering questions or being searched, but nobody ever gave any indication that they thought they had a right to insist in going on their way. People do feel that the police should have a reason for detaining them and (if it is not obvious already) should say what it is, but this is based on the idea that the police should be courteous and should make their behaviour intelligible and not on a notion of what the law is; it is based on the general assumption that if someone buttonholes you, you want to be told what it is about.

In the great majority of cases where people are stopped, the encounter is fairly relaxed and friendly. We have not attempted a rigorous classification of the stops we observed in this respect, because it would be very difficult to arrive at hard criteria for a classification. However, the proportion of cases where the person is clearly abusive or obstreporous is definitely small - perhaps five per cent. In a larger proportion of cases - perhaps 20 per cent - the person shows some resentment. (Of course, many of the incidents involve several people, and we are thinking of cases where any of them showed resentment or were abusive.) Resentment is most commonly shown by people who say they have been stopped repeatedly. This confirms the findings of the survey of Londoners, which shows that people who have been stopped repeatedly tend to be highly critical of the police.

Police officers seldom behave aggressively towards people they have stopped, and in a majority of cases they make attempts to placate the person or to give some explanation for the stop. The survey of Londoners shows that in about one quarter of cases the person stopped thought the police had given no explanation (where needed), and the findings from our observations were very much in agreement with this. That survey also shows that in 19 per cent of cases people stopped thought the police had not behaved in a fair and reasonable manner. From our observations, we judge that the police behave aggressively in a smaller proportion of cases than this, but what may underlie people's responses in some cases is a failure to give an explanation. DJS was with an inspector and a sergeant on one occasion when they made three stops in quick succession and completely failed to give any explanation in all three cases. This shows that a norm of giving an explanation is not being propagated by supervising officers.

It is important to recognise that stops that are made without 'reasonable suspicion' can produce results, and this is one of the main reasons for making them. For example, DJS was with two PCs in the early hours of the morning when they saw a car from a distance and decided to follow it purely on a whim. They could not see the occupants or even tell the make or age of the car when they made the decision to follow, and by the time they caught up with the car they had already decided to stop it. It turned out that the car was being driven by a black boy aged 15 who had stolen it earlier that day and changed the number plates. JG was with three officers who stopped a young man walking at an even pace along a pavement in the late afternoon and found some cannabis on him. Several more examples could be quoted.

Where they make a stop without reason, officers quite often say that they have a 'sixth sense' that leads them to suspect

497

someone. Some are undoubtedly skilled at noticing small behavioural cues that may indicate that a person is uncomfortable, worried or afraid. However, most decisions to stop can be understood in terms of the application of fairly straightforward criteria like the ones already quoted. In addition, many officers take particular interest in cars, know what makes and models are likely to be stolen and are able to notice small signs (for example, indications that the number plates are not the original ones). Cues of this kind are seldom enough to amount to a reasonable suspicion, in the sense that most cars that officers think 'might be dodgy' turn out to be 'straight'. Another reason for making stops is that the driver of a car seems too young for the vehicle, or not rich enough for it. Old and battered cars tend to be stopped, especially when they have youths in them.

As we have noted in our report on the survey of Londoners, the proportion of stops that lead to an arrest and charge (3 per cent) or to an offence being reported (5 per cent) is fairly low, but the number of offences detected in this way is substantial. From our observations, we find that 14 of the 129 stops (11 per cent) led to an arrest and charge or to an offence being reported, which is close to the figure produced by the survey of Londoners. However, this is somewhat misleading, since in 23 of the 129 cases the officer saw a motorist commit a traffic offence; in only four of these 23 cases did the officer report the motorist for the offence - in the remaining 19 cases he merely gave a verbal warning. This gives an indication of the massive scale of the exercise of discretion by police officers. In a considerable number of these cases, the offence was speeding, and the officer would not have had sufficient evidence to make a good case; but a considerable number of people were 'let off' for offences that could have been proved without difficulty. If we exclude the cases where the stop was made because of a traffic offence, we find that there was a charge or offence reported in ten out of the 106 cases (nine per cent).

We have mentioned that there are exceptional police officers who do not make stops without having what they regard as a reasonable suspicion. JG was with a WPC who carried out a stop for which there was a reason (but did not get a 'result'). Immediately afterwards she said, 'I won't stop people without reason, which is bad if you want crime arrests'. This illustrates the point we have made above: that a proportion of stops will result in the detection of crime, even if the stops are made without reason. Also, the WPC implied that her own practice was different from that of most police officers.

Police officers are required by Force procedures to take down the name and address of every person stopped and to record it in one of the 'stop books' at the police station. (There are separate books for those given verbal warnings of traffic offences and for those stopped under s.66 of the Metropolitan Police Act.) From the survey of Londoners we find that the person stopped thinks his name and address was taken in only 39 per cent of cases. Since we did not make contemporaneous accounts of our observations, we cannot quote a figure for the proportion of cases in which names and addresses were taken, but there are a substantial number of cases where we specifically recorded (afterwards) that this was not done. Our rough assessment is that names and addresses were taken in about half of cases, which would be broadly in accord with the survey. This is a good example of an 'inhibitory rule'. Most officers do not take the names and addresses down or make a record in the stop book as a matter of course, but they do so if resentment is shown or if they think the person might think of making a complaint later. The reason for this is that they will be in a weak position in any complaints investigation if the stop was not recorded. Although this matter is not particularly important in itself, it shows how ineffective management is at getting PCs to implement a procedure that they have introduced.

All of these findings highlight the weak relationship, in the field, between the formal rules and the actual behaviour of police officers. A broader question than this is the function performed, within the pattern of policing as a whole, by stop and search methods and how this relates to the actual objectives of police officers in making stops. At first sight, the function of stops is to detect offences, but to accept this would be to take a superficial view. The fact is that in about nine out of ten cases stops do not result in the detection of an offence, and the question must therefore arise as to what is the function of <u>these</u> stops. If the only function of stops is to detect offences, then these other stops must be regarded as disfunctional - they are merely the price that has to be paid for the one out of ten stops that are 'successful'. Ths is surely a very heavy price if the 'unsuccessful' stops have a bad effect on public opinion of the police. One response to this is to say that efforts must be made to make police officers more selective in their approach to stopping people, and thus to increase the 'strike rate'. While there is some scope for doing this, the criteria available to police officers in stopping people are too weak for there to be much hope of increasing the strike rate dramatically. As long as there is a policy of stopping people that bears any relation to present policy and practice, there are bound to be very many stops that produce no 'result'.

A second approach, which can be pursued in conjunction with trying to improve the 'strike rate', is to regard stops as having the proper function of improving public confidence in the police. What this means is that where a stop does not result in the detection of an offence, it may be considered as a potentially 'positive' encounter. It is an opportunity for a police officer to offer information, help or advice, to show that the police are making an effort to combat crime, and to engage in relaxed conversation.

On the whole, this view of the proper function of stops does not fit well with the informal objectives of police officers in initiating these encounters. Many or most police officers are capable of providing sympathy, help, information and advice and engaging in a relaxed conversation, but this is not the objective they have in mind when they carry out a stop. Having initiated an encounter in the effort to detect an offence they find it hard to switch to the contrasting objective of seeing if they can be of help. We have said that in a majority of the stops that we observed the officers were civil; it was rare for them to make an effort to be helpful. The exceptions when they did make such an effort are instructive.

JG was with two PCs in a police van when they stopped a teenage white boy who seemed to be carrying a number of rifles in an old dressing gown. The weapons turned out to be stage props which the boys was returning to the firm that lent them out. He immediately became exasperated and said, 'I've been expecting this'. The PCs accepted this explanation quickly, started to joke about what had happened, and gave the boy a lift to the firm's premises. On another occasion, JG was with members of a crime squad when he saw a white man in his late twenties carrying a television set and pointed him out. The detective constable he was with was delighted and thought there was a good chance of making an arrest. The officers stopped the man, who immediately became agitated, saying, 'Why are you bothering me? Bloody police, why don't you do something about the prostitutes and muggers round here?' and so on. He gave a satisfactory explanation (the set was defective, he was taking it to be mended), but still seemed upset and aggressive. The police officers cracked a few jokes, which calmed him down, as they took him to his home address to check it out and established that the set was not listed as stolen. They then gave him a lift to the repair shop, with the set.

DJS was with an area car crew when they saw two young looking girls walking slowly on the pavement in an area where prostitution is common. One of the girls (Cheryl) looked partly of West Indian origin, the other was white. The WPC in the crew questioned Cheryl, 'You look as if you might be, you know...' Cheryl understood immediately. 'We weren't. I wouldn't do it here. I wouldn't dare. You never know what might happen to you.' The WPC asked her whether she had done 'it' in the past. She answered, 'Just two or three times back home in Liverpool, but I've never done it here'. Cheryl had been obviously alarmed at first, but was now becoming more relaxed. The WPC said, 'We stopped you because we thought you looked very young'. Cheryl stepped out of her shoes and said, 'The trouble is I'm so small, see'. The WPC said, 'You want to put some manure in your shoes and see if you can shoot up a bit'. Cheryl said she had hoped to stay the night with some friends who lived in a flat nearby, but they were not in. She had no money left and did not know how she would get back to Liverpool. The WPC suggested that she should ring up her dad and get him to meet her at the station, because the railways would let you travel if there was someone to pay at the other end. She told her how to find out whether the coach company would do the same

(Cheryl thought the train would be too expensive). The WPC asked Cheryl about her elaborate hair style. She said she had spent £25 on having it done and the 'stuff' had trickled down her neck and given her a rash. The WPC said she must be mad to spend £25 on that. Cheryl replied, 'That's what me mum said'. She returned to 'it' and said she would be afraid to do 'it' around here. The WPC said, 'That's it, you take a risk of being beaten up every time you take a client'. The conversation went on in this vein for some time. By the end of it Cheryl's opinion of the police had probably changed greatly for the better, and she had been given some good advice (about getting home to Liverpool), though the WPC could have been more helpful, since there is a procedure for helping stranded persons which she could have used if she had known about it.

An example of the failure to make a positive encounter out of a stop was observed by JG when he was with an area car. The car went to assist a sergeant on foot who was chasing three black boys he had seen robbing an old lady of her handbag. He had lost them, but shortly after the arrival of the area car he appeared holding a young black boy by the arm. The boy was put in the van (which had also arrived) and as he climbed in said, 'Look, I've just been to Dicky Dirts (a clothes shop). I can show you the receipts'. He was quite calm. Three officers questioned and searched him, finding the receipt for the two new pairs of jeans he was carrying in a 'Dicky Dirts' bag. The boy answered all questions willingly. When asked where he lived, he said, 'Over there'. He was asked for his full name and address and said, 'Over there, I can show you, just round the corner'. The PC responded by saying 'Full address!' in a menacing tone. After further, abrupt questions, the officers let the boy go without a word of apology or explanation.

JG was with a different area car when a woman complained to them that three young motorcyclists had been riding about on the grass outside her flat. They found three motorcycles with the engines still warm and mud on the tyres outside a nearby council house, but took no further action at the time. Later they saw a boy riding ahead of them on a similar motorcycle, but were not sure whether it was one of the three they had seen earlier, not having taken the index numbers. They stopped him not because of the earlier incident, but because he was not displaying an L-plate and looked too young to have a full licence. When he stopped, he quickly retrieved his rear L-plate, which had become tucked up under the mudguard. The driver reprimanded him about the L-plate, then said, 'You're one of those little scrotes down at ---, aren't you? You said I'd never nick you, didn't you? Have you been riding around on the grass with all those other little scrote friends of yours tonight?' He denied it. The two officers went on making abusive remarks to him for a while, then left.

## Favours

We have said that any serious corruption would not be uncovered by research of the kind that we have done. However, our observations have established that it is common for police officers in London to accept food and other goods free or at a reduced price from tradesmen who give them this special treatment because they are police officers. Tradesmen who do this are referred to in police slang as 'GTP' ('good to police'). We were not aware, in any of these cases, that the tradesmen received special treatment of any kind in return. There are, of course, a number of other occupational groups whose members also tend to get preferential treatment.

There were 23 instances in all during our observations when officers obtained goods free or at a special price. In many of these cases the researchers also benefited. The commonest case is where officers in uniform go to buy meals at fast food restaurants. On one occasion an officer (in uniform) went to buy a television aerial with DJS; the shopkeeper insisted that he should not pay, while the officer made several attempts to pay before going away with the aerial for nothing. He was embarrassed and certainly did not look for special treatment.

When CID officers drink in pubs on duty they often get some of their drinks free.

## Other rules

Accidents involving police cars are generally investigated very thoroughly and fairly severe penalties are imposed where the police driver is found to be culpable. Police drivers will often find themselves disqualified from driving a police car for a lengthy period following an accident even when they were not guilty of an offence or liable in civil law. In spite of this, as we mentioned in Chapter XIV, many police officers routinely exceed speed limits for no apparent reason (when not answering a call).

There is a considerable apparatus of rules to do with booking on and off duty, and, for officers in plain clothes, keeping diaries of their movements and activities. There is considerable flexibility in the enforcement of these rules, especially in the CID. As we mentioned in Chapter XIV, CID officers often get others to 'book them off' and make arrangements to be 'shown' on duty when they are drinking or socialising. In certain circumstances, especially organised 'CID parties', this is done with the knowledge of senior officers such as the detective chief inspector.

It is also clear from the earlier chapter that drinking in CID offices is widely tolerated, while it remains formally against the rules. Nevertheless, the rule has not been wholly abandoned. DJS was with a CID officer during a visit by the Force Inspectorate. During this period the glasses and bottles were cleared away - the detective chief inspector explained that the Inspectorate would expect them to have the courtesy not to drink in the office while they were around and to remove the evidence. It was a matter of keeping up appearances rather than convincing the Inspectorate that drinking in the office did not happen. As soon as the

Inspectorate left, the regular drinking parties started again. This is not particularly important in itself, but again illustrates the tendency in the Force to regard certain rules as necessary, but merely 'presentational'.

# XVII SELECTION, TRAINING AND CAREERS

The nature of an organisation must partly depend on who enters it and on the structure of the internal pathways that lead individuals towards particular positions. The structure of the police force is unusual in that there is a single point of entry for everyone in the organisation, and everyone starts as a uniform constable on a relief. There are two broad paths of career development from that common starting point. One is by going into a specialism such as CID or traffic, or by acquiring a specialist skill, such as area car driver; the other is through promotion to more senior ranks. These two kinds of career development are not mutually exclusive, but they are often regarded as alternatives: an ambitious officer hoping for rapid promotion will probably not join traffic division or become a dog handler, while an officer who is keen to become an area car driver will probably put aside thoughts of promotion at least for several years. There is on the one hand a precise expression of levels of seniority through the hierarchy of rank, but on the other hand there are many specialisms and therefore different jobs to be done by people at the lower ranks: this provides an alternative system of rewards for officers who are not potentially senior managers.

One important consequence of this structure is that paths of advancement mostly lead away from the uniform relief, which therefore has a low status within the organisation although it carries out much of the most important police work. Another is that there is a single system of initial selection that must deal with a very wide range of applicants (from those without educational qualifications to those with degrees) and that must select potential commanders, detectives, home beat officers and dog handlers. In the first instance, people are being selected to work as constables on uniform reliefs, but this is the pool from which the specialists and senior managers will be drawn, so it is very important that potentially outstanding specialists or managers should not be excluded by the initial selection procedure.

A wide range of criteria and structures are involved in initial selection, selection for promotion and selection for specialist groups. These criteria are significant because they help to determine who does what and who becomes senior (and therefore powerful). They also have symbolic importance, as a statement by the organisation about the value of certain qualities and kinds of policing. To some extent, all officers will take their ideas about what kind of policing is valued from the criteria used in selecting people for promotion or specialisation, even if they themselves are not looking for promotion or hoping to enter a specialism.

### Initial selection
Chief criteria
The chief requirements and criteria applied in the initial selection procedure are as follows.

Nationality. Applicants must be British or Irish.

Age. The minimum age on entry into the Force is $18\frac{1}{2}$, but more mature applicants who have a variety of experience will tend to be favoured. Applicants are not considered over the age of 35 unless they have experience in the armed forces, in which case they may be considered up to the age of 39.

Educational standard. If applicants have a minimum of four 'O' levels including maths and English, they are exempt from taking a special test. Those who do not have these qualifications take a national test in English and maths (chiefly number). There is 'a national minimum of 80 out of 200 on this test as a requirement for entry into any police force, but individual forces may set their own minima above this level. Up to April 1981 the minimum for the Metropolitan Police was set at the national minimum of 80 (whereas some other forces had minima as high as 120), but since April 1981 the minimum was raised to 100 in the Met. Some applicants have much higher educational qualifications than the minimum required - there were 175 graduate entrants in 1982. It is not clear that those with high educational qualifications necessarily have a better chance of selection than those with lower ones (the point is discussed further below).

Physical qualifications. There is a minimum height requirement (5ft 8 for men and 5ft 4 for women) and a requirement that the applicant's build must fall within an acceptable range (as defined by height to weight ratio). Eyesight must be up to a defined standard (though glasses or contact lenses may be worn for the test). General fitness (as assessed by a fairly brief medical examination) must be up to a defined standard.

Personal circumstances. The Met does not generally accept applicants who are in the process of becoming divorced from their wives or husbands. They also reject people who are heavily in debt.

Good conduct of the applicant and close relatives. Applicants must be rejected if they have been found guilty of a criminal offence other than one of a list of minor offences not counted for this purpose. They will normally be rejected if their close relatives have been found guilty of serious offences, or if police intelligence suggests that the family associates with criminals. Under this head, checks are carried out with the Criminal Record Office, Special Branch and the local police collator who covers the applicant's current address. All of the addresses where the applicant has lived are checked to ensure that they have not been associated with illegal activities.

School and employment history. Where the applicant left school within the previous two years, a head teacher's report is obtained. This usually has little influence on the decision, but in a few cases it may alert the selectors to problems (for example, if a boy was suspended from school for fighting). Applicants provide details of their employment history, but references are taken up only where the applicant was dismissed from the last job or left after a disagreement. The selectors seem to disapprove of rapid job changes (as suggesting instability of character) but to approve of a smaller number of changes motivated by a desire to 'get on'. They look to the employment record for signs of initiative or persistence, or on the other hand, of instability and repeated failure. If the applicant was in the armed forces and did not get an exemplary discharge, the matter is take up with the force concerned: some minor disciplinary offences (such as absent without leave) may be overlooked.

Address check. A visit is made to the applicant's home address, partly to find out whether the accommodation is suitable for him to live there while a police officer (otherwise he would have to be lodged in a section house) and partly to get some information about the family background. The visiting police officer notes the sleeping arrangements (important if the applicant would be living at home while working shifts) and makes an assessment of the housekeeping standards and, roughly, the respectability of the family. Our impression is that it is only in a few cases that this criterion comes into play, and then as a reason for rejecting someone rather than a point in someone's favour.

Qualities assessed at the interview. About one-quarter of applicants are interviewed for about 15 minutes (the rest are excluded before that stage). Before recommending acceptance or rejection, the selection board rates these applicants on the following dimensions: appearance and bearing; clarity of speech; relations with other people; attitude to study; determination and persistence; knowledge of police work; maturity.

## The ideal applicant

When, in mid-1980, DJS interviewed the head of the branch responsible for recruitment, he asked what sort of person the branch was looking for. The administrator replied

> The ideal is a young man aged 24-25, 5ft 10 inches tall, weight 12-13 stone, having five 'O' levels including maths and English, physically fit, with perfect eyesight, having never had any physical problems at all or any diseases. He should come from a good working class background, be of good character. He must be of British nationality, be capable of absorbing information, show initiative, be alert and enthusiastic, have determination, be tolerant, slow-tempered, good humoured.

In practice the criteria of selection are complex and flexible, and a considerable variety of people enter the Force, but it is interesting that the administrator chose not to emphasise this variety and flexibility, but rather to talk in terms of a stereotype: a man (not a woman) from a 'good working class background' with five 'O' levels. One part of this stereotype that does seem to have an influence on actual selection is the sex of the ideal applicant.

## Women

In 1982 the Force received a large number of applications from women (3,693, or 24 per cent of all applications). The outcome of these applications from women is shown below alongside the figures for men.

|  | Men | Women |
|---|---|---|
| All applicants 1982 | 11,582 | 3,693 |
|  | % | % |
| Seen by a selection board | 30 | 12 |
| Recommended for acceptance | 17 | 7 |
| All seen by a selection board | 3,484 | 447 |
|  | % | % |
| Recommended for acceptance | 55 | 54 |

Most of those recommended for acceptance will have entered the Force, though a few will have been rejected following checks carried out after the selection board or will have withdrawn their applications. The table shows that 17 per cent of the men compared with 7 per cent of the women were recommended for acceptance: in other words, the chance of acceptance is two and a half times as high for male as for female applicants. The discrepancy arises entirely at the stages prior to the selection board, so that among those appearing before a board, the proportion recommended for acceptance is the same for men and women.

From the figures alone it is clear that the Force discriminates unlawfully against women applicants under the Sex Discrimination Act 1975. Undoubtedly, limited physical strength is a disadvantage for certain aspects of police work, but that does not affect the legality of Force policy, since physical strength and stamina cannot be a 'genuine occupational qualification' under the Act. In theory, the much lower success rate of women applicants could arise because they tend to be less well qualified, but an enormous difference in the quality of applicants between men and women would be required to explain the pattern of selection. It is most unlikely that there is a difference of this kind.

In any case, we have been told that it is 'unofficially' Force policy to keep the proportion of women in the Force down to about 10 per cent (which is roughly the present level). The reason given was that 'operational considerations' make this necessary. Since comparatively few women police officers are in specialist groups or in office jobs, the proportion of 'operational' police officers who are women will be higher than 10 per cent if the overall proportion is 10 per cent. For example, the survey of police officers shows that while 9 per cent of all officers up to the rank of inspector are women, 12 per cent of those on uniform reliefs are women. It is believed that it would be dangerous to allow this proportion to rise any further, on the ground that women are unsuited to handle public order events or incidents where violence is anticipated. Therefore, in order to keep the overall proportion of women in the Force to 10 per cent, stiffer criteria are applied to female than to male applicants at the stages of selection prior to the interview.

This is a very large and important issue which needs to be discussed more openly than it has been in the past. The logical consequence of the Sex Discrimination Act 1975 is that the proportion of women in the police force should be allowed to rise to a much higher level than the current one if enough suitable women applicants come forward. By failing to make the police force an exception to the Act, Parliament indicated that it was prepared to see this happen. On current trends the proportion of women in the Metropolitan Police would rise to about 25 per cent within 10 years if there were no discrimination in the selection procedure. It is quite clear that the Force considers that this would be unworkable. If Parliament is persuaded that the Force is right, then it should amend the legislation; if not, then the Force should bring its selection policy into conformity with the law and should consider at a fundamental level how a police force with a more even balance of the sexes can best be organised so as to meet operational requirements.

We have shown in Chapter XIV that there is a great deal of prejudice against women in the Force and that this is connected with a 'cult of masculinity'. It is possible to argue that a substantial increase in the number of women police officers would help to overcome some current problems and would increase the pool of certain resources that are currently scarce within the Force. At the same time, it would be a radical change, and there is no doubt that operational problems would be created, at least until new methods of organisation and ways of working had been established. This is therefore a matter that requires very careful consideration. In the short term the Force may be able to evade the issue by discriminating against women applicants, since arrangements for the enforcement of the legislation are weak. In the longer term it will have to consider its policy more deeply and discuss it within a wider forum.

Educational criteria
Consideration of the educational criteria in the selection process highlights the difficulty of having a common point of entry leading to jobs at so many different levels and requiring so many diverse skills and accomplishments. Literacy, numeracy and the ability to handle legal concepts are important to all police officers, but senior officers have to develop these skills to a much higher level than constables, and they also need to be able to assimilate large amounts of information quickly and to think analytically. At the stage of initial selection, therefore, it is important to ensure that everyone admitted to the Force has a basic minimum of literacy (and numeracy to a lesser extent) but it is also important to ensure that a proportion of those selected have the potential to develop these skills to the much higher level required if they are to become senior officers.

The survey of police officers shows there is a very wide range of educational qualifications among officers currently in the Force. Analysis in terms of the highest qualification held shows that 5 per cent of police officers up to the rank of inspector have a degree or postgraduate qualification; 18 per cent have 'A' levels or a qualification at a similar level; 16 per cent have at least four 'O' levels including maths and English; 32 per cent have other 'O' levels or CSEs; and the remaining 28 per cent have no educational qualifications.

| Year | Total no. of graduate entrants | Entered under national scheme |
|------|-------------------------------|-------------------------------|
| 1973 | 15 | 3 |
| 1974 | 14 | 3 |
| 1975 | 19 | 6 |
| 1976 | 38 | 4 |
| 1977 | 42 | 5 |
| 1978 | 50 | 3 |
| 1979 | 113 | 4 |
| 1980 | 116 | 7 |
| 1981 | 158 | 6 |
| 1982 | 175 | 8 |

A very small number of officers enter the Force each year through the national graduate entry scheme, which is highly competitive. These graduate entrants - on average about seven a year - go into a fast promotion stream. In recent years, a much larger number of graduates have entered by the normal route, which means that their status and promotion prospects are, in principle, the same as for non-graduates. The steep rise in the number of graduate entrants in recent years is shown in the table above.

This trend can be expected to continue, and will in time transform the composition of senior officers in terms of educational background. Even though most of the graduates are not in a fast promotion stream they are likely to gain promotion more quickly than non-graduates since promotion up to inspector rank is almost entirely on the basis of written examinations. This is one of the chief reasons why there is prejudice against graduates in the Force. However, if there is a justified criticism, it should be directed against the system of promotion by written examination, and not against the policy of admitting a larger number of graduates to the Force.

In addition, the Force acquires a small number of graduates each year by sending officers at inspector rank to take degrees; on average, this amounts to about ten officers a year, and the number has not been rising. The survey of police officers shows that of graduates in the Force up to the rank of inspector, 82 per cent took their degrees before joining, 13 per cent on leave of absence from the Force, and the remaining 5 per cent in their spare time while serving police officers.

We do not have good enough statistics to be able to analyse the weight placed on educational qualifications compared with other factors in the selection process. We do know that few applicants are excluded primarily because they do not meet the educational requirements. Out of 15,275 applicants in 1982, only 624 were required to take the PIR test and failed it (that is, scored less than 100), while 1,564 took it and passed. A total of 11,344 applicants were rejected without being interviewed, and the 624 who failed the PIR test are only 6 per cent of these rejected applicants. These statistics seem to imply that failure to meet the educational requirements is a comparatively infrequent reason for rejection and that other criteria are given far more importance. However, the statistics as they stand are not conclusive. It is possible that applicants are often rejected without being asked to take the test because it looks from their application forms and from other information that they would stand little chance of passing it. Also, the level of educational qualifications or the score on the test (where it is above the minimum) may be a factor weighing with selection boards when they make their assessment at a later stage. Even so, the indications are that the selection procedure places rather small weight on intellectual skills.

Our observations of police work suggest that a lack of writing skills is often a difficulty among those at constable rank. A considerable number of constables do not write fluently when taking down statements and recording interviews. There seems to be a good case, therefore, for placing more emphasis on writing skills in the selection procedure. It may be that steps already

510

taken in this direction will be sufficient. The minimum score required on the PIR test has been increased from 80 to 100 and all applicants are now being asked to take it regardless of their educational qualifications. Our observations relate almost entirely to officers who entered the Force before these changes were made.

## Selection boards

When we observed selection boards in mid-1980 they normally consisted of a commander and a chief-superintendent. However, boards seeing women applicants always contained at least one woman, often of a lower rank than chief-superintendent, since there are few high-ranking women officers in the Force. Boards now consist of rather more junior officers. Where men are being selected there is generally a chief-superintendent as 'president' and a superintendent. In 1980 the selectors were given no special training, but since then a small amount of training has been included in senior command courses; however, this does not include practice interviews with real applicants or sitting in on interviews carried out by experienced selectors. The boards are given some guidance in that they are asked to rate the applicants on specified dimensions, but they are not given specific guidance about what questions to ask or how to assess the results of the interview and the other information about the applicants that is available to them. The work of selection is not undertaken by a small number of officers who have been found to be good at it, but is shared between a large number of officers nominated by the recruiting branch. However, the branch has recently started trying to identify selectors who make bad choices so that they will not be invited to sit on boards again.

Research on interviews as a method of selecting people for jobs shows that they tend to be unreliable - that is, different interviewers select different people. The reliability of the method is increased if the qualities that the interviewers are looking for are closely specified, and if applicants are separately interviewed by different people. There is much less information about the validity of the interviewing method - that is, whether the people selected are actually better at the job than those who are rejected. However, reliability is a necessary condition of validity: if one selection board would accept and another would reject the same applicant, they cannot both be right. It is likely that the interviewing method presently used in the Force is unreliable, for a number of reasons. The interviews are short (about 15 minutes); although there are two interviewers, they see the applicant together, and the junior one tends to defer to the president, so that two distinct opinions are not expressed; and the qualities interviewers are looking for are not very closely specified -although the interviewers do rate the applicants on specified dimensions, they tend to make these ratings fit with a prior decision as to whether or not to recommend for acceptance.

Of course, these interviews are not just an opportunity for the Force to get more information about applicants; they are also an opportunity for applicants to gain an impression of what senior officers are like. Also, for both sides to be happy about making a commitment to each other, it is probably important that a formal exchange of this kind should take place. Therefore, even if interviews should prove to be extremely unreliable (which is quite likely) they should probably still be retained. At the same time, steps can be taken to improve their reliability to some extent.

## Increasing standards
The number of applicants to join the Metropolitan Police Force increased very rapidly from 3,000 to 4,000 a year in the mid 1970s to a peak of 20,000 in 1981; it then settled back to 15,000 in 1982 and will probably lie between 12,000 and 13,000 in 1983. Over the same period, the Force has reached full establishment, having been well below strength in previous years. Since there are now many more applications for fewer places than in the mid 1970s, the Force is able to be much more selective. It has responded by raising the required standards on the same criteria as those applied before. As already mentioned, the minimum score required on the PIR test has been increased from 80 to 100 and, more recently, all applicants have been required to take this test. Also, a requirement that applicants should score at least 50 per cent on the English parts of the test has lately been introduced. While the minimum height requirement has not been changed, the Force is now tending to give preference to people who are above average height. While the minimum age on entry to the Force is still $18\frac{1}{2}$, preference is now given to more mature applicants, especially those who have varied experience. The PIR test remains, and, as already mentioned, is being used more widely, but applicants with educational qualifications are preferred if they can also pass the test. This is the account that the recruiting branch gives of changes in policy: we do not have statistics that demonstrate a change in the criteria being applied.

## Weaknesses in the selection method
Because the Force is now able to be far more selective, it has the opportunity to review its selection criteria and procedures in a more fundamental way. Although there is little good information on the matter, the present procedures are probably very ineffective: one indication of this is that almost one-quarter of recruits drop out within the first two years, though it may be that some of those who leave are good recruits who have lacked encouragement or support. In the foreseeable future, selection will probably continue to be fairly inefficient, because too little is known about the qualities that successful police officers have, and there are no very reliable methods of identifying these qualities in young men and women. Although a wholly coherent approach to selection, along with reliable and valid methods, is probably a long way off, a

thorough review would probably lead to some useful improvements. A specific and detailed analysis of the skills required by successful police officers in various specialisms and at various ranks would be a good starting point for such a review. It is important that the skills required by senior officers should be considered as well as those required by constables, otherwise the Force may fail to select enough potential managers even if it succeeds in selecting good constables.

It is worth commenting on some of the limitations of the present selection method. There is a thorough procedure for checking the history of applicants for signs of criminality, instability or deviance, but there is much less emphasis on identifying personal qualities that would be of positive value in the police force. Many applicants are too young to have shown these qualities in what they have already done, so it may be worth trying to develop structured questioning methods or aptitude tests (to supplement the opinions of selection boards). The methods used in army officer recruitment, for example, include a fairly elaborate set of aptitude tests, some of a very practical kind, and similar methods might well be applied in the selection of police officers.

From our observations it is clear that in the past the selection procedure gave too little emphasis to reading and writing skills. Recent changes may make a substantial difference here, but two further steps could be taken at present. First, the recruiting branch could carry out analysis to show how much weight is actually given to educational criteria within the current selection procedure. Secondly, it could look for evidence about the later performance of recruits according to their educational qualifications and their score on the PIR test. This evidence would be a pointer to future policy.

It is likely that the selection tends to be more difficult when the applicants are young because they have done less, so that little is known about them. It also seems likely that very young people vary in their ability to tackle police work more than older people. The Force is in a position to make some assessment of the relation between age and performance, and such an assessment would make an important contribution to any review of the selection procedure. It might suggest that there is a good case for raising the minimum age on entry into the Force.

Various methods of improving the reliability of the interviews should be considered. A much closer definition of the criteria to be assessed at the interview would improve consistency. This does not mean that successful applicants should be required to conform to a rigid stereotype; the assessment would cover a variety of qualities, and successful applicants would be expected to have some, but not all of these qualities, so that a variety of people with contrasting personal strengths would be admitted to the Force. The reliability of selection interviews would be further improved if two officers saw the applicant separately rather than together. The selectors would then express genuinely independent opinions and there would be the added advantage that the encounter would be less intimidating to the applicant. Consistency would be further improved if the selectors received structured training and practice in life-like conditions. Regular monitoring of their interviewing with feedback of comments and suggestions would also be helpful.

This method would automatically produce information about the consistency of the assessments made by different interviewers, since each applicant would be separately assessed by two interviewers. Continuous monitoring of the level of agreement between the two interviewers would alert the recruitment branch to differences of approach between interviewers, and hence help to increase the level of consistency. It would be a reasonable policy to drop interviewers whose judgements seldom agreed with those of other interviewers. Some limited assessment of the validity of the assessments would also be possible, by comparing the performance of individual recruits in the early years of their careers with the judgements made about them during the selection procedure. Already the recruiting branch is carrying out analysis to show whether particular selectors tend to have chosen recruits who drop out during initial training. This kind of analysis should be extended in various ways. The early careers of recruits can be considered, and not just whether they drop out at training school; the analysis can be used to show how valid various kinds of assessment are as predictors of success in the job; and if the interviews are carried out by individual officers separately, the success of individual officers as selectors can be assessed.

The Force has moved towards using rather younger selectors by reducing the ranks of the two officers on a board to chief-superintendent and superintendent in the majority of cases. The argument for this is that officers who are closer to the recruits in age and who have more recent experience of dealing closely with constables may be better selectors than more senior officers. Whether there is a relationship between age and seniority and success as a selector is something that could be monitored within the framework of the more structured approach to selection that we are suggesting. It is, of course, quite possible that much more junior officers (such as inspectors) would make better selectors than chief-superintendents.

**Probationer training**
At the time when we observed the initial training (July to October 1980) recruits attended a 15-week residential course based at Peel Centre, Hendon. There they were taught in classes of about 20 by police officers at sergeant and inspector rank who were posted to training school as instructors usually for a period of years. Lessons in the classroom dealt with relevant aspects of the law and criminal procedure, with particular emphasis on the powers of the police; in addition there were 'social studies' classes which amounted to wide-ranging and often confusing discussions of broadly defined topics such as 'deviance' and 'community relations'.

An equally important part of the course was the 'practicals' held out of doors in which instructors acted out an incident and members of the class were asked to deal with it. These practicals were used to familiarise recruits with clerical and administrative procedures (such as filling in the incident report book), to help them to understand what their powers were in various specific situations, to give them practice in deciding broadly what action to take in a given set of circumstances, and to develop the social skills required in police work, though they were only a rough and ready method of doing this. The course included a substantial amount of physical training, but only very rudimentary training in self defence or methods of restraining a violent person. Assessment was by means of an intermediate and final exam (written papers and practicals) without any assessment of the work done by recruits during the course itself.

Recruits who passed out successfully at the end of the 15 weeks (over 90 per cent of the intake) were posted to Districts. During the remainder of their probationary period (the first two years) they regularly attended a continuation training centre for more classes much on the lines of those in the initial training course, and they had to pass a final exam before being 'confirmed' as constables at the end of the probationary period. Arrangements for 'training on the job' during the probationary period were very weak. At an earlier period, probationers used to be shown the job by 'parent constables' but this system had been allowed to lapse because not enough experienced officers were available in the mid 1970s. Each probationer had three-monthly meetings with his or her chief-superintendent, who had to be satisfied that the probationer had had experience of a suitable range of police work before recommending that he or she should be confirmed. Short attachments with specialist units such as beat crimes and the collator's office were arranged during the probationary period. However, probationers spent much of their first two years out on their own or with other inexperienced officers and with very little direct supervision or advice; they received no actual training in real policing situations.

However, changes were on the way. The Commissioner had set up a 'steering committee for the review of recruitment and training', which reported in 1980 (the year when we observed the as yet unchanged initial training). This report was highly critical of the existing system of probationer training and recommended radical changes. Some of these had already been put in hand by the time that Lord Scarman produced his report on the Brixton disorders. His report concluded

> Improvements in police training are in hand. But there is scope for further improvement. In particular the length of the present period of initial training for recruits is insufficient. I recommend that it be increased to a minimum of six months. More attention should be given, in an

515

extended curriculum, to training in the prevention, as well as the handling, of disorder, and in an understanding of the cultural backgrounds and the attitudes to be found in our ethnically diverse society.

The period spent by a recruit on probation after the initial training course is an essential and integral part of the recruit training process. It should include practical training and supervision in the handling of people in situations of potential conflict such as stops in the street, training provided either through a 'street duties course' or, preferably, through a tutor or parent constable scheme. An officer's period on probation should include a period in a city area where ethnic minorities form a substantial proportion of the population. Probationer constables should not, however, save in an emergency, go out alone on foot patrol in an inner city or any other racially sensitive area(1).

These recommendations gave an extra push to the changes that were already under way. There was no resistance to the recommendations - most senior officers agreed with them, except that they thought probationers should patrol alone in areas like Lewisham because there was no other way of giving them the experience of having to rely on themselves. Senior officers in charge of training welcomed the opportunity to increase the length of the initial course because they thought they needed a longer course to accommodate the new curriculum that they had in mind. While initial training for the other British police forces, which is centrally administered by the Home Office, is still confined to 10 weeks, the period in the Met went up to 16 weeks from April 1982 and then to 20 weeks from January 1983. At the same time there was a rethinking of the principles underlying probationer training, a reworking of the curriculum of the initial course and an attempt to reshape the training taking place on District after completion of the initial course.

The starting point for these changes was an analysis of the defects in the existing system. Most people seemed to agree about what these defects were: we came to much the same conclusions from our 1980 observations as did the steering committee for the review of selection and training. The course concentrated on imparting knowledge rather than skills (whereas it is much more important for police officers to learn how to do certain things and how to arrive at good decisions than to learn facts about the law and criminal procedure). There was an extraordinarily old-fashioned emphasis on rote learning of bits of statutes: recruits were regularly given 'star reports' (passages to be learnt word perfect) and 'A reports' (passages to be learnt in roughly the

---

(1)    The Brixton Disorders 10-12 April 1981, HMSO Cmnd. 8427.

516

original words). The practical lessons were unavoidably artificial, and were not supplemented by any teaching in real life situations. They were used to achieve too many objectives at once - for example, the recruit would be learning how to fill in an incident report book, how to apply his knowledge of police powers to a particular situation, how to decide broadly what action to take and how to control and adapt his manner, approach, speech and bearing, all at the same time.

In 'social studies' lessons, instructors conveyed little hard information, and they were not tough-minded enough to make the recruits think hard or reason closely about the issues under discussion. The intention behind these lessons was to challenge unthinking or reactionary views, for example on the treatment of offenders, on people who live unconventional lives, on ethnic minority groups. However, since the instructor's contribution to the discussion was generally weak, and since those holding reactionary views among the recruits would often be in a majority, the sessions could well have had the effect of reinforcing these views. Meanwhile, the recruits remained ignorant of basic facts about society. In the Autumn of 1980 we interviewed 40 recruits at around the tenth week of their initial training. Three-quarters of them thought the proportion of the London population who were 'coloured' was much higher than it actually is: the mean of the answers given was 22 per cent (the real figure is under 10 per cent on a reasonable interpretation of the National Dwelling and Housing Survey, 1977). Nearly one-third of these recruits thought that 30 per cent or more of the London population was 'coloured', and one thought the figure was 60 per cent. More than half of them had no idea what religions members of ethnic minorities belong to in Britain or what languages they speak: for example, only 20 per cent could think of the Sikh religion and 30 per cent of Hinduism; only 8 per cent thought of the Urdu language, and one person came up with Punjabi, while none thought of Gujerati or Bengali.

Perhaps the most obvious defect was that the initial course was not 'joined on' to the experience of real police work during the probationary period. Because the two phases were highly distinct, habits and attitudes acquired in the training were unlikely to carry over into policing behaviour on the streets. On the one hand, training school did not incorporate experience of real police work. On the other hand, when probationers did come to have experience of police work, they were little supervised, and there was little or no assessment of whether they were doing the job in the way they had been taught to do it; also, they were then subject to the influence of the informal objectives and norms of the relief, which would assume more importance in their eyes than the precepts of the initial training course.

The report of the working party on human awareness training for recruits and probationers, produced in 1981, signals a change in the thinking that underlies initial training. It begins

The Metropolitan Police Training philosophy stems from the Systems Approach to Training (SAT). It is new in the sense that SAT philosophy applies a logical approach to the design of training. It commences with an analysis of the job which the trained officer has to perform, proceeds to a statement of objectives which define clearly what the trainee must achieve to be successful, follows with decisions about assessment and methods, and closes with the establishment of feedback mechanisms which enable the training to be validated.

This is the starting point for a complete revision of the course content and of the materials used. A system of continuous assessment has been introduced, which (apart from any purely educational advantages it may offer) provides an immediate feedback of information about the success of particular elements of the course, so that methods can be continuously modified in the light of the results. It would be a far more difficult task to 'validate' the training, as promised in the opening paragraph quoted, in terms of the subsequent policing behaviour of trained officers: to show, that is, how far the training shaped their policing behaviour in the intended ways.

We have not had time to observe initial training since the process of change began to gain momentum. An evaluation by the Police Foundation is under way and will be published shortly. Early indications are that the results of this inquiry show the new initiatives in a very favourable light. If successfully implemented the proposed changes will clearly do much to overcome the inadequacies that we noticed and that were also identified by the Force's own steering committee on recruitment and training. There are two very general considerations which we believe should help to shape future policy in this field.

First, it is reasonable to be sceptical about the likely effect of formal initial training, away from the real policing environment. Attempts to assess the effect (as envisaged by the systems approach) are welcome, but they may well produce disappointing results. The difficulty is that the way police officers behave is influenced much more by the structure of opportunities, risks, rewards and punishments within which they work from day to day than by the models of good policing offered to them at training school, however attractively they may be packaged and however persuasively advertised. This is not to say that initial training has no influence or importance. In earlier chapters we have argued that police officers may behave badly, on occasion, because they lack the skills to handle the situation well. By beginning to equip young officers with more skills initial training would help to create conditions in which good policing would be more likely to flourish. Even so, unless the messages from training school are reinforced by the environment in which young officers find themselves when they are posted to a District, they will not be remembered for long. It is unrealistic to regard training as the leading edge of change, because changes in training, without far more general changes in the organisation, are unlikely to have much effect.

Secondly, because of this reasonable scepticism about the effect of the initial training at Hendon on its own, much greater emphasis should be placed on the rehearsal and reinforcement of the skills and habits taught at Hendon throughout the first two years of actual policing experience. This point was recognised by Deputy Assisant Commissioner Hunte, then in charge of training, when he told DJS in March 1982 that 'the key point is the bonding of recruit and probationer training: you have to look at the two-year probationary period as a whole'. People really learn to be police officers on District and not at training school. This process of learning cannot take place in the controlled conditions of the laboratory, but it can be controlled much more than it has been in the past. Important steps have already been made in this direction. Since July 1981 probationers have spent four weeks on a 'street duties course' at some time during their first twelve months on District. At the time when we carried out our observations, what was done on these courses varied considerably from one District to another, but in all cases probationers had the chance to do various kinds of police work themselves but under the eyes of an experienced PC or sergeant, who would correct or encourage them and give advice. Since October 1981, probationers have not been available for operational policing during the first 10 weeks of their posting to a District. For the first six weeks they go around with a senior PC, normally a home beat officer, and they then go on the four-week street duties course. At a fairly early stage they also spend two weeks on station duties (a good way to get a general picture of what is going on) and one week with the community liaison officer. There is a continuing movement towards standardising and formalising the sequence of activities during the probationary period, and towards extending the period of induction before the probationer becomes a part of the operational manpower.

Carrying the training through the whole probationary period must mean more direct supervision by officers who are attuned to the overall training objectives. Of course this means that, if they are to be effective, the changes in training must be linked with a more coherent and purposive approach to policing as a whole among the many officers who will have a supervisory responsibility for probationers at some point. If training cannot change much on its own, the need to train probationers better can perhaps highlight the current lack of objectives and of coherent thinking about policing among more experienced and supervisory officers. One way to change the way they approach their work is to insist that they accept an explicit responsibility for training others and to make that the opportunity for questioning what they are trying to achieve.

If much of the training - and perhaps the most important part - is to be integrated with actual police work, it follows that many of the training resources should be locally based and under the control of local commanders, and not concentrated at Hendon. In fact, the Force is moving towards the development of district training units which will bring together responsibility for all the training that takes place locally (continuation training and street duties courses for probationers, promotion classes, first aid training, courses for the special constabulary). These local units will be supported and advised by Peel Centre. Each will run a central core of courses closely specified by Peel Centre, will develop other courses in partnership with Peel Centre, and may devise other courses entirely on its own. For example, a district training unit could devise and run courses for station officers, although there was no central requirement to do so. The staff of the units will consist of an inspector, five sergeants and seven instructors who may be sergeants or constables. They will all be district officers who have done an instructor's course. It should be possible for the instructors to spend much of their time out doing police work, but training people at the same time. In that way there will be a much greater degree of integration between training and actual police work, and the process of training itself will lead to an increase in the amount of direct supervision. Also, because the training is carried out locally, information about individuals being trained can be efficiently fed back to the local management.

If these arrangements can be made to work, they will clearly be an enormous step forward. The point that needs to be emphasised most is that the increase in local training capacity, the decentralisation of training and the greater integration of training and actual police work are likely to be much more important steps forward than changes in the content and methods of the initial training course. In fact, if the district training units can be made to work, the length of the initial training course might usefully be reduced. The recruits whom we interviewed in the autumn of 1980 found the 15-week course at Hendon quite long enough: many regarded it as an ordeal to be undergone with stoicism; except for those who resigned at an early stage, all were looking forward to getting away from Hendon and getting to learn the real job on their posting to a District. Attitudes towards the new course are probably not fundamentally different. Any long residential course in artificial surroundings that keeps recruits away from actual police work is likely to be unpopular. In the context of the 'integrated' approach to training, the formal initial course should be shortened, not lengthened; when Lord Scarman recommended that it should be lengthened, he did not envisage the strengthening in local training of probationers on the job that is now planned.

Finally, there are two specific points to be made about the initial training course. When we observed the course, the training in self-defence and techniques for restraining a violent person was rudimentary. Since then, training in new techniques has been introduced into the initial training course, but there is still no continuation training except for the shield training courses. We assume that the objectives should be to ensure that police officers do not use force except when absolutely necessary, that when they do use force they achieve their objective quickly and effectively (quickly succeed in making an arrest or in stopping a fight), and that they cause the minimum of injury to others and expose themselves to the minimum danger of being injured. Assuming that these are the objectives, the question arises as to what training police officers should be given in techniques of unarmed combat and restraint. Two arguments can be put forward. The first is that if officers are trained in unarmed combat, they will act more aggressively and will cause more injuries, just as someone who has a gun will, at some time, fire it, and will be more likely to cause injury than someone who has no gun. However, there are many arguments on the other side of the question.

1. If people - especially young men - have no special training, they will revert, when threatened, to methods of fighting used in the school playground or in pub brawls. Not having any other fighting skills, they may, for example, punch someone in the face in circumstances where this makes the incident much more serious than it was and causes a risk that it will get out of control.

2. If police officers are not able to defend themselves reasonably well, they will lack physical self-confidence and will tend to be easily frightened by any physical threat. This may well cause them to act aggressively (to cover their fear) and to call up other officers to help them in circumstances where this could provoke a greater disturbance.

3. If police officers are to be sent, unarmed, to deal with people behaving violently, it is wrong that they should be exposed to more danger than necessary through not being trained to defend themselves.

4. We have argued elsewhere that women should be more fully integrated into the Force and that an increase in the number of women police officers would benefit the Force in a number of ways. However, these developments will not be possible unless women are adequately trained in self defence.

Taken together, these arguments amount to a very strong case for really effective training of police recruits in techniques for restraining violent people and for defending themselves without weapons. The danger that greater fighting skills will lead to more police violence remains. The danger can be contained in two ways. First, the training itself can be designed to emphasise restraint and control, and the actual techniques taught can be ones that carry the minimum risk of causing an injury. Secondly, local management can work towards attaching different values to the use of force from those that prevail at present.

Finally, we had many indications during the course of our research that both women and members of ethnic minority groups were badly treated at training school. Prejudice against the women was very noticeable in many of the classes that we observed. None of the recruits in these classes belonged to ethnic minority groups, but according to the accounts given later by black police officers, they were often picked on at training school. Instructors would justify their treatment of black and female recruits by saying they were getting them used to the treatment they should expect from other officers or members of the public. This argument is hollow. If training is to change anything, it cannot start by accepting the worst aspects of police culture. There should be a determined effort to change the approach at training school to the minorities within the police force itself.

## Promotion

We have argued in Chapter XIV that one of the most striking characteristics of the Metropolitan Police as an organisation is a concern with following a procedure rather than achieving an end result. A closely related characteristic is a failure to reward officers who do well. There are highly specific and limited arrangements for commending officers for bravery and for making good arrests. Entry into various specialist groups is dependent on a demonstrated ability to do relevant kinds of police work. Nevertheless, most police officers can probably achieve their career objectives merely by avoiding 'trouble' or serious mistakes without actually performing well. Of course, the underlying difficulty is that the proper objectives of police work have often not been clearly defined, and even where they have been defined, reliable methods of assessing whether particular officers are achieving the objectives have not been developed. A policy of reinforcing good policing by rewards must depend on the ability to identify good policing when it takes place.

The system for promotion up to the rank of inspector is the clearest example of a failure to reward those who do well as police officers. Within this system, the ability to pass examinations is given far more weight than any measure of performance. There is another reason for this, as well as the organisation's difficulty in defining and measuring good performance. We have shown in a previous section that there is a wide range of educational attainment among those coming into the Force. There is also a wide range in terms of ambition; some expect to remain constables during the whole of their service, while others expect to be promoted fairly rapidly to very senior ranks. All enter at the same point and must spend a fairly long period as constables (normally five years at least) before taking the first step onto the promotion ladder. But, while everyone has to start on the shop floor, it is assumed that not all constables have the intellectual accomplishments required by supervisory or senior officers. It is easy to see how this has led to the development of a system of promotion by examinations; having rejected the distinction between 'officers' and 'men', and having made all entrants start at the bottom, the Force then defines an 'intellectual elite' from which the senior officers will be drawn. It is quite understandable that this should happen, because supervisory and senior officers do need to know a great deal more than constables about the law, criminal procedure and the organisation of the Force, and they do need to have greater facility in absorbing information and marshalling facts; undoubtedly, a substantial proportion of constables would not be able to cope with the intellectual demands of the job at a more senior rank. Nevertheless, this can be fully recognised without making written examinations the chief criterion within the promotion system.

To illustrate the way in which the present system works, it is best to take the example of promotion from constable to sergeant among uniform officers on normal (not specialist) duties, since this is the case that applies to the great majority of officers. A written examination (two papers each of $1\frac{1}{2}$ hours) is held in January each year. Police regulations specify that these examinations will include questions on criminal law; evidence and procedure in criminal courts; public general statutes and statutory rules, orders and instruments; the structure of local and central government in relation to the administration of the Force; police powers and duties, and procedure in relation thereto. The first paper tests knowledge of facts, whereas the second tests the ability to reason about 'practical problems' while referring to the relevant facts.

Constables may take the examination as competitors or as qualifiers. Those who take it as competitors are competing for a pre-determined number of vacancies for promotion to sergeant; they are arranged in order according to their total marks on the examination, and if there are 300 vacancies, the first 300 in the list will gain promotion. (However, nobody can pass as a competitor without gaining the minimum marks of 60 per cent in aggregate and at least 40 per cent on each paper.) Between 75 per cent and 90 per cent of the vacancies each year are allocated to competitors. They may take the examination after two years' service, but if they pass they will not normally be promoted to sergeant until they have completed five years' service. The only other requirement is that the constable's commander must certify that the constable is 'fit' for promotion to the rank of sergeant. This does not mean that the commander recommends that the constable should be promoted, but only that he sees no over-riding reason why he should not be. The great majority of commanders and other senior officers whom we spoke to in the course of our research said that it was very unusual for a constable to be refused the certificate of fitness to sit the promotion examination. A few said that although a formal refusal was very rare, it was more common for a constable to be told informally that the certificate of fitness would not be granted, with the result that the constable would not apply to sit the examination that year. The survey of police officers shows that of all constables other than probationers, only 2 per cent have ever been refused permission to sit the promotion examination. Altogether, it is quite clear that assessment of performance in the job plays almost no part in selection for promotion of those who sit the examination as competitors - who amount to about four fifths of those promoted to sergeant.

Between 10 per cent and 25 per cent of anticipated vacancies are set aside for constables who have not passed the examination as competitors, but have reached the qualifying standard (60 per cent overall and at least 40 per cent on each paper) and who have completed 10 years' service. Selection from those who have reached the qualifying standard and have completed 10 years' service is by the commander's recommendation followed by a selection board. In the first instance, commanders recommend individuals 'by reason of their efficiency, energy and general suitability', then the recommended officers appear before a central selection board consisting of a deputy assistant commissioner and two commanders. We have not studied the basis on which commanders make the initial recommendations or observed the selection boards, but compared with selection by competitive examination, this method of selection is likely to place far more emphasis on demonstrated success in practical police work. However, it only accounts for about one-fifth of those promoted to sergeant. It is an alternative route, but only for those who will be promoted late, if at all, and who have little prospect of reaching a high rank.

Among those promoted to sergeant each year, a small number (on average about a dozen) are selected to attend the 'special course' at the national police college. At a first stage, those who obtain very high marks in the promotion examination attend a central selection board within the Metropolitan Police. At a second stage, this board selects candidates to go forward to an extended interview at the police college. At a third stage, some of these candidates are selected for the special course after the extended interview. Those selected for the special course go into a fast promotion stream. They may be promoted to sergeant after three years' service (instead of the normal five). If they successfully complete the special course, they will be promoted to inspector after completing one year's service as a sergeant on normal duties. This means that a few people become inspectors after only five years in the Force. Officers who attended an extended interview but were not selected for the special course may be promoted to sergeant after four years' service instead of the usual five.

The system of promotion from sergeant to inspector is similar in principle to the system for promotion from constable to sergeant. There is another examination on the same lines as before, and officers may be promoted as competitors or as qualifiers. Sergeants may be promoted as competitors after serving four years in the rank. They are eligible to be considered for promotion as qualifiers after serving eight years in the rank, or after 18 years' service in total, of which at least four years is in the rank of sergeant.

We have used the most common case of the officer on normal uniform duties to explain the system. There are some variations in the case of officers in some specialist groups. In the case of some of the uniform specialisms (mounted branch, Thames division and dog section) officers are generally promoted within the specialism by reaching the qualifying standard in the promotion examination and then being chosen by a selection board set up within the specialist group. This probably means there is a greater emphasis on performance in the job than within the mainstream promotion system. Officers in these uniform specialist groups may sit the promotion examinations as competitors, but they will then be applying for promotion on ordinary duty, and if they are successful they will move out of the specialist group.

CID officers who gain promotion as competitors to sergeant or inspector transfer to uniform on being promoted. After serving for one year as uniform sergeants or inspectors they 'will be considered' for return to CID duties. This 'interchange scheme' ensures that CID officers who achieve promotion by the faster route have some experience of uniform duties at the sergeant and inspector levels. However, there is no system to ensure that uniform officers obtain experience of CID duties as they move through the ranks, even though those who become senior will have to manage groups of CID officers: as we explained in Chapter II, the CID office in each Division is headed by a detective chief-inspector, who reports to the uniform chief-superintendent in charge of the Division.

Alternatively, CID officers may sit the promotion examinations as qualifiers. The length of service requirements are the same as for uniform officers. Those who qualify on the examination attend a CID selection board, which chooses the ones to be promoted: this replaces the central selection board for qualifiers on the uniform side. CID officers who are promoted as qualifiers do not transfer to uniform on being promoted.

Although the details of this system are complex, it is a fair summary to say that assessment of performance has only a small influence on selection for promotion up to the rank of inspector. In the case of competitors, about four-fifths of all those promoted, it has hardly any influence at all, yet senior officers (chief-inspector and above) are drawn almost entirely from those promoted as competitors. In adopting such a system, the Force misses the opportunity to show what kinds of approach to police work are most valued, and what counts as doing the job well. It also throws away some of the advantage of having all recruits start together at the same rank. Constables commonly think that senior officers are very distant from day-to-day policing and have very little influence on what happens on the ground. This is rather surprising, in that all senior officers do have lengthy experience of doing the constable's job. Part of the reason for the constables' attitude is that senior officers have not, in their view, become senior by showing that they are good police officers, but by passing examinations. The survey of police officers shows that constables have far more to say against the promotion system up to inspector rank than for it; 41 per cent spontaneously criticised the system on the ground that it takes no account of practical abilities.

The system of promotion to higher ranks (chief-inspector, superintendent and chief-superintendent) is entirely different. Officers can be considered for promotion provided they have been confirmed in their current rank by the time that the selection procedure starts. Selection boards are held for each rank, normally once a year. Officers appear before a board on the recommendation of their commanders, who 'review the merits of each eligible officer and recommend those considered most suitable for promotion to appear before the selection board'. Commanders' decisions about who to put up for promotion, and the decisions of the selection boards, are mostly based on an assessment of officers' experience and performance.

## A new approach to promotion
Our analysis of the promotion system up to the rank of inspector highlights what is perhaps the greatest weakness in the management of the Force: that the arrangements for continuously assessing the performance of police officers are weak. An annual qualification report is made for every police officer. In the case of constables and sergeants, the detailed assessment (ratings on each of 13 qualities) is made by the inspector; further comments are added by the superintendent or chief-superintendent after an appraisal interview, and the commander endorses the form and may add further brief comments. However, these reports do not have much influence on selection for promotion up to inspector rank, and this seems to imply that the Force lacks confidence in their value. The reports do not grow out of a structured system of continuous assessment. It is a common view among constables and sergeants that they are not based on a detailed and thorough knowledge of their work, and we see no reason to disagree with this view. We have listened to many descriptions by constables of the interview with the supervising officer that takes place annually when the qualification report is prepared, in which the proceedings were represented as a farce that served only to illustrate the supervising officer's ignorance about what the constable had been doing or even who he was. No doubt these descriptions are exaggerated: but they show that the system of assessment does not command confidence.

An improved system of continuous assessment should be

developed in conjunction with a reshaped promotion system. This must in turn be dependent on a clearer definition of policing objectives and hence of what counts as good performance. It is important that several supervising officers should independently assess each officer's performance: in the case of constables, these might be a sergeant, an inspector (as at present) and a chief inspector. Assessment by officers at these relatively junior ranks would have two advantages: it would increase the chance that the assessments were based on genuine knowledge of the constable's performance and it would strengthen the genuinely supervisory role of the more junior ranks - we shall argue in the next chapter that the supervisory role of sergeants and inspectors has not been fully realised. The use of several independent assessments would minimise the risk of relying too much on the judgement or prejudice of an individual officer. The most difficult aspect is the development of a varied set of dimensions of performance refined in a much more specific way than those used in the current system, and related to an evolving conception of the objectives of police work and of the skills required to work towards these objectives. They might include 'hard' measures of performance (especially of the actual amount of work done) and assessments or descriptions of performance on specific occasions when the officer's work was directly observed.

Of course, it would not be necessary to wait for the development of a system of continuous assessment before developing a new approach to promotion. The two should be developed together, and the development of the one would act as a stimulus to the development of the other. The following are the main elements of a new system of promotion up to the rank of inspector that we believe would be more appropriate to the needs of the Force than the present system.

1.  Not everyone wants to be promoted. As at present, the procedure would be started by the officer making a formal application to be considered for promotion to the next rank. Officers would be eligible to apply after completing a defined minimum period of service in the current rank, say four years as a constable before becoming eligible to be considered for promotion to sergeant.

2.  Continuous assessments of the officer's performance would be available and would be consulted. Those not reaching a defined standard (a considerable proportion) would be rejected.

3.  For those who had passed stage 2 a further assessment of performance would be made, on the usual pattern, by three officers independently. Again, a proportion of applications would be rejected on the basis of this

assessment. Officers whose application was rejected at stages 2 or 3 would be interviewed by their supervising officer (the chief-superintendent) who would explain the reasons for the rejection and engage in a constructive discussion with the applicant about ways in which his performance might be improved to help him to be considered for promotion the following year. In this way, the promotion system would be integrated with the management of police officers and the control of their behaviour. These interviews would also be an opportunity for the applicant to discuss ways in which he could be helped to gain experience of aspects of police work in which he was judged to be weak.

4. Applicants who qualified on the continuous assessment would take a test, for which no special study would be required. This would test knowledge and reasoning of the kind required at their current rank. It would also include a fairly stiff test of literacy and numeracy as applied to police work: for example, applicants might be required to write a report on a police matter and to reason from statistics on crime or police activities. The purpose of this test would be to establish whether applicants were capable of developing the knowledge and reasoning skills they would require at the new rank - not whether they already had them. A qualifying standard would be set, and applicants who failed to reach this standard would be rejected. They would be given a written assessment of their performance on the test with a diagnosis of weaknesses to help them to plan their career development.

5. The remaining applicants would appear before a central selection board, which would have copies of the applicant's career history, continuous assessments and marks on the test. The board would decide whether or not to recommend each officer for promotion after conducting a short interview. The reasons for rejection would be explained to unsuccessful applicants.

6. Applicants recommended for promotion would attend a residential course which would cover, intensively, the knowledge of the law and policing procedures required in the new rank, but would also make a start towards developing management skills. This course would replace both the present 'promotion classes' that officers attend before attempting the examination and the present pre-promotion courses that they attend after success in the examination. It should be a far more efficient method of study than the present promotion

classes and private study, which are spread out over a long period. Applicants would be continuously assessed during this course and would take a test (including a practical) at the end of it. They would be eligible for promotion to the new rank on successfully completing the course, and would be made up (as at present) as the vacancies arose. This course would not, however, be regarded as a stage in the selection process, since all officers selected by the board should be fully capable of successfully completing it. Anyone who failed the couse would be allowed to take it again the following year if they wished to.

Of course, this is only a framework for a new approach to promotion. Much would depend on the detailed working out of the various elements of such a system. However, even this sketch of a new approach is enough to show that a better system is possible. It would offer a number of advantages.

a)  By placing a much greater emphasis on performance, it would ensure that only those judged to be good police officers would be promoted.

b)  The system of management and control would be integrated much more fully than at present with the promotion system, so that the one would reinforce the other. This means that the promotion system would help to encourage the kind of policing that is desired, and would stimulate the organisation to develop better methods of assessing performance.

c)  The system should be less wasteful, because the study required by officers to be promoted would be concentrated and intensive, and there would not be a large number of officers who spend time studying, and attend classes, but who do not achieve promotion.

d)  There would be little or no loss of impartiality, compared with the present system. Assessment of some aspects of performance would be a matter of judgement, but this is better than failing to assess these aspects of performance at all; also, the judgements would be made independently by several supervising officers.

e)  While assessment of performance would be an important part of the system, use of an appropriate test would still ensure that officers would not be promoted without having the necessary intellectual skills.

## Career development

For many police officers, career development will not be through the promotion system. The survey of police officers shows that 41 per cent of constables have been in the Force for ten years or more; most of these will never be promoted. The survey also shows that only 33 per cent of constables definitely expect to try for promotion by sitting the sergeant's examination. Nevertheless, there is a great variety of jobs to be done at the constable level, many of them requiring specialist knowledge and skills. Some of these jobs are generally regarded as more desirable than others either because of their intrinsic interest or because they offer greater opportunities for overtime, or for both of these reasons. While some views about the prestige or interest of particular jobs and specialisms are widely shared within the Force, individuals may of course have sharply different interests and aptitudes.

The structure of the pathways by which constables move between particular jobs and specialisms may be as important as the structure of the promotion system. Everyone within the Force is eventually influenced by the criteria that decide promotion, because these criteria help to shape the 'culture' in which they move. However, constables who do not expect to be promoted - at least half of the total - are influenced only indirectly: they do not need to adapt their own behaviour to meet the criteria. On the other hand, all constables hope to achieve some kind of career development, and have considerable scope for doing so; in fact, many would argue that the interest, variety and job satisfaction provided by some kind of specialist job at constable rank can be much greater than the personal rewards of being a station sergeant. It follows that one of the chief means available to management of influencing and controlling the behaviour of constables is by helping those who perform well to develop their careers within their present rank.

Some of the opportunities available to constables are within their present operational unit, while others would involve moving to a different group. For example, there is considerable scope for career development within uniform reliefs through taking the successive driving courses which qualify officers to drive a panda or general purpose car, a van and finally an area car. An officer may also become an authorised shot. Some members of each relief are required to have training in using the VDU terminal connected to the police computer and in using the teleprinter. Thus, there is already considerable scope for career development within the uniform relief; with the growth of a more purposive and planned approach to policing by reliefs, the scope for career development should increase, because more specialist skills will be required.

Next, there are many moves available to an officer on a uniform relief to other jobs within the same Division. He may spend a period in the Immediate Response Unit, become a home beat officer or work on a divisional squad. If he is interested in CID work he may move to the divisional crime squad. Moves to less demanding or inside jobs are available for some older officers.

Finally, there is the possibility of a move away from the Division into a specialist group, such as the Traffic Division, the Special Patrol Group, the Dog Section, the Mounted Branch or the Thames Division. There is also, of course, the possibility of a move into the CID.

Whether or not a constable will be nominated to take a driving course is decided by his inspector in consultation with the senior officers at the Division - in other words, the decision is entirely a matter for the constable's current supervisory officers. Whether or not a constable will move to Traffic Division is, however, decided by Traffic Division more than by the constable's present supervisory officers. The same applies to other uniform specialisms, to central squads and to CID. It is natural and probably inevitable that these groups should operate their own selection systems. What is lacking at present is that these miniature selection systems are not related to a more general system for rewarding good performance assessed according to an agreed set of criteria.

Improvements in the career development system, as in the promotion system, must depend on the establishment of a more effective and sensitive method of continuously assessing the performance of officers. This would then be linked with a regular review of each officer's experience and of ways in which it might be extended. Something like this is done at present; every officer is seen by his chief-superintendent when the annual qualification report is prepared, and this is an opportunity for discussion of possible career moves. What we are suggesting is that the assessment should be more thorough and sensitive, and that career development should be more formally and explicitly considered and discussed every year. This would strengthen the links between performance and rewards, since officers would frequently be told that they would have the opportunity to go on a certain course or make a move to a specialist job only if their performance improved in certain specific respects. It would also lead to a better use of human resources and help officers to plan their careers in the light of a fuller knowledge of themselves and of the opportunities available. In such a large organisation with so many different kinds of jobs, managers need to perform the functions of a careers officer: that is, they need to give people relevant information about job opportunities within the organisation and, by providing an assessment of their experience and aptitudes, to help them decide what kind of job would suit them best.

The existence of miniature selection procedures run by various specialist groups is a difficulty if these groups are allowed to specify their requirements quite independently of a more general system for assessing officers' performance. It is important that a constable should be considered for entry to a specialist group only following a positive decision by his current supervising officer on the basis of his experience and continuous assessments.

Secondly, the selection procedures used by specialist groups should take place within a common framework for the assessment of performance, though particular specialisms will properly emphasise particular kinds of experience and aptitudes.

## The extent and nature of supervision

To the outside observer, one of the most striking facts about police work in the Met is that individual constables, including probationers, carry out their duties for the most part without any direct supervision by more senior officers.  There are some occasions when supervisory officers see constables doing police work, but these are exceptional and mostly confined to a limited range of policing activities, so that supervisory officers are seldom in a position to form a balanced judgement, based on their own observation, of how an individual officer approaches his job.  Sergeants and inspectors (and more rarely chief-inspectors and above) see constables dealing with prisoners and carrying out interviews inside police stations.  At events requiring a large police presence, senior officers see constables working, but this kind of activity is very different from most police work and forms only a small proportion of the total.  Where officers are working in a squad and cooperating very closely on a single task (as, for example, in a murder squad) there is more opportunity than usual for direct supervision. Generally speaking, however, it is rare for a constable to carry out police work outside in the company of a supervising officer.

On the whole, this lack of direct supervision is regarded within the Force as being natural and inevitable: so much so that it leads to a special use of words.  When a senior officer talks about 'supervision', he generally means looking at paperwork such as diaries, messages or log books and issuing reprimands when they have been wrongly or incompletely filled in.  It takes an effort of imagination for many senior officers to see that to call this supervision is to use words in a way that strikes people outside the Force as odd.

A second striking fact about supervision in the Force is that it tends very strongly to be negative: that is, supervisory officers criticise the officers under their command far more often than they praise or encourage them. The negative character of supervision is closely connected with the lack of direct supervision. Since senior officers are seldom on the spot, they get to know about things mostly when they have gone wrong. They often come to see their job, therefore, as dealing with mistakes and failures rather than forming constructive plans and nurturing success.

## Supervision by senior officers

It would not be reasonable to expect the District management team, who are typically in charge of about 1,000 officers, to do a significant amount of direct supervision themselves. When they do come into direct contact with constables, this is often in connection with a disciplinary matter or because they are carrying out a check. On the one occasion when we saw a commander directly impinge on a day-to-day policing matter, it was to see if something had gone wrong. DJS was in the front office of a police station when the commander's driver came in and spoke to one of the sergeants, saying that the commander had heard a call come out for the area car which had not been answered. The sergeant immediately checked up and found that the area car crew had 'booked off' because they were dealing with a prisoner. This check may have inspired some respect for the commander, but various officers on the relief pointed out that they never heard from him except when he had something to criticise; one added that he 'never had a friendly word' for anyone, and others agreed. In fact, this was not strictly true, because JG, working on a different Division within the same District, was shown a teleprinter message sent by the commander to congratulate a woman detective constable on passing the promotion exam. However, this gesture was not well received. The detective inspector thought that since the commander did not know the woman, the note was too impersonal and mechanical. 'The man never bothers to visit Sheila in person or ask her how her work is going or even accompany her. No, never does that but sends these condescending notes because he's been told that it's good man management on some command course.'

It would be more realistic to expect the Divisional management team, typically in charge of about 250 officers, to have some personal contact with each of them and to observe the work of at least some of them from time to time. In terms of size, this Divisional unit is comparable with a large primary school or a very small secondary school; in any such school, the head teacher will recognise and be able to name all of the children and (without consulting records) will be able to say something about how each one is getting on. Also, the head will take some classes and will probably teach every child (thus directly observe every child's work) at some point in the child's career. Chief-superintendents and superintendents do not have this kind of direct contact with the officers under their command. From the survey of police officers we find that only 15 per cent of constables had ever carried out normal police work outside the police station in the presence of their chief-superintendent, and an even smaller proportion (5 per cent) had done police work inside the police station in his presence. The survey shows that direct supervision by superintendents is only slightly more common.

These findings from the survey are underlined by our own observations and informal interviews. The very first time that he went out with an area car, DJS asked the crew who their chief-superintendent was: they did not know his name, or the names of most of the other senior officers on the Division. Our further research showed that this was not unusual. On the first occasion, the driver explained that the senior officers changed so often that it was hard to keep track of them, and he made it clear that he thought they had little relevance to the way that actual police work was carried out on the Division. He did know the commander, but made derisory comments about him. 'I wish you could be a fly on the wall as he was talking to us to see the way he talks to us.' Later, during an informal interview, DJS pressed the chief-superintendent of this Division on the subject of supervision.

> DJS: How effectively are you able to supervise the officers under your command? How far are they supervised by more junior officers?
>
> Chief-superintendent: There is little visual observation of what PCs do, but there is much supervision of a kind by sergeants and inspectors. They know the attitudes of their PCs, they are in radio communication with them, in general they know whether someone is doing any work or not. I see letters of thanks and complaints, I note the appearance of officers and the standard of their written work. But the duty officers know exactly what quality and amount of work everyone under their command does. They are a very close-knit group.
>
> DJS: PCs often say that they don't even know the names of officers at your level, that they change very often, that you have little to do with what actually goes on. Is it possible for you to supervise more directly or closely?
>
> Chief-superintendent: If you try, they think you are spying on them. In certain situations I do supervise directly. I take charge of public order events, raids, for example large-scale licensing and drugs raids. But on these occasions the operational chief-inspector will be in charge and I will be there to lend weight and will be careful not to interfere unless I have to.

It is worth isolating the separate points that emerge from this statement. In saying 'there is little visual observation of what PCs do' the chief-superintendent made it clear that PCs are directly supervised neither by him nor by the sergeants and inspectors. By mentioning radio communication as a method of supervision he showed that he thought remote observation and control of PCs by sergeants and inspectors was enough. His mention of letters of thanks and complaints and standards of written work showed that he thought he himself was expected to supervise 'on paper'. When pressed on the subject of direct supervision he said 'If you try, they think you are spying on them', which neatly sums up the quality of the relationship between the management and constables: the remark flows from the assumption that the two groups are separate and antagonistic. Finally, there is a refusal to face the facts in the assertion that 'the duty officers know exactly what quality and amount of work everyone under their command does'. From the rest of the chief-superintendent's remarks, this cannot be true unless the quality and amount of work can be defined purely in terms of radio communications and written records.

The chief-superintendent of another Division in the same District was interviewed by JG, who was much less abrasive in his questioning, and asked no specific question about supervision. However, the chief-superintendent spontaneously reflected on his role (along with his deputy). 'We're bogged down by so much administrative work that we don't get out and about enough. I'd like to occasionally travel around in the area car for an hour or two, but it's impossible ...' By this spontaneous remark, the chief-superintendent made it clear that he never goes out in a police car.

The attitudes of PCs, sergeants and inspectors towards supervision 'at a distance' by senior officers are mixed and, in some cases, ambivalent. It is quite common for constables to think that senior officers have their own job to do, which is distinct and separate from the job of the officers 'on the ground', and that it is better if they stick to their own job and 'interfere' as little as possible with the work of constables. At the same time, senior officers are often criticised for being distant, arrogant or unfriendly, for not communicating with the lower ranks and for being out of touch with what is going on. An area car driver put this latter view to JG at length while driving around his Division. He said that the chief-superintendent and superintendent were not well liked because they were not approachable. Whenever he went to the chief-superintendent's office (which he had done as an individual and as a Police Federation representative) the chief-superintendent did all the talking, which he thought was quite wrong. He thought there was no real channel through which the views of constables could be expressed to those at higher levels in the hierarchy, and he resented this. He criticised senior officers for 'playing safe', and described their supervision as a 'massive paperwork exercise' which had little effect on the policing that actually went on. What this method of supervision picked up, he explained, was any failures to follow the recognised procedures - forms not filled in, signatures not added, ticks not in the right boxes. He thought that senior officers were 'obsessed' with this kind of thing because it was failures of this kind that could affect their future careers. We also heard similar views expressed by sergeants and inspectors. For example, an inspector who was very popular with his own relief mentioned (spontaneously) that he thought communication was the most important part of his job. 'If I didn't communicate with my men and vice versa I wouldn't be able to run an effective relief.' By contrast he said (again spontaneously) that 'most senior officers are reluctant to communicate with anyone'.

The view that it is better for senior officers to 'interfere' as little as possible is common among the lower ranks, but it often goes with the idea that they should 'show and interest' and if any special operation has been organised should be present but only in a ceremonial capacity and without taking an active part. At an early stage during JG's visit to a CID office, a detective inspector said to him, 'Jones (the chief-superintendent) just lets the people who know about it (CID work) get on with it, which is quite right really'. Two weeks later, some constables in the crime squad, along with their sergeant, organised a raid on premises they had been observing for some time, and which they thought were used as a warehouse for stolen goods or for weapons. Senior officers were informed, and the chief-superintendent and detective chief-inspector turned up on the day. The chief-superintendent arrived after the search began, in full uniform. He was much respected for doing so, especially since he had avoided any 'interference' with the planning by not arriving until things were under way. One officer said, 'At least it shows he's interested', another 'It's good of him to make a showing, you've got to give him that'.

DJS was with a relief at one Division shortly after a new chief-superintendent had taken over. One day the main subject of conversation was that he had appeared at the parade of the early turn relief (just before 6 am). This was considered a remarkable and exceptional event. There was great speculation about what it meant and whether the chief-superintendent was planning sweeping reforms. On the whole, the response of the relief was one of reluctant approval; the PCs felt that 'at least the man made the effort', and he had not criticised anyone or caused any trouble. This shows that the lower ranks do not expect to be directly supervised by senior officers: but attempts by senior officers to become more directly involved in what the lower ranks are doing do not necessarily cause antagonism. There was a superintendent at one of the Divisions that we studied who was much more closely and actively involved in the day-to-day work of the lower ranks than any other senior officer we came across: he was also more popular with the lower ranks than any other. Some of the comments made by members of the relief were, 'He knows what he's doing', 'He's got a lot of bottle', and 'I have to admit, I like the man'. This PC was reluctant to admit that he liked the superintendent because he had been promoted rapidly and was young for his rank, and also just because he was a senior officer - he felt that to like a senior officer, as opposed to fearing or respecting him, was not entirely normal. This superintendent often took snacks or meals in the canteen and chatted to the constables there, was often to be seen in the charge room, and quite frequently went out with members of the reliefs (he did this twice when DJS was present). All this was thought to be very unusual, but improved his standing with the relief. An experienced PC said, 'You need to have someone upstairs who's a bit like God, but Mr Benson (the chief-superintendent) is like that, so between the two of them they make a team'.

## Sergeants and inspectors

At the time when we carried out the research, there was a shortage of sergeants in the Force (since then the numbers have risen). However, on some of the reliefs that we worked with the number of sergeants was up to establishment. There were, for example, four sergeants on a relief that DJS worked with. Three of these were normally on duty at the Divisional police station; one was looking after the sub-divisional station, but there was not much to do there and he was often to be seen at the Divisional station. Of the three sergeants based at the Divisional station, one was required to do the station officer's job, but that still left two. They tended to stay in the police station, sometimes helping the station officer. On occasion they went out in the 'section panda', normally the two sergeants together. There was only one occasion when DJS saw a sergeant go out with constables on this Division: this was in response to a call about an armed robbery, when one of the sergeants at the station jumped into a panda car and got a PC to drive him to the scene. Otherwise in all the time that DJS was out with constables at this Division he never saw a sergeant outside except passing by, normally with another sergeant, in the 'section panda'. During a very quiet night shift, DJS had a long conversation at the police station with the relief inspector, one of the sergeants and a PC. DJS pointed out that the PCs, including the probationers, were not directly supervised and the inspector and sergeant agreed. DJS then said he had noticed that on this relief sergeants were quite often available to go out, but they had not been with the constables he had been with. He asked bluntly what, in that case, the sergeants had been doing. At this point the PC looked embarrassed and moved away. The sergeant leaned over to DJS and said quietly, 'Resting'. DJS pointed out that the sergeants did go out in the section panda and asked why they did not go out with probationers and younger constables instead. The sergeant and inspector could not think of any answer to this. They made it clear that it was not traditional for sergeants to supervise on the streets, and that when they went out they expected to do their own work as a PC would. On the following shift, DJS raised the subject with the PC he was with, who said there were effectively no differences in rank among officers out on the street - they all did the same job and made their own decisions. He only qualified this by making an exception of public order events.

Later, DJS discussed the level of supervision with the chief-superintendent at the same Division.

DJS: How much information do you think you have about how individual PCs operate?

Chief-superintendent: We don't have enough. The great bulk of PCs I don't know personally, I only know about them through the relief inspector. Some are brought to my notice, usually because of a lack of vitality, because they don't do anything. This place suffers from a lack of continuity. I'm the third chief-superintendent in three years here. We are on our third superintendent in 18 months. John Stiles (the present superintendent) came in January. So at that point we had little knowledge of the men. Some of the relief inspectors have been here only a year.....

DJS: What about the relief inspectors, do they know their officers?

Chief-superintendent: Some do, some don't. Most of them know them by impressions, certainly by seeing how they behave in the charge room. They see them in the street on occasion, for example in the case of fatal accidents which have to be dealt with by an inspector. They see for example their pocket book reports. They get information from the sergeants. They are influenced by what they know about an officer's background. But it's true that they mostly work on the basis of what they see in the station and general impressions, and what they hear about the officer, rather than from direct observation or supervision on the streets.

DJS: In my time with the relief I did not see the sergeants directly supervising PCs or, in particular, probationers.

Chief-superintendent: I agree that the probationers are not well supervised by sergeants...

DJS: On the relief I was with there were four sergeants, and that was enough for some of them to have done more real supervision than they did.

Chief-superintendent: I agree that we don't use the sergeants enough.

DJS: Is it because the sergeant's job, before the creation of admin. units, used to be largely administrative, and it hasn't changed or adapted since?

Chief-superintendent: Yes. In my early days, sergeants used to deal with everything, for example with all the paperwork on process. They had no time for supervision. Now their pattern of work has not changed to meet the new circumstances. At the very best, PCs get taught by other PCs.

DJS pursued the point again with the superintendent.

DJS: What are sergeants actually supposed to do?

Superintendent: They should be supervising. The sergeant should be out and about as much as possible, but he has a considerable amount of paperwork and may have to help in the charge room. But on early turn and in the early part of the night shift he should be out and about.

DJS: In all the time I spent with Mr Barker's relief I was only once with a PC outside the police station when there was also a sergeant present.
Superintendent: I agree that they don't in fact supervise directly.

Finally, DJS put a similar question to the commander, who replied, 'Sergeants should go out in the section panda or on foot with PCs, but I accept that in practice it doesn't often happen'.

While there was some variation between Divisions and between individual sergeants, it was broadly true that there was little direct supervision by sergeants throughout the Divisions that we studied. In a number of cases there were fewer sergeants available than the three to four on the relief just described, and consequently there was often less opportunity for sergeants to supervise directly. However, it was clear that this was not the main reason for the lack of direct supervision. When DJS spent the early turn with a relief on a different Division, there were two sergeants on duty. They jointly engaged him in a long conversation at the police station. One took the opportunity to complain that the available manpower on the reliefs was quite inadequate, and that a high proportion of officers were taken away to deal with other matters without any appreciation of the problems of the reliefs, which were the real policemen doing the important work. Both sergeants also complained that the difference in pay between constables and sergeants was too small, so that with overtime a PC with long service could earn more than a young sergeant, which they thought was manifestly wrong. They said there was no incentive to become a sergeant and that the best people did not, therefore, go for promotion. DJS then asked the second sergeant (the one who was not acting as station officer) what he was supposed to be doing at that moment (he had been talking for about an hour). He said (with heavy irony), 'Supervising my two foot patrol officers'. His argument was that since there were only two it was not worth his while to do any supervision. It did not seem to occur to him that this would have been a good opportunity to take a thorough look at what these two officers were doing and how they were doing it. He stayed in the police station throughout the shift without doing any police work or supervision. Later DJS spent the night shift with a WPC on the same relief. There were again two sergeants on duty, one the station officer and the other 'section sergeant'. DJS asked the WPC what the section sergeant would be doing. She replied, 'Supervising us'. DJS said, 'Yes, but what is he actually doing at this moment?' (it was around midnight). She said, 'Going round in a car, probably'. Clearly, she did not expect the sergeant to be present when she did any police work. She had picked up one of the probationers, who was supposed to be walking, and she agreed that the other walkers had probably got into cars by now. The section sergeant made no attempt to stop this rearrangement of the postings given out at parade; all of the officers who were out were therefore in cars, and the sergeant was in a separate car on his own so that he had minimised the chance of directly supervising any police work.

There is little sense in the Met that the sergeants are in a position of authority over constables; sergeants and constables often treat each other in a familiar way without much indication that the sergeants can impose their authority when the need arises. This point was highlighted by officers who had served in other forces, where the distinction of rank is given more weight. A sergeant who had been a PC in another force told JG:

> In Loomshire, sergeants are next to God. If one tells you to do something and you don't do it, you are asked to produce a report which will explain why. If this is an unsatisfactory explanation, you're in trouble. For example, PCs never just wander in and out of the nick. They have to explain to the skipper (sergeant) why they're not on the streets. They have to ask permission to come in and write an incident up.

The commander of one of the Districts that we studied had transferred (at the rank of commander) from another force. He made just the same point as the sergeant who had served in Loomshire.

> DJS: What can be done to control and supervise what ordinary PCs do?
> Commander: Very little. They have to be self-disciplined. We can only supervise them en masse at public order events, or at the police station.
> DJS: Do you think sergeants are used for supervising and training the young PCs as much as they might be? My experience has been that they rarely accompany them on the streets or in cars.
> Commander: I agree that we have lost our way with the sergeant rank. Most of the time they are in the police stations doing charging and administration. At times that is inevitable because of the number of people passing through the station, but we could use them for supervision more. There is a difference between the Met and the provinces in this. Here the 'us and them' line is between the inspector and the chief-inspector. In the provinces it is between the PC and the sergeant. This means that the sergeant genuinely manages and supervises more. I disagree with the competitive examination system. It means that people do not get promoted for being good at the job. In the provinces sergeants and inspectors have more of a disciplinary role and are closer to the senior officers. Here it is far more common for PCs to use Christian names with sergeants and inspectors, whereas this is uncommon in the provinces.

Because of this lack of authority, sergeants may not feel that they are in a strong enough position to intervene when they see a constable doing something they disapprove of. On one night shift, JG saw a sergeant preparing to go out in a general purpose car on his own and decided to accompany him. The sergeant had quite strong views about how police work should be done and made it clear that he disapproved of officers who used excessive force. He made no particular effort to supervise the work of officers on the relief, but came into contact with several officers when answering calls throughout the shift. At about 2 am he and JG heard on the radio that the area car had come across a Ford Cortina being driven erratically with three youths inside and a man spreadeagled on the bonnet. They chased the car, the man on the bonnet was thrown off, and when two of the tyres burst as they hit the kerb the car ground to a halt. Two of the occupants ran away, but when the sergeant and JG arrived on the scene the third had been arrested and put into the area car. The sergeant asked on the PR for a description of the youths who had escaped. The area car driver replied that the youth who had been arrested was not 'coming across much at the moment'. The sergeant laughed wryly and said to JG that the information would be forthcoming soon enough, hinting that violence would be used. Before his own car drove off, JG saw one of the officers in the area car make a grab for the youth. The sergeant and JG looked around for the suspects for a while. Soon the area car driver said over the radio that they had got some information from the captured youth. The sergeant laughed again, saying, 'Sometimes it's better for me not to look'. At this point, the area car reappeared. The sergeant said, 'Ah, look, the boy is still holding his head'. One explanation of his attitude would be that he thought the area car crew had hit the youth to make him give a description of his friends, but did not disapprove. However, this did not fit in with his expressed views about the use of force. It seemed more likely that he would not have hit the youth himself, but did not think it appropriate to intervene when the area car crew did so.

These findings show that sergeants do not often supervise police officers outside the police station and that when they do observe incidents they may be reluctant to exert a direct influence. Even at the time of our observations, when there was a shortage of sergeants, there was enough capacity for much more direct supervision than actually took place. Now that numbers are increasing, there should be further capacity of this kind.

As the commander whom we have quoted pointed out, it is the station officer's job that has been most closely identified with the sergeant rank. In this capacity, sergeants do have heavy responsibilities, and at busy times they have to work very hard. As station officers they are felt to have genuine authority and certainly exert an influence. The most important reason for this is that the station officer has to decide whether a prisoner is to be released or held in custody, whether he is to be charged, and, if so, what the charge or charges will be. Also, the station officer has an influence because he regularly sees the constables dealing with prisoners and they see him dealing with prisoners. It is fairly common for the station officer to decide to release an arrested person without charge, and this has a considerable influence on the behaviour of constables, who may be in a difficult position if the station officer decides not to charge and there does not seem to have been a good reason to make the arrest. On the other hand, sergeants often fail to make full use of their authority in this respect. In Chapter IV we described a case where three black youths were arrested on suspicion of having stolen a handbag, but were eventually released without charge when the victim said they were not the culprits. Many aspects of the investigation and questioning were very badly handled; in particular, the youths were treated oppressively and were kept in custody long after it had become plain that there was no real evidence against them. The station officer did not intervene at all in the handling of this case: he accepted that the youths should be kept in custody and questioned without establishing what were the grounds for suspicion (they were flimsy), he did not check on the way the questioning was being conducted or what was emerging from it and therefore continued to hold the youths although there was no evidence against them, and he either did not notice or did not object to the oppressive way in which they were treated. More senior officers were also present during parts of the procedure, and they also failed to intervene. We cannot point to a case where a station officer did decisively intervene to prevent developments of this kind, but we did observe a number of cases where station officers refused to charge.

We have said that little use is made of the supervisory capacity of sergeants outside the police station, but that they do exert an important influence as supervisors when acting as station officers. In the case of inspectors it is more difficult to generalise. Certainly, relief inspectors are in a position to have a decisive influence because their responsibilities are well-defined: they are in charge of a group of about 40 officers (but usually about 20 or less on duty at a particular time) and, in principle, there is fairly wide scope for them to direct the pattern of work of the relief. They have a responsibility to ensure that probationers are given an appropriate balance of work and receive suitable advice and training on the job. The distinction of rank between constables and inspectors is felt to be real, yet constables usually feel that the inspector is 'on their side' whereas the senior officers (chief-inspector and above) are on the other side of the fence. One reason for this is that they come into regular contact, in the context of day-to-day policing, with their inspector, whereas they do not come into regular contact with chief-inspectors and above. Another reason is that above the rank of inspector there is a different system of promotion (by nomination and selection boards) so that senior officers appear rather like commissioned, as opposed

543

to non-commissioned officers in the armed forces. For all of these reasons, the inspector has a better opportunity than officers at other ranks to exert influence and authority over a small group of officers who will get to know him well and trust him.

Our observations suggest that there is a very wide variation in the extent to which inspectors make use of this excellent opportunity to supervise and manage. On some of the reliefs we worked with, the constables went out of their way to say that they respected and liked their inspector: on others they went out of their way to make derisory comments about him. When the inspector was criticised it was usually on the grounds that he knew little about what was going on, seldom went out on the streets and only intervened to criticise. Where the inspector was respected or praised it was because he 'took an interest', put himself in difficult or dangerous situations alongside other members of the relief, knew what was going on and provided help and support. There was sometimes a simple reason for a 'lack of interest' on the part of the inspector. For example, we came across two inspectors who had been obliged to transfer to uniform on promotion and hoped to return to CID after completing one year as a uniform inspector, and who regarded this year as a tiresome interruption to their CID careers. Also, we came across one inspector who had been promoted as a qualifier shortly before retirement and who regarded this promotion as chiefly a way of improving his pension. Another important factor is that some inspectors are not well-equipped to cope with the demands of the job: this happens because, as we have explained in the last chapter, promotion to this rank is not based on an assessment of ability in practical policing.

Although there are considerable variations, a majority of inspectors do spend a substantial amount of their time out on foot or in a car and in circumstances where they can supervise the work of constables. The survey of police officers shows that 63 per cent of constables on reliefs had been outside in the company of their inspector within the past month. (At the same time, 13 per cent said their inspector had never seen them do any police work outside.) On several of the reliefs with which we worked it was common for the inspector to go out in a car with a constable, and on most of them the inspector went out walking from time to time. The inspectors who were most respected would get into a car and go to the scene when they heard about a serious incident, even if they were doing something else at the station at the time. In Chapter XV we described in detail an incident that might have turned into a serious disturbance if the inspector had not taken charge at the scene.

On the other hand, the capacity of inspectors to plan the activity of their reliefs in a purposive way has been little developed. This is only one aspect of a failure to shape police work in the light of defined objectives, which applies throughout the ranks.

## Supervision of probationers

At the beginning of our research (the Autumn of 1980) arrangements for the supervision of probationers on Division were clearly inadequate, and a majority of supervising officers recognised that this was so. The parent constable system (whereby a probationer was shown the job by an experienced constable) had been allowed to lapse and nothing had been put in its place. One of the reasons for the breakdown was the large number of probationers in relation to the number of more experienced officers. From the survey of police officers we find that in the Autumn of 1982, one-third of constables on reliefs were probationers, and a substantial proportion of the confirmed constables were too inexperienced to act as parent constables. In the inner Divisions, the problem was still more acute, since these Divisions took more of the probationers than the outer ones. When DJS first spoke to a relief inspector, which happened to be on a busy inner London Division, the inspector immediately took the opportunity to complain about the difficulties caused by having such a large number of probationers on his relief. He said that out of the 42 officers on his relief, half were probationers, most of whom could not be given 'real police work' because they were not capable of doing it. DJS later raised this with the chief-inspector (operations) and the superintendent of the Division. They said that the inspector had been complaining about the low strength of his relief and that the only way they could build up the strength was to bring in more probationers which they thought was 'better than nothing'. They did not conceal their irritation with the inspector and his grumbles; far from making any constructive suggestions about training arrangements to get over the inspector's problem, they said that 'any probationer who is no good should be moved or asked to resign'. When DJS pointed out that any inadequate probationer who was moved would simply turn into someone else's problem, they said 'in the great majority of cases he would be asked to resign'. Thus, the inspector was acutely aware of the difficulty of supervising and training his probationers on the job, not necessarily because they were poor material, but because their abilities needed to be developed and there was too little capacity for supervision and training. The senior officers preferred to ignore the problem, although it would be immediately obvious to any intelligent observer after only an hour or two spent at the Division. Saying that inadequate probationers would be required to resign (in fact very few were) was a way of rejecting the need to develop the skills of young police officers. On another Division within the same District, a sergeant acting as station officer told JG that the relief continued to receive more recruits although there was supposed to be a ban on sending any more to the Division. 'You can have the young blokes as long as you increase the number of skippers (sergeants) and the amount of supervision. If you don't do that, it's madness having the younger blokes - we've been saying it for years.' Lord Scarman paid more attention to this view than did the senior officers at these inner Divisions.

Although the parent constable system had lapsed, there was an awareness of the need to help the probationers among some of the more experienced constables. For example, an area car driver raised the subject of the probationers on the relief with DJS. He said he thought that one of them in particular was a problem: he didn't speak unless he was spoken to and seemed reluctant to get involved in any police work. As it happened, DJS had been with this probationer when he had 'frozen up' completely and been unable to say anything to a girl who had been behaving suicidally. A few days later, the area car driver made a special effort to draw this probationer into conversation, formed a team with him at snooker, and went out walking with him. He made it clear to DJS that he thought it was the responsibility of the more experienced constables to help the probationers in this kind of way, but he also said that the sergeants should do more to help them than they actually did.

The consequences of the lack of proper arrangements for supervising probationers became obvious as soon as the researchers accompanied them on the streets. Some were extremely reserved or timid. Few of them had any sense of purpose in what they were doing, and tended to make random stops for the sake of engaging in at least some kind of activity. Some probationers tended to call for assistance whenever they had to deal with even the simplest matter. At the same time, there were other probationers who were full of confidence and who handled some incidents much better than some of the experienced constables. It was clear, therefore, that a suitable system of supervision would have to take account of the widely varying needs and accomplishments of individual probationers: it would have to start from an assessment of their performance.

Another consequence of the lack of an ordered system for supervising probationers was that they might easily be confirmed as constables without having achieved an acceptable level of competence. On one of the reliefs that he worked with, DJS had the opportunity to observe the work of a WPC who was coming to the end of her probationary period. She was very lacking in confidence, and tended to call for assistance if anything at all happened - on one occasion, for example, DJS was with a general purpose car which was called to help her with a stop, although nothing untoward had happened and the man she had stopped was behaving quite reasonably (he was allowed to go on his way). The men on the relief did not complain about helping her out because she was pretty and acted as a 'damsel in distress'. But she was far from being self-sufficient as a police constable. One night in the canteen, DJS overheard a conversation between her and one of the sergeants. She said she was anxious about whether she would pass her 'final' and be confirmed. At first, the sergeant said jokingly that she 'didn't have a hope in hell' and 'would have to be booted out'. Then he became more serious and said she would have to get together a statement of her 'figures', they would have a chat about it, then she would be confirmed without any trouble. What was striking about this was that the WPC did have problems, which the sergeant either didn't know about or chose to ignore. He saw the business of arranging for her to be confirmed as a matter of going through a procedure quite unconnected with any proper assessment of her performance. It was also notable that he asked when she had last made an arrest. She had to think very hard and then said there had been nothing in the past two months. The sergeant saw this as a minor obstacle to be overcome in arranging for her to be confirmed.

Half way through our research, the Force began to move towards improving the arrangements for supervising probationers and training them on the job. The first change (the only one we were able to observe) was the introduction of the street duties course in the Summer of 1981. This course seemed to be very generally welcomed both by probationers and by supervising officers. Some of the probationers who passed through too early to go on the course regretted that they had missed it. Since then, as explained in the last chapter, the whole of the first ten weeks spent on Division by probationers has been made into a period of induction and training. Structured arrangements for the supervision of probationers after the end of this ten-week period are still necessary. This does not mean that they should not go out by themselves. It does mean that their work should be regularly observed, their performance assessed, and that they should be given help and advice on an individual basis according to their needs.

### Divisional CID and crime squads
Each Divisional CID office is managed by a detective chief-inspector. Under him there are two detective inspectors who are each formally responsible for about half of the detective sergeants and detective constables. Again, each detective sergeant is formally responsible for a small group of detective constables. However, from observation of the work of these offices, it is hard to discern manifestations of this formal structure. It is not easy to tell which detective inspector a detective constable reports to, and there is so little distinction between the work of sergeants and constables that it is very hard to tell which are which. The detective inspectors are distinguishable because they seldom go out and generally take charge of only a few of the more important cases themselves. Otherwise, their job appears to be administrative. They rarely supervise the sergeants or constables directly.

There appears to be no good reason for the existence of detective sergeants as a separate rank from detective constables. After observing the work of a Divisional CID office for some weeks, DJS asked the uniform superintendent during an informal interview, 'Would you say that detective sergeants do a different job from detective constables?' He replied, 'No, they do the same job. They don't do any supervision at all'. We did not find anyone who seriously disputed this. A woman detective sergeant at the same Division pointed out that she had never been a detective constable, having got her promotion to sergeant while in uniform, and that when she started as a detective sergeant she had much less experience of CID work than most of the detective constables in the office, so it would have been absurd if she had been expected to supervise them. When DJS asked her whether detective constables and detective sergeants did the same job, she said she couldn't answer from her own experience, but certainly they did the same job. An inspector who was spending a year in uniform before transferring back to CID told DJS that people often got promoted out of the detective constable rank before they had got much experience of CID work and at this point (under the interchange system) transferred to uniform, so that when they went back to CID as sergeants they were in no position to supervise detective constables. A sergeant, currently in uniform but expecting to transfer back to CID shortly, told DJS that he was enjoying his year as a uniform sergeant, but was a bit worried about going back to the CID because he would have much less experience of CID work than most of the detective constables. He agreed that as a detective sergeant he would not be expected to supervise the detective constables, but would feel slightly uncomfortable about knowing less than them. He argued that detective constables did not require direct supervision because, unlike many uniform constables, they were mostly very experienced. What underlies these comments is the fact that promotion through the ranks and specialist experience of CID work do not go hand in hand. This may be a good reason why sergeants should not be used for supervision in the CID, but it leaves a vacuum, so that most CID officers are not directly supervised at all. The argument that they require no supervision because they are experienced cannot be taken seriously.

We feel that we do not have adequate information about what detective inspectors and detective chief-inspectors do. They spend a proportion of their time handling cases themselves; from the limited observation we were able to carry out we gained the impression that they often have considerably greater investigative and interviewing skills than more junior CID officers, so the time they give to handling cases may be well spent. However, a considerable proportion of their time seems to be spent in administrative matters connected with running a CID office and, in a limited sense, managing their staff. For example, in the Autumn of 1980 there was a sudden 'clamp down' on overtime throughout the Force, and for some time after that detective chief inspectors seemed to be somewhat preoccupied with checking and authorising overtime claims. At the same time, checks of this kind seem to be less than effective. We have pointed out in an earlier chapter that CID officers often 'bend' the rules on booking on and off duty, arrange to be paid overtime when they are drinking and organise their work so that it seems to be necessary for them to work overtime (when in fact it is not). The most characteristic form of supervision, as it is understood in the CID, is checking diaries. Detective chief-inspectors often claim that this takes up a substantial amount of their time. On the other hand, both DJS and JG have sat with detective chief-inspectors on several occasions engaging them in continuous conversation while they flipped through a pile of diaries and appended signatures without reading the contents. On one of these occasions, the detective chief-inspector apologised to DJS for 'doing the diaries' while talking to him, but explained that it hardly took any of his attention.

One of the difficulties of supervision and management on the uniform side is that much of the time officers are responding to immediate demands, so it is hard for supervising officers to plan the work of a relief or to allocate suitable jobs to different individuals: in practice, constables share out the work among themselves by their decisions as to whether to accept a call. In the case of CID work, there is much less of a difficulty, because an immediate response is not usually required. One of the main sources of work is cases entered in the crime book and which have to be investigated. It would be easy for the manager to review the new entries every day and allocate the work bearing in mind the work-load, aptitude and experience of individual officers and their need for new experience of various kinds. In practice, they do not seem to do this. At an early stage of the research, JG interviewed a detective inspector and asked him, 'How is work farmed out to individual officers?' He replied, 'I expect them to look in the crime book every morning and use their initiative. I expect them to look to do the job'. Later observation showed that this was what usually happened at all Divisions. Individual officers took on work if they wanted it or if they happened to be around when something came up; some were quite successful at avoiding work (notoriously so in a few cases).

There are occasions when CID officers mount an operation as a group. Whenever we have observed operations of this kind, the planning has been carried out by one or more junior officers who had the idea for the operation, but a senior officer was brought in at a late stage to take formal command on the day. For example, JG was with a group of CID and crime squad officers who organised a raid on a hotel which they had observed for some time and which they thought was used for trading in drugs. It was a detective constable and a crime squad PC who had got the information that led to the raid, and these two, along with the crime squad sergeant, did most of the planning. However, on the day, a more senior officer had to be brought in. The crime squad sergeant explained

> There's been a minor power struggle between Bulldog Drummond (a nickname for the detective chief-inspector) and the (uniform) chief-inspector over this one. Personally I'd rather neither of them were involved but when the chief-inspector started poking his nose in I decided it would be

better to have Bulldog Drummond. I told him that the chief-inspector was trying to grab the job and Bulldog Drummond did the rest. Actually, I don't expect him to do anything but strut about saying 'Carry on, chaps' and puffing at his pipe, but at least he won't get in the way too much.

The junior officers had organised everything well. They produced plans of the hotel and photographs of the people they were hoping to arrest with biographical information, and it was they who arranged for 40 officers to be available for the raid, including dog handlers whose dogs were trained to find drugs. They also obtained keys for the front door and for the interior doors of the hotel. They then briefed the detective chief-inspector about these arrangements (he had only known about them in very general terms) so that he could in turn give the formal briefing to the assembled officers on the day. He did this with aplomb, successfully creating the impression that he had organised the raid himself. He was also present when the raid took place. It was only on large operations of this kind that we ever saw a detective chief-inspector directly supervise police work.

In general crime squads work as a group to a considerable extent, and much of the work of individual constables in these squads is directly supervised by the uniform sergeant in charge. This is, of course, in marked contrast with the work of CID officers. There is a detective sergeant who (jointly with the uniform sergeant) has formal responsibility for the crime squad. In practice, we found that this detective sergeant was not closely involved with the work of the squad: at most he would act as a channel of communication with the CID officers and the detective chief-inspector.

## The negative emphasis of supervision
At an early stage of the research, a relief inspector said spontaneously to one of the researchers, 'In all the time I have been relief inspector I have never once received any praise, encouragement or constructive criticism. The only time you know the guvnors are around is when something goes wrong'. He added, rather intemperately, that most senior officers were 'ignorant and uneducated' and that they rarely, if ever, communicated with the lower ranks. He thought they had the opportunity to do much more because 'most of them don't have that much work to do'. A sergeant on the same relief, who was also present, put forward similar views. He said that he had spent $2\frac{1}{2}$ years as sergeant at the Division and had now 'had enough'. He was thoroughly disenchanted and cynical about the whole job and increasingly became 'fed up' with senior officers. They seemed to undergo 'some psychological change' when they were promoted from inspector to chief-inspector. From that point on they moved in different circles and forgot the problems of police work on the streets. On the same day, the researcher spoke to the superintendent of the Division. He mentioned the name of

the inspector whose relief he had been working with - this was not the inspector who had made the critical comments, but was one who worked very closely with his relief, engaged in much direct supervision, and was greatly respected. The superintendent immediately said when his name was mentioned, 'Oh, he's a bit of an old woman'. The researcher said he had been impressed with this inspector, who seemed dedicated to his job and happy enough to remain an inspector. The superintendent replied, 'Oh, he'd be chief-inspector soon enough if he thought he could get it. He's an old woman'. It later turned out that the reason for the superintendent's attitude was that this inspector was concerned about the number of probationers on his relief and the difficulty of supervising their work adequately, and that he had repeatedly pressed the senior officers to take some action to reduce the number of probationers or increase the supervisory capacity. This showed that there was some justification for the views of the inspectors about the senior officers at the Division. The superintendent did not want to know about their problems. An inpector who spoke to them about his problems was said to be carping, nagging or being an 'old woman'.

Morale was certainly low on this Division, which was facing difficult policing problems at the time. However, there was little evidence that senior officers were responding by trying to support and encourage those at lower ranks. Dissatisfaction with the attitude of the senior management team was not confined to the lower ranks. A chief-inspector at the Division said that when he had mentioned his worries about the behaviour of some police officers to the superintendent and chief-superintendent they had not taken it well: in fact, he felt that by persisting in voicing his anxieties, he could damage his career. He thought that senior officers could afford to give more time to considering the problems and difficulties that the lower ranks wanted to tell them about: in fact, he said that the senior officers 'did very little work', spent their day 'twiddling their thumbs', spent long periods in the pub and frowned on his own refusal to accompany them on these visits. Although this chief-inspector may have been exaggerating, it was clear that a failure by senior officers to listen and to offer support and encouragement had contributed to their currently very poor relationship with the lower ranks.

The most active and positive manager that we came across at inspector rank was the inspector of a relief that JG worked with. He was active in encouraging enthusiastic young officers. On one occasion, for example, a probationer PC who had been out on Division for about four weeks got involved in making lengthy enquiries following an arrest he had made. He had worked night duty, went to court at 9 am (for the appearance of the man he had arrested) and then came on duty for the late turn starting at 2 pm (since his relief had reached the 'quick change' from night shift to late turn). He was pursuing his enquiries with great enthusiasm. The inspector helped him with the paper work and showed him how to do each of the checks (for example, with Criminal Records Office and his local collator's records). Throughout the shift, the probationer returned to the inspector at frequent intervals to report on progress and get help and advice with the next step. He consistently refused to have time off to go home and get some sleep. The attention that the inspector gave to this matter was exceptional in our experience. As well as encouraging and helping enthusiastic officers, he also dealt firmly with those who were idle or behaved badly: for example, he strongly reprimanded officers (at parade) for using foul and racialist language over the radio, and he chased his relief out of the canteen when they lingered too long over tea. JG saw two examples of supervision of this inspector's work by senior officers. On the first occasion, the inspector was standing with four PCs in the front office at the police station when the superintendent came in and said, 'There are so many cars parked in the yard that are unauthorised that I can't park mine. Move them'. The inspector was (rightly) furious that the superintendent had reprimanded him in front of some of his PCs. His response was to make photocopies of the stickers carried by cars authorised to be parked in the yard and to fix a sticker to every car that was parked there. He said that the superintendent only ever spoke to him to pull him up on details of this kind. In spite of the fact that he was an outstanding inspector, he was given no encouragement in fact his good performance seemed to be resented by senior officers. A day later, JG saw him receive a memo from the commander which had the sole purpose of pointing out that he was failing to fill in two boxes in the 'radio book' (for keeping a record of the personal radios held at the station). These two incidents were, he said, typical of senior officers' communication with him.

It would be a gross exaggeration to say that all interventions by supervisory officers are in connection with things they think have gone wrong, or that they do not offer help, support and encouragement. Positive interventions by sergeants and inspectors are fairly common, though they could be much more common if there was more direct supervision. Also, some senior management teams make an effort to supervise in a positive way (there is considerable variation between senior management teams in this respect). However, the emphasis in supervision as a whole is negative rather than positive. It might be argued that this is an acceptable style of management - the kind described by some theorists as 'management by exception'. On this argument, managers should set up appropriate systems and should then intervene only when the systems break down or are faced with something they cannot cope with. However, this does not describe the way that management works in the Metropolitan Police, because the organisation does not have self-regulating systems that effectively control the pattern and quality of work. In order to facilitate the development of systems of this kind, a phase of active intervention by management would be required.

## The relationship between uniform and CID

The CID, which accounts for 14 per cent of officers in the Met, is the largest single specialism in the Force, and it has historically had a more important position in the organisation than the numbers would imply. Before the changes introduced by Sir Robert Mark and Sir David McNee, the chain of command for CID officers on Divisions was quite separate from that for uniform officers and led ultimately to a central Criminal Investigation Department. One effect of those changes, which were stimulated by the uncovering of widespread corruption among CID officers, was to make Divisional CID officers, under their detective chief-inspector, responsible to the uniform chief-superintendent in charge of the Division, so that the chain of command no longer led directly to the central Criminal Investigation Department. There is still a detective chief-superintendent attached to each District, but he is not in command of the Divisional CID officers within the District. He is in charge of general policy on CID matters within the District, and personally takes charge of certain major investigations (for example, into murders). A second change was the introduction of 'interchange' between uniform and CID branches, as described in the last chapter. Essentially, the effect of interchange is that CID officers spend at least a year in uniform on promotion to sergeant and to inspector. There have also been a more limited number of transfers of senior officers and inspectors between uniform and CID branches. The general intention behind these changes was to reduce the separate identity of the CID, to increase the level of understanding among CID and uniform officers of each others' work, and to encourage the two groups to work more closely together by binding them together in a single unit (the Division) under the command of one (uniform) officer. It is generally agreed by CID and uniform officers within the Force that these objectives have been only partially achieved.

People in the Force say that there used to be considerable tension and hostility between CID and uniform officers. Opinions differ about how far this has been reduced. A chief-inspector said to DJS, 'They (the CID) are still a force within the Force: they think we are wooden tops and thickos, we think they are drunken lechers and yobs'. It was quite common for PCs to complain to us about the attitude of CID officers at their Division, especially when they did not seem to be interested in helping them with a specific task (for example, interviewing a prisoner). However, it was also quite common for PCs to say that they got on reasonably well with local CID officers. Many people on the uniform side think their relations with CID have at any rate improved in recent years. One commander said that mutual resentment between CID and uniform was no longer serious, and that denigration of one group by the other was only banter. Whatever the attitudes on the uniform side, there is still much active resentment within the CID of the change in the command structure and the introduction of interchange. In our first few days in each CID office, we listened to a great deal of talk on this theme. Not all CID officers disapproved of the changes, but nearly all thought they had dealt a serious blow to the morale of 'the Department'.

In any case, the effect on actual working patterns is more important than the effect on attitudes. While there has been some change, there are still some obvious shortcomings in the way that the CID and the uniform branch fit together. Most uniform chief-superintendents have not themselves worked in the CID and do not have a detailed knowledge of CID work; in general, it is therefore more difficult for them to supervise the CID than the rest of their Division. As CID officers frequently point out, the interchange system is largely one-way: it does not ensure that most senior uniform officers spend a period working in the CID. Consequently, although new cohorts of senior officers will tend to have worked more closely with CID than in the past, they will not have worked in the CID and may still have some difficulty in supervising CID work. The position of the detective chief-superintendent, attached to the District, is clearly somewhat anomalous, and may in some cases weaken the control of the Divisional chief-superintendent over his CID office. Formally, the detective chief-inspector reports to the uniform chief-superintendent, but he should consult with the detective chief-superintendent, and may feel that he owes an equal loyalty to him. The detective chief-superintendent may be able to exert influence with the local management team and more widely within 'the Department' - for example, he may influence decisions about the promotion of CID officers. Local CID officers may therefore be responsive to requests made by the detective chief-superintendent even though they do not report to him. Within this management structure, there is therefore the potential for divided loyalties and weak control.

The point was illustrated in the course of an interview by JG of a detective chief-inspector in charge of a Divisional CID office.

> JG: How do you relate to senior officers?
> DCI: I report directly to the detective chief-superintendent and appraise him of the daily crime situation. If I was on any other Division on the District, I'd phone through to him rather than going upstairs. (The Divisional police station was in the same building as the District headquarters.)
> JG: Is he well-informed about CID matters?
> DCI: Yes, he's clued up. CID is very close-knit.
> JG: Don't you report to the uniform chief-superintendent?
> DCI: If I see him, yes.
> JG: What do you think of uniform command?
> DCI: Some uniform chief-superintendents are helpful and let you get on with the job within reason. Others stick their noses in. We're very fortunate here.

This detective chief-inspector made it quite clear that he reported, in practice, to the detective chief-superintendent attached to the District rather than to the uniform chief-superintendent in charge of the Division, and he also appreciated the tact shown by his uniform chief-superintendent in allowing this to continue and not taking a detailed interest in CID work. It was interesting that the uniform superintendent on the same Division criticised the existing command structure.

> The detective chief-superintendent acts as an adviser to the commander, deals with major investigations and coordinates CID on District. Of course, coordination by him can easily interfere with management and deployment by us. It's an unrealistic system. There is no need for the detective chief-superintendents at District level.

The detective chief-superintendent himself agreed that the CID officers on the Division had 'a divided responsibility', though he thought the system was workable. He said, 'Yes, there is a problem. They need a CID boss to talk to about CID matters. When I have heard from them, I go to the uniform chief-superintendent and make a suggestion. This does not usually lead to a conflict, because it usually relates to things that I clearly know more about, because they are CID matters'. Later in the interview, he said, 'Many chief-superintendents know nothing about crime, and let the CID officers get on with it. But after interchange has been going for a few years this will change'.

Within another District, the detective chief-inspector of one of the Divisions said that his clear-up rate was better than on a neighbouring Division, where the CID were in a bad state because of a clash of personalities between the chief-superintendent and the detective chief-inspector. He thought this illustrated how foolish it was to put CID under the command of uniform chief-superintendents, many of whom knew nothing about the work of CID officers and could not effectively supervise them. Nevertheless, he confessed that he himself had a good working relationship with his chief-superintendent.

More important than the anomalies in the command structure is the fact that uniform and CID officers on Divisions belong to separate organisational units which very rarely cooperate closely on the same tasks. Very occasionally, there may be a large-scale operation which is planned and executed by a team consisting of CID and uniform officers. For the most part, uniform and CID officers belong to separate teams which work different shifts, see themselves as having different objectives and communicate mainly by passing on forms. The best way of encouraging closer cooperation between CID and uniform would be to set up more working groups containing both CID and uniform officers. In practice, the only way to do this on a substantial scale would be to disperse some of the Divisional CID officers to the uniform reliefs, which would then become mixed CID and uniform reliefs. This would be a way of ensuring that CID officers were always available to interview prisoners, take statements and give help or advice to uniform officers. Also, reliefs would be in a much better position to form plans for crime prevention and detection if there were CID officers in the relief who would participate in the planning process.

The details of a structure bringing together CID and uniform officers on the same reliefs would have to be worked out after a careful analysis of what Divisional CID officers and members of uniform reliefs actually do and should do with their time. No doubt there are some tasks for Divisional CID officers that cannot easily be combined with membership of a joint CID/uniform relief, for example, handling lengthy or demanding investigations. This may mean that a small central pool of CID officers would have to be retained at each Division. However, we are not here concerned with the details, but with the general principles. The CID has traditionally been regarded as having a distinct function, and hence it seemed natural that it should be organised in working groups distinct from the uniform reliefs. We suggest that in fact many CID functions are similar or closely related to uniform functions. To the extent that this is so, the working groups can be combined. This does not remove the distinction between CID and uniform officers: but it means that instead of emphasising a difference of function, the Force should emphasise the distinct skills, resources and knowledge that detectives can bring to bear often on the same tasks as those tackled by uniform officers.

## Authoritarian and consultative styles of management
The style of management in the Force is shaped on a military model and is essentially authoritarian. A number of things are implied by this term. The emphasis on issuing instructions is allied to a reliance on set procedures rather than end results. It leads to control by checking that instructions have been obeyed and procedures followed rather than by attending to whether objectives have been achieved. The converse is a lack of a consultative approach to decision making. This lack of consultation leads to a failure to get officers to adopt goals and norms that are useful for the organisation as guiding principles of their own behaviour.

In the past, there has been very little consultation with the lower ranks about major or minor changes in the pattern of working, or about decisions affecting the individual's career. An example of a major change that was not discussed with the lower ranks was the withdrawal on 17 November 1980 of the 94 panda cars in central London and their replacement by 31 general purpose cars. Officers on reliefs got to know about this only days or hours before it happened, although it meant a radical change in the pattern of work of those accustomed to driving panda cars, many of whom were transferred to foot patrol. This example also illustrates the advantage of the authoritarian approach, which allows certain kinds of change to be implemented quickly and cleanly. The suggestion that panda cars should be withdrawn from central London was first seriously considered in February 1980.

556

The four Area DACs consulted their local commanders about the matter between February and July: three reported that their commanders were unequivocally and strongly opposed to the suggestion, while the fourth reported that his commanders supported the idea in principle but were unanimous in thinking that a substantial increase in manpower must come first. However, the new policy had the backing of the Commissioner. Local commanders quickly fell into line when they saw that a decision was to be imposed: a few of them contested some details of the implementation within their own Districts, but that was all. It is interesting that this change was imposed in an authoritarian manner both on commanders and on constables. Where the change involves the withdrawal of equipment, as in this example, the authoritarian method can work, but changes requiring people's active cooperation cannot be successfully introduced in this way.

A sudden change in the shiftwork pattern in one of the Districts that we studied provides an example of a minor change introduced without consultation. For some time, it has been the usual practice for the area car crews to change shifts one hour later than the rest of the reliefs, since otherwise all police vehicles would tend to be off the road at changeover times: thus, the late turn is 2 pm to 10 pm for the bulk of the relief, but 3 pm to 11 pm for the area car crew. On the relief that DJS was with, there was one officer who nearly always drove a panda car on the normal shiftwork pattern (that is, 2 pm to 10 pm and so on). He had been posted to a panda for the following month, and at parade on the first day was told he would be working the same hours as the area car (an hour later than usual) as from the following day. At first he thought it was a joke, but it turned out that it derived from a sudden instruction by the District commander.

Officers are frequently told in the most peremptory manner that they are being posted to another job on another Division maybe 20 miles away from where they are currently working. JG was once with a detective constable when he received a telephone call to tell him he was being transferred to a distant Division. At first he thought that one of his colleagues was playing a joke on him, but on asking his detective inspector about it he found it was serious. He did not want to transfer at all, but if he had to transfer he would have preferred to go to a different Division from the one nominated. He approached all of his supervisory officers in turn, but none of them was prepared to help in any way. This example is not untypical. It illustrates two points. First, decisions about postings are often made without discussion or even the show of consultation with the person concerned. Secondly, they are often communicated impersonally, tactlessly and without any explanation.

In most kinds of police work (with the exception of public order events) individuals and working groups are required to make plans, work towards objectives, take decisions and use discretion. Within this framework, an authoritarian method of management tends not to be successful, because individuals and groups cannot be told precisely what to do, but must have a degree of autonomy. Consequently, as we have shown in earlier chapters, compliance with instructions may be more apparent than real. Working groups are adept at finding ways of evading instructions so that they can pursue objectives they have informally set themselves. The way out of this impasse is a difficult one, but it must lie in getting working groups to understand and accept the objectives of the organisation as a whole, and ensuring that the objectives of working groups are identical with at least some of the objectives of the whole organisation. This can only be done by adopting a consultative style of management which allows the working groups to participate in discussion about methods of working and the definition of objectives.

The need for a more consultative style will be particularly evident if major changes in working patterns are contemplated (as they should be). For example, a very simple analysis is enough to show that the number of patrolling police officers remains fairly constant throughout the 24-hour cycle, though it is slightly higher than average in the middle of the night; at the same time, demand for police services varies very sharply through the 24-hour cycle, reaching a peak at some time between 8 and 12 pm and reaching a low point in the small hours of the morning. Clearly the resources (patrolling police officers) are not matched with the level of demand within the existing shift system. To vary the number of patrolling officers so as to match the pattern of demand would mean making radical changes in working patterns: the sequence of shifts for an individual officer would have to be more irregular than at present and the planning of duties more flexible, so that individuals would not know with certainty a long time in advance when they would be on duty. Changes of this kind could not be imposed in authoritarian style, because officers would not be obliged to accept them; the present shift system is the outcome of negotiations with the Police Federation. Senior management will have to adopt a more consultative style if they hope to introduce major changes like this. Police officers may agree to make radical changes in their working patterns if they have first come to see that the change is necessary so that their working groups can achieve their objectives, which are some part of the objectives of the organisation as a whole.

One consequence of the authoritarian style of management is that working groups tend to evade instructions if they find them inconvenient. This is an aspect of a more deep-seated tendency among the lower ranks to regard all initiatives with extreme scepticism. The attitude is that 'we've tried it all before and it didn't make any difference', that police work will always be essentially the same regardless of what senior officers say or do, and that all initiatives are based on false premises, are badly planned and don't work because senior officers don't know how the job is really done and won't listen to what the lower ranks have to say. In fact, the lower ranks protect and nurture this scepticism by not taking part in any decision-making and not expressing their views to senior officers in case they should be implicated in any decision and therefore lose the opportunity to grumble and complain. Thus, the counterpart of the authoritarian style of management is a grumbling acquiescence among the lower ranks, combined with a tendency to evade instructions when inconvenient and a refusal to accept any responsibility for the way the job is done. This helps to explain the enormous inertia that seems to exist in the system. One way of trying to overcome this inertia is to insist that working groups accept a greater responsibility for finding ways of achieving agreed objectives, so that some changes, at least, will come from the bottom upwards.

## Objectives

If senior officers are asked what they or the Division are trying to achieve they answer either in terms of the remote consequences of police work (for example, the crime rate) or in terms of crude indicators of policing activity. The answer given to JG by a superintendent is typical.

> JG: How do you measure the performance of your Division?
> Superintendent: You can't use business criteria. I would tend to judge my Division by the stops, charges PAS (persons at station). If they were low, it would suggest that morale had sagged or not enough work was being done. I would review those figures and compare them with the last three years. You've got to consider the figures against the number of officers. We lost 23 officers over three years, and at the same time crime went rampant.

This kind of answer betrays an extremely superficial view of the objectives of policing and measures of policing success; from conversations with senior officers, we find that it is this superficial view that predominates among managers in the Force. What the above superintendent essentially said was that he looks for indications that his officers are doing something rather than nothing: only if the level of activity, as measured by arrests and stops, goes down does he consider that something is wrong. He also made it clear, by his reference to the crime rate in the context of manpower, that he thought the level of crime was ultimately the measure of policing success. The simplifications inherent in these views are dangerous. There are many kinds of policing activity other than stops and arrests, some of them more difficult to count, but which may be equally important. According to the Instruction Book, 'The primary object of an efficient police is the prevention of crime'. The number of arrests and stops cannot possibly be an adequate measure of how well that object is being achieved. Secondly, to assume a direct relationship between the nature and extent of policing activity and the crime rate is to forget that the

559

police are only one of a number of related systems through which deviant behaviour is controlled. For most purposes it is not appropriate to assess the performance of a Division according to whether the <u>ultimate</u> objective (containing the increase in crime) has been achieved, because many factors outside the control or influence of the police affect the level of crime. Thirdly, it is foolish to think of objectives in such broad terms, without even distinguishing between different categories of crime. It makes little sense to assess a Division in terms of the crime rate: it makes considerably more sense to look at what it is doing about, say, vandalism or domestic burglaries. Fourthly, it seems remarkable that the quality of the relationships between police officers and local people and the level of satisfaction of local people with the police force were not mentioned as measures of success.

One way of visualising a new approach to policing is to try to define objectives that could be translated into tasks to be undertaken by working groups of police officers. This is the kind of approach that the new Commissioner has begun to adopt in his first year of office. It does seem to be a useful way of thinking about how to organise police work. It is important that the objectives should not be so remote from policing activities that the link cannot be clearly established. For example, there is evidence from American research that an increase in the number of police officers patrolling on foot and in the number of relaxed contacts between the police and the public tends to reduce people's fear of crime. In the light of this general evidence, it might be reasonable to make it an objective to increase the number of officers patrolling on foot and to increase the number of relaxed contacts they have with members of the public. It would be better to adopt those objectives than aim to reduce the fear of crime. In many cases it should be possible to define an objective in terms of something that 'ought to help' even though the ultimate outcome (in terms of the prevention of crime or the apprehension of criminals) would be very hard to identify. For example, it 'ought to help' if more officers are on duty at times of high demand and fewer at times of low demand, and if CID officers are available to carry out thorough interviews with all prisoners.

Plans and objectives can exist at many different levels in the organisation, but we suggest that the key levels are the Division and the working group (relief, crime squad, CID office, etc.). One of the chief ways in which Divisions could form objectives is by collecting information about the pattern of the demands being made on the police force locally. From this a Division might establish, for example, that there was extensive vandalism on certain council estates which caused deep concern to the people living there and seriously damaged their morale. An appropriate Divisional objective would be to do something useful about the problem of vandalism in these particular areas; doing something useful would include reducing the amount of new damage and defacement, but it would also include making good the damage, repainting or cleaning to get rid of graffitti, and making the local people feel that an effort was being made and that there was something they could do about the problem themselves. Thus, the objectives of a 'vandalism campaign' would certainly not be defined purely in terms of reducing the number of complaints or reported crimes. Any proper analysis of what could be done would show that agencies other than the police should be involved: facilitating action by other agencies should therefore be among the Divisional objectives. The following are some of the elements that the Division might put together to form a concerted campaign, involving several local agencies, to combat vandalism in the worst-hit areas.

1. Consultation with the local council, possibly through a specially constituted committee, to set up procedures for quickly making good criminal damage on the selected estates and for removing graffitti.
2. Strong advice given to the local council about the resiting of equipment (for example, telephone boxes) so as to make it less vulnerable to vandals. An analysis of criminal damage to vulnerable equipment would be required to form the basis for this advice.
3. Local police to establish close links with the council's planning and architect's departments and to ensure that their views, as law enforcement specialists, are taken into account in the planning of the built environment and the design of housing estates.
4. Find out when criminal damage occurs and which are the most vulnerable locations. Consider controlling patrolling patterns so as to increase police presence at the relevant times and places.
5. Consider a concerted public information campaign targeted at the areas worst affected. Local press, radio, doorstep visits, leaflets might be used to convey to people the cost of vandalism, where and when it is happening and what they can do about it (principally, provide information to the police and report damage to the council).
6. Police to attend meetings of tenants' associations to listen to what they have to say about the problem, to collect information, and to let them know what is being done in the current campaign.

Of course, there have been isolated campaigns of this kind in the past, though seldom involving such close cooperation with other agencies. Nevertheless, the pattern of policing would radically change if Divisions were regularly pursuing objectives of this kind in an ordered way, and if this activity was a substantial proportion of all policing activity on a Division.

Some of the objectives of working groups would follow

naturally from specific Divisional objectives: for example, if there was to be a campaign to combat vandalism, the reliefs and home beat officers would be set certain objectives within that overall campaign. However, there may be scope in addition for objectives identified by a particular working group and pursued by them alone. This happens at present to a limited extent. On one relief that DJS worked with, a group of four constables had decided to take an interest in the ponces and enforcers who frequented a particular club. When they were out on patrol they took every opportunity to observe the club and take down information about the men using it, the women they were with and the cars they used. Whenever they spoke to anyone who frequented the club (for example, if they stopped one of them or of course made an arrest) they took the opportunity to get as much information as possible about the ponces they were interested in. They checked the local collator's records for information about all the ponces they knew about, looked up their criminal records and checked out their cars on the computer records. They were hoping eventually to collect enough information to justify making a number of arrests, although they had not reached this point by the time DJS moved on. Supervisory officers were not involved at all: in fact the group tried to keep all the information to themselves, because they thought that if others got to know they might manage to take the credit.

Whether this was a reasonable choice of objectives, given the crime problems in the area, is open to doubt - but at least the officers involved were doing something useful at times when they would otherwise have been patrolling aimlessly. Of course, crime squads and CID officers often formulate plans of a broadly similar kind, but it is more unusual to find it happening among members of a uniform relief. There seems to be no reason why this kind of approach should not become much more common. The obvious difficulty is that members of reliefs (and to a lesser extent members of other working groups such as crime squads) need to be available to respond to calls. If they engage in a purposive activity of their own, they are liable to be interrupted. Now that the strength of the Force has increased, this difficulty might be reduced by dividing the relief officers on duty into those having the primary task of responding to calls and those having some other primary task during the current shift. Of course, the second group would be available to respond to urgent calls if necessary.

### Information
A bewildering range of records are kept in the Metropolitan Police, but largely as part of a system for getting things done and not for the purpose of providing information. The following are some of the available records.

1. Station messages, which give an indication of the extent and nature of the demands that the public are making on the police.

2. Incident report books, used by uniform officers to record incidents involving an arrest and most other kinds of incident except traffic matters ('accidents' and 'process').
3. Note books, used by CID officers to record most kinds of incident.
4. Diaries, kept by all officers working in plain clothes. They show, for example, arrests, interviews with prisoners and other tasks undertaken.
5. Person at station and charge sheets. A sheet is made out for every person brought into the police station under arrest, showing the circumstances of the arrest, a list of the prisoner's property, details of the charge or charges (if any).
6. Occurrents book, which is used to record various kinds of happening at the police station.
7. Stop book and verbal warning book, which are used to record stops under s.66 of the Metropolitan Police Act and stops of motorists who were not reported for an offence but given a verbal warning.
8. Crime sheets, used to record reported crimes together with details of the subsequent investigations.
9. Duty states, which show when individual officers booked on and off duty and (broadly) what they were doing during a given shift.
10. Complaints: details of every complaint and the subsequent investigation are recorded, and in addition complaints against an officer appear as part of his or her personal record.
11. Collator's records of local crime and offenders.

These records are little used by management as a source of information to feed into a planning process. Most of them were not designed to be used in this way. They may be seriously defective as raw data: we know, for example, that less than half of all stops are recorded in stop books and that many messages received at police stations are not recorded because no action is to be taken; it seems likely that many interviews carried out by CID officers are not recorded. Furthermore, these records are not organised in a way that would be convenient for analysis, so that attempts to use them as a source of information for management involve a great deal of extra work.

A central branch (G10) produces regular statistics (compiled from the forms filled in at police stations) on reported crimes and arrests classified according to the type of offence. In addition, each reported crime is shown as 'cleared up' or not, and statistics are produced showing the proportion of crimes in various categories that are cleared up. (Clear-up rates can be influenced by the extent to which prisoners are encouraged to admit to offences, because many of the clear-ups arise when someone arrested in connection with one offence admits to others, which will not be investigated thoroughly or be the subject of court proceedings, but will be 'taken into consideration'.) Senior management teams seem to make little, if any, use of these centrally produced statistics. One reason for this is that they think in terms of an immediate response rather than strategic planning, so that (in the words of a detective chief-superintendent) 'Statistics from G10 have often become history before you have had a chance to do anything about it'. Another point is that while the statistics are analysed by District, and some of them by Division, the raw figures are not related to anything that would make interpretation possible (for example, to the size of the local population or the number of police officers in the area). The Districts do produce a daily bulletin showing the number of reported crimes in certain categories (not all crimes are included). This bulletin is forwarded daily to a central CID branch, and the local management teams generally look at it, so they are quickly aware of any sudden rise in crimes of a certain type.

Divisions make efforts to look at the geographical distribution of certain kinds of crime from time to time. Quite often the distribution of burglaries or robberies is plotted on a map in the CID office, but this is not usually kept up consistently. Senior officers sometimes mentioned to us that they had noticed an increase in the number of crimes of a given type in a certain small area and occasionally took a localised initiative as as a result. However, these small plans were often based on an impressionistic or sketchy analysis of statistics, or on a reading through of individual entries.

It is difficult for management teams to make good use of information about reported crimes because they lack other information about the way in which manpower is being deployed, the amount and kinds of work done by different operational groups and the results of this activity. In addition, they are unable to set the information about reported crimes in the context of the total pattern of demands being made on the Division. Senior management teams generally look through a sample of the messages coming into the station, but they do this chiefly to check that messages are being dealt with appropriately; until recently, there has been no system for producing statistics that classify messages into categories and show the number in each category, though initiatives of this kind have been taken within the neighbourhood policing experiment and, in 1983, throughout London. Further improvements may be achieved in future if the message system can be computerised and the results tied in with the planning of the work of operational groups, especially the reliefs. The Force is planning to pilot a scheme of this kind. Senior management teams do not generally know how many officers belonging to various groups are patrolling on foot and in vehicles in different areas and at different times, although they are able to make checks from time to time. They do not generally know how many stops or arrests or interviews have been carried out by a particular operational group over a given period, though again they can extract this kind of information from the records from time to time. There is no regular record of the amount or nature of work undertaken by individual officers. Perhaps most important, it is very hard to find out from the available records what kind of policing activities produce various kinds of results. For example, a Divisional management team can find out fairly easily how many burglaries have been reported in a recent period and how many of these have been cleared up, but it is much more difficult for them to make a link between the clear-ups and the various kinds of policing activity - to find out what kinds of activity produced the clear-ups.

The development of a more measured and rational approach to the planning of the work of a Division poses a number of very complex and difficult problems. We do not suggest that the starting point should be to try to produce regular analyses of all of the available information from existing records. Information will not be used unless it is directly linked to the formation of practical plans and the evaluation of their success. The starting point, therefore, should be the definition of objectives and the formation of plans; but once this has been done, priority should be given to producing information that will feed in to the development of the plans and the evaluation of the success of the resulting initiatives. It is extremely important that information about these initiatives and their results should be disseminated to management teams elsewhere in the Force. Thus, appropriate information will only be produced in reponse to the pressure of demand from the planning process as it gets under way. Initially the need will have to be met by making better use of the existing records, but if planning becomes more general, we can expect the records themselves to be redesigned to take account of information needs as well as the need to chase progress and check that individual tasks have been properly carried out.

### Broad structure

There would be little disagreement within the Force with the view that certain aspects of its broad structure are unsatisfactory. It would be much more difficult to find agreement about what the broad structure should be, and still more difficult to find a way of moving towards a better structure. The following are defects in the existing structure that we have identified, but most of them have also been pointed out to us by senior officers.

1. The chain of command seems inordinately long. The disadvantages of this are that operational officers feel very distant from those making decisions, the responsibility of senior officers tends to be diluted by the existence of many intermediate ranks between them and those who will put plans into effect, it is difficult to arrive at a unity of purpose between the many different

ranks involved in any plan or operation, and individual officers can often evade responsibility for something by pointing to the other ranks that were also involved. The clearest responsibility rests with Divisional chief-superintendents, and the present Divisions are real and convenient units of organisation. The chain of command running from Divisional chief-superintendents in both directions (towards the constables and towards the Commissioner) seems too long.

2.   Working downwards from the Divisional chief-superintendents, what is broadly speaking required is a senior management team consisting of the chief-superintendent and deputies, then operational units directly responsible to the senior management team. For example, reliefs, immediate response units (jointly forming an extra relief), the CID office and any specialist squads would report directly to the senior management team. On the face of it, a structure of this kind would entail a reduction in the number of ranks from chief-superintendent downwards; otherwise, chief-inspectors would either have to become (full) members of the senior management team or run an operational unit. This second solution is a possibility, but it would mean using chief-inspectors in a flexible way.

3.   It is a constant and justified complaint, at all levels in the Force, that senior managers are moved about far too often. It is quite common for Divisional chief-superintendents and superintendents to stay in post for only six months. A number of the Divisions that we studied had no officer at the rank of chief-inspector or above who had been on the Division for more than a year. This instability wrecks attempts to formulate and implement even fairly short-term plans. It arises because there is a more or less exact match in the Force between the number of senior posts and the number of officers of the required ranks available to fill them. Any move at one point in the system therefore leads to a large number of moves elsewhere. Two kinds of action could be taken to reduce this instability. First, there can be greater flexibility in the rank of officer required to fill a particular post. For example, where a chief-inspector is promoted to superintendent, he could remain on the same Division as a member of the senior management team. This kind of solution would be natural if the definition of functions were to be separated, to some extent, from the definition of rank (or in other words seniority) as suggested in the last paragraph. Secondly, there should be more senior officers than are required to fill the available operational posts. It should be possible to find useful activities for the 'spare' senior officers -

activities that can be interrupted at short notice when an operational vacancy arises without causing serious instability and disruption.

4.    Moving upwards from the 75 Divisions, the next set of organisational units is the 24 Districts. After that, the next set of units is the four areas headed by deputy assistant commissioners. It is very hard to see why both of these levels are required. Detailed decisions are in any case taken and implemented at Divisional level, and the various Divisions within a District can be heterogeneous and may have sharply contrasting patterns of demand. Both the Districts and the Areas have functions connected with broad strategy and coordination. Neither have the capacity to engage in management of day-to-day police work on the ground, except in exceptional circumstances (such as the disturbances of 1981). We suggest that past plans (which were never implemented) to have one level of grouping only between the Divisions and the centre should be revived. An attractive plan, suggested in the past, is to group the 75 Divisions into eight Areas. Each of these areas would have a management team consisting of several senior officers (commanders or deputy assistant commissioners). If different members of these teams were to specialise it would be in terms of responsibility for particular projects, issues or problems, and not in terms of geography. Even if they did specialise, they would as a team accept joint responsibility for the policing of the Area.

5.    Moving upwards from the Areas, the problem is not that the chain of command is too long, but that there is no single chain. The four Departments are responsible for different aspects of the work of Areas, Districts and Divisions, and there is conflict of interest and competition between them. Also, the Departments partly exist to provide services to operational units, while at the same time having a direct responsibility for certain aspects of operations. There are two complementary approaches towards improving this structure. First, it is important that one Department should have full operational responsibility for Areas, Districts and Divisions. In practice, this means that 'A' and 'C' Departments should be combined into a single Department, and that the Areas should report to this Department alone. Secondly, the service functions of Departments should be clearly distinguished from their operational functions. For example, 'D' Department would continue to have operational responsibility for running all central training facilities. On the other hand, we have suggested in the last chapter that training should be

567

decentralised to a greater extent than at present: in other words, more training should take place on Divisions and be organised by Divisions. 'D' Department would have important service functions in relation to Divisional training, without having operational responsibility for it. This would mean that the Divisions could go to 'D' Department for advice about their training programmes, they might use teaching materials that had been developed by the Department, and they would use the Department as a source of information about training initiatives, materials and programmes in use on other Divisions. But their training programmes would not be subject to control by 'D' Department. By making this structure clear, the Force would ensure that responsibility for a particular training programme was firmly located within a single management team. The same principles would be applied to distinguish the service and operational functions of 'B' Department (which deals with traffic and technical support).

The main defects in the present broad structure of the Force can be summarised as excessive centralisation, a long chain of command, diffusion of responsibility and instability of senior management teams. There is nothing original about this analysis: these defects have been repeatedly pointed out to us by senior officers. At the same time, these senior officers often believe that nothing can be done about it. We have made some radical suggestions in order to show that, in principle, something could be done, and not because we expect the Force to adopt these particular suggestions. Proposals for change would have to evolve from a process of reassessment and planning within the Force. The Commissioner has recently set up a planning unit to provide a service to the policy committee. At present, this is a very small unit. If it can first achieve some small successes, a way forward might be to increase the size and seniority of its staff and to give it a brief to consider the broad structure of the Force.

## Methods of control

In earlier chapters we have pointed out that there is often a conflict between the informal objectives and norms of working groups of police officers and the formal objectives and rules of the organisation. The authoritarian style of management that we have described in this chapter tends to make the gap wider, because managers become distant from working groups and do not try to persuade them to adopt objectives that fit with the organisation's objectives. In extreme cases (we have quoted some examples) this leads to a double-think whereby a manager expects a working group to break formal rules but expects the groups to be careful to prevent him from getting to know about it, because if he got to know he would either have to back them up and be implicated, or would have to punish them for doing something he expects them to do. This pattern of management, and the attitudes that go with it among managers and the lower ranks, are extremely destructive of any attempts to improve the quality of policing.

The positive approach to controlling policing behaviour lies in seeking to create working groups that are motivated from within to achieve objectives that fit with those of the organisation and to use methods that the organisation considers to be acceptable. This involves a more consultative style of management, better methods of assessing the performance of groups and individuals, emphasis on rewarding groups and individuals that do well and a greater unity of purpose between different elements of the organisation. However, nothing that we have said about the positive approach should be taken to mean that there is no need for rules and effective sanctions. From the findings set out in Chapter XVI it should be clear that certain rules need to be much more consistently enforced. Increasing the level of supervision and simplifying the management structure, as suggested in this chapter, would make this easier.

Consistency on the part of management is probably more important than severity. A superintendent in one of the Divisions that we studied said that he went out of his way to 'get rid of' violent PCs. Yet he and a chief-inspector also went out of their way to persuade a person to withdraw a complaint which they knew to be justified about violent behaviour by an officer, who was not 'got rid of' or even disciplined or reprimanded. On another Division, a PC gave an account to DJS of an occasion when he was disciplined for a trivial matter. His inspector, who was also present, did not contest the facts. The PC said he had heard an urgent call over the radio before he had gone out at the beginning of a shift. He rushed to his panda car and set off, only to run out of petrol. The officer said that the matter was treated as a disciplinary offence and that he was suspended from driving as a punishment. This shows that an officer guilty of a serious offence may be let off, while an enthusiastic officer, doing the job to the best of his ability, may be disciplined for it.

An offensive aspect of the discipline system is that a CID officer who misbehaves may be 'returned to uniform'. Formally, this is not a punishment, but in practice it often is, and this is deeply resented by uniform officers.

The consistent application of sanctions against officers who are shown to have misbehaved must be an essential part of any strategy to improve policing behaviour. An increase in the level and quality of supervision and a shortening of the chain of command would make this much more possible.

# CONCLUSIONS AND RECOMMENDATIONS

# XIX   CONCLUSIONS AND RECOMMENDATIONS

Sir David McNee made a bold decision when he invited the Policy Studies Institute to carry out an independent study of 'relations between the Metropolitan Police and the community it serves'. Any good study of a large organisation and its relations with the public, particularly an organisation that deals with sensitive and controversial matters, is bound to show up defects and deficiencies, and there is the danger that when these are highlighted in a published report, the result will be to cause alarm and stimulate unreasonable attacks instead of laying the foundations for constructive change. But in asking for the study, the Metropolitan Police showed that it had enough confidence to expose itself to scrutiny and believed that public discussion and criticism, based on detailed and balanced information, was a necessary stage in its development in the 1980s and beyond. At an early stage, the Commissioner referred to the request that Oliver Cromwell made of his portrait painter, and said that he made the same request himself. 'Mr Lely, I desire you would use all your skill to paint my picture truly like me and not flatter me at all; but remark all these roughnesses, pimples, warts and everything as you see me, otherwise I never will pay a farthing for it.'

From the beginning, it was agreed that as well as carrying out research among the public, PSI would be granted access to police officers at all levels in the organisation and allowed to observe all kinds of police work. We are fully satisfied with the efforts made by senior officers to facilitate the research, and the difficulties that we sometimes encountered with officers at more junior ranks did not prevent us from carrying out our very detailed study substantially according to plan. The independence of the study was guaranteed by the agreement that the findings would be published in full and that, while drafts of the reports would be discussed with the Met in advance of publication, the final decision on drafting would rest with PSI. This agreement has been kept. This report is therefore PSI's. We hope that the Metropolitan Police will make full use of our findings and recommendations, but we do not expect them to agree with all of them.

In our original proposal, the chief subjects to be covered were defined as 'policing strategies, as officially prescribed and as carried out on the ground; the factual information, analysis and accepted wisdom on which they are based; how they affect relations with the public at large and with ethnic minority groups' and 'how the police actually behave in situations of contact with the public, and how people respond'. This was to be seen in the context of the attitudes of the police and the public towards one another, taking into account the differences among police officers doing different kinds of job and among people of different ages, living in different areas, and belonging to different groups. The proposal stated clearly that 'It will be an objective of the project to examine the current policies of the Metropolitan Police in the light of the findings ... and to make suggestions for changes of policy as appropriate'.

An outstanding problem for policy makers and managers in the police force is that there has to be a high level of consent, or at least compliance, if they are to carry out any of their duties effectively; there has to be a coherent set of policies and practices (interpreted with some flexibility at the local level and in particular circumstances); yet there can be sharp disagreements among the public about what these policies and practices should be. This is part of a wider political problem, and a very old one, which can again be illustrated by the words of Oliver Cromwell (in an interview with Edmund Ludlow in 1656). '"I am', said he, 'as much for a government by consent as any man; but where shall we find that consent? Amongst the Prelatical, Presbeyterian, Independent, Anabaptist, or Leveling Parties?' Then he fell into the commendation of his own government, boasting of the protection and quiet which the people enjoyed under it, saying, that he was resolved to keep the nation from being imbrued in blood."

But this research was not designed to help the development of an orthodoxy which is then to be imposed in the Cromwellian manner. Instead, it gives an account of police/public relations from the contrasting perspectives of the police, the public and an independent observer, and it gives particular attention to the differences in experience and views between different population groups. It is true that in making suggestions for changes in policy, we try to balance the sometimes conflicting experience, views and objectives that exist. But it is an essential aspect of our approach that such recommendations should be publicly discussed, together with the argument and information on which they are based. We have published the findings in great detail so that individuals and groups who have an interest may use them to develop their views in the light of information about what is actually going on.

## Police/public relations in London: a balance sheet
Our findings are based on four related studies: a survey of 2,420 Londoners including substantial sub-samples of people of Asian and West Indian origin, which was carried out in the Autumn of 1981; a

study, by participant observation, of a group of young black people based on a self-help hostel, which was carried out during the first half of 1981; a survey of 1,770 officers in the Metropolitan Police Force up to the rank of inspector, which was carried out in the late summer of 1982; and study of police work by lengthy observation, informal interviews and access to internal documents, which was carried out by two researchers over a two-year period starting in the late Autumn of 1980.

## Concern about crime and police performance

There are many forms of organisation and procedures that combine to control deviant behaviour. Among these, the police have a limited, yet decisive, role to play. In assessing the level of public confidence in the police it is therefore important to consider the level of public concern about crime and disorder, but it must not be assumed that action to combat crime is the responsibility of the police alone, or that police performance can be assessed purely in terms of the crime rate or the amount of public concern about crime.

Our findings show that people attach a high importance to safety on the streets and that there is a large body of opinion among Londoners generally, and among women in particular, that the streets of London are unsafe at night. A majority of Londoners believe that street robberies, burglary and vandalism are becoming more common, and very few think that any kind of crime is becoming less common. Even though fieldwork for the survey of Londoners took place soon after the riots of 1981, people were more concerned about street robberies, burglaries and vandalism than about riots and other disturbances. The riots of 1981 were, in fact, highly localised and were directly observed by only a small proportion of Londoners. Our findings show that the feeling that the police are losing the battle against street crime and burglaries is widespread, but they show a much higher, level of public confidence in police performance on other fronts. On these other matters, public confidence is not nearly as high as it could be, but it is still at a fairly high level. On the whole, these findings show that there is considerable public concern about certain kinds of crime combined with a belief that the police are failing to deal with these crimes effectively, but not that there is alarm about the level of crime or the failure of the police in general terms.

## Overall level of contact

More specific and detailed measures of the performance of the police are provided by people's descriptions and evaluations of the way they behaved in particular cases when they came into contact with them. The police come into contact with a large proportion of the population: just over half of Londoners say they have talked with a police officer for some reason or other in the past twelve months and 23 per cent have had three or more encounters. It is, therefore, not the case that most people form their impressions of the police entirely from hearsay, myth and rumour and the mass media, though of course the impressions that people get from their mostly mundane encounters with police officers may to some extent tend to fade into insignificance beside the more colourful and dramatic impressions they get in other ways. Also, the police have a good opportunity to create a favourable impression, since only 14 per cent of encounters are connected with an offence or suspected offence by the person or his child, and most are of a 'positive' or amiable kind in which the officer is helping the person in some way.

## Service given to victims of crime

Experience as a victim of crime is one of the major reasons for contact with the police: in fact, 27 per cent of Londoners say they have been the victims of some kind of crime in the past twelve months, and 52 per cent of these incidents became known to the police. However, most of the victim incidents were of a minor nature. Few of the personal offences resulted in the victim having medical treatment, and in only three out of one thousand cases did they result in the victim staying in hospital overnight. The median value of the loss in the case of property offences was £44 though in about one-quarter of cases the loss was of £200 or more. The more serious offences are more likely to be reported to the police than the less serious ones, and thefts from the person are less likely to be reported than several other kinds of offence, which suggests that they are not judged to be a uniquely damaging or disturbing kind of crime. The great majority of thefts from the person (wrongly equated with 'mugging' in most press reports) do not involve any violence or injury. Where the matter was reported to the police, the great majority of victims were happy with the way the officers spoke to them and expressed a high level of satisfaction with the way the matter was handled: this is in spite of the fact that in only 13 per cent of cases that came to police notice does the victim know that the offender was caught. These findings show that in the most important case where the police are providing a service - to victims of crime - this service is generally found to be very satisfactory.

However, the findings from our observational work on this point are not entirely in accord with those from the survey of Londoners just quoted - or perhaps they simply provide a different perspective. From observation we found that police officers vary very much in their ability to offer sympathy, support and advice (to victims of crime and others) and that whether they do so partly depends on whether the people involved seem to them to be normal and deserving rather than deviant, crazy or the cause of their own troubles. We have quoted two cases (page 381 onwards) where officers clearly failed to offer as much help as they could and should have done. It seems that the researchers expect more of police officers than victims do.

## Stops

Situations where there is an element of conflict between police officers and members of the public are a stiffer test of their performance. The two situations that we have studied in greatest detail are stops and arrests (along with the subsequent interviewing and 'processing' of the prisoners). Detailed information about both kinds of incident are available from three sources: the survey of Londoners, the survey of police officers and our own observations.

The powers of the police in London to stop and search people on foot and in vehicles (which are set out in detail on page 82 onwards) largely depend on the criterion of 'reasonable suspicion'. The question of what is the correct interpretation of this criterion is discussed on page 493 onwards. Two interpretations can be suggested. On the first interpretation, there must be a specific reason for suspecting the individual person concerned, while on the second interpretation it would only be necessary to show that there was a higher than average chance that the person had committed an offence, for example because the person belonged to a group within which offenders of a certain type were relatively common. It is not any part of the purpose of this report to arrive at a judgement as to the correct interpretation of the law on this point. If the narrower interpretation of 'reasonable suspicion' is adopted then a substantial proportion of stops are carried out where the criterion has not been met. If the broader interpretation is adopted, then the police are acting within their powers when making stops in the great majority of cases, but what this means is only that police officers rarely stop people belonging to groups for which the rate of arrest and conviction is <u>lower</u> than average and where there is no specific reason to suspect the individual concerned. In practice the criterion, on this broader interpretation, would be so weak that it would be difficult to discern its effect, since police officers would, in any case, have no motive for stopping people who are <u>less</u> likely than average to have committed an offence. For this reason we have evaluated the behaviour of police officers in stopping people against the first and narrower interpretation of the present powers.

Our findings from all three sources agree in showing that the criterion of reasonable suspicion does not act as an effective constraint on police officers in deciding whether to make a stop. In a substantial proportion of cases where stops were reported in the survey of police officers, the officer did not give what we judge to be a 'good' reason for making the stop. We could see no good reason for the stop in one-third of the cases recorded in the course of our observational work, and, closely in accord with this, the survey of Londoners shows that for 38 per cent of stops the person involved thinks the police had no good reason for making the stop. Further, it is clear from the way that police officers talk about stops that the question of what their legal powers may be does not enter into their decision-making except in the case of rare individuals. They do, of course, consider the chance of getting a 'result', but factors that they associate with the chance of getting a 'result' are often unconnected with the narrower interpretation of the concept of 'reasonable suspicion'. One reason why the legal powers have little relevance is that most people do not know what they are. We never saw anyone openly challenge the right of the police to stop, search and question them, nor did anyone ever refuse to answer questions.

A substantial minority of the population (16 per cent) have been stopped by the police one or more times in the past twelve months, but certain population groups are far more likely to be stopped than others; within certain groups, the chance of being stopped in a twelve-month period is well over 50 per cent, and a high proportion of these groups have been stopped several times in that period. The groups most likely to be stopped are young people, men and people of West Indian origin, and young men of West Indian origin have the highest chance of being stopped. Stops therefore bring the police into frequent contact with members of certain highly specific groups, but very rarely bring them into contact with the majority who do not belong to these groups. The policy is therefore, in a sense, divisive; if there is a price to pay in terms of police/public relations, it will be in relations with specific groups and in a sharp division of experience and opinion between the minority who are stopped and the majority who are not.

The two surveys are in agreement in showing that only a small proportion of the individuals who are stopped (between 3 and 5 per cent) are arrested as a result, and the survey of Londoners shows that a further 5 per cent are reported for an offence (generally a traffic offence). Overall, about 1 in every 12 stops leads to a 'result' (an arrest or report) if we take the individuals rather than the occasions as the base (several individuals may be stopped on the same occasion). This strike rate seems low: it certainly means that the great majority of people stopped must be presumed to be 'innocent persons'. On the other hand, our findings show that the stops made in London (amounting to at least $1\frac{1}{2}$ million a year) result in the detection of a very substantial number of offences - perhaps more than 100,000 a year. The survey of police officers suggests that about one-quarter of arrests arise directly from a stop.

Current practice runs the serious risk of 'causing offence to innocent persons', both because most people stopped are innocent and because they are unhappy about the way the police handle the incident in a substantial minority of cases (in 19 per cent of cases the person thought the police did not behave in a fair and reasonable manner). Our observations produced examples of a number of cases where officers behaved rudely or abusively to people they had stopped and who were not shown to have committed an offence. The survey of Londoners and the observations show that in a substantial minority of cases the officer gives the person no explanation of why he has been stopped (27 per cent of cases from the survey). At the same time, all three sources are in agreement in showing that a majority of stops are fairly amiable encounters. Nevertheless, people who have been stopped by the police, and especially those who have been stopped repeatedly, tend to be far more critical of the police than others. Taken together, these findings suggest that stops tend to have a poor effect on people's relations with the police even where (as in the majority of cases) they are fairly relaxed and amiable encounters. In a later section we shall recommend a number of changes in policy which would help to achieve a better balance between the costs and benefits of stopping and searching people and vehicles.

## Arrests

A very substantial minority of men have the opportunity to form an opinion of the police based on direct experience of being arrested and taken to a police station. As many as one out of five men, but only one out of 50 women, say they have ever been arrested. One out of ten men say they have been arrested within the past five years. Young people are, of course, much more likely than older people to have been arrested recently. A higher proportion of young people of West Indian origin than of young white people have been arrested in the past five years, but there is no difference of this kind for older people.

The findings of the survey of police officers show the enormous importance of cooperation by members of the public in the detection of offences: one-third of arrests directly arise from a call or approach by a member of the public; in addition, initiatives by members of the public must in many other cases make it possible for the police to make an arrest later. The findings also confirm that stops lead to a very substantial number of arrests: they lead directly to about one-quarter of all arrests made and, of course, information from stops may also contribute towards making other arrests possible. On the other hand, comparatively little crime is detected by the police being there when it happens: 14 per cent of arrests arise in this way, and a substantial number of these are for non-crime matters. It seems that very few arrests happen because of an incident that might have been caused by the presence of a police officer or the way he behaved, and a very small proportion of the total are made at 'public order events'.

The survey of Londoners provides accounts of 169 arrests over the previous five years. In 47 per cent of these cases people thought the police were behaving unreasonably in arresting them; in 59 per cent of cases, people had criticisms to make of the way the police behaved towards them; in 26 per cent of cases they thought a police officer said something rude or insulting to them; in 22 per cent of cases they said that police officers used force or hit them, in 18 per cent of cases unjustifiably in the person's opinion; in 20 per cent of cases people thought the police threatened them or put unfair pressure on them in some other way; and in 47 per cent of cases people thought they were treated unfairly overall in connection with the arrest. The accounts that informants give in their own words of the circumstances of their arrest and their treatment by the police give a much fuller picture than the statistics. In about one-half of cases the person freely admits that he had committed an offence, which shows that the answers given are not purely exercises in self-justification, and therefore suggests that some of the allegations made against the police should be taken seriously. It is impossible to summarise the accounts that people give (they are quoted in full from page 120 onwards) but it is clear that a substantial proportion of people who have been arrested make very specific allegations against the police, ones involving gross misconduct in many cases.

In 18 per cent of arrests reported in the survey of police officers, the officer said there was a struggle at some point between police officers and the person arrested, but in only $\frac{1}{2}$ per cent of cases did he think that the officer(s) used too much force. As to the facts of what happened, this is in close agreement with the findings of the survey of Londoners. But whereas most of the people who said that the police had used force thought that this had been unjustified, nearly all police officers thought that, where there had been a struggle in making an arrest, an appropriate amount of force (or too little) had been used. Thirty-nine per cent of police officers thought the person arrested was uncooperative.

In the course of the observational work, the researchers saw 100 arrests being made and saw a large number of people dealt with in the charge room, though it would not be appropriate to give a count since some of these prisoners were observed for short and some for long periods. In eight cases the researchers saw officers using excessive force and in a ninth case it was certain that this happened, though it was not observed. In addition, the researchers heard officers give fairly specific information about at least 20 other incidents where excessive force was used, but these were incidents that had stuck in the memory of police officers and may have taken place as long as two years before in some cases.

The great majority of arrests are made without a warrant. The police derive their powers of arrest without a warrant from a wide range of Acts of Parliament and from common law. The common principles underlying these powers are that the police may arrest someone who is in the act of committing a specified offence and that they may arrest someone whom they 'reasonably suspect' has committed a specified offence. The question of what amounts to proper grounds for reasonable suspicion is very complex, but the evidence required is much less than a court would require to convict. We conclude from our observations that when making arrests, most police officers do operate within 'working rules' which broadly approximate to powers of arrest defined by law. Among the 100 incidents involving arrests that we covered, there were four cases where officers exceeded their powers in making the arrest. In two of these cases, the officers arrested someone who they thought had not committed an offence, and therefore acted unlawfully. In each of these two cases the officers thought the person arrested knew something about an offence they were investigating and made the arrest in order to put pressure on the person to give evidence. According to their personal code, they thought they were acting fairly because, although they did not believe that the person arrested had committed an offence, this person was closely enough associated with it for the arrest to seem justifiable to them: also they thought they would have no difficulty in convincing a court that they did reasonably suspect that the person had committed an offence, although this was not, in fact, true. In a third case two aliens were arrested on insufficient grounds (because they did not have their certificate of registration with them); the officers thought this was 'fair' but their 'working rule' departed widely from their formal powers in the matter, probably because they thought the chance of any 'come-back' would be minimal. In a fourth case, three black youths were arrested on suspicion of having committed a street robbery, but there was no evidence at all to connect them with the offence. Thus there were four cases out of one hundred in which the powers of arrest were clearly exceeded. If we consider all arrests in a single lump, it is clear that the police were acting within their powers in the great majority of cases. However, we believe that the cases described in full from page 462 onwards are quite typical of their kind, and that people who are known not to have committed an offence but do have information about it would normally be arrested in order to bring pressure to bear on them to divulge the information. We also believe that anyone who is close to the seat of a major disturbance is at risk of being arrested, regardless of what he is actually doing as an individual: a clear example of this was the arrest of one of the researchers, which is described in volume II of the original edition. However, these generalisations are informed opinions rather than fully substantiated conclusions.

## The clientele of the police and their views

Like some previous studies, the survey of Londoners shows that victims of crime and offenders tend strongly to be the same people, and it shows an even stronger relationship between being a victim of crime and being stopped by the police (and therefore suspected of an offence). Also, both surveys show that there is a close fit between the characteristics of people stopped by the police and people actually arrested: although there is often no specific or sufficient reason for stopping a particular person or vehicle, police officers use criteria when deciding whom to stop (such as sex, age, ethnic group and type of car) which do increase the chance that an offence will be detected. It is particularly important to notice that unemployed men are much more likely than those in full-time work to be arrested, to be stopped and to be victims of crime. From this pattern it seems likely that there is a kind of person and style of life that is associated both with offending and with being a victim. According to this argument, some people are inadequate or accident-prone, have a style of life that is disorganised and uncontrolled, and tend to associate with others who live in the same kind of way. Within this 'sub-culture' criminality, mostly of a minor kind, is common, so that members of the group tend to be both offenders and victims. Also, our observations suggest that the police tend to concentrate their attention on people like this (a police word for them is 'slag') so that they come to deal with a limited clientele, both because of the social facts they are there to deal with and because of the criteria and priorities they use, which may be based on an exaggerated and simplified view of the facts.

The survey of Londoners shows that this 'clientele' is much more critical of the police than other people. There is a strong tendency for those who have been stopped by the police and for those who have been arrested to be critical, but other kinds of contact, where the person is not being treated as offender or suspect, are also associated with critical views. The lines of causation involved cannot be traced with confidence, but the following three conclusions seem likely to be correct. First, people who have been repeatedly stopped by the police tend very strongly to be critical of the police, and from this it seems likely that the experience of being stopped repeatedly causes them to be critical. Secondly, there is a group of people whose style of life tends to bring them into contact with the police (as victims, offenders and suspects) and who belong to a culture in which hostility to the police is the norm, so that the hostility of individuals is by no means entirely caused by their own personal experiences of contact with the police. Thirdly, it is likely that people who have had little or no contact with the police tend to have a somewhat unrealistic and idealised notion of what police officers and police work are like, so that any kind of contact tends to make them somewhat more critical.

## Standards of police conduct
One-third of Londoners think the police sometimes stop people in vehicles and one-fifth people on foot without sufficient reason. These answers should perhaps be regarded as mildly critical, since the question is about what 'sometimes' happens. A majority of Londoners think that the police never exceed their powers in this respect. Twenty-nine per cent of Londoners think there are groups or types of people who do not get fair treatment from the police; nearly half take the opposite view, and one-quarter have no definite opinion. More than three-quarters of those who think some groups are unfairly treated mention ethnic minorities as the victims (without any prompting); to a large extent, therefore, the notion of unfair treatment of particular groups by the police is synonymous in people's minds with unfair treatment of the ethnic minorities.

Over half of Londoners think that at least a few (and more than 'hardly any') police officers have accepted bribes, but only eight per cent think that 'quite a lot' or 'most' police officers have done so. The views expressed about accepting goods or favours are similar. Thus, it is a common view that there is some corruption in the police force, but not that it extends to more than a small minority of officers. The use of threats and unfair pressure in questioning people is the kind of misconduct that is thought to be most widespread. About half of informants think it happens at least occasionally, but perhaps more important, one-quarter think it often happens - that it is a usual pattern of behaviour by police officers. Fabrication of evidence, violence on suspects held at police stations, excessive use of force on arrest and false records of interviews are all thought to happen at least occasionally by a substantial proportion of Londoners, but by well under half; about one in ten Londoners think each of these kinds of misconduct often occurs. These findings suggest that there is a complete lack of confidence in the police among at least one in ten of Londoners, and that about half have serious doubts about the standards of police conduct, though in most cases they do not think there is a pattern of frequent or usual misconduct.

Nearly two-thirds of police officers surveyed think senior officers do everything they can to get rid of corrupt officers, and only 10 per cent think they try less than 'fairly hard'. There is much more criticism of senior officers' efforts to get rid of officers who use too much force. A substantial minority (9 per cent) think they don't make a genuine effort - a very strong criticism - and altogether 35 per cent think they try less than 'fairly hard'. Officers were asked a series of questions to find out how many police officers they think are often rude, often use excessive force and how many have ever accepted a bribe. The typical view is that there is a small but significant minority of police officers who show a pattern of repeated and frequent misconduct as regards rudeness and excessive use of force, that an extremely small proportion of uniform officers are corrupt and that a larger but still very small proportion of CID officers are corrupt. On average, officers think that 8 per cent of police officers are often rude, that 5 per cent often use more force than is necessary and that 1.4 per cent of uniform officers and 4.7 per cent of CID officers have ever accepted a bribe.

We cannot attach quantities to the findings of our observational research on these matters. This research could not provide any useful information about the extent of corruption in the Force. As already stated, we observed eight incidents in which excessive force was used and in a ninth case it was certain that this had happened, although it was not observed. We have already concluded that many officers routinely exceed their powers to stop and search and that while powers of arrest are not often exceeded in the main, there are certain circumstances in which it may be common for them to be exceeded.

Our findings from the observational work on police practice in obtaining and recording evidence are set out on pages 473-492. Our general conclusion is that outright fabrication of evidence is probably rare - that is, cases where an officer says he saw something he did not see or that a suspect said something that he did not say. This has to be qualified in three ways. First, our access to some aspects of the work of the CID was limited. Secondly, in order to share work, one officer frequently 'gives' an arrest to another, and this may often involve adjustment of evidence, but not usually in a way that the non-legal mind would think material (though, if known to the courts, it would often cause them to acquit). Thirdly, we believe that police officers will normally tell lies to prevent another officer from being disciplined or prosecuted, and this is the belief of senior officers who handle complaints and discipline cases.

However, our findings suggest that departure from rules and procedure affecting evidence are far more common than outright fabrication and have a far more significant effect on the quality of the evidence that goes before the courts (see page 473 onwards). At the time of arrest suspects are frequently neither cautioned nor told they are being arrested. Juveniles are often questioned without a responsible adult being present. While a degree of pressure is implicit in the fact of being arrested, it is not uncommon for officers to use bullying tactics in interrogation and to use threats, especially the threat of being kept in custody for a time. These kinds of pressure go well beyond what is necessary or inevitable within the current framework of procedure. In many cases, there is no record of the 'informal' interviews during which tough questions are asked, or merely a record to show that the interview took place. Statements are produced by a process of interaction between an officer and a suspect (or other person); they are generally not a record of what the suspect said in his own words. They may amount to a highly selective summary of what was said. We believe that it is common for officers to make 'bargains' with suspects in which an offer not to press charges or to help the suspect to get bail is traded for evidence or (perhaps more commonly) information. Taken as a whole, these findings show that a gap has opened up between the 'working rules' of officers and the formal rules of procedure affecting evidence. In many cases, however, a lack of skills may be the main reason for breaking rules, and an improvement in policing skills would often be a shorter way to better police behaviour than punitive action in connection with rule-breaking.

Willingness to cooperate with the police
Except in the case of domestic disputes, between two-thirds and three-quarters of Londoners say they would take the initiative in calling the police to a range of situations in which someone else might be at risk. Informants were also asked if they would help the police with inquiries into three imaginary incidents they had seen: youths smashing up a bus shelter, youths knocking a man down and taking his wallet, and a traffic accident in which someone was seriously hurt. In each case, people were asked whether they would

be prepared to tell the police what they had seen, to identify the culprits and to appear in court to give evidence. In all three situations, the great majority of people would be prepared to tell the police what they had seen. There are successively smaller proportion who would be prepared to help identify the culprits and to give evidence in court, but still the proportion who would be prepared to appear in court ranges from 70 to 90 per cent depending on the situation. These findings show that, in spite of the criticisms expressed by a substantial proportion of Londoners, the great majority are ready to cooperate with the police to a considerable extent.

## Views on policing policies and priorities

There is virtually no support among Londoners for the view that the police presence, from day to day, is oppressively high, though there is some support for the view that it is sometimes too high at certain special events. In fact, there would be wide support for an increase in the numbers of police patrolling in uniform. A majority of Londoners think that the police patrol mainly in vehicles and would like them to patrol more on foot. The survey of police officers shows that, in fact, the ratio of police time spent patrolling in vehicles to time spent patrolling on foot is of the order of 2:1.

While people place the strongest possible emphasis on the 'sharp end' of policing (catching robbers and burglars), they also think it is very important indeed for the police to cultivate regular, everyday contacts with people in the area and to make special efforts to establish relations with key members of ethnic minority groups. However, people do not attach a high priority to the 'social services' role of the police, especially where this seems to involve an intrusion into family life. There is no obvious conflict between the choice that Londoners make of the crimes it is most important for the police to combat and the actual priorities of the police force. Londoners attach a very low priority to combating illegal betting and gaming, prostitution and the sale of pornography, all types of offence against which the police in fact deploy very limited resources. There is, however, an important conflict of opinion about what action the police should take against the use of cannabis. A significant minority of Londoners think they should make this a high priority, but three times as many think they should make it a low priority. At the same time, a considerable amount of active policing, using stop and search methods, is (at least ostensibly) directed at catching people in possession of cannabis. The survey findings show that a considerable proportion of Londoners think this kind of police activity is inappropriate, while a significant minority strongly support it.

About three-quarters of Londoners are content with police policy on stops, or unconcerned about it, but groups that are likely to be stopped are aware of it, and are much more likely to be hostile to policy policy than other groups. This confirms the conclusion that a selective stopping policy is divisive: it meets with the support or indifference of the majority who are not affected, but tends to create opposition among the minority who are.

Just over half of Londoners say that marches and demonstrations are banned about as often as necessary. The balance of opinion among the remainder is strongly that these events are not banned often enough. Londoners generally think the police are successful in coping with marches and demonstrations. Whether people are in favour of more or fewer bans, they are usually thinking of events organised by right-wing rather than left-wing groups.

## Relations with the ethnic minorities and the young

What is left out of the general account just given is the very sharp differences in the nature of the relationship according to the age, sex and ethnic group of the people concerned. Women and older people are far less likely than men and younger people to be offenders or suspects, and the bulk of minor crime and disruptive behaviour is characteristic of boys and young men, most of whom grow out of it as they get older. For this reason, young men are far more likely to come into conflict with the police than other groups. Asians have much less contact with the police in all types of circumstance (as victims, offenders and suspects) than members of other ethnic groups. People of West Indian origin have substantially more contact with the police as offenders and suspects than members of other ethnic groups, and a markedly higher proportion of their contacts with the police are of a 'negative' kind (arise in circumstances where they are being treated as offenders or suspects). This is partly because people of West Indian origin are a young population, but substantial differences remain when young West Indians are compared with young white people; consequently, the proportion of young West Indian males who have come into conflict with the police is perhaps dangerously high, and the proportion of their contacts with the police that are negative is very high indeed (over 70 per cent, compared with 14 per cent for the general population). The differences shown are as large as any that ever emerge from social surveys, and they show that the nature of the relationship between the police and the public is fundamentally different for different population groups.

These differences in experience are accompanied by equally large differences in attitudes towards the police. Age has a stronger influence than ethnic group, but young people and people of West Indian origin tend very strongly to be more critical of the police in general terms than older people and whites, while Asians tend to be less critical than white people. There are similar differences in the proportion who would be prepared to cooperate with the police in various circumstances. In detail the findings are complex, but they certainly show that in some respects there is a dangerous lack of confidence in the police among substantial numbers of young white people and a disastrous lack of confidence among young people of West Indian origin. One-third of white people aged 15-24 think the police often use threats or unreasonable pressure in questioning and one-fifth think they often use excessive force on arrest and that they often unjustifiably use force on people held at police stations. Among people aged 15-24 of West Indian origin, 62 per cent think the police often use threats and unreasonable pressure in questioning, 53 per cent that they often use excessive force on arrest, 56 per cent that they often unjustifiably use violence on people held at police stations, 43 per cent that they often fabricate evidence and 41 per cent that they often make false records of interviews.

Nevertheless, these hostile views by no means amount to a complete rejection of the present policing system. Where people of West Indian origin are the victims of crime, they are just as likely as white people to report the matter to the police, which is a very important behavioural indication of a level of confidence that would not be suspected from the answers to attitudinal questions. While young people of West Indian origin are less likely than others to say that they would cooperate with the police in various circumstances, still a majority of them say they would cooperate to some extent (they do, however, show a particular reluctance to appear in court as witnesses). Young people of West Indian origin are markedly less likely than other groups to wish for an increase in the number of police on patrol, but still only one-quarter think there are too many police in the area. By and large, therefore, the views of young West Indians are not anarchic; they want a police force and in practice they make use of its services like everyone else while being highly critical of it in some respects.

The findings of the survey of Londoners show that the hostility of West Indians (and young West Indians in particular) to the police cannot be explained by the way in which they themselves were treated by the police in specific instances, though it may be explained, at least in part, by the large <u>number</u> of contacts they have had and by the very high <u>proportion</u> of contacts in which they were being treated as offenders or suspects rather than getting help or advice. Where West Indians were victims of crime in specific instances, they give a favourable assessment of the service provided by the police (only a slightly less favourable assessment than white people) and there is evidence that, in fact, the police tend to make more efforts on behalf of West Indian than on behalf of white victims. Where they were stopped by the police, West Indians (especially those aged 15-24) assess the behaviour of the officers less favourably than white people, but the difference is far smaller than the differences in answers to more general questions, and in 54 per cent of cases young people of West Indian origin thought the police behaved in a fair and reasonable manner in stopping and searching them. On specific occasions when they have been arrested, West Indians are no more likely than white people to think they were badly treated by the police; if anything, the answers given by people of West Indian origin are more favourable to the police.

We have shown that people who have a high level of contact with the police tend to be more critical of them, even when the contacts are broadly 'positive' ones. One reason for the hostility of young West Indians in general terms (though not in connection with specific incidents) must be that their level of contact is high and in a high proportion of encounters they are being treated as offenders or suspects. It is particularly important to notice that stops are an important element in this pattern. However, there is another, broader kind of explanation that is suggested by our study of a group of young black people in a self-help hostel. The hostility to the police which is shown by the survey was vividly expressed by nearly all members of this small group. At the same time, the locus of this hostility was not so much in specific personal experiences as in the sense of personal identity possessed by these young black people and their perception of themselves as members of a group that is struggling against sharply adverse economic circumstances and under attack from the institutions of a predominantly white society. These people have a sometimes overwhelming feeling that they are being persecuted, that their ambitions are always likely to be frustrated because of racial prejudice and discrimination and that they are deprived of the power to control their own lives. To a considerable extent, these feelings are justified by the objective facts of their social circumstances, as extensive research by PSI and others has shown. The latest national survey by PSI shows that the unemployment rate among young men of West Indian origin is of the order of 50 per cent, and all the evidence suggests that racial discrimination, especially in recruitment to employment, continues at a high level. To these people, the fact that they are black is the most important fact of their existence, and they respond to what they see as oppression by basing their sense of themselves, their past and their future on the ideas of blackness, the assertion of a distinct culture and struggle against the dominance of white people. Whatever the behaviour of the police on specific occasions, they seem like the most obvious symbol and representative of an oppressive white authority.

We have said that young people of West Indian origin tend to be hostile to the police in general terms but often assess their behaviour favourably in specific instances. In a complementary way, we find from our observational research that police officers tend to be hostile to black people in general terms, and certainly indulge in much racialist talk, but often have friendly and relaxed relations with individual black people in specific instances. Our first impression after being attached to groups of police officers in areas having a substantial ethnic minority population was that racialist language and racial prejudice were prominent and pervasive and that many individual officers and also whole groups were preoccupied with ethnic differences. At the same time, the degree of tension between them and black people from day to day was much less than might have been expected either from their

585

own conversation or from accounts in the newspapers and on television. Longer experience confirmed these initial impressions. Although there were variations in the extent of racial prejudice and racialist talk between different groups of officers and individuals and at different times (there was an increase at the time of the 1981 riots), these things are pervasive: they are, on the whole, expected, accepted and even fashionable. Senior officers seldom try to set a different tone (though they do on occasion) and there were some cases where they initiated racialist talk and kept it going. These attitudes are, to a large extent, a reflection of those in the wider society and especially in the social groups from which police officers are drawn, though they may be magnified within the closely-knit working groups within the Force. To some extent, they may be a response by police officers to the feeling that they are under attack from black people, and this was certainly the case in 1981.

At the same time it is our strong impression, from our observational research, that police officers rarely behave badly in such a way as to make it obvious that a person's ethnic group is the reason for their bad behaviour, and this conclusion is supported by the accounts given by black people in the survey of Londoners of their encounters with the police. Nevertheless, there are some officers for whom racial prejudice is the reason for their bad behaviour on occasion. We have described two cases (page 412 onwards) where police officers behaved badly, probably because the suspects were of West Indian origin. Some of the worst behaviour we have observed, in the second of these two examples, was towards black suspects.

Black people as classified by the police (broadly those of West Indian or African origin) account for 17 per cent of people arrested, according to the survey of police officers, but for only about 5 or 6 per cent of the population of London. Black people also form a similar proportion of alleged offenders described by victims in the survey of Londoners (for 24 per cent of offenders the victims were able to describe, though in two-thirds of cases they could not come up with a description). Also, a higher proportion of young people of West Indian origin than of young white people said they had been arrested in the past five years, according to the survey of Londoners. It is likely that the high proportion of people arrested who are black can be explained by a combination of demographic and social factors among which high unemployment may be the most important: unemployed men are much more likely to be arrested than those in full-time work and the rate of unemployment is extremely high among young black men. At the same time, the proportion of people arrested who are of Asian origin is lower than the proportion of the London population who are Asians, though Asians (like West Indians) are a young population and are experiencing high levels of unemployment. It is clear, therefore, that there are other factors which predispose Asians not to commit offences that bring them into contact with the police.

Among white people, fears about the safety of the streets and the belief that crime is prevalent in the locality are closely linked with the perception of the ethnic minorities as a threat. People in areas of high ethnic concentration are twice as likely as those in areas of low concentration to think the streets are unsafe for lone women at night, and nearly three times as likely to think that certain kinds of crime (street robberies in particular) are prevalent in the locality. The survey also shows that actual rates of victimisation are the same in areas of high and low ethnic concentration, except in the case of theft from the person (seldom involving violence) which is, indeed, much more common in areas of high ethnic concentration than elsewhere. Taken together, the findings show that the perception of the ethnic minorities as a threat is based only partially on fact. The prevalence of thefts from the person in areas of high ethnic concentration and the publicity given to these crimes, which falsely represents them as usually involving violence, has combined with more deep-seated and vaguer anxieties to make white people feel that black people are a threat.

In a variety of ways, Asians and West Indians in areas of high ethnic concentration seem to have a better relationship with the police than those in areas of low concentration: they are more willing to cooperate with the police, more likely to think the police are successful in various ways, and more likely to make a favourable assessment of the way they were treated when stopped by the police. The only exception to this pattern is that West Indians in areas of high concentration are more inclined than those elsewhere to think there are too many police in the area, but this is still the view of less than one-fifth of West Indians in all types of area. These findings show that tensions between the police and people of West Indian origin are not confined to areas like Brixton and Lewisham. If anything, the tensions are greater in mainly white areas, but they attract less attention because of the smaller number of West Indians there.

Just over half of Londoners think that more black and brown police officers would make no difference to police performance, and just over one-third think it would lead to an improvement; very few think that an increase in their numbers would have a bad effect. There is little difference between the views of white people, Asians and West Indians on this issue. These findings show that there is little public resistance to the current policy of increasing the numbers of officers belonging to minority groups, and a considerable body of public support for it. We also find that there is a considerable pool of potential applicants among the minority groups. However, two-thirds of white police officers and three-quarters of minority group officers think that black or brown officers face greater difficulties than white officers in doing the job. The difficulties most frequently mentioned are in dealing with members of the public belonging to ethnic minority groups, in dealing with the general population and in non-acceptance by (white) colleagues. From our observational work we can confirm that black and brown officers do have to cope with considerable strains and difficulties in their relationships both with the public and with their colleagues. It would be difficult to argue against the policy of recruiting more police officers from minority groups - at present these officers account for only $\frac{1}{2}$ per cent of the total - but it has to be recognised that these people will be facing a difficult task, and it seems unlikely that the modest increase in their numbers that can be achieved in the short term will make a fundamental difference to the relations between the police and the minority groups.

## Bringing about change

There is ample evidence, within this series of studies, of the need for change in the policing of London. In general, the level of public confidence in the police is reasonably high (though not nearly as high as it could be) but there is considerable anxiety about certain kinds of crime and a widespread belief that the police are not able to combat these crimes effectively. Objectively speaking, the clear-up rates for burglaries and thefts from the person are low. While the level of crime, especially violent crime, is very much lower than in large cities in some other countries, it is much higher than elsewhere in Britain and is probably rising (though perhaps not as fast as the statistics of recorded crime would suggest). Confidence in the police is dangerously low among certain sections of the population, especially young people of West Indian origin. At the same time, observational research and the accounts given by members of the public suggest that there is cause for serious concern about some aspects of police practice (rudeness, procedures affecting evidence, interpretation of powers of arrest and powers to stop and search, use of force and racial prejudice). Standards of conduct are probably higher than in many other police forces in developed countries and probably higher than they were, say, 50 years ago in London. But public expectations of the police are probably higher than before, and higher in Britain than in other countries. A rise in public expectations should be taken as an encouraging sign: it calls for a response from the Metropolitan Police.

This much would be accepted by most police officers and members of the public who have thought seriously about these issues. The most common response, among those outside the police force, is to suggest further or more tightly controlled constraints on policing through the law. The conclusions of the present study are entirely different. Of course, the police must continue to work within a framework of rules defined by the law. Arguments can always be put forward for changing some of the rules in certain ways, but the existence of rules does not necessarily have an important effect on actual policing behaviour. While discussion about the rules should continue, a much more important issue is how police officers may be brought to do their job in ways that are

588

more effective, more acceptable to the public and more likely to generate public confidence. This cannot be done by rules alone, since rules can only have an effect if they actually become governing principles of policing behaviour. It can only be done through a style of management and a structure within the Force that seeks to develop the appropriate patterns of policing in a positive way.

Some of the most important elements of a more positive approach by the management of the Force would be the attempt to define tasks and objectives for working groups of police officers or to help them define tasks for themselves; an emphasis on encouraging and rewarding good work for example by promotion or other career opportunities; regular evaluation of the performance of individual officers in the light of policing objectives and the tasks they have been set; a radical increase in the amount and quality of supervision by senior officers and by sergeants and inspectors; the introduction of a more consultative and less authoritarian style of management, so that officers at junior ranks have to accept responsibility for decisions about their pattern of work and so that their personal objectives become more closely identified with at least some of the objectives of the organisation as a whole; a drive to bring training and real police work much closer together, with far more training on the job; a major effort to tackle racial prejudice within the Force; a simplification of the management structure so as to shorten the lines of command and place a clear responsibility for particular matters on particular officers or management teams. This attempt to find a more positive approach is the thread that runs through the recommendations that have been made in preceding chapters and that will be briefly summarised here.

## Summary of recommendations
### Initial selection
Because of the sharp increase in the number of applicants in recent years and the decline in the number of places now that establishment has been reached, the Force has the opportunity to be far more selective than before. An immediate consequence has been a rapid rise in the educational standard of new entrants to the Force. However, in other respects the Force is probably not making the best use of the choice available because too little is known about the qualities that successful police officers have, and there are no very reliable methods of identifying these qualities in young men and women. Some modest improvements in the selection procedure can nevertheless be suggested (pages 511-513). The Force should try to identify the personal qualities that are of value in the police force and to develop structured questioning methods or aptitude tests to assess these qualities. The relevance of educational criteria should be studied and the appropriate action taken (low reading and writing skills have certainly been a problem in the past). If further study shows that selection tends to be ineffective

where applicants are very young, consideration should be given to raising the minimum age on entry into the Force. Various methods of improving the reliability of interviews should be considered, including more structured training and practice for interviewers, a closer definition of the qualities to be assessed at the interview and interviews by two officers separately rather than together (as at present). The Force should consider whether much more junior officers (such as inspectors) would make better selectors than chief-superintendents.

From the selection statistics it is difficult to escape the conclusion that the Force discriminates unlawfully against women applicants under the Sex Discrimination Act 1975. Independently of the statistics, we have reason to believe that it is 'unofficially' Force policy to keep the proportion of women in the Force down to about 10 per cent (which is roughly the present level). The logical consequence of the Sex Discrimination Act 1975 is that the proportion of women in the police force should be allowed to rise to a much higher level than the current one if enough suitable women applicants come forward. By failing to make the police force an exception to the Act, Parliament indicated that it was prepared to see this happen. On current trends the proportion of women in the Metropolitan Police would rise to about 25 per cent within 10 years if there were no discrimination in the selection procedure. The Force seems to consider that this would be unworkable. If Parliament is persuaded that the Force is right, then it should amend the legislation; if not, then the Force should bring its selection policy into conformity with the law and should consider at a fundamental level how a police force with a more even balance of the sexes can best be organised so as to meet operational requirements.

We find that there is a great deal of prejudice against women in the Force. It is possible to argue that a substantial increase in the number of women police officers would help to overcome some current problems and would increase the pool of certain resources that are currently scarce within the Force. At the same time, it would be a radical change, and operational problems would be created, at least until new methods of organisation and ways of working had been established. In the longer term, the Force will have to consider its policy on this matter more deeply and discuss it within a wider forum.

Probationer training
The Force's own steering committee on recruitment and training drew attention to a number of fundamental weaknesses in the training of probationers, and from 1982 onwards a complete revision of the initial training programme has been under way. Changes include a lengthening of the initial course at Hendon from 14 to 20 weeks, a revision of the content of the course to place a greater relative emphasis on skills (as opposed to knowledge), the use of continuous assessment with the possibility of modifying

elements of the course in the light of results and the introduction of a more structured method of introducing probationers to actual police work when they are posted to Divisions (including a 'street duties course'). Most of these changes are in the direction that we would have recommended, but because we are sceptical about the effect of the initial training at Hendon on its own, we believe that much greater emphasis should be placed on the rehearsal and reinforcement of the skills and habits taught at Hendon throughout the first two years of actual policing experience (see page 514 onwards). This point is accepted by the Force, but needs to be developed further. If much of the training - and perhaps the most important part - is to be integrated with actual police work, it follows that many of the training resources should be locally based and under the control of local commanders, and not concentrated at Hendon. In fact, the Force is moving towards the development of district training units which will bring together responsibility for all the training that takes place locally. The decentralisation of training and the greater integration of training and actual police work are likely to be much more important steps forward than changes in the content and methods of the initial training course. In fact, if the district training units can be made to work, the length of the initial training course might usefully be reduced. The recruits whom we interviewed in the autumn of 1980 found the 15-week course at Hendon quite long enough, and attitudes towards the new course are probably not fundamentally different. Any long residential course in artificial surroundings that keeps recruits away from actual police work is likely to be unpopular. When Lord Scarman recommended that the initial course should be lengthened, he did not envisage the strengthening in local training on the job that is now planned.

We believe that current self-defence training is inadequate and that there should be really effective training of police recruits in techniques for restraining violent people and for defending themselves without weapons. This will be particularly important if the number of women in the Force increases, as we believe it should.

Promotion and assessment of performance
Perhaps the most fundamental weakness of the organisation of the Force at present is that promotion up to the rank of inspector is basically dependent on passing examinations that test knowledge of law and regulations in a narrow sense and is very little related to proven ability, performance or standards of conduct. The survey of police officers shows that very few officers are refused promotion because of their performance or conduct. In page 522 onwards we outline a new approach to promotion that would place far more emphasis on assessment of performance while ensuring that only officers with the necessary intellectual skills could gain promotion. A pre-condition of this new approach to promotion is that an effective system of continuous assessment should be developed.

591

This must in turn be dependent on a clearer definition of policing objectives and hence of what counts as good performance. We recommend that several supervising officers should independently assess each officer's performance; that some of the assessors should be fairly junior officers who work closely with the person concerned; and that the assessments should be structured around a varied set of aspects of performance defined in a highly specific way. The results would be used within the promotion system and for other management purposes. Decisions about promotion would essentially depend on the assessments together with interviews by a selection board, but applicants would also be required to reach a minimum standard in a test (for which no special study would be needed) of knowledge and reasoning of the kind expected within the current rank. There would also be a fairly stiff test of numeracy and literacy as applied to police work. Applicants recommended for promotion would attend a residential course which would cover, intensively, the knowledge of the law and policing procedures required in the new rank, but would also make a start towards developing management skills. This course would replace both the present 'promotion classes' that officers attend before attempting the examination and the present pre-promotion courses that they attend after success in the examination.

Career development
For many police officers, career development will not be through the promotion system. Nevertheless, there is a great variety of jobs to be done at the constable level, many of them requiring specialist knowledge and skills. It follows that one of the chief means available to management of influencing and controlling the behaviour of constables is by helping those who perform well to develop their careers within their present rank. Improvements in the career development system, as in the promotion system, must depend on the establishment of a more effective and sensitive method of continuously assessing the performance of officers. This would then be linked with a regular review of each officer's experience and of ways in which it might be extended (see page 530). This would strengthen the links between performance and rewards, since officers would frequently be told that they would have the opportunity to go on a certain course or make a move to a specialist job only if their peformance improved in certain specific respects. It would also lead to a better use of human resources and help officers to plan their careers in the light of a fuller knowledge of themselves and of the opportunities available

Supervision
Our observational work shows that there is little direct supervision of the junior ranks by senior officers or of constables by sergeants and inspectors, and that there is scope for more direct supervision within the existing management structure. These conclusions are strongly confirmed by the findings of the survey of police officers.

If anything, they apply even more strongly to the Divisional CID than to the uniform side. Supervision tends to be 'on paper' rather than by direct contact, and supervising officers - certainly those above the rank of inspector - are not generally in a position to know much about the style or quality of work done by most of the officers under their command. Also, the emphasis in supervision is definitely negative: there is far more emphasis on criticising officers when things have gone wrong than on encouraging or rewarding officers when they have done well.

The move towards assessment of performance seems the best way of shifting the emphasis towards more positive supervision. Also, the Force could persuade officers to do more direct supervision by making this an important aspect of the assessment of their performance. While considerably more direct supervision would be possible within the present management structure, we shall recommend in a later section a simplification of management structures which would release some management resources from administrative tasks and make them available for direct supervision.

Management of Divisional CID officers
Before the changes introduced by Sir Robert Mark and Sir David McNee, the chain of command for CID officers on Divisions was quite separate from that for uniform officers and led ultimately to a central Criminal Investigations Department. One effect of those changes was to make Divisional CID officers, under their detective chief-inspector, responsible to the uniform chief-superintendent in charge of the Division. There is still a detective chief-superintendent attached to each District, but he is not in command of the Divisional CID officers within the District, though in practice they may feel that their loyalty is divided between him and the uniform chief-superintendent. A second change was the introduction of 'interchange' between uniform and CID branches, which means that CID officers spend at least a year in uniform on promotion to sergeant and to inspector. There have also been a more limited number of transfers of senior officers between uniform and CID branches. The general intention behind these changes was to reduce the separate identity of the CID, to increase the level of understanding among CID and uniform officers of each others' work, and to encourage the two groups to work more closely together by binding them together in a single unit (the Division) under the command of one (uniform) officer. It is generally agreed by CID and uniform officers within the Force that these objectives have been only partially achieved.

The position of the detective chief-superintendents attached to Districts is somewhat anomalous, but more important is the fact that uniform and CID officers on Divisions belong to separate organisational units which very rarely cooperate closely on the same tasks. At the same time, Divisional CID officers tend to be very little supervised: detective sergeants do not perform a genuinely supervisory function, and detective inspectors and detective chief-inspectors rarely even observe interviews of prisoners at the police station, though it would be very easy for them to do so. Furthermore, detective chief-inspectors often fail to perform the basic management function of allocating the work between their staff - they often leave it to them to sort it out for themselves. Also, our observational work shows that much of the time of Divisional CID officers is not productively used, and the findings of the survey of police officers are highly consistent with this conclusion. Interviewing suspects and witnesses at the police station is considered to be one of their principal tasks, yet it accounts for only 8 per cent of their time.

The best way of encouraging closer cooperation between CID and uniform and making better use of CID officers would be to set up more working groups containing both CID and uniform officers. We recommend that this should be done by dispersing some of the Divisional CID officers to the uniform reliefs, which would then become mixed CID and uniform reliefs. This would be a way of ensuring that CID officers were always available to interview prisoners, take statements and give help or advice to uniform officers. Also, reliefs would be in a much better position to form plans for crime prevention and detection if there were CID officers in them who would participate in the planning process (see pages 554-556).

## Consultative management
The style of management in the Force is shaped on a military model and is essentially authoritarian. In the past there has been very little consultation with the lower ranks about major or minor changes in the pattern of working, or about decisions affecting the individual's career. In most kinds of police work individuals and working groups are required to make plans, work towards objectives, take decisions and use discretion. Within this frame-work, an authoritarian method of management tends not to work, because individuals and groups cannot be told precisely what to do, but must have a degree of autonomy. Consequently, compliance with instructions may be more apparent than real. Working groups are adept at finding ways of evading instructions so that they can pursue objectives they have informally set themselves. The way out of this impasse is a difficult one, but it must lie in getting working groups to understand and accept the objectives of the organisation as a whole, and ensuring that the objectives of working groups are identical with at least some of the objectives of the whole organisation. This can only be done by adopting a consultative style of management which allows the working groups to participate in discussion about methods of working and the definition of objectives (see pages 556-559).

## Development of objectives
Much patrolling by police officers on foot and in vehicles is

apparently aimless. The officers are waiting for something to happen, which mostly means hoping they will have a call to respond to. Much of the time, there is no call to respond to and in the meantime the officers are not engaging in any purposive activity. They may therefore be getting very bored, and because of the tension produced by boredom, they may then tend to over-react when a call does come.

One way of visualising a new approach to policing is to try to define objectives that could be translated into tasks to be undertaken by working groups of police officers. This is the approach that the new Commissioner has begun to adopt in his first year of office. It does seem to be a useful way of thinking about how to organise police work, but it needs a great deal of development before it can become effective. Plans and objectives can exist at many different levels in the organisation, but we suggest that the key levels are the Division and the working group (relief, crime squad, CID office, etc.). One of the chief ways in which Divisions could form objectives is by collecting information about the pattern of the demands being made on the police force locally. From this a Division might establish, for example, that there was extensive vandalism on certain council estates which caused deep concern to the people living there and seriously damaged their morale. A coordinated plan might then be devised to do something useful about the problem. Any proper analysis of what could be done would show that agencies other than the police should be involved, so that facilitating action by these other agencies would have to be among the objectives (the 'multi-agency approach'). Of course, there have been isolated campaigns of this kind in the past, but the pattern of policing would radically change if Divisions were regularly pursuing objectives of this kind in an ordered way, and if this activity were a substantial proportion of all policing activity on a Division (see pages 559-562). Partly in response to the findings of our research, the Force has started to make major efforts to define Divisional objectives.

Some of the objectives of working groups would follow naturally from specific Divisional objectives. However, there may be scope in addition for objectives identified by a particular working group and pursued by them alone, as happens at present to a limited extent. The obvious difficulty with this planned approach to policing is that members of reliefs (and to a lesser extent members of other working groups such as crime squads) need to be available to respond to calls. If they engage in a purposive activity they are liable to be interrupted. Now that the strength of the Force has increased, this difficulty might be reduced by dividing the relief officers on duty into those having the primary task of responding to calls and those having some other primary task during the current shift. The second group would still be available to respond to urgent calls if necessary.

## Management information

A great number of records are kept in the Metropolitan Police, but largely as part of a system for getting things done and not for the purpose of providing information. In practice, managers have little information of a kind that allows them to assess and evaluate the pattern of policing activity in relation to definable objectives. They also tend to lack experience and skills in evaluating information, particularly when it is in a statistical form. The regular statistics that are centrally produced are little used at the local level because they do not correspond closely with the information needs of local managers. Locally collated information about crime and criminals is used much less and much less purposively by working groups of police officers than it could be. In particular, there is a lack of information that traces the links between particular kinds of policing activity and some sort of tangible results.

Information will not be used unless it is directly linked to the formation of practical plans and the evaluation of their success. The starting point, therefore, should be the definition of objectives and the formation of plans; but once this has been done, priority should be given to producing information that will feed into the development of the plans and the evaluation of the success of the resulting initiatives. It is important that information about these initiatives and their results should be disseminated to management teams elsewhere in the Force. Initially the need will have to be met by making better use of the existing records, but if planning becomes more general, we can expect the records themselves to be redesigned to take account of information needs as well as the need to chase progress and check that individual tasks have been properly carried out. A decentralised approach to the development of information systems, with strong participation by local management teams, is extremely important (see pages 562-565).

## Stops

The present policy of the Metropolitan Police involves stopping and questioning (and in many cases searching) a very large number of people in London each year. From the survey of Londoners we estimate that about $1\frac{1}{2}$ million stops are carried out over a twelve-month period. Because not all stops are recalled, this may be a low estimate: the survey of police officers tends to suggest that the true figure is higher.

There would be a substantial price to pay, in terms of crime detected, if this policy were to be suddenly abandoned and nothing put in its place. The proportion of stops that lead to the detection of an offence is low (3 per cent lead to an arrest and charge and 5 per cent to an offence being reported, according to the survey of Londoners). Nevertheless, a large number of offences (perhaps 100,000 per annum) are detected in this way, and the survey of police officers suggests that about one-quarter of arrests directly arise from a stop. At the same time, the cost of the policy, in its effects on the relationship between the police and the public, is substantial. People who have been stopped, and particularly those who have been stopped repeatedly, tend strongly to be more critical of the police than others; there is, therefore, strong evidence that the present stopping policy is one cause of hostility to the police among a substantial proportion of young people, and among young black people in particular.

Our findings in this field are relevant to two separate but related issues. The first is the balance to be struck by the law between individual liberty (particularly the liberty of innocent persons) and the need to prevent crime and catch offenders. The second is the balance to be struck by policing policy, within the framework of the law, between the use of powers to stop and search and alternative policing strategies.

On the balance to be struck by the law, we observe that a withdrawal of the present powers would deprive the police in London of a means which they currently detect a large number of offences. At the same time the inconvenience caused to people who are stopped is not very great, and in most cases people favourably assess the conduct and approach of police officers who stopped them. It is the fact of being repeatedly stopped that tends to cause hostility to the police rather than the conduct of the police on any particular occasion. On balance, therefore, our findings do not support the view that the present powers should be withdrawn. They do show that they are often exceeded by the police, if the criterion of 'reasonable suspicion' is interpreted to mean that there must be a specific reason for suspecting the individual person concerned. However, we can see no remedy for this within the law; it is hard to see how the criterion of reasonable suspicion could be made more clear cut while preserving the usefulness of the powers for the prevention and detection of crime. Furthermore, our findings show that by itself the law tends not to be an effective constraint on policing behaviour in this field, and it follows that detailed amendments to legislation are unlikely to have much effect. For the same reason, it seems unlikely that the proposed extension of the power to stop, contained in the current Police and Criminal Evidence Bill, to cases where a person is suspected of carrying an offensive weapon, would have much effect on policing behaviour in London, at least in the short term. This is not inconsistent with the view that it would have an effect in the longer term if it is thought that the extension would tend to dilute the concept of reasonable suspicion and encourage the acceptance of the broader interpretation of its meaning that we have referred to earlier. There is, however, some support in our findings for the usefulness of the Bill's proposal to require that a police officer who has stopped and searched someone should given a written state-ment of the reason for the stop. The survey of Londoners shows that people tend to be happier about a stop when a reason was given.

However, our more important conclusions relate to the

balance to be struck by policing policy between the use of powers to stop and search and alternative policing strategies. The starting point for a discussion of policing policy in this field must be that the powers exist and will continue to exist for the foreseeable future, and that the use of the powers does result in the detection of a substantial amount of crime. Nevertheless, it does not follow that the use of the powers on the present scale is wise or that it represents the most productive use of the available policing resources. Within the current framework of the law we believe there are ways in which the police could strike a better balance between the costs and benefits of stop and search.

First, we suggest that stopping practices should be tied in with the far more purposive policing that we recommend, and closely related to the defined objectives of working groups. The better use of information - particularly locally gathered information - is an important part of this. If police officers are more often trying to tackle a specific problem or pattern of crime, rather than randomly patrolling, they will more often be looking for something specific or for specific persons, and they will therefore tend more often to have a genuine and specific reason for stopping someone. Such a policy would lead to a substantial reduction in the total number of stops made. This kind of policy is likely to be more effective as well as more acceptable to the public. It is true that as the police become more discriminating in making stops, they will tend to concentrate on a smaller number of people who will be stopped repeatedly, and these people are likely to become hostile. However, if there is genuine reason to suspect that they have committed an offence, this is a price that has to be paid.

Secondly, there is a need for a change in the way that police officers handle stops, which can only be brought about by training on the job. We have pointed out (page 499) that police officers regard the nine out of ten stops that do not produce a 'result' as failures: as the price that has to be paid for the tenth that does. Even if the 'strike rate' can be increased, this is a very heavy price if (as we have shown) the 'unsuccessful' stops have a bad effect on public opinion. Instead, police officers should come to regard stops as having the proper function of improving public confidence in the police. This means that where a stop does not result in the detection of an offence, it should be considered as a potentially 'positive' encounter. It is an opportunity for a police officer to offer information, help or advice, to show that the police are making an effort to combat crime, and to engage in relaxed conversation. It is difficult for police officers to look at the matter this way because, having made the stop in the effort to detect an offence they find it hard to switch to the contrasting objective of seeing if they can be of help. In particular, the fear of being 'had over' (deceived) tends to weigh more heavily with them than other considerations. These difficulties can be overcome by a shift of values among police officers and a development of the (varied) social skills required to handle this kind of encounter more effectively.

## Home beat policing
One of the effects of the proposed changes would be to shift the balance in favour of positive policing as opposed to immediate responses to specific demands and events. But useful plans and objectives depend on officers having a detailed knowledge of fairly small neighbourhoods. At the time of our survey only 5 per cent of officers had continuous responsibility for a particular small area, and most working police officers covered a whole Division or District in a fairly random fashion. There is clearly a case for increasing the number of officers who work within a smaller area and get to know it well. Experience of a policing experiment in Lewisham suggests that this cannot be done at a stroke; also, it may not be necessary for officers to be confined to a small area permanently or for very long periods. However, a much greater degree of continuity can probably be gradually achieved. One method is to increase the number of 'home beat officers' as they are defined at present. Another is to reorganise the work of uniform reliefs on the lines already suggested. The two initiatives can be jointly pursued. These changes would have the effect of increasing the number of police officers going about on foot, an outcome that is desired by a majority of the public. However, this should be seen not so much as an end in itself as a consequence of the more purposive approach to policing.

## Complaints
The survey of police officers shows that a strengthening of the independent element within the complaints procedure would have substantial support among police officers in London, particularly those in supervisory ranks and those who have had many complaints made against them. There are divided opinions as to whether the independent body should deal with all complaints or only more serious ones. These findings should be taken into account by those now engaged in active discussions about the complaints procedure.

## Racial prejudice
Although it has less effect on policing behaviour than might be expected, the level of racial prejudice in the Force is cause for serious concern. No simple and straightforward solution to this problem can be offered, especially since many police officers do not see that racial prejudice makes it more difficult for them to achieve their policing objectives. However, we do have a general and a specific recommendation to make.

The general point is that the Force should make a major effort to stimulate explicit discussion and thinking about the ethnic dimension in policing at all levels in the organisation. One way of doing this is through training programmes; while initiatives are already being taken in this field, there is room for more, and in

599

particular there is a need to expose police officers to the views and attitudes of people outside the Force, especially members of ethnic minority groups. But there is also the need for the ethnic dimension to be explicitly discussed by all managers and working groups which are making or implementing plans. Open discussion and exposure to outside views is not a guarantee of progress, but it is a necessary condition.

Our more specific recommendation is that the Force should learn from the experience of local authorities which have set up groups of race relations advisers with a brief to review all aspects of policy in the light of their effects on members of ethnic minority groups and to work for changes in policy where these have been shown to be necessary. The present community liaison officers, attached to Districts, may be thought to have a role of this kind, but we have explained (page 427 onwards) that the area that they cover is too large and their responsibilities too diverse for them to have much effect on policing practices from day to day or on the attitudes of police officers. We suggest that more junior and more locally-based officers with a specific responsibility for race relations are required. A first step would be to create a post of this kind for an inspector on each Division in which ethnic minorities form a significant proportion of the population (which would include the majority of Divisions). This person would establish close relations with key individuals and groups belonging to minority groups, would make a direct input into locally-based training and would also review local policing activities and plans in the light of the ethnic dimension and advise accordingly. He or she would work with groups of police officers on operational policing tasks on occasion.

Broad structure
The main defects in the present broad structure of the Force can be summarised as excessive centralisation, a long chain of command, diffusion of responsibility and instability of senior management teams. There is nothing original about this analysis: these defects have been repeatedly pointed out to us by senior officers. At the same time, these senior officers often believe that nothing can be done about it. We have made some radical suggestions (pages 565-568) in order to show that, in principle, something could be done, and not because we expect the Force to adopt these particular suggestions. Proposals for change would have to evolve from a process of reassessment and planning within the Force.

Our first suggestion is that the Divisional structure should consist of a senior management team with operational units reporting to it directly. This would mean either a reduction in the number of ranks or the use of senior management teams, having joint responsibility for the running of the Divisions, but including officers at three different ranks (chief-inspector, superintendent and chief-superintendent). The second possibility implies a reduction in the importance of rank in determining management responsibilities instead of a reduction in the number of ranks.

Secondly, we suggest that senior officers (from chief-inspector upwards) should be moved about much less frequently than at present. This can be achieved by greater flexibility in the rank of an officer required for a particular post (so that a promotion does not inevitably imply a move) and by haveing more senior officers than are required to fill the available posts.

Thirdly, we strongly suggest that there is no need to have two levels between the Divisions and the centre, as at present (these two levels are the 24 Districts and the four Areas). An attractive plan, suggested in the past, is to group the 75 Divisions into eight Areas. Each of these Areas would have a management team consisting of several senior officers (commanders or deputy assistant commissioners). Different members of the team might have specialist interests, but would not have separate responsibility for a geographical sub-division of the Area: instead, the whole team would accept joint responsibility.

Fourthly, we suggest two changes in the central departmental structure. It is important that one Department should have full operational responsibility for the local police network. In practice, this means that 'A' and 'C' Departments should be combined into a single Department, and that the Areas should report to this Department alone (at present they report to different Departments depending on what aspect of police work is involved). Also, the service functions of Departments should be clearly distinguished from their operational functions. For example, 'D' Department would continue to have important service functions in relation to Divisional training, without having operational responsibility for it. At the same time, 'D' Department would continue to have operational responsibility for running all central training facilities.

## The future prospect

The conditions have not existed, in the past, in which there can be reasoned discussion in public of policing policies and practices. On the one hand police officers have tended to interpret any criticism from outside as an attack on their integrity and on the principle that law and order is necessary. On the other hand, civil libertarians have often put forward criticisms that are not informed by an understanding of the realities of policing and have often been unwilling to face up to the conflicts inherent in all attempts to reconcile the demand for liberty with the need for order. We see our research as part of an attempt to create the conditions in which people can discuss the issues with better information and more understanding. By initiating and supporting this research, the Metropolitan Police have shown that they wish to participate in a discussion of this kind. This is an atmosphere in which important changes in London's policing can be brought about.

Over the past year, while we have been engaged in the analysis and interpretation of our research, important initiatives have been set in motion within the Metropolitan Police. Some of these have developed out of preliminary discussions of our findings. There are now many initiatives within the Met at various stages of development that grow out of ideas contained in this report or from thinking that is parallel to it. While the general pattern of policing described and analysed in these reports cannot be expected to change rapidly, there are strong indications that the need for change is now recognised within the Force and that the organisation is beginning to change in directions suggested by our results and analysis.